Edited by

Niall Lucy   Postmodern
Literary Theory

An Anthology

BLACKWELL
Publishers

Copyright © Blackwell Publishers 2000

First published 2000

2 4 6 8 10 9 7 5 3 1

Blackwell Publishers Ltd
108 Cowley Road
Oxford OX4 1JF
UK

Blackwell Publishers Inc.
350 Main Street
Malden, Massachusetts 02148
USA

British Library Cataloguing in Publication Data

A CIP catalogue record for this book is available from the British Library.

Library of Congress Cataloging-in-Publication Data

Lucy, Niall.
   Postmodern literary theory : an anthology / Niall Lucy.
      p.   cm.
   Includes bibliographical references (p.) and index.
   ISBN 0–631–21027–X
   ISBN 0–631–21028–8 (pbk.)
   1. Literature—History and criticism—Theory, etc.   2. Postmodernism (Literature)   I. Title.
   PN98.P67 L83 1999
   801'.95—dc21   99–31612
                                                         CIP

Typeset in 10 on 12½ pt Sabon
by Ace Filmsetting Ltd, Frome, Somerset
Printed in Great Britain by MPG Books Ltd, Bodmin, Cornwall

This book is printed on acid-free paper.

Contents

Preface

You can 'say it with flowers', but you'd be saying something altogether different with lawn clippings. I guess that's why an anthology (from the Greek *anthos* flower + *logia* collection) is not, etymologically speaking, 'a bundle of twigs' or 'a clump of grass'. It's 'a bunch of flowers' for the simple reason that ideally an anthology is an arrangement of what it presents as the best examples of a certain type (never mind that flowers aren't always distinguishable from weeds).

Every arrangement – be it cultural or horticultural, as it were – is textual. Whether we're arranging flowers or words, the point is to establish orders of relation between the various elements of the arrangement. We put taller flowers behind shorter ones in a vase (daffodils in front of lilies, say), in the same way as if we wanted to compose a Shakespearean sonnet we'd be sure to arrange the words according to a standard rhythm (iambic pentameter) and to distribute them across three quatrains combined as twelve lines followed by a couplet. To varying degrees of flexibility, then, every arrangement has its rules.

But where do those rules come from? Who makes them?; how do they get passed on?; do they ever change? These are the sort of questions that this anthology is designed to raise, especially in relation to ideas concerning literature. One such idea might be that literature is a very different concept today (if not a different cultural practice and industry) from that of only a generation ago, and this idea – whether seen as invigorating or disruptive – is attributed usually to 'postmodernism' as a powerful signifier of the radically new and challenging or of everything that's gone wrong with the study of literature in recent times.

Most radical of all is the possibility that the very notion of literature is rendered untenable by postmodernism, in so far as literature's identity now is held to be no longer secure from the contaminations of literary theory and other 'external' interests and forces. Even so, this wouldn't be to say that postmodern literary theory (if that's what it might be called) is committed to such a view exclusively, as if the postmodern literary theoretical could be defined in terms of an archive and a method. Certainly, at any rate, what the present anthology marks as 'postmodern literary theory' is irreducible to a fixed set of ideas and practices deriving from a manifesto or constituting a school or a movement. Hence the title of this book is something of a misnomer, at least to the extent that, outside these pages, there isn't an institutionalized discipline or a self-proclaimed style of thought known as 'postmodern literary theory' as such. All the same there is, I think, a strong sense in which it does ring true that something out there might (or might as well) be called postmodern literary theory, as if it did have a certain identity of its own, and one that could be all the more in need of investigation precisely for seeming to be not such a well-kept secret.

Whatever the nature of that identity, though, it can't be understood in terms of a standard notion of genre. If, for example, you woke up one morning and decided to write a horror story, you'd probably have something to show for it by the time you went to bed. But what if you woke up and decided to write a postmodern literary theoretical essay (or, more likely, text)? Wouldn't you have to spend the rest of the day and well into the night asking the question, *what does a postmodern literary theoretical essay (or text) look like?*

And the answer is . . . ?

But of course there is no 'answer', which doesn't mean however that postmodern literary theory remains open to personal interpretation. When you think you can't find rules, it doesn't mean there *aren't* any. It doesn't mean that postmodern literary theory is absolutely open and therefore absolutely (and paradoxically, if not self-contradictorily) closed off to all possibility of being understood in terms of genre. It may mean rather that the *question* of genre is generic to postmodern literary theory, as I discuss at greater length in the Introduction.

For readers who may be familiar with my earlier discussion of these matters, I should mention that I haven't pursued the question of deconstruction's relations to postmodernism here. In a word, Derrida is a fairly minor figure in this anthology, for reasons that have to do with my earlier argument that Derrida and deconstruction are not quite within 'the post' at all. For clarity's sake, I have chosen not to return to that argument this time around, although traces of it do remain in a few of my additional notes. Most of these additional notes (on topics ranging from

Dasein to the Situationists, etc.) appear with my initials (NL), to avoid confusion with notes added by earlier editors and translators; none the less in many cases I have added a reference or a gloss inconspicuously, whenever it seemed uncontroversial, and likewise silently corrected a few typographical and other errors that I found in the originals.

This book took shape initially while I was a visiting scholar in the Philosophy department at the University of Wales, Cardiff, for a few months in 1997. I am very grateful to Christopher Norris and his Ph.D. students of the time for providing such an intellectually generous environment in which to work. I am also grateful to Stephen Knight, Dean of the School of English, Communications and Philosophy at Cardiff, for making me feel so welcome; and I thank Murdoch University for granting me the period of study leave. It was a long while before I had a chance to get back to the book, but I was fortunate in having many others to help me (by commenting on the manuscript, supplying a reference or checking a note) when I did. For all their help, rudely called on at impossibly short notice, I thank Abigail Bray, Robert Briggs, John D. Caputo, Julie Considine, Carolyn D'Cruz, Claire Colebrook, Peggy Kamuf, Alec McHoul, Jane Mummery, Horst Ruthrof and McKenzie Wark. I am grateful too to everyone at Blackwell, especially Andrew McNeillie.

Niall Lucy

Acknowledgements

The editor and publishers gratefully acknowledge permission from the following to reproduce material:

The authors, for Philippe Lacoue-Labarthe and Jean-Luc Nancy, 'Genre', trans. Lawrence R. Schehr, *Glyph* 7 (1980), pp. 1–14.

Blackwell Publishers, Stanford University Press and Editions Galilée, for Jean-François Lyotard, 'Something Like: "Communication . . . Without Communication" ', in *The Inhuman: Reflections on Time*, trans. Geoffrey Bennington and Rachel Bowlby (Stanford: Stanford University Press, 1988), pp. 108–18.

Columbia University Press, for Julia Kristeva, 'From One Identity to an Other' [Fr. 1975], in *Desire in Language: A Semiotic Approach to Literature and Art*, trans. T. Gora, A. Jardine and L. S. Roudiez; ed. L. S. Roudiez, pp. 124–47 (Columbia University Press, 1981, reproduced by permission of the publisher via Copyright Clearance Center, Inc.).

University of Minnesota Press and the Athlone Press, for Gilles Deleuze and Félix Guattari, 'Introduction: Rhizome', in *A Thousand Plateaus: Capitalism and Schizophrenia* [Fr. 1980], trans. B. Massumi (Minneapolis: University of Minnesota Press, 1987), pp. 3–25.

The author, for Steven Connor, 'Rewriting Wrong: On the Ethics of Literary Reversion', in *Liminal Postmodernism: The Postmodern, the (Post-)Colonial, and the (Post-)Feminist*, eds. T. D'Haen and H. Bertens, *Postmodern Studies* 8 (Amsterdam: Atlanta, 1994), pp. 79–97.

Oxford University Press, for Thomas Docherty, 'The Ethics of Alterity: Postmodern Character', in *Alterities: Criticism, History, Representation*, pp. 36–68; this selection, pp. 60–8 (Oxford: Clarendon Press, 1996, reprinted permission of Oxford University Press).

Columbia University Press and Editions de Minuit, for Luce Irigaray, 'The Three *Genres*' [Fr. 1987], trans. David Macey, in *Sexes et parentes* (Columbia University Press 1991/2, reproduced by permission of the publisher via Copyright Clearance Center, Inc.).

University of Minnesota Press, for Hélène Cixous, 'Writing and the Law: Blanchot, Joyce, Kafka, and Lispector', in *Readings: The Poetics of Blanchot, Joyce, Kafka, Kleist, Lispector, and Tsvetayeva*, edited, translated and introduced by Verena Andermatt Conley (New York and London: Harvester Wheatsheaf, 1992), pp. 1–27.

The author, for Kristin Ross, 'Watching the Detectives', in *Postmodernism and the Re-Reading of Modernity*, eds Francis Barker, Peter Hulme and Margaret Iversen (Manchester and New York: Manchester University Press, 1992), pp. 46–65.

Anne Balsamo, 'Feminism for the Incurably Informed', *South Atlantic Quarterly* 92 (4) (Fall 1993), pp. 681–712. Copyright © 1993, Duke University Press. All rights reserved. Reprinted with permission.

Duke University Press, for Brian McHale, 'POSTcyberMODERN-punkISM', in *Storming the Reality Studio: A Casebook of Cyberpunk and Postmodern Science Fiction*, ed. L. McCaffery, pp. 308–23. Copyright © 1991, Duke University Press. All rights reserved. Reprinted with permission.

The author, for Tony Thwaites, 'Miracles: Hot Air and Histories of the Improbable', in *Futur*Fall: Excursions into Post-Modernity*, eds E. A. Grosz, T. Threadgold, D. Kelly, A. Cholodenko and E. Colless (Sydney: Power Institute Publications, 1986), pp. 82–96.

Editions du Seuil and Farrar, Strauss & Giroux Inc., for Roland Barthes, 'From Work to Text' [Fr. 1971], in *Image Music Text*, trans. Stephen Heath (London: Fontana, 1977), pp. 155–64.

University of Oklahoma Press, for Ralph Cohen, 'Do Postmodern Genres Exist?', in *Postmodern Genres*, ed. Marjorie Perloff (Norman and London: University of Oklahoma Press, 1998), pp. 11–27.

John Barth, 'The Literature of Exhaustion' [1967], in *The Novel Today: Contemporary Writers on Modern Fiction*, ed. Malcolm Bradbury (London: Fontana, 1977), pp. 70–83. Copyright © 1967 by John Barth. Reprinted with the permission of The Wylie Agency, Inc.

Jenaro Talens, 'Writing Against Simulacrum: The Place of Literature and Literary Theory in the Electronic Age', *boundary 2*, 22 (1) (Spring 1995), pp. 1–21. Copyright © 1995, Duke University Press. All rights reserved. Reprinted with permission.

Editions Rodopi, for Catherine Burgass, 'Postmodern Value', in *Postmodern Surroundings*, ed. Steven Earnshaw, *Postmodern Studies 9* (Amsterdam: Atlanta, 1994), pp. 23–37.

The author and *New German Critique*, for William Rasch, 'In Search of the Lyotard Archipelago, or: How to Live with Paradox and Learn to Like it', *New German Critique* 61 (Winter 1994), pp. 55–75.

'Preface' by Michel Foucault, from *Anti-Oedipus: Capitalism and Schizophrenia*, by Gilles Deleuze and Félix Guattari, translated by Helen Lane, Mark Seem, and Robert Hurley. Translation copyright © 1977 by Viking Penguin Inc., English language translation. Used by permission of Viking Penguin, a division of Penguin Putnam Inc.

University of Nebraska Press, for Alec McHoul, 'Analytic Ethics', in *Semiotic Investigations: Towards an Effective Semiotics* (Lincoln and London: University of Nebraska Press, 1996), pp. 191–211. (Slightly revised by the author.)

Jean-François Lyotard, 'Note on the Meaning of "Post-" ', in *The Postmodern Explained to Children: Correspondence 1982–1985*, trans. Don Barry, Bernadette Maher, Julian Pefanis, Virginia Spate and Morgan Thomas; eds Pefanis and Thomas (Sydney: Power Publications, 1992), pp. 87–94. English translation copyright 1992 by Power Publications, Sydney, Australia. North American edition copyright 1993 by the Regents of the University of Minnesota. Original, French-language edition copyright 1988 Editions Galilée, Paris.

The author and the University of Chicago Press, for Jerome Christensen, 'The Romantic Movement at the End of History', *Critical Inquiry* 20 (Spring 1994), pp. 452–76.

Every effort has been made to contact all copyright holders. The publishers would be pleased to rectify any omissions brought to their attention at the earliest opportunity.

Introduction (On the Way to Genre)

Shock! Horror!

About a third of the way through one of Kathy Acker's novels, *Blood and Guts in High School* (1978), there appears a drawing (styled after the genre of lavatory graffiti) of – and let's get the grammar right – a cunt. A wide-open beaver. A full-page legs-apart close-up of a pussy. It is captioned, 'GIRLS WILL DO ANYTHING FOR LOVE'. On the facing page there is a drawing of a headless woman roped at the wrists and ankles, with the words (a quotation, the title of a poem by Keats) 'ODE TO A GRECIAN URN' printed underneath. Much earlier, and also taking up the whole page, there is a drawing of a drooping, possibly detumescing, cock, spurting a few last drops of come, or it could be piss (again, as always, the grammar and the details matter), below which the words 'TURN MY EYES INSANE' are written.[1] And so it goes . . . cocks and cunts, fondling and fucking, hard-ons and hot sex. The drawings are all there. But the point is that they are *drawings*; and they appear in a book whose cover labels it generically as 'a novel'. It is somewhat less the point for now that the drawings are lavatorially pornographic.

There is scarcely an aspect of *Blood and Guts in High School* that could not be said to raise the question, what is literature? What is literature if it may sometimes, for example, take the form of a drawing? One approach to such a question might be to situate Acker's novel within some sort of generic system or tradition, citing a few other examples of – let's call it – 'picture fiction'. For its proximity to *Blood and Guts*, Kurt Vonnegut's *Breakfast of Champions* (1973) springs to mind, a novel in which there is a drawing on almost every one of its 270-odd pages – see especially, for sake of comparison with Acker, those of an asshole and (choosing my words carefully) a wide-open beaver.[2] But of course the 'genre' of picture fiction is not confined to US literature of the 1970s; it is not simply a 'postmodern' or a proto-postmodern phenomenon, at least not as defined historically. For the locus classicus of the type is Lawrence Sterne's *The Life and Opinions of Tristram Shandy, Gentleman*, published in installments from 1759–67. Exceeding 600 pages in length, the 'novel' (and with *Tristram Shandy* one begins to understand why the term 'text' is often so precise – more on which in a moment) includes among its many non-linguistic elements blank pages, black pages and marbled pages; drawings of squiggly lines (representing various stages of plot development) and the flourish of a stick; along with such typographical superfluities as large blocks of asterisks and extended em-dashes.[3]

Nor is picture fiction a form of writing (or a mode of representation, as perhaps it should be expressed at this point) exclusive to fiction as such. In a now much-anthologized and very famous essay – 'POSTmodernISM: A Paracritical Bibliography' (you can see it, but you can't say it) – by the American literary critic Ihab Hassan, first published in 1971, all manner of typographical (visual, non-linguistic) apparatus is on display.[4] If *the look* of Hassan's essay is in one sense more reminiscent than prescient (more like *Tristram Shandy* than *Blood and Guts in High School*), the important point none the less is that its typography cannot be dissociated (and not only for reasons of legal violation) from its thematics. What 'POSTmodernISM' says, in short, is indissociable from how it looks.

What, then, is literature, that it may sometimes appear in its absences . . . as a blank page, a row of asterisks, a picture of a cunt – or a work of literary criticism?

After Joyce

If that question is understood today as characteristically postmodern, it should not be forgotten that the question has been asked before. Not only *Tristram Shandy*, but also many other eighteenth-century works of literature could be said to approach literature as a concept, and more so as a practice, that always overflows institutional, moral, political, aesthetic and other attempts to constrain it. Perhaps the eighteenth century was less anxious to know what literature is and more curious to find out what it could be. Perhaps too (although I don't quite think so) such curiosity might be said to have been rediscovered in recent times (in these 'postmodern' times) as a reanimating force within a concept of literature that was close to 'exhaustion' after Joyce. Come *Finnegans Wake* (1939) – what next?

While I don't believe the world had to wait almost half a century to get an answer, in the form of *Blood and Guts in High School,* I think it is still true that Acker's novel can be seen as a response (interesting or otherwise) to the *problem* of James Joyce, whose *Finnegans Wake* is the high point, or the end point, of modernist literary experimentation. The Joyce 'problem' was never entirely new, however, since it can be seen as a variation on the problem of what I have been calling picture fiction, a genre that goes back at least to *Tristram Shandy*. In other words, to the extent that *Finnegans Wake* is a work of literature it is first of all a piece of writing, and in so far as it is written it is also visual. As Darren Tofts has put it recently: 'the *Wake* is very aware of its own tactility, of visible punctures or marks made on a material surface that signify a unit of abstract value.'[5] As performed by *Finnegans Wake*, then, writing cannot be understood as a straightforwardly *linguistic* concept, easily separated from 'non-linguistic' signifying systems in the form of the tactile and the visual. Through its profuse references to writing systems of every kind ('from hieroglyphics to runes . . . [but] especially to forms of inscription that involve "paper wounds," the incising or puncturing of a material surface'),[6] moreover, Joyce's text enacts a kind of writing that is more disseminary than significatory in its manifold movements beyond any totalizing concept of literature or theory of writing as such. Yet in this way, in a sense, it is all the more 'ancient' for being so 'modern' – for '[t]he English word "write" is in fact derived from the Old Norse "rita," meaning to incise, and was coined within runic culture'.[7]

In Joyce – and this is the 'problem' – any word is capable of so *much* meaning, because it can appear in so many different contexts and is so overladen with the history of its different uses and nuances, that every word is forever on the verge of becoming gibberish. Each word is already an encyclopaedia (a text, as it were) long before it may be brought into association with other words to form something as complex as a novel. And if there is so much semantic indeterminacy in a word, how much more must there be in a novel – especially one of such disseminatory force as *Finnegans Wake*?

As with *Tristram Shandy*, then, *Finnegans Wake* stands against the traditional concept of the novel as a self-contained or closed system, a perfect little world from beginning to end. To call either *Finnegans Wake* or *Tristram Shandy* a 'novel' would be to suppose that each conforms to certain conventions and satisfies certain expectations within a totalizing *concept* of the novel; in short, that each belongs to a certain *genre* of writing. But what to call that genre? For in naming it, we would presume

to have enclosed (rounded up, shut down, closed off) the endless proliferation of meanings made possible by Joyce, certainly, if not also by
Sterne. We would presume that the identity of the named genre included
(enclosed) *Finnegans Wake* and *Tristram Shandy*'s 'lack' of an identity
from the viewpoint of a standard concept of the novel or a concept of
literature in general. If such a lack, however, were in fact *essential* to their
identities, then there could never be a name for the genre to which that
lack belonged, since the lack would always be particular to the text in
question and unable to be generalized except at the expense of that particularity (and hence of the text's very 'identity'). Only the term 'text', I
believe, allows Joyce and Sterne's writing the freedom to keep on the
move.

Nevertheless, if 'text' marks the necessary indeterminacy of all writing,
then it also threatens the identity of 'literature' by de-specializing it to
some extent. What is literature that it may sometimes be the unnameable,
what *cannot* be put into words? So one (doubtless extreme) response to
the threat of *Finnegans Wake* (the problem of Joyce) could be to regard
words as the very problem that literature must overcome. Literature would
then be understood to lie 'beyond' words – as a drawing, a blank page
and so on. After Joyce, what would be the point (so an argument might
go) of continuing to believe in the aesthetic ideal of a well-turned phrase
or a carefully-worded image, when it is clear from *Finnegans Wake* that
language leads to gibberish, and not to truth and beauty? Why bother
with literary niceties when you want to call a cunt, a cunt? And if that's
what you want to call it, why not say so – not in words but in pictures,
especially of the type requiring no particular skill to draw, like those
found on toilet walls?

Perhaps then it could be said that a text like *Blood and Guts in High
School* marks a loss of faith in a previously sustaining concept or ideal of
literature, which is seen now only as having perpetuated certain myths of
universal value and human nature based on a myth of 'good writing'. So
it may be that Acker's text is written in such a way that it could never be
mistaken for literature according to an ideal whose use-by date was reached
on that day in 1939 when *Finnegans Wake* was published!

If that were the case then it would raise a problem (still perhaps the
problem of Joyce) – what to call such a writing? However much *Blood
and Guts in High School* may be read as an expression of a lost faith in
grand ideals (of good writing, childhood innocence, individual autonomy,
historical progress, representative democracy and the like), the paradox is
that it's all the more a work of literature in its defiance of that name. If,

according to a certain ideal, that is, 'literature' stands for the right to defiance – to defy authority, common sense, religious and political orthodoxies, codes of moral conduct and sexual expression, laws governing desire and the imagination, whole systems of belief and thought dedicated to sustaining a certain picture of the world as the true image of reality and so on – then such a right must include (indeed it may even only be realized in) an attitude of defiance towards literature. But here's the rub: any 'genre' of writing that took up such an attitude (as represented perhaps by *Blood and Guts in High School*) would, in a seemingly impossible sense, be the very epitome of literature.

What must literature be, then, that it may be realized (perhaps even realized only) in its attempted negation?

Towards Postmodern Literary Theory

That is the sort of question which this anthology is intended to provoke and address. Hence my aim here is not to define 'postmodern literary theory', but rather to allow that putative category to act as a collecting term for relatively recent responses to the kinds of question raised above – and to many other questions, not all of which I am able to anticipate, to come.

Such questions belong to literary theory, as distinct (in a certain sense) from literary criticism. By the latter term I mean works of commentary on works of literature, where it is always understood in advance what literature means. Literary theory, though, marks an approach to 'literature' (in appostion to works of literature) that may be said to ask *the question of literature*. Literary theory does not deny that works of literature exist, nor even that (in a certain sense) there *is* something called literature in the world. It doesn't, moreover, deny that there *are* authors and publishers and books and readers and libraries and so on. While it prefers to talk about 'texts' than 'works' (see chapter 13, which I will discuss shortly), literary theory none the less does not refute the claims of some texts to be understood as better examples of writing than others. But if literary criticism is concerned with appreciating and understanding individual works of literature, literary theory is concerned to ask the root-and-branch – or better, rhizomatic (see chapter 4) – question of literature itself.

All the same, not every 'non-appreciationist' approach to literature is necessarily literary theoretical in the sense I have just given (several chapters here indeed may put the case in point). Marxist, New Historicist and a certain order of feminist 'literary theory', for example, see literature in terms of historico-political, cultural or gendered contexts, or as an effect of power relations, but not *as* the question of itself (which need not preclude – on the contrary – considerations of the shaping force of history, politics, culture, gender, power and the like). There are, to be sure, many questions that may be asked about literature; yet to ask questions *about* literature is not necessarily to ask the question of literature as such.

That doesn't mean, as I have argued elsewhere, that it is *postmodern* – certainly not exclusively or absolutely so – to ask the question of literature.[8] For if indeed the question of literature 'belongs' to postmodernism now, it none the less belonged in the beginning to the Romantics – and there may be good cause for thinking that it still does. Such cause is shown, I believe, in Philippe Lacoue-Labarthe and Jean-Luc Nancy's 'Genre' (chapter 1), where many of the themes of this anthology are introduced. Some of those themes may be listed here as follows:

- the search for a 'beyond' literature
- the question of genre
- the metaphysics of 'nothing'
- the limits of representation
- the dispersions of the subject
- the problem of origins

In order, then, to move towards an understanding of postmodern literary theory, we must first go back to the 'era' of Romanticism, which may yet be far from over.

Romanticism: An Unfinished Project

It was a 'group' of German Romantic philosopher-writers, according to Lacoue-Labarthe and Nancy, at the University of Jena in the 1790s who first broached the question of literature in a way that is recognizably literary theoretical. For this very loosely organized group, literature was the name of that textual activity which called to be understood in terms of the question, *what is it?* Such a conception of literature may be seen to have inaugurated an 'era' whose limits are yet to be reached – the era of a general romanticism. If today we are used to regarding literature as self-reflexive, then ours is still, on Lacoue-Labarthe and Nancy's account, a romantic conception of literature and so we remain, in a sense, within romanticism which itself remains – no less than the question of literature – unfinished and unfinishable.

One of the main questions posed by this anthology is whether the unfinished project of romanticism carries on today as postmodern literary theory. A strong argument for claiming that it does might turn on a certain continuity between romantic and postmodern approaches to the question of genre.

The Jena Romantics (and of course the English Romantics who came shortly after them) were never able to answer the question of what is the genre that is proper to romanticism, though they never tired of asking it. Yet it's not as if they should have thought more deeply about this question or tried harder in other ways to resolve it, on the assumption that if they had they would have been able to name 'the' genre of romanticism – instead of just calling it literature. The question is unanswerable. As Lacoue-Labarthe and Nancy argue, its unanswerability is an effect of romanticism's rejection of 'representation' – of the idea, that is to say, that thoughts and feelings (for example) are capable of being re-presented in literary or other textual forms. For romanticism, 'true' thoughts and feelings are incapable of representation: they are absolutely *unpresentable*. Nevertheless they *are* thoughts and feelings – and, in a sense, the impossibility of their presentation can be understood (thought and felt) only in the futile struggle to present them.

Unpresentability thus reveals itself, as it were, in the sense of failure or dissatisfaction that is left over after every attempt at (re)presentation. This is what 'literature' names, for romanticism. And it is this (im)possibility – that an understanding of the unpresentable, which it is impossible to present, is made possible through the attempt to present it – that romanticism inaugurates.

Now: what name should be given to the genre that is proper to the expression of the inexpressible, the presentation of the unpresentable? What name to give to the genre whose task it is to reveal the task of genre as the revelation of 'nothing'? For there is a sense, on this romantic view, in which every system of representation ('literature' as it is standardly conceived, for example) must end in failure because it cannot present the truth, which is unpresentable. Every system – or genre – of representation, then, turns out to reveal that it has nothing to reveal, since there is always something *more* to be revealed: that absolute revelation is impossible!

If this is the problem that romanticism inaugurates, and which inaugurates romanticism, how could it ever be 'inaugurated' again – by or as postmodernism, say?

The Postmodern Sublime

The structure of inauguration may not be as inviolable as a certain way of thinking leads us to suppose. Without suggesting for a moment that Lacoue-Labarthe and Nancy are wrong to see romanticism as having inaugurated the question of literature, it does not mean that the inauguration has to be seen as a fixed point of origin. Indeed it should also be seen as a form of repetition, in so far as so many of romanticism's ideas were anticipated by the eighteenth-century German thinker Immanuel Kant.

While Kant is not therefore the inaugurator of romanticism, and even less of postmodernism, his *Critique of Judgement* (Ger. 1790) is of fundamental importance both to the ideas of the Jena 'school' and to those of Jean-François Lyotard, the contemporary French philosopher (albeit who died last year, in 1998) whose work is at the forefront of postmodern thought. For Lyotard (see chapter 2) it is Kant who teaches us that aesthetic feeling is precisely a response to what every system or genre of representation lacks: the 'here-and-now' of *presentation*. For in any re-presentation, where is the something that must once have been *here* and *now*, in a certain place at a certain time? Within representation, that something must always appear as nothing. In a sense, it's the knowledge of this nothing that gives rise to aesthetic feeling, which would otherwise be a response simply to a formal idea or a concept. It is the knowledge that art 'contains' something (or nothing) – the uncontainable, unpresentable something that is no longer here and now – that brings forth aesthetic feeling.

Or rather what I have just called knowledge is in fact, for Kant, a sort of communicability, what Lyotard describes as 'communication without communication', or something like that. For it is essential to the Kantian understanding of the structure of aesthetic feeling that it is *communicable*, and not simply a personal response to art. In this way, crucially, aesthetic feeling is seen to arise from within a *community* whose members have agreed informally (agreement without agreement, as it were) to the conditions under which an object may count as art. So, as Lyotard puts it, 'every singular aesthetic feeling' – the singularity of which is not called into question by Lyotard, or by Kant – is also the expression of an 'assumed communicability'.

Here we may begin to see the emergence of certain similarities between Kant's ideas (as discussed through Lyotard) and those of the romantics, as discussed above. (And so we might say that romanticism inaugurates even as it repeats, which might also be true of postmodernism.) The idea that a concept or theory of communication misses something (the incalculability of the unpresentable) is analogous to the romantic idea that the concept of literature misses out what is perhaps most essential to literature – its non-conceptual unpresentability. To adapt (or re-inaugurate) an earlier question: what then would be the genre that is proper to communication-without-communication?

By now, surely, the answer is obvious: romantic literature! It is neither here nor there that Lyotard himself doesn't use this term, since its appearances within romanticism mark only the need for there to be a name for what must remain unnameable. What might be called the absolute of any concept of communication may be understood as having been reached at the point when it's felt that there is still something like communication going on, but non-conceptually. Kant calls this the sublime. As a response to the *lack* of form (the lack of genre, perhaps), the Kantian sublime describes, for Lyotard, today's (postmodern) experience of our encounters with telecommunications media, through which only communication without communication is possible. On this view (it can be inferred), to look at a painting is to feel its once-was here-and-nowness; but what is here and now about an email message, a television program or even a phone conversation? What is the time and place of an internet connection, a satellite broadcast and so on?

This may be to ask, what is the *genre* of tele-communication? For while it may be true, in a sense, that today's communications technologies are responsible for the possibility of *virtual* communities, as against 'immediate' communities that give rise to aesthetic feeling, this would not be to say that 'postmodern' communication makes it impossible to experience art. Perhaps it is simply that immediate communities engender so-called aesthetic feeling, while virtual (postmodern) communities can recognize art only in terms of what Kant called 'an outrage on the imagination'. Hence art is recognizable today only through an experience of the sublime. Postmodern 'art', then, could be only what *lacks* beauty (form, genre) in so far as it does not con-form to a communal ideal of art as such – the atrocious (disturbing, outrageous) formlessness of *Blood and Guts in High School*, for example.

By the same token, if the postmodern inaugurates the sublime as the proper response to what continues to be called – for want of a better word – 'art' today, it also repeats the romantic problem of what to call a genre that is always in excess of genre (generally and in particular)? The genre then of communication-without-communication is analogous to the romantic genre of literature as the name of what can never be present either in or to itself, and is therefore strictly unnameable. But Lyotard's mistake (if not the postmodern mistake) could be to suppose that unpresentability is proper only to forms of telecommunication rather than communication generally. It's as if for Lyotard (if not for Kant, too) the 'immediacy' of aesthetic feeling derives from a certain concept of face-to-face communication understood as actual or authentic. Against this concept, telecommunication must appear 'virtual' since it occurs in the absence (the virtual absence, as it were) of geo-temporally locatable corporeal beings. 'Perhaps,' Lyotard writes in chapter 2, 'we should set ourselves to the work of mourning the body.' Like that of romantic literature, then, the problem of telecommunication is one of presence. Romantic literature never comes: it is always be-coming. It never arrives 'in' the present, or is never quite present as such. So too with telecommunication, which occurs (if that's the right word) somewhere that is never present – never 'in' the present – as a so-called actual time and place that might be said to mark the space of a certain presence as such. On a romantic reckoning, though, genre is always 'beyond' genre, unpresentably other than or outside itself. Its essence is to remain absolutely incomplete, forever in the process of becoming – or of being *not-present*.

Could it be that 'postmodernism' names not the discovery but the affirmation of this 'not', in the form of what is either or both an inaugural repetition or a repetitive inauguration?

Starting Out/Starting Over

Again, the resources for an answer to that question may be found in chapter 1. The argument there is that the romantic genre of literature (call it what one will) is not in the power of any author (conceived either as 'textual function' or 'real historical subject') to control. Literature/genre is 'beyond' mastery, including the mastery of any subject. It is what always remains to come.

How then to define the identity of what never actually *is* because 'it' is always coming to be? In asking that question, romanticism (though it has never been able to answer it) might be said to have inaugurated a certain way of approaching or understanding literature (which is not quite the same as saying that romanticism invented *a new genre* of literature) such that literature could be understood in terms of the necessity of that question. In a word, the question of literature is inseparable from the concept of literature.

Yet this romantic 'inauguration' is also a repetition of what literature 'is' already. The romantic double-bind is that there could be no romantic *theory* of literature that was independent of literature as such. Self-questioning ('theoretical') literature was not something that started being written around the time of the Jena Romantics but is rather what literature (albeit conceived romantically) has always been, as a condition. By virtue of this condition, literature has always been unstable as regards semantic communicability, syntactic expression, aesthetic value, moral reckoning, political utility and so on. Hence, for example, while the genre of romantic poetry is 'the only one', according to the Jena Romantic Friedrich Schlegel (cited in Lacoue-Labarthe and Nancy), 'that is more than a genre', it is also *at the same time* 'the very art of poetry: in a certain sense, all poetry is or should be Romantic.'

And so no poet could ever hope to control, in a poem or a genre, the becoming of poetry, the still to come of literature. As what must always lie ahead of itself, (romantic) literature is always absolutely out of control – beyond communicability, intention or consciousness. A text like *Finnegans Wake* then is not, on this view, the end point but the starting point of literature, both the time and the place from which everything begins . . . again and again and again . . .

Not 'I'

Such a scene is played out (re-run) by Julia Kristeva in chapter 3, though she does not attribute it directly to romanticism. For her the origins of what might be called communicative instability (or indeterminacy) are historically closer to home, arising out of Saussurean linguistics, Russian Formalism and the structural anthropology of Claude Lévi-Strauss. Even so, Kristeva's account of the 'questionable subject in process' relies heavily on the Formalist notion of 'poetic language' whose characteristics are strongly analogous to romantic literature.

In poetic language we encounter – once more, for the umpteenth but never for the last time – the romantic problem of genre. What is language that its essence (as 'poetry') is revealed in the non-linguistic 'echolalias of infants' and through 'glossalalias in psychotic discourse'? By grounding her linguistic theory on the non-ground of a radical heterogeneity, Kristeva opens (or re-opens) the question of where to locate the subject ('I') within a signifying process that is so unstable as to deny any support for an ideal of 'thetic consciousness' or individual mastery? Together with the 'speech' of infants and psychotics, it is the 'genre' of romantic literature (although Kristeva doesn't call it that) which communicates without communicating the crises within 'meaning, subject, and structure' today. Such crises are a necessary part of any discourse, Kristeva argues, in so far as they testify to the force of nonsensical, ungrammatical and, to an extent, non-discursive elements (rhythm, intonation, babble and so on) which no language can hope to do without or overcome. These elements belong to what Kristeva calls the 'semiotic' order of signification, which comprises everything that might otherwise be regarded as accidental, insignificant or extraneous to a positive theory of signification as such, especially a linguistic theory. By comparison she terms 'symbolic' that order of signification (as understood in its routine or positive sense) which results in meanings that are comprehensible and communicable, because they derive from signifying systems (or genres, we might say) whose principles of sense-production have been agreed to, and may from time to time be altered, by a community. The symbolic order is not ahistorical, in other words, although it may (perhaps even must) appear so at any given moment in time. Much more radical than mere historical change, however, is the unsettling, irruptive, unpredictable and dynamic force of the semiotic order or function, whose effects could arise from an ellipsis, a grammatical infelicity, a tonal inflection, an unexpected cadence or even a typographical 'error' (where – in a novel, for example – is the place of a 'misprint'?).

And of course, in terms of any literary text, what could be more 'semiotic' than a drawing? So we might say that the drawings in *Blood and Guts in High School* are indicative of that text's affirmation of the semiotic function, which could be to say that they indicate its refusal to be understood according to the genre of the novel or a certain concept of literature. Yet let's be clear about this: even if we thought of *Blood and Guts in High School* as bad, uninteresting or offensive literature, it would press against all limits of sense to think of it as a scientific treatise or a shopping trolley. In so far as it is made from words (albeit supplemented by pictures), it is not a shopping trolley; in so far as it is made from words that have been put together in a certain way, it is not a scientific treatise. However semiotic *Blood and Guts in High School* might be, that is to say, it cannot but be symbolic at the same time. If it were absolutely semiotic (absolutely non-symbolic), it could never signify. The semiotic, in short, is an order of signification; it is not absolutely outside, but absolutely within, signification. Or to put this another way: the (romantic) problem of genre is that there is no absolute of genre, and no absolute opposite of genre.

One could say that *Blood and Guts in High School* is a lousy novel, but that wouldn't be the point. The point is that it can't be said that *Blood and Guts in High School* is *not* a novel, that it doesn't belong to a genre (and so to genre), because its 'semiotic' (or, perhaps, unpresentable) features are generically unclassifiable and therefore *Blood and Guts in High School* is 'beyond' genre or outside, in Kristeva's terms, symbolic signification.

All the same, despite the necessity of the symbolic function in *Blood and Guts in High School*, it is through the unsettling power of poetic language that the unpresentability of a signified object is revealed (as it were) beyond the limits of knowledge or the comprehension of any critical discourse or metalanguage. In this way, too, the novel's signifying identity (the authorial or narratorial 'I') is unable to close on a stable referent, whether in the form of an individuating consciousness, a transcendental ego or a thinking subject. For Kristeva, though, this is all the more reason not to give up on theory, 'but to compel it to increase its power by giving it an object beyond its limits', which she claims it is 'probably necessary to be a woman' to fully appreciate. In other words the 'lack' accorded to feminine identity, on the imputed ground that women are more instinctual and emotional (more semiotic) and less rational (symbolic) than men, is the very means by which women are better positioned to confront rather than recede from what is always heterogeneous to symbolic signification. In a word, women are the best metaphysicians of 'nothing' (as what the symbolic understands must lie beyond it) and so it may be that the only fully responsive theory of poetic language could be feminist. If 'I' is a symbolic and therefore possibly masculine concept or position, then perhaps it is only through what might be called the not-'I' of a certain order of the feminine poetic that an identity without identity could be fashioned in response to the crisis within signification.

In its neo-romantic/proto-postmodern guise of 'poetic language', however, what must literature be that we can't even say for sure who writes the stuff?

Crash!

And so it may seem that, by this point, none of literature's traditional supports – genre, author, meaning and so on – is left standing. But we ain't seen nothin' yet.

If all along we have been waiting for an answer to the question, 'What is literature?', only to keep on finding that the question keeps on coming back to us, always in another, slightly different form, perhaps it is time we took a look at this phenomenon. Or so, at any rate, we might conclude from Deleuze and Guattari's 'Rhizome' (chapter 4). If the general form of our question has been, 'What is literature that it may sometimes etc., etc. . . .', then perhaps we ought to start to pay more attention to these etceteras. Maybe literature 'is' only in the miscellany that attaches to it.

This is the approach Deleuze and Guattari take in chapter 4. For them, literature is not so much an abstract concept as an assemblage of concrete objects – books – whose workings are revealed through 'the exteriority of their relations'. Some books may be written or approached in such a way as to appear tree-like, but for Deleuze and Guattari the essence of the book is rhizomatic. An arborescent book would be assumed to have roots (hidden meanings) and a hierarchical structure that resembled a tree, with so many subplots branching out from the trunk of the narrative. A rhizomatic book (or simply a rhizome), however, would resemble grass. Unlike a tree, grass is always on the move, always forming alliances with the world outside itself as it keeps on spreading across and across the surfaces of things. Grass doesn't grow up; it spreads out. Trees settle; grass roams.

As another instance of heterogeneity, then, the rhizome is also another name for romantic literature and the question of genre. For if, as Deleuze and Guattari write, 'any point of a rhizome can be connected to anything other, and must be', this is no less true of Schlegel's understanding of romantic poetry, as cited by Lacoue-Labarthe and Nancy in chapter 1, which 'includes everything poetic from the largest system of art, itself containing other systems, down to the breath or kiss that the child-poet exhales in an artless song'. It is therefore of little wonder that the famous fragment 116 of the *Athenaeum*, the Jena group's journal, should define the genre of romantic poetry as 'still in the process of becoming, and it is its proper essence that it is always only becoming, and that it is never capable of completing itself.' Or as Deleuze and Guattari put it, only somewhat differently, more than a century-and-a-half later: 'A rhizome ceaselessly establishes connections between semiotic chains, organizations of power, and circumstances relative to the arts, sciences, and social struggles.'

Postmodern Ethics

In the eternal return of romanticism that characterizes Part I of this anthology, however, could it be that the many recurrences of the question of genre overshadow another, possibly more important, question – of ethics? For what is the point of being able to say that *Blood and Guts in High School* is a work of romantic literature or postmodern literature, when it might be that you want to say it's a lousy book (or indeed that it's a great one)? What's the point of postmodern literary theory (if that's what we've been doing here) if all it can do is to provide us with another – whether familiar or radical – metaphysics, when maybe we should have been looking for an *ethics* all along?[9]

That is not an easy question to answer, though at least one point can be made for now. The question assumes there to be a fundamental difference between metaphysics and ethics. On this assumption, one might think it is metaphysical to ask the question of literature and ethical to ask questions about individual works of literature. Hence metaphysics has to do with impractical abstractions, while ethics has to do with pragmatic particularities.

Well, yes . . . but not quite. Particularities are not simply just available to us in terms of what they ideally 'are', outside all consideration of mediating contingencies. We could not even recognize a particularity in the first place if we didn't see it as something other than itself – an instance of a general category of related particularities, each of which is therefore all the less particular for being able to be generalized.

Doesn't this repeat the question of genre once again, however? For what is particular to *a* genre, the romantics may have asked, if every genre always turns out to exceed what are supposed to be its particularities? Or, to take this back to chapter 2, what is particular to telecommunication (as against communication generally) such that Lyotard appears to regard it as 'post-communicative'?

The point is that what might be called the ethical question still remains within the question of genre, the romantic question of literature. No more nor less than genre, there may be no general system of ethics; but that is not to say that every ethical response or action is entirely unmediated, completely devoid of exterior relations and absolutely singular unto itself. Ethics may well be a pragmatics, although not in the sense of being opposed to metaphysics. Indeed, any ethics that presents itself as anti-metaphysical (the ethics of a certain affirmation of the 'beyonds' of literature, genre, signification and so on could mark an interesting case in point) should be called by its proper name – a morality.

In turning to ethics in Part II, then, we are not therefore turning away from genre. This is clear from chapter 5 where Steven Connor argues that the postmodern preference for parody and pastiche is not at all an obviously unambiguous sign of ethical irresponsibility. His concern is with the contemporary genre of rewriting, as it might be called, in which a well known work of literature (*Dr Jekyll and Mr Hyde, Lord of the Flies* and *Robinson Crusoe* are the relevant examples here) is 'rewritten' to form a new work (Emma Tennant's *Two Women of London*, Marianne Wiggins' *John Dollar* and J. M. Coetzee's *Foe*, respectively). And so the question arises: should this practice – or as we might want to say, this genre – be lauded or decried? The point for Connor is rather more to explain than to judge the genre of rewriting (at least in so far as it involves the examples he has chosen), although it cannot go unnoticed that his explanations are inseparable, in the end, from his estimation of the ethics of rewriting, or at any rate from the ethics of the rewritings he chooses to discuss. The further point for us might be that a question should arise at all in respect of 'rewriting', given that it could be based only on an imagined concept of generic purity – as if romanticism had never happened! Certainly it seems scarcely credible that the genre of rewriting (or surely by now, the genre of writing) calls for either approval or disavowal, which would be absurd (or ungrammatical) if directed at the genre of tragedy, say, or the genre of poetry. It would seem ridiculous to ask whether we *approved* of tragedy, for example. Hence it must be that for the legitimacy of 'rewriting' to be called into question, its generic standing has to be refuted. Without genre there can be no writing, in other words. On that score rewriting is not a genre, and cannot therefore be understood as writing.

What the hell is it, then? Once more, this is to ask the question of genre. For romanticism, the essence or identity of a genre (and of genre) always remains to come, since there is no end to the miscellaneous exteriorities to which a genre (or genre) could find itself in relation. The identity of the romantic genre thus remains a kind of mystery, which would seem to be self-defeating of the whole point of genre. Why 'genre' if its limits are indeterminate, especially if the absolute of genre *is* this (its) indeterminacy? But to recoil from the idea that genre is unsettling would be to suppose that it could be otherwise, that genre is a way of distinguishing between different types of writing and between what absolutely is and isn't 'writing' in the first place. In which case, why should a rewriting of *Robinson Crusoe* be any more troublesome to a concept of writing than the appearance of a blank page in *Tristram Shandy*, the semantic indeterminacy of *Finnegans Wake*, the lascivious cartoons of *Blood and Guts in High School* – or even the typographical heterogeneity of Hasan's early essay on postmodernism?

If each of those texts participates in a certain order of generic hybridity, can it be said that there is anything unusual about that? The view put by Thomas Docherty in chapter 6 is that generic hybridity is indeed exceptional, the knowledge of which is what distinguishes postmodern literature as a genre in its own right. For Docherty, postmodern narrative tends 'towards an endlessly proliferating heterogenerity' such that characterization is never finally revealed but always 'deferred as the proliferation of information about the character leads into irrationality, incoherence, or self-contradiction'. Hence postmodern literature 'knows' *nothing*, or it knows that there is no representational form of characterization that could hope to account for or capture a character's 'identity', whose essence is to remain unpresentable. Such knowledge is an ethics, Docherty maintains, because it substitutes a search (on the reader's part) for the ontology of character (identity) with the need to respond pragmatically to the non-totalizing particularities of the alterity of character (difference). This is an ethical substitution because it locates the reader, like a character, as a marginalized subject-in-process within textuality, such that through his or her decentered subjectivity a reader might begin to understand some of the difficulties of being 'other'. Hence it may be that, following Kristeva, the ideal postmodern reading position is a feminized one.

This point is taken even further by Luce Irigaray in chapter 7. In French, the word 'genre' carries the sense of 'gender', and so for Irigaray the question of genre is unavoidably rent by sexual difference. However, despite the existence of a 'third' genre (the feminine), most discourse is positioned as masculine even when it is supposedly neutral. 'Man gives his *genre* to the universe', Irigaray argues, 'just as he wants to give his name to his children and his property.' The feminine genre is thus 'always subordinated to the principal *genre*', thereby repressing the operations of sexual difference. So what is at stake ethically, as Irigaray sees it, is the need to develop a *style* of discourse which acknowledges the productive force of the differences between the sexes. Such a style would remain irreducible to its content and to structures of opposition (for example, masculine/feminine); in its hybridity it would always exceed the limitations of genre. Irigaray gives the example of her own writing style, in which 'its language is already allied with other languages'. In its alliances, then, which cannot easily be understood as linguistic in themselves, her style might be said to be rhizomatic (and therefore romantic) through its refusal to settle down into a totality. By its very multiplicity, such a style resists the hermeneutic demand to make sense according to laws of cognition that deny the multiplicity of genre (gender). In short, an ethics of sexual difference (as opposed to a traditional morality of the sexes) can be achieved only through styles of discourse that embrace the power of genre to always go beyond attempts to systematize or historicize differences between genres. It is not differences between but the difference within genre that releases sexual difference, and which is at the same time produced by sexual difference.

Perhaps an example of what Irigaray means by ethical ('sexuate') writing is discussed by Hélène Cixous in chapter 8, in the form of Clarice Lispector's *Near to the Wild Heart* (Braz. 1943). This text is distinguished by its *incompletion*, according to Cixous, a characteristic she associates also with the writings of Joyce, Maurice Blanchot and Franz Kafka. By this she means that such writing is closer to 'the origin of the gesture of writing' than to writing as such – as if such writing were an expression of a pure *desire* to write, unencumbered by a desire to mean. In its incompletion – marked for example by the informality, if not the ungrammaticality, of its prose and by the immaturity of its author (who was only seventeen) – Lispector's text is yet another reminder that the question of literature always positively lacks a definitive answer or totalizing signified. Above all, though, *Near to the Wild Heart* is closest to an Irigarayan ethics for its complete indifference (as it were) to an oppositional or binary way of thinking. It is this (what might be called its morality without morality) that strikes Cixous as most remarkable about the text, such that its ethics can be understood as an affirmation of *living* outside the law. For Lispector, Cixous notes, 'it is bad to steal if one steals while being afraid', since fear can arise only from within the determinations of moral law. But outside or beyond that law, although not in *opposition* to it, it is possible to 'steal' without stealing: 'To steal without fear is not to steal at all.' In this way Lispector's text offers 'a critique of metaphysics', Cixous argues, rather than a counter-morality in its refusal to endorse a moral code which is always at the same time political. And the target of that critique is no less a notion of the finality of writing (or of genre) than a system of moral injunctions and inducements. Lispector's ethics, then, are inseparable from a certain style of writing, as a style of living, which manifests a disregard for laws – including, if not above all, the law of genre.[10]

Postmodern Space

But in order for all this not to sound like so much grandiose theorizing, perhaps we should ask in what kind of dimensions or space the subject of such an ethics might exist? This is to some extent the question asked by

Kristin Ross in chapter 9. For her, although she does not quite put it like this, what might be called the ethical turn associated with postmodernism may not so much reveal as obfuscate contemporary reality. If so, this may have to do with a conception of ethics that sees it as a namby-pamby middle-class excuse for politics, a wishy-washy refuge from the rough-and-tumble effects of systematic corporate, institutional, governmental, class and other forms of real power that no theoretical agonies over 'the question of genre' or 'the question of woman' could ever hope to address, let alone begin to help to overcome. On this view, if politics belongs to times and places (Vietnam in the 1960s, Bosnia in the late 1990s, the ongoing struggles of labour movements everywhere since around the mid-nineteenth century), ethics 'belongs' only to a virtual or cyber 'space', whose historical and class origins in the English-speaking world are obscured from within but none the less derive from the 'French'-envy of a post-1960s knowledge elite, indifferent to the actual inequalities of life and obsessed, perversely if not obscenely, with the insignificant vagaries of metaphysics, rather than a grass-roots all-join-in passion for nuts-and-bolts social change in the here and now!

Writing on behalf of a cultural studies agenda, Ross sees the problem of postmodernism precisely in terms of its 'effacement of the historical', such that the notion of a sort of all-encompassing 'cyberspace' (which is not a term she employs) has been substituted for a geo-political sense of time and place. This substitution begins to occur, for Ross, in the mid twentieth-century American 'takeover' of the meaning of culture from its centuries-long guardianship by Europeans. Significantly, the takeover starts out with the Americanization – the rewriting, as it were – of the European (predominantly British) *genre* of detective fiction, as perhaps the great American crime writer Raymond Chandler was the first to suggest in a famous essay, published in 1949, called 'The Simple Art of Murder'. It is there that Chandler differentiates between the superficial, plot-driven formalism of British detective fiction of that time and the hard-boiled, 'shocking' truth of the life-imitating American variety. Whereas British detective fiction was mostly rustic in setting, its US counterpart was exclusively urban – and this is a key point in the cultural takeover, or changeover, that Ross describes (if only in a sense to debunk). Working against Fredric Jameson, she argues that a certain myth of alienation (exemplarized especially in the LA sprawl of Chandler's novels) passed through and out of American crime writing to take hold as a kind of global (Westernized) origin myth of the decentered 'postmodern' subject. For Ross, however, such a 'myth' of decentring obscures, if not obliterates, the ongoing class-historical positionings of subjects by and within 'the national state apparatus'. Despite a widespread notion that culture has been 'internationalized' (turned into a sort of frozen no-place of the eternal now), Ross stands up for an old-fashioned regionalism in which she believes that most of us still live out (or experience) our everyday lives. Nevertheless, 'lived experience' now ain't what it used to be, and there is no question for Ross that experiences of suburbia today cannot be explained as distorted or impoverished forms of an earlier, 'authentic' mode of life or 'structure of feeling' (as Raymond Williams famously put it). Whether real or imagined, as it were, postmodern alienation is *felt*, and this alone is sufficient cause for taking 'the post' seriously – not necessarily as the truth about the present historical moment, but as a way of explaining it.

This explanation – of the tension between and within the internationalized (pan-American, placeless) postmodern subject and the 'real-historical' subject, as it were – is played out today, Ross argues, not in post-Chandleresque detective fiction from the US but in the crime novels of French writer Didier Daeninckx, whose chosen genre is the one that Chandler made over so forcibly into his own. Hence the genre of detective fiction has undergone many geographical to-ings and fro-ings across the past century-and-a-half: beginning as a new-world genre (with Edgar Allan Poe as its progenitor), it found fame in the UK (through Arthur Conan Doyle and afterwards, Agatha Christie), was later re-made in the US as a distinctively urban form and has now come back (via the reworkings of Chandler and other American writers of the 1930s to 1950s) to the old world, to be rewritten yet again! For Ross, the significance of this latest make-over is that Daeninckx's novels raise the political stakes of Chandler's reinvention of detective fiction as an authentic representation of modern everyday life. In a way, though, Chandler might be said to have faked it: his famous LA 'mean streets' of the 1940s belong, Ross quotes others to observe, to a real-world LA of the 1930s, on which score it could be argued that Chandler didn't so much authenticate as romanticize the lived reality he claimed to have set out to represent. This is pretty much the line that Ross takes, though of course it holds only on the basis of a certain theory of representation which it might be well to set against some of the points I made earlier, especially concerning chapters 1 and 2.

Nevertheless, given an implied distinction in chapter 9 between 'virtual authenticity' (Chandler) and 'actual authenticity' (Daeninckx), it's clear that the higher value accrues to the latter on account of Daeninckx's success in representing the here-and-nowness of everyday life at the metropolitan edges of Paris in the 1980s, specifically in the region of 'the

banlieux', a run-down knocked-up urban wilderness of developmental planning gone amok, allotted to the poor as their 'place' in the city. But for
most Parisians, Ross argues, the *banlieux* comprise only a virtual 'space'
somewhere far away from the experiences of their own daily lives. And so
it turns out that there is a higher value still (beyond just representational
authenticity) to Daeninckx's writing – namely, its political motivation to
give readers an *experience* of the *banlieux* as a *place* which is here, right
now. As Ross tells it, Daeninckx understands his purpose as a writer of
detective fiction to be one of 'tricking' his readers 'into encountering the
intolerable effects of uneven development in their own immediate surroundings by the allure of a fairly traditional and suspenseful murder plot.'

From this we might be tempted to draw the moral that writing about
place is good, but writing about space is bad. Yet everything we have
come across to do with writing so far should caution us (and I see no
reason not to think of this as a 'postmodern' caveat, although it could go
by other names) to wonder whether the very idea of 'place' (as a some
'thing' before it is a some 'where') isn't made possible *within* writing? The
unpresentable, after all, is not simply what exists *prior* to representation,
which cannot be re-presented. It is what is given us to experience or
contemplate from within representation. The unpresentability of genre,
for example, is not pre-existent to genre, but simultaneous to it. Instead
of opposing 'place' to 'space', then, we could say that 'space' is a concept
which acknowledges the unpresentability (or, in a sense, the always already virtuality) of 'place', whereas 'place' presupposes its own presentability and so lends itself to more apparently down-to-earth 'political'
discourses on dispossession, inequality and suffering.

POSTcyberGENDERpunkPOLITICS

In chapter 10, however, which is also written from a cultural studies
perspective (albeit at the same time a feminist one), Anne Balsamo takes
a rather different approach from Ross to the politics of postmodern
space. Balsamo is interested in science fiction, rather than crime fiction,
and particularly in the contemporary subgenre of cyberpunk, an SF
make-over that could be likened to the hard-boiled detective novel
in terms of its generic reinventiveness. (For an excellent potted history of
SF, with particular attention to the interconnections of cyberpunk and
postmodernism, see chapter 11, by Brian McHale.) From a certain
feminist perspective, though, one problem with cyberpunk could be that

most of it is written by men, which is perhaps why Balsamo is so interested in the work of one of the very few women writing in the genre, Pat
Cadigan.

On Balsamo's reading, Cadigan's *Synners* (1991) suggests a number of
feminist insights into the gender politics of cyberspace that complexify
rather than deny women's relationships to the 'materiality' of their bodies. As with Kristeva in chapter 3 and Irigaray in chapter 7, then, the
recognition of female corporeality as a site of powerful drives and expressions is affirmed in Cadigan, or at any rate in Balsamo's reading of her. As
Balsamo sees it, the female body appears in *Synners* as 'a body that
labours', while men's bodies are represented as 'repressed or disappearing
[into cyberspace]'. The assumption seems to be that men are socialized to
feel uncomfortable with themselves (in their bodies) and are therefore
more likely to seek out virtual (that is, socially escapist) relationships with
and through technology. On this assumption the cyberpunk imagined-
world of cyberspace would be the ultimate men's fantasy. Women's better understanding of the materiality of their bodies (which one is tempted
to call an 'authentic' understanding), however, allows them to see technologies for what they are – tools for getting things done. Historically,
moreover, women have rarely been in positions of power over technologies, either being superseded by them in the workplace or relegated to the
role of bottom-level users. For Balsamo, this makes women the best *critics* of technology (the resonance with Kristeva's claim that women are the
best theorists of language, although undoubtedly unintended, cannot go
unremarked), and so they are more likely than men to develop highly
complex relations to postmodern space – instead of wanting simply to
escape into it for the sake of getting away from it all.

Even so, despite a more genuine engagement with 'space' than Ross
evinces, Balsamo still comes down on the side of 'place'. Hers may be the
place – or the ground – of feminine corporeality rather than Parisian
poverty, but it would seem to be no less fundamental (on the contrary, no
doubt) for being gendered than for being classed. On such firm footing
(the absolutes of women's bodily emplacement or of the Parisian poor's
cultural displacement), perhaps it's all too easy to be political.

After Pynchon

Among the most common charges levelled at 'the post' is its lack of
political conviction – a charge that may arise out of a certain metaphysi-

cal faith in a pre-romantic *genre* of political ideas and actions. But if (as we might say that postmodernism believes, regardless of whether it does so knowingly) romanticism unsettled the concept of genre for evermore, then how could other concepts – such as 'politics' – go on being presentable in the wake of that disturbance, when it is precisely the question of representation that the unsettling of genre opened up to endlessly experimental forms of speculation and signification?

These forms are irreducible to a classical understanding of genre, and the rhizomatic process of their borrowings from and overlappings with each other cannot be credited as a postmodern invention. This is McHale's point in chapter 11, where he argues that not even a distinction between so-called 'high' and 'low' orders of generic production is sustainable. In his words, 'the constant traffic between low and high – the high art appropriation of pop art models and the reciprocal assimilation by pop art genres of "cast-off" high art models – is one of the universal engines driving the history of literary (and, more generally, cultural) forms.' Following this, perhaps an interesting comparison between *Tristram Shandy* and *Blood and Guts in High School* remains to be drawn in terms of how each exploits a different set of popular (literary and non-literary) genres, despite the canonical status of the one and the high art pretensions of the other, though that is somewhat by the by for now.

In tracing the transferences and interferences between genres, McHale is able to build a picture of cyberpunk that could be described as interactive or hypertextual. But it could also be described as romantic in so far as it relies on a concept of genre that takes into account such elements as accidents and atmospheres in the production of genres, elements which therefore in a sense 'belong' to genre. For cyberpunk, such an element is the work of American novelist Thomas Pynchon whose *Gravity's Rainbow* (1973) in particular is a source of many in-jokes, scenes and subplots in cyberpunk fiction, as McHale notes. Over and above the documentable evidence, though, Pynchon's influence on the genre is undeniable, if also unpresentable, to the point even where McHale wonders whether the celebrated opening sentence of William Gibson's *Neuromancer* (1984), the most famous of all cyberpunk novels, may not be an allusion to a sentence from Pynchon's *The Crying of Lot 49* (1965) – never mind the lack of any strong formal similarities between them.

McHale is right all the same to see Pynchon behind almost every word of cyberpunk, even though he isn't. His unpresentability within the genre is Elvis-like in proportion, and it's this (a quality more of admiration than direct influence) that belongs to the genre, rather than a set of factual correspondences. Indeed, Pynchon's unpresentability within or to postmodernism generally (especially in the US) is often remarked upon, frequently in relation to *The Crying of Lot 49*. Usually what is held to mark out this notoriously enigmatic little book as an exemplary (if not inaugural) postmodern text is its supposed theme of paranoid subjectivity, understood as a condition or an effect of the contemporary disbelief in metanarratives. As Tony Thwaites argues in chapter 12, however, paranoia is not quite containable as part of the thematics of Pynchon's novel, belonging only at the level of content; it belongs rather to the style or structure of the text (the genre of writing) and is therefore irreducible to the sign of an underlying disorder 'within' the subject's psyche.

Psych, Out!

If Pynchon's heroine, Oedipa Maas, is paranoid, it's not because she lacks order within herself, but because she lacks a guarantee that there is any order in the world outside and all around her. Nor is this merely a crisis of faith on her part, as though some way could be found of restoring Oedipa's confidence in the orderly regulations of history and everyday life. Her whole problem is that she can't decide the nature – or the genre – of the problem facing her; worse, she can't even be sure if she *is* faced with a problem . . . outside the problem of the fact that she thinks she might be. For Oedipa, then, the whole problem is that she doesn't quite know if there is a whole problem, which, understandably enough, she finds pretty terrifying.

Yet her further problem, which could be the real problem (or the problem of the real), is that she can't quite locate the source of her terror. It could be the result of an unconscious disturbance, or the fact that reality as it appears is completely the opposite of what it seems. But it could also be that someone (probably her ex-lover, Pierce Inverarity) has set her up to think that reality is topsy-turvy, or to think she's mad. Or of course it could be that her very contemplation of the possibility that reality is really otherwise, or her contemplation of the possibility that someone has set her up to think it could be, is the very proof that she's gone hopelessly insane, which may of course be true. But how to tell?

Faced with that dilemma (namely, of whether she's found or imagined a dilemma, stumbled across it or made it up), Oedipa's whole identity is open to endless speculation, but so too is what might be called the identity of identity. Nothing is absolutely what it seems (or at any rate there's no absolute certainty that anything is) in *The Crying of Lot 49*, and so even the identity of what might count as a 'fact' remains indeterminate. In this way the novel may be said to posit a sort of cyberspace in which the representation of reality is so convincing as to make it seem irrelevant to ask, what are its grounds? As Thwaites argues, though, this would be to presuppose that *prior* to representation (or before the postmodern cyber, as it were), reality was just there . . . in all its gloriously unmediated, non-representational, a-signifying, neutered self-identity. It would be as if, in Thwaites's heavily ironic words, there is no reality now, within the postmodern condition, 'but once, somewhere and sometime, somehow, before representation began its insidious curvature back onto itself as simulation, there might, just might, have been a real upon which the successive negations of the image could act.' It would be as if a metaphysical notion of 'space', that is, had supplanted a historical notion of 'place' – as if the structures of belonging and identity were once absolutely outside representation (the question of genre) as the un-pretextual basis of everyday life.

It is clear from chapter 12 that some of the claims of postmodernism – especially those of Jean Baudrillard, whose ideas come in for some astute questioning by Thwaites – are a bit over the top. Hence the cautionary approaches of Ross and Balsamo in chapters 9 and 10 are entirely warranted, even if there is room for disagreement with their understandings of postmodernism. In Ross's case, for example, one could say that her position depends (as, ironically, does Baudrillard's) on the priority of place over representations of place. Place is prior, simulation is post. A 'good' representation, then, doesn't stray too far from its referent (and so much the better if its referent is 'downtrodden class'), which is the quality that Ross admires in Daeninckx's writing. By contrast, the worst representation of all (pure empty signifier) is of the type that conveys all the *appearance* of a good representation, but in fact has nothing to represent except its own representational power (or perhaps its delight in that power). So Raymond Chandler's representation, in the 1950s, of 1930s LA is 'bad' because it convincingly passes itself off as a representation of LA in the 1950s. This is representation as *simulation* (postmodern representation, as it were), and Ross differs from Baudrillard in her relation to it only in so far as she disapproves of simulation whereas he is all in favour of it. Good forms of representation (good genres of representation) are, on this view, historically and politically grounded; they convey a sense of place. Bad representation (bad genre) is so all over the place, however, that it refers only to an imagined world of cyberspace, in which all identity markers (of sex and gender, race and ethnicity, history, culture, politics and so on) have no location outside the text.

The TeXt-Files

What if, however, there is 'nothing' outside the text? Far from this having to be an overwhelmingly metaphysical question, it may be that it's a perfectly mundane one – albeit the fact of its mundanity could be the sign of its belonging to the postmodern condition. This might be to say that if postmodernism marks a return to romanticism, it does so in the absence of the possibility of a sense of being overwhelmed. For postmodernism, then, the sublime would *be* its absence, in so far as the very mundanity of the sublime could be nothing but the simulacrum of 'an outrage on the imagination'. A perfect example of this (the 'dumbing down' of the sublime, as it were) might be the ordinariness of the paranormal as shown each week on *The X-Files*, where the invariably dead-pan response to the latest conspiratorial cover-up of world-historical proportions may be all that separates it from the still incredulous disbelief of Oedipa Maas, in *The Crying of Lot 49*, towards the possibility that history has been tampered with. Yet in that separation or difference, however slight and equivocal, perhaps a certain historical metaphysics of the sublime is revealed: in Pynchon there remains the possibility of being confounded, even if its source (a secret postal system going back to the Middle Ages) is seemingly preposterous; by the time of *The X-Files*, though (and this is not to argue for a distinction between 'early' and 'late' forms of postmodernism, albeit some may see it that way), the preposterous has taken over from the real, defining it in terms of whatever it's most apparently not. And once reality becomes all but unbelievable (which is where, in more than one sense, *The X-Files* comes in and *The Crying of Lot 49* goes out), why get worked up about it?

If, moreover, there's no hope of hermeneutic closure from within a text like *The X-Files* or *Lot 49*, what hope could there be of finding a space outside the text from which to assert the mastery of a critical discourse (a metalanguage) over the text's own anticipation, and subsequent undermining, of seemingly every possible interpretive move and counter-move? As Roland Barthes argues in chapter 13, any theory of what he calls 'the text' (as against 'the work', marked by a certain order of linguistic and – for us especially – generic stability) 'cannot be satisfied by a metalinguistic exposition: the destruction of meta-language, or at least (since it may be necessary provisionally to resort to meta-language) its calling into doubt, is part of the theory itself'.

Barthes' famous essay on what has since come to be known again as the unpresentability of text (and so it would be well to compare his 'text' with romantic 'literature') may be seen to repeat, or perhaps to inaugurate once more, the question of genre. What is the genre of the text, in other words, and what is the genre proper to its commentary? For Barthes the answer lies in an understanding of the text not as object, but as process. In its irreducible multiplicity (and not merely its generic hybridity) the text calls for a response that goes beyond a standard sense of reading (the space of commentary), as if the text were after all a kind of finished product able to be classified (or objectified) as literature according to a system of differences imposed on writing. But what if the text (or indeed writing) is the name of what resists being systematized or classified? What genre would then be proper to a theory of the text conceived in terms of its impenetrability to theory (at any rate in the sense of being thematized)? Here again it would be necessary to return to Lacoue-Labarthe and Nancy, but let it suffice for now that Barthes' response is that any theory of the text 'can coincide only with *a practice of writing*' (emphasis added).

No doubt this is not the sort of response that everyone would have hoped for.

Postmodern Writing

Judging from chapter 14, certainly, Ralph Cohen might have hoped for more. For him, there is just no getting away from genre, despite what he sees as postmodern attempts at doing so. Hence it would be impossible to have a non-generic understanding of writing, for example (as though this were what 'writing' intimates). On Cohen's account, the concept of genre already accommodates notions of hybridity and heterogeneity, whether as 'multiple discourses and discontinuous structures' or 'the foregrounding of literary artifice' and so on. What postmodern theories of generic 'blurring' or 'intertextuality' forget, then, is that 'every text is a member of one or more genres', as Cohen puts it. But while every text must be generically mixed or hybrid, it doesn't follow necessarily that every genre is always already impure or divided from itself, rent or contaminated from within. And perhaps it's this latter point about the irreducible multiplicity or the irreducible heterogeneity of genre that belongs to postmodern literary theory (albeit after, or still as, romanticism), rather than the far less radical point about generic hybridity being a necessary feature of actual instances of writing or of every text-in-particular. In that case Cohen could be said to mistake postmodern genre (or postmodern writing) for an affirmation of generic hybridity, when perhaps it should be understood as a reaffirmation of the romantic question of literature as the unpresentability of what 'it' is.

All the same, Cohen's insistence on the mundanity of hybridity is a useful counter against a certain tendency within postmodernism (if only by attribution) to regard all its ideas and practices as radically new and unsettling. This is true as well of John Barth's 'The Literature of Exhaustion' (see chapter 15), which makes the point that what we might think of now as postmodern writing is not at all lacking in historical precedents. Barth's argument (already partially glimpsed through our discussion of *Tristram Shandy* above) is not simply that certain works of literature from the past can be seen in terms of metafictive or postmodern writing today; it's that, from the beginning, literature was always already self-reflexive or self-questioning about what 'it' is. The genre of the realist novel, then, would be, on this argument, merely a passing phase in a discontinuous history of representation, a phase marked by its aberrant (and in a sense non-literary) belief in the presence and presentability of the real. The problem of Joyce, then, or, for us, the problem of postmodern writing, might be said to re-engage with the question of literature precisely in so far as it re-opens the question of genre.

For all that, Barth remains in no doubt as to the qualities of good literature, however much he might be in favour of a certain order of experimental or 'self-imitating' writing. For him, those qualities reside in a notion of the writing subject as an expressive and technical genius capable of producing 'the kind of art that not many people can *do*: the kind that requires expertise and artistry as well as bright aesthetic ideas and/or inspiration'.

Perhaps, though, it is precisely 'the nostalgia of representation', as Jenaro Talens calls it in chapter 16 and of which Barth's faith in a grounding concept of authorial sovereignty is an example, that postmodern writing may be said to try to work – or to write – against. The nostalgia that Talens has in mind can be identified as a belief in 'the idea of a centred subject whose life the literary text refers to', suggesting that John Barth's critique of realist representation is not, in our terms, a critique of representation as such. Nevertheless, if Barth still holds to an ideal of good writing based on the writing subject's mastery over representation, it should be noted that Talens too is deeply vested in that ideal, although for him good writing conveys a sense of political consciousness exhibited as an understanding of the subject's bodily emplacement within social history. As with Kristin Ross in chapter 9, then, Talens is opposed to what he sees as a certain *excessive* decentring of the postmodern subject resulting in its dis-location. It's as if postmodern writing's resistance to 'the nostalgia of representation' can sometimes go too far, as Talens tells it, leaving absolutely nothing except 'the bodiless subject of the simulacrum' in its wake.

Say Something!

What might be called 'bad' postmodern representation (simulation) often stands accused therefore of relativism. The charge seems to be that too much representational activity or self-reflexivity (a sort of hyper-obsessiveness with the question of genre, as it were) can result in all too little in the way of value judgements, a case of much ado about nothing. This is the view of Catherine Burgass in chapter 17, in which she argues that the challenge facing postmodern writing now is 'to repoliticize postmodern discourse after the radical relativism perceived as a necessary apolitical and quietistic consequence of deconstruction'.

As I have argued elsewhere, especially in my *Postmodern Literary Theory: An Introduction*, there really are no good reasons for regarding deconstruction (or poststructuralism) as 'apolitical'; hence the alleged 'radical relativism' of postmodern writing cannot be a 'consequence of deconstruction'. Be that as it may (and there's no room here to go back over those arguments, which others have made as well),[11] the conflation of the two 'posts' under the collecting nomenclature of 'the' post is all too common, leading to the absurdly unprofessional view that the ideas of Lyotard, Baudrillard, Lacan, Kristeva, Barthes, Irigaray, Deleuze, Foucault and Derrida (not to mention Heidegger and Nietzsche) are all virtually the same! These figures' indistinguishability from each other is seen, certainly from an Anglo perspective, usually to result from their alleged indifference to statements of positive value, unless in the 'apolitical' guise of performative statements *about* value.

The post's 'evacuation of evaluation', as it were, is traced by Burgass (via Barbara Hernstein Smith) to the Enlightenment split between fact and value, the one belonging as the proper object of the sciences and the other of the humanities. Within literary studies, however, a certain wrong turn occurred in the early part of the twentieth century such that a kind of

'science envy' took hold as the driving force of literary-critical investigation, making evaluation obsolete. Later, when literary studies went 'post',
there was even less need of evaluative work because now there wasn't
even a fact/value distinction any more, not after Lyotard explained to
everybody they no longer believed in 'metanarratives' like science and so
we all came to understand at last what Nietzsche meant when he said,
'There are no facts, only interpretations'.[12] (This is of course what Derrida
means by 'there is nothing outside the text'!)

On this (by no means exclusively Burgass's) account, the post's only
hope of rediscovering 'good' representation is to stop asking the question of genre and return (though by now we may feel justified in asking,
to where? to when?) to an acceptance *of* genre, that there simply *are*
genres, at least for all intents and purposes, as Cohen argues in chapter
14. Hence for Burgass, Steven Connor's recent support, in his *Theory
and Cultural Value*, for 'the imperative of value (the value of value
itself)' just isn't enough, although at least it does count as a 'post' recognition of the need for evaluative judgement. A theory of 'the value of
value', however, is still too close to a romantic theory of literature as the
theory of itself. What is needed instead is for the post to move on to
become a critical practice rather than to go on being a theoretical one –
and the proper genre of criticism is concerned with the production of
'positive value judgements'.

While there is certainly cause for questions to be asked of postmodern
evaluation, Burgass's account of the post may be too broad a category
(though others would surely disagree) to allow her questions to be effective. This is not the case in chapter 18, however, where William Rasch
asks very similar questions to those of Burgass, but directs them at the
work of Jean-François Lyotard instead of an all-encompassing 'post'.

In particular, Rasch is interested in Lyotard's insistence on the self-
referentiality of utterances, the claim being that what an utterance 'says'
cannot be dissociated from what it says about itself. Yet there is nothing
especially new or postmodern about this 'paradox', according to Rasch,
for indeed it's as old as modernity. Take away the transcendental grounds
of utterance (in the form of God, the divine right of kings and so on) and
what you're left with is 'self-reference in the guises of historicism (all
statements, including this one, are historically conditioned), psychoanalysis (all statements, including this one, are the result of sublimation), political philosophy (all philosophy, including this one, is ideological), and
rhetorical analysis (all statements, including this one, are rhetorical)'. The
paradox of self-reference may indeed be paradoxical, but that doesn't

make it postmodern (at least not in the sense of *belonging* to the post except in the form of a return or repetition).

Lyotard's mistake, for Rasch, is to suppose that because the utterances of modernity lack a transcendental basis, therefore they don't really *say* anything. Instead they conform simply to the rules of particular 'language games', a concept that Lyotard derives from the Austrian philosopher Ludwig Wittgenstein. Where Lyotard goes wrong is in attributing to each language game a 'strict autonomy', almost as if (in our terms) the romantic question of genre had never been asked, as if each language game comprised an order of absolute generic purity or singularity.[13] Due to their absolute differences from one another, modes of communication (language games) could never hope to express what might be called the injustice of an injustice, or the injustice of any singular instance of injustice (injustice-in-particular). Hence it could be only by means of communication without communication (from outside or beyond communication as such) that an injustice could ever hope to speak or be heard to have spoken. It is here, as Rasch explains, in the gaps and silences between language games, that Lyotard locates what he calls the differend, an adaptation of the Kantian sublime. But the problem of the differend may be that its appeal to an outside is recognizable only from within the space to which it is supposedly external. Or as Rash (paraphrasing Niklas Luhmann) puts it, 'paradoxical circularity cannot be avoided by appeals to the outside; what escapes the system can only be observed, and therefore communicated, from within the system, and that which can be communicated is, by definition, part of the system.'

Politics and Friendship

Yet for all that Rasch's critique of Lyotard is astute and challenging, it has to be said that its force depends on a certain faith in the (transcendental) stability of a certain notion of 'system' in general. Such faith, judging from Michel Foucault's reading (in chapter 19) of Deleuze and Guattari's *Anti-Oedipus*, may not simply be unwarranted – it may be fascist! On Foucault's account of his friends' project, any idea of system (genre, for example) would be 'fascist' in so far as the ultimate aim of systems is to discipline human desires by subjecting them, subtly or otherwise, to regimes of prohibitions. In this light, a text such as *Blood and Guts in High School* might be seen as 'political' (in the terms Foucault uses here) for the force of its resistance to a notion of genre conceived as a system of limits governing a set of practices and expectations. Perhaps, then, Acker's text is an indirect or asystematic response to Foucault's entreaty to '[p]refer what is positive and multiple, difference over uniformity, flows over unities, mobile arrangements over systems', which he takes to be the political lesson – or the ethics – of *Anti-Oedipus*.

And so it may be that, as Foucault sees it, Deleuze and Guattari announce not so much a new genre of politics as a new concept of genre, albeit one that in its asystematic pragmatics (a sort of genreless micropolitics of the everyday, which is what Foucault seems to mean by 'ethics' here) is as far from a concept as could be. But it would not, if so, be without certain problems.

Some of these are addressed in chapter 20, by Alec McHoul. For him the question might be put as follows: before deciding on political intervention or action, what is the basis for deciding? Deleuze and Guattari's point (at least as Foucault makes it) is that we cannot afford to allow our decisions to be decided by a system – whether of literature or politics, or whatever – because in doing so we give ourselves over to a higher power, if not to power itself. If every decision belongs to a system (or a genre), then it does not belong to anyone – it's no one's responsibility at all.[14] If it's just *true* that *Jane Eyre* is a superior work of literature to *Blood and Guts in High School*, then we may want to wonder how, if we were to accept the 'truth' of that comparison, we'd be able to find the resources to object to instances of racism, say, which are always grounded in the 'obviousness' of a superior/inferior distinction. If 'decisions' about the superiority of one literary text to another, or of one ethnic group to another, are merely the result of a *system* of differences, then they are not decisions.

By the same token it may not have to be that the singularity of every decision is absolutely opposed (all the way down, as it were) to any notion of system whatsoever. If it were, and if the structure of that opposition were held to be indicative (indeed, a *requirement*) of the post, then surely the sort of anarchic 'mobility' that Foucault advocates in chapter 19 would be less an ethics (in the sense of a radical pragmatics) than a politics of avoidance, an all too familiar relativism. What this may suggest is that Foucault sets up a choice between life-denying self-discipline (the politicized body of the system) and life-affirming self-experimentation (the desiring body as an ethics), as if in the space outside the structure of genre absolutely anything goes!

As McHoul points out, however, 'anything goes' includes the possibility that 'everything stays', such that an ethics of 'pure' affirmation cannot rule out affirmations of 'conservatism, non-intervention and a politics of zero transgression'. For us, this would mean that an absolute affirmation of *Blood and Guts in High School*, based on a notion of the sublimely non-generic signifying power of that text to 'signify' outside any *system* of writing or signification whatsoever, would be powerless to challenge an opposing view of Acker's novel as a completely uninteresting text (precisely because of being seen, or wanting to be seen, as 'non-generic') or, because of its lavatorial depictions of sexuality, a morally distasteful one. The absolute affirmation of non-genre could never be a basis for deciding whether the apparent refusal of Acker's writing to conform to any standard of literature is an expression of a radical ethics, a gynaecological intervention into the gender of genre, perhaps, or simply a vacuous attempt to be shocking and therefore nothing but 'a politics of zero transgression'.

What then *would* be a basis for deciding? The problem, though, in asking this question is that it risks a return to a certain notion of system or genre that would take out of our hands any responsibility for making decisions, which would never always remain to be made because they would always in a sense have been made already. To say, in other words, that *Blood and Guts in High School* shouldn't be undervalued for not meeting a standard of literature defined by novels like *Jane Eyre* would not be to say that, simply because of its nonconformity, therefore it represents a radical challenge to that standard or exposes the oppressive illusion that literature could ever be understood in terms of standards. (Sometimes a cigar is just a cigar, and the nonconformity of Acker's novel could just be a consequence of bad rather than transgressive writing. Or of course it could just be dreadfully unpostmodern to wonder either way.) The question of what to say or think about *Blood and Guts in High School*, and therefore what to say and think about (postmodern) literature and literary theory, cannot be systematically generalized into a position independent of the particularities of contexts and other forces; nor could it be so contingently singular as to exist outside every conceivable and unimaginable effect of a general system. This could be to suggest, as I think McHoul can be read as suggesting, that a certain order of deconstructive 'pragrammatology', rather than the sort of 'postmodern ethics' that seems to be the inevitable outcome of a certain return to the romantic question of literature as the question of itself, could point the way to the possibility of a 'new' ethics of textual analysis. Since it would not be new in the sense of bearing no traces at all of historical and disciplinary pasts (or of bearing no relation to metaphysics), such an ethics, or such analysis, might indeed be described as 'post' – though the question of what to call 'it', like the question of what to call romantic 'literature' or 'the' genre of romanticism, must remain open even as it must have a name.

Beyond Postmodern Literary Theory?

To ask after the relations of chapter 20 to postmodern literary theory might be to suppose that there *is* a genre of the postmodern literary theoretical such that chapter 20 seems not to belong to it. At this late stage, however, surely it can't be necessary to put the question – what does that genre look like?

This would not be to say that postmodern literary theory is 'beyond' genre, except in the perfectly routine and not at all exclusively postmodern sense in which every instance of a genre cannot be fully identical with itself. Genres always remain to come; they are always on the way to genre. Even so it would be stretching things to imagine the write-up of a chemistry experiment as an example of postmodern literary theory, but I suppose it could be said that things are there to be stretched. After all, if the concept of literature can stretch to accommodate a blank page and a picture of a cunt as instances of itself, who knows what the genre of postmodern literary theory may go on becoming? Or is it precisely there – in attributing to theory the sort of creative license that belongs only, as it were, to literature – that the genre of postmodern literary theory takes on its identity? Precisely *as* a genre, in other words, postmodern literary theory remains open to creative experimentation, both stylistically and thematically, even to a point of appearing 'genreless'?

This seems to be the view of Lyotard in chapter 21, which is included here, along with chapter 22, not as an afterthought but in response to the sorts of question that have just been raised. For Lyotard, the 'post' (he doesn't use the term 'postmodern literary theory') is first of all a continuation of the *work* of modernist avant-garde painters, writers and thinkers (Picasso, Joyce, Freud et al.) – the work of questioning 'expressions of thought'. (But interestingly he fails to mention the 'work' of modernist filmmakers, an absence I wish merely to note in passing here, though perhaps much remains to be made of it.) Now while Lyotard admits to a certain discomfort with the term 'avant-garde', it is none the less for him through 'the true process of avant-gardism' that was carried out 'a long, obstinate and highly responsible work concerned with investigating the assumptions implicit in modernity'. Today, this is the work of the post.

Yet the work of the post is not, or not quite, the work of the past. Lyotard insists that today's work has to be seen in its own historical right or identity, and not as a nostalgic return to questions put to modernity by the avant-garde *per se*. All the same it can't be incidental that it's the modernist avant-garde (and not, say, the Enlightenment *philosophes*) that Lyotard cites as an analogue of the post, for perhaps the obvious reason of the avant-garde's experiments at breaking free from the 'strangulations' of genre. On this account the post is certainly in some kind of relation with the avant-garde affirmation of what might be called 'genres-without-genre', but not in the sense of being in receipt of fully worked-out attitudes, thoughts and practices. Indeed, each historical moment, although it has to be concerned with the work of questioning expressions of thought, has to do so in its own terms, and so there could be no sense in which the workings of the past could simply work again, without being reworked and therefore worked anew, in another (always different) historical context. For this reason, *Blood and Guts in High School* could never be an avant-garde hand-me-down: even if Acker's novel were seen as a pastiche, say, of Joyce, Ferdinand Céline, Anaïs Nin, William Burroughs and Lou Reed – it would still, for and because of all that, be an original *text*.

If the nature of its originality were to be understood as postmodern, this would not, on Lyotard's account, be due to any movement of repetition (quoting, copying, returning), but rather to a double movement of what he calls 'a procedure in "ana-"', meaning both 'again' and 'anew' (hence 'analysis', 'anamnesis', etc.). Perhaps then it is precisely because of postmodernism's understanding of 'writing' as 'rewriting' (and here we might want to go back – afresh – to chapters 4, 5, 8, 13 and 15, especially) that the postmodern question, and the question of postmodernism, seems to be the question of genre.

If (other than plagiarism) there *is* a genre of rewriting, what then is genre that it may sometimes appear as its own imitation?

The Last Post

That, it might be said, is a question bearing on 'a problem in identification and in practice', to cite the words of Jerome Christensen in the final chapter, albeit in relation to what he sees as the true nature of romanticism.

And so in returning to romanticism at the finish, we begin again. This time out we encounter a romanticism that is everywhere engaged with, if only to pre-empt, the question of the post rather than the question of genre, which is where we began before. But what's the difference?

As Christensen tells it, romantic writing is indissociable from a form of romantic living, which in turn cannot be separated from a deeply political approach to being in the world. By romantic politics (and therefore writing), though, Christensen refers to 'spontaneous anti-systematic impulses' rather than an organized structure of ideological beliefs and practices. Indeed, for him, romanticism is characterized as a 'movement' (a point that might be set in comparison with chapter 4 perhaps) driven by its opposition to ideologies and systems, as if the contemporary disbelief in metanarratives – an assumption so crucial to Lyotard's designation of 'the postmodern condition' – were in fact not so contemporary after all.[15]

Or perhaps (and this could be the rub) the contemporaneity of that disbelief is not postmodern, but romantic. If this turned out to be the case, indeed, we might then say that the last 'post' was not the moment of avant-garde modernism but in fact the era of romanticism, whose time may be far from up. According to a certain concept (or a certain genre) of the historical, of course, romanticism was well and truly all used up by about the middle of the nineteenth century. Come the industrial revolution and all those dark satanic mills, why should anybody care about the question of genre anymore?

To ask the question of genre again today, in the nuclear age, may therefore seem anachronistic. But perhaps it seems so only in the belief that a *system* of genres (if not a certain idea of system in general, if not of genres-in-particular) is a post-romantic phenomenon, such that the *question* of genre (or the question of literature, which literary theory is concerned to speculate on) can appear now only as metaphysical or nostalgic, which is to say apolitical either way. Perhaps too the 'apoliticism' of such a return is itself only an effect of *not* having asked, or of not allowing to be asked, for so long, the romantic question of literature.

Above all, perhaps, the critical force of postmodern literary theory can be measured in the apparent lack of a genre which defines and contains that force. No doubt the radical import of that lack is often absurdly exaggerated, as several chapters in the present volume assert (though for different reasons and purposes). But at least the affirmation of such a lack goes some way towards releasing literature from a certain order of historicity that would see it in terms only of self-contained periods and genres. To be sure, that affirmation may be totalizing in its *negation* of historicity (and therefore of a certain metaphysics of representation), and to that extent it could be only an inversion of, rather than a radical departure from, the history of representation it opposes.

Even in the impossible form of an absolute affirmation, though, postmodern literary theory's reopening of the question of genre is at least a first move (again, for another first time) in a struggle to think and be outside the constraints of systems. Maybe therefore it owes as much to British punk as to Continental theory or European romanticism, in so far as a novel like *Blood and Guts in High School*'s defiance of literary standards may be said to give the impression that anyone can be a writer (because anything can be writing), just as The Sex Pistols made it seem that anyone could be a rock star![16]

Politically that is a very dangerous sentiment, of course, since it points as strongly to fascism as to democracy. But in its openness it's no more dangerous than the idea that canonical texts (whether of literature or pop music) leave nothing to be decided about their genericity because their canonicity decides everything! According to that idea it would be simply wrong, for example, to say that the following lines from Shelley's celebrated poem 'To a Skylark' are among the most embarrassing ever to be published, certainly by a famous poet:

> Hail to thee, blithe Spirit!
> Bird thou never wert

If that's poetry, then I'm very happy to think of *Blood and Guts in High School* as a novel.[17]

But so what?

That might be the question of postmodern literary theory, pertaining to the irrelevance of naming works of literature – or instances of writing – in terms of generic identities.

The question for us, however, might be whether 'irrelevance' is too strong a term.

Notes

1 Cf. Kathy Acker, *Blood and Guts in High School* (New York: Grove Press, 1978), pp. 62, 63 and 30.

2 Cf. Kurt Vonnegut Jr., *Breakfast of Champions* (Frogmore, St Albans: Panther, 1975), pp. 14 and 31.

3 Cf. Lawrence Sterne, *The Life and Opinions of Tristram Shandy, Gentleman*, ed. Graham Petrie (Harmondsworth: Penguin, 1967).

4   Cf. Ihab Hassan, 'POSTmodernISM: A Paracritical Bibliography', in *From Modernism to Postmodernism: An Anthology*, ed. Lawrence Cahoone (Oxford: Blackwell, 1996), pp. 382–400. From this it becomes clear that the title of Brian McHale's essay in the present volume (chapter 11) is a quotation, albeit what is quoted is irreducible simply to words.

5   Darren Tofts and Murray McKeich, *Memory Trade: A Prehistory of Cyberculture* (North Ryde, Sydney: Interface, 1998), p. 91. While on the topic of picture writing, McKeich's stunning (if not disturbing) digital artwork in this text cannot go unremarked.

6   Ibid. The embedded reference is to James Joyce, *Finnegans Wake* (London: Faber, 1975), p. 124.

7   Tofts and McKeich, *Memory Trade*, p. 91.

8   See my *Postmodern Literary Theory: An Introduction* (Oxford: Blackwell, 1997). Hereafter cited as *PomoIntro* throughout.

9   By 'metaphysics' I mean a way of thinking which is understood as *the* way of thinking, as if thought were independent of historical and other forces. This is not to suppose, however, that a 'counter-' or (worse) 'post-metaphysics' is conceivable on the basis of an 'anti-metaphysical' stance against received habits of thought. It is not that easy to escape thought, certainly not simply by thinking (and there's the difficulty right there) to oppose it. Such an account of the problem caused by and as metaphysics derives largely from Derrida. For discussions of Derrida's rendering of the problem of metaphysics and how to work (or live) through it, as it were, see my *Debating Derrida* (Carlton: Melbourne University Press, 1995), esp. pp. 64–70, and my *PomoIntro*, pp. 113–20, 212–19 and 236–45.

10   On Derrida's account, the law of genre is in fact 'the law of the law of genre', which refers to a principle of irreducible impurity or hybridity. A text may be said to belong without belonging to a genre, in so far as the signs of its belonging do not themselves belong to the genre they designate. For example: the sign 'a novel' on the cover of *Blood and Guts in High School* is not itself unproblematically within that text, but functions rather to frame it according to a certain generic designation. In this way, perhaps, one should not so much refer to 'the law of genre' as to 'the law *enforcement* of genre'. See Jacques Derrida, 'The Law of Genre', trans. Avital Ronell, *Glyph 7* (1980), pp. 202–32; and beware the misreading of this paper in chapter 14 of the present volume.

11   There are many examples that could be given here, but these are three of my favourites: Christopher Norris, *Derrida* (London: Fontana, 1987); Drucilla Cornell, *The Philosophy of the Limit* (London: Routledge, 1992); and John D. Caputo, *Deconstruction in a Nutshell: A Conversation with Jacques Derrida* (New York: Fordham University Press, 1997).

12   So far as I know, Nietzsche never quite said as much, although these words are commonly attributed to him; hence they are often 'quoted': see for example Susan Sontag, *Against Interpretation and Other Essays* (New York: Farrar,

Straus and Giroux, 1978), p. 5. What Nietzsche actually wrote was this (from *The Will to Power*): 'In opposition to Positivism, which halts at phenomena and says, "There are only *facts* and nothing more," I would say: No, facts are precisely what is lacking, all that exists consists of *interpretations*', *The Complete Works of Friedrich Nietzsche*, ed. Oscar Levy (New York: Russell and Russell, 1964), p. 12.

13 See my *PomoIntro*, pp. 57–80, for further discussion of Lyotard's 'mistake' with respect to a theory of language games.

14 I am mixing genres here: the question of the relations of responsibility to structures of decision-making is asked explicitly by Derrida rather than by Foucault or Deleuze and Guattari. See for example Jacques Derrida, 'Afterword: Toward an Ethic of Discussion', trans. Samuel Weber, in *Limited Inc*, ed. Gerald Graff (Evanston: Northwestern University Press, 1988), pp. 111–60.

15 See Jean-François Lyotard, *The Postmodern Condition: A Report on Knowledge*, trans. Geoff Bennington and Brian Massumi, *Theory and History of Literature* 10 (Manchester: Manchester University Press, 1986).

16 For the view that 'rock is a vulgar adaptation of nineteenth-century Romanticism', the Pistols being a prime example, see Robert Pattison, *The Triumph of Vulgarity: Rock Music in the Mirror of Romanticism* (New York and Oxford: Oxford University Press, 1987).

17 There are, I think worse examples of 'poetry' than Shelley's, albeit by less famous poets. See especially anything by Richard Brautigan, a US West Coast writer of the 1960s and 1970s who shot himself in the head in the 1980s, no doubt because it was still full of poems like the following (called 'Melting Ice Cream at the Edge of Your Final Thought'):

> Oh well, call it a
>   life.

See the Brautigan collection (one of many), *Rommel Drives on Deep into Egypt* (New York: Delta, 1970) – perfect for passing around at dinner parties!

Part One **Genre**

Chapter One **Genre**

Philippe Lacoue-Labarthe and Jean-Luc Nancy

What then, is the question?

Quite simply, it is *the* question: 'What is literature?'

In Romanticism's own terms, and especially in those peculiar to the very well-known fragment 116 [quoted below – NL] (on which, from all indications, the *Lessons* and the *Conversation* are, after all, the commentary)[1] a certain question arises: 'What is Romantic poetry?' To be more precise: 'What is the Romantic genre?' Consequently, this question is nothing less than what, in condensed form, we called the question of the 'literary genre'.

In any case, the important thing is that the question be precisely this question. That is to say that first of all, the question must persist and be maintained – and obviously, that we must wait for the answer. It does not only mean that Romanticism is, strictly speaking, the locus at which this question appears, nor even that Romanticism inaugurates the era of literature. Nor does it only mean that, as a result, Romanticism can find no other definition than that of the perpetual introversion of the question, 'what is Romanticism', or 'what is literature?' It means rather that Romanticism, as such, dates literature as its constant auto-implication, and as the ever-repeated asking of its own question. It means therefore that there is and can be no answer either to the Romantic question or to the question of Romanticism. Or at least, that the answer could only be interminably deferred, a constantly deceptive answer which always recalls the question (if only by denying that it is still necessary to ask the question). This is why Romanticism, which comes into being at a given moment, the moment of its question, will always be more than just an

Philippe Lacoue-Labarthe and Jean-Luc Nancy, 'Genre', trans. Lawrence R. Schehr, *Glyph* 7 (1980), pp. 1–14.

'era', or, on the other hand, why, even now, it has not stopped in-completing the era it began. And this is something of which Romanticism was perfectly conscious: 'The genre of Romantic poetry is still in the process of becoming; it is its true essence to be always only becoming and never to be capable of completing itself'. (*Ath.* 116: 'Die romantische Dichtart ist noch im Werden; ja das ist ihr eigentliches Wesen, daß sie ewig nur werden, nie vollendet sein kann.')[2]

Romanticism finds itself in an impossible situation where it cannot answer the very question with which it is confused, or in which it is entirely caught up. This inherent impossibility within Romanticism is, of course, the reason why the question is actually an empty one, and why, under the rubric of Romanticism or of literature (or of 'Poetry', '*Dichtung*' [versification – NL], 'Art', 'Religion', etc.), the question only comes to bear on something indistinct and indeterminate, something that indefi-nitely recedes as one gets closer to it. It is something susceptible to being called (almost) any name, but not able to tolerate any one of these names: it is an unnameable thing without shape or form – in the end, this some-thing is 'nothing'. Romanticism (literature) is that which has no essence, not even in its inessentiality. And this, after all, is perhaps the reason why the question is never really asked, or else, why it is asked an incalculable number of times – and why the Romantic texts, in their fragmentation or even in their dispersion, are only the interminable answer (always ap-proximate, neither here nor there) to the question that is really unformable, i.e., always too quickly, too lightly and too easily formulated, just as if the 'thing' worked all by itself.

Moreover, neither the fragments (for 'form'), nor religion, for example (for 'contents'), unless it be vice versa, could adequately answer or ask the question of literature (of Romanticism), since, in any case, all of these only came to be by removing what they had sought to enclose; or, to state it another way, they were only the *Darstellung* [representation – NL] of what was refused to every presentation in itself, in the exact ratio of its will to appear. 'Literature' did not start to devote itself just yesterday to swerving from the truth. If one noticed that the term 'mystical' designated the specular itself for Schlegel,[3] it remains nevertheless clear that, quite understandably, he signalled thereby the negative theology of Jacob Boehme. This was necessary then, as it will always be, if one dares to say 'another turn'. And in many ways, this is what the *Conversation* repre-sents here.[4]

There are two reasons for this, the first one being, of course, the fact that the *Conversation* once again seems to attack the question head on. It has to do quite openly with 'poetry' (literature); of all the texts that appeared in the *Athenaeum*, it is the only essay of any depth devoted to poetry. Or at least, it is the most ambitious of them. Most importantly, it is auto-referential by its own method of exposition, its *Darstellung*: it is a dialogue, and that fact alone is sufficient to bring to the fore the same question of literature, brought into play here until the time that it becomes witness to its own impossibility. But we know all too well that this question will never be brought into play except by means of the 'formalist' inversion, by the endless interreflection (*mise-en-abyme*) that is inseparably specular and speculative. And it is not quite certain that, in this interreflection, the question is always capable of losing that very thing (what thing?) it claimed was the question.

But here it is necessary to decompose.

And to note, first of all, that the dialogue, no more than the letter or the aphorism, is not a stranger to fragmentation. Moreover, it will be recalled that this was unequivocally announced in *Ath*. 77: 'A dialogue is a chain or a crown of fragments. An exchange of letters is a dialogue on a greater scale, and memorabilia are a system of fragments.' ('Ein Dialog ist eine Kette, oder ein Kranz von Fragmenten. Ein Briefwechsel ist ein Dialog in vergrössertem Maßstabe, und Memorabilien sind ein System von Fragmente.) We have spoken of the 'necessity of fragmentation'.[5] The words could not be more appropriate when they refer to the *Ideas* and to the *Letter to Dorothea*.

On the whole, Friedrich never yielded one bit on this early demand of Romanticism. If we may make a conjecture, he would even rather have 'increased' its role (– think, for example, of the fact that the *Conversation* itself does not fail to contain a letter). As we shall see momentarily, this is doubtless the explanation for the rather singular fashion in which he conceives and creates dialogue, not at all comparable to that of August (who had strongly encouraged him along this line),[6] nor to that of Novalis (whom Friedrich in turn, with his usual strategy, had more or less encouraged to follow the same path).[7]

The essentially fragmentary nature of the dialogue has at least one consequence (among many others which we cannot examine here): the dialogue, no more than the fragment, does not properly constitute a genre. This is the reason why, in fact, the dialogue, like the fragment, is a privileged battlefield for the question of genre as such. But let us not be too hasty.

The fact that the dialogue is not a genre means first of all (by means of an equivalency to which we are already accustomed) not that the dialogue lacks something *vis-à-vis* genre, but rather that it can, by definition, contain all genres. The dialogue is the 'non-genre', or the 'genre' that is a mixture of genres. The dialogue thus takes us back not only to its own origin (i.e., for Schlegel, a Platonic one, but also to the Roman satire, and, in general, to all the late literature of the Alexandrine era in which all the forms of ancient poetry, including philosophy, of course, came together, reflecting each other, thereby fulfilling themselves. From this fact is also issued the very tight link forged between dialogue (and the fragment as well, but in a more immediate manner for the former) and the spirit of society (the social, the urban[e]), the *Witz*, great culture, popularity, lively intellectualism, virtuosity, etc.: in short, all those values and qualities that Romanticism took from the tradition of the Enlightenment and from English or French moral philosophy, qualities which, by the way, the dialogue had not failed preferentially to cultivate.[8]

We are now in well-charted territory. This also explains how the dialogue, by perpetuating the necessity of fragmentation, allows for the appearance of several contradictions, which no genre (or 'genre') theretofore used by Schlegel in the *Athenaeum* had permitted. In distinction from the letter in particular, which was based quite emphatically on the opposition between writing and speech (that is to say as well, as we have mentioned, between masculinity and femininity), and which, because of that, carried to its most acute point the problem of popularity.[9] The dialogue (and we are not twisting things around in order to state matters in this fashion) is actually in the position of a relief (*relève*) inasmuch as, in the *Conversation*, it is explicitly given as the transcription (a more or less exact one, to which point we shall return) of real conversations. Moreover, to see women, in fact, oppose the spontaneous practice of simple conversation (though it be brilliant) and call rather for reports, that is, for the reading of written texts, is not one of the lesser paradoxes of this text. This exchange of roles is revealing as well, and we shall soon see, in the most minute fictional creation of the *Conversation*, that the male protagonists' observation of this female injunction allows the dialogue's author to realize the wish he had previously expressed in the *Letter to Dorothea*, and to write, by mixing styles and genres (thus including the 'letter' itself) these little essays whose number he hoped to increase. He no longer feared the proliferation of 'projects' in which the rapid change of subject inherent in a lively conversation was cause for worry, and which essays were a necessary step to be taken on the road to true popularity. In this way, the dialogue, once and for all, attained the position of what we have called the 'moral genre of the fragment', and, if it does not wholly fulfill this (we shall see why), it actually only misses the mark by very little. From this point on, the reader is not astonished when, under the rubric of 'didascalic genre', or, what comes to the same thing, under the rubric of the 'reciprocal transfers between poetry and philosophy', he finds that one of the reports especially insists on the gnomic aphorisms (and the philosophical dialogues).[10] Nor is he astonished when he finds that one of its substitutes (in this case, the 'letter') refers, with the intercalation of Rousseau, to the tradition of the confession, or to that of 'subjective literature' in general.[11] The dialogue is, above all, the 'genre of the Subject'.

And paradoxically, this brings the dialogue back to its origin, that is to say, to Plato. In fact, all the themes that we have briefly outlined above interweave and intersect around what fragment 42 of the *Lyceum* calls 'the exalted urbanity of the Socratic muse' ('die erhabne Urbanität der sokratischen Muse'). For modern metaphysics, it follows once again that Socrates (the person and the character) has always represented the projected incarnation or prototype of the Subject itself. For Schlegel, at least, the reason is that Socrates (i.e., Plato's Socrates; the Socrates in Plato's works) is, in a wholly privileged way, what could be termed the ironic subject; in other words, Socrates is the locus at which the very exchange that defines irony ('logical beauty,' [*logische Schönheit*] according to *Lyceum* 42) operates both figuratively and in practice. This is the exchange of form and truth, or, in what amounts to the same thing, of poetry and philosophy. Socrates is thus made the subject-'genre' whereby – and wherein – literature begins (and begins with all the power of reflection, because irony is that as well: the very power of infinite reflection or reflexivity, which is another way of saying specularity). In a rigorous argument, Socrates would thus be called the formal or figurative Subject (the exemplary Subject) and would thereby be considered to be the eponymous 'genre' of literature, that is, philosophy. Consequently, this is a 'genre' beyond all genres, including a theory of this very 'beyond': in other words, it is a general theory of genres, and of itself as well.

It is precisely at this point that the novel is called into question.

But it is necessary to be patient a little longer in order to unfold these matters in a methodical fashion, hoping of course that they are in fact unfoldable. There are actually three elements that are put into play; to put it efficaciously: the name, the author, the reflection. This in turn supposes three questions: that of genre, of subject, and finally of theory, questions which are inextricably linked with one another. As is always the case in Romanticism, there is no privileged position that might afford a bird's eye view; there is no fixed point (*ancrage*) beginning at which one might categorize (*arrimer*); and thus arrange, if not organize, a system. This is the reason why fragment 42 of the *Lyceum*, always in the name of irony, proffers the dialogue as a pure and simple substitute for the system. 'Wherever people philosophize, not only in a systematic fashion, but also in either oral or written dialogues, irony must be both demanded and used' ('. . . denn überall wo in mündlichen oder geschriebenen Gesprächen, und nur nicht ganz systematisch philosophiert, soll man Ironie leisten und fordern . . .').

However, in order to see a bit more clearly, ironically or not, one must resolutely begin with this platitude: the *Conversation*, deliberately (it remarks on this at least twice) takes the Platonic dialogue as a model. And it is not just any dialogue, but rather the one which, more than any other, by its agonistic nature, connotes the social: that is to say, the *Symposium*. This does not mean, of course, that the *Conversation* presupposes a fictional symposium. Unlike Hemsterhuis, for example, who pushed the cult of genre (or of 'genre') to the point at which he claimed to have been able to retranscribe a Platonic dialogue that he had miraculously 'discovered', Schlegel only copied the model's structure, that of a dialogue with intercalated reports or 'discourses', in an appropriate format. More precisely, as we shall soon understand, the only thing that interests him is the complexity of the structure of something like the *Symposium*: that is to say, that, the question is not at all of a dialogue, but rather of a story including, or recalling, a dialogue, which in turn, contains intercalated discourses.

We know that, since antiquity, this type of structure has been the reason for the true originality of the Platonic mode of writing. It is this structure as well that we in fact find in varying degrees of complexity in most of the major dialogues of Plato, from the *Republic* to the *Sophist*, and including the *Theaetetus*. We know too that this very structure was not only 'reflected' on and condemned by Plato in the *Republic* (in the light of the epic structure, and under the name, if name it be, of a mixed diegesis, that is to say, of a mixture of pure story and of 'mimetic' or dramatic form).[12] But also it is this structure which proved to be of great consternation to Aristotle in his attempt at creating a taxonomy in the *Poetics*. This was so much the case that he was forced to yield and leave a blank, or anonymous space (ἀνώνυμος) – for lack of a common term (κοίνον ὄνομα), a concept lacking for a single genre (between prose and poetry, according to Diogenes Laertius), in which he could have placed the mimes of Sophon and Xenarch, the *Sokratikoi Logoi*, and didactic poems, such as those of Empedocles.[13] Added to that and thereby giving justice to the inventor of this 'art without a name' is the fact that Plato's condemnation of 'genre' (or the 'self-criticism', as it were, of Plato) devolved upon the general putting into question (*mise-en-cause*) of mimesis, that is to say, as far as writing is concerned, the putting into question of 'apocrypha', of the dissimulation and the dispersion of the author (or of the subject of discourse) behind the figures (characters or narrators) of dialogical narration. For Schlegel, this mimetic power had always been the lot (or appanage) of the genius, and particularly, of the great writer.[14] We therefore understand that, in the aftermath of the Greeks that Romanticism would wish itself to be, the Platonic dialogue appears as the very model of the union of the poetic and of the philosophical, and consequently, as the original matrix of the novel, that is, of that thing for which the Moderns had finally found a name.[15]

Lyceum 26: 'Novels are the Socratic dialogues of our time'. ('Die Romane sind die sokratischen Dialoge unserer Zeit'.)

Athenaeum 252: 'A philosophy of poetry in general . . . would hover between a unification and separation of philosophy and poetry, of praxis and poetry, of poetry in general and the various genres and species. . . . A philosophy of the novel, whose first foundations are seen in Plato's political theory, would be the keystone. ('Eine Philosophie der Poesie ilberhaupt . . . wiirde zwischen Vereinigung und Trennung der Philosophie und der Poesic, der Praxis und der Poesie, der Poesie überhaupt und der Cattungen und Arten schweben. . . . Eine Philosophie des Romans, deren erste Grundlinien Platos politische Kunstlehre enthält, wore der Schlußstein'.)

This is actually what the *Conversation* proposes.

Or at least, it is what allows for the explanation of its own *Darstellung*, or, in other words, its own method of fictional creation.

Irony, of course, is both its rule and its principle.

First of all, that which constitutes order in the *Conversation*, or, in other terms, the fiction-making (*mise-en-fiction*) – in order not to say incorrectly, the staging (*mise-en-scène*) – is ironic in a strict sense, and down to the smallest detail. Here it would be necessary to take the time to dissect carefully the 'fabrication' of the text. Failing that, we shall be satisfied to point out two major characteristics, which are, by the way, practically inseparable.

The first one is obviously (if we do not forget that we are still in the realm of the 'necessity of fragmentation') the reunion, as if 'through the looking glass', of the group itself, and, as if by mere chance, in its most 'critical' phase – that is to say, the phase that, in the fall of 1799, began with the last great meeting at Jena, where all the members of the 'alliance', except Schleiermacher,[16] had a reunion. In fact, many people have spoken a bit too rashly about the *Conversation*, for it is not very difficult to illuminate the identities of the protagonists of the *Conversation*: the whole *Athenaeum* is there, everyone with his own preoccupations (from the 'new mythology' to the 'characteristic of Goethe'), his quirks of tongue and mind (particularly evident in the 'reports' where Friedrich gives free rein to his genius at pastiche and to his virtuosity). There are the salient features of each one's character or personality (from good humor to guarded caution, from playfulness to rivalry or to quick retorts). And the simple interrelations of everyone within the group show, like an open book, the seeds of the group's impending dissolution. It is doubtless correct to emphasize the fact that, whatever the 'realism' of the *Conversation*, it is basically only the author of the text who speaks or gives his theoretical views.[17] That, by the way, is the second major characteristic of this 'fiction-making' to which we shall return momentarily. But it is obvious that the latter characteristic does not preclude the former; on the contrary, that is precisely the logic of mimetic behavior where the more the differences (that is to say, the dissimulation) are accentuated, the more the identity is reinforced, and vice versa. Schlegel was less aware than any other member of the group of this fact, Schlegel, who had made a career as a virtuoso, and who recognized in this principle (which is, from at least one point of view, the principle of the self-constitution of the Subject) the basis of the power of the novel, and as we shall see further on, of characterization.[18] That is why it is hardly valid not to see in the two women's roles in the *Conversation* – Amalia and Caimilla – Caroline and Dorothea[19] respectively. As for the men's roles, one can see the philosopher of the meeting, and the author of the *Discourse on Mythology*, Schelling, in Ludoviko; in Lothario, whose pseudonym is borrowed from Goethe[20] and who, in this case, represents the poet who always announces a work to come, we see Novalis. In Marcus, the Goethe 'specialist' obsessed by the problems of the theater, is Tieck; in Andrea, the philologist who begins the series of reports with his recapitulation of the history of literature (the *Eras of Poetry*), can be seen August. Finally, giving every man his due, in Antonio (which, in *Lucinde*, was Schleiermacher's pseudonym, for he was the one who knew about sailing), we see Friedrich himself, or 'himself', whose prestation is at the center of the *Conversation* (this *Letter on the Novel*, which is precisely not a report, which was not even supposed to have been divulged, and which actually re-marks, this

time on the literary level, all that is at stake in the *Letter to Dorothea*).[21]
This prestation, which is a proposition for a 'theory of the novel', is
actually the keystone of this 'philosophy of poetry' that actually determines the extent of the former.

Nevertheless, the *Letter on the Novel* does not occupy the center of the
text. For that to be the case, it would be necessary, at least if we follow the
series of reports,[22] for Marcus's essay on Goethe's styles to have been
followed by Lothario's reading of the work, which, from the beginning,
he has attempted to create, and for which, at the end, he settles for a
repeated promise.

The 'theory of the novel' would be the center of the *Conversation*, were
it not for the absence of the work – the 'poem,' the '*Dichtung*' (for at the
moment, the genre matters little). In which case, again as a result of irony,
the re-mark would be doubly impeccable: first, by the author, or 'novelist', insofar as he projects himself and disperses himself in the multiplicity
of characters or 'personalities' he creates (and we know he does this in
order to reassure himself of his power); that would be the second characteristic of the 'fiction-making' of which we spoke earlier. But it would
also be the re-mark (and this time a new step is taken, marking a greater
degree of complexity in the *Darstellung*, in the broadest sense) of the
'fiction-making' itself – that is to say the Platonizing, if not really Platonic, re-mark of the infinite power of introversion that is characteristic
of 'literary' mimesis.

This, however, is not the case. Certainly, there are allusions to the
'fabrication' of the *Conversation* which subtly 'reflects' itself (Schlegel is
a master in underhanded manipulation, and in any case the Platonic
model is the *law*). Just as the *Conversation* would be the transcription of
real conversations, in the beginning of the text there is a short passage on
the division between truth and fiction; in the same way, the first discussion, during which the rules of play for this modern 'symposium' are
adopted, is concerned with – and this comes as no surprise – the theater,
and precisely with the *theater* (which, according to Plato, was the purely
mimetic genre) and not with the novel. Similarly, Lothario's missing work,
which places the *Conversation* in a state of disequilibrium, or more precisely, puts it off-center, should have been a tragedy. Here, the power of
irony is at a disadvantage. That is to say as well that it is reinforced. For
there is nothing in the whole work left to chance or to quick improvisa-
tion; for you can't judge a book by its cover.

That nothing is left to chance means exactly that the *Letter on the Novel*
cannot be at the center of the *Conversation* because the *Conversation*

is not itself a novel. To put it another way, borrowing a formula from the self-same *Letter on the Novel*, with the proviso that the terms be inverted: only a novel is equal to the task of containing its own reflection and of including the theory of its own 'genre'. Once more, with the terms in their correct order: there can be no theory of the novel that is not a novel. And neither the *Conversation* nor the *Letter on the Novel* contained in it is a novel. But *Lucinde* could very well be a novel,[23] unless, in this game of funhouse mirrors (*cette fausse mise-en-abyme*) which is the ultimate ironic barb, the incomplete aspect of *Lucinde* (upon which the Letter offers much commentary) is sought and reflected; unless the dialogue is the form of renunciation, the *Darstellung* of the impossibility of self-constitution, and that the parody of Plato (or the multiple pastiche, already present, of the Romantic 'style') is the admission of the insufficiency and failure of the work; unless, quite possibly, it is the 'out of work quotient' (*l'indice du désoeuvrement*). In which case, beyond (or rather aside from), the question of literature there would be a sort of uncanny writing secretly at work in this apparatus. But where then would the difference go, and would irony still be able to control such an obliteration of the mark (*un tel démarquage*)?

This is perhaps the basic reason why the *Conversation* is never quite able to define or delimit the Romantic genre, that is to say, the literary genre – and most certainly not, though we often think in this fashion, in (or like) the novel.[24] This does not mean that the novel is not the 'genre' that was obstinately sought for by Romantic theory; the contrary is the case. But it means rather that the inability to be defined or delimited is probably part of the essential nature of this genre. Without a doubt, genre is the completed, differentiated, and identifiable product of an engenderment or of a generation; even in German, where the etymology of the word is completely different,[25] *Gattung* is not unrelated to congregation in general, indeed, to marriage. However, the process of generation or of assembly obviously presupposes interpenetration and confusion; that is to say, a mixture (*gattieren*, in German, means 'to mix'). This would seem to be precisely what the Romantics sought as the very essence of literature: union, in the satire (another name for mixture) or in the novel (or even in the Platonic dialogue), the union of poetry and philosophy, the confusion of all the genres that had previously been delimited by ancient poetics, the interpenetration of the old and the new, etc. But is that sufficient to define the nature of the mixture? What is, in fact, the nature of the fusion or union? And, all told, what is a genre? Or to be more precise, Genre?

The answer is quite simple and well-known to us besides. Simple and unfathomable: Genre is 'more than a genre' ('Die romantische Dichtart ist die einzige, die mehr als Art . . .' *Ath*. 116). It is an Individual and an organic Whole capable of self-engenderment (*Ath*. 426); it is a World, the absolute *Organon*. In other words: generation is dissolution (*Auftösung*) in the sense of Kant's intussusception,[26] that is to say, that the idealist step in the properly speculative sense of the term, has in fact been taken. Not only is there dissolution like decomposition or resolution, but also, beyond a simple chemism (again, *Ath*. 426), there is a dissolution like organicism itself or like the process of auto-formation. This is actually a far cry from being able to delimit a genre, but is completely equivalent to Genre *in toto* (in the absolute), in the dissolution of all limits and the making absolute of all individuality. The literary Genre is Literature itself, the *Literary Absolute* (*L'Absolu littéraire*); it is 'true literature', Schlegel would say several years later,[27] that is to say, literature that is not 'one genre or another, willing to content itself, as if by whimsy, with a specific formation, but rather that literature is a great totality, with complex connections and organization, which encompasses in its unity many worlds of art – it is a unitary work of art' ('. . . so daß nicht etwa nur diese oder jene Cattung, wie es das Glück will, zu einiger Bildung gelangen, sondern daß vielmehr die Literatur selbst ein Großes durchaus zusammenhägendes und gleich organisiertes, in ihrer Einheit viele Kunstwelten umfassendes Ganzes und einiges Kunstwerk sei . . .'). Reread fragment 116, or look at the *Essence of Criticism*:[28]

Romantic poetry . . . should not only unite the divers genres of poetry and make poetry, philosophy and rhetoric join together. It intends to, and has to, both mix and meld poetry and prose, genius and criticism, artistic and natural poetry, poetic life and society, poeticize the *Witz*, fill to the brim all the various forms of art with basic cultural materials, and inspire them with flashes of humor. Romantic poetry includes everything poetic from the largest system of art, itself containing other systems, down to the breath or kiss that the child-poet exhales in an artless song. . . . It is more than adequate to the greatest and most universal formation . . . ; for each whole that its products should form, it adopts a similar organization of its parts, and is thereby given to a perspective that allows for a limitless classificatory system. . . . Other poetic genres are complete and can now be fully dissected. . . . Only Romantic poetry is infinite as only it is free. . . . The genre of Romantic poetry is the only one that is more than a genre: it is, in a way, the very art of poetry: in a certain sense, all poetry is or should be Romantic.

Just as one must look to mythology for the origin and common source of all poetic genres, it is equally true that . . . poetry is the tallest cyme of all, found in the flower from which, once perfect (*sich vollendet*), the spirit of all the arts and sciences is resolved (*sich auflöst*).

It is understandable then, how in this situation, Literature, or Poetry, the 'Romantic genre', insofar as the thing exists at all, is always sought for as a kind of 'beyond' of literature itself. In actuality, this is what prohibits the *Conversation* from producing the promised concept. The process as such of absolutization or infinitization exceeds, in all senses of the word, the theoretical or philosophical power in general of which it is, after all, the fulfillment. The 'auto' movement, if it can be called that – auto-formation, auto-organization, auto-dissolution, etc. – is always in a state of excess with itself. In a certain way, this is also what fragment 116 marks: 'The genre of Romantic poetry is still in the process of becoming, and it is its proper essence that it is always only becoming, and that it is never capable of completing itself. No theory can exhaust it, and only a clairvoyant sort of criticism could dare to characterize its ideal'. ('Die romantische Dichtart ist noch im Werden; ja das ist ihr eigentliches Wesen daß sie ewig nur werden, nie vollendet sein kann. Sic kann durch keine Theorie erschöpft werden, und nur eine divinatorische Kritik dürfte es wagen, ihr Ideal charakterisieren zu wollen').

Notes

1   The famous 'fragment 116', the *Lessons* and the *Conversation* refer to works by Friedrich Schlegel (see details below) that represent the ideas of a loosely comprised group of philosopher-poets at the German town of Jena in the 1790s. Schlegel himself was a part of it, as were Friedrich Schelling, Friedrich Novalis and several others, all of whom contributed to the group's journal *Athenaeum* in which the text of fragment 116 appears. For a brief discussion of the Jena Romantics and a summary of Lacoue-Labarthe and Nancy's argument of their importance, see my *PomoIntro*, pp. 32–6. (NL)

2   Friedrich Schlegel, *Athenäums Fragmente*, in *Kritische Friedrich-Schlegel-Ausgabe*, vol. II, ed. Hans Eichner (Munich: Verlag Ferdinand Schöningh). (Trans.)

3   Cf. *Athenaeum* 121.

4   *Conversation* refers to *Gespräch über die Poesie*, Schlegel, *Kritische Ausgabe*. (Trans.)

5   Cf. the authors' *L'Absolu littéraire* (Paris: Seuil, 1978), pp. 198ff. (Trans.)

6   Cf. in the *Athenaeum* the two dialogues signed by August, with the collabo-

ration on the second of Caroline: *Languages: A Dialogue on the Grammatical Dialogue of Klopstock, and Paintings*. Both of them, notwithstanding the fact that the second is interspersed with long reading passages, are simple dialogues, that is to say, without a story. This is why, in reference to them, we use the term 'dialogue' (*dialogue*) and not 'conversation' (*entretien*) even though the same German word is used in both cases: *Cespriäch*.

7   Cf. The Dialogues (1 to 5) which Novalis intended for the *Athenaeum*. In the last section of *L'Absolu littéraire*, pp. 428–33, the first two can be found. Here again, these are simple dialogues.

8   We refer the reader here to our 'Dialogue des genres', in *Poétique* 21 for the historical analyses that we cannot develop here. Insofar as the relationship between the dialogue and Roman satire, and consequently the novel, is concerned, see *Lyceum* 42, and *Athenaeum* 146, 148, 239, and 448, among others, as well as the *Eras of Poetry* in the *Conversation*.

9   Cf. On Philosophy and the analyses developed in *L'Absolu littéraire*, pp. 181–205. One can also refer to *Lucinde* (*Kritische Fr.-Schlegel-Ausgabe*, vol. V), pp. 74–8 (also, in the French translation by J. J. Anstett [Paris: Aubier-Flammarion, 1971], pp. 22lff. [Julius to Antonio]).

10   Cf. *The Eras of Poetry*.

11   That is to say, to the tradition which we have followed back to Montaigne, and which the Romantics knew essentially by English 'literature' or that of eighteenth-century France.

12   Cf. Gérard Genette's 'Frontières du récit,' in *Figures II* (Paris: Seuil, 1966).

13   *Poetics*, 1447b – Since these pages were written we have been made aware of Gèdrard Genette's essential study, 'Genres, "types", modes,' in *Poétique* 32. In a decisive manner, from the point of view of the history of poetics, this study illuminates the process whereby Romanticism, while completing a movement begun at the least by the Abbé Batteux, tended to project on ancient poetics (Plato and Aristotle) a distinction of genres (lyric, epic, dramatic) which: (1) does not appear as such either in the *Republic* or in the *Poetics* (nothing is in fact determined for the lyric); (2) actually conceals a distinction between the modes of enunciation (direct, or in the first person: *diegesis*; indirect, or by an interposed person: *mimesis*)
It is thus understandable that that which Romanticism calls, or desires, under the name of 'genre' is actually the result of this double distortion. It is also understandable that, as we mention at the end of *L'Absolu littéraire*, Romanticism's 'generic speculation' bumps up against the problem of the lyric. In the following discussion it is taken for granted that the word 'genre' is used with the meaning the Romantics gave it.

14   Cf. in the *Conversation*, for example, the developments concerning Goethe's *Wilhelm Meister* (*Essay on Goethe's Various Styles* . . .): the first quality of *Wilhelm Meister* is that 'the individuality that appears there is divided among different rays of light and distributed among several persons'. ('Erstlich daß die Individualität, welche darin erscheint, in verschiedne Strahlen gebrochen,

unter mehrere Personen verteilt ist'.)

15 Cf. Nietzsche, *The Birth of Tragedy*: Plato is the inventor of the novel in antiquity (chapter 14).

16 Cf. Roger Ayrault, *Genèse du romantisme allemand*, 4 vols. (Paris: Aubier-Montaigne, 1961–76), III, pp. 74ff.

17 Ibid., IV, 294ff.

18 Cf. *Athenaeum* 22 and 418 as well as 'The Formation of Character' in *L'Absolu littéraire*, pp. 371–93.

19 Amalia was already used as Caroline's pseudonym in August Schlegel's *Four Letters on Poetry, Metrics and Language*.

20 As Ayrault (IV, p. 290) reminds us, Lothario in *Wilhelm Meister* is the figure who symbolizes the problems of economic activity, and who is, for Schlegel, 'the most interesting character in the entire work'.

21 At least it re-marks some of its important themes, beginning with that of the 'erotic' pedagogy. It is clear that the relation with Catherine is not at all the same as the one glimpsed in *On Philosophy* or in *Lucinde* (where, by the way, the 'Platonic' love of Friedrich for Caroline is recalled in the chapter, 'The Learning-Years of Masculinity' (*Kr. Aus.* V, 35–59); this is why there is no trace here of the theme of initiation. Curiously, the *Conversation* is a *Symposium* without Diotima.

22 Herewith, for expediency, is the plan of the *Conversation*, the first pagination being that of *L'Absolu littéraire*, the second referring to vol. II of the *Kritische Ausgabe*:
    1) Prologue: pp. 289–91; pp. 284–7.
    2) Story; Play production: pp. 291–4; pp. 287–90.
    3) Andrea's report; *Eras of Poetry*: pp. 294–306; pp. 290–303.
    4) First Discussion: pp. 306–11; pp. 303–11.
    5) Ludviko's report; *Discourse on Mythology*: pp. 311–17; pp. 311–22.
    6) Second Discussion: pp. 317–21; pp. 321–8.
    7) Antonio's text; *Letter on the Novel*: pp. 321–30; pp. 329–38.
    8) Third Discussion (Summary): p. 330; pp. 338–9.
    9) Marcus's Report; *Essay on Goethe's Various Styles in his Earlier and Later Works*: pp. 331–7; pp. 339–47.
    10) Fourth Discussion: pp. 337–40; pp. 348–51.

23 *Lucinde* actually does contain a chapter entitled 'Allegory of Impudence', and in the form of a 'waking dream' there is a sort of theory of the novel. It would not be difficult to show that the whole text of *Lucinde* is built on the principle of self-engenderment; however, this important point still remains: the book was never completed, or, as it were, was aborted.

24 It is best to refer the reader here to Szondi's seminal study, 'La Théorie des genres poétiques chez Friedrich Schlegel', in *Poésie et poétique de l'idéalisme allemand*, trans. Jean Bollack (Paris: Minuit, 1975), pp. 117ff. By concentrating on the posthumous 'fragments' in particular, collected in the *Kritische Friedrich-Schlegel-Ausgabe*, and the *Literary Notebooks*, edited by Eichner,

Szondi attempts to recreate a 'system' of Schlegel's poetics, which wavers between a 'critique of poetic reason' and a sort of pre-Hegelian synthesis which, both in and like the novel, would reconcile subjective and objective poetry. In light of the above, it remains true that Szondi's analysis stops at a recognition of Schlegel's contradictions and a paraphrase of fragment 116. Moreover, the editor of the French edition notes, on p. 120, that 'Peter Szondi was not indifferent to the objections made to him about the validity of placing the category of the novel in the genre that Schlegel had defined as objective/subjective, as well as on his imposition of the oppositions: poetry of nature/poetry of art, and antiquity/modernity'. On the other hand, Walter Benjamin, in his *Der Begriff der Kunsthritik in der deutschen Romantik* (Bern: Francke, 1920), pp. 94ff., demonstrated that the novel is not an ideal, insofar as it permits poetry to fulfill itself as prose ('The idea of poetry is prose.'), that is to say, poetry, which for Novalis was that which should define 'the Romantic rhythm'. In addition, this theme will be found quite explicitly in A. Schlegel's *Lessons* (published in *L'Absolu littéraire*, pp. 341–68): 'In Romantic poetry, a genre blossomed which not only can do without verse, but also, in many situations, actually prohibits versification: this is the novel.' One must attach this ideal for prose of the *oratio soluta* to what we have called 'the necessity of fragmentation', that is to say as well, to everything seen to devolve on the speculative theme of the Ab-solute (cf., on the Absolute, Heidegger, *Schelling*, trans. J. F. Courtine (Paris: Gallimard, 1977), pp. 82–3).

25   The root *ghedh-* is found in *gatten* (to join, to assemble) and in the pair *Gatte/Gattin* (husband/wife), which refers as well to the idea of joining or connecting. Perhaps to the idea of system?

26   Cf. 'L'Exigence fragmentaire' in *L'Absolu littéraire*, pp. 57–80.

27   In 'Of the Combinative Spirit' ('Vom kombinatorischen Geist') in the introduction to the second part of *Lessing's Thoughts and Beliefs* (1804), *Kr. Aus.* III, p. 83.

28   Friedrich Schlegel, *Schriften und Fragmente*, ed. Ernst Behler (Stuttgart: A. Kröner, 1956). For the French translation, see *L'Absolu littéraire*, pp. 407–16. (Trans.)

Chapter Two Something Like: 'Communication ... Without Communication'

Jean-François Lyotard

With a view to dramatizing the question laid down [at the conference], 'Art and Communication', I would just like to recall the regime of representation which is proper, or which has been thought proper, at least since Kant, to aesthetic reception; and, in order to pick out this regime, I will just quote two sentences, aphorisms, which appear to contradict one another perfectly:

> No work of art should be described or explained through the categories of communication.

> One could even define taste as the faculty of judging what renders our feeling, proceeding from a given representation, universally *communicable* without the mediation of a concept.

The first is from Theodore Adorno (*Aesthetic Theory*), the second from Immanuel Kant (*Critique of Judgement*, § 40).[1]

These two aphorisms appear to be contradictory, one saying that art has nothing to do with communication, and the other that the reception

Jean-François Lyotard, 'Something Like: "Communication ... Without Communication"', in *The Inhuman: Reflections on Time*, trans. Geoffrey Bennington and Rachel Bowlby (Stanford: Stanford University Press, 1988), pp. 108–18.

of art presupposes and demands a universal communicability without concept. The philosopher is used to contrary theses. The Adorno passage is one of the objections he makes to the Hegelian reduction of the work to the dialectic of the concept. Adorno, not without premonition, discerns in Hegelian thought the beginnings of something like a *communicationalist* ideology, and probably – here we come back to Kant's formulation – for the very reason that in Hegel's speculative philosophy there is an absolute hegemony of the concept.[2] Now in what Adorno calls *communication*, the idea is also implicitly required that if there is a communication in art and through art, it must be without concept. So much so, that in spite of the apparent contradiction, Adorno is at this point inserting himself into a tradition of thinking about art which we get from Kant. There is a thinking about art which is not a thinking of non-communication but of non-conceptual communication.

The question I want to dramatize is this: what about communication without concept at a time when, precisely, the 'products' of technologies applied to art cannot occur without the massive and hegemonic intervention of the concept? In the conflict surrounding the word *communication*, it is understood that the work, or at any rate anything which is received as art, induces a feeling – before inducing an understanding – which, constitutively and therefore immediately, is universally communicable, by definition. Such a feeling is thereby distinguishable from a merely subjective preference. This communicability, as a demand and not as a fact, precisely because it is assumed to be originary, *ontological*, eludes communicational activity, which is not a receptiveness but something which is managed, which is done. This, in my view, is what governs our problematic of 'new technologies and art', or, put differently, 'art and postmodernity'. This communicability, as it is developed in the Kantian analysis of the beautiful,[3] is well and truly 'anterior' to communication in the sense of 'theories of communication', which include communicative pragmatics (*pragma* is the same thing as *Handeln*). This assumed communicability, which takes place immediately in the feeling of the beautiful, is always presupposed in any conceptual communication.

By showing that the feeling of beauty differs from the other affects or affections with which it is tempting to confuse it, including the feeling of sublimity, Kant signifies that it *must be made transitive* immediately, without which there is no feeling of beauty. The requirement that there be such an assenting, universal in principle, is constitutive of aesthetic judgement. So if we keep to a psychological or social or pragmatic or generally anthropological kind of description, we give up on according to art a specific status as to its reception, and basically, we grant that there is no art. If we abandon this transitivity – potential, immediate, capable of being demanded in the judgement of taste and, simultaneously, demanded in order for there to be art – by the same token we abandon the idea of a community deriving from what Kant calls *sensus communis*, which is to say from an immediately communicable *sentimentality*.

And it cannot be said of a feeling that it must gather everyone's agreement without mediation, immediately, without presupposing a sort of *community of feeling* such that every one of the individuals, placed before the same situation, the same work, can at least dispose of an identical judgement without elaborating it conceptually. In the analysis of aesthetic feeling, there is thus also an issue of the analysis of what goes on with a community in general. In the reception of works of art, what is involved is the status of a sentimental, aesthetic community, one certainly 'anterior' to all communication and all pragmatics. The cutting out of intersubjective relations has not yet happened and there would be an assenting, a unanimity possible and capable of being demanded, within an order which cannot 'yet' be that of argumentation between rational and speaking subjects.

The hypothesis of another type of community thus emerges, irreducible to theories of communication. If we accept that assumed communicability is included in the singular aesthetic feeling, and if we accept that this singular aesthetic feeling is the immediate mode, which is no doubt to say the poorest and the purest, of a possibility to space and time, necessary forms of *aesthesis*, then can this communicability persist when the forms which should be its occasion are conceptually determined, whether in their generation or in their transmission? What happens to aesthetic feeling when *calculated* situations are put forward as aesthetic?

The opposition between linear system and figurative system indicated in the conference's rubric, not to mention the hopes invested in the calculated production of figures, seems to me irrelevant in relation to the one I am trying to state between *passibility* and activity. Passibility as the possibility of experiencing (*pathos*) presupposes a donation. If we are in a state of passibility, it's that something is happening to us, and when this passibility has a fundamental status, the donation itself is something fundamental, originary. What happens to us is not at all something we have first controlled, programmed, grasped by a concept [*Begriff*]. Or else, if what we are passible to has first been plotted conceptually, how can it *seize us*? How can it test us if we already know, or if we can know – of what, with what, for what, it is done? Or else, if such a feeling, in the very radical sense that Kant tries to give this term, takes place, it must be admitted that what happens to us disconcerts us. When Kant speaks of the *matter* of sensation, which he opposes to its form, its formation, it is precisely to do with what we cannot calculate. We have nothing to say about what it is that administers this matter to us, gives it to us. We cannot conceptualize this sort of *Other* with a capital O which Kant calls a big X. It must certainly be granted that the donation proceeds from an X, which Heidegger called *Being*.[4] This donation which is experienced before (or better, in) any capture or conceptualization gives *matter* for reflection, for the conception, and it is *on it*, for it, that we are going to construct our aesthetic philosophy and our theories of communication. There does have to be something which is given first. The feeling is the immediate *Welcoming* of what is given. Works produced by the new *techne* necessarily, and to quite diverse degrees, and in diverse parts of themselves, bear the traces of having been determined to be one or more *calculations*, whether in their constitution and/or their restitution, or only in their distribution. And by 'calculation' I don't only mean the kind that occupies the time of computer engineers, but also taking in the inevitable measurability of spaces and times, of all the times, including those dubbed 'working' times, expended in the production of these works and their distribution.

Any industrial reproduction pays homage to this profound and funda- mental problematic of *re*-presentation, and aesthetic feeling presupposes something which necessarily is implied, and forgotten, in representation: presentation, the fact that something is *there now*. All representations presuppose space and time as that by and in which something happens to us and which is always here and now: the place and the moment. It has to do not with concepts but simply with modes of presentation. As soon as we are within the arts of representation, the question of the here-and-now is hidden. How can there be an *aesthetic* feeling issuing from calculated re-presentation alone? How could the traces of the conceptual determina- tion of the forms proposed by the new *techne* leave free the play of reflexive judgement which constitutes aesthetic pleasure? How could the communicability constitutive of this pleasure, which remains potential, promised and not affected, not be excluded by the conceptual, argumen- tative and techno-scientific – 'realistic' – determination of what is com- municated in the product of these new technologies?

In urging this strange problematic of aesthetic feeling in Kant, in its im- mediacy and its demand for universal communicability, without which it's not art we're dealing with, I only mean to suggest the following hypothesis: what is hit first of all, and complains, in our modernity, or our postmodernity, is perhaps space and time. What is attacked would be space and time as forms of the donation of what happens. The real 'crisis of foundations' was doubtless not that of the foundations of reason but of any scientific enterprise bearing on so-called real objects, in other words given in sensory space and time.

There are already two aesthetics in Kant, two senses of the word *aesthetic*. In the first Aesthetic (*Critique of Pure Reason*), the question posed is restricted to the elaboration of the sensible (its 'synthesis') through which it is knowable by concept. How is it that concepts can find application in reality? It must be that there are already, in the sensible as it is given to us, types of syntheses of elements, sensible unities, which prepare it for its being taken into intelligibility under concepts. There is an affinity between what is given in the sensible and what the concept is going to do with it. For example in the temporal series of sounds, there is what permits the application of the numerical series. It is this first synthesis which Kant calls *schema* and which, in the sensible, prepares for the conceptual application. We can know the sensible because it has an affinity with the intelligence. In the third Critique [the *Critique of Judgement*], the Aesthetic elaborates the question of the forms. The object at this point is not to understand how science is possible but to understand how it is that in the here-and-now of donation a feeling is produced such that it is only the affective transcription of the forms which float freely in space and time. Kant attributes this feeling to the inscription on the subject of the forms attributable to the productive imagination. The syntheses which take place in the sensible are no longer conceived here by Kant as preparing for science but as permitting *feeling* which is itself preparatory to all knowledge. It is the way that the forms are received by a subject which interests him; he also calls them *monograms*.

There is thus first of all this schema/form problem, but there is further the division of the apprehension of the forms into two aesthetic feelings: the feeling of the beautiful and the feeling of the sublime. This last, whose Analytic Kant introduces without any sort of justification, contrary to rule, has the interesting property of including no immediate communicability. The feeling of the sublime is manifested when the presentation of free forms is lacking. It is compatible with the form-less. It is even when the imagination which presents forms finds itself lacking that such a feeling appears. And this latter must go via the *mediation* of an Idea of reason which is the Idea of freedom. We find sublime those spectacles which exceed any real presentation of a form, in other words where what is signified is the superiority of our power of freedom *vis-à-vis* the one manifested in the spectacle itself. In singling out the sublime, Kant places the accent on something directly related to the problem of the failing of space and time. The free-floating forms which aroused the feeling of the beautiful come to be lacking. In a certain way the question of the sublime is closely linked to what Heidegger calls the retreat of Being, retreat of donation. For Heidegger, the welcome accorded something sensory, in other words some meaning embodied in the here-and-now before any concept, no longer has place and moment. This retreat signifies our current fate.

In *The Principle of Reason* and *The Age of the World Picture*, the opposition is at its greatest between the poetic, receptivity in the sense of this Kantian sentimentality, and the *Gestell* [untranslatable: enframing?], which is to be credited to techno-science. For Heidegger, techno-science at its height was nuclear science; we have done much better in *Gestell* nowadays. It is clear that the in-stallation [same 'root' as *stellen*] of the concept as far as space-time is infinitely more fine in the new technologies than it was in what Heidegger was familiar with. Opposition between two forms of reception: on one side the poetic form which he imputes to the Greeks, and on the other techno-scientific reception (it is still an ontological reception) which occurs under the general regime of the principle of reason and whose explicit birth he sees in Leibniz's thought. It is clear that the idea of the combinatory, and thus of all that governs computer science and communication, is one of the things whose birth is in this, including the infinitesimal.

This problematic should be taken up again, revised and corrected: it seems to me central in the question of 'art and communication'. In Hölderlin's *Remarks* on Oedipus, which it would be necessary for us to ponder, the poet notes that the true tragedy of Oedipus is that the god has categorically turned away from man. The real tragedy is not *Oedipus Tyrannos* (the plot, the murder, the misunderstanding) but *Oedipus at Colonus*, in other words when fate is accomplished and nothing more happens to the hero, nothing is destined for him any more. The loss of all destiny is the essential feature of the drama and in this 'nothing happens' also lies the essential feature of our problematic. It is clear that what is called communication is always, in every case, that nothing happens, that we are not destined. And in this connection Hölderlin adds this quite remarkable sentence: 'At the extreme limit of distress, there is in fact nothing left but the conditions of time and space.'

At the horizon of what is called the 'end of art', which Hegelian thought discovers at the start of the nineteenth century, we find the melancholy of 'there is nothing left but the conditions of time and space', which tends and bandages itself in that immense work of mourning, that immense remission which is Hegelian dialectical thought. Not only is it going to be necessary to absorb the fact that 'there is nothing left but time and space' as pure conditions (which is done from the start of the first great work, the *Phenomenology of Spirit*, where it is demonstrated that space and time have their truth not in themselves but in the concept, that there is no here-and-now, that the sensible is always already mediated by the under-standing), but the theme of the end of art reveals on another level the persistence of the theme of the retreat of the donation and the crisis of the aesthetic. If there is no time, if time is the concept, there is no art except by mistake, or rather the moment of the end of art coincides with that of the hegemony of the concept. We should connect this problematic back with the one we are immersed in nowadays, generalized logocentrism, and show that the art-industry belongs indirectly to this way of finishing art off. The art-industry would be a completion of speculative metaphys-ics, a way in which Hegel is present, has succeeded, in Hollywood. To be elucidated through Paul Virilio's remarks on the problem of space and time which he calls *critical*, in a strategic sense: that of the Pentagon.[5] The position of Husserl in the face of the crisis of the sciences in Europe should also be elaborated.

A study of the advant-gardes is imperative. Their movement is not only due to the end of art. If they are in a problematic analogous to the one through which Hegel thematizes the end of art, they have 'exploited' this 'there remains only' in an exemplary way. If there remain only the condi-tions of space and time, in other words, basically, if representation, the staging of plots, are not interesting and what is interesting is Oedipus without a fate, then let's elaborate a painting of the fate-less. The avant-gardes get to work on the conditions of space and time. Attempts which have been going on for a century without having finished yet. This prob-lematic makes it possible to resituate the real issue of the avant-gardes by putting them back in their domain. They have been inflexible witnesses to the crisis of these foundations of which theories of communication and the new technologies are other aspects, much less lucid ones than the avant-gardes. They at least had the sense of drama, and in this they are completely analogous in their own field to what has happened in the sciences.

From the end of the nineteenth century, there has been an immense amount of discussion under the heading of 'crisis of the sciences' – bearing on arithmetic, in other words the science of number which is the science of time; on geometry, the science of space; and on mechanics, the science of movement, which is to say the science of space and time. It is very hard to believe that what has been being discussed between scientists and philosophers for a century must be of no interest to the little ideology of communication. The problems out of which emerged non-Euclidean geometry, axiomatic forms of arithmetic and non-Newtonian physics are also those which gave rise to the theories of communication and information.

Is it the case that in this crisis, which bears on the conditions of space and time (with its two expressions: modern – there no longer remains anything but space and time; and postmodem – we no longer *even* have space and time left) – is it the case that in this work, which we take up under the aspect of communication, there is simply the loss of something (donation or presentation) without there being some gain? We are losing the earth (Husserl), which is to say the here-and-now, but are we gaining something and how are we gaining it? Can the uprooting which is linked to the new technology promise us an emancipation?

As is indicated in the conference's programme, the question of the body comes up here; but we must not put too much trust in this word, for if space and time are hit and attacked by the new technologies, then the body is too and has to be. Perhaps we should also set ourselves to the work of mourning the body.

About the confusion between passible and passive. These two problems are distinct: passivity is opposed to activity, but not passibility. Even further, this active/passive opposition presupposes passibility and at any rate is not what matters in the reception of works of art. The demand for an activity or 'interactivity' instead proves that there should be more intervention, and that we are thus through with aesthetic feeling. When you painted, you did not ask for 'interventions' from the one who looked, you claimed there was a community. The aim nowadays is not that sentimentality you still find in the slightest sketch by a Cézanne or a Degas, it is rather that the one who receives should not receive, it is that s/he does not let him/herself be put out, it is his/her self-constitution as active subject in relation to what is addressed to him/her: let him/her reconstitute himself immediately and identify himself or herself as someone who intervenes. What we live by and judge by is exactly this will to action. If a computer invites us to play or *lets* us play, the interest valorized is that the one receiving should manifest his or her capacity for initiative, activity, etc. We are thus still derivatives from the Cartesian model of 'making oneself master and possessor . . .' It implies the retreat of the passibility by which alone we are fit to receive and, as a result, to modify and do, and perhaps even to enjoy. This passibility as *jouissance*[6] and obligatory belonging to an immediate community is repressed nowadays in the general problematic of communication, and is even taken as shameful. But to take action in the direction of this activity which is so sought-after is only to react, to repeat, at best to conform feverishly to a game that is already given or installed [*gestellt?*]. Passibility, in contrast, has to do with an immediate community of feeling demanded across the singular aesthetic feeling, and what is lost is more than simple capacity, it is propriety. Interactional ideology is certainly opposed to a passivity but it remains confined in a completely secondary opposition.

The true issue is to know whether or not are maintained the actuality and immediacy of a feeling which appeals to the co-belonging to a 'ground' presupposed by concept and calculation in their eluding of it. The work is only first *received* in the name of this immediate community, even if afterwards it can be presented in a gallery, at a distance. We are dealing with a problem of the modality of presence and not a problem of content or simple form. The question of unanimity of feeling bears not on what is presented or on the forms of presentation, but on the modality of reception, as demand for unanimity. It is not a matter of situating passibility as a moment, even a brief one, in a process of appropriation of the work, it is a matter of saying (and this is what is meant by *transcendental critique* in Kant) that without this dimension, we are incapable of so much as recognizing a work *of art*. It is an a priori condition even if it is never marked in a perceptible way in the psycho-social process.

What is absolutely specific in art? What do space and time have to do with it? What is the gain from techno-science? What will become of our body? It is not in the discourse of techno-science, which *de facto* and *de jure* takes place outside this situation, but in the quite different field of the will to identification, that we will be able so much as to broach these questions.

Passibility: the opposite of 'impassibility'? Something is not destined for you, there is no way to feel it. You are touched, you will only *know* this afterwards. (And in thinking you know it, you will be mistaken about this 'touch'.) We imagine that minds are made anxious by not intervening in the production of the product. It is because we think of presence according to the exclusive modality of masterful intervention. Not to be contemplative is a sort of implicit commandment, contemplation is perceived as a devalorized passivity.

In Kant, passibility does not disappear with the sublime but becomes a passibility to *lack*. It is precisely the beautiful forms with their destination, our own destiny, which are missing, and the sublime includes this sort of pain due to the finitude of 'flesh', this ontological melancholy.

The question raised by the new technologies in connection with their relation to art is that of the here-and-now. What does 'here' mean on the phone, on television, at the receiver of an electronic telescope? And the 'now'? Does not the 'tele-' element necessarily destroy presence, the 'here-and-now' of the forms and their 'carnal' reception? What is a place, a moment, not anchored in the immediate 'passion' of what happens? Is a computer in any way here and now? Can anything happen with it? Can anything *happen* to it?

Notes

1 Cf. Theodor Adorno, *Aesthetic Theory*, trans. C. Lenhardt (London: Routledge and Kegan Paul, 1984); and Immanuel Kant, *The Critique of Judgement*, trans. James Creed Meredith (Oxford: Clarendon Press, 1952). It is worth noting that Lyotard consistently opposes his own views on art to those of Adorno, for whom art today is the guarantee of a 'critical theory'. That is, for Adorno, art manifests the historical loss of a grand theory of everything, but in doing so maintains the critical necessity of compensating for that loss. Art, then, plays the negative role of marking loss *in order to* continue playing out the historical promise of emancipation. What this 'negative aesthetics' cannot see, on Lyotard's account, is that art's negative work (its exposure of the role of asystematic, irrational forces within history and human subjectivity, for example) is in and of itself *affirmative*, without any recourse to a myth – another grand theory – of historical emancipation. For Lyotard, 'art' is the name of what always resists historical resolution or metanarratives of any kind, such that art is the affirmation of a resistance to 'theory' in general. In place of an aesthetic theory, Lyotard proposes a 'libidinal economy' based on the Kantian beautiful and a certain notion of *jouissance* (see note 6 below). (NL)

2 Philosophy, for Hegel, incorporates art: the figure is contained within the concept, which is therefore higher than it or more absolute. But for Lyotard the figural is what cannot be conceptualized; art is what always remains outside knowledge as defined philosophically or dialectically. In other words, because art cannot be communicated *to* philosophy (or any 'critical theory'), it most certainly cannot be communicated *through* it. (NL)

3 Cf. Kant, *Critique of Judgement*, Bk I. In a nutshell, this (in Kant's words) is Lyotard's point: 'In all judgements by which we describe anything as

beautiful, we tolerate no one else being of a different opinion, and in taking up this position we do not rest our judgement upon concepts, but only on our feeling. Accordingly we introduce this fundamental feeling not as a private feeling, but as a public sense' (§ 22). (NL)

4   There could be no neat definition of what Heidegger means by 'Being', but here goes: There is a world; this alone is cause for unsurpassable wonder; such wonder is Being. Yet Being senses not only that there is a world but also that it's made up of differences (between beings, between the particularities of entities); hence Being senses both the *that* and the *way* of the world. See Martin Heidegger, *Being and Time*, trans. J. Macquarie and E. Robinson (Oxford: Blackwell, 1962). (NL)

5   Cf. Paul Virilio, *The Lost Dimension*, trans. Daniel Moshenberg. New York: Semiotext(e), 1991. (NL)

6   *Jouissance*, with at least three senses in French, is notoriously tricky to translate into English. The term refers to orgasmic pleasure, to pleasure generally and to the enjoyment of certain privileges (such as legal rights) or of ownership or belonging (the enjoyment of belonging to a class or community or of owning a certain professional rank or social status). Roland Barthes is to be credited with thinking the importance of *jouissance* to a theory of reading or, in Lyotard's terms here, to any form of communication in general. See Barthes' chapter in the present volume and especially his *The Pleasure of the Text*, trans. Richard Miller (New York: Hill & Wang, 1975). The key point perhaps is that *jouissance*, certainly as sexual excitement, is located in the body; hence communication is not simply an effect of signifying systems as structural or formal abstractions, since it involves a corporeal dimension which is incalculable from the vantage of any communication 'system' but is none the less essential to any instance of 'communication' as such. (NL)

Chapter Three **From One Identity to an Other**

Julia Kristeva

I shall attempt, within the ritual limits of a one-hour seminar, to posit (if not to demonstrate) that every language theory is predicated upon a conception of the subject that it explicitly posits, implies, or tries to deny. Far from being an 'epistemological perversion', a definite subject is present as soon as there is consciousness of signification. Consequently, I shall need to outline an epistemological itinerary: taking three stages in the recent history of linguistic theory, I shall indicate the variable position these may have required of the speaking subject-support within their object language. This – on the whole, technical – foray into the epistemology of linguistic science will lead us to broach and, I hope, elucidate a problem whose ideological stakes are considerable but whose banality is often ignored. Meaning, identified either within the unity or the multiplicity of subject, structure, or theory, necessarily guarantees a certain transcendence, if not a theology; this is precisely why all human knowledge, whether it be that of an individual subject or of a meaning structure, retains religion as its blind boundaries, or at least, as an internal limit, and at best, can just barely 'explain and validate religious sentiment' (as Lévi-Strauss observed, in connection with structuralism).[1] Second, I shall deal with a particular signifying practice, which, like the Russian Formalists,[2] I call 'poetic language', in order to demonstrate that this kind of language, through the particularity of its signifying operations, is an unsettling process – when not an outright destruction – of the identity of meaning and speaking subject,[3] and consequently, of transcendence, or, by derivation, of 'religious sensibility'. On that account, it

Julia Kristeva, 'From One Identity to an Other' [Fr. 1975], in *Desire in Language: A Semiotic Approach to Literature and Art*, trans. T. Gora, A. Jardine and L. S. Roudiez; ed. L. S. Roudiez (Oxford: Blackwell, 1981), pp. 124–47.

accompanies crises within social structures and institutions – the moments of their mutation, evolution, revolution, or disarray. For if mutation within language and institutions finds its code through this signifying practice and its questionable subject in process that constitutes poetic language, then that practice and subject are walking a precarious tightrope. Poetic language, the only language that uses up transcendence and theology to sustain itself, poetic language, knowingly the enemy of religion, by its very economy borders on psychosis (as for its subject) and totalitarianism or fascism (as for the institutions it implies or evokes). I could have spoken of Vladimir Mayakovsky or Antonin Artaud; I shall speak of Louis-Ferdinand Céline.

Finally, I shall try to draw a few conclusions concerning the possibility of a *theory* in the sense of an *analytical discourse* on signifying systems, which would take into account these crises of meaning, subject, and structure. This for two reasons: first, such crises, far from being accidents, are inherent in the signifying function and, consequently, in sociality; secondly, situated at the forefront of twentieth-century politics, these phenomena (which I consider within poetic language, but which may assume other forms in the West as well as in other civilizations) could not remain outside the so-called human sciences without casting suspicion on their ethic. I shall therefore and in conclusion argue in favor of an analytical theory of signifying systems and practices that would search within the signifying phenomenon for the *crisis* or the *unsettling process* of meaning and subject rather than for the coherence or identity of either *one* or a *multiplicity* of structures.

Without referring back to the stoic sage, who guaranteed both the sign's triad and the inductive conditional clause, let us return to the congruence between conceptions of language and of subject where Ernest Renan [the nineteenth-century French philologist and historian – NL] left them. We are all aware of the scandal he caused among nineteenth-century minds when he changed a theological discourse (the Gospels) not into a *myth* but into the *history* of a man and a people. This conversion of *theological* discourse into *historical* discourse was possible thanks to a tool (for him, scientific) whose omnipotence he never ceased praising – philology. As used by Renan or Eugene Burnouf in Avestic Studies, for example, philology incorporates the *comparativism* of philologists Franz Bopp or August Schleicher. Whatever the difference between comparativists seeking those *laws* unique to *families* of languages and philologists deciphering the *meaning of one* language, a common conception of language as an *organic identity* unites them. Little does it matter that, as comparativists believed, this organic identity articulates itself thanks to *a law* that crosses national and historical language borders making of them one family (cf. Jacob Grimm's phonetic laws); or that, as philologists believed, this organic identity articulates itself thanks to *one meaning* – singular and unique – inscribed into a text still undeciphered or whose decipherability is debatable. In both cases *this organic identity* of law or meaning implies that language is the possession of a *homo loquens* within history. As Renan writes in *Averoés et l'Averroïsme*, 'for the philologist, a text has only one meaning' even if it is through 'a kind of necessary misinterpretation' that 'the philosophical and religious development of humanity' proceeds.[4] Closer to the objectivity of the Hegelian 'consciousness of self' for the comparativists, embodied into a singularity that, be it concrete, individual, or national, still owes something to Hegel for the philologists; language is always one system, perhaps even one 'structure', always *one meaning*, and, therefore, it necessarily implies a subject (collective or individual) to bear witness to its history. If one has difficulty following Renan when he affirms that 'rationalism is based on philology' – for it is obvious that the two are interdependent – it is no less obvious that philological reasoning is maintained through the identity of a historical subject: a subject in becoming. Why? Because, far from dissecting the internal logic of sign predication (sentence grammar), or syllogism (logic), as did the universal grammar of Port Royal, the comparativist and philological reason that Renan exemplifies considers the signifying unit in itself (sign, sentence, syllogism) as an unanalyzable given. This signifying unit remains implicit within each description of law or text that philologists and comparativists undertake: linear, unidimensional descriptions – with no analysis of the sign's density, the logical problematic of meaning, etc. – but which, once technically completed, restore structural identity (for the comparativists) or meaning (for the philologists); in so doing they reveal the initial presupposition of the specifically linguistic undertaking as an ideology that posits either the people or an exceptional individual as appropriating this structure or this meaning. Because it is in itself unanalyzable (like the sign, sentence, and syllogism, it has no density, no economy), this subject-support of comparativist laws or of philological analysis does not lend itself to change, that is to say, to shifting from one law to another, from one structure to another, or from one meaning to another, except by postulating the movement of becoming, that is, of history. In the analysis of a signifying function (language or any 'human', social phenomenon), what is censured at the level of semantic complexity re-emerges in the form of a becoming: that obliteration of the density that constitutes sign, sentence, and syllogism (and consequently, the speaking subject), is compensated for by historical reasoning; the reduction of the complex signifying economy of the speaking subject (though obliquely perceived by Port Royal) produces without fail an opaque 'I' that makes history. Thus, philological reasoning, while founding history, becomes a deadlock for language sciences, even though there actually is in Renan, beyond countless contradictions, an appreciation of universal grammar, a call for the constitution of a linguistics for an isolated language (in the manner of the ancient Indian grammarian Panini), and even surprisingly modern proposals that advocate the study of crisis rather than normality, and in his semitic studies the remarks on 'that delirious vision transcribed in a barbaric and undecipherable style' as he calls the Christian gnostic texts, or on the texts of John the Apostle.[5]

Linguistic reasoning, which, through Saussure, succeeded philological reasoning, works its revolution precisely by affecting the constitutive unity of a particular language; a language is not a system, it is a system of signs, and this vertically opens up the famous gap between signifier and signified, thus allowing linguistics to claim a logical, mathematical formalization on the one hand, but on the other, it definitely prevents reducing a language or text to one law or one meaning. Structural linguistics and the ensuing structural movement seem to explore this epistemological space by eliminating the speaking subject. But, on a closer look, we see that the subject they legitimately do without is nothing but the subject (individual or collective) of historico-philological discourse I just discussed, and in which the Hegelian consciousness of self became stranded as it was concretized, embodied into philology and history; this subject, which linguistics and the corollary human sciences do without, is the 'personal identity, miserable treasure'.[6] Nevertheless, a subject of enunciation takes shape within the gap opened up between signifier and signified that admits both structure and interplay within; and structural linguistics ignores such a subject. Moreover, because it left its place vacant, structural linguistics could not become a linguistics of speech or discourse; it lacked a grammar, for in order to move from sign to sentence the place of the subject had to be acknowledged and no longer kept vacant. Of course, generative grammar does reinstate it by rescuing universal grammar and the Cartesian subject from oblivion, using that subject to justify the generative, recursive functions of syntactic trees. But in fact, generative grammar is evidence of what structural linguistics omitted, rather than a new beginning; whether structural or generative, linguistics since Saussure adheres to the same presuppositions, implicit within the structuralist current, explicit in the generative tendency that can be found summed up in the philosophy of Husserl.

I refer modern linguistics and the modes of thought which it oversees within the so-called human sciences back to this founding father from another field, but not for conjunctural reasons, though they are not lacking. Indeed, Husserl was invited to and discussed by the Circle of Prague;[7] indeed, Jakobson explicitly recognized in him a philosophical mentor for post-Saussurian linguists; indeed, several American epistemologists of generative grammar recognize in Husserlian phenomenology, rather than in Descartes, the foundations of the generative undertaking. But it is possible to detect in Husserl the basis of linguistic reasoning (structural or generative) to the extent that, after the reduction of the Hegelian consciousness of self into philological or historical identity, Husserl masterfully understood and posited that any signifying act, insofar as it remains capable of elucidation by knowledge, does not maintain itself by a 'me, miserable treasure' but by the 'transcendental ego'.

If it is true that the division of the Saussurian sign (signifier/signified), unknown to Husserl, also introduces the heretofore unrecognized possibility of envisioning language as a free play, forever without closure, it is also true that this possibility was not developed by Saussure except in the very problematic *Anagrammes*.[8] Moreover, this investigation has no linguistic followers, but rather, philosophical (Heideggerian discourse) and psychoanalytic (Lacan's signifier) contemporaries or successors, who today effectively enable us to appreciate and circumscribe the contribution of phenomenological linguistics from a Husserlian perspective. For post-Saussurian structural linguistics still encloses the signifier, even if nonmotivated, within patterns of a signification originally destined for faultless communication, either coinciding with the explicit signified or set off a short distance from it, but still fastened to the unalterable presence of meaning and, similarly, tributary to phenomenological reason.

It is therefore impossible to take up the congruence between conceptions of language and of subject where Renan left off without recalling how Husserl shifted ground by raising it above empiricism, psychologism, and incarnation theories typical of Renan. Let us examine for a moment the signifying act and the Husserlian transcendental ego, keeping in mind that linguistic reason (structural or generative) is to Husserl what philological reason was to Hegel: reduction perhaps, but also concrete realization, that is, failure made manifest.

As early as *Logical Investigations* of 1901, Husserl situates the sign (of which one could have naively thought that it had no subject) within the act of expressing meaning, constituted by a judgment on something: 'The articulate sound-complex, the written sign, etc., first becomes a spoken word or communicative bit of speech, when a speaker produces it with the intention of "expressing himself about something" through its means.'[9]

Consequently, the thin sheath of the sign (signifier/signified) opens onto a complex architecture where intentional life-experience captures material (hylic) multiplicities, endowing them first with noetic meaning [pertaining to the intellect], then with noematic meaning [pertaining to understanding], so that finally the result for the judging consciousness is the formation of an *object* once and for all signified as real. The important point here is that this real *object*, first signified by means of hylic data, through noesis and noemis, if it exists, can only be transcendental in the sense that it is elaborated in its identity by the judging consciousness of transcendental ego. The signified is transcendent as it is posited by means of certain concatenations within an experience that is always confined to judgment; for if the phenomenologist distinguishes between intuiting and endowing with meaning, then perception is already *cogitation* and the *cogitation* is transcendent to perception.[10] So much so that if the world were annihilated, the signified '*res*' would remain because they are transcendental: they 'refer entirely to a consciousness' insofar as they are signified *res*. The *predicative* (syntactic) operation constitutes this judging consciousness, positing at the same time the signified *Being* (and therefore, the object of meaning and signification) and *the operating consciousness* itself. The ego as support of the predicative act therefore does not operate as the ego-cogito, that is, as the ego of a logically conceived consciousness and 'fragment of the world'; rather, the transcendental ego belongs to the constituting operating consciousness, which means that it takes shape within the predicative operation. This operation is *thetic* because it simultaneously posits the thesis (position) of both Being and ego. Thus, for every signified transcendental object, there is a transcendental ego, both of which are givens by virtue of thetic operation – predication of judgment.

'Transcendental egology'[11] thus reformulates the question of the signifying act's subject: (1) the operating consciousness, through predication, simultaneously constitutes Being, the (transcendent) signified real object, and the ego (in so far as it is transcendental); the problematic of the sign is also bound up in this question; (2) even if intentionality, and with it, the judging consciousness, is already a given in material data and perceptions, as it 'resembles' them (which allows us to say that the transcendental ego is always already in a way given), *in fact*, the ego constitutes itself only through the operating consciousness at the time of predication; the subject is merely the subject of predication, of judgment, of the sentence; (3) 'belief' and 'judgment' are closely interdependent though not identical: 'The syntheses of belief (Glaubenssynthesen) find their 'expression' in the forms of stated meaning'.[12]

Neither a historical individual nor a logically conceived consciousness, the subject is henceforth the operating thetic consciousness positing correlatively the transcendental Being and ego. Thus, Husserl makes clear that any linguistic act, insofar as it sets up a signified that can be communicated in a sentence (and there is no sign or signifying structure that is not already part of a sentence), is sustained by the transcendental ego.

It is perhaps not unimportant that the rigor of Judaism and the persecution it has been subjected to in our time underlie Husserl's extraordinarily firm elucidation of the transcendental ego, just as they are the foundation of the human sciences.

For the purposes of our discussion, we can draw two conclusions from this brief review:

1. It is impossible to treat problems of signification seriously, in linguistics or semiology, without including in these considerations *the subject thus formulated as operating consciousness*. This phenomenological conception of the speaking subject is made possible in modern linguistics by the introduction of logic into generative grammar and, in a much more lucid manner, through a linguistics (developing in France after Benveniste) which is attuned to the *subject of enunciation* and which includes in the latter's operating consciousness not only logical modalities, but also interlocutory relationships.

2. If it is true, consequently, that the question of signification and therefore of modern linguistics is dominated by Husserl, the attempts to criticize or 'deconstruct' phenomenology bear concurrently on Husserl, meaning, the still transcendental subject of enunciation, and linguistic methodology. These criticisms circumscribe the metaphysics inherent in the sciences of signification and therefore in the human sciences – an important epistemological task in itself. But they reveal their own shortcomings not so much, as some believe, in that they prevent serious, theoretical or scientific research, but in that such 'deconstructions' refuse (through discrediting the signified and with it the transcendental ego) what constitutes one function of language though not the only one: to express meaning in a communicable sentence between speakers. This function harbors coherence (which is indeed transcendental) or, in other

words, social identity. Let us first acknowledge, with Husserl, this thetic character of the signifying act, which establishes the transcendent object and the transcendental ego of communication (and consequently of sociability), before going beyond the Husserlian problematic to search for that which produces, shapes, and exceeds the operating consciousness (this will be our purpose when confronting poetic language). Without that acknowledgment, which is also that of the episteme underlying structuralism, any reflection on significance, by refusing its thetic character, will continually ignore its constraining, legislative, and socializing elements: under the impression that it is breaking down the metaphysics of the signified or the transcendental ego, such a reflection will become lodged in a negative theology that denies their limitations.

Finally, even when the researcher in the field, beginning with what is now a descriptive if not scientific perspective, thinks he has discovered givens that may escape the *unity* of the transcendental ego (because each identity would be as if flaked into a multiplicity of qualities or appurtenances), the discourse of knowledge that delivers this multiplied identity to us remains a prisoner of phenomenological reason for which the multiplicities, inasmuch as they signify, are givens of consciousness, predicates within the same eidetic unity: the unity of an object signified by and for a transcendental ego. In an interpretive undertaking for which there is no domain heterogeneous to meaning, all material diversities, as multiple attributes, revert to a real (transcendental) object. Even apparently psychoanalytic interpretations (relationship to parents, etc.), from the moment they are posited by the structuring learning as particularities of the transcendental real object, are false multiplicities; deprived of what is heterogeneous to meaning, these multiplicities can only produce a plural identity – but an identity all the same, since it is eidetic, transcendental. Husserl therefore stands on the threshold not only of modern linguistics concerned with a subject of enunciation, but of any science of man as signified phenomenon, whose objecthood, even if multiple, is to be restored.

To the extent that poetic language operates with and communicates meaning, it also shares particularities of the signifying operations elucidated by Husserl (correlation between signified object and the transcendental ego, operating consciousness, which constitutes itself by predication – by syntax – as thetic: thesis of Being, thesis of the object, thesis of the ego). Meaning and signification, however, do not exhaust the poetic function. Therefore, the thetic predicative operation and its correlatives (signified object and transcendental ego), though valid for the signifying economy of poetic language, are only one of its *limits*: certainly constitutive, but not all-encompassing. While poetic language can indeed be studied through its meaning and signification (by revealing, depending on the method, either structures or process), such a study would, in the final analysis, amount to reducing it to the phenomenological perspective and, hence, failing to see what in the poetic function departs from the signified and the transcendental ego and makes of what is known as 'literature' something other than knowledge: the very place where social code is destroyed and renewed, thus providing, as Artaud writes, 'A release for the anguish of its time' by 'animating, attracting, lowering onto its shoulders the wandering anger of a particular time for the discharge of its psychological evil-being'.[13]

Consequently, one should begin by positing that there is within poetic language (and therefore, although in a less pronounced manner, within any language) a *heterogeneousness* to meaning and signification. This *heterogeneousness*, detected genetically in the first echolalias of infants as rhythms and intonations anterior to the first phonemes, morphemes, lexemes, and sentences; this heterogeneousness, which is later reactivated as rhythms, intonations, glossalalias in psychotic discourse, serving as ultimate support of the speaking subject threatened by the collapse of the signifying function; this heterogeneousness to signification operates through, despite, and in excess of it and produces in poetic language 'musical' but also nonsense effects that destroy not only accepted beliefs and significations, but, in radical experiments, syntax itself, that guarantee of thetic consciousness (of the signified object and ego) – for example, carnivalesque discourse,[14] Artaud, a number of texts by Mallarmé, certain Dadaist and Surrealist experiments. The notion of *heterogeneity* is indispensable, for though articulate, precise, organized, and complying with constraints and rules (especially, like the rule of *repetition*, which articulates the units of a particular rhythm or intonation), this signifying disposition is not that of meaning or signification: no sign, no predication, no signified object and therefore no operating consciousness of a transcendental ego. We shall call this disposition *semiotic* (*le sémiotique*), meaning, according to the etymology of the Greek *sémeion* (σημεῖον), a distinctive mark, trace, index, the premonitory sign, the proof, engraved mark, imprint – in short, a *distinctiveness* admitting of an uncertain and indeterminate articulation because it does not yet refer (for young children) or no longer refers (in psychotic discourse) to a signified object for a thetic consciousness (this side of, or through, both object and consciousness). Plato's *Timeus* speaks of a *chora* (χώρα), receptacle (ὑποδοχεῖον), unnamable, improbable, hybrid, anterior to naming, to the One, to the father, and consequently, maternally connoted to such an extent that it merits 'not even the rank of syllable'. One can describe more precisely than did philosophical intuition the particularities of this signifying disposition that I have just named semiotic – a term which quite clearly designates that we are dealing with a disposition that is definitely heterogeneous to meaning but always in sight of it or in either a negative or surplus relationship to it. Research I have recently undertaken on child language acquisition in the pre-phonological, one could say pre-predicative stages, or anterior to the 'mirror stage',[15] as well as another concomitant study on particularities of psychotic discourse aim notably at describing as precisely as possible – with the help of, for example, modern phono-acoustics – these semiotic operations (rhythm, intonation) and their dependence *vis-à-vis* the body's drives observable through muscular contractions and the libidinal or sublimated cathexis that accompany vocalizations. It goes without saying that, concerning a *signifying practice*, that is, a socially communicable discourse like poetic language, this semiotic heterogeneity posited by theory is inseparable from what I shall call, to distinguish it from the latter, the symbolic function of significance. The symbolic (*le symbolique*), as opposed to the semiotic, is this inevitable attribute of meaning, sign, and the signified object for the consciousness of Husserl's transcendental ego. Language as social practice necessarily presupposes these two dispositions, though combined in different ways to constitute *types of discourse*, types of signifying practices. Scientific discourse, for example, aspiring to the status of metalanguage, tends to reduce as much as possible the semiotic component. On the contrary, the signifying economy of poetic language is specific in that the semiotic is not only a constraint as is the symbolic, but it tends to gain the upper hand at the expense of the thetic and predicative constraints of the ego's judging consciousness. Thus in any poetic language, not only do the rhythmic constraints, for example, perform an organizing function that could go so far as to violate certain grammatical rules of a national language and often neglect the importance of an ideatory message, but in recent texts, these semiotic constraints (rhythm, phonic, vocalic timbres in Symbolist work, but also graphic disposition on the page) are accompanied by nonrecoverable syntactic elisions; it is impossible to reconstitute the particular elided syntactic category (object or verb), which makes the meaning of the utterance undecidable (for example, the nonrecoverable elisions in *Un Coup de Dés*).[16] However elided, attacked, or corrupted the symbolic function might be in poetic language, due to the impact of semiotic processes, the symbolic function nonetheless maintains its presence. It is for this reason that it is a language. First, it persists as an internal limit of this bipolar economy, since a multiple and sometimes even uncomprehensible signified is nevertheless communicated; secondly, it persists also because the semiotic processes themselves, far from being set adrift (as they would be in insane discourse), set up a new formal construct: a so-called new formal or ideological 'writer's universe', the never-finished, undefined production of a new space of significance. Husserl's 'thetic function' of the signifying act is thus re-assumed, but in 'different form: though poetic language unsettled the position of the signified and the transcendental ego, it nonetheless posits a thesis, not of a particular being or meaning, but of a signifying apparatus; it posits its own process as an undecidable process between sense and nonsense, between *language* and *rhythm* (in the sense of linkage that the word 'rhythm' had for Aeschylus's *Prometheus* according to Heidegger's reading),[17] between the symbolic and semiotic.

For a theory attuned to this kind of functioning, the language object itself appears quite differently than it would from a phenomenological perspective. Thus, a phoneme, as distinctive element of meaning, belongs to language as symbolic. But this same phoneme is involved in rhythmic, intonational repetitions; it thereby tends towards autonomy from meaning so as to maintain itself in a semiotic disposition near the instinctual drives' body; it is a sonorous distinctiveness, which therefore is no longer either a phoneme or a part of the symbolic system – one might say that its belonging to the set of the language is indefinite, between zero and one. Nevertheless, the set to which it thus belongs exists with this indefinition, with this fuzziness. It is poetic language that awakens our attention to this undecidable character of any so-called natural language, a feature that univocal, rational, scientific discourse tends to hide – and this implies considerable consequences for its subject. The support of this signifying economy could not be the transcendental ego alone. If it is true that there would unavoidably be a speaking *subject* since the signifying set exists, it is none the less evident that this subject, in order to tally with its heterogeneity, must be, let us say, a questionable *subject-in-process*. It is of course Freud's theory of the unconscious that allows the apprehension of such a subject; for through the surgery it practiced in the operating consciousness of the transcendental ego, Freudian and Lacanian psychoanalysis did allow, not for (as certain simplifications would have it) a few typologies or structures that might accommodate the same phenomenological reason, but rather for heterogeneity, which, known as the unconscious, shapes the signifying function. In light of these statements, I shall now make a few remarks on the questionable subject-in-process of poetic language.

1. The semiotic activity, which introduces wandering or fuzziness into language and, *a fortiori*, into poetic language is, from a synchronic point of view, a mark of the workings of drives (appropriation/rejection, orality/anality, love/hate, life/death) and, from a diachronic point of view, stems from the archaisms of the semiotic body. Before recognizing itself as identical in a mirror and, consequently, as signifying, this body is dependent *vis-à-vis* the mother. At the same time instinctual and maternal, semiotic processes prepare the future speaker for entrance into meaning and signification (the symbolic). But the symbolic (i.e., language as nomination, sign, and syntax) constitutes itself only by breaking with this anteriority, which is retrieved as 'signifier', 'primary processes', displacement and condensation, metaphor and metonomy, rhetorical figures – but which always remains subordinate – subjacent to the principal function of naming-predicating. Language as symbolic function constitutes itself at the cost of repressing instinctual drive and continuous relation to the mother. On the contrary, the unsettled and questionable subject of poetic language (for whom the word is never uniquely sign) maintains itself at the cost of reactivating this repressed instinctual, maternal element. If it is true that the prohibition of incest constitutes, at the same time, language as communicative code and women as exchange objects in order for a society to be established, *poetic language would be* for its questionable subject-in-process the *equivalent of incest*: it is within the economy of signification itself that the questionable subject-in-process appropriates to itself this archaic, instinctual, and maternal territory; thus it simultaneously prevents the word from becoming mere sign and the mother from becoming an object like any other – forbidden. This passage into and through the forbidden, which constitutes the sign and is correlative to the prohibition of incest, is often explicit as such (Sade: 'Unless he becomes his mother's lover from the day she has brought him into the world, let him not bother to write, for we shall not read him', – *Idée sur les romans*; Artaud, identifying with his 'daughters', Joyce and his daughter at the end of *Finnegans Wake*, Céline who takes as pseudonym his grandmother's first name; and innumerable identifications with women, or dancers, that waver between fetishization and homosexuality). I stress this point for three reasons:

(a) To emphasize that the dominance of semiotic constraint in poetic language cannot be solely interpreted, as formalist poetics would have it, as a preoccupation with the 'sign', or with the 'signifier' at the expense of the 'message'; rather, it is more deeply indicative of the instinctual drives' activity relative to the first structurations (constitution of the body as self) and identifications (with the mother).

(b) To elucidate the intrinsic connection between literature and break-ing up social concord: because it utters incest, poetic language is linked with 'evil'; 'literature and evil' (I refer to a title by Georges Bataille) should be understood, beyond the resonances of Christian ethics, as the social body's self-defense against the discourse of incest as destroyer and generator of any language and sociality. This applies all the more as 'great literature', which has mobilized unconsciousnesses for centuries, has noth-ing to do with the hypostasis of incest (a petty game of fetishists at the end of an era, priesthood of a would-be enigma – the forbidden mother); on the contrary, this incestuous relation, exploding in language, embracing it from top to bottom in such a *singular* fashion that it defies *generaliza-tions*, still has this common feature in all outstanding cases: it presents itself as demystified, even disappointed, deprived of its hallowed function as support of the law, in order to become the cause of a permanent trial of the speaking subject, a cause of that agility, of that analytic 'competency' that legend attributes to Ulysses.

(c) It is of course possible, as Lévi-Strauss pointed out to Dr André Green, to ignore the mother–child relationship within a given anthropo-logical vision of society; now, given not only the thematization of this relationship, but especially the mutations in the very economy of dis-course attributable to it, one must, in discussing poetic language, consider what this presymbolic and trans-symbolic relationship to the mother in-troduces as aimless wandering within the identity of the speaker and the economy of its very discourse. Moreover, this relationship of the speaker to the mother is probably one of the most important factors producing interplay within the structure of meaning as well as a questioning process of subject and history.

2. And yet, this reinstatement of maternal territory into the very economy of language does not lead its questioned subject-in-process to repudiate its symbolic disposition. Formulator – logothete, as Roland Barthes would say – the subject of poetic language continually but never definitively assumes the thetic function of naming, establishing meaning and signifi-cation, which the paternal function represents within reproductive rela-tion. Son permanently at war with father, not in order to take his place,

nor even to endure it, erased from reality, as a symbolic, divine menace and salvation in the manner of *Senatspräsident* [President of the Senate] Schreber. But rather, to signify what is untenable in the symbolic, nominal, paternal function. If symbolic and social cohesion are maintained by virtue of a sacrifice (which makes of a soma a sign towards an unnamable transcendence, so that only thus are signifying and social structures clinched even though they are ignorant of this sacrifice) and if the paternal function represents this sacrificial function, then it is not up to the poet to adjust to it. Fearing its rule but sufficiently aware of the legislation of language not to be able to turn away from this sacrificial-paternal function, he takes it by storm and from the flank. In *Maldoror*, Lautréamont struggles against the Omnipotent. After the death of his son Anatole, Mallarmé writes a Tombeau, thanks to which a book replaces not only the dead son, his own father, mother, and fiancée at the same time, but also hallowed humanism and the 'instinct of heaven' itself. The most analytical of them all, the Marquis de Sade, gives up this battle with, or for, the symbolic legislation represented by the father, in order to attack the power represented by a woman, Madame de Montreuil, visible figurehead of a dynasty of matrons toward whom he usurps, through writing, the role of father and incestuous son; here, the transgression is carried out and the trans-symbolic, transpaternal function of poetic language reaches its thematic end by staging a simultaneously impossible, sacrificial, and orgastic society – never one without the other.

Here we must clearly distinguish two positions: that of the rhetorician and that of the writer in the strongest sense of the word; that is, as Céline puts it, one who has 'style'. The rhetorician does not invent a language; fascinated by the symbolic function of paternal discourse, he *seduces* it in the Latin sense of the verb – he 'leads it astray', inflicts it with a few anomalies generally taken from writers of the past, thus miming a father who remembers having been a son and even a daughter of his father, but not to the point of leaving cover. This is indeed what is happening to the discourse of contemporary philosophers, in France particularly, when, hemmed in by the breakthroughs in social sciences on the one hand, and social upheavals on the other, the philosopher begins performing literary tricks, thus arrogating to himself a power over imaginations: a power which, though minor in appearance, is more fetching than that of the transcendental consciousness. The stylist's adventure is totally different; he no longer needs to seduce the father by rhetorical affectations. As winner of the battle, he may even drop the name of the father to take a pseudonym (Céline signs with his grandmother's first name), and thus, in the place of the father, assume a different discourse; neither imaginary discourse of the self, nor discourse of transcendental knowledge, but a permanent go-between from one to the other, a pulsation of sign and rhythm, of consciousness and instinctual drive. 'I am the father of my imaginative creations,' writes Mallarmé at the birth of Geneviève. 'I am my father, my mother, my son, and me', Artaud claims. Stylists all, they sound a dissonance within the thetic, paternal function of language.

3. Psychosis and fetishism represent the two abysses that threaten the unstable subject of poetic language, as twentieth-century literature has only too clearly demonstrated. As to *psychosis*, symbolic legality is wiped out in favor of arbitrariness of an instinctual drive without meaning and communication; panicking at the loss of all reference, the subject goes through fantasies of omnipotence or identification with a totalitarian leader. On the other hand, where *fetishism* is concerned, constantly dodging the paternal, sacrificial function produces an objectification of the pure signifier, more and more emptied of meaning – an insipid formalism. Nevertheless, far from thus becoming an unpleasant or negligible accident within the firm progress of symbolic process (which, in the footsteps of science, would eventually find signified elements for all signifiers, as rationalists believe), these borderline experiences, which contemporary poetic language has undergone, perhaps more dramatically than before or elsewhere, show not only that the Saussurian cleavage (signifier/signified) is forever unbridgeable, but also that it is reinforced by another, even more radical one between an instinctual, semioticizing body, heterogeneous to signification, and this very signification based on prohibition (of incest), sign, and thetic signification establishing signified object and transcendental ego. Through the permanent contradiction between these two dispositions (semiotic/symbolic), of which the internal setting off of the sign (signifier/signified) is merely a witness, poetic language, in its most disruptive form (unreadable for meaning, dangerous for the subject), shows the constraints of a civilization dominated by transcendental rationality. Consequently, it is a means of overriding this constraint. And if in so doing it sometimes falls in with deeds brought about by the same rationality, as is, for example, the instinctual determination of fascism – demonstrated as such by Wilhelm Reich – poetic language is also there to forestall such translations into action.

This means that if poetic economy has always borne witness to crises and impossibilities of transcendental symbolics, in our time it is coupled with crises of social institutions (state, family, religion), and, more profoundly, a turning point in the relationship of man to meaning. Transcendental mastery over discourse is possible, but repressive; such a position is necessary, but only as a limit open to constant challenge; this relief with respect to repression – establishing meaning – is no longer possible under the incarnate appearance of a providential, historical, or even rationalist, humanist ego (in the manner of Renan), but through a *discordance* in the symbolic function and consequently within the identity of the transcendental ego itself. This is what the literary experience of our century intimates to theoretical reason, thereby taking its place with other phenomena of symbolic and social unrest (youth, drugs, women).

Without entering into a technical analysis of the economy specific to poetic language (an analysis too subtle and specious, considering the purpose of this specific paper), I shall extract from Céline, first, several procedures and, second, several themes, which illustrate the position of the unsettled, questionable subject-in-process of poetic language. I shall not do this without firmly underlining that these themes are not only inseparable from 'style', but that they are produced by it; in other words, it is not necessary 'to know' them, one could have heard them by simply listening to Céline's staccato, rhythmic discourse, stuffed with jargon and obscenity.

Thus, going beyond semantic themes and their distributions, one ought to examine the functioning of poetic language and its questionable subject-in-process, beginning with constitutive linguistic operations: syntax and semantics. Two phenomena, among others, will become the focus of our attention in Céline's writing: *sentential rhythms* and *obscene words*. These are of interest not only because they seem to constitute a particularity of his discourse, but also because, though they function differently, both of them involve constitutive operations of the judging consciousness (therefore of identity) by simultaneously perturbing its clarity and the designation of an object (objecthood). Moreover, if they constitute a network of constraints that is added to denotative signification, such a network has nothing to do with classic poeticness (rhythm, meter, conventional rhetorical figures) because it is drawn from the drives' register of a desiring body, both identifying with and rejecting a community (familial or folk). Therefore, even if the so-called poetic codes are not recognizable within poetic language, a constraint that I have termed semiotic functions in addition to the judging consciousness, provokes its lapses, or compensates for them; in so doing, it refers neither to a literary convention (like our poetic canons, contemporary with the major national epics and the constitution of nations themselves) nor even to the body *itself*, but rather, to a signifying disposition, pre- or trans-symbolic, which fashions any judging consciousness so that any ego recognizes its crisis within it. It is a jubilant recognition that, in 'modern' literature, replaces petty aesthetic pleasure.

Sentential rhythms. Beginning with *Death on the Installment Plan* [Fr. 1936], the sentence is condensed: not only does Céline avoid coordination and embeddings, but when different 'object-phrases' are for example numerous and juxtaposed with a verb, they are separated by the characteristic 'three dots'. This procedure divides the sentence into its constitutive phrases; they thus tend to become independent of the central verb, to detach themselves from the sentence's own signification, and to acquire a meaning initially incomplete and consequently capable of taking on multiple connotations that no longer depend on the framework of the sentence, but on a free context (the entire book, but also, all the addenda of which the reader is capable). Here, there are no syntactic anomalies (as in the *Coup de Dés* or the glossalalias of Artaud). The predicative thesis, constitutive of the judging consciousness, is maintained. By using three dots to space the phrases making up a sentence, thus giving them rhythm, he causes connotation to rush through a predication that has been striated in that manner; the denotated object of the utterance, the transcendental object, loses its clear contours. The elided object in the sentence relates to a hesitation (if not an erasure) of the *real object* for the speaking subject. That literature is witness to this kind of deception involving the object (object of love or transcendental object); that the existence of the object is more than fleeting and indeed impossible: this is what Céline's rhythms and syntactic elisions have recently evidenced within the stern humor of an experiment and with all its implications for the subject. This is also true of Beckett, whose recent play, *Not I*, spoken by a dying woman, sets forth in elided sentences and floating phrases the impossibility of God's existence for a speaking subject lacking any object of signification and/or love. Moreover, beyond and with connotation, with the blurred or erased object, there flows through meaning this 'emotion' of which Céline speaks – the nonsemanticized instinctual drive that precedes and exceeds meaning.

The exclamation marks alternating with three dots even more categorically point to this surge of instinctual drive: a panting, a breathlessness, an acceleration of verbal utterance, concerned not so much with finally reaching a global summing up of the world's meaning, as, to the contrary, with revealing, within the interstices of predication, the rhythm of a drive that remains forever unsatisfied – in the vacancy of judging consciousness and sign – because it could not find an other (an addressee) so as to obtain meaning in this exchange. We must also listen to Céline, Artaud, or Joyce, and read their texts in order to understand that the aim of this practice, which reaches us as a language, is, through the signification of the nevertheless transmitted message, not only to impose a music, a rhythm – that is, a polyphony – but also to wipe out sense through nonsense and laughter. This is a difficult operation that obliges the reader not so much to combine significations as to shatter his own judging consciousness in order to grant passage through it to this rhythmic drive constituted by repression and, once filtered by language and its meaning, experienced as jouissance. Could the resistance against modern literature be evidence of an obsession with meaning, of an unfitness for such jouissance?

Obscene words. Semantically speaking, these pivotal words in the Célinian lexicon exercise a *desemanticization* function analogous to the fragmentation of syntax by rhythm. Far from referring, as do all signs, to an object exterior to discourse and identifiable as such by consciousness, the obscene word is the minimal mark of a situation of desire where the identity of the signifying subject, if not destroyed, is exceeded by a conflict of instinctual drives linking one subject to another. There is nothing better than an obscene word for perceiving the limits of a phenomenological linguistics faced with the heterogeneous and complex architectonics of significance. The obscene word, lacking an objective referent, is also the contrary of an autonym – which involves the function of a word or utterance as sign; the obscene word mobilizes the signifying resources of the subject, permitting it to cross through the membrane of meaning where consciousness holds it, connecting it to gesturality, kinesthesia, the drives' body, the movement of rejection and appropriation of the other. Then, it is neither object, transcendental signified, nor signifier available to a neutralized consciousness: around the object denoted by the obscene word, and that object provides a scanty delineation, more than a simple context asserts itself – the drama of a questioning process heterogeneous to the meaning that precedes and exceeds it. Childrens' counting-out rhymes, or what one calls the 'obscene folklore of children', utilize the same rhythmic and semantic resources; they maintain the subject close to these jubilatory dramas that run athwart the repression that a univocal, increasingly pure signifier vainly attempts to impose upon the subject. By reconstituting them, and this on the very level of language, literature achieves its cathartic effects.

Several themes in Céline bring to light the relationships of force, at first within the family triangle, and then in contemporary society, that produce, promote, and accompany the particularities of poetic language to which I have just referred.

In *Death on the Installment Plan*, the most 'familial' of Céline's writings, we find a paternal figure, Auguste: a man 'of instruction', 'a mind', sullen, a prohibitor, prone to scandal, full of obsessional habits like, for example, cleaning the flagstones in front of his shop. His anger explodes spectacularly once, when he shuts himself up in the basement and shoots his pistol for hours, not without explaining in the face of general disapproval, 'I have my conscience on my side', just before falling ill. 'My mother wrapped the weapon in several layers of newspaper and then in a cashmere shawl ... "Come, child ... come!" she said when we were alone ... We threw the package in the drink.'[18]

Here is an imposing and menacing father, strongly emphasizing the enviable necessity of his position, but spoiling it by his derisive fury: undermined power whose weapon one could only take away in order to engulf it at the end of a journey between mother and son.

In an interview, Céline compares himself to a 'society woman' who braves the nevertheless maintained family prohibition, and who has the right to her own desire, 'a choice in a drawing room': 'the whore's trade doesn't interest me'; before defining himself, at the end: 'I am the son of a woman who restored old lace ... [I am] one of those rare men who knows how to distinguish batiste from valencienne ... I do not need to be taught. I know it.'

This fragile delicacy, heritage of the mother, supports the language – or if you wish, the identity – of him who unseated what Céline calls the 'heaviness' of men, of fathers, in order to flee it. The threads of instinctual drive, exceeding the law of the paternal word's own mastery, are nonetheless woven with scrupulous precision. One must therefore conceive of another disposition of the law, through signified and signifying identity and confronting the semiotic network: a disposition closer to the Greek *gnomon* ('one that knows', 'carpenter's square') than to the Latin *lex*, which necessarily implies the act of logical and legal judgment. A device, then, a regulated discrimination, weaves the semiotic network of instinctual drives; if it thus fails to conform to signifying identity, it nevertheless constitutes another identity closer to repressed and gnomic archaisms, susceptible of a psychosis-inducing explosion, where we decipher the relationship of the speaker to a desiring and desired mother.

In another interview, this maternal reference to old lacework is explicitly thought of as an archeology of the word: 'No! In the beginning was emotion. The Word came next to replace emotion as the trot replaces the gallop. They pulled man out of emotive poetry in order to plunge him into dialectics, that is, into gibberish, right?' Anyway, what is *Rigodon* if not a popular dance which obliges language to bow to the rhythm of its emotion.

A speech thus slatted by instinctual drive – Diderot [a leading figure of the French Enlightenment] would have said 'musicated' – could not describe, narrate, or theatricalize 'objects': by its composition and signification it also goes beyond the accepted categories of lyric, epic, dramatic, or tragic. The last writings of Céline, plugged in live to an era of war, death, and genocide, are what he calls in *North*, 'the vivisection of the wounded', 'the circus', 'the three hundred years before Christ'.

While members of the Resistance sing in alexandrine verse, it is Céline's language that records not only the institutional but also the profoundly symbolic jolt involving meaning and the identity of transcendental reason; fascism inflicted this jolt on our universe and the human sciences have hardly begun to figure out its consequences. I am saying that this literary discourse enunciates through its formal decentering, more apparent in Artaud's glossalalias, but also through the rhythms and themes of violence in Céline, better than anything else, the faltering of transcendental consciousness: this does not mean that such a discourse is aware of such a faltering or interprets it. As proof, writing that pretends to agree with 'circus' and 'vivisection' will nonetheless find its idols, even if only provisional; though dissolved in laughter and dominant non-sense, they are nevertheless posited as idols in Hitlerian ideology. A reading of any one of Céline's anti-semitic tracts is sufficient to show the crudely exhibited phantasms of an analysand struggling against a desired and frustrating, castrating, and sodomizing father; sufficient also to understand that it is not enough to allow what is repressed by the symbolic structure to emerge in a 'musicated' language to avoid its traps. Rather, we must in addition dissolve its sexual determinations. Unless poetic work can be linked to analytical interpretation, the discourse that undermines the judging consciousness and releases its repressed instinctual drive as rhythm always turns out to be at fault from the viewpoint of an ethic that remains with the transcendental ego – whatever joys or negations might exist in Spinoza's or Hegel's.

Since at least Hölderlin, poetic language has deserted beauty and meaning to become a laboratory where, fading philosophy, knowledge, and the transcendental ego of all signification, the impossibility of a signified or signifying identity is being sustained. If we took this venture seriously – if we could hear the burst of black laughter it hurls at all attempts to master the human situation, to master language by language – we would be forced to re-examine 'literary history', to rediscover beneath rhetoric and poetics its unchanging but always different polemic with the symbolic function. We could not avoid wondering about the possibility, or simultaneously, the legitimacy of a theoretical discourse on this practice of language whose stakes are precisely to render impossible the transcendental bounding that supports the discourse of knowledge.

Faced with this poetic language that defies knowledge, many of us are rather tempted to leave our shelter to deal with literature only by miming its meanderings, rather than by positing it as an object of knowledge. We let ourselves be taken in by this mimeticism: fictional, para-philosophical, para-scientific writings. It is probably necessary to be a woman (ultimate guarantee of sociality beyond the wreckage of the paternal symbolic function, as well as the inexhaustible generator of its renewal, of its expansion) not to renounce theoretical reason but to compel it to increase its power by giving it an object beyond its limits. Such a position, it seems to me, provides a possible basis for a theory of signification, which, confronted with poetic language, could not in any way account for it, but would rather use it as an indication of what is heterogeneous to meaning (to sign and predication): instinctual economies, always and at the same time open to bio-physiological sociohistorical constraints.

This kind of heterogeneous economy and its questionable subject-in-process thus calls for a linguistics other than the one descended from the phenomenological heavens; a linguistics capable, within its language object, of accounting for a nonetheless articulated *instinctual drive*, across and through the constitutive and insurmountable frontier of *meaning*. This instinctual drive, however, located in the matrix of the sign, refers back to an instinctual body (to which psychoanalysis has turned its attention), which ciphers the language with rhythmic, intonational, and other arrangements, nonreducible to the position of the transcendental ego even though always within sight of its thesis.

The development of this theory of signification is in itself regulated by Husserlian precepts, because it inevitably makes an *object* even of that which departs from meaning. But, even though abetting the law of signifying structure as well as of all sociality, this expanded theory of signification cannot give itself new objects except by positing itself as nonuniversal: that is, by presupposing that a questionable subject-in-process exists in an economy of discourse other than that of thetic consciousness. And this requires that subjects of the theory must be themselves subjects in infinite analysis; this is what Husserl could not imagine, what Céline could not know, but what a woman, among others, can finally admit, aware as she is of the inanity of Being.

When it avoids the risks that lie in wait for it, literary experience remains nevertheless something other than this analytical theory, which it never stops challenging. Against knowing thought, poetic language pursues an effect of *singular truth*, and thus accomplishes, perhaps, for the modern community, this solitary practice that the materialists of antiquity unsuccessfully championed against the ascendance of theoretical reason.

Notes

Originally a paper read at a seminar organized by Jean-Marie Benoist and directed by Claude Lévi-Strauss at the Collège de France, January 27, 1975; first published in *Tel Quel* 62 (Summer 1975); reprinted in *Polylogue* (Paris: Seuil, 1977), pp. 149–72. 'D'une identité à l'autre', the original title of Kristeva's essay reflects and makes use of the title of Céline's novel *D'un château à l'autre*. Although this has been translated as *Castle to Castle*, the more literal 'From One Identity to an Other' has been chosen in order to keep the ambiguous feeling of the French as well as the word 'other', an important one in philosophy since Hegel and also in Kristeva's work. (Ed.)

1   Claude Lévi-Strauss, *L'Homme nu* (Paris: Plon, 1971), p. 615.
2   Russian Formalism (heavily influenced by the ideas of Swiss linguist Ferdinand de Saussure, the founder of semiotics) flourished in St Petersburg and Moscow in the 1920s, marking a 'scientific turn' in the study of literary language which it took to be measurably different from other linguistic phenomena. The main idea is that literary texts are open to inspection for the devices they use in the service of *ostranenie*, the 'making strange' or 'defamiliarization' of language. (NL)
3   Kristeva's French phrase is *mise en procès*, which, like *le sujet en procès*, refers to an important, recurring concept – that of a constantly changing subject whose identity is open to question. Cf. Leon S. Roudiez, 'Introduction', in Kristeva, *Desire in Language: A Semiotic Approach to Literature and Art*, ed. Leon S. Roudiez, trans. T. Gora, A. Jardine and L. S. Roudiez (Oxford: Blackwell, 1981), p. 17, and n. 8 below. (Ed.)
4   Ernest Renan, *Oeuvres complètes* (Paris: Calmann-Lévy, 1947–58) 3, p. 322.
5   Ernest Renan, *The Future of Science* (Boston: Roberts Brothers, 1891), p. 402.
6   Lévi-Strauss, *L'Homme nu*, p. 614.

7   The Prague Circle, active throughout the 1930s and 1940s, succeeded Russian Formalism in accounting for literary meaning as an effect of 'functional' semiotics, against the 'appreciationist' view of literature as an expression of external realities or inner truths. One of its leading lights, Roman Jakobson, had been a member of the formalist group at Moscow. (NL)

8   See Jean Starobinski, *Les Mots sous les mots* (Paris: Gallimard, 1971). (Ed.)

9   Edmund Husserl, *Logical Investigation*, trans. J. N. Findlay (London: Routledge & Kegan Paul, 1970), pp. 276–7.

10   Edmund Husserl, *Ideas: General Introduction to Pure Phenomenology*, trans. W. R. Boyce Gibson (London: Collier-Macmillan, 1962), pp. 93–4 and 101.

11   Edmund Husserl, *Erste Philosophie*, VIII, in *Husserliana* (The Hague: Hrsg. von R. Boehm, 1956).

12   Husserl, *Ideas*, p. 313.

13   Antonin Artaud, 'L'Anarchie sociale de l'art', in *Oeuvres complètes* (Paris: Gallimard), 8: 287.

14   'Carnivalesque' is a term associated with Mikhail Bakhtin, a Russian critic of formalist and semiotic approaches to literature – and an important influence on Kristeva's thinking – whose major works were written in the 1920s and 1930s. For Bakhtin, poetic language is not simply different from ordinary language; it challenges the normalizing effects of ordinary language's grammatical and semantic codes. In its very playfulness, poetic language operates at the limit of official practices of linguistic sense-making and therefore can be seen as a protest against them, just as the playfulness of a carnival can be taken for a social protest against official codes of public conduct. (NL)

15   The 'mirror stage' is a concept of Jacques Lacan's referring to the process by which a child, on seeing a reflection or representation of itself in a mirror, begins to develop an understanding of its own identity. Previously that 'identity' was bound up in 'imaginary' relations between the child and other objects, so that the mirror stage brings about an enabling separation (of self and other, I and you etc.) through which we pass into the 'symbolic' (cultural) order of laws and language. See Barthes, 'From Work to Text', n. 1, in the present volume. For a discussion of the mirror stage and other aspects of Lacan's thought, see my *PomoIntro*, esp. pp. 22–30. (NL)

16   See Kristeva, *La Révolution du langage poétique* (Paris: Seuil, 1974), pp. 274ff. (Ed.)

17   As far as I know, there is no reference to Aeschylus in any of Heidegger's works that have been translated into English. (NL)

18   Louis-Ferdinand Céline, *Death on the Installment Plan*, trans. Ralph Manheim (New York: New Directions, 1966), p. 78.

Chapter Four **Rhizome**

Gilles Deleuze and Félix Guattari

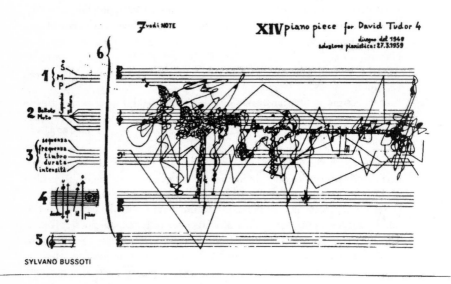

SYLVANO BUSSOTI

The two of us wrote *Anti-Oedipus* together. Since each of us was several, there was already quite a crowd. Here we have made use of everything that came within range, what was closest as well as farthest away. We have assigned clever pseudonyms to prevent recognition. Why have we kept our own names? Out of habit, purely out of habit. To make ourselves unrecognizable in turn. To render imperceptible, not ourselves, but what makes us act, feel, and think. Also because it's nice to talk like

Gilles Deleuze and Félix Guattari, 'Introduction: Rhizome', in *A Thousand Plateaus: Capitalism and Schizophrenia* [Fr. 1980], trans. B. Massumi (Minneapolis: University of Minnesota Press, 1987), pp. 3–25.

everybody else, to say the sun rises, when everybody knows it's only a manner of speaking. To reach, not the point where one no longer says I, but the point where it is no longer of any importance whether one says I. We are no longer ourselves. Each will know his own. We have been aided, inspired, multiplied.

A book has neither object nor subject; it is made of variously formed matters, and very different dates and speeds. To attribute the book to a subject is to overlook this working of matters, and the exteriority of their relations. It is to fabricate a beneficent God to explain geological movements. In a book, as in all things, there are lines of articulation or segmentarity, strata and territories; but also lines of flight, movements of deterritorialization and destratification. Comparative rates of flow on these lines produce phenomena of relative slowness and viscosity, or, on the contrary, of acceleration and rupture. All this, lines and measurable speeds, constitutes an *assemblage*. A book is an assemblage of this kind, and as such is unattributable. It is a multiplicity – but we don't know yet what the multiple entails when it is no longer attributed, that is, after it has been elevated to the status of a substantive. One side of a machinic assemblage faces the strata, which doubtless make it a kind of organism, or signing totality, or determination attributable to a subject; it also has a side facing a *body without organs*,[1] which is continually dismantling the organism, causing asignifying particles or pure intensities to pass or circulate, and attributing to itself subjects that it leaves with nothing more than a name as the trace of an intensity. What is the body without organs of a book? There are several, depending on the nature of the lines considered, their particular grade or density, and the possibility of their converging on a 'plane of consistency'[2] assuring their selection. Here, as elsewhere, the units of measure are what is essential: *quantify writing*. There is no difference between what a book talks about and how it is made. Therefore a book also has no object. As an assemblage, a book has only itself, in connection with other assemblages and in relation to other bodies without organs. We will never ask what a book means, as signified or signifier; we will not look for anything to understand in it. We will ask what it functions with, in connection with what other things it does or does not transmit intensifies, in which other multiplicities its own are inserted and metamorphosed, and with what bodies without organs it makes its own converge. A book exists only through the outside and on the outside. A book itself is a little machine; what is the relation (also measurable) of this literary machine to a war machine, love machine, revolutionary machine, etc. – and an *abstract machine* that sweeps them along? We have been criticized for overquoting literary authors. But when one writes, the only question is which other machine the literary machine can be plugged into, must be plugged into in order to work. Kleist and a mad war machine, Kafka and a most extraordinary bureaucratic machine. . . . (What if one became animal or plant *through* literature, which certainly does not mean literarily? Is it not first through the voice that one becomes animal?) Literature is an assemblage. It has nothing to do with ideology. There is no ideology and never has been.

All we talk about are multiplicities, lines, strata and segmentarities, lines of flight and intensifies, machinic assemblages and their various types, bodies without organs and their construction and selection, the plane of consistency, and in each case the units of measure. *Stratometers, deleometers, BwO units of density, BwO units of convergence*: Not only do these constitute a quantification of writing, but they define writing as always the measure of something else. Writing has nothing to do with signifying. It has to do with surveying, mapping, even realms that are yet to come.

A first type of book is the root-book. The tree is already the image of the world, or the root the image of the world-tree. This is the classical book, as noble, signifying, and subjective organic inferiority (the strata of the book). The book imitates the world, as art imitates nature: by procedures specific to it that accomplish what nature cannot or can no longer do. The law of the book is the law of reflection, the One that becomes two. How could the law of the book reside in nature, when it is what presides over the very division between world and book, nature and art? One becomes two: whenever we encounter this formula, even stated strategically by Mao or understood in the most 'dialectical' way possible, what we have before us is the most classical and well reflected, oldest, and weariest kind of thought. Nature doesn't work that way: in nature, roots are taproots with a more multiple, lateral, and circular system of ramification, rather than a dichotomous one. Thought lags behind nature. Even the book as a natural reality is a taproot, with its pivotal spine and surrounding leaves. But the book as a spiritual reality, the Tree or Root as an image, endlessly develops the law of the One that becomes two, then of the two that become four. . . . Binary logic is the spiritual reality of the root-tree. Even a discipline as 'advanced' as linguistics retains the root-tree as its fundamental image, and thus remains wedded to classical reflection (for example, Chomsky and his grammatical trees, which begin at a point S and proceed by dichotomy).[3] This is as much as to say that this system of thought has never reached an understanding of multiplicity: in order to arrive at two following a spiritual method it must assume a strong principal unity. On the side of the object, it is no doubt possible, following the natural method, to go directly from One to three, four, or five, but only if there is a strong principal unity available, that of the pivotal taproot supporting the secondary roots. That doesn't get us very far. The binary logic of dichotomy has simply been replaced by biunivocal relationships between successive circles. The pivotal taproot provides no better understanding of multiplicity than the dichotomous root. One operates in the object, the other in the subject. Binary logic and biunivocal relationships still dominate psychoanalysis (the tree of delusion in the Freudian interpretation of Schreber's case), linguistics, structuralism, and even information science.

The radicle-system, or fascicular root, is the second figure of the book, to which our modernity pays willing allegiance. This time, the principal root has aborted, or its tip has been destroyed; an immediate, indefinite multiplicity of secondary roots grafts onto it and undergoes a flourishing development. This time, natural reality is what aborts the principal root, but the root's unity subsists, as past or yet to come, as possible. We must ask if reflexive, spiritual reality does not compensate for this state of things by demanding an even more comprehensive secret unity, or a more extensive totality. Take William Burroughs' cut-up method: the folding of one text onto another, which constitutes multiple and even adventitious roots (like a cutting), implies a supplementary dimension to that of the texts under consideration. In this supplementary dimension of folding, unity continues its spiritual labor. That is why the most resolutely fragmented work can also be presented as the Total Work or Magnum Opus. Most modern methods for making series proliferate or a multiplicity grow are perfectly valid in one direction, for example, a linear direction, whereas a unity of totalization asserts itself even more firmly in another, circular or cyclic, dimension. Whenever a multiplicity is taken up in a structure, its growth is offset by a reduction in its laws of combination. The abortionists of unity are indeed angel makers, *doctores angelici*, because they affirm a properly angelic and superior unity. Joyce's words, accurately described as having 'multiple roots', shatter the linear unity of the word, even of language, only to posit a cyclic unity of the sentence, text, or knowledge. Nietzsche's aphorisms shatter the linear unity of knowledge, only to invoke the cyclic unity of the eternal return, present as the nonknown in thought. This is as much as to say that the fascicular system does not really break with dualism, with the complementarity between a subject and an object, a natural reality and a spiritual reality: unity is consistently thwarted and obstructed in the object, while a new type of unity triumphs in the subject. The world has lost its pivot; the subject can no longer even dichotomize, but accedes to a higher unity, of ambivalence or overdetermination, in an always supplementary dimension to that of its object. The world has become chaos, but the book remains the image of the world: radicle-chaosmos rather than root-cosmos. A strange mysti-fication: a book all the more total for being fragmented. At any rate, what a vapid idea, the book as the image of the world. In truth, it is not enough to say, 'Long live the multiple', difficult as it is to raise that cry. No typographical, lexical, or even syntactical cleverness is enough to make it heard. The multiple *must be made*, not by always adding a higher dimen-sion, but rather in the simplest of ways, by dint of sobriety, with the number of dimensions one already has available always $n - 1$ (the only way the one belongs to the multiple: always subtracted). Subtract the unique from the multiplicity to be constituted; write at $n - 1$ dimensions. A system of this kind could be called a rhizome. A rhizome as subterra-nean stem is absolutely different from roots and radicles. Bulbs and tu-bers are rhizomes. Plants with roots or radicles may be rhizomorphic in other respects altogether: the question is whether plant life in its specificity is not entirely rhizomatic. Even some animals are, in their pack form. Rats are rhizomes. Burrows are too, in all of their functions of shelter, supply, movement, evasion, and breakout. The rhizome itself assumes very diverse forms, from ramified surface extension in all directions to concretion into bulbs and tubers. When rats swarm over each other. The rhizome includes the best and the worst: potato and couchgrass, or the weed. Animal and plant, couchgrass is crabgrass. We get the distinct feeling that we will convince no one unless we enumerate certain approxi-mate characteristics of the rhizome.

1 and 2. Principles of connection and heterogeneity: any point of a rhizome can be connected to anything other, and must be. This is very different from the tree or root, which plots a point, fixes an order. The linguistic tree on the Chomsky model still begins at a point S and pro-ceeds by dichotomy. On the contrary, not every trait in a rhizome is necessarily linked to a linguistic feature: semiotic chains of every nature are connected to very diverse modes of coding (biological, political, eco-nomic, etc.) that bring into play not only different regimes of signs but also states of things of differing status. *Collective assemblages of enuncia-tion* function directly within *machinic assemblages*; it is not impossible to make a radical break between regimes of signs and their objects. Even when linguistics claims to confine itself to what is explicit and to make no

presuppositions about language, it is still in the sphere of a discourse implying particular modes of assemblage and types of social power. Chomsky's grammaticality, the categorical S symbol that dominates every sentence, is more fundamentally a marker of power than a syntactic marker: you will construct grammatically correct sentences, you will divide each statement into a noun phrase and a verb phrase (first dichotomy ...). Our criticism of these linguistic models is not that they are too abstract but, on the contrary, that they are not abstract enough, that they do not reach the *abstract machine* that connects a language to the semantic and pragmatic contents of statements, to collective assemblages of enunciation, to a whole micropolitics of the social field. A rhizome ceaselessly establishes connections between semiotic chains, organizations of power, and circumstances relative to the arts, sciences, and social struggles. A semiotic chain is like a tuber agglomerating very diverse acts, not only linguistic, but also perceptive, mimetic, gestural, and cognitive: there is no language in itself, nor are there any linguistic universals, only a throng of dialects, patois, slangs, and specialized languages. There is no ideal speaker-listener, any more than there is a homogeneous linguistic community. Language is, in Weinreich's words, 'an essentially heterogeneous reality'.[4] There is no mother tongue, only a power takeover by a dominant language within a political multiplicity. Language stabilizes around a parish, a bishopric, a capital. It forms a bulb. It evolves by subterranean stems and flows, along river valleys or train tracks; it spreads like a patch of oil.[5] It is always possible to break a language down into internal structural elements, an undertaking not fundamentally different from a search for roots. There is always something genealogical about a tree. It is not a method for the people. A method of the rhizome type, on the contrary, can analyze language only by decentering it onto other dimensions and other registers. A language is never closed upon itself, except as a function of impotence.

3. Principle of multiplicity: it is only when the multiple is effectively treated as a substantive, 'multiplicity', that it ceases to have any relation to the One as subject or object, natural or spiritual reality, image and world. Multiplicities are rhizomatic, and expose arborescent pseudo-multiplicities for what they are. There is no unity to serve as a pivot in the object, or to divide in the subject. There is not even the unity to abort in the object or 'return' in the subject. A multiplicity has neither subject nor object, only determinations, magnitudes, and dimensions that cannot increase in number without the multiplicity changing in nature (the laws of combination therefore increase in number as the multiplicity grows).

Puppet strings, as a rhizome or multiplicity, are tied not to the supposed will of an artist or puppeteer but to a multiplicity of nerve fibers, which form another puppet in other dimensions connected to the first: 'Call the strings or rods that move the puppet the weave. It might be objected that *its multiplicity* resides in the person of the actor, who projects it into the text. Granted; but the actor's nerve fibers in turn form a weave. And they fall through the gray matter, the grid, into the undifferentiated. . . . The interplay approximates the pure activity of weavers attributed in myth to the Fates or Norns'.[6] An assemblage is precisely this increase in the dimensions of a multiplicity that necessarily changes in nature as it expands its connections. There are no points or positions in a rhizome, such as those found in a structure, tree, or root. There are only lines. When Glenn Gould speeds up the performance of a piece, he is not just displaying virtuosity, he is transforming the musical points into lines, he is making the whole piece proliferate. The number is no longer a universal concept measuring elements according to their emplacement in a given dimension, but has itself become a multiplicity that varies according to the dimensions considered (the primacy of the domain over a complex of numbers attached to that domain). We do not have units (*unité*) of measure, only multiplicities or varieties of measurement. The notion of unity (*unité*) appears only when there is a power takeover in the multiplicity by the signifier or a corresponding subjectification proceeding: This is the case for a pivot-unity forming the basis for a set of bi-univocal relationships between objective elements or points, or for the One that divides following the law of a binary logic of differentiation in the subject. Unity always operates in an empty dimension supplementary to that of the system considered (overcoding). The point is that a rhizome or multiplicity never allows itself to be overcoded, never has available a supplementary dimension over and above its number of lines, that is, over and above the multiplicity of numbers attached to those lines. All multiplicities are flat, in the sense that they fill or occupy all of their dimensions: we will therefore speak of a *plane of consistency* of multiplicities, even though the dimensions of this 'plane' increase with the number of connections that are made on it. Multiplicities are defined by the outside: by the abstract line, the line of flight or deterritorialization according to which they change in nature and connect with other multiplicities. The plane of consistency (grid) is the outside of all multiplicities. The line of flight marks: the reality of a finite number of dimensions that the multiplicity effectively fills; the impossibility of a supplementary dimension, unless the multiplicity is transformed by the line of flight; the possibility and necessity of flattening all of the multiplicities on a single plane of consistency or exteriority, regardless of their number of dimensions. The ideal for a book would be to lay everything out on a plane of exteriority of this kind, on a single page, the same sheet: lived events, historical determinations, concepts, individuals, groups, social formations. Kleist invented a writing of this type, a broken chain of affects and variable speeds, with accelerations and transformations, always in a relation with the outside. Open rings. His texts, therefore, are opposed in every way to the classical or romantic book constituted by the inferiority of a substance or subject. The war machine-book against the State apparatus-book. Flat *multiplicities of n dimensions* are asignifying and asubjective. They are designated by indefinite articles, or rather by partitives (*some* couchgrass, *some* of a rhizome . . .).

4. Principle of asignifying rupture: against the oversignifying breaks separating structures or cutting across a single structure. A rhizome may be broken, shattered at a given spot, but it will start up again on one of its old lines, or on new lines. You can never get rid of ants because they form an animal rhizome that can rebound time and again after most of it has been destroyed. Every rhizome contains lines of segmentarity according to which it is stratified, territorialized, organized, signified, attributed, etc., as well as lines of deterritorialization down which it constantly flees. There is a rupture in the rhizome whenever segmentary lines explode into a line of flight, but the line of flight is part of the rhizome. These lines always tie back to one another. That is why one can never posit a dualism or a dichotomy, even in the rudimentary form of the good and the bad. You may make a rupture, draw a line of flight, yet there is still a danger that you will re-encounter organizations that re-stratify everything, formations that restore power to a signifier, attributions that reconstitute a subject – anything you like, from Oedipal resurgences to fascist concretions. Groups and individuals contain microfascisms just waiting to crystallize. Yes, couchgrass is also a rhizome. Good and bad are only the products of an active and temporary selection, which must be renewed.

How could movements of deterritorialization and processes of reterritorialization not be relative, always connected, caught up in one another? The orchid deterritorializes by forming an image, a tracing of a wasp; but the wasp reterritorializes on that image. The wasp is nevertheless deterritorialized, becoming a piece in the orchid's reproductive apparatus. But it reterritorializes the orchid by transporting its pollen. Wasp and orchid, as heterogeneous elements, form a rhizome. It could be said that the orchid imitates the wasp, reproducing its image in a signifying fashion (mimesis, mimicry, lure, etc.). But this is true only on the level of the strata – a parallelism between two strata such that a plant organization on one imitates an animal organization on the other. At the same time, something else entirely is going on: not imitation at all but a capture of code, surplus value of code, an increase in valence, a veritable becoming, a becoming-wasp of the orchid and a becoming-orchid of the wasp. Each of these becomings brings about the deterritorialization of one term and the reterritorialization of the other; the two becomings interlink and form relays in a circulation of intensities pushing the deterritorialization ever further. There is neither imitation nor resemblance, only an exploding of two heterogeneous series on the line of flight composed by a common rhizome that can no longer be attributed to or subjugated by anything signifying. Rémy Chauvin expresses it well: 'the *aparallel evolution* of two beings that have absolutely nothing to do with each other'.[7] More generally, evolutionary schemas may be forced to abandon the old model of the tree and descent. Under certain conditions, a virus can connect to germ cells and transmit itself as the cellular gene of a complex species; moreover, it can take flight, move into the cells of an entirely different species, but not without bringing with it 'genetic information' from the first host (for example, Benveniste and Todaro's current research on a type C virus, with its double connection to baboon DNA and the DNA of certain kinds of domestic cats). Evolutionary schemas would no longer follow models of arborescent descent going from the least to the most differentiated, but instead a rhizome operating immediately in the heterogeneous and jumping from one already differentiated line to another.[8] Once again, there is *aparallel evolution*, of the baboon and the cat; it is obvious that they are not models or copies of each other (a becoming-baboon in the cat does not mean that the cat 'plays' baboon). We form a rhizome with our viruses, or rather our viruses cause us to form a rhizome with other animals. As François Jacob says, transfers of genetic material by viruses or through other procedures, fusions of cells originating in different species, have results analogous to those of 'the abominable couplings dear to antiquity and the Middle Ages'.[9] Transversal communications between different lines scramble the genealogical trees. Always look for the molecular, or even submolecular, particle with which we are allied. We evolve and die more from our polymorphous and rhizomatic flus than from hereditary diseases, or diseases that have their own line of descent. The rhizome is an anti-genealogy.

The same applies to the book and the world: contrary to a deeply rooted belief, the book is not an image of the world. It forms a rhizome with the world, there is an aparallel evolution of the book and the world; the book assures the deterritorialization of the world, but the world effects a reterritorialization of the book, which in turn deterritorializes itself in the world (if it is capable, if it can). Mimicry is a very bad concept, since it relies on binary logic to describe phenomena of an entirely different nature. The crocodile does not reproduce a tree trunk, any more than the chameleon reproduces the colors of its surroundings. The Pink Panther imitates nothing, it reproduces nothing, it paints the world its color, pink on pink; this is its becoming-world, carried out in such a way that it becomes imperceptible itself, asignifying, makes its rupture, its own line of flight, follows its 'aparallel evolution' through to the end. The wisdom of the plants: even when they have roots, there is always an outside where they form a rhizome with something else – with the wind, an animal, human beings (and there is also an aspect under which animals themselves form rhizomes, as do people, etc.). 'Drunkenness as a triumphant irruption of the plant in us.' Always follow the rhizome by rupture; lengthen, prolong, and relay the line of flight; make it vary, until you have produced the most abstract and tortuous of lines of n dimensions and broken directions. Conjugate deterritorialized flows. Follow the plants: you start by delimiting a first line consisting of circles of convergence around successive singularities; then you see whether inside that line new circles of convergence establish themselves, with new points located outside the limits and in other directions. Write, form a rhizome, increase your territory by deterritorialization, extend the line of flight to the point where it becomes an abstract machine covering the entire plane of consistency. 'Go first to your old plant and watch carefully the watercourse made by the rain. By now the rain must have carried the seeds far away. Watch the crevices made by the runoff, and from them determine the direction of the flow. Then find the plant that is growing at the farthest point from your plant. All the devil's weed plants that are growing in between are yours. Later . . . you can extend the size of your territory by following the watercourse from each point along the way.'[10] Music has always sent out lines of flight, like so many 'transformational multiplicities', even overturning the very codes that structure or arborify it; that is why musical form, right down to its ruptures and proliferations, is comparable to a weed, a rhizome.[11]

5 and 6. Principle of cartography and decalcomania: a rhizome is not amenable to any structural or generative model. It is a stranger to any idea of genetic axis or deep structure. A genetic axis is like an objective pivotal unity upon which successive stages are organized; a deep structure

is more like a base sequence that can be broken down into immediate constituents, while the unity of the product passes into another, transformational and subjective, dimension. This does not constitute a departure from the representative model of the tree, or root-pivotal taproot or fascicles (for example, Chomsky's 'tree' is associated with a base sequence and represents the process of its own generation in terms of binary logic). A variation on the oldest form of thought. It is our view that genetic axis and profound structure are above all infinitely reproducible principles of *tracing*. All of tree logic is a logic of tracing and reproduction. In linguistics as in psychoanalysis, its object is an unconscious that is itself representative, crystallized into codified complexes, laid out along a genetic axis and distributed within a syntagmatic structure. Its goal is to describe a de facto state, to maintain balance in intersubjective relations, or to explore an unconscious that is already there from the start, lurking in the dark recesses of memory and language. It consists of tracing, on the basis of an overcoding structure or supporting axis, something that comes ready-made. The tree articulates and hierarchizes tracings; tracings are like the leaves of a tree.

The rhizome is altogether different, a *map and not a tracing*. Make a map, not a tracing. The orchid does not reproduce the tracing of the wasp; it forms a map with the wasp, in a rhizome. What distinguishes the map from the tracing is that it is entirely oriented toward an experimentation in contact with the real. The map does not reproduce an unconscious closed in upon itself; it constructs the unconscious. It fosters connections between fields, the removal of blockages on bodies without organs, the maximum opening of bodies without organs onto a plane of consistency. It is itself a part of the rhizome. The map is open and connectable in all of its dimensions; it is detachable, reversible, susceptible to constant modification. It can be torn, reversed, adapted to any kind of mounting, reworked by an individual, group, or social formation. It can be drawn on a wall, conceived of as a work of art, constructed as a political action or as a meditation. Perhaps one of the most important characteristics of the rhizome is that it always has multiple entryways; in this sense, the burrow is an animal rhizome, and sometimes maintains a clear distinction between the line of flight as passageway and storage or living strata (cf. the muskrat). A map has multiple entryways, as opposed to the tracing, which always comes back 'to the same'. The map has to do with performance, whereas the tracing always involves an alleged 'competence'. Unlike psychoanalysis, psychoanalytic competence (which confines every desire and statement to a genetic axis or overcoding structure, and makes infinite, monotonous tracings of the stages on that axis or the constituents of that structure), schizoanalysis rejects any idea of pretraced destiny, whatever name is given to it – divine, anagogic, historical, economic, structural, hereditary, or syntagmatic. (It is obvious that Melanie Klein has no understanding of the cartography of one of her child patients, Little Richard, and is content to make ready-made tracings – Oedipus, the good daddy and the bad daddy, the bad mommy and the good mommy – while the child makes a desperate attempt to carry out a performance that the psychoanalyst totally misconstrues.)[12] Drives and part-objects are neither stages on a genetic axis nor positions in a deep structure; they are political options for problems, they are entryways and exits, impasses the child lives out politically, in other words, with all the force of his or her desire.

Have we not, however, reverted to a simple dualism by contrasting maps to tracings, as good and bad sides? Is it not of the essence of the rhizome to intersect roots and sometimes merge with them? Does not a map contain phenomena of redundancy that are already like tracings of its own? Does not a multiplicity have strata upon which unifications and totalizations, massifications, mimetic mechanisms, signifying power takeovers, and subjective attributions take root? Do not even lines of flight, due to their eventual divergence, reproduce the very formations their function it was to dismantle or outflank? But the opposite is also true. It is a question of method: *the tracing should always be put back on the map.* This operation and the previous one are not at all symmetrical. For it is inaccurate to say that a tracing reproduces the map. It is instead like a photograph or X-ray that begins by selecting or isolating, by artificial means such as colorations or other restrictive procedures, what it intends to reproduce. The imitator always creates the model, and attracts it. The tracing has already translated the map into an image; it has already transformed the rhizome into roots and radicles. It has organized, stabilized, neutralized the multiplicities according to the axes of signifiance and subjectification belonging to it. It has generated, structuralized the rhizome, and when it thinks it is reproducing something else it is in fact only reproducing itself. That is why the tracing is so dangerous. It injects redundancies and propagates them. What the tracing reproduces of the map or rhizome are only the impasses, blockages, incipient taproots, or points of structuration. Take a look at psychoanalysis and linguistics: all the former has ever made are tracings or photos of the unconscious, and the latter of language, with all the betrayals that implies (it's not surprising that psychoanalysis tied its fate to that of linguistics). Look at what happened to Little Hans already, an example of child psychoanalysis at its purest: they kept on BREAKING HIS RHIZOME and BLOTCHING HIS MAP, setting it straight for him, blocking his every way out, until he began to desire his own shame and guilt, until they had rooted shame and guilt in him, PHOBIA (they barred him from the rhizome of the building, then from the rhizome of the street, they rooted him in his parents' bed, they radicled him to his own body, they fixated him on Professor Freud). Freud explicitly takes Little Hans' cartography into account, but always and only in order to project it back onto the family photo. And look what Melanie Klein did to Little Richard's geopolitical maps: she developed photos from them, made tracings of them. Strike the pose or follow the axis, genetic stage or structural destiny – one way or the other, your rhizome will be broken. You will be allowed to live and speak, but only after every outlet has been obstructed. Once a rhizome has been obstructed, arborified, it's all over, no desire stirs; for it is always by rhizome that desire moves and produces. Whenever desire climbs a tree, internal repercussions trip it up and it falls to its death; the rhizome, on the other hand, acts on desire by external, productive outgrowths.

That is why it is so important to try the other, reverse but nonsymmetrical, operation. Plug the tracings back into the map, connect the roots or trees back up with a rhizome. In the case of Little Hans, studying the unconscious would be to show how he tries to build a rhizome, with the family house but also with the line of flight of the building, the street, etc.; how these lines are blocked, how the child is made to take root in the family, be photographed under the father, be traced onto the mother's bed; then how Professor Freud's intervention assures a power takeover by the signifier, a subjectification of affects; how the only escape route left to the child is a becoming-animal perceived as shameful and guilty (the becoming-horse of Little Hans, a truly political option). But these impasses must always be resituated on the map, thereby opening them up to possible lines of flight. The same applies to the group map: show at what point in the rhizome there form phenomena of massification, bureaucracy, leadership, fascization, etc., which lines nevertheless survive, if only underground, continuing to make rhizome in the shadows. Deligny's method: map the gestures and movements of an autistic child, combine several maps for the same child, for several different children.[13] If it is true that it is of the essence of the map or rhizome to have multiple entryways, then it is plausible that one could even enter them through tracings or the root-tree, assuming the necessary precautions are taken (once again, one must avoid any Manichean dualism). For example, one will often be forced to take dead ends, to work with signifying powers and subjective affections, to find a foothold in formations that are Oedipal or paranoid or even worse, rigidified territorialities that open the way for other transformational operations. It is even possible for psychoanalysis to serve as a foothold, in spite of itself. In other cases, on the contrary, one will bolster oneself directly on a line of flight enabling one to blow apart strata, cut roots, and make new connections. Thus, there are very diverse map-tracing, rhizome-root assemblages, with variable co-efficients of deterritorialization. There exist tree or root structures in rhizomes; conversely, a tree branch or root division may begin to burgeon into a rhizome. The coordinates are determined not by theoretical analyses implying universals but by a pragmatics composing multiplicities or aggregates of intensifies. A new rhizome may form in the heart of a tree, the hollow of a root, the crook of a branch. Or else it is a microscopic element of the root-tree, a radicle, that gets rhizome production going. Accounting and bureaucracy proceed by tracings: they can begin to burgeon nonetheless, throwing out rhizome stems, as in a Kafka novel. An intensive trait starts working for itself, a hallucinatory perception, synesthesia, perverse mutation, or play of images shakes loose challenging the hegemony of the signifier. In the case of the child, gestural, mimetic, ludic, and other semiotic systems regain their freedom and extricate themselves from the 'tracing', that is, from the dominant competence of the teacher's language – a microscopic event upsets the local balance of power. Similarly, generative trees constructed according to Chomsky's syntagmatic model can open up in all directions, and in turn form a rhizome.[14] To be rhizomorphous is to produce stems and filaments that seem to be roots, or better yet connect with them by penetrating the trunk, but put them to strange new uses. We're tired of trees. We should stop believing in trees, roots, and radicles. They've made us suffer too much. All of arborescent culture is founded on them, from biology to linguistics. Nothing is beautiful or loving or political aside from underground stems and aerial roots, adventitious growths and rhizomes. Amsterdam, a city entirely without roots, a rhizome-city with its stem-canals, where utility connects with the greatest folly in relation to a commercial war machine.

Thought is not arborescent, and the brain is not a rooted or ramified matter. What are wrongly called 'dendrites' do not assure the connection of neurons in a continuous fabric. The discontinuity between cells, the role of the axons, the functioning of the synapses, the existence of synaptic microfissures, the leap each message makes across these fissures, make the brain a multiplicity immersed in its plane of consistency or neuroglia, a whole uncertain, probabilistic system ('the uncertain nervous system'). Many people have a tree growing in their heads, but the brain itself is much more a grass than a tree. 'The axon and the dendrite twist around each other like bindweed around brambles, with synapses at each of the thorns.'[15] The same goes for memory. Neurologists and psychophysiologists distinguish between long-term memory and short-term memory (on the order of a minute). The difference between them is not simply quantitative: short-term memory is of the rhizome or diagram type, and long-term memory is arborescent and centralized (imprint, engram, tracing, or photograph). Short-term memory is in no way subject to a law of contiguity or immediacy to its object; it can act at a distance, come or return a long time after, but always under conditions of discontinuity, rupture, and multiplicity. Furthermore, the difference between the two kinds of memory is not that of two temporal modes of apprehending the same thing; they do not grasp the same thing, memory, or idea. The splendor of the short-term Idea: one writes using short-term memory, and thus short-term ideas, even if one reads or rereads using long-term memory of long-term concepts. Short-term memory includes forgetting as a process; it merges not with the instant but instead with the nervous, temporal, and collective rhizome. Long-term memory (family, race, society, or civilization) traces and translates, but what it translates continues to act in it, from a distance, off beat, in an 'untimely' way, not instantaneously.

The tree and root inspire a sad image of thought that is forever imitating the multiple on the basis of a centered or segmented higher unity. If we consider the set, branches-roots, the trunk plays the role of *opposed segment* for one of the subsets running from bottom to top: this kind of segment is a 'link dipole', in contrast to the 'unit dipoles' formed by spokes radiating from a single centre.[16] Even if the links themselves proliferate, as in the radicle system, one can never get beyond the One-Two, and fake multiplicities. Regenerations, reproductions, returns, hydras, and medusas do not get us any further. Arborescent systems are hierarchical systems with centers of significance and subjectification, central automata like organized memories. In the corresponding models, an element only receives information from a higher unit, and only receives a subjective affection along pre-established paths. This is evident in current problems in information science and computer science, which still cling to the oldest modes of thought in that they grant all power to a memory or central organ. Pierre Rosenstiehl and Jean Petitot, in a fine article denouncing 'the imagery of command trees' (centered systems or hierarchical structures), note that 'accepting the primacy of hierarchical structures amounts to giving arborescent structures privileged status. . . . The arborescent form admits of topological explanation. . . . In a hierarchical system, an individual has only one active neighbour, his or her hierarchical superior. . . . The channels of transmission are preestablished: the arborescent system preexists the individual, who is integrated into it at an allotted place' (signifiance and subjectification). The authors point out that even when one thinks one has reached a multiplicity, it may be a false one – of what we call the radicle type – because its ostensibly nonhierarchical presentation or statement in fact only admits of a totally hierarchical solution. An example is the *famous friendship theorem*: 'If any two given individuals in a society have precisely one mutual friend, then there exists an individual who is the friend of all the others'. (Rosenstiehl and Petitot ask who that mutual friend is. Who is 'the universal friend in this society of couples: the master, the confessor, the doctor? These ideas are curiously far removed from the initial axioms.' Who is this friend of humankind? Is it the philosopher as he appears in classical thought, even if he is an aborted unity that makes itself felt only through its absence or subjectivity, saying all the while, I know nothing, I am nothing?) Thus the authors speak of dictatorship theorems. Such is indeed the principle of roots-trees, or their outcome: the radicle solution, the structure of Power.[17]

To these centered systems, the authors contrast acentered systems, finite networks of automata in which communication runs from any neighbor to any other, the stems or channels do not preexist, and all individuals are interchangeable, defined only by their *state* at a given moment – such that the local operations are coordinated and the final, global result synchronized without a central agency. Transduction of intensive states replaces topology, and 'the graph regulating the circulation of information is in a way the opposite of the hierarchical graph. . . . There is no reason for the graph to be a tree' (we have been calling this kind of graph a map). The problem of the war machine, or the firing squad: is a general necessary for n individuals to manage to fire in unison? The solution without a General is to be found in an acentered multiplicity possessing a finite number of states with signals to indicate corresponding speeds, from a war rhizome or guerrilla logic point of view, without any tracing, without any copying of a central order. The authors even demonstrate that this kind of machinic multiplicity, assemblage, or society rejects any centralizing or unifying automaton as an 'asocial intrusion'.[18] Under these conditions, n is in fact always $n - 1$. Rosenstiehl and Petitot emphasize that the opposition, centered–acentered, is valid less as a designation for things than as a mode of calculation applied to things. Trees may correspond to the rhizome, or they may burgeon into a rhizome. It is true that the same thing is generally susceptible to both modes of calculation or both types of regulation, but not without undergoing a change in state. Take psychoanalysis as an example again: it subjects the unconscious to arborescent structures, hierarchical graphs, recapitulatory memories, central organs, the phallus, the phallus-tree not only in its theory but also in its practice of calculation and treatment. Psychoanalysis cannot change its method in this regard: it bases its own dictatorial power upon a dictatorial conception of the unconscious. Psychoanalysis's margin of maneuverability is therefore very limited. In both psychoanalysis and its object, there is always a general, always a leader (General Freud). Schizoanalysis, on the other hand, treats the unconscious as an acentered system, in other words, as a machinic network of finite automata (a rhizome), and thus arrives at an entirely different state of the unconscious. These same remarks apply to linguistics; Rosenstiehl and Petitot are right to bring up the possibility of an 'acentered organization of a society of words'. For both statements and desires, the issue is never to reduce the unconscious or to interpret it or to make it signify according to a tree model. The issue is *to produce the unconscious*, and with it new statements, different desires: the rhizome is precisely this production of the unconscious.

It is odd how the tree has dominated Western reality and all of Western thought, from botany to biology and anatomy, but also gnosiology, theology, ontology, all of philosophy . . . : the root-foundation, *Grund*, *racine*, *fondement*. The West has a special relation to the forest, and deforestation; the fields carved from the forest are populated with seed plants produced by cultivation based on species lineages of the arborescent type; animal raising, carried out on fallow fields, selects lineages forming an entire animal arborescence. The East presents a different figure: a relation to the steppe and the garden (or in some cases, the desert and the oasis), rather than forest and field; cultivation of tubers by fragmentation of the individual; a casting aside or bracketing of animal raising, which is confined to closed spaces or pushed out onto the steppes of the nomads. The West: agriculture based on a chosen lineage containing a large number of variable individuals. The East: horticulture based on a small number of individuals derived from a wide range of 'clones'. Does not the East, Oceania in particular, offer something like a rhizomatic model opposed in every respect to the Western model of the tree? André Haudricourt even sees this as the basis for the opposition between the moralities or philosophies of transcendence dear to the West and the immanent ones of the East: the God who sows and reaps, as opposed to the God who replants and unearths (replanting of offshoots versus sowing of seeds).[19] Transcendence: a specifically European disease. Neither is music the same, the music of the earth is different, as is sexuality: seed plants, even those with two sexes in the same plant, subjugate sexuality to the reproductive model; the rhizome, on the other hand, is a liberation of sexuality not only from reproduction but also from genetality. Here in the West, the tree has implanted itself in our bodies, rigidifying and stratifying even the sexes. We have lost the rhizome, or the grass. Henry Miller: 'China is the weed in the human cabbage patch. . . . The weed is the Nemesis of human endeavor. . . . Of all the imaginary existences we attribute to plant, beast and star the weed leads the most satisfactory life of all. True, the weed produces no lilies, no battleships, no sermons on the Mount. . . . Eventually the weed gets the upper hand. Eventually things fall back into a state of China. This condition is usually referred to by historians as the Dark Age. Grass is the only way out. . . . The weed exists only to fill the waste spaces left by cultivated areas. *It grows between*, among other things. The lily is beautiful, the cabbage is provender, the poppy is maddening – but the weed is rank growth . . . : it points a moral'.[20] Which China is Miller talking about? The old China, the new, an imaginary one, or yet another located on a shifting map?

America is a special case. Of course it is not immune from domination by trees or the search for roots. This is evident even in the literature, in the quest for a national identity and even for a European ancestry or genealogy (Kerouac going off in search of his ancestors). Nevertheless, everything important that has happened or is happening takes the route of the American rhizome: the beatniks, the underground, bands and gangs, successive lateral offshoots in immediate connection with an outside. American books are different from European books, even when the American sets off in pursuit of trees. The conception of the book is different. *Leaves of grass*. And directions in America are different: the search for arborescence and the return to the Old World occur in the East. But there is the rhizomatic West, with its Indians without ancestry, its ever-receding limit, its shifting and displaced frontiers. There is a whole American 'map' in the West, where even the trees form rhizomes. America reversed the directions: it put its Orient in the West, as if it were precisely in America that the earth came full circle; its West is the edge of the East.[21] (India is not the intermediary between the Occident and the Orient, as Haudricourt believed: America is the pivot point and mechanism of reversal.) The American singer Patti Smith sings the bible of the American dentist: Don't go for the root, follow the canal. . . .

Are there not also two kinds of bureaucracy, or even three (or still more)? Western bureaucracy: its agrarian, cadastral origins; roots and fields; trees and their role as frontiers; the great census of William the Conqueror; feudalism; the policies of the kings of France; making property the basis of the State; negotiating land through warfare, litigation, and marriages. The kings of France chose the lily because it is a plant with deep roots that clings to slopes. Is bureaucracy the same in the Orient? Of course it is all too easy to depict an Orient of rhizomes and immanence; yet it is true that in the Orient the State does not act following a schema of arborescence corresponding to preestablished, arborified, and rooted classes; its bureaucracy is one of channels, for example, the much-discussed case of hydraulic power with 'weak property', in which the State engenders channeled and channelizing classes (cf. the aspects of Wittfogel's work that have not been refuted).[22] The despot acts as a river, not as a fountainhead, which is still a point, a tree-point or root; he flows with the current rather than sitting under a tree; Buddha's tree itself becomes a rhizome; Mao's river and Louis's tree. Has not America acted as an intermediary here as well? For it proceeds both by internal exterminations and liquidations (not only the Indians but also the farmers, etc.), and by successive waves of immigration from the outside. The flow of capital produces an immense channel, a quantification of power with immediate 'quanta', where each person profits from the passage of the money flow in his or her own way (hence the reality-myth of the poor man who strikes it rich and then falls into poverty again): in America everything comes together, tree and channel, root and rhizome. There is no universal capitalism, there is no capitalism in itself; capitalism is at the crossroads of all kinds of formations, it is neocapitalism by nature. It invents its eastern face and western face, and reshapes them both – all for the worst.

At the same time, we are on the wrong track with all these geographical distributions. An impasse. So much the better. If it is a question of showing that rhizomes also have their own, even more rigid, despotism and heirarchy, then fine and good: for there is no dualism, no ontological dualism between here and there, no axiological dualism between good and bad, no blend or American synthesis. There are knots of arborescence in rhizomes, and rhizomatic offshoots in roots. Moreover, there are despotic formations of immanence and channelization specific to rhizomes, just as there are anarchic deformations in the transcendent system of trees, aerial roots, and subterranean stems. The important point is that the root-tree and canal-rhizome are not two opposed models: the first operates as a transcendent model and tracing, even if it engenders its own escapes; the second operates as an immanent process that overturns the model and outlines a map, even if it constitutes its own hierarchies, even if it gives rise to a despotic channel. It is not a question of this or that place on earth, or of a given moment in history, still less of this or that category of thought. It is a question of a model that is perpetually in construction or collapsing, and of a process that is perpetually prolonging itself, breaking off and starting up again. No, this is not a new or different dualism. The problem of writing: in order to designate something exactly, anexact expressions are utterly unavoidable. Not at all because it is a necessary step, or because one can only advance by approximations: anexactitude is in no way an approximation; on the contrary, it is the exact passage of that which is under way. We invoke one dualism only in order to challenge another. We employ a dualism of models only in order to arrive at a process that challenges all models. Each time, mental correctives are necessary to undo the dualisms we had no wish to construct but through which we pass. Arrive at the magic formula we all seek – PLURALISM = MONISM – via all the dualisms that are the enemy, an entirely necessary enemy, the furniture we are forever rearranging.

Let us summarize the principal characteristics of a rhizome: unlike trees or their roots, the rhizome connects any point to any other point, and its traits are not necessarily linked to traits of the same nature; it brings into play very different regimes of signs, and even nonsign states. The rhizome is reducible neither to the One nor the multiple. It is not the One that becomes Two or even directly three, four, five, etc. It is not a multiple derived from the One, or to which One is added ($n + 1$). It is composed not of units but of dimensions, or rather directions in motion. It has neither beginning nor end, but always a middle (*milieu*) from which it grows and which it overspills. It constitutes linear multiplicities with n dimensions having neither subject nor object, which can be laid out on a plane of consistency, and from which the One is always subtracted ($n - 1$). When a multiplicity of this kind changes dimension, it necessarily changes in nature as well, undergoes a metamorphosis. Unlike a structure, which is defined by a set of points and positions, with binary relations between the points and biunivocal relationships between the positions, the rhizome is made only of lines: lines of segmentarity and stratification as its dimensions, and the line of flight or deterritorialization as the maximum dimension after which the multiplicity undergoes metamorphosis, changes in nature. These lines, or lineaments, should not be confused with lineages of the arborescent type, which are merely localizable linkages between points and positions. Unlike the tree, the rhizome is not the object of reproduction: neither external reproduction as image-tree nor internal reproduction as tree-structure. The rhizome is an anti-genealogy.

It is a short-term memory, or anti-memory. The rhizome operates by variation, expansion, conquest, capture, offshoots. Unlike the graphic arts, drawing, or photography, unlike tracings, the rhizome pertains to a map that must be produced, constructed, a map that is always detachable, connectable, reversible, modifiable, and has multiple entryways and exits and its own lines of flight. It is tracings that must be put on the map, not the opposite. In contrast to centered (even polycentric) systems with hierarchical modes of communications and preestablished paths, the rhizome is an acentered, nonhierarchical, nonsignifying system without a General and without an organizing memory or central automaton, defined solely by a circulation of states. What is at question in the rhizome is a relation to sexuality – but also to the animal, the vegetal, the world, politics, the book, things natural and artificial – that is totally different from the arborescent relation: all manner of 'becomings'.

A plateau is always in the middle, not at the beginning or the end. A rhizome is made of plateaus. Gregory Bateson uses the word 'plateau' to designate something very special: a continuous, self-vibrating region of intensifies whose development avoids any orientation toward a culmination point or external end. Bateson cites Balinese culture as an example: mother-child sexual games, and even quarrels among men, undergo this bizarre intensive stabilization. 'Some sort of continuing plateau of intensity is substituted for [sexual] climax', war, or a culmination point. It is a regrettable characteristic of the Western mind to relate expressions and actions to exterior or transcendent ends, instead of evaluating them on a plane of consistency on the basis of their intrinsic value.[23] For example, a book composed of chapters has culmination and termination points. What takes place in a book composed instead of plateaus that communicate with one another across microfissures, as in a brain? We call a 'plateau' any multiplicity connected to other multiplicities by superficial underground stems in such a way as to form or extend a rhizome. We are writing this book as a rhizome. It is composed of plateaus. We have given it a circular form, but only for laughs. Each morning we would wake up, and each of us would ask himself what plateau he was going to tackle, writing five lines here, ten there. We had hallucinatory experiences, we watched lines leave one plateau and proceed to another like columns of tiny ants. We made circles of convergence. Each plateau can be read starting anywhere and can be related to any other plateau. To attain the multiple, one must have a method that effectively constructs it; no typographical cleverness, no lexical agility, no blending or creation of words, no syntactical boldness, can substitute for it. In fact, these are more often than not merely mimetic procedures used to disseminate or disperse a unity that is retained in a different dimension for an image-book. Technonarcissism. Typographical, lexical, or syntactic creations are necessary only when they no longer belong to the form of expression of a hidden unity, becoming themselves dimensions of the multiplicity under consideration; we only know of rare successes in this.[24] We ourselves were unable to do it. We just used words that in turn function for us as plateaus. RHIZOMATICS = SCHIZOANALYSIS = STRATOANALYSIS = PRAGMATICS = MICROPOLITICS. These words are concepts, but concepts are lines, which is to say, number systems attached to a particular dimension of the multiplicities (strata, molecular chains, lines of flight or rupture, circles of convergence, etc.). Nowhere do we claim for our concepts the title of a science. We are no more familiar with scientificity than we are with ideology; all we know are assemblages. And the only assemblages are machinic-assemblages of desire and collective assemblages of enunciation. No signifiance, no subjectification: writing to the nth power (all individuated enunciation remains trapped within the dominant significations, all signifying desire is associated with dominated subjects). An assemblage, in its multiplicity, necessarily acts on semiotic flows, material flows, and social flows simultaneously (independently of any recapitulation that may be made of it in a scientific or theoretical corpus). There is no longer a tripartite division between a field of reality (the world) and a field of representation (the book) and a field of subjectivity (the author). Rather, an assemblage establishes connections between certain multiplicities drawn from each of these orders, so that a book has no sequel nor the world as its object nor one or several authors as its subject. In short, we think that one cannot write sufficiently in the name of an outside. The outside has no image, no signification, no subjectivity. The book as assemblage with the outside, against the book as image of the world. A rhizome-book, not a dichotomous, pivotal, or fascicular book. Never send down roots, or plant them, however difficult it may be to avoid reverting to the old procedures. 'Those things which occur to me, occur to me not from the root up but rather only from somewhere about their middle. Let someone then attempt to seize them, let someone attempt to seize a blade of grass and hold fast to it when it begins to grow only from the middle.'[25] Why is this so difficult? The question is directly one of perceptual semiotics. It's not easy to see things in the middle, rather than looking down on them from above or up at them from below, or from left to right or right to left: try it, you'll see that everything changes. It's not easy to see the grass in things and in words (similarly, Nietzsche said that an aphorism had to be 'ruminated'; never is a plateau separable from the cows that populate it, which are also the clouds in the sky).

History is always written from the sedentary point of view and in the name of a unitary State apparatus, at least a possible one, even when the topic is nomads. What is lacking is a Nomadology, the opposite of a history. There are rare successes in this also, for example, on the subject of the Children's Crusades: Marcel Schwob's book multiplies narratives like so many plateaus with variable numbers of dimensions. Then there is Andrzejewski's book, *Les portes du paradis* (The gates of paradise), composed of a single uninterrupted sentence; a flow of children; a flow of walking with pauses, straggling, and forward rushes; the semiotic flow of the confessions of all the children who go up to the old monk at the head of the procession to make their declarations; a flow of desire and sexuality, each child having left out of love and more or less directly led by the dark posthumous pederastic desire of the count of Vendôme; all this with circles of convergence. What is important is not whether the flows are 'One or multiple' – we're past that point: there is a collective assemblage of enunciation, a machinic assemblage of desire, one inside the other and both plugged into an immense outside that is a multiplicity in any case. A more recent example is Armand Farrachi's book on the Fourth Crusade, *La dislocation*, in which the sentences space themselves out and disperse, or else jostle together and coexist, and in which the letters, the typography begin to dance as the crusade grows more delirious.[26] These are models of nomadic and rhizomatic writing. Writing weds a war machine and lines of flight, abandoning the strata, segmentarities, sedentarity, the State apparatus. But why is a model still necessary? Aren't these books still 'images' of the Crusades? Don't they still retain a unity, in Schwob's case a pivotal unity, in Farrachi's an aborted unity, and in the most beautiful example, *Les portes du paradis*, the unity of the funereal count? Is there a need for a more profound nomadism than that of the Crusades, a nomadism of true nomads, or of those who no longer even move or imitate anything? The nomadism of those who only assemble (*agencent*). How can the book find an adequate outside with which to assemble in heterogeneity, rather than a world to reproduce? The cultural book is necessarily a tracing: already a tracing of itself, a tracing of the previous book by the same author, a tracing of other books however different they may be, an endless tracing of established concepts and words, a tracing of the world present, past, and future. Even the anticultural book may still be burdened by too heavy a cultural load: but it will use it actively, for forgetting instead of remembering, for underdevelopment instead of progress toward development, in nomadism rather than sedentarily, to make a map instead of a tracing. RHIZOMATICS = POP ANALYSIS, even if the people have other things to do besides read it, even if the blocks of academic culture or pseudoscientificity in it are still too painful or ponderous. For science would go completely mad if left to its own devices. Look at mathematics: it's not a science, it's a monster slang, it's nomadic. Even in the realm of theory, especially in the realm of theory, any precarious and pragmatic framework is better than tracing concepts, with their breaks and progress changing nothing. Imperceptible rupture, not signifying break. The nomads invented a war machine in opposition to the State apparatus. History has never comprehended nomadism, the book has never comprehended the outside. The State as the model for the book and for thought has a long history: logos, the philosopher-king, the transcendence of the Idea, the inferiority of the concept, the republic of minds, the court of reason, the functionaries of thought, man as legislator and subject. The State's pretension to be a world order, and to root man. The war machine's relation to an outside is not another 'model'; it is an assemblage that makes thought itself nomadic, and the book a working part in every mobile machine, a stem for a rhizome (Kleist and Kafka against Goethe).

Write to the nth power, the $n - 1$ power, write with slogans: Make rhizomes, not roots, never plant! Don't sow, grow offshoots! Don't be one or multiple, be multiplicities! Run lines, never plot a point! Speed turns the point into a line![27] Be quick, even when standing still! Line of chance, line of hips, line of flight. Don't bring out the General in you! Don't have just ideas, just have an idea (Godard). Have short-term ideas. Make maps, not photos or drawings. Be the Pink Panther and your loves will be like the wasp and the orchid, the cat and the baboon. As they say about old man river:

> He don't plant 'tatos
> Don't plant cotton
> Them that plants them is soon forgotten
> But old man river he just keeps rollin' along

A rhizome has no beginning or end; it is always in the middle, between things, interbeing, *intermezzo*. The tree is filiation, but the rhizome is alliance, uniquely alliance. The tree imposes the verb 'to be', but the fabric of the rhizome is the conjunction, 'and . . . and . . . and . . . '. This conjunction carries enough force to shake and uproot the verb 'to be'. Where are you going? Where are you coming from? What are you heading for? These are totally useless questions. Making a clean slate, starting or beginning again from ground zero, seeking a beginning or a foundation – all imply a false conception of voyage and movement (a conception that is methodical, pedagogical, initiatory, symbolic . . .). But Kleist, Lenz, and Bilchner have another way of traveling and moving: proceeding from the middle, through the middle, coming and going rather than starting and finishing.[28] American literature, and already English literature, manifest this rhizomatic direction to an even greater extent; they know how to move between things, establish a logic of the AND, overthrow ontology, do away with foundations, nullify endings and beginnings. They know how to practice pragmatics. The middle is by no means an average; on the contrary, it is where things pick up speed. *Between* things does not designate a localizable relation going from one thing to the other and back again, but a perpendicular direction, a transversal movement that sweeps one *and* the other away, a stream without beginning or end that undermines its banks and picks up speed in the middle.

Notes

1   Deleuze and Guattari derive the notion of a 'body without organs' (BwO) from Antonin Artaud, for whom the body 'is all by itself/and has no need of organs' (cited in Gilles Deleuze and Félix Guattari, *Anti-Oedipus: Capitalism and Schizophrenia*, trans. R. Hurley, M. Seem and H. R. Lane (Minneapolis: University of Minnesota Press, 1983), p. 9. The BwO is always outside any systematic account of bodies (through legal, philosophical, medical or other discourses) and therefore outside the disciplining of bodies via such accounts. Whereas the body is what always belongs to a subject (the rational, the political, the psychoanalytic subject and so on), for Deleuze and Guattari the BwO has nothing to do with belonging but only with becoming. The body without organs is never the property of a subject (a person or a discourse); it is always in the process of becoming a body which is unable to be controlled by totalizing discourses about the body. The BwO is the body 'all by itself' (not yours or mine), with its own desires and energies and in its own relationships to and impacts on other bodies (yours and mine, as well as those of animals, plants and things). (NL)
2   The 'plane of consistency' refers to the *style* by which a BwO holds itself together, dynamically and precariously; it is the 'mode of composition' by which elements come to be assembled (neither purely by chance nor wholly by choice) into and as a body without organs, such as a book, which is 'all by itself' in its connections to exteriorities. In short, a book's plane of consistency is the style of its connections to other books. A book may be said to be

'all by itself', then, in terms of such a style, and not in terms of its 'interiorities' in the form of themes, contents and meanings. (NL)

3   See, for example, Noam Chomsky, *Aspects of the Theory of Syntax* (Cambridge, Mass.: MIT Press, 1965). (NL)

4   U. Weinreich, W. Labov, and M. Herzog, 'Empirical Foundations for a Theory of Language', in W. Lehrnann and Y. Malkeiel, eds, *Directions for Historical Linguistics* (1968), p. 125; cited by Françoise Robert, 'Aspects sociaux du changement dans une grammaire générative', *Langages*, 32 (Dec. 1973), p. 90. (Trans.)

5   Bertil Malmberg, *New Trends in Linguistics*, trans. Edward Carners (Stockholm: Lund, 1964), pp. 65–7 (the example of the Castilian dialect).

6   Ernst Jünger, *Approches; drogues et ivresse* (Paris: Table Ronde, 1974), p. 304, § 218.

7   Rémy Chauvin in *Entretiens sur la sexualité*, eds M. Aron, R. Courrier, and E. Wolff (Paris: Plon, 1969), p. 205.

8   On the work of R. E. Benveniste and G. J. Todaro, see Yves Christen, 'Le rôle des virus dans l'évolution', *La Recherche* 54 (March 1975): 'After integration-extraction in a cell, viruses may, due to an error in excision, carry off fragments of their host's DNA and transmit them to new cells: this in fact is the basis for what we call "genetic engineering". As a result, the genetic information of one organism may be transferred to another by means of viruses. We could even imagine an extreme case where this transfer of information would go from a more highly evolved species to one that is less evolved or was the progenitor of the more evolved species. This mechanism, then, would run in the opposite direction to evolution in the classical sense. If it turns out that this kind of transferral of information has played a major role, we would in certain cases have to *substitute reticular schemas (with communications between branches after they have become differentiated) for the bush or tree schemas currently used to represent evolution*' (p. 271).

9   François Jacob, *The Logic of Life*, trans. Betty E. Spillmann (New York: Pantheon, 1973), pp. 291–2, 311 (quotation).

10 Carlos Castaneda, *The Teachings of Don Juan* (Berkeley: University of California Press, 1971), p. 88.

11 Pierre Boulez, *Conversations with Célestin Deliège* (London: Eulenberg Books, 1976): 'a seed which you plant in compost, and suddenly it begins to proliferate like a weed' (p. 15); and on musical proliferation: 'a music that floats, and in which the writing itself makes it impossible for the performer to keep in with a pulsed time' (p. 69 [translation modified]).

12 See Melanie Klein, *Narrative of a Child Analysis* (London: Hogarth Press, 1961): the role of war maps in Richard's activities. [Deleuze and Guattari, with Claire Parnet and André Scala, analyze Klein's Richard and Freud's Little Hans in 'The Interpretation of Utterances', in *Language, Sexuality and Subversions*, trans. Paul Foss and Meaghan Morris (Sydney: Feral Publications, 1978), pp. 141–57. (Trans.)]

13 Fernand Deligny, *Cahiers de l'immuable*, vol. 1, *Voix et voir, Recherches*, 8 (April 1975).

14 See Dieter Wunderlich, 'Pragmatique, situation denunciation et Deixis', in *Langages*, 26 (June 1972), pp. 50ff.: MacCawley, Sadock, and Wunderlich's attempts to integrate 'pragmatic properties' into Chomskian trees.

15 Steven Rose, *The Conscious Brain* (New York: Knopf, 1975), p. 76; on memory, see pp. 185–219.

16 See Julien Pacotte, *Le réseau arborescent, schème primordial de la pensée* (Paris: Hermann, 1936). This book analyzes and develops various schemas of the arborescent form, which is presented not as a mere formalism but as the 'real foundation of formal thought'. It follows classical thought through to the end. It presents all of the forms of the 'One-Two', the theory of the dipole. The set, trunk-roots-branches, yields the following schema:

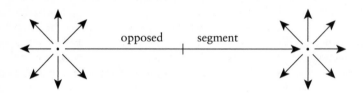

More recently, Michel Serres has analyzed varieties and sequences of trees in the most diverse scientific domains: how a tree is formed on the basis of a 'network'. *La traduction* (Paris: Minuit, 1974), pp. 27ff.; *Feux et signaux de brume* (Paris: Grasset, 1975), pp. 35

17 Pierre Rosenstiehl and Jean Petitot, 'Automate asocial et systèmes acentrés', *Communications*, 22 (1974), pp. 45–62. On the friendship theorem, see H. S. Wilf, *The Friendship Theorem in Combinatorial Mathematics* (Welsh Academic Press); and on a similar kind of theorem, called the theorem of group indecision, see K. J. Arrow, *Choice and Individual Values* (New York: Wiley, 1963).

18 Rosenstiehl and Petitot, 'Automate asocial'. The principal characteristic of the acentered system is that local initiatives are coordinated independently of a central power, with the calculations made throughout the network (multiplicity). 'That is why the only place files on people can be kept is right in each person's home, since they alone are capable of filling in the description and keeping it up to date: society itself is the only possible data bank on people. A naturally acentered society rejects the centralizing automaton as an asocial intrusion' (p. 62). On the 'Firing Squad Theorem', see pp. 51–7. It even happens that generals, dreaming of appropriating the formal techniques of guerrilla warfare, appeal to *multiplicities* 'of synchronous modules . . . based on numerous but independent lightweight cells' having in theory only a minimum of central power and 'hierarchical relaying'; see Guy Brossollet, *Essai sur la non-bataille* (Paris: Belin, 1975).

19 On Western agriculture of grain plants and Eastern horticulture of tubers, the opposition between sowing of seeds and replanting of offshoots, and the contrast to animal raising, see André Haudricourt, 'Domestication des animaux, culture des plantes et traitement d'autrui', *L'Homme* 2 (1) (Jan.–April 1962), pp. 40–50, and 'Nature et culture dans ta civilisation de l'igname: l'origine des clones et des clans', *L'Homme* 4 (1) (Jan.–April 1964), pp. 93–104. Maize and rice are no exception: they are cereals 'adopted at a late date by tuber cultivators' and were treated in a similar fashion; it is probable that rice 'first appeared as a weed in taro ditches'.

20 Henry Miller, in Henry Miller and Michael Fraenkel, *Hamlet* (New York: Carrefour, 1939), pp. 105–6.

21 See Leslie Fiedler, *The Return of the Vanishing American* (New York: Stein and Day, 1968). This book contains a fine analysis of geography and its role in American mythology and literature, and of the reversal of directions. In the East, there was the search for a specifically American code and for a recoding with Europe (Henry James, Eliot, Pound, etc.); in the South, there was the overcoding of the slave system, with its ruin and the ruin of the plantations during the Civil War (Faulkner, Caldwell); from the North came capitalist decoding (Dos Passos, Dreiser); the West, however, played the role of a line of flight combining travel, hallucination, madness, the Indians, perceptive and mental experimentation, the shifting of frontiers, the rhizome (Ken Kesey and his 'fog machine', the beat generation, etc.). Every great American author creates a cartography, even in his or her style; in contrast to what is done in Europe, each makes a map that is directly connected to the real social movements crossing America. An example is the indexing of geographical directions throughout the work of Fitzgerald.

22 Karl Wittfogel, *Oriental Despotism* (New Haven, Conn.: Yale University Press, 1957). (Trans.)

23 Gregory Bateson, *Steps to an Ecology of Mind* (New York: Ballantine Books, 1972), p. 113. It will be noted that the word 'plateau' is used in classical studies of bulbs, tubers, and rhizomes; see the entry for 'Bulb' in M. H. Baillon, *Dictionnaire de botanique* (Paris: Haehette, 1876–92).

24 For example, Joëlle de La Casinière, *Absolument nécessaire. The Emergency Book* (Paris: Minuit, 1973), a truly nomadic book. In the same vein, see the research in progress at the Montfaucon Research Center.

25 *The Diaries of Franz Kafka*, ed. Max Brod, trans. Joseph Kresh (New York: Schocken, 1948), p. 12.

26 Marcel Schwob, *The Children's Crusade*, trans. Henry Copley (Boston: Small, Maynard, 1898); Jersy Andrzejewski, *Les portes du paradis* (Paris: Gallimard, 1959); Armand Farrachi, *La dislocation* (Paris: Stock, 1974). It was in the context of Schwob's book that Paul Alphandéry remarked that literature, in certain cases, could revitalize history and impose upon it 'genuine research directions'; *La chrétienté et l'idée de croisade* (Paris: Albin Michel, 1959), vol. 2, p. 116.

27   See Paul Virilio, 'Véhiculaire', in *Nomades et vagabonds*, ed. Jacques Bergue (Paris: Union Générale d'Editions, 1975), p. 43, on the appearance of linearity and the disruption of perception by speed.
28   See Jean-Cristophe Bailly's description of movement in German Romanticism, in his introduction to *La légende dispersée: Anthologie du romantisme allemand* (Paris: Union Générale d'Editions, 1976), pp. 18ff.

Part Two **Ethics**

Chapter Five Rewriting Wrong: On the Ethics of Literary Reversion

Steven Connor

Contemporary fiction seems marked by the imperative of the eternal return. Whether assembled under the rubric of Barth's 'literature of exhaustion', Genette's 'literature to the second degree', Kristeva's 'intertextuality', or Baudrillard's 'regime of the simulacrum', or instanced by Beckett's obsessive auto-iterations, Barth's sequels to the *Odyssey* and *Don Quixote* in *Tidewater Tales*, Robert Coover's skilful parodies of movie genres in *A Night at the Movies* and his extrapolation of the Pinocchio story in *Pinocchio in Venice*, Alain Robbe-Grillet's reworking of the Oedipus story in *The Erasers*, Gert Hoffman's literary reworking of Breughel's painting in *The Parable of the Blind*, D. M. Thomas's reworking of Freudian case-history in *The White Hotel*, Peter Ackroyd's literary replications in *The Last Testament of Oscar Wilde* and *Chatterton*, Angela Carter's rewritings of fairy tales in *The Bloody Chamber*, and her brilliant vaudevillian travesty of Shakespeare in *Wise Children* or feminist reappropriations in general of the genres of science fiction and the detective story, it is plain that, in contemporary fiction, telling has become compulsorily belated, inextricably bound up with retelling, in all its idioms: reworking, translation, adaptation, displacement, imitation, forgery, plagiarism, parody, pastiche. This phenomenon has tended to produce two opposed critical responses. The first unconditionally celebrates

Steven Connor, 'Rewriting Wrong: On the Ethics of Literary Reversion', in *Liminal Postmodernism: The Postmodern, the (Post-)Colonial, and the (Post-)Feminist*, eds T. D'Haen and H. Bertens, *Postmodern Studies* 8 (Amsterdam: Atlanta, 1994), pp. 79–97.

the procreative abundance of a narrative able to replenish itself ceaselessly out of its own forms and energies. The second mourns the loss of
normative stability in a world in which forms seem to slide frictionlessly
over each other, proliferating a difference that is really indifference. This
second attitude is perhaps evidenced in Fredric Jameson's rejection of the
culture of pastiche: 'Pastiche is, like parody, the imitation of a peculiar
mask, speech in a dead language; but it is a neutral practice of such
mimicry, without any of parody's ulterior motives, amputated of the
satiric impulse, devoid of laughter, and of any conviction that alongside
the abnormal tongue you have momentarily borrowed, some healthy
linguistic normality still exists'.[1]

In recent years, there have been a number of highly particular instances
of the culture of pastiche which ought, I think, to complicate this dichotomous structure of response, *either* celebration of polyphilo-progenitiveness,
or disapproval of the vacuity of pastiche without purpose or moral grounding. I have in mind the practice of fictionally *rewriting* well-known or
culturally central texts. Such rewriting can take different forms and have
different effects, but a characterizing feature that allows it, at least provisionally, to be distinguished from other forms of cultural mimicry, is that
it consists of a particularized and conscientious attachment to a single
textual precedent, such that its departures from the original must be
measured in terms of its dependence upon it. I have in mind here such
texts as Jean Rhys's reworking of *Jane Eyre* in her *Wide Sargasso Sea* (to
name what is probably the most well-known example), or Sue Roe's
reworking of *Great Expectations* in *Estella: Her Expectations*. In such
rewritings, there is something different and more complex at work than
the mere reduplication or replenishment of narratives. If rewriting com-
promises the cultural authority of the original text, then this never amounts
to a simple denial of it; for the degree of its attention to its original, its
fidelity-in-betrayal, must always submit to the authority of an ethical
imperative, whose complexity is not well described by either side of the
critical dichotomy I have just now evoked.

I want in this essay to look briefly at three instances of such rewriting:
they are Emma Tennant's rewriting of Stevenson's *The Strange Case of
Dr Jekyll and Mr Hyde* (1886) in her *Two Women of London: The
Strange Case of Ms Jekyll and Mrs Hyde* (1989), Marianne Wiggins's
rewriting of William Golding's *Lord of the Flies* (1954) in her *John Dollar* (1989) and J. M. Coetzee's rewriting of Defoe's *Robinson* Crusoe
(1719) in his *Foe* (1987).[2] In each case, the rewriting is of a well-known
and canonical text (in this kind of rewriting, there would hardly be any

point in taking as one's object a text that were not thus well-known). The cultural centrality of these texts has to do with the fact that they are all in different ways myths of origin and/or reversion. In all three cases, *Robinson Crusoe*, *Dr Jekyll and Mr Hyde*, and *Lord of the Flies*, a certain form of extreme experience produces a reversion to origins. The stranded Robinson Crusoe is forced to invent himself from nothing on his island, building from the ground up his self, his culture, his history, spelling out, as many have noted, a powerful Puritan lesson of individual self-making. *Lord of the Flies* is, of course, already a rewriting of this myth, since here being stranded on an island produces not the slow climb back to civilization, but a dramatic slither into savagery. Of course, one of the most striking differences between *Lord of the Flies* and *Robinson Crusoe* is that the former presents a vision of collective life under conditions of isolation and extremity; though there is also a sense in which the concentration of the group's experience in Ralph (and the homing in on Ralph's conscious-ness at the end of the book) makes it a novel about a certain kind of self-making which is similar to *Robinson Crusoe*. *Dr Jekyll and Mr Hyde* does not depend upon isolation from society in order to produce its condition of extremity and its action takes place, not on an island, but in London. But, like the two other novels, *Dr Jekyll and Mr Hyde* does indeed involve extremity, in the form of that Romantic Faustianism in which a single inspired scientist is impelled to reach beyond the limits of conventional knowledge and morality. Dr Jekyll's 'transcendental medi-cine' is the metaphorical equivalent of the shipwreck, which separates him from ordinary life, by revealing to him a certain truth about man's primitive nature. Henry Jekyll actually uses the metaphor of the ship-wreck to describe his own history: 'I thus drew steadily nearer to that truth by whose partial discovery I have been doomed to such a terrible shipwreck: that man is not truly one, but truly two' (*JH*, 82).

When such texts are subject to rewriting, the question of origin is interestingly redoubled. If all three 'original' novels concern the reversion to different sorts of origin, then the return to such texts for the purposes of rewriting may be seen as a reversion of a similar kind. In each case the originality of the original cultural myth of origin is doubled and divided by the act of the rewriting, the reversioning of the reversionary text. But there is one further crucial feature of these three rewritings. In all of them, female authors are rewriting myths of male origin. (All of them? Well, yes, since, although J. M. Coetzee is not in fact a female author, the whole purpose of *Foe* is nevertheless to substitute a female narrative for the male narrative of Daniel Defoe. Or to substitute an attempted narrative, which does and does not displace the male narrative; to write the narrative which the male narrative must have displaced in order to represent itself as original.) In all three rewritings, the substitution of a female narrative draws attention to the remarkable absence of the female in the originals, revealing the ways in which myths of extremity and origin, literary and otherwise, have often been bound up with a male myth of, and profound desire for, parthenogenetic self-authoring.

Emma Tennant's *Two Women of London* is probably the closest rewriting of the three that I am looking at, for it follows with deliberation most of the stages of the narrative of *Dr Jekyll and Mr Hyde*. The difference is that where Stevenson's tale has a male narrator and a cast of characters who are exclusively male, the narrator and characters of *Two Women of London* are female. Dr Jekyll has become the beautiful, cultured and affluent Eliza Jekyll, whose opulent apartment backs on to the miserable rooms where dwells the slatternly and violent Mrs Hyde. The narrative takes the form of an elaborate reconstruction of the case of Ms Jekyll and Mrs Hyde, by an unnamed editor-narrator, who stitches together video footage, taped interviews, letters and other forms of testimony from a number of middle-class women inhabiting Nightingale Crescent in West London. During the period dealt with by the narrative, the area has been tyrannized by a serial rapist. The crucial event in the narrative is the killing of a man thought to be the rapist by Mrs Hyde, a man who turns out to be the innocent local businessman and magistrate, the Hon. Jeremy Toller – an event corresponding to the motiveless killing of the MP Sir Danvers Carew by Mr Hyde in Stevenson's story. Just as in the original, the story ends with the testimony of the Jekyll-figure. This reveals the single most important difference between the first and the second versions. Henry Jekyll is driven initially by the desire to confront his other, to separate out the good and evil constituents fused together so incongruously in a single human nature. Having released the figure of Mr Hyde from his psychic confinement, he then finds it more and more difficult to return to his 'true' self. In *Two Women of London*, it is Mrs Hyde who finds that the fortuitous combination of a tranquillizer and the drug Ecstasy can transform her into her idealized self-image, Ms Eliza Jekyll. In Stevenson's story, the singular, expansive ego attempts to give birth to its not-self. In Tennant's version of this story, it is the disintegrating ego, the suffering and atrophied not-self that Mrs Hyde has become, which craves the drug which will restore her self-possession. Here, self-possession is a derived rather than an original effect, the transformation wrought is not a reversion but a projection.

In feminizing Stevenson's version of the male split self, Tennant actually compels attention to the ways in which the apparently absent female is in fact present in his story. For although there are no leading female characters in Stevenson's story, women are important to its structural scheme. There are three females who feature in it briefly. The first is the little girl who is trampled underfoot by Hyde in the opening episode of the story. The second is the maidservant who witnesses Hyde's murder of Sir Danvers Carew (*JH*, 46–7). The one is the victim of Hyde's motiveless violence, the other is the helpless spectator of it, and both of these stand for a pure, mute innocence, the exact and abstracted antithesis to the evil represented by Hyde. There is something extraordinarily deliberated in Stevenson's account of the foolish and childish innocence of the maidservant: 'Never (she used to say with streaming tears, when she narrated that experience), never had she felt more at peace with all men or thought more kindly of the world. And as she so sat, she became aware of an aged and beautiful gentleman with white hair drawing near along the lane; and advancing to meet him, another and very small gentleman, to whom at first she paid less attention' (*JH*, 46). Here woman is on the side of goodness and of self-identity, but only because her identity is a pure abstraction, part of that neurotic separation of the male and female spheres and values in Victorian ideology. Here the female is not only defined according to ideological and psychic processes of distinction, she seems to guarantee distinctiveness as such, the boundary between the inside and the outside, law and criminality, virtue and licence.

But, according to a well-documented psycho-cultural process, woman can also stand for loss of identity, and the reversion to indistinction. The third female who features in *Dr Jekyll and Mr Hyde* is Hyde's housekeeper, who mirrors the indefiniteness of her master: she is 'ivory-faced and silvery-haired', but with 'an evil face, smoothed by hypocrisy' (*JH*, 49). This figure connects in a complicated way with the theme of appearance in Stevenson's story. The woman resembles Hyde not so much in her appearance of being evil, as in the fact that her face is 'smoothed by hypocrisy'. Although Jekyll thinks that Hyde's face 'seemed more express and single, than the imperfect and divided countenance, I had been hitherto accustomed to call mine', and attributes this to the fact that Hyde is 'pure evil' (*JH*, 84–5), the people who meet Hyde are perplexed by being unable to give a name to their feelings of disgust for him. This means that the evil of Hyde consists as much in his uncertainty of definition as in the more comfortable doctrine that he is pure evil. This contradiction perhaps arises from a psychic economy in which evil is characterized precisely as the not-self, the indefinite, the impure (the female); an economy which makes it impossible to maintain consistently the notion of 'pure' evil.

There are one or two occasions when Mr Hyde is characterized in Stevenson's story not only as a kind of evolutionary throwback (he is said on several occasions to be 'apelike') but also as female.[3] Dr Lanyon writes of Edward Hyde that 'he paused, and put his hand to his throat, and I could see, in spite of his collected manner, that he was wrestling against the approaches of the hysteria' (*JH*, 78). In a passage towards the end of Henry Jekyll's deposition, Hyde is characterized as between life and death, as the embodiment of a Sartrean vision of the female *visqueuse*: 'This was the shocking thing: that the slime of the pit seemed to utter cries and voices; that the amorphous dust gesticulated and sinned; that what was dead, and had no shape, should usurp the offices of life' (95). Jekyll then suddenly genders this terrifying liminality: 'And this again, that this insurgent horror was knit to him closer than a wife' (*JH*, 95). It is the female that here must name the indistinct union of self and not-self, the joining of joining and dissolution.

By making the doubling take place between the two versions of woman offered by Stevenson – the degraded and the idealized – rather than within the single person of a man, Emma Tennant makes manifest the latent anxieties about gender that are encoded within *Dr Jekyll and Mr Hyde*. At the same time, she substitutes for the series of male narrators (Mr Enfield, Mr Utterson, Dr Lanyon, Dr Jekyll), a network of female narrators (though they are marshalled together by a single, authoritative and unnamed narrator). The substitution of network for series means that Tennant's rewriting designedly sacrifices the sense of development towards closure. In particular, the dispersal of the narrative of Mrs Hyde among a number of witnesses and narrators prevents that final authoritative act of self-immolation with which Henry Jekyll closes his – and Stevenson's – account of his life: 'Here then, as I lay down the pen, and proceed to seal up my confession, I bring the life of that unhappy Henry Jekyll to an end' (*JH*, 96). In Emma Tennant's version, Jekyll/Hyde does not die, but escapes, perhaps to the continent, nor does Jekyll have the final word. Although the narrator surmises that 'perhaps she has at last been able to find herself' (*TW*, 129), the final words of the book are the narrator's describing the lawyer Jean Hastie's determination to keep the wholesome and the murderous separate, by protecting Mrs Hyde's children from knowledge of their mother:

I'll make sure they don't find the other side of this tragic victim of our new Victorian values: the word, scrawled across the pad under a list of household essentials –

> Ajax
> fishfingers
> ketchup
> Mother's Pride
>   KILL
>
>   (*TW*, 121)

But Jean Hastie's conviction that some irreducible and, it seems, metaphysical evil lies within Jekyll/Hyde represents a partial retraction of the critique which she has made throughout the novel of Stevenson's ethical determinism. Jean Hastie is the author of an academic work on the Gnostic Gospels which aims radically to revise the Augustinian doctrine of Original Sin, arguing that 'The message of the story of Adam and Eve in the Garden of Eden is that we are responsible for the choices we freely make, good or evil, just as Adam was' (*TW*, 73). This doctrine of ethical self-determination and self-authorship stands against the demonizing impulses both of Stevenson's story, which denies women's self-determination by identifying the female merely as the inhibiting or corrupting materiality from which the freely self-determining male must extricate himself, and of the women in *Two Women of London* who demonize men in something of the same way. But in refusing the determining force of Stevenson's myth of self-determination, Tennant also reproduces it. Stevenson's fear of reversion into the female resurfaces as a fear of reversion *in the female* into pure and unrepresentable 'evil'. In reversing Stevenson's premises, Tennant reverts to them. Here, difference and repetition, reversal and reversion, change places.

Marianne Wiggins's *John Dollar* also claims for the female an experience of extremity which in both *Robinson Crusoe* and *Lord of the Flies* had been represented as male. In this story, a number of colonial schoolgirls are shipwrecked on a Burmese island in 1918, after a tidal wave washes away all the adults but two – their schoolteacher Charlotte, who has gone blind and disappeared into the forest, and her lover, the adventurer John Dollar, who is paralysed and dying after breaking his spine. Like the schoolboys in *Lord of the Flies*, the girls slide slowly into chaos and brutality. In the final scenes of the novel, the girls, who have witnessed their fathers being burnt and eaten by a tribe of cannibals who visit their island, begin ritually to eat the flesh of John Dollar from his still-living body. We learn from the retrospect which actually opens the novel that Charlotte, her sight suddenly restored, and a little Indian girl called Monkey, have killed the last remaining girls, and buried the body of the now-dead John Dollar.

The parallels with *Lord of the Flies* are insistent. Like the boys, the girls begin with instituting laws which soon collapse; where the boys experience a visit from the adult world, in the quasi-divine personage of the dead parachutist, the girls tend and ritually consume their own adopted God, John Dollar. Both novels use the experience of children to chart the swift giving way of the order and rationality associated with the patriarchal British Empire. The fact that it is girl children who undergo the reversion into savagery makes for some interesting complexities however. The experience of reversion in *Lord of the Flies* takes place within a structure of polar alternatives: reason, order, science and law (embodied in the persons of Ralph and Piggy) on the one hand or savagery, chaos, violence and ecstasy on the other. The fact that the boys share a common class and national background makes this symbolic bifurcation all the more clear and emphatic. If the novel's official thematic truth is the inferiority of 'evil', the fact that the dark or primitive other is always within the self, this is finally measured from the viewpoint of Ralph's grief which can still detect the distance between the values of civilization and what the boys have descended to on the island: 'Ralph wept for the end of innocence, the darkness of man's heart, and the fall through the air of the true, wise friend called Piggy' (*LF*, 223).

The schoolgirls on the island in *John Dollar* are much more diverse than the boys in *Lord of the Flies*, each being named and supplied with a kind of biography. More importantly, they do not conceive of themselves and are not presented as the allegorical bearers of Western values and cultural identity. The party includes not only colonial girls, but a number of marginals and misfits, including Menaka (Monkey), the Indian servant girl, Gaby, the Portuguese daughter of a highly unconventional kitemaker, Jane, whose brother has been killed in the First World War, reducing her life to a kind of sham or nonexistence ('He held a sort of radiance. He was their hope. What she was was *jane*, something that came after 'Hope' – an afterthought; a lapse. . . . When she looks into the mirror, which she seldom does, she's surprised to find she owns a body. *It's I who go here, sir*, she often needs to say. just jane' (*JD*, 55–6), and Charlotte, who travels to Rangoon in an attempt to escape the miserable half-life of being a war widow, and is fascinated by the images of negativity offered by the East: 'She, too, longed to live in a non-world, outside existence of the law and literature, of the King's Own Version of the text' (*JD*, 33). It is men, and especially boys who seem to inhabit a stable world of meanings, partly because their lives are organized around the violent enforcement of such meanings – the giving of names, the charting of the unknown, the maintaining of differences, the fixing of the indefinite. The first part of the novel is taken up with the expedition to the island first named by Marco Polo, which the party intends to rename 'King George's Island' in honour of the king's birthday. The collusion of kingship, birth and naming is appropriate; landing on the island is equivalent for the men and boys to the retelling of a story of an origin already many times told, the myth of man's self-making in existential emptiness:

> Everyone who stepped ashore that day (except the bearers) had either read or heard the story of *The Life and Adventures of Robinson Crusoe* so there was that, that sense of exhilaration which comes when one's life bears a likeness to the fictions one's dreamed; plus there was the weighty thrill of bringing light, the torch of history, into one more far-flung reach of darkness. (*JD*, 75–6)

After the dissolving force of the tidal wave, the girls must try to inhabit a world where names do not cohere with what they name, where time has become indefinite and immeasurable, and identity is frighteningly fluid; a world perhaps more aptly encompassed in the stories that Monkey dares not tell, stories which 'were less like stories that the english knew and more like lengthy stratagems exaggerated to fantastic lengths' (*JD*, 174). The lethargic life of superstition, magic and ritual into which the girls relapse is in fact a new, displaced version of the proportion and rationality they have left behind, rather than its opposite. Deprived of fathers and their law, the girls are in a sense forced to become the authors of themselves, but, without any clearly formed sense of identity, their acts of self-authorship are parasitic upon the absent law of the father. Nolly rewrites the Christianity she has learned and lived by as demonism; and Nolly and Amanda together replace their murdered fathers by John Dollar, the ritualized father whom they both depend upon helplessly and gruesomely punish for his failure to be the God they demand: 'They desired him to evidence omniscience, a higher wisdom than their own – they believed in his capacity to right their wrongs, to lead them, to resist their natural predilection for defiance. A state of subjugation makes its own revolt when the object of its worship fails to stimulate belief in its omnipotence' (*JD*, 225).

If being and identity come from naming and narrating in this novel, then they also, crucially, come from eating. Deprived of their fathers, and unable to reconstitute their scattered, cannibalized bones, the girls attempt to assuage their loss by eating all that remains to them, the flesh that has become the faeces that the cannibals have left on the shore (*JD*, 204–5). In doing so, they are simultaneously transgressing the most important of laws, and affirming a sacrificial principle upon which law seems to be inaugurated. The girls leave the beach after having made a shrine of their fathers' remains, going back to worship their substitute father, John Dollar:

> Without speaking, they withdraw from it, understanding it is never to be touched, the bones, never to be broken, that perimeter, its ultimate offence, obscenity, its inviolability. They are different now. Even those whose fathers were not massacred are different. They are silent, changed, contaminated, beyond grief, ecstatic. Day is dawning. John is waiting for them. Blacked with shit and whitened with the sand, they gather things they hope will please him – pretty shells, a rock, a shrimp, a cinder. Flies descend. Flies follow on them. Flies are living in their skin. (*JD*, 205)

This absolute collusion of the sacred and the profane, of law and transgression, resembles and differs from the dominion of the Lord of the Flies in Golding's novel. For there, as we have seen, although the message of the Lord of the Flies is that the evil is in man himself, it is still possible to distinguish depravity and evil from rational good. John Dollar proposes a much more radical intertwining of civilization and its opposite. For both seem founded indifferently upon eating, upon the oral rage of a civilization that simultaneously wishes to absorb everything other to itself, and to maintain laws to regulate this collapse of distinctions. Having carried Charlotte's dead body down from the Cornish moors where they have been living for long years after their rescue (the fact that the rescue is left undescribed in the novel increases our sense of the continuity between the castaway and civilized conditions), Monkey is forbidden by a priest to give Charlotte burial without authorization. The reflections prompted in her by this compound death, law, eating and naming in strangely engendered series:

> The english makes laws. He makes one law for men. He makes one law for women, a law for his children. Laws for his dogs. A law for bats. This law, exclusive, ecclesiastic, for keeping the dead from the dead, under ground. Very good, she translated. The english would never fill rivers with corpses,

he hides them instead in the ground. He eats with sharp knives. He chews with a knife and fork. He buries his dead so the other white castes will not cook and eat them. Worms and the maggots are better than teeth of one's enemies, that's why the white caste is always at table. He eats and he eats. He eats mountains and ore. He eats diamonds and rubies, blue sky. He eats cities, chews names. He eats people. Her name was something a long time ago that the English had chewed from its whole state of 'Menaka' into a word they said 'Monica' into the status of 'Monkey', for short. He translated her person, he chewed and he chewed. (*JD*, 7–8)

In a sense, the girls' recapitulation of a society based upon killing and sacrificial eating itself recapitulates what happens in *Lord of the Flies*. There, too, the savage killing and eating of the pig (at one point clearly represented as a female object of male lust) is both a transgression of the rules of civilization, but also, as Luce Irigaray has put it in an essay on the relationship between gender and sacrifice, 'an immolation that brings the social space into being'.[4] This sacrifice marks out the region of the sacred, the pig's head who becomes Beelzebub, the Lord of the Flies, and of the profane, for the pig is identified with the scapegoat and the outsider – first of all, the visionary Simon, and then the Promethean Piggy.

Not to reproduce the idea of a social order based upon acquisition, consumption and sacrifice would entail producing a civilization in which, as Luce Irigaray has put it, women would be able to exchange among themselves, rather than being the sacrificial objects of male exchange.[5] It would also involve rewriting the myths of male inauguration of social life, myths which systematically exclude the female:

> doesn't the founding sacrifice precisely correspond to this extradition from the celebration of religion, this exile from the places where the ultimate social decisions are taken? As long as we live in sacrificial societies, the choice of who will be victim and of the form of the rite are essential, both during the rite and afterwards. Now women aren't allowed to have anything to do, with it. They shouldn't want to? Perhaps not. But they don't have any other societies, at least not yet. They are therefore reinserted into a form of sociality that has been determined by sacrifice. They haven't been included in it and they're still excluded from it. At this level they remain an inert body, paralysed in and through cultural bonds which aren't their own.[6]

Though Irigaray only hints at this, it seems that myths of founding male sacrifice not only exclude women, but in that very action include them, as the figurative if not the literal object of the sacrifice. Expelled from social life, women are sacrificed by myths of originary sacrifice. There may be no girls on the island in *Lord of the Flies*, but the assertion of self in actions of primal sacrifice recalls and enacts the expulsion and punishment of the female. If we glimpse another law, another way of living in *John Dollar*, other than by the economy of sacrifice and consumption, it lies in the images of fluidity which multiply through the book, the fluidity which *John Dollar* remembers of Charlotte, who was 'like the sea itself, an even wash across his senses, sometimes merciful, expansive, never calculating, often violent, never still' (*JD*, 168), or the redemptive stream discovered by Monkey which 'tasted like a breath of heaven, like the story and meaning of her life-like joy' (*JD*, 217). This water is associated both with her care for Jane, based not upon appetitive individualism but upon nurture, and with her discovery of Charlotte. But if *John Dollar* does point to any civilization beyond sacrifice, it is with no great confidence, for most of the novel seems to confirm its inescapable force. Unlike *Lord of the Flies*, which does indeed still repose hope in a form of knowing, *John Dollar* seems to suggest that civilization can only survive by continuing and repeated acts of violence and sacrifice.

Since it deliberately eschews the didactic and allegorical mode which so effectively governs *Lord of the Flies*, it is hard to be sure whether *John Dollar* is intended to *demonstrate* the failure to escape the mythology of sacrificial origin (and therefore to suggest the need for some revision of that mythology), or whether it is itself the victim of the repetition compulsion it represents. If it were the latter, then Wiggins's revision of the narrative of reversion to origin would have to be seen as itself a reversion to that narrative, in a way that would resemble Emma Tennant's *Two Women of London* in its failure to escape from the originary force of its literary antecedent. But in both cases, it is not a matter of a simple choice between literary originality or derivativeness, since the relations between these two are precisely what are put at stake in the rewritings of reversion. If neither narrative achieves anything that we could define as full, unprecedented originality, this is precisely because the repetitions of each narrative so thoroughly perturb the idea of self-origination.

Of the three rewritings with which I am concerned here, J. M. Coetzee's *Foe* pays the most explicit attention to the interrelations of subjectivity, origination and narrative. The novel is centred around Susan Barton, a woman who is shipwrecked on an island with Robinson Cruso and his slave Friday, and her attempts to get their, or, more properly, her story written by one Daniel Foe.[7] Indeed, although it is a rewriting of *Robinson*

Crusoe, *Foe* must also be seen as a 'prequel', whose main concern is not with the events which have taken place on the island, but with the struggles over the narrative of those events. On the island, it is Susan who urges Cruso to think of the future, to extend himself beyond his sterile dominion over his kingdom, she who urges him to keep some record of his stay on the island; but, once returned to England, Cruso having died on the journey, Susan becomes marginal to her own narrative: 'When I reflect on my story I seem to exist only as the one who came, the one who witnessed, the one who longed to be gone: a being without substance, a ghost beside the true body of Cruso. Is that the fate of all storytellers?' (*F*, 51). Her urgent desire to repeat the truth about her stay on the island with Cruso is what gives Foe the narrative material which enables him to construct the myth of Cruso's self-construction. If *Robinson Crusoe* is a cultural myth of the birth of social life in male individuality, then Coetzee's narrative shows the necessary (non)participation of the female in, and as, the sacrifice that enables this supplementary, revisionist myth of origin to be generated. In one episode in the narrative, she travels to Bristol with Friday, in order to get him a passage on a ship back to Africa. Her shabby appearance and unconventional companion mean that she is mistaken for a gipsy, make her wonder, indeed, 'Am I become a gipsy unknown to myself?' (*F*, 109). Here, her condition seems the exact reverse of Crusoe's; where, in Defoe's account, he creates social life out of his own resourceful solitude, Susan discovers her solitude and marginality in the very midst of social life.

Temporarily abandoned by Foe when, like his historical original, he flees London to escape his creditors, Susan tries to write her own story, to take possession of her own life, declaring 'I am a free woman who asserts her freedom by telling her story according to her own desire' (*F*, 131). In so doing, Susan is attempting to rewrite the story of male self-origination of which *Robinson Crusoe* is the archetype, even sitting at Foe's desk and supplanting him as controlling author: 'I have your table to sit at, your window to gaze through. I write with your pen on your paper, and when the sheets are completed they go into your chest. So your life continues to be lived, though you are gone' (*F*, 65). Endeavouring, as she puts it, 'to be father to my story', Susan must also resist the deceitful fatherhood of Foe, who sends to her a young girl whom he has primed with the plausible story that she is her long-lost daughter, also named Susan Barton. Susan tells her, '"I do not know who told you that your father was a brewer from Deptford who fled to the Low Countries, but the story is false. Your father is a man named Daniel Foe . . . I will vouch he is the author of the story of the brewer"' (*F*, 90–1). But, in resisting the false paternity of Foe,

Susan also deprives the girl of her maternal origin, ironically confirming the sacrifice of the female which she is attempting to resist: '"You are father-born. You have no mother. The pain you feel is the pain of lack, not the pain of loss"' (ibid.).

In fact, Susan increasingly risks falling into the same desire for authoritative self-possession as that apparently guaranteed in *Robinson Crusoe*. 'I was intended not to be the mother of my story, but to beget it', she says to Foe, reversing their genders. 'It is not I who am the intended, but you' (F, 126). But the acknowledgement of the joint parentage of her narrative brings her slowly to recognize the ghostly indeterminacy of its issue. Dedicating her life to the telling of her story, but compelled to deliver that story through another, story and life become interchangeable and interchangeably indefinite:

> 'In the beginning I thought I would tell you the story of the island and, being done with that, return to my former life. But now all my life grows to be story and there is nothing of my own left to me. I thought I was myself and this girl a creature from another order speaking words you made up for her. But now I am full of doubt. Nothing is left to me but doubt itself. Who is speaking me?' (F, 133)

The transferential effect of narrating, of speaking for oneself as another, or speaking for another as oneself, means that the responsibility of narration can never be one's own alone; narration can never be self-authorship, or pure paternal self-begetting. It is for this reason that Susan Barton's narrative, or the narrative of how her narrative comes to be silenced, joins with another, even more profound loss of voice – that of the tongueless Friday. Foe is confident that he and Susan can decipher the nonspeech of Friday, can penetrate to his heart. In this, of course, Coetzee is meditating on the possibility, and the unending responsibility, of those who narrate to speak on behalf of those who have had no voice, or no words that can be heard. To rewrite the narratives of the past is to allow and foster the remission of that 'eternal and inhuman wakefulness' of self-present consciousness, to allow those blinks of the eye, 'the cracks and chinks through which another voice, other voices speak in our lives' (F, 30). But such rewriting must also beware of the danger that it admit the voice of the other only in that self's terms: the image for this in *Foe* is the document that Susan writes and hangs around Friday's neck to say that he is free, the very linguistic form of the manumission signalling Friday's continuing exclusion from its terms. To hear, or to speak the voice of the other, for Coetzee, may only be possible in artfully contrived, ethically sustained disruption of the self-possession of narrative, may only be possible therefore in the ethical interval of transference, as narrative passes from author to author, rather than in the proprietary self-begetting of narrative. Either to speak the self, or to speak the other in the self's terms, is to do violence to the transferential ethics of narrative, which always expels the self from centrality, compelling it to ask, in the words of Emmanuel Levinas, 'if the *Da* of my *Dasein* is not already the usurpation of somebody else's place'.[8]

Coetzee offers an image of this commitment to the other, in the final episodes of *Foe*. In these episodes an 'I', who may be Foe, or Defoe, or Susan, or Coetzee himself, or some compound of them all, begins to rewrite the rewritten narrative which Susan Barton has already provided. The dreamlike quest of this 'I' is for the speech of Friday, a speech below, or before the speech which always drowns his speech. It takes the 'I' deep in dream or vision, first to Foe's room, where he lies with Susan, Friday asleep at their feet, and then into the waters off Cruso's island, where Susan Barton and her captain lie drowned, along with Friday. Somehow, an unimaginable utterance passes from Friday, through his interlocutor and out into history, an urgent, ceaseless, speechless speech:

> His mouth opens. From inside him comes a slow stream, without breath, without interruption. It flows up through his body and out upon me; it passes through the cabin, through the wreck; washing the cliffs and shores of the island, it runs northward and southward to the ends of the earth. Soft and cold, dark and unending, it beats against my eyelids, against the skin of my face. (*F*, 157)

To make the voice of Friday articulate would be to betray it sentimentally into self-present intelligibility, for the comfort of the guilty self; but not to articulate its silencing would be an even worse treachery.

In attempting to speak with, or give a voice to one who would speak from the condition of linguistic sacrifice, Coetzee's novel attempts to resist the reversion to sacrificial myths of origin which in some respects characterizes Emma Tennant's *Two Women of London* and Marianne Wiggins's *John Dollar*. For the voice that it ends up speaking with belongs to no one, consists in, or occupies the space of its giving, the sacrifice of itself. In a sense, the decision not to offer a wholly new or other narrative in a wholly new and self-possessed voice is what confirms *Foe*'s radical novelty. Of course, making this judgement of (in this case) a male author as opposed to (in this case) two female authors risks reinstating the very myth that is supposed to be put at risk in these rewritings, that of the greater originating powers of the male as opposed to the non-original dependency of the female. And we do indeed need to specify the originality of *Foe*'s apparent sacrifice of self-possession carefully. For is it not possible to judge *Foe*'s combination of the gift of voice to the other with the refusal to credit that other as anything but a negativity, as a certain curbing of the gift, as a donation which reverts to the credit of the self seemingly dispossessed? If, as we have already seen, Coetzee's novel itself provides an image of just such a recursive structure, in Susan's document of manumission hung like a yoke round the neck of Friday, the gift of freedom given in a language the exclusion from which marks the very impossibility of freedom for Friday, making him 'the helpless captive of my desire to have our story told' (*F*, 150), such acknowledgement of the difficulty of giving freedom unconditionally on Susan's and Coetzee's part guarantees no immunity for the novel itself against the dangers of reversion to the mentality of the slave-owner, the colonist, the self-originator.

But perhaps there is no such immunity. If it is impossible to begin again, to write entirely anew the false story of the parthenogenetic origin of man, culture, and language, then this is because narrative begins and prevails in a process of transference and contamination which is the very impossibility of such ethical immunity. For what is rewritten in these three narratives is precisely the wrong of the issueless insulation of the self from the other. No revision can entirely avoid reversion; no attempt to rework the myths of self-possessed beginning can entirely avoid becoming possessed by the desire for self-possession on which it lays hands; but it is only by taking the risk of reversion that it may be possible to imagine, diversely, collectively, intermittently, myths of founding and finding instituted otherwise than on sacrifice and silence.

Notes

1 'Postmodernism: or, the Cultural Logic of Late Capitalism', *New Left Review* 146 (1984), pp. 53–92.
2 Quotations from these texts are from the following editions, abbreviated as indicated and incorporated in my text: Robert Louis Stevenson, *The Strange Case of Dr. Jekyll and Mr. Hyde* (Harmondsworth: Penguin, 1979), *JH*; Emma Tennant, *Two Women of London: The Strange Case of Ms Jekyll and*

Mrs Hyde (London: Faber and Faber, 1989), *TW*; William Golding, *Lord of the Flies* (London: Faber and Faber, 1988), *LF*; Marianne Wiggins, *John Dollar* (Harmondsworth: Penguin, 1989), *JD*; Daniel Defoe, *Robinson Crusoe* (London and Toronto: J. M. Dent, 1906), *RC*; J. M. Coetzee, *Foe* (Harmondsworth: Penguin, 1987), *F*. I am very grateful to Gillian Beer for pointing out to me the connection between *Foe* and *John Dollar*.

3   For an exhaustive account of the cultural connections between women and degeneracy in the late nineteenth century, see Bram Dijkstra, *Idols of Perversity: Fantasies of Feminine Evil in Fin-de-Siècle Culture* (New York and Oxford: Oxford University Press, 1986).

4   'Women, the Sacred and Money', *Paragraph* 8 (1986), p. 6.

5   Ibid., p. 10.

6   Ibid., pp. 8–9.

7   Coetzee distinguishes 'his' castaway from Defoe's by calling him 'Cruso' rather than 'Crusoe', and distinguishes his author by calling him 'Foe' rather than 'Defoe'. I will try, wherever possible, to maintain this orthographical distinction between the two castaways and the two authors.

8   'Ethics as First Philosophy', trans. Seán Hand and Michael Temple, in *The Levinas Reader*, ed. Seán Hand (Oxford: Blackwell, 1989), p. 85. [*Dasein* (literally, 'there-being') is a term of Heidegger's that both stands in for and pushes aside such standard philosophical terms as 'subjectivity' or 'consciousness'. It refers to the specificity of who we are now (what kind of beings are we?), which is something that we need to know in order to engage with the question of the meaning of Being. The nature of *Dasein*, as opposed to the nature of a hippopotamus, is simply not given biologically; the kind of beings that we are has come about within culture, and so it cannot be regarded as other than essential to *Dasein* that the nature of human beings incorporates an array of differences unknown to hippos. The nature of hippopotamus being is such that it does not divide into, say, medieval hippo being and contemporary Parisian, Iraqi or former-Soviet hippo being. But *Dasein* does so divide, and of course far more complexly than that. *Dasein*, then, is not 'man' or 'humanity'; it is a way of being, which is both enabling and limiting. By the same token, it is unique to the being of *Dasein* to question its ways of being, and so to ask the question of the meaning of Being as such. See also the following chapter for Docherty's discussion of *Dasein* in relation to a notion of postmodern characterization. (NL)]

Chapter Six The Ethics of Alterity

Thomas Docherty

A Different Economy

Postmodern characterization, then, advances an attack on the notion of identity, or of an essential Selfhood which is not traduced by a temporal dimension which threatens that Self with heterogeneity. In short, it leads to the elaboration of 'characters' (if they can still be called such, given their confusing ontological status) whose existence (rather than essence) is characterized by *difference* (rather than identity). Postmodern figures are always differing, not just from other characters, but also from their putative 'selves'. Whereas previously characters were considered as entities 'present-to-themselves' or, to put this in existentialist terms, finally reduced to the status of an essential selfhood and thus reified as *en-soi*, exchangeable as commodities, postmodern characters always dramatize their own 'absence' from themselves.

Postmodern characters typically fall into incoherence: character-traits are not repeated, but contradicted; proper names are used, if at all, inconsistently; signposts implying specific gender are confused; a seemingly animate character mutates into an inanimate object; and so on. At every stage in the representation of character, the finality of the character, a determinate identity for the characters is deferred as the proliferation of information about the character leads into irrationality, incoherence, or self-contradiction. There is never a final point at which the character can be reduced to the status of an epistemologically accessible essential qual-

Thomas Docherty, 'The Ethics of Alterity: Postmodern Character', in *Alterities: Criticism, History, Representation* (Oxford: Clarendon Press, 1996), pp. 36–68; this selection, pp. 60–8.

ity or list of qualities or 'properties'. What is at stake in this is the entire notion of 'representation'. As in most art-forms and cultural practices, the postmodern impetus is almost synonymous with the questioning of representation.

Following in the wake of an existentialist philosophical tradition, many postmodern characterizations seem to argue that there is always a discrepancy between the character who acts and the character who watches herself or himself acting. There is, as it were, a temporal distance between agency and self-consciousness regarding that agency, a fine example of which is John Barth's fiction, 'Menelaiad'. This text enacts the continual deferral of coincidence between the narrating subject and the subject narrated, even though these are ostensibly identical, namable as 'Menelaus'. As a result, 'Menelaus', paradoxically, is 'identified', or better characterized, as that which is always differing from himself. There is a series of confusions about the ontological presence of the character, such that at any moment in the text when it seems that 'Menelaus' *is* somewhat, immediately a difference is produced, and an alternative or new narrative is released.

The voice of Menelaus (for that is all there is in this tale) begins to relate the story of his life to Telemachus, Peisistratus, and a hypothesized listener (actually, of course, the ear of the reader). During the tale, he tells of meeting Helen, who demanded the tale of his life; within this tale, now on a different level and in a different temporal frame, he met Proteus, who asked for the tale of his life, and so on. There are, then, a number of *hommes-récits* identified under the sign of Menelaus; but this fiction begins to unravel or untangle that supposed self-identical sign or identity, to release all the different figures, masquerading under the identical proper name which supposedly offers them a non-temporal, non-historical identity, and produces a multi-layered narrative. In characterological terms, the result is that the consciousness that identifies itself as 'Menelaus' is always out of step or non-identical with the voice of Menelaus and with the actions which Menelaus supposedly performed. The very telling of the tale of his life, an act which is supposed to proffer and guarantee identity, in fact produces this radical *décalage* or self-difference as the constituent of the being of 'Menelaus'. Menelaus is thus never fully present-to-himself; every time he identifies himself, he has to do so by adverting to a different Menelaus, one who exists in a different temporal and narrative frame and one who exists, therefore, at a different ontological level from the narrating consciousness. Worse than this, within one of the tales Menelaus indicates his fully temporal predicament. He changes places and times on every occasion at which he tries to fix or identify himself, as is fully seen in his encounter with Proteus:

> ' " 'My problem was, I'd leisure to think. My time was mortal, Proteus's im-; what if he merely treed it a season or two till I let go? What was it anyhow I held? If Proteus once was Old Man of the Sea and now Proteus was a tree, then Proteus was neither, only Proteus; what I held were dreams. But if a real Old Man of the Sea had really been succeeded by real water and the rest, then the dream was Proteus. And Menelaus! For I changed too as the long day passed: changed my mind, replaced myself, grew older. How hold on until the "old" (which is to say the young) Menelaus rebecame himself? . . . ' " . . . '[1]

Menelaus is, if anything, the character as Heideggerian *Dasein*; the 'being' of Menelaus, such as it is, is endlessly deferred, endlessly seeming otherwise and reiterating itself in an altered figuration. Its identity is characterized by this potentially endless differing from itself, the perpetual deferring of an essential selfhood: 'the thing I am' is replaced – or, indeed, *constituted* – by a 'seeming otherwise'. The character is constantly disappearing from its own surface, constantly escaping the parameters which the text implies for its figuration: in short, the character is constantly 'being there', constantly evading the fixity of a definite or identifiable and single 'place' for itself. To this extent, it becomes the merest series of instantiations of subjectivity, rather than a characterological entity: it has no place, but a series of dispositions (moods, ethics), as the parameters of its figuration shift and metamorphose in temporal sequence.

There is a difficulty with the very notion of 'representation' of a character whose condition is that it is never present to itself in the first place but is always 'ec-statically' escaping the constraints of self-presence.[2] Yet it is precisely here that the politics of a 'different economy' or an economy of difference can enter into a consideration of postmodern characterization. Previous theories of characterization are all, as I have stressed, dependent upon the paradigmatic dichotomy of appearance and reality; and their narratives are always 'apocalyptic' in the sense that they move from mystification to enlightenment and revelation as to the 'truth' of the character and its identity. The narrative trajectory is from the heterogeneity of different appearance to a presumed homogeneity of a real identity. It follows from this that what we can call the 'economy of identity' is based upon a supposed equality between the self of a character, on the one hand, and that character's narrative of the self, on the other: this is the *homme* as *récit* in Todorov's terms.[3] The character is adequately 're-presented' in the narrative; the self-presence of an identity reiterated in its mimetic relaying in the tale. Further, this equation is commutable. For it is not simply the case that characters in fiction are the mimetic echoes or representations of selves in history; on the contrary, as I argued above, characters in fiction are, proportionately to the extent that they are 'representative' of a supposed human nature, models upon whom selves in history must fashion themselves if they are to have a claim on being a 'reasonable' or 'enlightened' individual – a legitimate individual – within human nature. It is in these terms that the economy of identity assumes a political cast, for 'representation' here assumes the burden also of political representation. It transpires that characters, acting on behalf of selves (functioning as 'representatives' in a manner akin to bourgeois parliamentary representation), act as the legislators for certain kinds of political practice. As Davis indicated, the novel reduces all political action to moral action undertaken by and on behalf of individuals; character, operating according to an economy of identity in which the character is assumed to function as the mimetic representation of a self which is equally assumed to be fully present to itself, fully self-identical, is the means whereby this morality of individualism supplants the possibility of political praxis in narrative.

However, postmodern narrative disturbs the neat equations of the economy of identity, reversing the trajectory described by earlier narratives. In postmodern characterization, the narrative trajectory is from the assumed homogeneity of identity (as in the nameable identity of Menelaus, say) towards an endlessly proliferating heterogeneity, whereby identity is endlessly deferred and replaced by a scenario in which the 'character' or figure constantly differs from itself, denying the possession of and by a self and preferring an engagement with Otherness. Every mention of the same proper name, for instance, operates to release a new narrative, one which is typically at odds with the narratives previously ascribed to that proper name in the fiction. Rather than the self being identified with one narrative (biography), in this postmodern model the self disappears under a welter of proliferating narratives, 'forking paths', which never cohere or become exactly commensurable with one another. *Vivre* does not equal *raconter* here, at least not in the sense that a life has one story: rather, there is the production of an *excess*, a *surplus* of narrative, and it is this surplus which disturbs the neat equalities of the economy of identity and which calls into question the function of representation in postmodern narrative. Representation is no longer conceivable as a simple 'duplication' or substitutive mimetic doubling: representation is now 'excessive' or economically dysfunctional.

We have thus a different economy, an 'economy of difference'. Postmodern narrative enacts the character as *Dasein*, the character who constantly escapes the fixity of identity by existing in and through the temporal predicament whereby the assumed or desired totality of a real self is endlessly 'dispositioned', always a 'being *there*', as opposed to a being here, a being present to itself. This is not so much a character, more a series of fleeting instantiations of subjectivity, a series of 'appearances' which do not act as the cover for a 'deeper' reality, for it is that very notion of a material or essential reality which postmodern characterization denies. At best, then, the progression of a postmodern narrative cannot move from appearance to the enlightenment of a reality, but only from appearance to disappearance to *different* appearance and so on. In such characterization, the idea of a reciprocity, according to which the character is seen as a representative of the self of the historical reader, becomes impossible, since it is just this notion of a totalized real and essential selfhood that the texts deny. The simplicity of a seemingly 'democratic' mode of characterization, based upon a liberal individualism and the category of 'representation', is called into question. Postmodern narrative reveals that it is not simply the case that earlier modes of reading fiction reduce the political to the moral; more importantly, in their delineation of social and political formations through the medium of 'representative' characters, they confuse a political category of representation with an aesthetic mode of mimesis. Criticism has always prioritized this aesthetic component, in its endless discussion of 'well-rounded', or 'vividly realized' or 'fully depicted' characters in fiction. In brief, there has been in this area a dangerous 'aestheticization of politics'.[4]

But postmodern narrative does not easily reverse this orientation. Instead, it introduces, through its mode of characterization, the category of *ethics*. The reader of postmodern narrative, as allegorized in Calvino's *Se una notte d'inverno un viaggiatore*,[5] is fully implicated in the proliferation of narratives. However, unlike the reader of earlier fictions, she or he is denied the possibility and solace of producing a totalized self for the characters being processed in the reading; the totality of a supposedly enlightened truth or real essence of character is denied as a result of the proliferation of narratives which contradict such a totality. This also means that postmodern narrative attacks the possibility of the reader herself or himself becoming a fully enlightened and imperialist subject

with full epistemological control over the fiction and its endlessly different or altered characters. In order to read postmodern narrative at all, the
reader must give up such a singular position, for she or he will be endlessly 'disposed', displaced, in figuring a number of different narratives
and different characters. She or he has to be seduced from the occupation
of one position ('Othello's occupation's gone') into many positions; she
or he has to give up a quasi-authorial position of a supposed access to the
singular truth of character and move instead into a series of dispositions
(ethics) in trying to deal with the proliferating narratives she or he hears.
The reader, then, is denied access to a totalizing narrative which will
allow her or him to identify herself or himself against the stable 'other' of
a mysterious character. Rather, the reader replaces such a totalized enlightened narrative, proposing access as it does to a singular monotheistic
truth, with the multiplicity of singularities, the multiplicity of different
local narratives, having no claims on truth in any absolute sense at all.
The reader becomes nothing more or less than an excuse for the proliferation of yet further narratives, further dispositions. The reader thus
becomes as imbricated in a temporal or historical predicament as the
characters in postmodern narrative, and, like those characters, has no
access to a totalized narrative of a true or essential selfhood according to
which she or he orients her or his present being. The reader's 'temporality' or historical condition in the act of reading postmodern characterization is itself characterized by the notion of disposition, of being seduced
or disposed from one position to another in the construction and
deconstruction of a series of narratives. In this, there is no final or overall
single position which would allow for a systematic ranging of the narratives; there is only an economy which, in its basic orientation to heterogeneity, endlessly produces more and more different narratives. Where the
economy of identity produces a single totalized narrative or a priority
among narratives which allows for the formulation of a narrative of the
stable self, it also arrests the temporality of narrative and the notion of
temporal change which is axiomatic to narrative. Postmodern characterization keeps the narratives going.

In so doing, postmodern narrative lures a reader into 'disposition', a
translation of the Greek *ethos*. To this extent, the category of the ethical
is introduced; and through this, which involves the reader in the search
for 'the good' (as opposed to the mere subscription to a monotheistic
truth), the political does in fact return. As MacIntyre indicates, there is a
distinction between the ethical and the political, but it cannot be drawn
too sharply:

Such a distinction depends upon there being a distinction between private and public life of such a kind that I can consider what it is best for me to do without considering in what political order it is requisite for me to live, either because I treat the political order as a given and unalterable context of private action, or because I think the political order irrelevant for some other reason.[6]

Postmodern narrative of characterization, of course, in attacking not only the notion of a self but also the dichotomy on which it is based (inferiority of 'reality' versus external ostension of 'appearance'), eradicates the distinction between the ethical and the political. A fundamental ontology is replaced by a first philosophy of ethical demands. To read postmodern characterization is to reintroduce the possibility of politics, and importantly of a genuinely historical political change, into the act of reading; and this reintroduction is generated from the category of the ethical, from the disposition (mood, ethics) of the reading subject.

Seeming Otherwise

What is at stake, then, in postmodern characterization is, first, the confusion of the ontological status of the character with that of the reader; secondly, the decentring of that reader's consciousness, such that she or he is, like the character, endlessly displaced and 'differing'; and, thirdly, the political and ethical implications of this 'seeming otherwise', shifting from appearance to different appearance in the disappearance of a totalized selfhood. The reading subject in postmodern characterization is, thus, exactly like Kristeva's 'subject-in-process' [see chapter 3 of the present volume], a subject whose very subjectivity is itself endlessly deferred, endlessly differing. The explicit political dimension of reading postmodern characterization is now clear: it involves a marginalization of the reader from a centralized or totalized narrative of selfhood, thus rendering the reading subject-in-process as the figure of the *dissident*. Among her types of dissident, Kristeva locates both the experimental writer, working with the 'diaspora of those languages that pluralize meaning and cross all national and linguistic barriers', and, crucially, *women*: 'And sexual difference, women: isn't that another form of dissidence?' What these two groups share is the impetus towards marginalization and indefinition; they are in a condition of 'exile' from a centred identity of meaning and its claims to a totalized Law or Truth. And she writes: 'Our present age is one of exile. How can one avoid sinking into the mire of common sense, if not by becoming a stranger to one's own country, language, sex and identity? Writing is impossible without some kind of exile.'[7] Exile, further, is itself a form of dissidence, since it involves the marginalization or decentring of the self from all positions of totalized or systematic Law (such as imperialist nation, patriarchal family, monotheistic language), and 'if meaning exists in the state of exile, it nevertheless finds no incarnation, and is ceaselessly produced and destroyed in geographical or discursive transformations.'[8]

In the terms which concern us here, those of experimental writing, the major source of such exile and its consequential political disposition towards dissidence is in the questioning of the system of language itself (though, as is clear now, this is not easily to be distinguished from the concerns of empire, family, and so on). Postmodern characterization, construed as a writing in and from exile, serves to construct the possibility, for perhaps the first time, of elaborating the paradigmatic reader of these new novels as feminized. Woman, as 'that which cannot be represented, that which is not spoken, that which remains outside naming and ideologies',[9] is always 'dispositioned' towards otherness, alterity. To read postmodern characterization is thus to begin to construct the ethics of alterity, to replace a philosophy of Identity with that of Alterity, to discover what it means – without yet *representing* what it means – to speak always from the political disposition of the Other, and hence to find *presentation* as itself a disposition (mood, ethics) towards alterity.

Notes

1   John Barth, *Lost in the Funhouse* (New York: Doubleday, 1968), p. 142.
2   For this notion of 'ecstasy', see Docherty, *Reading (Absent) Character: Towards a Theory of Characterization in Fiction* (Oxford: Clarendon, 1983).
3   Cf. Tzvetan Todorov, *The Fantastic: A Structural Approach to a Literary Genre*, trans. Richard Howard (Ithaca, NY: Cornell University Press, 1975). (NL)
4   For the implication of such a state of affairs, see, of course, Walter Benjamin, 'The Work of Art in the Age of Mechanical Reproduction', trans. Harry Zohn, in *Illuminations*, ed. Hannah Arendt (Glasgow: Fontana, 1973).
5   Italo Calvino, *Se una notte d'inverno* (Torino: Einaudi, 1979).
6   Alasdair MacIntyre, *A Short History of Ethics* (London: Duckworth, 1967), p. 129.
7   Julia Kristeva, *The Kristeva Reader*, ed. Toril Moi (Oxford: Blackwell, 1986),

pp. 299, 296, 298; cf. also Kristeva, *Étrangers à nous-mêmes* (Paris: Gallimard, 1988).

8 Kristeva, *Reader*, p. 298.

9 Ibid., p. 163.

Chapter Seven The Three *Genres*

Luce Irigaray

The Notion of *Genre*

The structure of discourse and its impact on meaning, the truth it translates and transmits, is still quite rarely analysed as an *instrument* in any of the sciences. We find debates about content which give little consideration to the *vehicle* of their message.

The sciences are constantly polishing new instruments, new machines (and very expensive ones, at that!) but the technique that is language [*langage*], the tool that is language [*langue*] are still rarely investigated in any research. Except for computer-programming purposes?

We were taught that man was the speaking animal. Today, man appears to be surrendering to the possibilities of the brains of machines for his present and his future – biological, affective, intellectual, social....

A curious epoch in which 'cold' hypertechnicity goes hand in hand with rustic magical passions, with a rather worrying irrationality. With medicine, and all its resources, being called in to help. And religion as such?

Shouldn't we be seeing, in this crisis of the dispossession of reason, signs of the mutation of an era in culture? An incentive to work towards the elaboration of a new discourse, especially in relations between microcosm and macrocosm? Between the universe and us, but also in us and between us, another world must be thought.

Hence my project of working on *genre* in discourse:

Genre as index and mark of the *subjectivity* and ethical responsibility of the speaker. *Genre* is not in fact merely something to do with physiology, biology or private life, with the mores of animals or the fertility of

Luce Irigaray, 'The Three *Genres*' [Fr. 1987], trans. David Macey, in *The Irigaray Reader*, ed. Margaret Whitford (Oxford: Blackwell, 1991), pp. 140–53.

plants. It constitutes the irreducible differentiation *internal to the 'human race'* ['*genre humain*']. *Genre* represents the site of the nonsubstitutable positioning of the *I* and the *you* and of their modalities of expression. Should the difference between the *I* and the *you* disappear, so do demand, thanks, appeals, questions. . . .

It seems that, rather than becoming more human by developing the sexuate morphology of his discourse, man now wants to absent himself from language [*langage*], no longer saying *I*, *you* or we. Here, the sciences, technologies and certain regressions to religiosity appear to go hand in hand. In taking over from the *I* (here and now), from the subject and from a possible *you*, these truths seem to have the force of law.

Which brings me to my second question. Not saying *I* implies leaving speech, voice, to that which is supposed to be more worthy of articulating our truth. What is the status of this something that could speak better than us? In a *universal* and *neutral* manner? Does neutrality exist? Where? How?

When I question discourse – starting with the language [*langue*] I speak, which made me a subject – I observe, first of all, that the neuter is apparently something to do with *nature*. *Il pleut, il neige, il vente, il tonne* (it is raining; it is snowing; it is windy; it is thundering) . . . express forces [*puissances*] that resist human power [*pouvoir*], its formalization. This is not an inert matter which imposes itself upon or is distinct from man, this is an *animate* nature whose language [*langage*] is spoken more or less capriciously and is now expressed in the *neuter*: in its movements, its manifestations, its rhythms, but also when we grasp it through our sense-perceptions: it shines [*ça brille*], it's bright [*ça lust*], it smells good [*ça sent bon*], it's beautiful [*c'est beau*], it's thundering [*ça tonne*]. The sense which could invert things is basically *touch*, our body as *tactile tool* for apprehending and manipulating the world, ourselves, the other. This tool is a hand-tool, but also a speech-tool: translation, relay, creation. This work of man – and I say man because man, the people of men, has for centuries been the active worker manipulating and transforming the world with his hands, his tools and language – wants to behave like [*faire comme*] nature? Mimic it? Impose itself as a force [*puissance*] without any subjective mark of gender? So we would move from *il fait beau* (it is fine) or *il pleut* (which corresponds to a rhythm and not a formal dichotomous opposition) to *il faut* (it is necessary to), *c'est vrai* (it is true), *c'est ainsi* (it is so) *ou pas* (or not). This order of laws claims to be neutral, but it bears the marks of he who produces them. Between 'the weather today' [*le temps qu'il fait*] and 'the time of history' [*le temps de l'histoire*], there

is the time of the creation of words, of the establishment of their economies, and of gods or a God speaking in nature.

Three '*il*', three so-called 'neuters' which are worth questioning, especially in their intervention between the two human *genres*: the language
of nature, the word(s) of exclusively made god(s), the cultural order and
its discourse through things. Through machines? Things of our era that
speak a language that sometimes swamps us, erases us, and whose noise
superimposes itself on the noise or silence of the natural world.

This can be put differently: most of the time, language [*langage*] serves
to convey a meaning, a content. How did discourse permit this content,
this signification, this culture? How can it replace them with others?
These aspects of the message are not usually investigated.

Hence my decision to question the structure of discourse, the language-
tool, so as to interpret its sexuation and to attempt to effect a change in its
order. This work must be carried out at two levels of discourse:

1 that of the formalization, automatic or conscious, of its means, its
   powers;
2 that of the style, of the subjective involvement of he or she who is
   speaking, of his/her relationship with the body, with the sexuate body.

It is in fact necessary to analyse the relationship within discourse between:

1 that which can be formalized: passively/actively; popularly/scientifi-
   cally, etc.
2 that which, as style, resists formalization.

This is a matter of elaborating the problem of ethical responsibility in
relation to formalization, but also of the expression or translation of
identity in style. Is one dissociable from the other? Is not the sexuate the
brake and the *reserve* in the face of a life-threatening formalization, a
heedless development of sciences and technologies, and the subsequent
atrophies or paralyses of the body? The issue is not simply a matter of
justice for one sex, but of responsibility for the preservation, organization, consciousness and creation of life, of the world. Such a task demands that we consider the responsibility of the speaker and question any
discourse which claims to be indifferent to the subject – in its dimensions
of perception, sensitivity, understanding and sex –, which calls itself universal and neutral. What does the neutral conceal? Where in the economy
of discourse does the sexuate lie hidden? How to discover it?

It is not enough to talk of content, especially historical content. To approach the sexuate dimension of discourse, change its rules, we must analyse quite rigorously the forms that permit that content. If the ethical, or simply cultural, transformation concerning sexual difference is not brought about, or is brought about badly, it is for want of an *active* mutation in the laws and order of discourse.

The Unconscious Translation of *Genre* in Discourse

I insist upon the fact that I am not going to define an ideal model of language [*langue*]. This means that I do not claim to be indicating in an *absolute* manner the most important elements of the language spoken by men and women. I can say what I have observed. Nor do I wish to establish a *fixed* and *immutable* schema for the production of discourse; I want to show that the generation of messages is not neutral, but sexuate. Sexual difference has always been used for procreation. For a long time, it has not been used for the *creation of culture*, except in a division of roles and tasks which does not permit both sexes to be subjects. We thus find ourselves faced with a certain *subjective pathology* on both sides of sexual difference. This pathology appears with varying degrees of clarity in social behaviour. It is covered up by different masks, and there is a great reluctance to analyse it, even to admit its existence, either because language [*langage*] is considered an ideal alien to the body which produces it or because it is asserted to be reducible to the superstructure of a restricted economy. There are other possible hypotheses, notably that of repression or censorship being exercised on a sexuate language [*langage*]. Even those who profess sexual liberation (in the therapeutic mode or in a more directly political mode) often deny the fact that language is sexuate. They, men or women, stick to content, to certain sexual representations, but overlook the fact that sexuation corresponds to a general structure of discourse.

The sexuation of discourse does not in fact correspond to a few words more or a few words less, even though the non-existence of terms in the *vocabulary* may be structurally significant. Nor does the *mark of gender* in language [*langue*] (masculine, feminine, neuter) exhaust the meaning of a sexuate generation of messages. It is often revelatory of social and historical phenomena. It shows how one sex has subordinated the other or the world. Thus, in French at least, the masculine gender always takes syntactic precedence: a crowd of one thousand people made up of 999 women and one man will be described as *ils étaient* ('they were'); it will be said of a couple that *ils s'aiment* ('they love one another'); a woman telling the story of her love must employ the masculine form *'nous nous sommes aimés'* ('we loved each other'), etc. What is more, the neuter is expressed by the same pronoun as the masculine: *il tonne, il faut*, and not *elle faut, elle tonne.* These syntactic laws reveal the dominance of one sex over the other.

This sex has, besides, appropriated the most highly valued truths: *God* is now masculine in most, if not all, languages; so is *sun*; in countries where the *moon* is important, it is masculine in gender, etc. Man gives his *genre* to the universe, just as he wants to give his name to his children and his property. Anything which seems valuable to him must belong to his *genre.* The feminine is a secondary mark, always subordinated to the principal *genre.* The neuter is reserved for certain domains that vary from language to language. An analysis of its origins often reveals that it stems from an erased sexual difference. Thus, cosmic phenomena which where once the attributes of gods *and goddesses* are now expressed in the neuter form: *il tonne, il fait soleil, il pleut* etc. This necessity was once bound up with sexuate acts. Similarly, the *'ananke'* [*il faut* or *il est nécessaire*] of the Greek philosophers, or derived from the Greeks, probably conceals a sexual necessity associated with a destiny at once human and divine.[1] This necessity was later subordinated to the Roman juridical order. But laws were then decreed by men alone. Necessity [*il faut*] signifies a duty or an order established by one sex, one *genre.* It is only apparently neutral and, once more, it is expressed, in French at least, by the same *genre* as the masculine.

Our social organizations and the discourse that stems from them are therefore regulated by a neuter governed by the masculine *genre.* A place of respite from wars and polemics between men, this neuter does not resolve the problem of the hierarchy of masculine and feminine genres, of its injustices and of the pathogenic neutralization of languages [*langages*] and values that ensues.

For this long-standing taboo on a truly sexuate morphology of and in culture leads to repressions, compensations and pathologies. Hence the invention of various individual or collective therapies. Psychoanalysis is the most obvious example. Given the conventions of the analytic session, it is also the site where language disorders are seen most clearly, quite apart from the fact that language is the means used in treatment. It is in this non-social context that the difference between subjects at the level of the structure of the utterance is manifested at its simplest. If I start with traditional classifications, it becomes apparent that so-called hysterics and obsessionals do not produce a discourse in accordance with the same structures. Hysterics (or at least women hysterics) generate messages of the type: (I) (You love me?) (you) or (I) (I love what you love) (you). Obviously, they do not produce sentences in precisely this form. This sentence model is derived from the analysis of several samples, from their reduction to kernel sentences and so on.[2] The male obsessional, for his part, produces a discourse of the type: (I) (I say to myself that perhaps I am loved) (you) or (I) (I wonder if I am loved) (you). In the first case, the message, the object exchanged, the world view or perspective often belong to *you*; in the second, it often belongs to *I*. The objection that there are hysterical men and obsessional woman is not valid as a counter-interpretation. The model of the male hysteric is different to that of the female hysteric. The same applies to the obsessional structure.[3]

But sexual difference can also be observed within so-called homogeneous groups. Thus, female *schizophrenics* do not elaborate the same neocodes as male schizophrenics. Women tend mainly to structure a corporeal geography; men, new linguistic territories.

The sexuate structure of discourse is also found in cases other than those specifically identified as pathological. Students of different sexes do not, for instance, produce the same sentences on the basis of given inductor words. This is not simply a matter of the content of the messages, but also of their form. In the sentences I analysed, the words were, for example: marriage, celibacy, motherhood, fatherhood, femininity. The samples were collected by a team working on obstetrical psychoprophylaxis.[4] The findings obtained by the authors differed considerably from mine. It is true that they were concerned with a study of content and not an analysis of the structure of discourse. In my view, the sentences produced by men and women differ in their choice of subjects, verbs, tenses, modes, transformations of the predicate, etc. This can be interpreted as a different positioning of the subject generating the message in relation to language [*langage*], the object of discourse, the world, the other. Contrary to what is usually said or thought, women construct more objective sentences whose meaning or denotation is often supported by an extra-linguistic context. Men connote their messages much more. They assert their subjective mark in somewhat impassioned terms ('I claim the paternity of these sentences' was one man's response to the word paternity), whereas women, reputedly incapable of neutrality, reply in a much more impersonal manner, in a more 'scientific' style. These findings may be a source of surprise. They are, however, related to those obtained in the psychoanalytic situation. With men, the *I* is asserted in different ways; it is significantly more important than the *you* and *the world*. With women, the *I* often makes way for the *you*, *the world*, for the objectivity of words and things. From that point of view, women appear to be more capable of listening to, discovering or accommodating the other and the world, of remaining open to *objective* invention or creation, provided that they can also say I.[5]

I have just given two examples of the sexuation of discourse. I have approached the question of the sexual order of discourse in various ways: the discourses of the hysteric and the obsessional, the production of sentences by men and women students, Freud's theory *on* Dora, the text addressed by Schreber to his wife, the sexual language of fairy tales and legends, the sexuate determination of the discourse of science, philosophy, art, religion, etc.[6]

What becomes apparent when we analyse the expressions of the subject in language, representations, art, legends and myths is that *sex [sexe] is a primal and irreducible dimension of subjective structure*. We are sexuate and we produce sexuate forms. We know little about this production – and not merely reproduction – in difference, but, more so than ever, we need to safeguard ourselves against a technocratic imperialism that often cares little for the regeneration of living beings, for freedom and the future. This also means that we need it if we are to be capable of using our technical powers to construct, and not destroy, human values.

For me, working on language does not correspond to a matter of mere statistical surveys, nor to the registration of a de facto state. I use the scientific apparatus to bring out certain tendencies that we habitually misrecognize, forget. But can we speak and be conscious of the form, the forms, of our discourse? Not necessarily. Indeed, it seems impossible in the immediate. Hence the need for an investigation.

Its project is to reveal who is speaking, to whom, about what, with what means. In technical terms, this means that it is a matter of uncovering the dynamics of the utterance [*énonciation*] underlying the statements [*énoncés*] produced. Beneath what is being said, it is possible to discover the subject, the subject's economy, potential energy, relations with the other and the world. The subject may be masked, bogged down, buried, covered up, paralysed, or may be engendered, generated, may become, and grow through speech [*en parlant*].

Working on language in its sexuation therefore means bringing out who *I*, *you*, *he*, *she* are in the discourses of men and women. That allows us to interpret the misunderstandings and impasses to which their sexual relations, both in the strict sense and in the social, cultural sense, are often reduced. This type of work allows us to analyse the symptom, to name and understand the problem, to find the openings that allow us to modify the economy of the utterance [*énonciation*], of exchanges in general. A formalism undergone, unconsciously produced, can thus become a style.

The Expression of *Genre* in a Style

This work may seem austere to some, even if it does have its intellectually amusing and stimulating side. I therefore want to state another reason why it seems to me indispensable. No narrative, and no commentary on a narrative is enough to bring about a change in discourse. They may, moreover, establish a moralizing repression of sexual and affective freedom, unless they create a style, transcend the statement [*énoncé*] in the creation of new forms. I am thinking in this connection of all the contemporary autobiographical narratives which are not transposed into novels, poems, tales, legends, theories. The transformation of the autobiographical I into another cultural I seems to be necessary if we are to establish a new ethics of sexual difference. To avoid turning it into a traditional morality, abstract norms of feeling, formal frameworks or a truth resulting from the personal experience of an *x* or *y* who can shout louder than the rest, it is also important not to reduplicate this ethics by *explaining* what is being invented, discovered by way of gestures of creation, love and freedom. Two approaches are important for the establishment of different norms of life: the analysis of the formal structures of discourse, and the creation of a new style. Thus, in *Ethique de la différence sexuelle*, which presupposes a lot of cultural analyses,[7] there is no basic narrative and no possible commentaries by others, in the sense of an exhaustive deciphering of the text. What is said in this book is conveyed by a double style: a style of amorous relations, a style of thought, exposition, writing. Consciously or unconsciously, the two are connected; on the one hand, there is a more immediately corporeal and affective side and, on the other, a more socially elaborated side. But its language [*langage*] is already allied with other languages. And an alliance is an act which cannot easily be transposed. Nor can an alliance with language [*langue*].

Gestures made in accordance with a style do not constitute a formal model. Even if fashion does try to take it over, even if irritation does caricature it or use part of its content, a style remains irreducible. It cannot be reduced to a grid that can be transposed or imposed elsewhere.

A style resists coding, summarizing, encrypting, pigeon-holing in differently programmed machines. It cannot be reduced to oppositions like sensible/intelligible, poetic/conceptual . . . or the masculine/feminine, as presented to us by all these dichotomies. A style will not let itself be reduced to bipolar alternatives: positive/negative, better/not so good, etc. It may permit them, especially in the form of (digestive? and) in one way or another contradictory commentaries, but it escapes them insofar as it creates and is neither resolved nor dissolved into dichotomies, however refined.

Hence the resistances. What is it all about? What exactly is she saying? What is its, already given, meaning? The answers to these questions are not forthcoming, especially out of context, which sometimes leads to the objection that the thought is esoteric. But any text is esoteric, not because it conceals a secret, but because it constitutes the secret, the not-yet-revealed or the never-exhaustively-revealable. The only reply that can be given to the question of the meaning of the text is: read, perceive, feel. . . . *Who are you?* would be a more pertinent question, provided that it does not collapse into a demand for an identity card or an autobiographical anecdote. The answer would be: *and who are you?* Can we meet? Talk? Love? Create something together? Thanks to which milieu? What between us [*entre-nous*]?

We cannot do that without the horizon of sexual difference. No world can be produced or reproduced without sexual difference. Everything is sexuate: plants, animals, the gods, the elements of the universe.

Whether or not the force of matter alone (which? and what are we calling matter?) engenders organized beings remains an insistent question, especially in relation to the origins of our life. Although research has gone a very long way, in every sense and direction, in an attempt to prove it, it sometimes overlooks our most elementary realities and needs. But, to date, no one has been able to assert that they belong to a monosexuate or asexuate universe. Except in fiction? And in certain formal truths of science, abstracted from life and said to be neutral?

Man appears to have forgotten this destiny in its most universal, and most creative, dimensions. In the beginning, 'God' (or some animal, vegetable pair) created us naked, man and woman, in a garden that sufficed us for our shelter, our food. Working to make a living, and especially procreating in pain, signify *exile* from that garden. What have become our duties, *our only horizon*, may be no more than exile as we wait to return, the taboo on the flesh, the obligation to work, and to suffer, representing the reverse of, the fall from, our first birth. Man is now excavating his mythical archaeology, when he is not looking for himself on the most distant planets, being still bound here and now to a *fault* from which he cannot deliver himself, which he cannot manage to replace with a third element such as: love, grace, jubilation in the flesh, and therefore their sharing in the word.

An apocryphal gospel reports Christ saying to Salome that happiness will not return to earth until women cease procreating! That can be understood as the discovery of a love in which the child is no longer *necessary*. But the text, the texts, add that sexual difference will then be erased. One might as well say that it existed only for or through the child, and in hierarchy: there will be neither man nor woman, master nor slave.

If sexual difference is to be transcended, must it not first find its ethics? If we are to be as *one*, isn't it necessary for us first to be *two*? Lest we lapse into some empty, formal *one*, into the hierarchies we know or into a nostalgia for intra-uterine regression where the other is no more than a place, food, a conveyance. Hasn't man, on his travels, confused what is most archaic on earth with what is most celestial in heaven?

How has the sexual ethic been neglected to this extent? Why does it make so many detours: animal ecology, the sexuation of plants, the more or less pathological language of our cells, the sex of our chromosomes of our brain, etc.? Sexuality appears to have become little more than an issue of power, and pain. . . . Man no longer even takes the time for any courtship display [*parade*]. He must work faster, ever faster. As for woman, her gestures as lover seem yet to be invented. She has become lost in the mother, or in a display of adornment [*parade*] which does not describe her space for either encounter or embrace. She may perhaps express her need-desire to be loved, but not her own love. Why? The woman with a value in her own right [*la femme valable*] has been reduced to giving birth to the son, to mothering and to the corresponding language [*langage*]. Man, who, thanks to his labour, has a monopoly on the symbolic, has not thought his body or his flesh. And, quite apart from the need to think himself, perhaps he would have some difficulty in saying what constitutes the singularity of the feminine sexual world: a different energy and morphology, a particular relationship with the mucous and the threshold that goes from outside to inside the body, from the exterior to the interior of the skin (and the universe?) without a wound.

For women, it is therefore a matter of learning to discover and inhabit a different magnetism and the morphology of a sexuate body, especially in its singularities and mucous qualities. But this flesh (and aren't the mucous membranes the very stuff of flesh for many?) has remained ignored, often imagined as chaos, abyss or dregs. Raw material, or a cast-off from what has already been born, it has yet to find its forms, to flower in accordance with its roots. It has still not been born into its own growth, its subjectivity. The feminine has not yet deployed its *morphology*. Yoked to the maternal, reduced to the womb or to seductive adornment, the feminine has been used only for the conception, growth, birth and rebirth of the *forms* of the other.

But how to espouse that which has no *forms*, no edges, no limits? No style of nuptials and alliance to propose? In this absence of her self-assertion, man drowns, consumes or undertakes some nostalgic odyssey. Woman mothers her little one, her externalized one; she makes him grow and flourish in her place. As a wife, she masks herself, adorns herself. Yet when she has no intention of her own, adornment leads only to disappointments. Clothes that are only *for the other*, that are not an expression of my flesh, unveil a sort of void once they are taken off: woman's inability to love herself, to care for herself, to become an *other* partner, irreducible to what man expects, and therefore still desirable, attractive. Then she is beautiful, not only with the beauty of more or less artificial appearances, but with the radiance of an inferiority, an intimacy. These words make us smile today, but in many traditions they are weighty. In other traditions, they designate an energy that can be conserved.

In ours, don't women suffer from not having known and lived *together* an initiation to their sexuality? In certain societies, men live through the rites of their transition to manhood together in groups. In one way or another, that persists in our cultures. For women, initiation, even when it is marked as a stage, remains solitary. The little girl becomes a woman and a mother alone, at best with her mother or a substitute. This burden of solitude still weighs upon women. Even when they are together, they rarely know how to live and speak this transition from one state to another. They do not go beyond criticizing existing situations, beyond rivalry, beyond their complaints and cares. They are rarely initiated together into their becoming women. They may, perhaps, talk about their pregnancies or their mothers. They almost never speak of their sexual needs and desires as women. If they do, they rarely go beyond describing their sufferings, the damage suffered. They exchange scraps of games that have already been played. They rarely invent new games, their games.

Language [*langage*] seems to have paralysed our gestures, including our verbal gestures. As adults, we no longer have any mobility. Once childhood is over, our moving trajectories are limited to poetry, art, prayer. Does not the still silent understanding of the feminine signify *movements* to be liberated? This is not a matter of women outbidding technology, even if they can, but of their discovering forgotten, misrecognized gestures, and also verbal gestures other than those of mothering, shedding a different light on corporeal generation in the strict sense.

The most forgotten symbol in the universe and in our cultures is the sexual symbol, *the living symbol*. In their failure to recognize this living symbol, men – men alone – exchange women, children, products of labour, tokens, money (often struck in the image of the feminine?). They exchange something instead of exchanging love, god(s), art, thought, language [*langage*]. Any assertion stating that God constitutes the most noble of human exchanges, its celestial cornerstone, the basis of language, is redundant if God is not really exchanged. And he has for centuries been the focus of a monopoly on truth(s), rites. But one apparently negative predicate still remains to him: that of invisibility. Invisible too, to a large extent, our sexual relation, our carnal act especially through the mediation of woman. What birth takes place, is yet to come, between these two poles of invisibility? How can we discover and interpret its traces in discourse? How can we remodel existing languages [*langages*] so as to give rise to a sexuate culture? That is what is at issue in my researches.

Notes

1 Irigaray does not give the Greek term signifying 'necessity'; '*ananke*' is in fact feminine. (Ed.)
2 Cf. 'Grammaire de l'énonciation de l'hystérique et de l'obsessionnel', in *Parler n'est jamais neutre*, Paris: Minuit, 1985.
3 Cf. 'L'Ordre sexuel du discours', in *Langages*, March 1987: *Le Sexe linguistique*.
4 Cf. *Bulletin de la Société nationale de Psychoprophylaxie obstétricale*, 1971, pp. 21-40.
5 Cf. *Langages*, March 1987.
6 Cf. the texts in *Sexes et parentés* and my other work. The studies of Dora and Schreber remain unpublished.
7 Cf. *Speculum, This Sex Which is Not One, Marine Lover, L'Oubli de l'air*, and most of the texts in *Parler n'est jamais neutre*.

Chapter Eight Writing and the Law: Blanchot, Joyce, Kafka, and Lispector

Hélène Cixous

I want to work on texts that are as close as possible to an inscription – conscious or unconscious – of the origin of the gesture of writing and not of writing itself. Writing is already something finished, something that follows the drive to write. Such texts could be expected to be among the writer's firstborn that are not afraid to be so. Clarice Lispector's *Near to the Wild Heart* is just such a text.[1] Its title is a quotation from Joyce's *Portrait of the Artist as a Young Man*.[2]

What does it mean to work on texts that are 'near to the wild heart'? Reading Clarice's text, I was struck by its extraordinary power. It is a text that has the audacity to let itself be written close to the very drive to write. At the same time, it gives the impression of being poorly written. It does not display a mastery of form or language and does not raise the question of art. It is the contrary of Flaubert. Clarice's first movement as a child was to put herself at the *écoute* of, in tune with, writing, of something that happens between the body and the world. One has to have a touch of something savage, uncultured, in order to let it happen. It is the contrary of having been so much of a student, of a scholar, that one thinks that a

Hélène Cixous, 'Writing and the Law: Blanchot, Joyce, Kafka, and Lispector', in *Readings: The Poetics of Blanchot, Joyce, Kafka, Kleist, Lispector, and Tsvetayeva*, ed. and trans. Verena Andermatt Conley (New York and London: Harvester Wheatsheaf, 1992), pp. 1–27.

book is a book, and that, if one vaguely has the desire to write, one says: I have to write a book.

Clarice's text comes from within. It is written from an unformulated hypothesis that writing is something living. It is not the book as sacred object. *Near to the Wild Heart* is a kind of germination where these problems are irrelevant. It stands out by contrast with other texts, such as Flaubert's. Yet, at the same time, something makes me give Flaubert a thought, because he is one of those important beings who have a vocation – the word has to be taken in its strong meaning, in relation to something of the order of a calling, and, of course, he answers it. Flaubert answered it when he was very young and said yes, definitely. He organized the totality of his material, psychological, and affective life in such a way that he became forever the lover of writing. He called it art, not writing. I said writing because I did not want to place him in a kind of unconscious pederasty. But art was his love object and it was inscribed in pederastic fashion. In a certain way, he was a monster. He made love with art throughout his entire life. In itself that would not be so bad if it were not done by a choice that excludes human beings. Flaubert was never in a relation of living and livable love with other human beings. His relation with Louise Collet was monstrous. Flaubert fixed a rendezvous with her only after completion of such and such a chapter. Living entirely in the universe of production of writing, he was one of its most arduous crafts-men. Like his successor, James Joyce, he thought of creation in extraordinary fashion. His 'savage heart' can be found in his correspondence, a kind of *mise à nu* (laying bare) of a tyrannic drive, of an incredible rigor of the *bien écrire* (the beautifully written).

He is of interest as one of those beings who paid the price of their wager without concession. This presupposes that first one pays the price oneself, then one makes others pay. Is there a possibility of a half-gesture that would be less cruel? What does one have to pay to stay close to the savage heart? Flaubert did not give the answer, he died of it. We can see Joyce and Kafka appear in the same field.

Writing pushed to an absolute degree differs from that of human and mercantile dimensions. We can verify this by taking as the main question the locus of *writing* and not that of art. Flaubert advanced in this dilemma to the point of madness. For him, the question is not who but where, from where? In the course of the journey, Flaubert – like Kafka – got lost. Flaubert wanted people to burn all the papers he did not specifically authorize for publication and, in any case, Kafka was a dying man. Did Kafka finish something because he himself knew he was dying? All of his gestures were morbid gestures. Kafka's strongest writings are those that are unfinished, that he was only beginning, over and over again, and the same can be said of Flaubert.

James Joyce's *Portrait of the Artist as a Young Man* can be put side by side with Clarice Lispector's *Near to the Wild Heart*. Though Joyce is still quite young when he writes the novel, it is not his first, but a portrait of the primitive portrait. Joyce shows extraordinary formal mastery in this text, which is a kind of organized mobile that takes off from a very precise and coded architecture. Where Flaubert worked only on the sentence, Joyce goes further to work also on articulations.

Of importance for a reading concerning our *questions-femmes*, or woman's questions, is the place of origin and the object. What is a writer looking for? What are the stakes in the text? How does one search for something? The movements of the body are determined by what one is looking for and the object one seeks depends on the kind of body one has. We have to work on the first and most primitive pleasure, that is to say, on orality. Rather than give answers, we have to follow the questions, the woman-questions: How does one write as woman? have pleasure as woman? We have to be transgrammatical, the way one says to be transgressive, which does not mean that we have to despise grammar but we are so used to obeying it absolutely that some work has to be done in that direction. I find it important to work on foreign texts, precisely because they displace our relationship to grammar. I will use caution too in relation to what I call trap-words (*motscages*). One has to be audacious in one's reading, so that it becomes an intense deciphering. We need not be afraid of wandering, though one should read in terms of a quest. There always has been femininity from time immemorial but it has been repressed. It has never been unnamed, only suppressed. But it constantly reappears everywhere. Of course, one finds more femininity in texts that are written 'close to the savage heart', in texts that are still close to sources, springs, to myth and to beginnings of literary movements before they become institutionalized. Literature is like history. It is organized so as to repress and hide its own origin which always deals with some kind of femininity.

Joyce's *Portrait of the Artist as a Young Man*: Silence, Exile, and Cunning

The work Joyce produced in *Portrait of the Artist*, his *Künstlerroman*, his formative novel, is not without ambivalence. In one of the first scenes, he who will become the artist is in open opposition to the law and to author-ity. We have to look at the word 'law' and render it more flexible. We have to analyze who lays down the law and who is in the law's place. In this respect, there is a difference between Joyce and Kafka. In Kafka, the law is not figured by anyone. In Joyce there are specific authorities. In the first page of his novel, the women threaten him with castration but, as in Clarice Lispector, the question of the father is important too. In Clarice's 'Sunday, before falling asleep', the father is really a father/mother and everything is organized in the direction of the father.[3] Genesis takes place in a maternal and paternal mode of production. In Joyce, something analogous is related to the very possibility of the formation of the artist. Which father produces the artist? The question is related to the superego. Yet it is not always the same self that has a repressive figure.

The first two pages of *Portrait of the Artist* can be approached through a kind of multiple reading, which is what Joycean writing asks for. We read word for word, line by line, but at the same time it has to be read – because that is how it is written – as a kind of embryonic scene. The entire book is contained in the first pages, which constitute a nuclear passage. The ensemble of Joyce's work is here like an egg or an opaque shell of calcium. An innocent reading will lead us to believe that these pages are hermetic. One understands everything and nothing; everything because there is really nothing obscure, nothing because there are many referents. Perhaps Irish people would find it more accessible, at least if they know their history well. Here, we have something of a *coup d'écriture* with many signs of the ruse of the artist. The text is presented in an apparent näiveté – like Clarice's 'Sunday, before falling asleep' – but nothing is more condensed, or more allusive. It is already a cosmos.

Joyce denied using psychoanalysis in his work, yet he was impregnated by it. It is as if Joyce, though writing when Freud's texts were not yet well known, was in a kind of intellectual echo with him.

The story of *A Portrait of the Artist* is both that of a portrait being made and that of a finished portrait. The title indicates this kind of permanent duplicity. The reader is told that it is the portrait of an artist, not of a young man, which raises the question of the self-portrait of the artist, of the coming and going of the look, of the self, of the mirror and the self in the mirror.

A Portrait of the Artist is a genesis, like Clarice's text. But hers was a genesis as much of the artist as of the world, and the artist-world relation went through that of father-daughter. In *Portrait of the Artist*, one first sees a series of births, inscribed through the motif of evasion, of flight, and that is how the artist is made. The first and the fifth chapters resemble each other most. In those chapters, writing is much more disseminated, dislocated, than in the others. The successive stories of birth are stories of the breaking of an eggshell, in relation with a parental structure. In the first scene, there is a kind of elementary kinship structure. The scene opens little by little. In this story of the eye and of birds, not the real but the symbolic father marks the artist as genetic parent.

The text begins with an enormous *O* that recurs in the first pages. It can be taken as a feminine, masculine, or neuter sign, as zero. The *o* is everywhere. One can work on the *o–a*, on the *fort–da*.[4] I insist on the graphic and phonic *o*'s because the text tells me to do so. With all its italics and its typography, the text asks the reader to listen. There is also a series of poems. The last one, with its system of inversions and inclusions and exclusions, ends in an apotheosis with 'apologise'.

In these two pages we have everything needed to make a world and its history, in particular that of the artist. The text begins with: 'Once upon a time . . . baby tuckoo' (3). We are in the animal world. *I* begins with a moocow. Daedalus constructed his maze not without relation to a cow. It was built to contain the Minotaurus, the child of a (false) cow. We are in the labyrinth. There is no sexual hesitation and the first structure puts Oedipus in place. A cow and a little boy form a dual structure. We go on rapidly to the formation of the subject through the intervention of a third term. We go through the history of the mirror stage and of the cleavage, which is much funnier in Joyce than in Lacan.

In 'His father told him that story:' the colon and the organization of the sentence are important since they speak at all levels. 'His father looked at him through a glass:' a window separates without separating. With mirror and glasses we are already in the complex space of the history of blindness and of identificatory images. His father told him this story. The reader waits to hear what the father thinks but at that very moment the father is seen: 'He had a hairy face.' This is brought about by the father's look cast upon the boy. We are reminded of Kafka's keeper of the law, who was also said to have a hairy face. Our first perception of the father focuses on the glasses and on hair.

'He was baby tuckoo': not cuckoo, but tuckoo, a failed bird linked through its double o to the moocow that is walking down the road. His song falls from the sky, in the guise of a failed phonic signifier.

We go on to a succession of personal pronouns and adjectives: 'His mother put on the oilsheet.' She functions as an anal mother. She is at the centre of a moment of corporeal perceptions: cold, warm, wet, smell. The bottom of the body and the odor are feminine but the mother is on the side of a certain orality as well.

'She played on the piano' so that he would dance. The mother is equally on the side of a kind of eroticism and makes things move.

Uncle Charles and Dante (whose double-entendre of 'Auntie' and 'Dante' is exploited by Joyce on the side of writing) open up the value of young and old at play throughout the entire text. It can be said that the subject in Joyce is structured by a series of oppositions: young, old; weak, strong. The symbolic father toward whom one regresses through a series of signifiers is treated as 'Old Father', 'Old Artificer'. The real father is always in rivalry with the son, expressed in such statements as 'I am beating him, I run faster than he, the women are mine'.

With Dante and her two brushes we enter into the world of mathematics. The number two introduces sexual difference. The two brushes are very different in this scene, written as it is perceived by the child. High and low resemble each other.

The relation between naming and not-naming has to be noted. In chapter 2 (72–86), in the scene with Heron, his classmate and rival who wants to make Stephen confess to having a girlfriend, the girl is not named. She is simply called 'the girl'. The motif of naming comes about in a central way, beginning with the name of the main protagonist: Stephen, which echoes the first Christian martyr, and Dedalus, a foreign name, the strangeness of which is erased but which remains unexplainable. To put oneself under the sign of Dedalus is to play the card of the signifier.

Proper names are stressed. Parnell has no first name. A Protestant, he was worshiped and called the 'uncrowned king of Ireland'. He died trying to lead the first Irish revolution and, at that moment, Ireland lost its exemplary battle. The men of the Dedalus family themselves – and Joyce keeps on saying it in all of his work – killed Parnell. The old, archaic, Catholic Ireland turned against him who was called its liberator. Parnell had been unjustly accused of being the instigator of the assassination of Phoenix Park. The falsifier who had fabricated the letter supposedly written by Parnell was discovered later through a spelling mistake. This (happy) mistake joins the Augustinian motif *felix culpa*. Luckily there was a fault, so there could be redemption. Everything is owed to a fault. In a play of signifiers, Joyce works on *Phoenix/Felix* around the happy fault, which, since he hates the theological perspective, is a subversive theme. In 'Phoenix' read across French and German there is also *fait nichts*, 'does not do anything'. Parnell is innocent. His fault is not to have done anything. The artist, however, is going to take his place in the happy, subversive fault. 'I did well to do what I did'. Joyce touches upon an interdict, a prohibition, the first of which is that of sexuality. We can say that Joyce's work is owed to an immense spelling error. It is nothing but orthography playing infinitely. The letter plays with the letter, from the very beginning.

'The Vances lived in number seven', has to be heard in a childish way: in the number itself. 'They had a different father and mother'. In the child's view, there is an inside and an outside. 'They' includes mother and father. That is when Eileen, the feminine respondent in the undifferentiated 'they', appears.

> 'When they were grown up he was going to marry Eileen. He hid under the table. His mother said:
> – O, Stephen will apologise'. (8)

The position of hiding becomes his definitive position. Is it the fact of hiding that is prohibited? The reaction – 'secret', 'defense' – precedes in writing the statement that signifies there has been a fault. This demonstration of fear, the necessity of hiding before the cause, refers the reader to Kafka's keeper in 'Vor dem Gesetz' ('Before the Law').[5] Joyce is going to do what big people do since he identifies with them. Everyone is 'they'. We can deduce that getting married is also prohibited. Did Freud not say, in *Totem and Taboo*, you must not do like your father'?

Yet the symbolized threat comes from the mother. At the level of the body, we have seen the father's hair. But hair does not speak. Stephen's own name appears for the first time in a reductive scene where the mother speaks for him. She announces what he will do. Throughout the whole text, Stephen will have a relation as loving and compassionate son with his mother. At some point, in a protective gesture, he is going to buy a coat for her. In other words, he covers the mother uncovered by the father, who, in Irish fashion, drinks away her coat. He covers the very mother who had forced him to cover himself. Yet the mother is a good person and not the aggressive Dante with her two brushes. She is the typical uterine mother with ten children who is repressed by her husband.

During the Christmas dinner, the scene of communion the child had desired is carried off and transformed by political arguments. In a typical Dublin scene, both clans are present. The Parnellites and the men are Joyce's father's legacy to him. Dante had been a Parnellite but has turned against him. The mother is between the two. Being on the side of submission, she tries to be conciliatory. When she speaks for Stephen, the latter goes under the table that serves him as an eggshell and whence he will not come out again.

And Dante adds:

' – O, if not, the eagles will come and pull out his eyes – '. (8)

The reader does not know where the little poem 'Pull out his eyes, Apologise', comes from. It substitutes itself for the wild rose but now there are eagles. It is inscribed in a terrifying threat of enucleation that cannot not be in relation with the Oedipal scene.

At the same time, there is a displacement through rhythm and we can say that the artist is being born. At the beginning there was the Verb and everything else slides surreptitiously over this dictum. At the beginning there was a scene where rhythm and music, coming from the mother, were inscribed. And the mother makes him dance. Something happens between music and the words on music. When enucleation threatens, resistance is produced in a most ruseful way. The child under the table recuperates. He appropriates what frightens him; and a division takes place between the law, the utterance of the law, and the noise that this utterance makes. At the beginning there was the noise of the word, the noise of the law. Everything is inscribed phonically, the more so as there is the couple eye, ear, and the artist is somebody who has problems with his eyesight. Joyce theorizes this problem early in his work. He analyzes his relation to language in relation to his myopia. A tremendous ambivalence is put in place. The law that horrifies him also gives him pleasure. The name of the law frightens, but 'apologise' has a nice sound. The text plays obviously on the phonic confusion between 'eye' and 'I'. 'Apologise' is the last word of this short introduction and the first word with which Joyce played, which he rolled on his tongue. Quite unlike Kafka, Joyce, as a Catholic, is never done with the law. His unconscious is completely taken into the Christian space of the fault. The debate is carried out in a way quite different from Kafka, who wanted to be outside the space of the law. Instead of giving up the law, Joyce puts in place an enormous system of transgression. And there can be no transgression without law. It all remains very masculine. At the end, in *Finnegans Wake*, Joyce even managed to make of transgression his law.

In 'apologise', the question is between asking and forgiveness. The mother's force is to be identified with the Church. There is a cleavage that does not coincide. The young boy is taken between two different images: his father is rebellious but he is a scoundrel; his mother is a great soul but a slave, and she asks slavery of him. He is caught in complete ambivalence toward both parents. In Joyce, as well as in his fictional characters, everything is played out in a dramatic rapport with the mother. Joyce never stops wanting to kill her since she asked for his submission. He is going to work on all that is being played out on the body of the mother and on the enormous scene where a relation to the body of woman ensues. It is most classical and not classical at all, since, at the same time, Joyce analyzes it. The question of sexuality has to be followed from one end to the other, from Eileen who is legitimate since she is named to relations with women that begin to be prohibited when they are no longer named. The boy, full of sadistic phantasms, begins to have very violent relations with women.

In addition to 'apologise', in the scene with Heron in chapter 2, there is another word: 'admit' (58), which means to interiorize the fault. In chapter 3, there is yet another: 'amend' (135). This lexical system can be followed. Forgiveness has different forms, different colours, establishes different rapports. And the answer is always 'no'. The law is active in the Catholic world. It imposes upon those who resist it a negative position. Joyce's first motto reads *non serviam*, 'I will not'. He is obliged to begin from a refusal, from a retreat. This movement is going to be transformed into Joyce's theory of the artist. He is going to have to work on the interiorization of the fault. The three virtues of the artist's behavior – silence, exile, cunning – are related to stories of interiorization and duplicity.

Joyce situates the structure that can produce what is called 'the artist' at an important archetypal level. He puts the artist into rivalry with God since both are creators. What are the conditions that produce this artist? I am interested quite generally in the structure that makes the artist write, and in analysing it, I want to see if there are sexual differences that can be theorized as well. What structure produces the woman and the man who write? Is it as daughter, as son of the father, of a certain father that they do so? Joyce, in answer to such questions, has elaborated a rapport with castration, something inevitable for a boy. Generally, men are caught in this space; some women too, but only through identification. As Freud described it, the boy begins to symbolize from the threat of castration, from resistance to castration, and what appears, what is described in a more than illuminating näiveté, is what Joyce calls the artist. At a certain moment, there is an encounter, and a law is interiorized in a certain mode. It has to do with inhibition, with the staging of a limit right where Stephen's body is small, weak, and marked by bad eyesight. There, at once, a physical weakness, the system of prohibitions, and the violence of history produce prohibiting knots. It is at these very points of encounter that something will disengage itself and produce the artist.

One should keep in mind the primal scenes from Joyce's *Portrait of the Artist*, Lispector's *Near to the Wild Heart*, Kafka's 'Before the Law', and Blanchot's *The Writing of Disaster*. *Near to the Wild Heart* is the portrait of the artist as a young woman. It is a primitive, archaic, unique text. When Clarice was seventeen, she did not write the portrait of the artist; she wrote the portrait of the subject in formation, a feminine subject that reveals at the same time all the traits of the artist. It is the portrait of someone abnormal – that is, of someone who is outside norms and who continuously gathers moments of the real, just the way Stephen had done it under the name 'epiphanies'.

I want to put Joyce's primal scene side by side with Clarice Lispector's from *Near to the Wild Heart*. Clarice's scene, on the side of a feminine fault, also begins with a relation to the father, soon after the latter's death. In Lispector, the father always has to be dead. There is going to be a scene with a real aunt in relation to the story of a theft.

On two different sides of sexual difference, *Portrait of the Artist* and *Near to the Wild Heart* stage the same scene. Young Stephen's fixation on language is the main element of the text that is marked by a succession of short poems punctuated by the word 'apologise'. Clarice is into chickens and worms, Joyce into roses and eagles. The system of thought of the young artist is put in place. From thinking about things the artist ends up understanding them. Joyce says this along these lines: If one reflects on words, if one warms them like a hen, one ends up understanding them. The little boy is constantly before a secret constituted by signifiers or by words. Over hundreds of pages, for Stephen Dedalus it is but a question of enigmas. Where there is a primal scene, there are also primal words, since the two are equivalent. The words hold back, they bind the future artist as young man. On the first page, the subversion of the law in the form of ambivalence, fear/pleasure, had taken place. When Stephen hears the threat:

> Apologise,
> Pull out his eyes

he is afraid, yet he feels an auditory pleasure. What the law says frightens but its noise is pretty. Joyce is fixated by the noise of the law. He is someone for whom the secret is audible, which is not the case of Blanchot or of Kafka. Joyce writes to the ear, whose secret he tries to surprise. This goes with the fact that he is very myopic. And, with his poor eyesight, the question of the law always returns. A drive is displaced because at that very moment the look is related to something specular. There is insistence. The look is in relation with space and opens upon a system of meaning that allows appropriation in distance and is the closest to symbolization. The sense of smell is the most primitive and relates to objects close up. The more one is elevated intellectually, the less one smells, the more one sees, farther and farther. One enters into an intellectual dimension. Hearing is much closer to the body, to the ear. In this way, the artist is quite explicitly in relation with femininity. At a certain moment when he goes over to the side of creation, or when, after all the emotions of childhood, he begins to be the one who produces, the metaphoric systems alluding to the soul of the artist as the Holy Virgin keep recurring. Femininity is all the stronger as it surges in an imaginary, Catholic space. The ideal figure of the Virgin is not an archaic, primitive femininity but a much re-elaborated femininity, that of the Virgin Mary as desired by the artist.

Near to the Wild Heart: How Not to Appear before the Law

I am going back to my chickens. The first pages of *Portrait of the Artist* are the embryo of the whole work. In *Near to the Wild Heart*, the phonic obsession is magnetized by the words 'never' (*nunca*) and 'yes' (*sim*). When Joyce wrote *Portrait of the Artist*, he was a sly old fox, while Clarice was seventeen years old when she wrote her text. The dinner in the third chapter of *Near to the Wild Heart* can be related to Joyce's Christmas dinner, where what should be a scene of orality is symbolized right away. Orality is displaced, carried off, through a great political struggle in a story where politics and food clash. In Clarice, the scene of the meal turns around chickens. We have a certain story of cannibalism that she experiences when she is eating the chickens to whom she gives the names of daughters. She epiphanizes a certain femininity in the chickens. They are body. In Clarice's writing about the naked chicken, there is a strong feeling of sacrificial, erotic violence. The scene is all the stronger as it happens between the father and one of his friends, that is to say among men. Suddenly a naked chicken lies on the table and Clarice notes:

The father and the man were drinking wine, and the man was saying from time to time: I cannot even believe that you have found yourself a daughter. (20)

We are on the side of elementary formation.

A few pages later, the reader learns that Joana is an orphan and that she is now at her aunt's. With an artist or a writer, one has to think of the structure that gives birth to, that produces, the strange being whose life is divided and who lives in a kind of duplicity, permanently torn between living and writing. The question was lived mortally by Kafka, but the necessity of a choice is always present. To write is a more or less solitary activity. For Kafka, it was total solitude. For Joyce, three main words – silence, exile, cunning – are the development of the theme of isolation and of a solitude needed to write.

Writers inhabit both the living and the writing worlds. They navigate with difficulty between the two, of which one will always be emphasized more than the other. To be the inhabitant of two worlds brings about a feeling of betrayal. Every exile cannot but think this way since one cannot change countries without being from two countries. This double appurtenance, this double focus is going to lead to the theme of betrayal, a dominant problem in Joyce. It is put into place by the institution of a double world.

The two worlds – of presence and absence – are formalized. They name, yet are lived, inscribed in the body. In *The Uncanny*, Freud tells us that death is a late discovery of mankind. Writers carry within themselves their own disquieting strangers, like Kafka who felt that he had been on Mount Sinai and had experienced another world. The variable of this structure is that death is lived necessarily as if it were one's own. The supreme case is to have made the experience of one's own death, of one's own castration. It can be played like the death of the other, but of an other so close that it is interiorized. In any event, it is being played in relation to a certain loss, which then has to be sublimated.

Clarice inscribes the death of the father. The latter is at the origin of the movement of reconstruction, of a writing as resistance to castration. This is the thematic of Freud's *Totem and Taboo*. For the boy, the threat of castration is of an extreme simplicity, as we can see in *Portrait of the Artist*: If you do not behave so as to be forgiven, the eagles will come and pull out your eyes. For Clarice, the threat of castration is displaced and symbolized rather late through the loss of the living phallus, the father. In *Near to the Wild Heart*, in a chapter entitled 'The Aunt' (that is, after her father's death), she has to succeed in interiorizing a certain reality of that death. In an extraordinary scene, Clarice takes refuge from her aunt and her vulgar femininity. She tells the story of the latter's breasts, enormous and fatty, that look at the girl as if they were about to swallow her. The little girl runs toward the sea. In a moment of savage communion, she arrives at the following thoughts:

> Her happiness increased, it united itself in her throat like a sack of air. She understood that it was over with her father. That was all. (32)

And Kafka? After all, his father was not dead. Kafka's story is obviously written in relation to his father, but human beings are not made of blocks of cement. Kafka was composed of his father, which was not very amusing because the latter was a tall, thin man whom he could not contain. He dies from his father, but an interiorized father. In Clarice, the father-daughter relation is mediated by the sea. The chapter ends with a short poem the father had made up when she had said to him: But what am I going to do now? It reads as follows:

> Daisy and Violet knew
> One was blind, the other lived very crazily,
> The blind one knew what the crazy one said,
> And ended up seeing what no one else saw. (40)

That is the father's testament.

The chapter entitled 'The Bath' begins with these words:

> At the moment when the aunt went to pay for her purchase, Joana took out the book and stuck it carefully between the others under her arm. The aunt turned pale. (42)

In the street, the aunt tries to make Joana feel guilty:

> – Do you know what you did?
> – I know . . .
> – You know . . . and you know the word?
> – I stole the book, isn't that it? (42)

And in answer to the aunt's question about whether Joana thinks that one can steal, she answers:

I can.

    – You?! – screamed the aunt.

    – Yes, I stole because I wanted. I will only steal when I want.

This scene can be put side by side with Stephen's. The little girl in this scene does not enter into the space of the fault. Clarice puts herself in a special rapport with the story of forgiveness. In the scene that follows, the little girl, glued to the door, hears her aunt complain to her uncle, saying: 'She is a viper' (44). In a truly comic scene, the aunt opposes Joana, the artist, and Amanda, the daughter of the house. The uncle claims that Amanda would also be capable of stealing books. But the aunt continues to scream that this is different. Even if she did, she would remain a person.

The power of Clarice's remark, which reveals her moral law, has to be underlined: It is not bad because I am not afraid. She is not under the spell of transgression, while in the Joycean dilemma, nothing can function without transgression. There must be law so it can be transgressed.

Joyce – and all that comes through him – is going to say: Tell me no. Whereas Clarice – and this marks the totality of her text – does the contrary. Clarice does not respond to the calling of the law. Her relationship to the inside of the law is different. She does not enter though the aunt with her big breasts would like to make her do so. Clarice produces the inverse of this gesture. Her aunt tells her: Do you know what you did and what it is called? The sentence goes through an entire system of naming. Joana, the protagonist, is not ignorant. Yes, she knows that in a certain vocabulary and in a certain world, it is called 'to steal'. There is a displacement of values – something more than simply Nietzschean – or a reversal, but elsewhere. Joana does not appear before the law.

When Stephen says in chapter 5 that it is as Icarus that he will leave Ireland, we may think, on the one hand, that he will fall into the sea, and on the other hand, we may read it as an allusion to the trajectory of the Luciferian fall. Lucifer is the one who said no to God. He is the creator as anticreator, the rival. Is he not the son? The equivalent of the relation Lucifer-God, is the already human character of Prometheus, who is announced in the first page with the appearance of the eagles. Prometheus's eagle did not tear out his eyes but his liver. Joyce plays as if he were mixing the cards of mythology. There is some Prometheus in the motifs of punishment, of the eagle and enucleation. Under Prometheus and behind the eagles, Oedipus appears. We could speak of a composite myth, the way we could speak of a composite kinship. According to Marx, Prometheus is the first martyr of the philosophical calendar. One could say that Stephen Dedalus is the first martyr of the literary calendar. Joyce touches on this kind of subversion with a Promethean character who resists but does not give in. Hephaistos introduces a supplementary link since he had been forced by Zeus to chain Prometheus to the Caucasus. The scene is cruel, because, in a certain way, Hephaistos likes Prometheus in whom he sees himself. The motif of the chain, of links and of linking, is introduced. Hephaistos is taken in the chain of chains, be it the conjugal chains he tries to protect, or the weave of the net in which he captures adults. He is someone who forges.

If we look ahead to Kafka's texts, we see that links are everywhere. They are Kafka's very drama. We can see it in the famous story of his impossible engagements. Kafka spent his time getting engaged and disengaged, indefinitely. He was playing with his own life and death. His major engagements were those he tied and untied the most, as the one with Felice, a kind of first *felice culpa*. Felice Bauer, whose name, across German, insists on peasant and construction, marks Kafka's texts under the initials F.B., which one finds constantly in *The Trial*. Through these engagements and disengagements, linkings and unlinkings, something important is going to be played out in relation to the law. As with Joyce, though, written quite differently, the statement that can be read in filigrane throughout Kafka's adventure is: Tell me no. Kafka needs someone to tell him yes in order to be able to say no. The most solid person in this respect was Felice.

Kafka's last tragic scene took place just before his death. His last fiancée, Dora Diamant, was nineteen and Kafka was forty-one. It was a completely incestuous relationship. We have been told that Kafka wanted to live until the very last minute. He was so caught in the death drive that at the moment of agony which lasted several weeks, he was overcome by a terrible desire to live. In his last moments, he did what he had done during his entire life; that is, he asked Dora's parents, since she was so young, if he could marry her. He wrote to Dora's father who, as an orthodox Jew of the Hassidic sect, venerated an old, saintly rabbi. The father showed the rabbi a letter in which Kafka asked: Will the marriage take place? Before this sphinx-like question, the rabbi shook his head. The answer came back descriptive rather than written, the supreme mark of Kafka's destiny. At that moment, he had all he ever wanted. His demand for 'no' and exclusion had its ultimate answer.

Compared to Joyce, the difference would be in the way the artist says no. Joyce hears real and not imaginary voices, voices of authority – like his father's – which call him and make certain propositions to him. In *Portrait of the Artist*, the most obvious example is the proposition the rector makes to induce Stephen to enter the Jesuit order. He is chosen. It is an enormous proposition of legitimation. Yet after a slight manifestation of seduction, he refuses.

There are also several scenes of exclusion. The first one takes place when he hides under the table. Another defensive exclusion occurs right afterward, during a childhood scene at school. The boy constantly describes himself as the little young-weak one, he who always remained on the edge:

> He kept on the fringe of his line, out of sight of his prefect, out of the reach of the rude feet, feigning to run now and then. (8)

This marks the beginning of the theme of appearances. There is an explanation:

> He felt his small and weak body amid the throng of players and his eyes were weak and watery. (8)

The first violent interpellation is:

> – What is your name?
> Stephen had answered: – Stephen Dedalus.
> Then Nasty Roche had said:
> – What kind of a name is that?
> And when Stephen had not been able to answer, Nasty Roche had asked:
> – What is your father? (8–9)

All the elements are here. The question of appearance, of its value, opens the system of a vicious circle or of a double-bind. In this classical scene, we can see the defensive posits on of the little weak one who only pretends he is running. At the level of the body, he makes a simulated gesture in order to pretend that he is part of it, in order not to be interpellated any more. Difference is marked by a negative sign. He is less strong, weaker, smaller. Everyone has known such power relations. They are the first inscriptions of a threat of castration, of an exclusion inscribed spatially. We are on the edge, at the outer limit, which is going to be the metaphor of something that will be the exclusion caused by inverse reasons. He is excluded as corporeally weak. But he is on both sides of the barrier.

Intellectually stronger, he is the one who is most threatened. He who is below can be looked at, he who is above cannot be seen. He disappears, becomes invisible. He who knows more, who has a greater score, cannot be understood. Literally, he cannot be included since he is in excess. When he is below, he can be caught and understood by images in the order of representation. But he becomes unrepresentable when he begins to exceed the limit.

Kafka's 'Before the Law': How to Go before One's Door

In *The Passion according to G.H.*, Clarice uses the metaphor of cutting meat into small pieces to produce form. There must be form but there also can be something formless that can be given a positive value. What has no form totalizes, and the unlimited suscitates the necessity of making distinctions. How can it allow for otherness? It is all and nothing and has to be organized, which does not necessarily mean to lay down the law. It can also mean to shape a body. Form is needed in order to give it to the other.

A text calls for, provokes, calls for a certain reading. In 'Before the Law', in two pages, Kafka, the hunger artist, wrote something immense. The text is but writing, the sublimation of a paradox. It is not the *body* that prevents the man from the country from going through the door, but the *word*. The law is but a word, not a real being, and from this Kafka draws certain effects. In his diary, on November 6, 1913, we can read: 'Whence the sudden confidence? If it would only remain! If I could go in and out of every door in this way, a passably erect person. Only I don't know whether I want that.'[6]

The text is situated in a space where the distinction between reason and madness is impossible. We are in a paradox, where when we think one thing, the thing itself thinks the opposite of what we think that it thinks. What does it mean to be outside the law or to be in the law?

Let us take what Clarice called, in her novel with the same title, 'an apple in the dark'. We can imagine that it is a candle. With the 'apple in the dark', we go into the labyrinth. The first narrative of a series of interdictions is the story of Eve and the apple. The poor man from the country is before the apple, except that there is no apple. In Kafka, it is a question of differences. The story takes place between city and country, nature and culture, while knowing that the opposition never has an absolute value and that nature and culture are always in contact and in exchange. One has to shuttle back and forth between the enunciation – the statement – and the locus of reading.

Does the law come first? There is already an implicit paradox in the fact that the text begins with 'Before the law'. The text says it, and imposes on the reader a law that consists in making it impossible to put into question the existence of the law.

From the beginning, we are interpellated by the word 'law'. Kafka's genius is to put everything in place in the first three words. Then, with the man from the country, we are going to wait before the door and learn to be patient. We become old and deaf. We share the destiny inaugurated by the word 'law', while throughout the text, we are in a relation of desire along with the man who wants to enter the law. We are not supposed to ask him what the law is. The law is treated like a place one thinks one is going to enter. From the beginning, we are prohibited from going in, and from asking ourselves what it means to enter the law. The law is inscribed as spatialized, localized, even if it is so in an indefinite way. If, instead of 'law', I would say, with echoes of Clarice, 'before the apple', I would not be so crazy. But, in fact, I should say 'before the word'. Is the man before the law not already in the law? The man arrives, desiring to enter in the law. His desire already belongs to the law. It does not come while he desires to transgress the law. However, to want to enter into the law is transgressive. The man from the country is in this strange situation where from the moment he wants to enter in the law, he is not there. In order not to transgress the law, he has to remain in the immobile situation before the law. One has to want to enter. It is enough to become mad and deaf.

To whom does he address his desire to enter the law? To the guardian, to the *Türhüter*. Etymologically, *hüten*, 'to keep', is also *bewahren*, as in *wahr*, 'true'. The keeper is posted before the law in order to maintain its truth, in order to keep it for himself. One falls into a terrifying microscene where, as in every story, one finds oneself answering the question of the man from the country with: What do you want to know? But he does not know what he wants to know. This sends us back to a childhood scene: Why? – Because! What do you want to know? A cruel question, the answer to which is: I want to know.

What are the evident themes? The text begins with: 'Before the law stands a doorkeeper'. *Türhüter*, 'doorkeeper', is in one word, which doubles the effect of the keeper.

> To this doorkeeper, there comes a man from the country and asks for admittance to the Law.

The story takes place between two men, the doorkeeper and the man from the country who is marked by his origin. He will never get over coming from the country.

The text is in a glacial present tense that carries us into the level of something eternal, definitive: the text is the law.

But the keeper tells the man from the country that he cannot grant him entrance. The text is about entering. The door is not there, except in its composition with the keeper. The man asks to enter. It all remains very abstract.

The game of entering and not entering which will be solved with a 'You have not entered!' reminds us of the Biblical exclusion from paradise, an echo of which is going to be played out again in the story of Moses, who loses something before entering. You will not enter into the Promised Land because you were not already there, or, to put it another way: You would not look for me, if you had not already found me. This is the reassuring motto of the Christian quest. Judaism is much more tragic. Christ came and he remains to be found. Moses' law is: you will not enter because you are not in it. The man from the country is Moses' imperceptible double. 'You will not enter into the Promised Land' promises negatively and positively. It promises that he will not enter, but it promises the earth. Moses, contrary to the man from the country, saw it from a distance. It is a story to be put side by side – though at opposite ends – with Moses' story.

The keeper does not tell the man from the country that he will not enter. It is less a question of entering into an outside than into an inside that is difficult. There are three points of view: that of the man from the country, Kafka's, and ours. In his diary, Kafka lets us know that he insists on 'entering'. Nothing is inscribed in a nonparadoxical way. The entrance is not that of Moses. It is not a question of entering into a forbidden place, because that would be related to desire. But we do not know if there is an inside. In an arrested and terrifying movement, reducing the space between the two men, the text relates that there is no inside. It is the story of a man and the law. Perhaps the drive to enter is similar to that of wanting to enter the body of the mother. But the similarity is at the level of the drive only, because the object is not feminine. The law, *das Gesetz*, in German is neuter and we have to stay with the word.

The relation between the two protagonists, described in concrete terms, is going to last a lifetime. The positions of the bodies are important. The keeper, described physically with his fur coat, is before the law in such a way that he has the law behind him. The man to whom the keeper assigns a place before the door, on a little stool – an inverse description of the Oedipal enigma – arrives upright, then sits down, shrivels up, and finally reverts back to childhood, even from the point of view of language. He does not know if darkness is inside or outside. But he recognizes a glorious glimmer, somewhat of a contradiction, that eternally shines forth from the door of the law. Here we have a key for the use of tenses. The man is in eternity.

'Now he does not have very long to live' is paradoxical. If he sees eternity, is he still alive? These two sentences hint at the question of mortality and immortality. At the moment of 'nun lebt er nicht mehr lange (now he does not have much longer to live)', there is no more separation between life and death. The sentence tells us that we are already in eternity. All is concentrated in the one and only question he did not ask. The man is already in a state of rigor mortis and his body is stiff. The difference in size between the two is modified to the disadvantage of the man from the country.

What do you want to know? You are insatiable.

The man's essence is insatiability.

All aspire to the law. How is it that all these years, no one has asked to go in?

The man himself happens to enunciate the law as a universal utterance. And he obeys the law. One can ask the question of what he asked himself without asking the question. He is at the end of his life. Am I the law myself? Perhaps only I asked to go in. What anguish! And what if he made a mistake? He is going to die reassured.

The keeper recognizes that he is already at the end.

Not only because he goes out like a flame but because he did ask the final question. He approached the truth of the law in the very terms of the law: If everyone, then why me alone? He is crossing the extreme limit. The following question can be asked only if there is still some breath left: Did I make a mistake? This would question the scene of the law, which cannot be separated from the law. Worse, perhaps, he could not say: If there is only I, then I am wrong because truth is universal. But where could the error be? In the door, in the moment, in the keeper?

There has been no doubt until now, but it occurs with the *doch* (but). The keeper recognizes that the man is going to die, for one cannot doubt the law during one's lifetime. One cannot doubt death, since one is no longer here to doubt it.

> The doorkeeper recognizes that the man has reached his end, and, to let his failing senses catch the words, roars in his ear: 'No one else could ever be admitted here, since this gate was made only for you. I am now going to shut it'.

The man from the country arrives and the keeper leaves: 'I am now going to shut it [*ihn*]', that is to say, the entrance. He can only close the entrance, since there is nothing inside. The *ihn*, 'it', is the key to the text. It means that the keeper himself cannot say anything about the inside. He cannot say but what he knows, that is to say, the entrance.

I come back to the main threads of interpretation.

At the level of the dilemma that can be read throughout the text, we begin to see in the last conversation that the law is forbidden. It prohibits because it is prohibited. What the man wants to know touches on the law itself. It is prohibited like everything that is inaccessible or unapproachable. This paradox can be found in everything of the order of defense. There is no gesture of defense that does not have this kind of ambivalence, that does not push toward the outside and the inside, that does not have this double trait: to defend toward the inside, while defending against the outside. From the very beginning, the movement of the text itself is: You will not enter. It is prohibited. There is a no-trespassing sign. The law prohibits and is prohibited.

But the secret of the law is that it has no material inside. The text is diabolical and puts down the law of the reader. One cannot contest that one is before the law, even if one does not know it. The law cannot be defined. It is neither man nor woman. It is known only as a verbal construct and is designated to come and go, in relation with a concrete object, be it the apple or the mother's body.

The imperceptible *tour de passe-passe* (sleight-of-hand) of this text is that it begins with a keeper and it ends with: 'This door was only meant for you.' Hence, I, the keeper, was only for you, since there is not one without the other. In a very definite way, everything happened inside the man from the country.

The law especially defends its own secret, which is that it does not exist. It exists, but only through its name. As soon as I speak about it, I give it a name and I am inside Kafka's texts. The law is before my word. It is a verbal rapport. The entire force of the law consists in producing this scene so that it be respected. How? The police force is concrete and we are on the side of the state. 'Before the Law' is a story of symbolization in relation to the unconscious since it does not have recourse to the police force. From the beginning, we have a mechanism that says: It is possible, but not now. The text raises the question of a narrative instance. Like Kierkegaard's Abraham,[7] Kafka's man came to his rendezvous with the law alone, with his provisions. The door is open. The system of repression is put in place. He leans forward to look inside but he does not see. We are not told this because the keeper begins to speak. The man thinks the law. The reality of the law is in the keeper who acts and prohibits. Hence, he also institutes the possibility of transgressing. The scene is comical. The keeper is seen like the father in *Portrait of the Artist*: he is hairy, with a beard and a long nose. The keeper opposes the man's desire verbally and there is no bodily struggle. 'You can enter if you want', translated into elementary Freudian terms would read: 'If you want, you can.' But Kafka would say: I can but do I want to? I can go in and out of all the doors but am I sure that I want to? Kafka expressed it as a desire, but a split desire. The man from the country desires himself as wanting. True desire is: I can and I want. The keeper's presence splits the man's desire into: If only I could want what I want. This is the instance of the law. Nothing prevents me, except the law transformed into the self. I, the law. That is what psychoanalysis calls the superego, which is an inner instance. The law is *in* the man so how can he enter the law? The law is the divided desire inside him. There are antidotes to this; for example, apples and oranges à la Clarice.

In Kafka's text, there is a monstrous opening without inside. Something has to be opened. If the law existed, the man would have entered. The stakes of his desire were situated between the opening and closing of something that does not take place. The entrance is the very step the man does not take. He did not come to enter but in order to ask for entrance. But the law is truly a French *pas*, which is both a step and its annulment, a step-not. It opens or closes. Everything happens in relation to an originary given, to the law of the law: I exist. The definition of the law can unfold only in relation to the question of the origin of the law. In order to get out of Kafka's text, we must ask: Where does the law come from? and not think that it has always been there.

Blanchot, *The Writing of Disaster: Nothing Is What There Is*

In Blanchot's *Writing of Disaster* there is also an important primal scene. Blanchot, Kafka's phantom and vampire, preys upon the latter incessantly. However, he distilled something and pushed the Kafkaesque dilemma toward an algebraic formulation. Blanchot, who is not without psychoanalytic knowledge, has a different style. The passage I chose to read on page 72 is taken up again on page 114.[8] The second version becomes a remainder through a kind of explosion, or decomposition, hence through a kind of analysis. The scenes could be juxtaposed, critically, to Clarice's text 'Sunday, before falling asleep'. The second, exploded version contains certain small motifs that are like signifying, partial objects, for example, a tree, reminiscent of what we read in Clarice's story. We can distinguish between common and differential elements in both texts and make a kind of montage with the different images of the body. In Blanchot, a child is standing upright while lifting the curtains, and looks out of the window. In Clarice's 'Sunday, before failing asleep', the child is in bed, looking out of the window. In a system of relations between body and self, self and world, there are differences and similarities. In the first version of the primal scene, Blanchot directs himself to 'You who live later'. With Blanchot, everything is always posthumous. The scene reads:

(A primal scene?) *You who live later, close to a heart that beats no more, suppose, suppose it: the child – is seven years old, or eight perhaps?* (translation modified)

'Suppose it' refers to the heart. But afterward, there is a colon. And then there follows the child. The text is being organized around the child and the heart. There is a masculine, grammatical chain with le (the and it). However, Blanchot does not say 'the boy'. The originary scene takes place when the child is about seven or eight years old (hence late), but the child, masculine and not masculine, is still on the side of a certain neuter.

What happens then: the sky, the same sky, suddenly open, absolutely black and absolutely empty, revealing (as though the pane had broken) such an absence that all has since always and forevermore been lost therein – so lost that therein is affirmed and dissolved the vertiginous knowledge that nothing is what there is, and first of all nothing beyond.

The short text, located in the middle of *The Writing of Disaster*, is also the heart of the book. The entire book does nothing but retell this scene referring to the writing of disaster. We see here a disaster, as dis-aster (*dés-astre*), as that which is without *astres*, without stars.

'What happens then: the sky', has to be questioned at the syntactical or grammatical level. Of importance is the interpellation of the sky, a matrix that is disseminated in the whole paragraph. The sky, *le ciel*, by disseminating itself in expressions like *s'y est, s'y affirme*, signals its own annullment as '*s'y*'.

A primal scene always refers to the parental coitus. *Finnegans Wake* can be read as a primal scene. People do nothing but listen at doors while something is happening. Therefore we are voluntary or involuntary witnesses, something that is difficult to analyze, but a sign of destiny for us. The child is always in the position of a third, excluded term, behind doors or behind the window. There is usually a displacement toward the look, since in the originary scene, something not seen is given to be seen, or something that is not to be seen is staged.

Blanchot writes the scene with a question mark: 'A primal scene?' Is it or is it not? What is it? In Blanchot, something is happening that is nothing. We are at the limit of a 'happening', of presence and absence.

We have to recall the conceptual frame. In a classical analytic space, the discovery of the nothing takes place in a formidable scene for the child which is the impossible discovery of the mother's castration and the entire articulation of the mechanism that is going to be described in the constitution of fetishism. When one says 'the discovery that the mother does not have a penis', one already states it in a Freudian way. One discovers that she does not have something. Obviously that is not the way it is said in Blanchot. That would be too simple. It is not written in the form of lack. Very subtly, two coordinates are at work: the originary scene and the mother without a penis. All illusions have to be kept.

A theme, borrowed from Kafka, keeps recurring in Blanchot:

> *Absolutely black and absolutely empty, revealing (as though the pane had been broken) such an absence that all has since always and forevermore been lost therein.*

The utterance is paradoxical. There is not nothing, there *is*: nothing. At the end of the text, if, as Blanchot suggests, the flood is infinite, what does the reader do with 'He will weep no more'? Is it to be read as an opposition? No, because the flood is not of the same nature as in 'He will weep no more'.

According to Freud, it is from the discovery of the absence of the mother's penis that fear of castration and masculinity are constituted. Something is being symbolized where there is interiorization of the threat of castration and resistance to castration. Something is being symbolized there. Resistance to castration is often figured in the form of petrifaction, as in the story of Medusa. Here, in Blanchot, to the contrary, we have an infinite flood. It cannot not be heard on the side of femininity. On the side of masculinity, it could be heard as an endless ejaculation but that does not mean anything. Hence, it can be said that it is really a resistance to castration put in place by a kind of femininity.

'He says nothing. He will live henceforth in the secret. He will weep no more.' 'Says' is a present to be questioned. Henceforth, he will live in secret, indefinitely. If one moves in the direction of writing, a lot can be said about the various floods and their drying up. 'He says nothing' and 'He will weep no more' are related to desiccation and can be associated with the secret. What is before the secret but helps keep it? He says nothing because he cannot. He is somewhat in the same situation as Kierkegaard's Abraham. What he has to say is unspeakable and inaudible. Beginning with the space of misunderstandings, on the side of the parents, he is being comforted for something that has no consolation. He is considered by others to be afflicted with grief, while he is submerged by joy. The experience he has had in the primal scene cannot be transmitted. Where does it lead? Either one is in the space of Abraham, on the side of the knight of the absolute, of the unique experience – hence we cannot understand either, and that is part of the paradox – or one is prey to easy symbolization and the material constitution of the space of exclusion. In *Portrait of the Artist*, the scene is constituted ambiguously. The experience of the artist is not absolute but belongs to a level of communication. Artists are supposed to communicate, at least among themselves. Dedalus, for example, can communicate with the Ancient Fathers.

Most often we do not deal with the law but only with its representatives, its incarnations and figures. All of *Portrait of the Artist* occurs in a classical Oedipal space because there is someone who laid down the law for him who puts down the law. Generally we are before a hairy father and an aunt with brushes. But in life we encounter representatives of the law who are mistaken for the law because we do not look behind them. The force of Kafka's text is that he does not deceive the world. The first sentence reads, 'Before the Law . . . '. There is a representative of the law, hence we have an Oedipal scene and the space in which it is inscribed which begins with the law. But we do not see the law that is *behind* the text.

If we come back to Blanchot's primal scene in *The Writing of Disaster*, the look is related to respect for the law, to the nonvisibility of the law: 'Nothing is what there is' (72). It is also a story of respect. The child leads us through the window and into the garden:

> The child – is he seven years old, or eight perhaps? – standing by the window, drawing the curtain and, through the pane, looking. What he sees: the garden, the wintry trees, the wall of a house.

The child looks up toward the sky. The narrator sees what the child sees: nothing (*rien*). He sees the sky and then the same sky. He respects the sky, he looks (*re-garde*) in the sense of keeping, of appropriating the sky. In this text, which is a sequel, a kind of commentary on Kafka's 'Before the Law', what *happens* is that the child has seen the law. He has seen 'nothing'. He has seen the sky, absolutely black and absolutely empty.

> *The sky, the same sky, suddenly open, absolutely black and absolutely empty, revealing (as though the pane had broken) such an absence that all has since always and forevermore been lost therein – so lost that therein is affirmed and dissolved the vertiginous knowledge that nothing is what there is, and first of all nothing beyond.* (72)

This is what Blanchot wrote on the tomb of the man from the country who did not die seeing nothing, but who died of seeing 'Nothing'. He died from wanting to see something that was really nothing. And the child, not yet all shriveled up, at the age of seven or eight, pushed the keeper aside and looked. He saw the law, even the sky. Can one say that he did not die of it?

> *The unexpected aspect of this scene (its interminable feature) is the feeling of happiness that straightaway submerges the child, the ravaging joy to which he can bear witness only by tears, an endless flood of tears.*

He cannot be a witness other than through tears. He makes his testimony through his tears, through a kind of sexual gesture and also through writing, but a silent writing. He cannot bear witness through words because that is what the law does. 'An endless flow of tears ... he said nothing'. Is he dead or not from having seen nothing? He is like someone who does not live. He says nothing. He does not say 'nothing'. Silence, as we know, is the metaphor of death. 'Hence he will live in secret.' He keeps the secret and is kept secret. 'You who live in the future' is a reading among many. All this to say that in a certain way it is possible to see the law. I need a basket full of quotation marks not to be, henceforth, in the secret of the law which is ordinary, black, absolutely empty, and which is nothing. But Blanchot's child is a masculine child. For him, there is not nothing but nothing is what there is.

If I go back to Kafka, I read: 'Now he has not very long to live'. The short sentence cannot be replaced. He comes from the country and is insatiable. But let us go back to a general philosophical territory. On a philosophical level, the text is about respecting the law as an expression of the moral law, or of the law as moral. If the man had wanted, he could have entered. He would have transgressed but obeyed the law in a different, negative way. But he does not and thus puts down the law for himself. He decides to wait to receive permission, instead of granting it to himself, something he could have done. The mechanism of the law is to ask us to lay down the law. If we do not, as we can read in Joyce, 'the eagles will come and tear out our eyes'.

One arrives at something enormous, unthinkable. One knows nothing about the law. One can only respect the law, that is, be content with knowing nothing. All human beings have been exposed to this. Not to know anything is difficult. By definition, humans, children of cows, as Joyce tells us, are curious about the origin, about the inside, the belly. Hence the importance of the gaze in relation to the body. The body starts close to the ground then gets up and looks into the distance, toward the inaccessible. It occupies a moral position. But it is also the body's erect position that plunges us into the abyss of the sky. The law is related to *non-savoir*, to not-knowing, but the originary scene is related to a desire to know. Curiosity is a feminine fault because men who respect themselves do not have that vice. The man from the country had this kind of feminine curiosity. Respect implies a distance from the law. The trace of femininity in the man is that he *wants* to know. He does not, since he is from the country, respect the unthinkable fact that nothing is what there is to know. He thinks – and this is rather comical – that there is something. He *imagines* the law which means that he is always outside the law. He has always wanted to see God face to face, as if God had a face. The supreme respect, the pure law, would be more than to accept. It would be not to know in Christian terms, but to be in a kind of quiet knowledge, without feeling anxiety.

If we are like the child, and look from the tomb of the unhappy man, we see the sky. Blanchot writes in the perspective of a certain knowledge, with a memory of philosophical and psychoanalytic references. The text can be read as a metaphor of a primal scene. And the sky is empty, absolutely black. It cannot not be put in relation with a traditional background that surrounds the dilemma of the moral law the way it has been analyzed, unfolded in texts by Kant and taken up again by Heidegger.[9] We have to recall Kant's sentence dealing with the origin of the moral law. He writes his own relationship to the moral law as the starry sky above his head and the moral law in his heart. This produces feelings of moral respect. Admiration and fear produce a moral feeling of respect. What is extraordinary in Kant is the mention of the starry sky.

In *The Writing of Disaster* Blanchot writes of a sky without stars. It is the critique, the passage to the limit of the Kantian or Freudian moral, but it is not at all immoral. Blanchot's strength is to have said not just 'the sky', but the '*same* sky', 'absolutely black' and 'absolutely empty'. It is a kind of philosophical profession or a poetics of atheism. What he sees is of such absence that 'everything has always lost itself in it and has been lost forever'. If, for example, he had seen the stars – because Blanchot does not say that he sees God, he is not mad, he is a philosopher, hence he sees something sublime. If he had seen the stars or a satellite, if he had had an Einsteinian vision or if he *had* seen God, the world would have had its limit. Of course, what he sees is, as he says, 'nothing'. Henceforth he will have to live knowing that there is nothing beyond. He tolerates what is intolerable for the human imagination, that is to say the absence of limit, or of limiting transcendence. Why is this despair? We all know that civilization, limits and laws, are practical. We need them. If the law is not imposed on us, we have to impose it on ourselves. Is it possible not to lay down the law for ourselves? In other words, can we live without law, and if so, what does it mean?

One has to begin with the first three words in Kafka's story. In fact, we do not think, say, or articulate anything that is not 'before the law'. In banal psychoanalytic terms, one would say that it is symbolization, in the name of the father, that is the law.

Philosophy, psychoanalysis, have worked on the history of the origin of the law, of morals. Freud studied these problems in texts that are at the basis of his whole edifice, like *Totem and Taboo*. Kant produced a gigantic work on this question: Where does the moral law, outside the police and the armies, come from? He worked philosophically, pre-analytically, in a passionate search, and arrived at an impasse because he was not a theologian. For him the law was not given by Moses and the moral law did not depend on God. It had to be in relation with a finite human being.

He arrives where we would also arrive if we followed the path of reason. Going back from generation to generation, we arrive at Adam and Eve and there everything breaks down. Every time one breaks down with Kant, one ends with the aporia of: 'There is neither origin, nor beginning'. There is no first example; all is pure, immediate. And Kant's conclusion is well known: There is pure law, pure moral law.

There is a gap between Kant's and Kafka's texts. Kafka asked the real question of a law that was only for him, while Kant, turning like a rat in a labyrinth, had to send everything back into a reflexive mode. One cannot say that respect for the law is only intimate. The law is here to be respected the same way that radishes are here to be eaten. Kant turns in circles he can close only through a categorical imperative. For him, it is yes or no and those who say no will be decapitated.

Freud took up this problem and arrived at the same impasse. Working on the origins of the prohibitions upon which civilization is founded, he invented the story of the murder of the father, both a Freudian hypothesis and a phantasm. It is the murder of a very heavily symbolized father – Freud did not choose to explicate the original fault – which leads to the formation of the subject, subjectivity, and repression.

In *Totem and Taboo*, Freud tells a story that is forever unfinished. We barely come upon the father, and then upon the moral place of the father, and, quickly, we fall into remorse. Freud touches on fascinating and terrifying problems resembling Kafka's as well as Lispector's. From what moment on can we say that a gesture is bad? Generally, this is not asked since the law is affirmative. The law first designates something and then limits it right away. Freud is turning, interminably around the question: What if one says that the murder of the father is bad? He declares that at the origin there is the murder of the father. Then there is punishment, fault, guilt. But to feel guilt, one needs a feeling of guilt. Where does it come from? Freud cannot break out of the closure of guilt. Kafka and Blanchot do not leave it either. Explicitly, I have seen only Clarice Lispector produce utterances that do not deal with the law or what goes with it, that is, transgression. She does it, as we have seen, in the episode of theft by putting herself at the origin of what could be the law. She herself decides the value of such and such a gesture. She had the incredible strength to resist the ready-made in the world with its finished laws ordered by a system of moral values, hierarchized into good and bad. The ready-made laws are always hierarchized from an anthropomorphic point of view, instituting a god, then angels, men, women, animals, plants, always in a descending order. Clarice dehierarchizes. She does not accept that the law is systematically anthropomorphic. It is always andromorphic. Clarice takes as law, the law of the living. She takes it 'as' the law. Because there is an absolute without law, all depends on the content one puts into the word 'law'. Clarice infuses this word with a content completely subversive in relation to what has been transmitted by it since time immemorial. The secret of the law, of the categorical imperative, of the Oedipal prohibition, and of all the laws under which we live, is that there is no secret, there are no stars. If the law tricks us, it is because we internalized its interdiction. We are always inside the social, and history began before us with the law. We are inside the narrative of the law and we cannot help it. The law tells us a story. Is there an author? That is the question. Given a masculine consensus, I have to say that the author of the law, transmitted from father to son, is 'they'. Blanchot's story is exemplary. He saw that there was nothing. And since he was a boy, he died of it. After having shed all the tears in his body, he precipitated himself into the silence of the law and into the secret. And he has a lot to cry about. Kafka's man from the country kept on thinking that there was somebody or something inside. He thought there was an inside. Blanchot's little boy has seen nothing and does not betray. He obeys nothing. The horror of his fate is expressed in the last sentence: 'He will weep no more.' He sees that there is no transcendence. One cannot wait for the law to fall from the sky. He has to be autonomous and make someone lay down the law for him. There is, of course, something supreme, something difficult, that is to say, love, about which he says nothing. He leaves others with these illusions. He only knows that there is no starry sky, no sublime origin of morals. He says nothing and lies. He does not say anything of the truth but spares others. He keeps the secret for those who have not understood him yet, but his fate is sealed. He will not cry anymore because he has no grief. The sole passion of his life will have been this feeling of ecstatic happiness, once and for all. That is because in Blanchot, we stay in the space of the classical moral law and of the categorical imperative.

But there are always variants. In Kafka, it is not as clear as in Blanchot where it is written in a kind of a scintillating black and white. In Kafka, everything is very ambiguous. The man is insatiable and he still cries. A key for understanding is given too late. There are continuous slippages. It is either as if Kafka could not tolerate such cruelty or as if he told himself the story.

Clarice Lispector completely displaces the dilemma. She never did enter the world of the law as it is described here. This does not mean that she is absolutely without law. If we look at the different positions, we can say that where Blanchot discovers that there are no stars in the sky and that he is going to be his own executioner, he stays under the influence of the starry sky. But he does not even have the stars to console himself. He is in the enigma of human destiny, which is one of being in the law without knowing why. He is not an atheist, he is nontheistic. Like Freud and other men, he is still inside the closure.

Without theorizing, Clarice Lispector says that there are no laws other than those imposed on us by institutions, religion, morals. At seventeen, she already writes that she is going to stay far from this kind of thinking. She says in *Near to the Wild Heart* that it is bad to steal if one steals while being afraid. It is bad to steal inside the law. She refers stealing back to the word with its negative connotation. To steal without fear is not to steal at all. She is not on the side of delinquency but, to the contrary, on the side of a critique of metaphysics. This is carried to its extreme refinement in *The Passion according to G.H.* In *The Passion*, we can read her legal tablets. They are those of another law. This means that without being regressive, there can be another law, of the order of the living. Clarice is neither mad nor under an idealistic or aesthetic illusion. She fully recognizes the death drive. She deconstructs. She is neither crazy nor idealistic. She does not reject a current vocabulary but goes through it. That is why, in *The Passion according to G.H.*, there is a step-by-step deconstruction of morals and of metaphysics. Otherwise she would be in magic or in madness. But she says – and this is why her gesture is so important – that we are not hysterical, or mad, or anything at all, if we do not legitimate the system of moral laws that is in reality already a system of political laws upon which civilization, as Freud had described it, is founded. One has a choice between the moral law, the asylum, or being asocial. Or one can have recourse to another logic altogether. Where morals are concerned, everything has always been done in the name of reason and reason did not fall from the sky. It is the very discourse of half of humanity. But one can have another reason, another logic. One can have interest in something that again does not interest half of humanity. There is a kind of creation of the world, a cosmos having nothing to do with the classical creation that is immediately hierarchized. Clarice obeys the laws of the living, of pleasure, in a very realistic mode. She never ignores the limit, death or pain. She is not a partisan of excess. She embodies another economy. That is what is of interest to women. One can ask the question of why this happens and why half of humanity continues to be caught in the vicious circle described so remarkably by Kant and Freud. Why do they say that everybody thinks that way, and why do they include everyone? Is there really something else, something that could be called feminine and that disengages itself from the Kantian or Freudian structure? One has to come back once more to the old question of libidinal economies. All morals must go back to these questions. There is such an attachment to the moral law and to what it may represent as cruel, intolerable, rationalizing, including the imposition of all that is nonexistent, such as 'nothing is what there is'. Such an economy is in relation with a certain need, for if it were not it would be inexplicable. For most men it is not possible to think, to want, to desire a life that would not be structured by the moral law and by its functioning of prohibition that supports sublimation, restriction, immobility, and all that can be seen in Kafka's text.

I said that the system of putting a keeper in front of the law the secret of which is life, the secret of which is that there is no secret, is symbolized perfectly in the scene where a sentence is placed like a legend to a vignette. There would be a legend before the apple that says: 'You will not go in.' It is the other side of the law because if you touch, you will discover that the apple has an inside and that it tastes good. You will go over to a pleasure that goes through the mouth. Such a feminine libido is stronger than anything and Eve will go in. The law in Kafka says: 'You will not enter', because if you do, you will discover that I do not exist. One has to do everything so that the law will be respected, so that one stays in front of the word, so that the word will be the law, as it says in all the books. But it has to be a ruseful law because there are always men from the country with a little bit of femininity who feel like going in to see nevertheless. But the word is always stronger. That is why men were believers and women were witches. Something happens constantly at the level of the body that is related to libidinal economies. True, men know how to sublimate, they have a libidinal interest in sublimation, and women do not. That is where we women have our political problems. These are real differences. There is something of the other that cannot be transmitted unless there is a political revolution such that a masculine man will let go of his phallic position and accept, even without understanding, the possibility of something else.

Notes

1   Clarice Lispector, *Perto do coraçao selvagem* (*Near to the Wild Heart*) (Rio de Janeiro: Livraria Francisco Alves, 1943), p. 163. All translations mine, with the help of Claudia Guimarães; further references are indicated in the text.
2   James Joyce, *A Portrait of the Artist as a Young Man* (New York: Viking

Press, 1969); further references are indicated in the text. [Cixous's reading deals especially with the opening passage, pp. 7–10. (Trans.).]

3 See 'Sunday, before falling asleep', in Hélène Cixous, *Reading with Clarice Lispector*, ed. and trans. Verena Andermatt Conley (Minneapolis: University of Minnesota Press, 1990).

4 'Fort' ('gone') and 'da' ('there') are supposedly the 'words' that Freud's grandson uttered while playing a 'game' in his cot: tossing away a reel of thread, the child would say 'fort'; then, on drawing it back, he would say 'da', appearing to be happy. For Freud, the game was a way of acting out the child's traumatic experience of his mother's frequent absences, since it involved a terrifying loss of mastery ('fort') counterbalanced by the reassuring pleasure of always being able to regain control ('da'). From this (already an act of massive speculation) Freud speculates that the 'fort-da game' is indicative of human cultural life generally, showing that our time is spent in warding off the death-drive (absolute loss of control, 'fort') by means of the pleasure-principle (absolute self-gratification and hence self-mastery, 'da'). Without the freedom to express 'da', in other words, we would be utterly captive to the self-destroying effects of external forces (a parent who comes and goes, despite how we might feel about it; a social institution which demands our self-denial by insisting we conform to standard – impersonal – rules of self-comportment; and so on). But of course it is only in relation to the threat of losing our self-mastery ('fort') that such 'freedom' has any meaning. See Sigmund Freud, *Beyond the Pleasure Principle*, vol. XVIII of *The Standard Edition of the Complete Psychological Works of Sigmund Freud*, trans. and ed. James Strachey (London: Hogarth, 1986), pp. 7–64. On the pleasure principle and other aspects of Freudian psychanalysis, including discussion of a paper by Strachey, see my *PomoIntro*, esp. pp. 2-7. (NL)

5 Franz Kafka, 'Before the Law', in *The Complete Stories*, ed. Naham N. Glatzer (New York: Schocken, 1983), pp. 3–4.

6 Franz Kafka, *The Diaries, 1910–13*, ed. Max Brod, trans. Joseph Kresh (New York: Schocken, 1948), p. 30.

7 The nineteenth-century Danish philosopher Sören Kierkegaard was extremely fond of retelling, again and again, the biblical story of Abraham. See, for example, his *Fear and Trembling*, vol. VI of *Kierkegaard's Writings*, trans. H. Hong and E. Hong (Princeton: Princeton University Press, 1983), esp. pp. 9–14. On Kierkegaard's several Abrahams, as well as many other Abrahams, see John D. Caputo, *Against Ethics: Contributions to a Poetics of Obligation with Constant Reference to Deconstruction* (Bloomington: Indiana University Press, 1993). (NL)

8 Maurice Blanchot, *L'écriture du désastre* (Paris: Gallimard, 1980), pp. 117 and 176; *The Writing of Disaster*, trans. Ann Smock (Lincoln and London: University of Nebraska Press, 1986), pp. 72 and 114–15.

9   See especially Immanuel Kant, *Grounding for the Metaphysics of Morals* [Ger. 1785], trans. James. W. Ellington (Indianapolis: Hackett, 1981); *Critique of Practical Reason* [Ger. 1788], trans. Lewis White Beck (New York and London: Garland, 1976); and *The Metaphysics of Morals* [Ger. 1797] trans. Mary J. Gregor (Cambridge: Cambridge University Press, 1991). On morality as indistinguishable from metaphysics, see Martin Heidegger, *An Introduction to Metaphysics*, trans. Ralph Manheim (New Haven: Yale University Press, 1959) and also his 'Letter on Humanism', in *Basic Writings*, ed. David Farell Krell (New York: Harper & Row, 1977), pp. 193–242. (NL)

Part Three **Cyber**

Chapter Nine **Watching the Detectives**

Kristin Ross

I

the literature which concerned itself with the disquieting and threatening aspects of urban life was to have a great future ... Walter Benjamin

In his last work, *The Politics of Modernism* (1989), Raymond Williams proposes a history of modernism constructed through different experiences of exile and emigration. By concentrating on the social formations of modernist artists, their lived experience of isolation and *dépaysement* in the transnational capitals of the new imperialism, he locates the decisive factor of modernism in the experience of the metropolis on form and language: 'Their self-referentiality, their propinquity and mutual isolation all served to represent the artist as necessarily estranged, and to ratify as canonical the works of radical estrangement.'[1]

Certainly the modernist geographic trajectory of Rimbaud, a poet Williams doesn't mention, would seem to fit his argument: moving first from the provinces (the 'accidental forests' as he called them) to Paris, Rimbaud's preliminary migration prepares that even greater geographic displacement: from the metropolis to the colonies. Yet his final works offer something closer to a prophecy of Williams's argument. In one of his last poems, an *Illumination* entitled 'Démocratie', Rimbaud parodies the speech of a mobile and imperialistic bourgeois class, expanding out

Kristin Ross, 'Watching the Detectives', in *Postmodernism and the Re-Reading of Modernity*, eds Francis Barker, Peter Hulme and Margaret Iversen (Manchester and New York: Manchester University Press, 1992), pp. 46–65.

from the capitals to the 'languid, scented lands', feeding. as the poem says, 'the most cynical whoring', and 'destroying all logical revolt'. The *Illuminations* stand on the brink of the forward movement of late nineteenth-century European spatial hegemony; in them Rimbaud foresees the culmination of that movement in, as he puts it in one poem, a 'little world, pale and flat', or in 'the same bourgeois magic wherever your baggage puts you down'. Many of the *Illuminations* can be read in the light of a prophetic denunciation of that compact but undifferentiated space that would soon become the globe. Others – I'm thinking here of poems like 'Métropolitain', 'Barbare' and 'Soir historique' – serve as exemplary illustrations of the many ways in which the middle-class imagination seeks to intoxicate itself with apocalyptic images of its own death. In a panoramic vision Rimbaud presents the cancelled future of a vanished colonial and imperial destiny: crystal and fantastic cityscapes rejoin ancient prefigurations of the end of the world in geological cataclysms of exploding ice and flame; intertwining webs of bridges and highways lie flanked by barbarian tribes; a recurring planetary apocalypse, at once polar and fiery. How can the future be imagined after the demise of the Commune? Perhaps nothing less than an apocalyptic reversal of the forward colonizing movement of 'Démocratie' is sufficient: a cataclysmic break in the continuum of history that can only be figured in the late poems as the earth exploded, as frozen or crystallized cities. Having lived the first great experiment in revolutionary urbanism and its bloody demise, faced now with the 'swamp', as he called it, of the French middle classes consolidating the colonial impetus that would propel them through the next several decades faced, that is, with a class that resists and continues to resist precise analysis and precise representation, Rimbaud chooses to prefigure both the triumph and the death of that class in a series of fantastic and futuristic prose-poems (imagery courtesy of Jules Verne) – the triumph of that class in a progressive, virtually postmodern *planification* of the planet, its death in an exploded earth. No longer able to *represent* the middle classes as he had done in his earlier, satirical Charleville poems, he instead *spatializes* their global image. And something like the global ('transnational capitals as an art without frontiers'[2] or universal was certainly, according to Williams, the political and cultural scope modernism set for itself. In his most concise formulation, Williams defines modernism as 'the metropolitan interpretation of its own processes as universals'.[3]

If we take Williams' definition of modernism as our own, what then has changed, if anything, in the move to postmodernism? To what extent is postmodernism a continuation of, rather than a significant break with, 'the metropolitan interpretation of its own processes as universals?' Or do postmodern urban intellectuals and artists no longer interpret their own processes as universals? Has the nature of the metropolis changed, so that the city is no longer central, no longer a point of origin? Or is the shift rather one in the international balance of cultural power, a shift in dominant cities – Los Angeles, say, taking the place of Paris – but still continuing a modernist, universalizing project? To what extent is postmodernism (including the *theorizing* of postmodernism) synonymous with Americanization, its particularity based on the difference in urban 'structures of feeling' experienced in North American versus European cities?

Williams and Rimbaud are not the first to analyse the privileged temporal language of modernism in terms of world realignment, nor to show that the nineteenth-century European middle-class discovery of – and obsession with – time and history, was at one and the same time its production of space as colonial space. Williams is not the first to approach modernism spatially – that is, to use the analytic tools and co-ordinates we have learned to associate with *post*-modernism. Walter Benjamin provided the most influential version of French modernism by meditating on the role of lyric poetry and the emergence of the detective story – a genre which takes as one of its principal tasks the representation of the ordinary, everyday entanglement of people with their surroundings – in the modernist capital of Paris. Commenting on Williams's affinity to Benjamin, Tony Pinkney writes that 'Modernism can now be located, not on the "inside" of its self-validating ideologies nor in the "outside" of a political trauma of the order of 1848, but in the *intermediate zone of urban experience* . . . in a "structure of feeling" that has not yet assumed the relatively formalized shape of aesthetic doctrine or political act.'[4] It was precisely by raising to the status of a concept such an 'intermediate zone of urban experience' or ('everyday life' as he called it) – that Henri Lefebvre [see note 21] arrived at his own conception of the modernist period.

My interest in writers and theorists who approach modernism through a primarily spatial perspective has its counterpart in a preference for contemporary writers who confront, engage directly with the problem of history, whose work, in some sense, tries to 'save the narrative'. I think it is important at this point to work towards recasting the productive but now hardened-into-stone opposition that has resulted from the periodizing of postmodernism – an opposition variously conceived as the present moment's general substitution of spatial coordinates for the privileged temporal coordinates (the lags and anticipations, the deferrals, the promise of future reconciliations) of modernism; or, the society of consumption (production organized for a market) replacing a society of production; with its concomitant replacement of the political figure of the citizen by today's figure of the quotidian: the consumer. We must begin to determine the ways in which such a periodization may in fact obscure, not illuminate reality. For such a reified opposition in fact takes the point of view of consumption, thereby masking the relations of production that have by no means disappeared in contemporary society. It ignores the fact that industrialization remains the primary propulsive force in development everywhere in the world, and it often denies the contradictions that arise from an increasingly international division of labour. 'From time to time events of the moment', as Jacques Rancière points out, 'make it all too clear that nine-tenths of humanity, or a little more, suffer from what postmodernism has long since moved beyond: archaic stories of hunger, of faith, and of the people.'[5]

The overemphasis on consumption issues has also had baleful effects on much of recent cultural studies intent on charting the 'dominant cultural logic of postmodernism' within an ever more narrowly conceived present moment. Often taking the form of a kind of catalogue or 'shopping list' of current cultural and consumer practices or images, these studies have rapidly become symptomatic of the very practices they seek to analyse – precisely, some would argue, the postmodernism effect (or trap) itself. For postmodernism, as writers like J. G. Ballard began to inform us in the early 1970s, is about the effacement of history, the loss of the past, the inability to conceive of a before or beyond to the vast condominium or shopping mall of Being:

> Just as the past itself, in social and psychological terms, became a casualty of Hiroshima and the nuclear age (almost by definition a period where we were all forced to think prospectively), so in its turn the future is ceasing to exist, devoured by an all voracious present. We have annexed the future into our own present, as merely one of those manifold alternatives open to us. Options multiply around us, we live in an almost infantile world where any demand, any possibility, whether for lifestyles, travel, sexual roles and identities, can be satisfied instantly.[6]

Postmodernism is a conceptualization of the present that seeks to historicize the effacement of the historical – thus, in some ways eternalizing itself, freezing the movement of time. An enormous sense of 'period' competition or envy must be at work here – generated, no doubt, by the extraordinary success of modernism. For modernism was a period so powerful that it was able to make all of the rest of history nothing but its own precedent or antecedent. The least postmodernism can do is become eternal.

II

You cannot have art without a public taste and you cannot have a public taste without a sense of style and quality throughout the whole structure. Curiously enough this sense of style seems to have very little to do with refinement or even humanity. It can exist in a savage and dirty age, but it cannot exist in the Coca-Cola age ... the age of the Book-of-the-Month and the Hearst press. Raymond Chandler

In 1970, while living and teaching in southern California, Fredric Jameson published an essay – his first about American literature – on detective novelist and Hollywood screenwriter Raymond Chandler. I want to consider 'On Raymond Chandler' at some length, for it contains many elements – a fascination with Los Angeles, a reflection on nostalgia, a concern with periodization, a centrality given to the category of reification and to the figure of Warhol – that would resurface in what remains the most important and influential theorization of postmodernism, Jameson's widely read 1984 essay, 'Postmodernism, or the Cultural Logic of Late Capitalism'.[7] In fact Chandler, in the first essay, becomes the vehicle for Jameson to talk about what he really wants to talk about: a set of cultural phenomena that had not yet been theorized as the postmodern.

At a moment in the history of literary studies when allusion to biographical data about an author was singularly unfashionable, Jameson begins the essay by underscoring two facts about Chandler's life: that he worked for fifteen years as an oil company executive in Los Angeles before beginning writing, and that he spent his childhood and adolescence in England. The essay in its entirety builds on the opposition suggested by the two phases of Chandler's life: European art, writes Jameson, is 'metaphysical and formalistic', while 'any picture of America is bound to be wrapped up in a question and a presupposition about the nature of American reality.'[8] America, then, is situated on the side of realism, and, moreover, on the side of a reflection about the nation, a particularly

American reality.

To situate America on the side of realism is firmly in keeping with the object of Jameson's study, for it was Chandler's well-known essay, 'The Simple Art of Murder', first published in 1949, that definitively established the opposition between the formal, game-playing ratiocination of the classical, generally British detective story, its 'mechanical', 'artificial', 'superficial' aspects, versus the 'authenticity', 'reality', and 'life' of the American product, which strives for 'the authentic flavor of life as it is lived'.[9] In this essay, and throughout his letters, Chandler delights in the national stereotype: 'The English may not always be the best writers in the world, but they are incomparably the best dull writers.'[10] Because the English formula still, according to Chandler, 'dominates the trade', much of the energy of the essay is spent asserting the generic superiority of Hammett, and in establishing for him a national genealogy passing through Dreiser, Lardner, Anderson and Walt Whitman.

Jameson is less concerned with evaluative judgement. Rather, he uses Europe and European literature to provide a backdrop of social cohesion against which the atomized and fragmentary nature of American society can emerge. The well-known vertical social organization of Parisian apartment houses in Zola's *Pot bouille* provides the contrast for Los Angeles's horizontal urban sprawl. The episodic, 'picaresque' form taken by the detective's quest (duplicated, to a certain extent by Jameson's own form in 'On Raymond Chandler'; to a much greater extent by his form in the postmodernism essay), is explained by the centreless, fragmented city he moves through:

> In European countries people no matter how solitary are still somehow engaged in the social substance; their very solitude is social. . . . But the form of Chandler's books reflects an initial American separation of people from each other, their need to be linked by some external force (in this case the detective) if they are ever to be fitted together as part of the same picture puzzle. (p. 131)

Chandler's Los Angeles – its shabby rooming houses and hotel lobbies, its private clubs set back on long driveways in the hills, its gambling ships, its dry-out spas in the desert, its manzanita trees, its dingy office interiors, the juxtaposition of its clearly demarcated dreary and luxurious zones – all this is no mere background scenery to some more crucial drama unfolded on its stage: for Jameson the very *content* of Chandler's novels is a scenic one. The divided scenic content conjures up the figure of the detective, Marlowe, who alone can unite the disparate parts of the city into a social whole.

Many of Chandler's readers have described his Los Angeles as already 'dated'; his novels, set in the 1940s and 1950s, seem to unfold in an early 1930s Los Angeles of crime and power and money. Leigh Brackett, for example, author of the screenplay of *The Long Goodbye*, writes in 1969: 'The Los Angeles Chandler wrote about was already long gone.'[11] Jameson, however, writing at the same time, sees a more futuristic, prophetic Los Angeles in Chandler's books, one whose paradigmatic status of the country as a whole was already certain:

> But already the Los Angeles of Chandler was an unstructured city. . . . (p. 133)

> . . . his social content anticipates the realities of the fifties and sixties. For Los Angeles is already a kind of microcosm and fore-cast of the country as a whole: a new centerless city, in which the various classes have lost touch with each other because each is isolated in his own geographical compartment. (p. 127)

By a kind of accident then, Chandler's modernist detective finds himself in a postmodern city, one which forecasts the social organization of the country as a whole. By the 1980s, Jameson's Los Angeles would have an even greater paradigmatic power; its downtown, crowned by the Bonaventure hotel, would prophesy the vast new multinational hyperspace of postmodernism.[12] While Marlowe moved horizontally between the isolated class compartments, Jameson as postmodern critic stands above, high atop the Bonaventure tower, adopting a panoramic perspective that excludes the intricacies or conflicts of social relations surrounding the hotel: the communities of Central American immigrants nearby, the potentially *conflictual* urban geography of a post-Fordist political economy. The hotel for Jameson, denuded of its historical and geographic context, stands as symbolic icon of postmodernism: 'it [the elevator] gives us the chance at a radically different, but complementary, spatial experience, that of rapidly shooting up through the ceiling and outside, along one of the four symmetrical towers with the referent, Los Angeles itself, spread out breathtakingly and even alarmingly before us' (p. 83). But by adopting at once a more 'horizontal' and a more historical perspective, Mike Davis offers an important corrective to Jameson's iconic reading of the Bonaventure.[13] Davis's analysis highlights the dialectical and contradictory urban geography resulting from two separate macro-processes: the multinational accumulation of bank and real estate capital (Jameson's unique concern) and another, equally important: the reflux of low-wage manufacturing and labour-intensive services provided by unprecedented Central American mass immigration. Taking the latter into account undermines the cultural dominance of Jameson's postmodernism: 'The great Latino shopping streets – Broadway in Downtown and Brooklyn in Boyle Heights – have more in common with the early twentieth century city, with the culture of Ragtime than they do with a death-wish post-modernity.'[14]

Another point of conjuncture between Jameson's two essays occurs around the figure of Andy Warhol. A long section of the essay on Chandler deals with nostalgia; not with Chandler himself producing nostalgic writing, but rather with the taste for Chandler among contemporary readers being a nostalgic one. Chandler, Jameson writes, 'evokes a world similar enough to our own to seem very distant' (p. 141), and he argues this – in effect, a periodization of Chandler – by way of historicizing the relationship of consumers to the commercial object world. In this literary history, Chandler, with his 'stable products', his 'permanent industrial background which has come to resemble nature itself', lies somewhere between the inventive, creative energies of Balzac's manufactured objects and the fetishized nostalgia of Warhol's soup cans. (Chandler, then, is a true modernist, in accordance with Jameson's later tripartite periodization of realism-modernism-postmodernism.) But consider the difference between the Warhol who emerges in this essay and the Warhol of 1984:

> The Warhol image . . . [is] a fetish representing the will to return to a period when there was still a certain distance between objects . . . [it] is a way of making us stare at a single commercial product, in hopes that our vision of all those around us will be transformed, that our new stare will infuse *those also* with depth and solidity, with the meaning of remembered objects and products, with the physical foundation and dimensions of the older world of need. (p. 139, emphasis added)

The Warhol image here is endowed with depth and solidity; it entertains a powerful redemptive relation to the exterior world, both present and past. It instils desire in the viewer to extend the image's solidity to the object world around it; it is even capable of conjuring up a formerly meaningful, past, but still accessible, object world. In the 1984 postmodernism essay, however, Warhol's objects have lost any resonance to either a past world or to a context larger than themselves; they are no longer synechdochal:

> Here, however, we have a random collection of dead objects, hanging together on the canvas like so many turnips, as shorn of their earlier life-world as the pile of shoes left over from Auschwitz, or the remainders and tokens of some incomprehensible and tragic fire in a packed dancehall. There is therefore in Warhol *no way* to complete the hermeneutic gesture, to restore to these oddments that whole larger context of the dance hall or the ball, the world of Jetset fashion or of glamour magazines.[15]

Warhol in the 1980s represents 'the supreme formal feature' of post-modernism: 'the emergence of a new kind of flatness or depthlessness, a new kind of superficiality in the most literal sense.'

Whether or not it is true that the hermeneutic gesture can no longer be completed, it is clear that Jameson in the 1980s chooses not to complete it. In the Chandler essay, of course, the hermeneutic gesture is alive and well, embodied in the figure of Marlowe the detective, whose cognitive function, as we saw earlier, is rendered necessary by the proto-postmodernist space of Los Angeles:

> Since there is no longer any privileged experience in which the whole of the social structure can be grasped, a figure must be invented who can be superimposed on the society as a whole, whose routine and life pattern serve somehow to tie its separate and isolated parts together. . . . (p. 127)

Even the incorruptible, chivalric purity of Marlowe, his ability to circulate amidst the human detritus of Los Angeles without being in any way tainted by it, his solitary, heroic, and exemplary purity in the face of social corruption, that quality that Chandler (and Jameson) refer to as Marlowe's 'honesty', all this is granted by Jameson a purely cognitive, rather than moral, function: 'the honesty of the detective can be understood as an organ of perception', and:

> the detective in a sense once again fulfills the demands of the function of knowledge rather than that of lived experience: through him we are able to see, to know, the society as a whole, but he does not really stand for any genuine close-up experience of it. (pp. 127–8)

Is Marlowe then the functional equivalent of the 'cognitive cartographer' Jameson calls for at the end of the postmodernism essay – the cognitive cartographer who is none other than the essay's author himself? Can the figure of Marlowe help us understand Jameson's own ill-defined location within postmodernist culture? Marlowe is a modernist hero cut adrift in a postmodernist cut-and-paste world; ironic distance keeps the beautiful soul of the detective pure in a corrupt universe, a universe granted depth precisely by the detective's own ironic detachment from it. 'Down these mean streets', Chandler begins a famous passage describing his detective, 'a man must go who is not himself mean, who is neither tarnished nor afraid. . . . He is the hero, he is everything. He must be a complete man and a common man yet an unusual man. . . .'[16] Jameson's relation to his own attempt to 'tie the separate and isolated parts' of postmodernism together raises questions. Is Jameson's desire Marlowesque, that is, does he stand outside postmodernism to explain and judge it? And isn't this an impossible task under postmodernism, when, according to Jameson, all critical distance or perspective collapses? Where does this desire come from, the desire to 'give a genuinely historical and dialectical analysis' of a period defined by its sheer discontinuity and eradication of historical depth? It could not flourish, presumably, within the monolithic contours of postmodernism outlined by Jameson. Or could such a desire be nourished, as one critic suggests, 'by certain appositional forces alive within postmodernism',[17] residual or emergent forces Jameson chooses in this context to downplay ('one would want to begin to wonder a little more seriously about the possibilities of political or critical art in the postmodern period of late capital')[18] or to treat, as he has indeed done at great length elsewhere?[19] What very different account of postmodern cultural dominance would follow if the work on Third World literature was included in the panoramic perspective Jameson adopts here?

III

The work of Henri Lefebvre during the 1970s helped provide Jameson with his theory of postmodern space. It was Lefebvre who went so far as to proclaim the 'urban' or spatial particularity of our time to be no mere epiphenomenal or superstructural change, but rather proof of what recent economists like Alain Lipietz have designated as a decisive shift in the way capital is working, a transition in the 'regime of accumulation' and its associated mode of social and political regulation. During a mutually beneficial collaboration with the Situationists in the early 1960s, Lefebvre had begun to argue that in late capitalism practices of consumption act to legitimate and reproduce the system, regardless of an individual or group's particular beliefs or values.[20] Since the Second World War and the Marshall Plan in France, everyday life practices – and not abstract ideas or philosophies – had come to play the functional role of ideology. In a series of books written in the 1960s and 1970s (*La révolution urbaine* [1970]; *Le Droit à la ville* [1972]; *La Production de l'espace* [1974]), Lefebvre takes up his initial concept of everyday life and reworks it in spatial terms under the rubric of what he calls 'the urban'. The everyday, the urban, the production of social space become in his work a constellation of concepts recoding the same basic idea: that the reproduction of the social relations of production is the central and hidden process of capitalist society, and that this process is inherently spatial. The conflictual, lived contradictions of space, and not the economic in general, constitute the level at which neocapitalism is established.

What then has become of the diachronic, the historical, the dialectic in such a schema? The dialectic, effectively relegated to the dustbin of history by poststructuralism, has not, according to Lefebvre, disappeared. History, like politics, has not come to an end. The dialectic has simply been displaced – and it is this very displacement that informs what is new and paradoxical about our times.[21] No longer attached to temporality, no longer clinging to historicity or the temporal mechanics of thesis, antithesis, synthesis, the dialectic is to be resumed and recognized in the real, effective contradictions of space, in those lived, uneven developments that alone, for Lefebvre, have consequences – consequences like May 1968, which erupted, as he likes to remind us, in a suburban functionalized university *cité* constructed in the middle of *bidonvilles*.

Lefebvre begins by analysing the increasing 'planification' of space under capitalism as a movement toward global homogeneity – Rimbaud's prophetic 'same bourgeois magic wherever your baggage sets you down' – the unification of a planetary state system with centres or points of strength whose domination over peripheral weaker points serves to guarantee the production of homogeneity. Simultaneous with the move to homogeneity, though, is one of fragmentation: space is divided up like graph paper into autonomous, Taylorized parcels with distinct, localized functions. Fragmentation occurs when the historical big city of the nineteenth century – that defined and definite object – explodes in the twentieth. The urban is not the classical city-monster defined in opposition to village or rural life but rather the ghost of that city, what hovers along its outskirts; the 'urban', then, for Lefebvre, is closer to what others would call the suburban or periurban. For with the emergence of global space, the city, the cradle of accumulation, the locus of wealth, the subject of history, the centre of historical space, shatters, spawning in its wake a host of doubtful protuberances: *banlieux*, a vacation home, an autoroute, a supermarket or factory in the middle of the countryside, housing developments, *pavilions*, whole satellites of thickening small and medium-sized cities, semi-colonies to the metropolis. And amidst this motley accumulation, Lefebvre's third category of hierarchy comes to light, as an increasingly conscious and treacherous strategy divides this suburban space into more or less favoured zones, destined either for a great industrial and urban future, or for controlled, closely supervised decline. Guy Debord, writing at the same time, describes a similar movement:

> Economic history, which developed entirely around the city/country opposition, has succeeded to such a point that it has annihilated both terms at once. The contemporary *paralysis* of total historical development, at the profit of the sole pursuit of the independent movement of the economy, makes of the moment when city and country begin to disappear, not the *overcoming* of their division, but their simultaneous collapse.[22]

For Lefebvre the most important spatial contradiction of our time – and this is where his dialectical method resides, in the reading of spatial contradictions – can be detected in the deterioration of urban life that has accompanied the urbanization of society. The dominant class and the state act to reinforce the city as the centre of power and political decision, while the very dominance of that class and the state causes the city to explode. The boundary line is no longer to be drawn between city and country but *within* the urban phenomenon between a dominating centre and a dominated periphery: the eventual 'banlieuization' of a great part of the world, no less true in Paris than in the Third World, where peasants dispossessed as a result of the decomposition of agrarian structures pour into cities and constitute the *bidonvilles*, the shantytowns of Dakar, the *favellas*, the *ciudades perdidas* of Mexico City.

Lefebvre's discovery and analysis of this spatial structure in large part accompanied its production, at least in Paris. The decade between 1960 and 1970 marked a systematic and overt programme of Parisian urban renewal that led to a more and more pronounced social division of urban space. Between the years of 1954 and 1974 Paris underwent the demolition and reconstruction of 24 per cent of its buildable surface[23] – a transformation equivalent in scale to the better known and more fully analysed Hausmannian reconstruction of the city a hundred years earlier. As in the nineteenth century, when recently arrived provincial unskilled day labourers – the future Communards of 1871 – laboured on the urban renewal projects, thus constituting both the instruments and the main victims of the transformation, the 1970s projects employed a large percentage of recently arrived foreign immigrants as an 'instrument of manoeuvre' in the strategy of reconquest of central areas by the upper classes.[24] The government offered incentives to employers to move what industrial jobs remained in Paris to the *banlieux*, while the redevelopment of substantial areas of the city, notably the Place d'Italie, eliminated most of Parisian low-income housing, causing a steady forced migration of French and immigrant workers to the outer suburbs. Algerian independence played a significant role in the 'grands ensembles' boom in the early 1960s – the boom responded to the demands of a mass influx of *pieds noirs* into France and a simultaneous surge in immigration. By 1969 one in six inhabitants of the greater Paris region lived in a 'grand ensemble'.[25] Paris *intra-muros*, peopled by the upper and upper-middle classes, became more and more a power site at the centre of an archipelago of *banlieux* inhabited by mostly working-class people with the occasional wealthy enclave thrown in.

Substantial budgetary restrictions in the planning of the suburban communities became apparent in 1968, and many housing developments were halted in mid-construction, awaiting government subventions which all but categorically dried up after the 1973 economic crisis. Entire *cités* were left isolated and stranded in a state best described as half-built ruins, encircled by vague terrains that at one time were supposed to support an entire cultural and commercial infrastructure. The rusted carcasses of abandoned aeroglisseurs, and the supports for never-to-be-completed autoroutes in Nanterre and Gennevilliers testify to the endless deferment of a plan that never materialized: that of a transportational network that would link *banlieu* to *banlieu* without passing through Paris. Better to take the TGV to Lyons, as the saying goes in Paris, than the bus to Mantes-lajolie.

What are the generic options available to today's working artist that might best render the spatial dialectic described by Lefebvre, the particular kind of uneven development characteristic of our time of which the 'banlieu' is perhaps the exemplary locus? Is there a space within postmodernist culture for a consciously realist mode of writing, what Jameson calls 'genuine historicity', and a conception of space that is lived and historical? How, in other words, does the writer within postmodernism make history emerge – not, perhaps, so much a *representation* of history, easily subsumable into the special form of spectacle known as the 'lifelike reproduction', the 'image of the past' or the period piece', but rather something quite different and jarring, namely, the *concept* of history?

French writer Didier Daeninckx has published a number of detective novels throughout the 1980s in the French 'Série noire'. In the great Chandleresque division between the 'formulaic' and the 'authentic', Daeninckx, whose childhood reading veered between Aragon and American noir, has cast his lot with authenticity. His setting of choice, more fully realized in his books than in any I know of, is the irregular settlements, vague terrains, and experimental decaying *cités* of what Blaise Cendrars called in the 1940s the 'banlieu noire': the north-east Parisian periphery of Seine-Saint-Denis. What interests Daeninckx is the here and now of daily life in the *banlieux*; his gamble is that his French readership, who rarely if ever see that reality, can be tricked, so to speak, into encountering the intolerable effects of uneven development in their own immediate surroundings by the allure of a fairly traditional and suspenseful murder plot.

The real content of Daeninckx's work then, like that of Chandler's, is a scenic one: the reader's hermeneutic activity winds its way through ramshackle buildings thrown up in three months on hasty foundations, mazes of prefabricated cubes that will lose their air of newness after the first rains; through suburbs where the Municipal Council thought to soften the impression of misery people feel entering the sector by giving the streets the names of Brueghel (without saying which one), Picasso, Van Gogh and Rembrandt; through variously densely populated ruins:

> The *cité* République bordered the F2 highway. Its dozen or so buildings seemed to serve as an anti-noise screen for a recently constructed enclave of *pavilions*. The central building, designated B2, was a mass of 15 floors that sheltered at least 150 families. The orange and red frescoes covering the concrete walls didn't manage to confer on the mastodon the light and engaging allure desired by the decorator; the cells on the ground-floor, destined in some past life to welcome shops, had been transformed into so much debris, vague surfaces . . . the square entry hall with its alignment of elevator doors recreated rather faithfully the ambiance of a metro station. . . .[26]

The detective, Cadin, visits the parents of a victim who live:

> in Saint-Ouen, in a bizarre building with a facade made of gangways whose metallic handrails, when glimpsed from the péripherique, imitated the contours of automobiles. The city government had relocated them there after the patched-up pavilion they had practically built with their own hands was included in a zone destined for renovation. They had gotten used to it little by little, the dog much less so. He had become idiosyncratic and only pissed against the entry-hall wall.[27]

But these desolate terrains are not the only setting; often just a line of trees, or some other makeshift 'anti-noise' protector separates the workers' *cité* from the privileged zone of the *pavilions*, designed to make the most of the 'green world' fantasy of the suburbs: 'The Codman-Bret *pavilions*, named after their promoter, were grouped at the centre of the village, near the grade school and the shopping centre. Each of these houses disposed of a vast garden agreeably planted with trees and flowers.'[28] The detective in most of the stories, Cadin, is, like his continental predecessors Gaboriau, Le Coq and Maigret, a cop; but like Chandler's private detective Marlowe, Cadin's circuit takes him, often with dizzying rapidity, back and forth between the unevenly developed zones of the suburbs, between *bidonville* and *pavilion* – through him we have access to the social territory as a whole. The detective's function, his movements, show us that the separation between zones – what Lefebvre calls fragmentation – is at once *fictive* (for one cannot completely separate the functions even though each localized function is represented as being autonomous), and *real* (for all the parcels of space, with their functions divided and Taylorized like jobs in a factory, obtain and preserve an autonomy).

In *Lumière noire*, for example, transport police murder an airline worker by mistake and launch an elaborate cover-up that extends even to Africa. For the only witness to the murder may well be a Malian worker spending the night before his expulsion from France on the seventh floor of an airport hotel reserved for those purposes by the Bobigny prefecture and the Ministry of the Interior. Investigating the murder involves a tour of the suburbs surrounding the airport; it also retraces another *international* geographical axis: the transit connecting the *foyer immigré* of Aubervilliers and the outlying districts of Bamako in Mali – *quartiers* that have more in common than not.

In Daeninckx the detective moves frequently *between* declining and thriving areas: the juxtaposition occurs at both the urban (rich and poor suburbs) and the international (France and its former colonies) levels. And from out of this frequent displacement comes the solution to the murder, to the mystery: a *national* crime, an ancient fact successfully repressed, a past injustice whose contamination threads its way into the present. The detective's privileged access to spatial contradictions of the present allows history to emerge: not with the purpose of giving the French 'images' of their past – but rather to defamiliarize and restructure their experience of their own present.

Perhaps the most striking facet of Daeninckx's response to the postmodern crisis in narrative, is that in all of his novels the solution to the mystery rests on authentic facts, whether these be, in the case of *Lumière noire*, French Minister of the Interior Pasqua's 1986 decision to brutally deport hundreds of Malian workers, or, in his best novel, *Meurtres pour mémoiré* (1984), the Tienanmen Square-like 'disappearance' of the traces of the massacre of hundreds of Algerian demonstrators by the CRS in Paris in October 1961.[29] The contemporary murder masks a bloody, past crime, but the crime is not, as in the novels of Chandler or Ross Macdonald, a family affair, an Oedipal crime, a fictional, incestuous dirty secret: it is a *national* crime, an actual moment of French history the authorities – usually the police, zealous and not so zealous bureaucrats, and the Ministry of the Interior working in tandem – have gone to great lengths to bury.

Most popular mysteries, especially of the English variety, are devoted to solving rather than examining a problem. The detective is presented with a situation surrounded by misleading or ambiguous information; the story is an exercise in revolving ambiguity; the final scenes read with all the conclusive, reassuring clarity of *explanation*. The very *velocity* of the form, the feverish acceleration in pace of hermeneutic frenzy that plummets the reader head forward to the final moments demands a solid, reliable closure, a reaffirmation of some comforting order and stability in the world. In Daeninckx a different, longer temporality – deep history – comes to light in the course of the investigation that acts to prevent such closure; a past crime, often only tangentially related to the contemporary one, disrupts the hygiene of the initial national fiction. If one corpse can be properly buried at the end of the story, dozens of others have been unearthed along the way.

Le Bourreau et son double is set in a suburb called Courvilliers, located in the zone that was called in the 1930s and 1940s the 'redbelt', and dominated by a single factory, Hotch. A new municipal government has been recently elected on the heels of the old communist *mairie* by promising a security to its wealthier inhabitants that depends on forgetting that immigrants exist. A husband and wife are found dead in an HLM – murder/suicide by all appearance. But the husband, Cadin discovers, worked undercover as a literacy and housing activist outside the CGT[30] and against the house syndicate at the factory, and the story, in fact, is a double one: the murder victim and the new head of security at Hotch, it seems, knew one another quite well ten years earlier in a bled outside Oran in Algeria, and the reasons for the murder pertain as much to this earlier story as they do to the present. Is it coincidental that the two men should end up in the same place ten years later? Not if we recall that the companies of French conscripts in Algeria were composed in large part of men drafted from the Parisian *banlieux*, men who worked at Babcock or Simca, who traded in a factory uniform for that of the army. Nor when we remember that successful French officers in the Algerian war, returning in 1962, could make a painless transition back into a big growth sector: security assistance in the burgeoning post-war suburban factories.

And what of Daeninckx's detective, Cadin? In some ways Cadin recalls his predecessor Marlowe: anonymous, somewhat blank, with only vague memories of a personal life the events of which are not part of any of the novels. But the distance separating Marlowe from Cadin is the distance separating incorruptible modernist perfection of an essentially ironic hero from something like postmodern neutrality. Cadin makes his home in the transient zones he investigates without becoming fully integrated into the life there; in no way an activist or an anti-police crusader, nor, like Marlowe, imbued with chivalric purpose, he is much more a 'hired man', a worker whose métier, at least in the early books, is an end in itself. But as his discoveries of police and state activities pile up, he is consequently assigned to more and more obscure suburbs, finally turning up in one of the last novels as a minor character, effectively silenced by the central administration, having resigned from the force after a career trajectory that increasingly came to resemble that of an immigrant worker. 'Ils m'ont fait visiter la France,' he explains to his successor in a bar, 'Six mois ici, trois mois ailleurs. . . . '[31]

The example of Daeninckx allows us to propose a number of conclusions about the possibility of history in contemporary narrative. I take from Lefebvre and Benjamin the suggestion that the moments when everyday life becomes the most vivid or tangible are the moments when most people find themselves living more than one life. Baudelaire, for Benjamin, presided over and embodied the accelerated entry of Paris into modernism. But it was Rimbaud, as I have argued elsewhere, whose peculiar adolescent and provincial position, whose essentially *regional* perspective, allowed him to write something like the critical history *and prophecy* of that entry into modernism. Baudelaire, in other words, was in modernism, Rimbaud sufficiently askew from it to be able to see it.[32]

Daeninckx, I think, occupies a similarly regional perspective, and it is this vantage point – as well as his choice of a mass genre which immerses the reader in everyday life – that facilitates the synthesis of urban and global in his works. His peripheral perspective on Paris and environs allows the new 'world city' of postmodernism – the urban condensation of the restructured international division of labour – to emerge in all the intricacy of its lived, daily, social relations.

To argue for something like a 'critical regionalism' in cultural studies is fraught with dangers – not the least of which, perhaps, is the obvious one that the discourse and rhetoric of regionalism has been a mainstay of the right for decades, and has only recently begun to be reappropriated by the left.[33] A 'regionalist' position also runs the risk of coinciding with the recent separatist tendency to 'barricade oneself within one's own subculture' of the various vernacular, regional, 'identity' movements of the left – movements whose fetishism of locality, place, or social groupuscule tends to coincide with denying or masking the totality of practices that constitute capitalism. Daeninckx's work, perhaps, suggests a limit to left fragmentation. For the moment of political accountability in his novels takes place, as we have seen, on the *national* level, and what we are shockingly jarred into realizing is a factor which everything in postmodernist culture encourages us to forget: the powerful mediating role of the national state. Economist Alain Lipietz has underlined the contradiction between the more and more internationalized character of production and the world market, and the *national* character of the 'modes of regulation' that, since Fordism, have allowed for stabilization. Despite the state's need, in other words, to create a business climate conducive to attracting transnational and global finance capital, interventionism on the part of the state, particularly regarding labour control, is more crucial now than ever before. If the lived realities of postmodernism, its patterns of immigration and displacement, tend to highlight the perception of local and international experience, if the role of the state apparatus, at least in the West, seems to dwindle under the onslaught of a capitalism multinational in its scope, it is still at the national level, the level of the state apparatus, Daeninckx reminds us, that crime is being committed. Critical regionalism, it would then seem, not only represents the privileged vantage point from which to mediate between the local and the global: it does so without losing sight of the workings of the national state apparatus.

Notes

1   Raymond Williams, *The Politics of Modernism: Against the New Conformists*, ed. Tony Pinkney (London: Verso, 1989), p. 35.
2   Ibid.
3   Ibid., p. 47.
4   Tony Pinkney, 'Editor's Introduction: Modernism and Cultural Theory', in

Williams, *Politics of Modernism*, p. 11.

5   Jacques Rancière, 'Après quoi', *Confrontation* 20 (1989), p. 191. Author's translation.

6   J. G. Ballard, 'Some Words About Crash! 2: Interview', *Foundation: The Review of Science Fiction* 9 (Nov. 1975), p. 4.

7   Fredric Jameson, 'Postmodernism, or the Cultural Logic of Late Capitalism', *New Left Review* 146 (1984), pp. 53–92. In what follows I will refer to this particular essay rather than to any of Jameson's more lengthy, subsequent meditations on postmodernism. This essay has had an enormous effect within cultural studies; with the possible exception of Laura Mulvey's 'Visual Pleasure and Narrative Cinema', *Screen*, 16, 3 (1975), I can think of no more widely read and cited single essay in the last twenty years.

8   Fredric Jameson, 'On Raymond Chandler', *Southern Review* 6 (1970); rpt. in Glenn Most and William Stowe, eds, *The Poetics of Murder: Detective Fiction and Literary Theory* (San Diego: Harcourt Brace Jovanovich, 1983), p. 126. Further references cited in the text.

9   Raymond Chandler, 'The Simple Art of Murder: An Essay', (1949); rpt. in *The Simple Art of Murder* (New York: Ballantine, 1988), p. 11.

10 Ibid.

11 Cited in Peter Wolfe, *Something More Than Night: The Case of Raymond Chandler* (Bowling Green: Bowling Green University Press, 1985), p. 46.

12 Jameson is certainly not alone in putting Los Angeles and southern California at the centre of postmodernist culture. The most important precursor to the flood of 1980s writing about Los Angeles is Reyner Banham's *Los Angeles: The Architecture of Four Ecologies* (1971). Most recently, Edward Soja's *Postmodern Geographies* (1989), concludes its theoretical argument with a culminating chapter entitled: 'It All Comes Together in Los Angeles'. Soja and Manuel Castells, both students of Henry Lefebvre, live and work in California; indeed, it was a visit to the Bonaventure by the trio of Lefebvre, Soja and Jameson that provided the 'fieldwork' for Jameson's essay. We must also note the importance of the Californian landscape both in the texts and the travel itineraries of European theorists of postmodernism such as Eco, Baudrillard and Marin. Even an early text like Michael Herr's *Dispatches* (1968), which Jameson reads as the paradigmatic evocation of the space of postmodern warfare, has a central theme something like the Americanization – read Californianization – of the rest of the world: 'You'd stand there nailed in your tracks sometimes, no bearings and none in sight, thinking, Where the fuck am I?, fallen into some unnatural East–West interface, a California corridor cut and bought and burned deep into Asia, and once we'd done it we couldn't remember what for.' [*Dispatches* did not in fact appear until 1977, although Herr's reports on the war in Vietnam, to which Ross must be referring, began appearing in *Esquire* and *Rolling Stone* soon after he arrived in Saigon in 1967. The quotation is from Michael Herr, *Dispatches* (London: Pan, 1978), p. 42. (NL)] Herr also reminds us that Los

Angeles declared Saigon to be its 'sister city' during the war, in order to provide photo opportunities for then LA mayor, Sam Yorty. For a critical history of the place of Los Angeles in twentieth-century intellectual and political life, see Mike Davis, *City of Quartz* (1990).

13   See Mike Davis, 'Urban Renaissance and the Spirit of Postmodernism' *New Left Review* 151 (May/June 1985), pp. 106–14; and 'Chinatown, Part Two? The "Internationalization" of Downtown Los Angeles' *New Left Review* 164 (July/Aug. 1987), pp. 65–86.

14   Davis, 'Chinatown, Part Two?', p. 78.

15   Jameson, 'Postmodernism', p. 61; emphasis added.

16   Chandler, 'Simple Art', p. 18.

17   Lambert Zuidvervaart, 'Realism/Modernism/The Empty Chair', in *Postmodernism/Jameson/Critique*, ed. Douglas Kellner (Washington: Maisonneuve Press, 1989), p. 217.

18   Jameson, 'Postmodernism', p. 60.

19   See for example his 'Third-World Literature in the Era of Multinational Capital', *Social Text* 15 (1986), pp. 65–88.

20   The Situationists were among the earliest theorists of postmodernism to focus on Los Angeles, specifically on the 1965 Watts riots, which they viewed as less a race riot than a 'rebellion against the commodity': 'How do people make history under conditions preestablished to dissuade them from intervening in it? Los Angeles blacks are better paid than any others in the United States, but they are also the most separated from that high point of flaunted affluence, California. Hollywood, the pole of the global spectacle, is in their immediate vicinity' (Ken Knabb, 'The Decline and Fall of the Spectacle-Commodity Economy', in *Situationist International Anthology*, ed. and trans. Ken Knabb (Berkeley: Bureau of Public Secrets, 1981), p. 156). [The Situationist International (previously the Lettrist International) was founded in Italy in 1957 by a small group of European avant-garde artists and writers who wanted to change the future by destroying the present. For the Situationists, whose leading figure was Guy Debord (see below), small-scale revolutions around the world were proof of a global discontent with the quality of life – and so their plan was to use art to oppose everything! By opposing all civic, moral, political, aesthetic, institutional and other rules of order, the Situationists hoped to show that it was those very rules that were the cause of peoples' unhappiness. Without rules, people would be free to experience each situation in life as it happened and for what it was. The situation that finally overcame the Situationists themselves was the 'defeat' of the Left in the wake of the student riots in Paris in May 1968. For the view that 'situationism' came back to life in London a decade later, in the form of The Sex Pistols, see Greil Marcus, *Lipstick Traces: A Secret History of the Twentieth Century* (Harmondsworth: Penguin, 1993). (NL)]

21   Henri Lefebvre, *The Survival of Capitalism: Reproduction of the Relations of Production*, trans. Frank Bryant (London: Allison and Busby, 1976),

p. 17. [Lefebvre, one of the preeminent Marxist intellectuals in France in the 1950s, became a close companion of the Situationists and a strong advocate of their work, only to have his own work condemned by them, in the early 1960s, as plagiarism. See Marcus, *Lipstick Traces*, pp. 146–7. (NL)]

22 Guy Debord, *La société du spectacle* [1968] (Paris: Buchet/Chastel, 1971), p. 115. Author's translation.

23 Norma Evenson, *Paris: A Century of Change, 1878–1978* (New Haven: Yale University Press, 1979), pp. 309–10.

24 Jacques Barou, 'Immigration and Urban Social Policy in France: The Experience of Paris', in *Migrant Workers in Metropolitan Cities*, ed. John Solomos (Strasburg: European Science Foundation, 1982).

25 Evenson, *Paris*, p. 238.

26 Didier Daeninckx, *Le Bourreau et son double* (Paris: Gallimard, 1986), p. 22. Author's translation.

27 Didier Daeninckx, *Lumière noire* (Paris: Gallimard, 1987), p. 41. Author's translation.

28 Daeninckx, *Bourreau*, p. 193. Author's translation.

29 Daeninckx's version of this event – what was effectively the largest massacre of workers in the capital since the fall of the Commune in 1871 – remains one of the few that question the official police version of the October 1961 peaceful demonstration of 30,000 Algerians in Paris. Contemporary investigations into police conduct were largely suppressed; a film made about the subject, *Octobre à Paris*, was never allowed to be released. For more information, see one of the few history texts to give a (very brief) account: Bernard Droz and Evelyne Lever, *Histoire de la guerre d'Algérie (1954–1962)* (Paris: Gallimard, 1982), pp. 324–5. In 1990 the first commemoration of the event took place in Paris; historian Benjamin Stora notes: 'We had to wait for the political emergence of the youth produced by Algerian immigration for that date to reappear' (*Libération*, 22 Oct. 1990). *Meurtres pour mémoiré* has been translated into English (Didier Daeninckx, *Murder in Memorium*, trans. Liz Heron (London: Gallimard, 1991)).

30 Activities which apparently duplicate, to a certain degree, those of the author; Daeninckx worked for many years as a cultural and literacy activist in immigrant communities in Seine-Saint-Denis.

31 Daeninckx, Bourreay, p. 140.

32 We should recall, in this light, Rimbaud's well-known critique of Baudelaire: 'Baudelaire is the first seer, king of poets, a real god! But he lived in too artistic a world; and the form so highly praised in him is trivial. Inventions of the unknown call for new forms.' Arthur Rimbaud, *Oeuvres complètes*, eds Rolland de Renéville and Jules Mouquet (Paris: Gallimard, 1967), p. 273.

33 Edward Soja, *Postmodern Geographies: The Reassertion of Space in Critical Social Theory* (London: Verso, 1989), pp. 188–9.

Chapter Ten Feminism for the Incurably Informed

Anne Balsamo

All we ever want (ever wanted) was to be on that mailing list.
Ron Silliman, *What*

My mother was a computer, but she never learned to drive. Grandmother was an order clerk in a predominantly male warehouse; she did all the driving for the family, having learned to drive almost before she learned to speak English; her first car was a 1916 Model T Ford equipped with a self-starter.[1] Both my mother and grandmother worked for Sears and Roebuck in the 1940s; mother entered orders on a log sheet, grandmother filled those orders in the warehouse.[2] When an opening in payroll came through, my mother enrolled in night school to learn to be a computer. Within two years she received a diploma from the Felt and Tarrant School of Comptometry that certified her to operate a comptometer – one of the widely used electromechanical calculating machines that preceded electronic calculators.[3] She worked at Sears for two more years before she was replaced by a machine.

My sister and I both work for the technostate – it seems only natural. In 1991, my sister was deployed to the borderland between northern Iraq and southwest Turkey as part of the US military's humanitarian effort, called 'Operation Provide Comfort', to give medical attention to the Kurdistani refugees exiled during and after the technologically hallucinogenic Gulf War.[4] About the same time, I was deployed to a technological

Anne Balsamo, 'Feminism for the Incurably Informed', *South Atlantic Quarterly* 92 (4) (Fall 1993), pp. 681–712.

institution to teach gender studies (their term) or feminism (mine). Situated within different histories, biographical as well as cultural, these technological encounters suggest several topics of investigation for feminist studies of science and technology.

These working-class histories will span one hundred years before they're finished, and even that is an arbitrary span of time, determined more by the mangling of immigrant names and the near impossibility of extrapolating from today into tomorrow than by any formal sense of narrative closure. I do not want to invoke an experiential framework for the elaboration of this essay; I have no stories to tell here about the subjective experiences of a mother, sister, or grandmother using technology, displaced by it, or even cleaning up after it. Instead, I use these autobiographical notes as a platform upon which to stage a feminist reading of the current (cyber)cultural moment. This scene, which Pat Cadigan's main hacker-girl, Sam, says is gripped by an 'information frenzy', is the present context for those of us who pride ourselves on being plugged in, on-line, and living on the New Edge.[5] Like the hackers and domestic exiles who populate Cadigan's cyberpunk novel *Synners*, we too qualify as 'incurably informed'.[6]

If my opening remarks were about working-class histories, Cadigan's second novel *Synners*, published in 1991, is much more about the postindustrial present; as a particular kind of science fiction novel – a cyberpunk narrative – it offers a techno-mythology of the future right around the corner.[7] When *Synners* is discussed as a cyberpunk novel, it is usually mentioned that Cadigan is one of the few women writing in that subgenre. Textually, *Synners* displays the verbal inventiveness and stylistic bricolage characteristic of the best of the new science fiction, but in Cadigan's case her verbal playfulness invokes Dr Seuss, and the plot melds a Nancy Drew mystery with a Kathy Acker-hacked Harlequin romance. The mystery plot includes familiar cyberpunk devices, such as illegal corporate manoeuvers and heroic hacking; the Acker-hacked romance plot offers a gentle critique of women's propensity to fall for men who can't be there for them: in this case, though, it's because the guy has abandoned his meat (the body) for the expanse of cyberspace. More interesting is the manner in which her refrain 'Change for the machines?' morphs from a literal question at a vending machine to a philosophical comment about the nature of the technologized human.

One way to investigate the interpretive and ideological dimensions of contemporary cyberculture is to situate cyberpunk mythologies in relation to the emergence of a new cultural formation built in and around cyberspace.[8] Although we could map the discursive terrain of cyberpunk science fiction through an analysis of the lists of (best) book titles, author anecdotes, critical interpretations, readers' reviews, and the contradictions among them, this would only partially describe the practices of dispersion and interpretation that serve as the infrastructure of a much broader formation.[9] To fully investigate the cultural formation of what *Mondo 2000* calls 'the new edge' would require an investigation of related discursive forms, such as comic books, 'zines, and other forms of popular print culture, as well as new hybrid social-textual forms, such as electronic newsgroups, bulletin boards, discussion lists, MUDs (multi-user domains), on-line journals, E-zines, and IRChats.[10] Given that these textually mediated social spaces are often constructed and populated by those who participate in related subcultural practices, such as CONS, raves, body alteration, smart drugs, computer hacking, and video art, what is needed for a more developed and historically specific analysis of the New Edge as a cultural formation is a multidisciplinary analysis of other spaces of popular culture where material bodies stage cyberpunk identities.[11] Although constructing such a multiperspectival analysis is a challenging task, my intent is to demonstrate that such a project is already under way. In synthesizing this material, I want to suggest what is needed to produce a critical analysis of a specific socio-historical conjunction that attends both to the expressive practices of cyberpunk SF and to the political aims of feminist cultural studies, and that can draw meaningful connections between them. My goal, then, is to read *Synners* as both cognitive map and cultural landmark.

Teresa de Lauretis anticipated the critical response that cyberpunk science fiction enjoys from postmodern readers when she provisionally suggested in 1980 that in 'every historical period, certain art forms (or certain literary forms . . .), have become central to the episteme or historical vision of a given society. . . . If we compare it with traditional or postmodern fiction, we see that SF might, just might, be crucial from now on.'[12] In one of the first reports on cyberpunk as a new SF subgenre, Darko Suvin, quoting Raymond Williams, argues for its cultural significance by claiming that cyberpunk novels (especially those by William Gibson) articulate a new structure of feeling: 'a particular quality of social experience and relationship . . . which gives the sense of a generation or of a period.'[13] Several critics have discussed the details of the relationship between cyberpunk and a postmodern sensibility.[14] For example, in her essay 'Cybernetic Deconstructions: Cyberpunk and Postmodernism', Veronica Hollinger reads cyberpunk through a poststructuralist antihumanism to claim that 'cyberpunk [is] an analysis of the postmodern identification of human and machine'.[15] Her main point is that cyberpunk participates in the (postmodern) deconstruction of human subjectivity. According to her reading, cyberpunk narratives radically decenter the human body, the sacred icon of essential self, in the same way that the virtual reality of cyberspace works to decenter conventional humanist notions of an unproblematic 'real'. By the end of her analysis, though, we discover that the antihumanist critique of cyberpunk doesn't hold. Cyberpunk collapses under the weight of its own genre determinations. It is still, Hollinger argues, about the 'reinsertion of the human into the reality which its technology is in the process of shaping'.[16] In support of Hollinger's conclusion, it is more useful to think of cyberpunk as offering a vision of post-human existence where 'technology' and the 'human' are understood in contiguous rather than oppositional terms.

As an example of the cyberpunk meditation on the posthuman condition, *Synners* posits a world populated by 'Homo datum', people whose natural habitat is 'the net', for whom disconnection from the information economy is not an option. This leads one character to speculate that there are three species of technological humans: 'synthe*sizing* humans, synthe*sized* humans', and the 'bastard offspring of both' – artificial intelligences (pp. 386–7). The original syn, in this case, is neither an act nor a transgression, but rather the posthuman condition of being 'incurably informed'. Death, according to this logic, is defined as an EEG flatline.

To the extent that we read cyberpunk through postmodern social theory, one of the most obvious thematic connections between the two is the way that each discourse configures the space of the social as a landscape structured by the network of relations among multinational capitalist corporations. As Fredric Jameson suggests, the generic structure of cyberpunk science fiction represents an attempt to 'think the impossible totality of the contemporary world system'.[17] This space of 'the decentered global network', metaphorically known as cyberspace, is a bewildering place for the individual/subject who is left to his/her own devices to construct a map of the relationship between a corporeal locale and the totality of 'transnational corporate realities'.

The focal tension in *Synners* concerns the multinational Diversifications' takeover of two small companies: Eye-Traxx, an independent music-video production company, and Hall Galen Enterprises, a company that employs the medical researcher who invented and patented the procedures for brain socket implants. As a result of the takeover, two of the four main characters, Gina and Visual Mark, become Diversifications' corporate property. Visual Mark was one of Eye-Traxx's original *Synners*, a human synthesizer who is now nearing the age of fifty: 'It was as if he had a pipeline to some primal dream spot, where music and image created each other, the pictures suggesting the music, the music generating the pictures, in a synthesic frenzy' (p. 109). Diversifications intends to market its new brain sockets by offering virtual reality rock videos: Visual Mark is the best music-video synner in the business. Diversifications' brain sockets not only allow music-videos to be fed into a receiving brain: they also provide a direct interface between a brain and a computer. This type of brain-to-computer connection proves to have dire consequences. While Diversifications tries to corner the market on a lucrative new form of electronic addiction – by providing the sockets and what is fed into the sockets – their socket clients encounter a fatal side effect: 'intercranial meltdown' in the form of a cerebral stroke.

In elaborating the distinctions between cyberpunk SF and its generic antecedents, namely, New Wave and feminist SF from the late 1960s and 1970s,[18] Fred Pfeil writes: 'I am tempted to say [cyberpunk novels have] no "political unconscious": [but are rather] a kind of writing in which, instead of delving and probing for neurotic symptoms, we are invited to witness and evaluate a relatively open acting out.' That a cyberpunk work's neurotic symptoms are easily identified does not disqualify it as an interesting cultural text; on the contrary, Pfeil argues that this is a productive, creative mutation:

> this new SF hardly requires the literary analyst's ingenuity in order for us to find or fathom its real social content; the collective anxieties and desires that fuel it are relatively openly evoked and worked through. And the shift from formal and aesthetic experimentation back to experiments in social thought itself suggests that in at least some senses and sectors we have indeed moved on from that earlier humanist debate on freedom, power and order to some new or at least mutated social and ideological ground, which is once again open and fresh enough to be explicitly tried on and explored.[19]

In the case of *Synners*, the 'real social content', according to Pfeil's formulation, is not simply the plottings of a hostile corporate takeover, but also what we can read on/off its textual surface about the technological configuration of human life in multinational capitalism. Several topics nominate themselves as experiments in thinking through the social consequences of new technologies, any one of which could serve as the organizing perspective for the elaboration of an interpretive map of Cadigan's cosmology: the capitalist production of electronic addictions, the recording practices of video vigilantes, or the multiplication of television channels devoted to new forms of pornography – disasterporn, medporn, foodporn. In addition to speculating about the dynamics of new communication technologies, *Synners* also offers a critical account of the commodification of information:

> Truth is cheap, but information costs. . . . 'Besides being rich,' Fez said, 'you have to he extra sharp these days to pick up any real information. You have to know *what* you're looking for, and you have to know how it's filed. Browsers need not apply. Broke ones, anyway. I miss the newspaper.' (pp. 52–3)

This subtext also includes a political critique of the availability of information and of the difficulty of determining relevance in the midst of the 'Instant information Revolution'.

> 'Good guess, but the real title is *Need to Know*,' said the same voice close to his car. 'It's an indictment of our present system of information dispersal. You're allowed to know only those things the information czars decide that you need to know. They call it "market research" and "efficient use of resources" and "no-waste," but it's the same old shit they've been doing to us for more than one-hundred years – keep 'em confused and in the dark. You gotta be a stone-ham super-Renaissance person to find out what's really going on.' (p. 194)

Pfeil is right when he says that isolating passages such as these hardly requires literary ingenuity to identify expressions of collective anxieties. Indeed, such skeptical statements about information overload and manipulation resonate strongly with Baudrillard's reading of the postmodern scene: 'We are in a universe where there is more and more information, and less and less meaning.'[20] And yet, in contrast to the reading Baudrillard offers, Carolyn Marvin argues that 'information cannot be said to exist at all unless it has meaning, and meaning is established only in social relationships with cultural reference and value'.[21] In her critique of the dominant notion of information-as-commodity (a notion that is at the heart of the ideology of the information age), Marvin redefines information not as a quantifiable entity, but rather as a 'state of knowing', which reasserts a knowing *body* as its necessary materialist foundation. This embodied notion of information is at the heart of *Synners*. Moving around a postmodernist reading of cyberpunk SF that would focus on its figuration of multinational capitalism and the technological deconstruction of human identity, I would like to elaborate an alternative reading of *Synners* that reflects a slight mutation of these thematic preoccupations. In this case, the focus is on the relation of the material body to cyberspace.

In the course of developing an ideological critique of a capitalist information economy, Cadigan focuses attention on an often-repressed dimension of the information age: the constitution of the informed body. The problem is not just that information 'costs', or even that it replicates exponentially, but rather that information is never merely discursive. What we encounter in the Cadigan novel is the narrativization of four different versions of cyberpunk embodiment: the repressed body, the labouring body, the marked body, and the disappearing body. In this sense, the four central characters symbolize the different *embodied* relations one can have, in theory and in fiction, to a nonmaterial space of information access and exchange. The following figure roughly illustrates how Sam, Gabe, Gina, and Visual Mark represent four corners of an identity matrix constructed in and around cyberspace:

Sam (the body that labours)   Gina (the marked body)

Gabe (the repressed body)   Visual Mark (the disappearing body)

Where Sam hacks the net through a terminal powered by her own body, Visual Mark actually inhabits the network as he mutates into a disembodied, sentient artificial intelligence (AI). Although both Gina and Gabe travel through cyberspace on their way to someplace else, Gabe is addicted to cyberspace simulations, and Gina endures them. Each character plays a significant role in the novel's climactic confrontation in cyberspace: a role determined, in part, by their individual relationships to Diversifications and, in part, by their bodily identities.

Sam, Gabe's daughter and the only real hacker among the four, is a virtuoso at gaining access to the net. She is the character who best describes the labour of computer hacking and the virtual acrobatics of cyberspace travel: 'if you couldn't walk on the floor, you walked on the ceiling. If you couldn't walk on the ceiling, you walked on the walls, and if you couldn't walk *on* the walls, you walked *in* them, encrypted. Pure hacking' (p. 351). As competent as she is in negotiating the cyberspatial landscape of the net, Sam tries to live her embodied life outside of any institutional structure. Her only affiliations are to other punks and hackers who form a community of sorts and who live out on 'the Manhattan-Hermosa strip, what the kids called the Mimosa, part of the old postquake land of the lost' (p. 7). Sam trades encrypted data and hacking talents for stray pieces of equipment and living necessities. In what proves to be a critically important 'information commodity' acquisition, Sam hacks the specifications for an insulin-pump chip reader that runs off body energy. When every terminal connected to 'the System' is infected by a debilitating virus, Sam's insulin-pump chip reader is the only noninfected access point to the net. Connected by thin needles inserted into her abdomen, the chip reader draws its power from Sam's body. Seventeen-year-old Sam is a cyberspace hacker of considerable talent who shuns the heroic cowboy role. And for the most part, she is content to provide the power while others, namely, Gina and Gabe, go in for the final showdown.

Recoiling from a real-time wife who despises him for his failure to live up to his artistic potential, Gabe spends most of his working time, when he should he designing advertising campaigns, playing the role (Hotwire) of a *noir* leading man in a computer simulation built from pieces of an old movie thriller; his two female cyberspace sidekicks are 'templates [that] had been assembled from two real, living people' (p. 41). Where Visual Mark cleaves to cyberspace because the world isn't big enough for his expansive visual mind, Gabe becomes addicted to cyberspace because the world is just too big for him. He retreats to the simulation pit for the safety and familiarity it offers. 'He'd been running around in simulation for so long, he'd forgotten how to run a realife, real-time routine; he'd forgotten that if he made mistakes, there was no safety-net program to jump in and correct for him' (p. 239). Throughout the novel, Gabe moves in and out of a real-time life and his simulated fantasy world. In real time his body is continually brought to life, through pain, intoxication, and desire caused by Gina, first when she punches him in the face with a misplaced jab intended for Mark, then later when he gets toxed after she feeds him two LotusLands (a 'mildly hallucinogenic beverage'). After they make love for the first time, Gina wonders if Gabe has ever felt desire before: 'She didn't think Gabe Ludovic had ever jumped the fast train in his life. Standing at the end of fifteen years of marriage, he'd wanted a lot more than sex. The wanting had been all but tangible, a heat that surprised both of them' (p. 243). After a climactic cyberspace struggle, his repressed body reawakens; Gabe learns to feel his body again (or for the first time) with Gina's help. Like Visual Mark, Gina is a synner who synthesizes images, sound, and special effects to produce virtual reality music videos. For all her disdain and outright hostility toward other people and institutions, 'Badass Gina Aiesi' has an intense emotional connection to Mark, her partner of twenty years, that she romanticizes in an odd way:

> They weren't smooch-faces, it didn't work that way, for her or for him. . . .
> One time, though . . . one time, three-four-five years into the madness,
> there'd been a place where they'd come together one night, and it had been
> different. . . . He'd been reaching, and she'd been reaching, and for a little
> while there, they'd gotten through. Maybe that had been the night when the
> little overlapping space called *their life* had come into existence. (p. 213)

Gina's body, marked by its colour, 'wild forest hardwood', and her dreadlocks, figure prominently in the narrative description of her sexual encounters, first with Visual Mark and then with Gabe. After both she and
Visual Mark have brain sockets implanted by Diversifications' surgeon-
on-contract, they jack in together and experience a visual replay of shared
memories: 'The pov [point-of-view] was excruciatingly slow as it moved
across Mark's face to her own, lingering on the texture of her dreadlocks
next to his pale, drawn flesh, finally moving on to the contrast of her deep
brown skin' (p. 216). The characteristics that mark Gina are her anger,
her exasperated love for Mark, and the colour of her skin.

Like others who have bought the new means for jacking in, Visual
Mark begins to spend less and less time off-line and more and more time
plugged into the global network known as 'the System'. This leads him to
reflect on the metaphysical nature of his physical body: 'he lost all awareness of the meat that had been his prison for close to fifty years, and the
relief he felt at having laid his burden down was as great as himself' (p.
232). After suffering a small stroke (one of the unpleasant side effects of
brain sockets) when he was jacked in, Visual Mark prepares for 'the big
one' – a stroke that will release his consciousness into the system and
allow him to leave his meat behind.

> He was already accustomed to the idea of having multiple awareness and a
> single concentrated core that were both the essence of self. The old meat
> organ would not have been able to cope with that kind of reality, but out
> here he appropriated more capacity the way he once might have exchanged
> a smaller shirt for a larger one. (p. 325)

And sure enough, while his body is jacked in, Mark strokes out. He tries
to get Gina to pull his plugs, but she is too late. As his meat dies, both his
consciousness and his stroke enter 'the System'. In the process, his stroke
is transformed into a deadly virus (or spike) that initiates a worldwide
network crash.

Like the dramatic climax in recent cyberpunk films, such as *Circuitry
Man*, *The Lawnmower Man*, and *Mindwarp*, the final showdown in

Synners takes place in cyberspace.[22] Working together, a small community of domestic exiles, hackers, and punks assembles a workstation (powered by Sam's insulin-pump chip reader) that enables Gina and Gabe to go on-line to fight the virus/stroke – an intelligent entity of some dubious ontological status that now threatens the integrity of the entire networked world. Like a cyberspace Terminator, the virus/stroke is rationally determined to infect/destroy whoever comes looking for it. In the course of their cyberspace brawl, Gabe and Gina confront the virus's simulation of their individual worst fears. Gabe's enemy is a simple construct: the fear of embodiment. 'I can't remember what it feels like to have a body', he repeats obsessively during his final confrontation. A 'reluctant hero' till the very end, he learns through the encounter that his whole body is a hot suit; that is, he learns to feel the body that he has technologically repressed.

Gina's struggle is with an embodiment of her own deepest fears about missed chances, lost love, and suffocating commitment. Her cyberspace showdown replays her obsessive twenty-year-long search for Mark: 'Old habits, they do die hard, don't they. That's yours, ain't it – looking for Mark' (p. 400). 'Who do you still want to love?' she is asked by the omniscient virus. In one sense her struggle is to confront the fact that she loves an addict and still wants to save him. The crucial decision Gina faces is whether to stay in cyberspace – where there is no pain, no separation – or to renounce him and return to the real world, where such love is impossible. In the end, Gabe and Gina defeat the virus, and the global network shortly reestablislies connections. But when Gina finally wakes to reunite with Gabe, we find out that although *they* have changed for the machines, the machines didn't change for them. 'The door only swings one way. Once it's out of the box, it's always too big to get back in. Can't bury that technology. . . . Every technology has its original sin. . . . And we still got to live with what we made' (p. 435).

Darko Suvin asks two additional questions about the shape of a cyberpunk sensibility: 'whose structure of feeling?' and 'to what ideological horizons or consequences does it apply?' As if in response, Fred Pfeil suggests that most cyberpunk SF 'remains stuck in a masculinist frame', in that cyberpunk dramas, like most video game narratives, remain 'focused on the struggle of the male protagonist . . . to wend his lonely way through the worlds'.[23] Andrew Ross concurs with Pfeil's assessment and adds: 'One barely needs to scratch the surface of the cyberpunk genre, no matter how maturely sketched out, to expose a baroque edifice of adolescent male fantasies.'[24]

In reading *Synners* as a feminist text, I would argue that it offers an alternative narrative of cyberpunk identity that begins with the assumption that bodies are always gendered and always marked by race. Cadigan's novel is implicitly informed by Donna Haraway's cyborg politics: the gendered distinctions between characters hold true to a cyborgian figuration of gender differences whereby the female body is coded as a body-in-connection and the male body, as a body-in-isolation.[25] *Synners* illuminates the gendered differences in the way that the characters relate to the technological space of information. Sam and Gina, the two female hackers, actively *manipulate* the dimensions of cybernetic space in order to communicate with other people. Gabe and Visual Mark, on the other hand, are *addicted* to cyberspace for the release it offers from the loneliness of their material bodies. But the novel's racial politics are more suspect; racial distinctions between characters are revealed through its representation of sexual desire. Gina is the only character who is identified by skin colour. She is also the focal object and subject of heterosexual desire, for a moment by Mark, and more frequently by Gabe; and we know both men's racial identities by their marked difference from Gina's. The unmarked characters are marked by the absence of identifying marks. In different ways and with different political consequences, *Synners* reasserts gender and race as defining elements of posthuman identity so that, even as *Synners* discursively represents different forms of technological embodiment, it also reasserts the critical importance of the materiality of bodies in any analysis of the information age.

Maybe Pfeil is right to claim that cyberpunk novels have no political unconscious in that their symbolic preoccupations are relatively easy to access. But in constructing this reading of *Synners* not to emphasize its cyberpunk characteristics, but rather to point to its feminist preoccupations, I am implicitly arguing that it entails some form of allegorical narrative; as a work of the feminist imagination, it narrativizes certain tensions and obsessions that animate feminist thinking across cultural discourses. I've argued that Cadigan's narrative symbolically represents the female body as material, as a body that labours. The male body, in contrast, is represented as repressed or disappearing. This reading suggests a slight revision of Arthur Kroker's theory of the postmodern body, in which he argues that the signal form of postmodern embodiment is 'the disappearing body'.[26] In offering gendered descriptions of *multiple* forms of postmodern embodiment, *Synners* sets the stage for the elaboration of a feminist theory of the relationship of material bodies to cyberspace and of the construction of agency in technological encounters. But even in saying this, I must assert that the final horizon of this reading is not Cadigan's novel, but rather the insights it offers for a feminist analysis of the politics of new information technologies. To this end, *Synners* suggests a starting point for the elaboration of a map of contemporary cyberculture, where technology serves as a site for the reinscription of cultural narratives of gendered and racial identifies.

This reading of *Synners* also implies that a political judgement of any technology is difficult to determine in the abstract. For example, several news articles about the phenomenon of virtual reality boldly assert that VR applications, such as 'Virtual Valerie', and 900-number phone sex services are technologies of safe (fluidless) sex; one Atlanta-based sex expert goes so far as to say that VR will be a mainstream sex aid by the end of the decade, stimulating yet pathogenically prudent. The very same phenomenon enables new forms of social and cultural autism. Brenda Laurel, a VR researcher and designer, reports: 'I've had men tell me that one of the reasons they got into this business was to escape the social aspects of being a male in America – to escape women in particular.[27] Sandy Stone studies electronic communities and the bodies that labour in cyberspace – including VR systems engineers as well as phone-sex workers. In her analysis of the virtual body, she concludes that cyberspace both disembodies and re-embodies in a gendered fashion: 'the desire to cross the human/machine boundary, to penetrate and merge, which is part of the evocation of cyberspace . . . shares certain conceptual and affective characteristics with numerous fictional evocations of the inarticulate longing of the male for the female.' But, as she goes on to argue, 'to enter cyberspace is to physically put on cyberspace. To become the cyborg, to put on the seductive and dangerous cybernetic space like a garment, is to put on the female.'[28] Even as she elaborates the gendered dimensions of cyberspace connection, Stone sees an inherent ambiguity in cyberspace technologies that is tied to the facticity of the material body. For as much as they offer the opportunity for new forms of virtual engagement, Stone rightly asserts that 'no refigured virtual body, no matter how beautiful, will slow the death of a cyberpunk with AIDS. Even in the age of the technosubject, life is lived through bodies'.[29]

If, on the one hand, new communication technologies such as VR create new contexts for knowing/talking/singing/fucking bodies, they also enable new forms of repression of the material body. Studies of the new modes of electronic communication, for example, indicate that the anonymity offered by the computer screen empowers anti-social behaviours, such as 'flaming' (electronic insults), and border line illegal behaviours, such as trespassing, email snooping, and MUD rape (unwanted, aggressive, sexual-textual encounter in a multi-user domain).[30] And yet, for all the anonymity they offer, many computer communications reproduce stereotypically gendered patterns of conversation.[31]

In The Jargon File, the entry on 'Gender and Ethnicity' claims that although 'hackerdom is still predominantly male,' hackers are gender- and colour-blind in their interactions with other hackers because they communicate (primarily) through text-based network channels.[32] This assertion rests on the assumptions that 'text-based channels' represent a gender-neutral medium of exchange and that language itself is free from any form of gender, race, or ethnic determination. Both of these assumptions are called into question not only by feminist research on electronic communication and interpretive theory, but also by female network users who particiapte in cyberpunk's virtual subculture.[33] This was dramatically, or rather textually, illustrated in an exchange that occurred on FutureCulture, an electronic discussion list devoted to cyberpunk subculture. The thread of the discussion (which took place over several days in the late months of 1992 and included a dozen participants, most of whom signed their postings with masculine handles) concerned a floating utopia called 'Autopia'. The exchange about women in 'Autopia' began innocently:

From the cyberdeck of student . . .

It may just be my imagination, but it seems that the bulk of the people participating in the Autopia discussion are men.

And hasn't anyone else noticed that most people on FutureCulture are men? Not to mention the overall population of the net, generally speaking. I'd like to get women into this discussion, but I'm not even sure if there are any women on FC.

Are there?

In response, a male participant pointed out:

IF you haven't noticed, the bulk of the people on these networks are men. It is about 80% male, with higher percentages in some places.

Yeah, Clearly, the Internet is dominated by men. It just seems that some outreach to women might be in order. Hanging out on on a ship with hundreds of male computer jocks isn't exactly my idea of utopia. :)

A female participant wrote back:

> Now, this is a loaded question. A lot of women will not open themselves to possible net harassment by admitting they are listening. Of course, if they've come this far, they are likely to be the more bold/brave/stupid type.

> Which leaves me where?

> Cuz, yes, I am a woman & I hang out on the Internet, read cyberpunk, do interesting things with locks and computers. I don't program, I don't MU*/D/SH. I do technical work/repair. I write. I read. I'm a relatively bright individual.

This posting was followed by a self-acknowledged sexist statement from a male participant who asked others if they too found that women on the net were extremely unattractive. He was flamed by several other men in the discussion, one of whom posted this rebuke:

> Concepts of physical beauty are holdovers from 'MEAT' space. On the net, they don't apply. We are all just bits and bytes blowing in the phospor stream.

Concepts of physical beauty might be a 'meat' thing, but gender identity persists in the 'phospor stream' whether we like it or not. Eventually, the thread returned to the question of what a woman might say about 'Autopia', the floating-utopia idea. Several postings later, the original female participant responded:

> And, would you like to know why, overall, I am uninterested in the idea of Autopia? Because I'm a responsible person. (Over-responsible, if you want to get into the nit-picky psychological semantics, but that's another point.) As a responsible person, I end up doing/am expected to do all the shit work. All the little details that others don't think of; like setting up laundry duty, dishes, cooking, building, repairs, and handling garbage. This is not to say that I fall into the typical 'FEMALE' role, because both women and men have left these duties to fall into my lap. And, it's not a case that, if I leave it, it will eventually get done either – you'd be amazed at how long people will ignore garbage or dishes; at how many people can't use a screwdriver or hold a hammer correctly.

Plus, how about security? There is a kind of assumption that goes on, especially on the net, that folks on whatever computer network are a higher intelligence, above craven acts of violence. If you end up with 50 men for every woman, how are you going to ensure her safety?

So, talk about security issues, waste disposal, cooking and cleaning duties, the actual wiring of whatever ship for onboard computers, how you're planning on securing hard drives for rough seas, how you're going to eat, in what shifts are you going to sleep, who's going to steer, how you are going to get navigators.

Where will you get the money for the endeavor? If you decide against a ship, and go for an island, how are you going to deal with overrunning the natural habitat? What are you going to do if you cause some species that only lived on *that* island to become extinct? What are you going to do with refugees from the worlds of hurt on this planet, who are looking for someplace to escape to?

As one other (male) participant in the discussion pointed out, these are eminently practical concerns, but not ones that were raised until the female participant emerged from the silence she was lurking in. Her original point was passed over quickly, even as it was enacted in the course of the subsequent discussion: electronic discussion lists are governed by gendered codes of discursive interchange that are often not hospitable to female participants. This suggests that on-line communication is structured similarly to communication in other settings and is overtly subjected to gender, status, age, and race determinations.

Hoai-An Truong, a member of Bay Area Women in Telecommunications (BAWIT), writes: 'Despite the fact that computer networking systems obscure physical characteristics, many women find that gender follows them into the online community, and sets a tone for their public and private interactions there – to such an extent that some women purposefully choose gender-neutral identities, or refrain from expressing their opinions.'[34] This is a case where the false denial of the body requires the defensive denial of the body in order to communicate. For some women, it is simply not worth the effort. For most men, it is never noticed.

In *Landscape for a Good Woman*, a genre-bending theoretical critique of psychoanalysis and working-class social history, Carolyn Steedman asserts that autobiography is useful for the production of cultural criticism because '[p]ersonal interpretations of past time – the stories that people tell themselves in order to explain how they got to the place they currently inhabit – are often in deep and ambiguous conflict with the official interpretive devices of a culture.' Steedman describes the conflict she experiences when she takes cultural theory personally:

> the structures of class analysis and schools of cultural criticism . . . cannot deal with everything there is to say about my mother's life. . . . The usefulness of the biographical and autobiographical core of the book lies in the challenge it may offer to much of our conventional understanding of childhood, working-class childhood, and little-girlhood.[35]

In 'writing stories that aren't central to a dominant culture', specifically the story of her working-class childhood and a de-authorized father, Steedman simultaneously revises the insights of psychoanalytic theory and the discursive conventions of cultural criticism. More specifically, she links an autobiographical account of her working-class childhood with a biographical account of her mother's class determinations to serve as the context for a narrative critique of a classic psychoanalytical case study (Freud's story of Dora);[36] her intent is to articulate the relationship between narratives of the self and narratives of history. Her broader point is to demonstrate that working-class histories, in whatever form they are found, as case studies or autobiographical narratives, will often contradict the official 'interpretive devices' of a dominant culture. Implicit in Steedman's work is the argument that provoking such a conflict creates the opportunity to interfere with the ongoing codification of official interpretations.

Although different accounts of this conflict could be written, I suggest that the 'ambiguous conflict' between the autobiographical notes I opened with and the dominant, if not exactly official, interpretive theory of our era – postmodernism – concerns the penchant to celebrate the perpetual present. Steve Best and Doug Kellner identify this tendency as 'radical presentism' and argue that the 'erasure of depth also flattens out history and experience, for lost in a postmodern present, one is cut off from those sedimented traditions, those continuities and historical memories which nurture historical consciousness and provide a rich, textured, multidimensional present.'[37] Presentism augments two ideological projects of the information age: the construction of social theories narrated by disembodied virtual minds, and the construction of technological histories written without women, without workers, and without politics.[38] The issue I would like to conclude with concerns the gendered aspects of the development of those technologies that have been identified as central to the New

Edge and the age of information: microelectronics, telecommunications networks, and other forms of computer technologies. To read accounts of the development of information technologies, for example, one might conclude that women have only just begun to show an interest in and aptitude for technological knowledge, innovation, and employment. This signals yet another pervasive myth of the information age: namely, that everything that is important to know is transparently accessible with the right access codes. Feminist thinkers know differently.

Gathering even basic biographical material about the women who participated in traditionally male-domniated technical and professional fields, including the physical and natural sciences, engineering, mathematics, military science, and astronomy, is not an easy project. The historical material that is available illuminates the daunting structural barriers that many women had to overcome in order to pursue their interests and research in scientific and technological fields. The structural barriers ranged from formal prohibitions against women's education to the legal restrictions on women's property rights which caused many women inventors to patent their inventions under their brothers' or husbands' names. In reporting on her analysis of the treatment of gender and women's subjects in the twenty-four-year history of the journal *Technology and Culture* – the journal of the Society for the History of Technology – Joan Rothschild asserts that one of the reasons for the lack of discussion about gender in the historiography of technology is a 'literal identification of the male with technology'.[39] This association has been seriously challenged by recent feminist studies that not only seek to recover women's contribution to the historical development of different technologies, but also to rethink the history of technology from a feminist perspective. Autumn Stanley, for example, argues that the history of technology omits women in part because of a categorical exclusion of the technology that women were specifically instrumental in developing as not 'proper': here she lists food preparation, nursing and infant care, and menstruation technologies.[40] Other feminists investigate social arrangements that reproduce the masculinist identification with technologies that intimately affect women's lives, such as domestic technologies, as well as specific domains that are still dominated by male scientists, engineers, and medical researchers, such as the new reproductive technologies.[41]

As I implied in the opening remarks about my mother's computer employment history, women's relationship to the technology of the workplace has been a troubled one. The expansion of clerical occupations after World War I resulted in the feminization of such occupations; women were preferentially hired over men because they were less expensive to employ. This kept the costs of expansion contained. After World War II, many forms of female office work were subjected to the analysis of scientific management. Tasks were routinized and rationalized; bookkeepers and other office workers became 'machine attendants who performed standardized repetitive calculating operations'.[42] This repetitive work was the perfect material for automated calculators. Although some labour historians assert that the introduction of electronic calculators and computers occurred during a time of economic expansion, and thus had the effect of actually increasing the number of clerical jobs available for displaced workers, the new jobs were often sex-stratified such that better-paying data-processing positions were staffed by men. I offer this brief outline to point to the fact that women have been involved with the implementation of information technology in US business and industry since at least World War I. This technology had contradictory effects on women's employment: it increased the opportunity for new jobs, but at the same time it downgraded the skill level of office workers who were employed to attend to the new machines.[43] In forming a judgement about the impact of these technologies on women's lives, it is important to remember that it is likely that the women who were displaced from their bookkeeping positions in the 1950s by the introduction of electronic technology did not necessarily experience this as an employment failure. No doubt some of them, like my mother, were eager to get on with the real business of their lives, which was getting married, having children, and raising families.

In the ten years since the personal computer became widely available as a mass-produced consumer item, it has become an entirely naturalized fixture in the workplace, either at home or at the business office.[44] It is also becoming common to criticize the claims that computers increase office worker productivity – the primary marketing line for the sale of PCs to businesses and industries. Some critics protest that the real impact of computers and word-processing systems has been to increase the quantity of time spent producing documents, while others argue that the computerized office decreases the quality of work life due to physical discomfort and information overload.[45] Sociological studies of the gendered aspects of computer employment focus on the de-skilling and displacement of female clerical workers in different industries. While these studies on women as labourers are vital for an understanding of the social and economic impact of computers, there is less research available about women's creative or educational use of information technologies or their role in the history of computing. But there is also a class bias reflected in these investigations due to the fact that, by focusing on women's computer use in the workplace, such studies restrict their critical investigation to those women who have access to what remains a costly technology that is out of the reach and the skill level of most women in the United States today. The question of women's employment and computer technology can be asked another way. For example, Les Levidow studies the women who make the tiny silicon chips that serve as the electronic guts for cheap computer gadgets. Both in affluent (until recently) Silicon Valley and in a relatively poor Malaysian state (Penang), the large majority of chip makers are poorly paid immigrant women.[46]

Yet another way to approach the question of women and technological histories, more sensitive to class-related issues, is to ask 'Who counts?' This leads to the investigation of both those who determine who counts as instances of what identities and also those who are treated as numbers or cases in the construction of a database. The politics of databases will be a critical agenda item for the 1990s as an increasing number of businesses, services, and state agencies go 'on-line'. Determining who has access to data, and how to get access to data that is supposedly available to the 'public', is a multi-dimensional project that involves the use of computers, skill at network accessing, and education in locating and negotiating government-supported databases. Even a chief data coordinator with the US Geological Survey asserts that 'data markets, data access, and data dissemination are complicated, fuzzy, emotional topics right now.' She 'predicts that they likely will be the major issues of the decade.'[47] Questions of public access and the status of information in the computer age are just now attracting public attention. As Kenneth B. Allen argues, the same technologies that enable us to 'create, manipulate, and disseminate information' also, ironically, 'threaten to diminish public access to government information'. The issue of citizens' rights to information needs to be monitored by computer-savvy citizen advocates. The question is: Where will such advocates come from?[48] Two answers immediately arise: they will be either educated or elected. Feminist scholars and teachers can contribute to both processes by encouraging women students to address information policy issues in their research projects and by supporting women candidates who will serve on the federal and state boards that govern information access.[49] These candidates and policy students will certainly face several difficult issues involving bodies, information, and criminal charges. The Council for State Governments describes one item of state legislation that may be voted on during 1993: 'The Prenatal

Exposure to Controlled Substances Act'. This act would require 'substance abuse treatment personnel to report to the state department of children and family services any pregnant woman who is addicted to drugs or alcohol.'[50] The positive consequence of such an act would be requiring states to 'bring treatment services to alcohol and/or substance abusing pregnant women.' Negative consequences, such as the criminalization of pregnant women for delivering controlled substances to minors, are not mentioned. This act could, as Jennifer Terry suggests, serve as a 'technology of surveillance' whereby the unborn fetus is guaranteed certain rights denied to the pregnant woman: for 'poor women, interventions into daily life through social welfare and the criminal justice system render recourse to the right to privacy somewhat moot.'[51]

In telling the cyberpunk story of the coordination between technology and technical expertise and how it becomes subject to corporate control, *Synners* offers a counter-mythology of the information age – not that information wants to be free, but rather that access to information is going to cost, and cost a lot. Through its post-feminst portrayal of empowered female bodies who play off and against repressed or hysterical male bodies, *Synners* offers an alternative vision of technological embodiment that is consistent with a gendered history of technology: where technology isn't the means of escape from or transcendence of the body, but rather the means of communication and connection with other bodies. *Synners* also raises questions about the meaning of race in a technological age. How is technological disembodiment also a comment on the desire to transcend racial identities? How are material bodies race-marked through technological encounters? How are racial identities articulated by myths of technological progress?[52] Despite our condition of being incurably informed, we don't have enough information about the embodied aspects of new information technologies. Simply put, we need a great deal more in order to construct the type of analyses of the information age that can serve as a foundation for a critical political agenda.

Synners also suggests the importance of a cyberpunk mythology for the construction of feminist cultural studies of scientific and technological formations. Gina and Sam make interesting subjects for feminist theory in that their technological competencies and synner talents emphasize the need for feminist activists to encourage women to develop technological skills, and for feminist teachers to promote educational efforts to increase technological literacy. The challenge is to harness the power of technological knowledge to a feminist agenda while struggling against an increasing industrial imperialism that eagerly assimilates new techno-workers to labour in the interests of private enterprise.[53] The question is how to empower technological agents such that they work on behalf of the right kind of social change. Determining exactly what constitutes a feminist technological agenda is another matter entirely.

Notes

Thanks to Michael Greer for the Ron Silliman line and for reading and discussing this paper during its various stages of construction. I would also like to thank Pat Cadigan, Sene Sorrow, Stuart Moulthrop, Jay Bolter, Tom Foster, Alan Ranch, Chea Prince, and Robert Cheatham for many discussions that contributed to this essay. A much earlier draft of this paper was presented at the Modern Language Association meetings, San Francisco, 1991.

1 In her historical study of the gendering of the automobile, Virginia Scharff reports that the first woman in the US to get a driver's license was Mrs John Howell Phillips of Chicago in 1899. See her *Taking the Wheel: Women and the Coming of the Motor Age* (New York: Free Press, 1991), p. 25.

2 Jumping thirty years in this abbreviated history leaves several threads hanging. From World War I to the end of World War II, Chicago was the scene of several significant industrial and cultural transformations. Like thousands of other new immigrants, one set of my grandparents emigrated from southern Italy, the other set from Lithuania. Each settled in an ethnic-identified Chicago neighbourhood and began working for one of several large corporate employers already dominating Chicago politics and economics: Grandfather Balsamo at International Harvester, Grandmother Martins at Hart, Schaffner and Marx, and Uncle Barnes at the Swift stockyards. See Lisbeth Cohen, *Making a New Deal: Industrial Workers in Chicago, 1919–1939* (Cambridge: Cambridge University Press, 1990). Cohen's project enacts a cyborgian logic to investigate a historical pattern of recombinant social identity, whereby we can read how mass culture played a significant role in the unification of previously disparate groups.

3 According to Sharon H. Strom, 'The comptometer, developed by Felt and Tarrant in Chicago, was often more popular than the calculator because it was key-driven, lightweight, and inexpensive. . . . Its chief drawback was that it was non-listing; that is, there was no printed tape which showed each item entered, only a window in which a running total appeared' (p. 70). See '"Machines Instead of Clerks": Technology and the Feminization of Bookkeeping, 1930–1950', in *Case Studies and Policy Perspectives*, ed. H. I. Hartmann (Washington, DC: National Academy Press, 1987), vol. 2, pp. 630–97.

4 Rose Balsamo was one of the 800 troops assigned to the Headquarters Com-

pany Fourth Aviation Brigade; she was assistant to the NCO in charge of medical support for the other US troops and Kurdistani refugees.

5   The 'New Edge' is one of the most recent labels for a particular arrangement within contemporary culture. See James R. Beniger, *The Control Revolution: Technological and Economic Origins of the Information Society* (Cambridge, Mass.: Harvard University Press, 1986).

6   Pat Cadigan, *Synners* (London: Grafton, 1991), p. 3; hereafter cited in the text. Cadigan's first novel, *Mindplayers* (1989), and most recent one, *Fools* (1992), also belong to the genre of cyberpunk SF. *Fools* is experimental in its narrative construction in a way similar to Joanna Russ's *The Female Man*, where the identity of the narrative 'I' is fluid and fragmented. [For a brief discussion of Cadigan's *Fools*, see my *PomoIntro*, p. 231. (NL)]

7   Teresa de Lauretis writes: 'Hence SF as a mode of writing and reading, as a textual and contextual production of signs and meanings, inscribes our cognitive and creative processes in what may be called the technological imagination. In tracing cognitive paths through the physical and material reality of the contemporary technological landscape and designing new maps of social reality, SF is perhaps the most innovative fictional mode of our historical creativity.' See her 'Signs of Wa/onder', in *The Technological Imagination: Theories and Fictions*, eds Teresa de Lauretis, Andreas Huyssen, and Kathleen Woodward (Madison, Wis.: Coda Press, 1980), p. 169.

8   In describing the structural definition of a cultural formation, Lawrence Grossberg states that a 'formation is a historical articulation, an accumulation or organization of practices. The question is how particular cultural practices, which may have no intrinsic or even apparent connection, are articulated together to construct an apparently new identity. . . . It is not a question of interpreting a body of texts or tracing out their intertextuality. Rather the formation has to be read as the articulation of a number of discrete series of events, only some of which are discursive.' See his *We Gotta Get Out ot This Place: Popular Conservatism and Postmodern Culture* (New York: Routledge, 1992), p. 70.

9   If we broaden the dimensions of a discursive formation such that it includes the way in which readers read the work and discuss it, reproduce it and detourn it, then the possibility of producing archemedian criticism of any form of popular fiction is all the more improbable. In this way, cyberpunk illustrates one of the key issues at the heart of our information-obsessed culture. As Darko Suvin argues, 'an encompassingly extensive survey of cyberpunk SF looks . . . not only materially impossible but also methodologically dubious' (see his 'On Gibson and Cyberpunk SF', *Foundation* 46 (1989), p. 41). It has become increasingly difficult to claim any sort of mastery *vis-à-vis* a discursive dispersion or a properly historical genealogy because of the rate of publication and the shelf life of science fiction publications. Not only is it very difficult to keep track of all the writers of a particular style, it is equally difficult to keep

track of a single author's output. Few libraries archive pulp science fiction novels; even fewer catalogue the early science fiction magazines or any of the numerous fanzines that have appeared in the past decade. As with the situation for small press literature and poetry, the economics and politics of publishing and library archiving have more to do with the evaluation of the work in question than with any meta-literary notions of 'value', 'unity', or 'genre'. The field exists as an unpatterned dispersion – like the Internet, it is impossible to map exhaustively. Users who read the Internet newsgroup report that several lists of cyberpunk fiction have circulated in the past three years. I have one compiled by Jonathan Drummey, dated 23 February 1992, that lists 91 authors, including some who only write nonfiction. The *Beyond Cyberpunk* hypercard stack lists over two hundred books, stories, and anthologies, whereas the FutureCulture list maintained by Andy Hawkins includes over three hundred. I cite these fan bibliographies to illustrate how a community of readers constitutes a discursive field; it would be interesting to study how and why they determine who's in and who's not.

10   *Mondo 2000* has an interesting publishing history, having begun as a hacker's magazine, only to be transformed more recently into a slick, visually dense, technopop fanzine with high production values. Selections from the first eight issues have been collected in *The Mondo 2000 User's Guide to the New Edge*. Chapter topics include all the defining preoccupations of New Edge cyberpunks: smart drugs, computer graphics, chaos theory, electronic music/freedom, hip-hop, robots, street tech, VR, V-sex, wetware, multimedia, and the net (among other things). The book includes a bibliography under the title 'The Shopping Mall', which is a list of products, programs, music, journals, and books where you can 'read/hear all about it'. See *The Mondo 2000 User's Guide to the New Edge*, eds Rudy Rucker, R. U. Sirius, and Queen Mu (New York, 1992).

11   Although clearly beyond the scope of this paper, such an analysis would also need to trace the enabling conditions for the emergence/convergence of the New Edge as cultural formation, notably, the phenomenon of Star Trek fandom, the affective structure of punk rock & roll, phone phreaking, and the computerization of fantasy RPGs (role-playing games). Mixing in with these popular forms is a range of new technologies that are themselves being studied as important cultural phenomena; here I'm thinking of Brenda Laurel's work, *Computers as Theater* (Reading, Mass.: Addison-Wesley, 1991) and Benjamin Woolley's study of virtual reality, *Virtual Worlds: A Journey in Hype and Hyperreality* (Oxford: Blackwell, 1992).

12   Having identified the key periods in science fiction's literary history, Teresa de Lauretis puts the issue of periodization aside in favor of discussing the sign work of SF as a 'mode of writing [and] a manner of reading'. She points out two modes of signification unique to science fiction as an art form: (1) 'SF uses language and narrative signs in a literal way', and (2) 'technology is its diffuse landscape'. See her 'Signs of Wa/onder', pp. 160, 167 and 170.

13   Suvin uses Gibson's novels to identify the genre conventions of 'the best works' of cyberpunk SF, while Sterling's work serves as an 'unworthy' example. However, Suvin's polarization of the two is somewhat reversed when he considers the two writers' more recent novels. Suvin claims that Gibson's third novel, *Mona Lisa Overdrive*, 'confirms and solidifies his trajectory from critical to escapist use of cyberspace'. See 'On Gibson and Cyberpunk SF', p. 48.

14   Much of this work has focused on the postmodern qualities of Gibson's novels in particular: see, for example, David Porush, 'Cybernauts in Cyberspace: William Gibson's Neuromancer', in *Aliens: The Anthropology of Science Fiction*, ed. George Slusser (Carbondale: Southern Illinois Press, 1987), pp. 168–78; and Peter Fitting, 'The Lessons of Cyberpunk', in *Technoculture*, ed. Constance Penley and Andrew Ross (Minneapolis: University of Minnesota Press, 1991), pp. 295–315. Other writers elaborate the connection between cyberpunk and popular media: Brooks Landon, 'Bet On IT: Cyber/video/punk/performance', *Mississippi Review* 16 (1988), pp. 245–51; and George Slusser, 'Literary MTV', *Mississippi Review* 16 (1988), pp. 279–88.

15   Veronica Hollinger, 'Cybernetic Deconstructions: Cyberpunk and Post-modernism', *Mosaic* 23 (Spring 1990), pp. 29–44. If Hollinger misses anything in her careful reading, it is the multiplication of capitalist space, where the mise-en-scène of cyberpunk landscapes (cybernetic as well as the urban sprawl) doesn't just signify an excess of surface, but also an excess of corporate territorialization. In this sense, Gibson's compulsive use of brand names is a testimony to the cybernetic expansion of multinationalist capitalism. On this point, see Pam Rosenthal, 'Jacked In: Fordism, Cyberpunk, Marxism', *Socialist Review* 21 (1991), pp. 79–103. [For a way of seeing poststructuralism as other than 'antihumanist', and not the same as postmodernism, see my *PomoIntro*. (NL)]

16   Hollinger, 'Cybernetic Deconstructions', pp. 33 and 42.

17   Fredric Jameson, *Postmodernism, or, The Cultural Logic of Late Capitalism* (Durham: Duke University Press, 1991), p. 38.

18   'New Wave' science fiction refers to SF writing of the 1960s which 'rebelled' against a certain mood of 'middle classness' that was felt to have settled on the genre, restricting its potential for imaginative growth. Figures associated with the New Wave include Thomas Disch, Roger Zelazny, Ursula Le Guin and J. G. Ballard, while the 'movement' (as it may loosely be called) can be said to have begun in the UK under Michael Moorcock's editorship of the magazine *New Worlds*, extending thereafter to the US sci-fi mags *Amazing Stories* (during Cele G. Lalli's editorial reign) and *If* (edited by Frederik Pohl). For a discussion of feminist science fiction, see Marleen S. Barr, *Lost in Space: Probing Feminist Science Fiction and Beyond* (Chapel Hill: University of North Carolina Press, 1993). (NL)

19   Fred Pfeil, *Another Tale to Tell: Politics and Narrative in Postmodern Culture* (London: Verso, 1990), p. 38.

20   Jean Baudrillard, *In the Shadow of the Silent Majorities . . . or The End of the Social*, trans. Paul Foss, Paul Patron, and John Johnston (New York:

Semiotext[e], 1983), p. 95.

21   Carolyn Marvin, 'Information and History', in *The Ideology of the Informa-tion Age*, ed. Jennifer Daryl Slack and Fred Fejes (Norwood, NJ: Ablex, 1987), pp. 49–62.

22   Hollywood representations of technological hallucinations show an amazing visual similarity over time, using out-of-focus shots, swirling images that involve a p.o.v. sequence that moves through a worm hole, rapid edits, and illogically juxtaposed shots to suggest a technologically induced subjective state. See especially *The Trip* (1967), *Brainstorm* (1983), *Circuitry Man* (1989), *Freejack* (1992), *Till the End of the World* (1992).

23   Pfeil, *Another Tale*, p. 89. In his study of Nintendo video games, Eugene Provenzo reports that when women are included as characters in video games they 'are often cast as individuals who are acted upon rather than as initiators of action'. They are depicted as the princess or girlfriend in distress who must be rescued by the male hero acting alone or as the leader of a team of fighters/magicians. Female characters may obliquely serve as the animating motive for the video search, journey, and fight narratives, but they do so only as victims who are unable to rescue themselves. Video games designed for other gaming systems show a similar stereotyping of female characters. In the Sega Genesis game *Phantasy Star III*, for example, the video player can choose female cyborgs as members of his team of adventurers; in the course of this game the hero's team encounters many powerful monsters depicted as seductive women. Even when the games include women characters on the fighting/journeying team, they still serve at the behest of the male warrior figure who is the real agent in the gaming narrative. Girls who play video games have no other choice but to play the male main character who rescues the pretty princess or, in the case of *Maniac Mansion* (Nintendo), Sandy the Cheerleader. 'Thus the games not only socialize women to be dependent, but also condition men to assume dominant gender roles.' See Eugene F. Provenzo, Jr., *Video Kids: Making Sense of Nintendo* (Cambridge, Mass.: Harvard University Press, 1991), p. 100.

24   Andrew Ross, *Strange Weather: Culture, Science, and Technology in the Age of Limits* (London: Verso, 1991), p. 145.

25   Cf. esp. Donna J. Haraway, 'A Manifesto for Cyborgs: Science, Technology, and Socialist Feminism in the 1980s', *Socialist Review* 15, 2 (1985), pp. 65–108; and also her *Primate Visions: Gender, Race, and Nature in the World of Modern Science* (London and New York: Verso, 1992). (NL)

26   According to Arthur Kroker, the female body has always been postmodern in that it has always been saturated with the signs of capitalism; the male body, in turn, becomes hysterical when it encounters this condition of satu-ration for the first time. See Arthur and Marilouise Kroker, eds., *Body In-vaders: Panic Sex in America* (New York: St Martin's Press, 1987). I develop a fuller analysis of Kroker's treatment of the disappearing body in postmodern theory in *Technologies of the Gendered Body* (Durham: Duke University Press, 1996). [For more on the relations of Kroker's work (especially in

collaboration with David Cook) to a certain version of the post, see my *PomoIntro*, pp. 88–90. (NL)]

27 For an insightful discussion between Susie Bright and Brenda Laurel on the erotic possibilities of virtual sex, see 'The Virtual Orgasm', in Bright's *Sexual Reality: A Virtual Sex World Reader* (Pittsburgh: Cleis Press, 1992), pp. 60–70.

28 Allucquere Rosanne Stone, 'Will the Real Body Please Stand Up?: Boundary Stories about Virtual Cultures', in *Cyberspace: First Steps*, ed. Michael Benedikt (Cambridge, Mass.: MIT Press, 1992), p. 109. See also Sally Pryor, 'Thinking of Oneself as a Computer', *Leonardo* 24 (1991): pp. 585–90.

29 Stone, 'Real Body', p. 113. I would argue that the repression of the material body is discursively accomplished in part because of the very intelligence of the technobody: just as driving a car becomes physiologically intuitive, so too does using a VR rig. As a newly emergent popular cultural form, embodied encounters with VR are more virtual than real at this point. See Anne Balsamo, 'The Virtual Body in Cyberspace', *Journal of Research in the Philosophy of Technology* (Spring 1993).

30 For a discussion of the ethical/policy dimensions of computer communication, see Jeffrey Bairstow, 'Who Reads Your Electronic Mail?', *Electronic Business*, 16 June 1990, p. 92; Pamela Varley, 'Electronic Democracy', *Technology Review* (November/December 1991), pp. 40–3; and Laurence H. Tribe, 'The Constitution in Cyberspace', *The Humanist* 51 (Sept./Oct. 1991), pp. 15–21.

31 For a discussion of the gendered nature of communication technologies, see especially Lana Rakow, 'Women and the Telephone: The Gendering of a Communications Technology', in *Technology and Women's Voices: Keeping in Touch*, ed. Cheris Kramarae (London: Routledge & Kegan Paul, 1988).

32 The Jargon File, version 2.0.10, 1 July 1992. Available on-line from ftp.uu.net.

33 See Sherry Turkle and Seymour Papert, 'Epistemological Pluralism: Styles and Voices with the Computer Culture', *Signs* 16 (1990), pp. 128–57; and Dannielle Bernstein, 'Comfort and Experience with Computing: Are They the Same for Women and Men?' *SIGCSE Bulletin* 23 (Sept. 1991), pp. 57–60.

34 Hoai-An Truong, 'Gender Issues in Online Communication', CFP 93 (version 4.1). Available on-line from ftp.eff.org.

35 Carolyn Kay Steedman, *Landscape for a Good Woman: A Story of Two Lives* (London: Virago, 1986), pp. 6–7.

36 Cf. Sigmund Freud, *Case Histories 1: 'Dora' and 'Little Hans'*, trans. Alix and James Strachey, ed. James Strachey, vol. 8 of *The Pelican Freud Library* (Harmondsworth: Penguin, 1977). The 'Dora' study (or, officially, 'Fragment of an Analysis of a Case of Hysteria') is one of Freud's most controversial texts. The teenage Dora is diagnosed a 'hysteric' for not taking pleasure in the sexual advances of one of her father's male friends, who covets Dora in exchange for his wife who has been sleeping with Dora's father who is not opposed to the 'exchange'! (NL)

37 Steven Best and Douglas Kellner, *Postmodern Theory: Critical Interrogations* (New York: Guilford, 1991), p. 274. [The vexed question of 'the

post-historical' is taken up throughout my *PomoIntro*, but see esp. ch. 3. (NL)]

38   In one account of the history of the computer, the identity of the 'world's first programmer' is left out of the chapter title: 'Charles Babbage and the World's First Programmer'. We discover on the next page that '[t]hough Babbage was a lonely man obsessed with his vision of a programmable computer, he developed a liaison with the beautiful Ada Lovelace, the only legitimate child of Lord Byron, the poet. She became as obsessed as Babbage with the project and contributed many of the ideas for programming the machine, including the invention of the programming loop and the subroutine.' Apparently Lovelace translated a description of Babbage's machine, 'The Analytical Engine', and 'included extensive discussion on programming techniques, sample programs, and the potential of this technology to emulate intelligent human activities.' Lovelace was honored by the US Defense Department when it named its programming language after her: ADA. Lovelace and Captain Crace Murray Hooper (who is credited with the development of the programming language COBOL) are usually the only two women who appear in histories of the computer. See Raymond Kurzweil, *In the Age of Intelligent Machines* (Cambridge, Mass.: MIT Press, 1990), p. 167. For a brief biography of Ada Byron Lovelace (1815–52), see Teri Perl, *Math Equals: Biographies of Women Mathematicians* (Menlo Park: Addison-Wesley, 1978).

39   Joan Rothschild, 'Introduction', in *Machina Ex Dea: Feminist Perspectives on Technology* (New York: Pergamon Press, 1983), p. xviii. In her 1982 review of women and the history of American technology, Judith McGaw identifies Ruth Schwartz Cowan's address to the 1976 meetings of the Society of the History of Technology as a significant founding moment for the feminist study of technology. It was also a literal founding moment for the organization of Women in Technological History (WITH). See Judith A. McGaw, 'Women and the History of American Technology', *Signs* 7 (1982), pp. 798–828.

40   Autumn Stanley, 'Women Hold Up Two-Thirds of the Sky: Notes for a Revised History of Technology', in Rothschild, ed., *Machina Ex Dea*, pp. 5–22. See also Judy Wajcman's discussion of how women are 'hidden from histories of technology': *Feminism Confronts Technology* (North Sydney: Allen & Unwin, 1991). A more popularized treatment of the topic is Ethlie Ann Vare and Greg Ptacek, *Mothers of Invention: From the Bra to the Bomb, Forgotten Women and Their Unforgettable Ideas* (New York: Morrow, 1987).

41   See esp. Cynthia Cockburn, *Machinery of Dominance: Women, Men and Technical Know-How* (London and Sydeny: Pluto, 1985); Gina Corea, *The Mother Machine: Reproductive Technologies from Artificial Insemination to Artificial Wombs* (New York and Sydney: Harper & Row, 1985); and Michelle Stanworth, ed., *Reproductive Technologies: Gender, Motherhood, and Medicine* (Cambridge: Polity Press, 1987).

42   See the chapter, 'Historical Patterns of Technological Change', in *Computer Chips and Paper Clips: Technology and Women's Employment*, eds Heidi I.

Hartmann, Robert E. Kraut, and Louise A. Tilly (Washington, DC: National Academy Press, 1986), p. 40.

43 Other studies of women and workplace technology include Margery Davis, *Woman's Place Is at the Typewriter: Office Work and Office Workers, 1870–1930* (Philadelphia: Temple University Press, 1982); Judith S. McIlwee and J. Cregg Robinson, *Women in Engineering: Gender, Power and Workplace Culture* (Albany: SUNY Press, 1992); and Uma Sekaran and Frederick T. L. Leong, eds, *WomanPower: Managing in Times of Demographic Turbulence* (Newbury Park: Sage, 1992).

44 As a more recent contribution to the study of women's relationship to the technology of the workplace, Ruth Perry and Lisa Greber edited a special issue of *Signs*, published in 1990, on the topic of women and computers. The scholarship that they review considers the impact of the computer on women's employment and the structural forces that limit women's access to computer education. See Ruth Perry and Lisa Greber, 'Women and Computers: An Introduction', *Signs* 16 (1990), pp. 74–101.

45 See ch. 5, 'Conclusions and Recommendations', in Hartmann, Kraut, and Tilly, eds, *Computer Chips and Paper Clips.*

46 Levidow explores the 'price paid for cheap chips' in terms of the harassment and forms of control that Malaysian women endure. See Les Levidow, 'Women Who Make the Chips', *Science as Culture* 2 (1991), pp. 103–24. See also Aihwa Ong's ethnographic study, *Spirits of Resistance and Capitalist Discipline: Factory Women in Malaysia* (Albany: SUNY Press, 1987).

47 The quotation is from Nancy Iosta, chief of the Branch of Geographic Data Coordination of the National Mapping Division, US Geological Survey in Reston, Virginia ('Who's Got the Data?', *Geo Info Systems* (Sept. 1992), pp. 24–7). Iosta's prediction is supported by other statements about the US government's efforts to build a Geographic Information System (GIS): a database system whereby 'all public information can be referenced by location', the GIS is hailed as 'an information intergrator'. The best use of GIS would be to support the coordination of local, regional, and national organizations – both governmental and private. See Lisa Warnecke, 'Building the National GI/GIS Partnership', *Geo Info Systems* (April 1992), pp. 16–23. Managing data, acquiring new data, and safeguarding data integrity are issues of concern for GIS managers. Because of the cost of acquiring new data and safeguarding data integrity, GIS managers sometimes charge a fee for providing information. This process of charging 'has thrown [them] into a morass of issues about public records and freedom of information: the value of data, privacy, copyrights, and liability and the roles of public and private sectors in disseminating information.' See Nancy Iosta, 'Public Access: Right or Privilege?' *Geo Info Systems* (Nov./Dec. 1991), pp. 20–5.

48 Kenneth B. Allen, 'Access to Government Information', *Government Information Quarterly* 9 (1992), p. 68.

49 Teola P. Hunter, for one, argues that African-American women must seek

out potential political candidates who are already 'appearing in city council seats, on county commissions, on school boards, in chambers of commerce and on many advisory boards at all levels of government.' The key for success that these women hold is their connection to 'civil rights groups, education groups, and church groups'. Hunter goes on to argue that when 'minority women use these contacts and these bonds, they have a support base that is hard to match'. See Teola P. Hunter, 'A Different View of Progress – Minority Women in Politics', *Journal of State Government* (April/ June 1991), pp. 48–52.

50   Council of State Governments, *Suggested State Legislation 51* (1992), pp. 17–19. There are a number of pieces of legislation that women in particular should he aware of: Breast Cancer Education, Detection, and Screening Standards Acts, Battered Woman Syndrome Defense Act, and a new Domestic Violence Act.

51   Jennifer Terry, 'The Body Invaded: Medical Surveillance of Women as Reproducers', *Socialist Review* 39 (1988), pp. 13–43.

52   An advertisement that appeared in *Essence* magazine in 1991 publicizes Garrett Morgan's invention of the traffic light. This ad also illustrates the subtle appropriation of a black agent to support the ideological myth of technological progress, whereby a racist system can somehow be vanquished through a technological fix. The advertisement is sponsored by Amtrak, and includes a picture of a traffic light and the caption: 'How do you see the road in front of you?' The rest of the ad copy reads:

> The opportunity to get ahead isn't always a matter of red or green. Historically, it's often been a question of black and white. Luckily, Garrett A. Morgan didn't see color as an obstacle. Instead, this son of a former slave overcame tremendous prejudice to become one of the most important American inventors of this century. His creations ranged from a hair straightening cream to the gas mask which saved thousands of lives during WWI. But it was Mr. Morgan's development of the traffic signal which perhaps best symbolizes his life. In 1923, automobiles were increasing in number, and so, unfortunately, were automobile accidents. After witnessing one down the street from his house, he developed and sold his patent for a traffic safety light to General Electric – the forerunner of the traffic light we see on practically every corner in the world. It typified his concern for the safety of people everywhere. His perseverance, and his refusal to let the color of his skin color anyone's perception of his ability. Which brings us the true lesson of Garrett A. Morgan. He may have invented the traffic signal. But he never saw a red light. (*Essence*, Feb. 1991, p. 95)

53   For a discussion of the technological takeover of higher education in Britain – a discussion that offers insights into the shift away from the humanities and social sciences and toward technological and managerial fields going on right now in the United States – see Kevin Robins and Frank Webster, 'Higher Education, High Tech, High Rhetoric', in *Compulsive Technology: Computers as Culture*, eds Tony Solomenides and Les Levidow (London: Free Association Books, 1985), pp. 36–57.

Chapter Eleven
POSTcyberMODERN-
punkISM

Brian McHale

These are days of lasers in the jungle . . .

Paul Simon

Suppose a reader, in search of a reliable and authoritative account of con-temporary fiction in the United States, were to consult the *Columbia Liter-ary History of the United States* (1988), edited by Emory Elliot with nine distinguished Americanists listed as associate and advisory editors. What could be more reliable and authoritative? Opening to the chapter titled 'The Fictions of the Present', this reader would immediately encounter an epigraph from *Neuromancer* (1984) by William Gibson. William who? William Gibson, the cyberpunk science fiction writer, of course. Reading on, she or he would find that the author of this chapter, Larry McCaffery, considers science fiction to be 'arguably the most significant body of work in contemporary fiction',[1] and ranks science fiction's 'emergence . . . as a major literary genre first among the 'most significant new directions in recent American fiction'.[2] Moreover, McCaffery's judgements are reflected in his allocation of space in what must have been a very tightly budgeted essay: of its twenty-two paragraphs, two full paragraphs are devoted to SF in general, another to women SF writers, two more to Ted Mooney's *Easy Travel to Other Planets* (1981) (not 'hard' SF but SF-related), and parts of two other paragraphs to the SF novelists Samuel R. Delany and (of course) William Gibson.

Brian McHale, 'POSTcyberMODERNpunkISM', in *Storming the Reality Studio: A Case-book of Cyberpunk and Postmodern Science Fiction*, ed. L. McCaffery (Durham and London: Duke University Press, 1991), pp. 308–23.

The *Columbia Literary History* represents, if not a breakthrough, at least a striking advance in the process of science fiction's legitimation. What explains this new 'official' acceptability of SF? Perhaps after all it is just a matter of quality: SF writers are now able to meet the standards that we expect 'serious' writing to meet. But there have always been critics willing to maintain that SF has already achieved such standards, and there have always been at least a few SF writers who could measure up to even the most demanding literary criteria; anyway, the notion that there exists some absolute threshold of quality which candidates for legitimation must cross seems dubious, to say the least.

This is not, in any case, the explanation that the *Columbia Literary History* gives. Here and elsewhere McCaffery views the new cyberpunk SF in the light of a general postmodernist phenomenon, the alleged collapse of genre distinctions, including the distinction between 'genre' fiction (such as SF) and 'serious' fiction.[3] The underlying thesis, in other words, is the one associated with Fredric Jameson and Andreas Huyssen, among others: namely, that postmodernism is characterized by the collapse of hierarchical distinctions between high and low art, between 'official' high culture and popular or mass culture.[4] So attractive and influential is this thesis that we ought to be more than a little wary of it. For one thing, as E. Ann Kaplan has observed, just because certain high culture texts happen to mingle high culture and popular culture elements, there is no reason to conclude that the boundaries between high and popular culture have been effaced in the culture at large. In fact, of course, the institutions for the production, distribution, and consumption of high culture continue to be distinct from those for popular culture, regardless of whatever promiscuous minglings of cultural strata may occur inside texts.[5]

McCaffery also proposes this thesis of the collapse of cultural distinctions in an interview with William Gibson, who unreservedly endorses it: 'This process of cultural mongrelization seems to be what postmodernism is all about. . . . I know I don't have a sense of writing as being divided up into different compartments. . . .'[6] Nevertheless, it is easy to demonstrate that Gibson's own writing relies on the continuing viability of cultural compartmentalization. Gibson's fiction functions at every level, even down to the 'micro' structures of phrases and neologisms, on the principle of incongruous juxtaposition – juxtapositions of American culture with Japanese culture, of high technology with the subcultures of the 'street' and the underworld, and so on. The term 'cyberpunk' has been constructed according to this incongruity principle. There is an example in the

McCaffery interview itself, when Gibson gives as an instance of 'cultural mongrelization' people who like punk and Mozart, and who will 'invite you to mud wrestling or a poetry reading'.[7] The effect of incongruity here and elsewhere in Gibson's writing obviously depends on the persistence of hierarchical cultural categories: a poetry reading belongs to high culture and mud wrestling to low culture. If the distinction were effaced, the effect would be lost; no compartmentalization, no effect of incongruity. As Ralph Cohen remarks, in the context of a discussion of the persistence of genres in postmodernism, the very possibility of transgression presupposes the existence of generic (or, more generally, categorial) boundaries.[8]

Furthermore, the thesis of postmodernism's effacement of the 'great divide' between high and low culture depends for much of its potency and persuasiveness on a particular construction of modernism. Historical 'high modernism', by this account, sought to seal high culture off from 'contamination' by mass culture. This particular construction of modernism is obviously tendentious, designed partly to throw into high relief the novelty and difference of postmodernism. A little reflection will show, however, the degree to which even the most self-assertively 'artistic' modernist writers exploited popular art models and genres, and not just by ironically quoting or parodying them: think of James's reliance on melodrama and romance, or Conrad's on adventure story models; Faulkner's exploitation of historical 'costume' romance, detective fiction, horror stories, pornography, and just about every other currently available pop art genre; and the almost universal impact of cinematic models and strategies, especially in the United States (Hemingway, Faulkner, Dos Passos, Fitzgerald, Nathanael West). This is not to say that there is no significant difference between modernism and postmodernism on this issue, for of course there is, but it is mainly a difference of their respective self-descriptions: where the modernists repudiated and sought to camouflage their reliance on pop art models, the postmodernists have tended openly to advertise theirs. But we must try not to confuse polemics with actual practice.

In fact, it would be utterly astonishing if modernist writing had failed to exploit pop art models, for the constant traffic between low and high – the high art appropriation of pop art models and the reciprocal assimilation by pop art genres of 'cast-off' high art models – is one of the universal engines driving the history of literary (and, more generally, cultural) forms. Thus, while modernist writers were quarrying popular genres for materials with which to revivify their own high art productions, they were also supplying, directly or through intermediaries, popular writers with materials to replenish their stock. For example, we can trace the diffusion of a certain avant-garde minimalist prose style from its innovator (Gertrude Stein, about 1914) through her epigones (especially Sherwood Anderson, about 1920, and Hemingway, about 1925) to certain intermediaries (especially Dashiell Hammett), and from them to a wide range of mass-market media – a sort of 'trickle-down' modernism.[9]

What is distinctive of postmodernism, then, is not the fact of 'contamination' of high culture by mass culture, since that turns out to be a universal of cultural history (and as characteristic of modernism as it is of postmodernism), but rather the technologically enhanced speed of the traffic in models between the high and low strata of culture. Pop art models are assimilated by high art (and vice versa) more quickly now than ever before, and this has the further consequence of producing an ever more intimate interaction, an ever-tighter feedback loop, between high and low. Such speed and intimacy of interaction is not, however, to be confused with the collapse or effacement of hierarchical distinctions. For the engine to continue to turn over, the high culture/low culture distinction must persist, in however problematic or attenuated a form.

Science fiction is a case in point. A number of critics have noted the 'convergence' or 'cross-fertilization' between recent science fiction and 'serious' or 'mainstream' postmodernist fiction.[10] Yet, so steadily has the tempo of this interaction accelerated from decade to decade that at the same time we were making these observations the youngest generation of science fiction writers, the so-called cyberpunks, were both corroborating our observations and pre-empting them, in a sense rendering them obsolete. In any case, the trajectory of convergence we had begun to map can now be extended through the 1980s.

Samuel Delany contends, in his contribution to the *Mississippi Review* 'Forum',[11] that only in the context of the internal history of the SF genre do cyberpunk's themes and styles acquire their full significance. Delany makes a strong case; but I want to argue that the SF tradition is not the only relevant context for cyberpunk, and that, on the contrary, part of cyberpunk's significance derives from the changing relationship between SF and 'mainstream' fiction in recent decades.

For SF is not a genre in a vacuum, of course, but belongs to an entire system of genres, popular entertainment genres as well as high art genres, within the overall system of systems, or polysystem, of the culture.[12] In order to describe some of the systemic relations relevant to cyberpunk, we need to make a few preliminary distinctions. First of all, if we continue to operate with the distinction, current in SF criticism and polemic, between SF and 'mainstream' fiction, we do so only with the severest reservations. Obviously too crude for most theoretical uses, indeed more a caricature than a descriptive tool, this opposition nevertheless does capture economically some of the most salient facts about SF's systemic relations. In particular, it captures the orientation of all species of 'genre' fiction – including SF, detective fiction, women's's gothic romance, horror stories, and so on – toward the central or mainstream genres, and their functional 'indifference' to one another. That is, each of these popular genres defines itself in terms of its differences from the central system of mainstream fiction, perceived (from the position of these peripheral genres) to be relatively homogeneous, and not in terms of its differences from other popular genres. The functionally relevant distinctions for SF are not the ones that differentiate it from, say, detective fiction, but the ones that differentiate it from the mainstream. And, of course, this opposition between 'genre' writing and the mainstream is faithfully reflected by the practice of the book marketing industry, which helped to produce the opposition in the first place, and continues to maintain it.

So we can retain the familiar opposition between SF and mainstream fiction as a kind of convenient shorthand, on the condition, however, that we introduce a functional distinction within the 'mainstream' category. In order to make the mainstream/SF opposition more fully adequate to our purposes, we need to discriminate between (aesthetically) conservative mainstream genres and (again, aesthetically) progressive genres, between norm-observant writing and norm-violating or innovative writing. We could call the conservative wing of mainstream writing 'bestseller' fiction, and its progressive wing 'advanced' or 'state-of-the-art' fiction.[13]

In the earliest phases of SF history, from the 1920s through the 1940s, SF and mainstream fiction existed in mutual isolation from one another, mutually incommunicado. Modern SF crystallized and developed as a 'ghetto' enclave, largely out of touch with both contemporary bestselling fiction and advanced mainstream fiction, just as these latter were in turn largely unresponsive to SF. The first important interspecies contacts, so to speak, occurred in the 1950s, with the 'leveling up' of SF to something approaching the stylistic norms of mainstream bestseller fiction. Heinlein, Asimov, Clarke, Sturgeon, Bester, and others of their generation modeled their prose style and narrative structures on those of bestseller fiction, while a few mainstream bestsellers in turn adopted typical SF motifs, themes, and materials (for example, Nevil Shute's *On the Beach* (1957),

Walter Tevis's *The Man Who Fell to Earth* (1963)).[14] It is partly due to the success of the SF novelists of this generation that the poetics of the leveling-up phase has come to be perceived as the SF norm. No doubt it is the poetics of this phase that critics such as Christine Brooke-Rose have in mind when they describe SF as an essentially realist discourse.[15]

There had as yet, however, been little if any interaction between SF and advanced or state-of-the-art mainstream fiction. That interaction began in the next phase, in the 1960s and early 1970s, with New Wave SF and the first wave of postmodernist mainstream fiction. What is striking here is that, when this mutual interaction finally did get under way, it had an oddly regressive character, with each partner in the exchange returning to an earlier historical phase of its opposite number. That is, SF in this phase began to absorb models from state-of-the-art mainstream fiction of an earlier period, not the advanced fiction contemporaneous with itself, while advanced mainstream fiction in the 1960s and early 1970s drew on the SF of an earlier phase of its development, not the concurrent phase.[16]

Thus, postmodernist fiction in those decades began to exploit motifs and materials drawn from early, long outdated SF sources: the space operas and bug-eyed-monster fiction of the early pulp magazines (William Burroughs, Kurt Vonnegut, Thomas Pynchon), superhero comics (Italo Calvino's *Cosmicomics*, Pynchon's Rocketman, Plasticman, and other superheroes), SF disaster and monster movies (Sam Shepard's early plays, *Operation Sidewinder* and *Angel City*, and Pynchon's use of King Kong), and so on.[17] Meanwhile, SF in its New Wave phase 'modernized' itself, absorbing elements from the poetics of the high modernists of the 1920s and 1930s, not its postmodernist contemporaries. In most New Wave writing the model involved is that of a kind of generalized high modernist poetics, but in some cases specific indebtednesses or homages can be traced: to Conrad in the case of J. G. Ballard, to Dos Passos in the case of John Brunner, to Thomas Mann in the specific case of Thomas Disch's *Canip Concentration* (1968), and so on.[18]

Only in the course of the 1970s did SF and postmodernist mainstream fiction really become one another's contemporaries, functionally as well as chronologically, with each finally beginning to draw on the current phase of the other, rather than on some historically prior phase. It is during this period that we encounter SF that incorporates elements of postmodernist poetics, such as the later novels of Philip K. Dick, especially *Ubik* (1969); J. G. Ballard's novels beginning with *Atrocity Exhibition* (1969) and *Crash* (1973); Samuel R. Delany's big SF novels of the 1970s and early 1980s, *Dhalgren* (1974), *Triton* (1976), and *Stars in My*

Pocket Like Grains of Sand (1984); and the late, linguistically playful SF novels of Alfred Bester. It is also during this period that mainstream postmodernist fiction opens itself up to motifs and materials from SF of the New Wave and later. Indicative of this new openness to contemporary SF is an essay, by the mainstream novelist Joseph McElroy (1975) in which J. G. Ballard is credited as an influence alongside such state-of-the-art postmodernists as Butor, Robbe-Grillet, and Pynchon.[19]

As this phase of the interaction prolongs itself into the 1980s, a feedback loop begins to operate between SF and postmodernist fiction. That is, we find postmodernist texts absorbing materials from already 'postmodernized' SF, and SF texts incorporating models drawn from already 'science-fictionized' postmodernism, so that certain elements can be identified which have cycled from SF to mainstream postmodernism and back to SF again, or from mainstream fiction to SF and back to the mainstream again. A case in point would be William S. Burroughs's 'lost civilization' motifs (see, for example, 'The Mayan Caper' in *The Soft Machine* (1966)). Burroughs combined formulaic motifs from jungle adventure thrillers and pulp magazine SF to create a new motif complex, recontextualizing the original materials and literally reprocessing them, that is, subjecting them to his cut-up and fold-in techniques. When this particular bundle of motifs, bearing traces of Burroughs's characteristic obsessions and emphases, reappears in 1980s SF (for example, Lucius Shepard's *Life During Wartime* (1987) or Lewis Shiner's *Deserted Cities of the Heart* (1988)), this is clear evidence of the circulation of motifs from SF sources back to SF again by way of a postmodernist intermediary.[20]

It is this latest phase of the interaction that, on the SF end of the feedback loop, has acquired the label of 'cyberpunk'. In this systemic perspective, cyberpunk can be seen as SF which derives certain of its elements from postmodernist mainstream fiction which has already been 'science-fictionized' to some degree.[21] When questioned, cyberpunk writers typically acknowledge the influence of non-SF writers in about equal proportion with that of their SF predecessors, and the non-SF writers most frequently named are Burroughs and Pynchon, state-of-the-art mainstream writers heavily indebted to earlier forms of SF for themes, motifs, and materials.[22] Burroughs's role in recycling transformed SF elements back to cyberpunk SF has already been noted. Pynchon's position in this loop is, if anything, even more crucial.

The presence of Pynchon's texts, *Gravity's Rainbow* (1973) in particular, is pervasive in cyberpunk, ranging from plot structure and large-scale world elements down to fine verbal details. For example, the Slothrop plot of *Gravity's Rainbow* would appear to have provided the model for Shepard's *Life During Wartime*, in which a soldier with psychic talents is trained by military intelligence for special operations, escapes from his handlers, and undergoes picaresque and fantastic adventures traversing a war zone. Traces of this same plot-structure (perhaps fused with that of a SF precursor, Bester's *The Stars My Destination*, 1956) may be detected in Michael Swanwick's *Vacuum Flowers* (1987), while the plot of Pynchon's *The Crying of Lot 49* (1966) surely underlies the adventures of Bruce Sterling's heroine Laura in *Islands in the Net* (1988).

Pynchon's worlds contributed even more than his plots have to the cyberpunk repertoire. The paranoid vision of a world controlled by multinational corporations, who are controlled, in turn, by the self-actuating technologies upon which their power depends – this world-view, so pervasive a feature of cyberpunk extrapolation, certainly derives, at least in part, from Pynchon. Thus, for example, in Walter Williams's *Hardwired* (1986), in which the multinationals have abandoned the planet surface and now exert their control from orbiting platforms, the ultimate source of this extrapolated world is signaled by the names of two of the orbital cartels, Yoyodyne and Pointsman Pharmaceuticals A.G., both 'borrowed' from Pynchon.[23] Similarly, Pynchon's motif of conditioning – control internalized and made inseparable from individual identity – appears in the many cyberpunk variations on the zombie theme. Pynchon may even be partly responsible for what is arguably the most characteristic of all cyberpunk motifs, that of human–computer symbiosis, and the associated motif of the 'Electroworld' (Pynchon's term), the computer-generated parallel world or paraspace of Gibson's 'Matrix' trilogy and other cyberpunk texts.[24]

Finally, Pynchon's presence may be traced even at the 'micro' level, in fine details of cyberpunk world-texture and language. Pynchon is the source for, among other details, the fictional plastic, 'Imipolex G', in Rudy Rucker's *Software* (1982) and *Wetware* (1988); the unwholesome sexual habits of the executive officer of an orbiting station in John Shirley's *Eclipse* (1985); a disgusting dinner-table conversation intended to discourage enemies in Swanwick's *Vacuum Flowers*; a spooky episode in an empty nightclub in Gibson's *Count Zero* (1986a); unauthorized research into the corporate structure of a multinational cartel in Williams's *Hardwired*; sex with the television on in Sterling's *Islands in the Net*; a 'smart bomb' (in the original it was a can of hairspray) caroming around a room in Rucker's *Wetware*; and the angels in both *Wetware* and

Sterling's *Schismatrix* (1985). Pynchon may even have contributed to-ward the notorious opening sentence of Gibson's *Neuromancer*: 'The sky above the port was the color of television, tuned to a dead channel.'[25] Do we catch here an echo, however subliminal, of a sentence from the first page of *The Crying of Lot 49*? Pynchon wrote: 'Oedipa stood in the living room, stared at by the dead eye of the TV tube. . . . '[26]

On one end of this feedback loop, then, we find a mode of SF that exploits the already 'science-fictionized' postmodernism of Burroughs, Pynchon, and other state-of-the-art mainstream writers; on the other end of the loop, we could expect to find advanced mainstream writers who exploit the already 'postmodernized' SF of the cyberpunks. One post-modernist writer who fits this description is Kathy Acker. Already in Acker's *Don Quixote* (1986), SF sources figured among the materials feeding into her mix of pastiches and appropriations. Here the source was Japanese SF monster movies (Megalon, Godzilla), and Acker's treatment of them[27] seems likely to have been influenced by Susan Sontag's well-known essay (1966) on post-Hiroshima SF films.[28] In other words, *Don Quixote* belongs to an earlier phase of interaction, in which advanced mainstream fiction draws upon historically prior and already outdated SF models.

By *Empire of the Senseless* (1988), however, Acker is already aware of cyberpunk, and of Gibson's *Neuromancer* in particular.[29] She appropri-ates and extensively reworks the episode in which the female ninja Molly, backed up by her hacker partner Case and a gang of high-tech terrorists, the Panther Moderns, raids the corporate headquarters of the Sense/Net communications system in order to steal a storage unit housing the 'con-struct' of a dead hacker's personality. A close comparison of Gibson's original with Acker's reworking of it would reveal much about Acker's methods and priorities.[30] For one thing, the episode she has selected, in which the male hacker Case has access to the sensory experience of the female ninja Molly, literally shifting in and out of her point of view, is a highly congenial one for her thematics of gender and identity. Acker changes names (the Panther Moderns become simply the Moderns, Sense/Net becomes American Intelligence, Wintermute, the name of an artificial intelligence in Gibson, becomes Winter, and so on), shifts passages from one context to another, and faithfully duplicates certain details while displacing and confusing others (for example, the immediate purpose of the break-in is to steal a code, not a personality construct as in the origi-nal, Gibson's construct motif having been displaced to a different point in Acker's story). She sometimes rewrites Gibson's prose entirely, transposing it into her characteristic anti-literary register of 'bad writing', but at other times preserves much of his verbal texture intact.[31]

Nor is this the only episode Acker pirates from *Neuromancer*. She also lifts the story (told in Gibson's original by his favourite narrator of inset stories, the Finn) of the fence who runs afoul of a shadowy organization – in Gibson, the powerful Tessier-Ashpool; in Acker, American Intelligence, or AI (which is of course the acronym, in Gibson, for Artificial Intelligence, not American Intelligence; another example of Acker's displacements).[32] More generally, Acker's criminal partners, Abhor and Thivai, the former evidently herself a 'construct', the latter the son either of an alien or a robot (pp. 34, 154–5), echo not only Gibson's Molly and Case but also the cyberpunk thematics of human–computer symbiosis. More generally still, the world of *Empire of the Senseless*, dominated by omnipotent multinationals and intelligence organizations, is that of cyberpunk (but also, as we have seen, that of Pynchon), while its cityscapes of post-apocalyptic ruin mingle cyberpunk models (for example, Shirley's *Eclipse*) with those of mainstream postmodernist fiction and film (Fuentes's *Terra nostra*, Goytisolo's *Paisajes despues de la batalla* (1982), Frears's *Sammy and Rosie Get Laid* (1987)). Postmodernized SF mingling with postmodernism: here we see just how tight the feedback loop has become, just how rapid the traffic between high and low.[33]

Traffic between cultural strata, however, is not the only factor involved in the apparent convergence of cyberpunk and mainstream postmodernism in the 1980s. Apart from the feedback mechanism, one might also take into consideration the phenomenon of independent but parallel developments in SF and postmodernist fiction. This phenomenon accounts for the appearance, in an earlier phase, of a text such as Beckett's *The Lost Ones* (1972; in French, *Le Dépeupleur*, 1971), which seems to exploit SF formulas (that of the multigeneration space voyage, for instance) but almost certainly does not, its true sources being high culture models (Dante) and Beckett's own individual repertoire of motifs and procedures.[34] Especially striking in this context is the emergence in the 1980s of what might be called postmodernist fiction of the cybernetic interface, texts which register the first, often traumatic encounters between 'literary' culture (high culture generally) and the transformative possibilities of computer technology.[35] Christine Brooke-Rose's *Amalgamemnon* (1984) and *Xorandor* (1986), two-thirds of a 'computer trilogy' completed by *Verbivore* (1990), are exemplary in this regard. In the first the encounter with computers is tentative and anxious, but by the second the literary repertoire has been reconfigured so as to begin to accommodate – right down to the 'micro' level of verbal detail – the *realia* of computer technology.

Some of these cybernetic interface motifs emerge directly from earlier postmodernist topoi, in particular the topos of the act of writing, or what Ronald Sukenick calls 'the truth of the page'.[36] This topos involves the insc+-

ysical act of writing in the written text itself, and amounts to a kind of postmodernist hyperrealism involving the breaking of the fictional frame and the collapse of ontological levels. Of all the topoi in the postmodernist repertoire, this is the one most directly responsive to changes in the technology of writing, for obvious reasons. Thus, earlier versions of the topos (Beckett's *Stories and Texts for Nothing* (1967), early texts of the surfictionists Sukenick, Federman, and Katz) reflect traditional, lowtech writing practice – the writer at his desk, pen or pencil in hand. Later versions register the changes in the physical act of writing produced by electric typewriters (Federman's *The Voice in the Closet* (1979)) and tape recorders (stories in Sukenick's *Death of the Novel and Other Stories* (1969) and *The Endless Short Story* (1986), and in Barth's *Lost in the Funhouse* (1968)). From here it is an obvious extension of the topos to adapt it so as to reflect the newest writing technology, that of personal computers and word-processing, as in such texts as Russell Hoban's *The Medusa Frequency* (1987), James McConkey's *Kayo* (1987), William Vollman's *You Bright and Risen Angels* (1987), and Umberto Eco's *Pendolo di Foucault* (*Foucault's Pendulum*, 1988).[37]

In such texts computers typically serve the function of literalizing and updating traditional literary elements – ancient topoi, for instance, or conventions of narrative structure. For example, the topos of the Muse is liberalized and brought up to date in Hoban's *The Medusa Frequency* and McConkey's *Kayo*, in which 'voices' from beyond (the Kraken and the Medusa in Hoban, an extraterrestrial narrator in McConkey) manifest themselves on the computer monitor, literally dictating (parts of) the text before us. Files accessed on a personal computer function in Eco's *Foucault's Pendulum* to literalize and motivate such conventional narrative structures as the inset story, the flashback, and shift of point of view. A more complicated (but not entirely unprecedented) narrative situation is actualized by means of the cybernetic interface in Vollmann's *You Bright and Risen Angels*. Here two narrators, one a computer programmer, the other his superior, who can freely intervene to alter his underling's input into the computer system, compete for control of the narration.[38]

But such updatings and literalizations do not begin to exhaust the full postmodernist potential of cybernetic interface fiction. There are other, more radical possibilities to be exploited. For instance, in Eco's *Foucault's Pendulum*, the computer Abulafia, apart from its functions as surrogate narrator, also and more interestingly functions as a literal *combinatoire*, a device (in both the literary and the mechanical senses) for generating unforeseen combinations from elements of a fixed repertoire. Here Eco approaches the distinctively postmodernist combinatorial poetics of the OuLiPo group (including Raymond Queneau, Italo Calvino, Georges Perec, Harry Mathews, and others) and that of their precursor Raymond Roussel, originator of this entire tendency.[39] Perhaps more radical still are the possibilities recognized by Brooke-Rose in *Xorandor*, where the computer serves as the narrative motivation or alibi for a wall-to-wall reconfiguration of language and where the reconfiguration of language serves as a kind of global metaphor for the impact of cybernetic technology. Working out in their own postmodernist terms the literary implications of computers, *Xorandor* and other mainstream fictions of the cybernetic interface have in effect arrived independently at a position parallel to the one occupied by the cyberpunks in the adjacent SF tradition.

As a consequence of all these developments – the ever-tightening feedback loop between SF 'genre' fiction and state-of-the-art mainstream fiction, together with certain independent but parallel developments in SF and the mainstream – the poetics of mainstream postmodernism and the poetics of the latest wave of SF overlap to an unprecedented degree. It is this high degree of overlap, this shared repertoire of motifs and strategies, that justifies, if anything else, the new legitimacy granted to SF by canonical authorities such as the *Columbia Literary History*.

Notes

1   Larry McCaffrey, 'The Fictions of the Present', in *Columbia Literary History of the United States*, gen. ed. Emory Elliot (New York: Columbia University Press, 1988), p. 1167.
2   Ibid., p. 1162.
3   Ibid., p. 1174; see also Larry McCaffrey, 'The Desert of the Real: The Cyberpunk Controversy', *Mississippi Review* 47/48 (1988), p. 13.
4   Fredric Jameson, 'Postmodernism, or The Cultural Logic of Late Capitalism'

New Left Review 146 (July–Aug. 1984), pp. 54–5 and 'Postmodernism and Consumer Society', in *Postmodernism and Its Discontents: Theories, Practices*, ed. E. Ann Kaplan (London and New York: Verso, 1988), p. 14; and Andreas Huyssen, *After the Great Divide: Modernism, Mass Culture, Postmodernism* (Bloomington: Indiana University Press, 1986).

5 See Kaplan, ed., *Postmodernism*, p. 4; see also Istvan Csicsery-Ronay, 'Cyberpunk and Neuromanticism', in *Storming the Reality Studio: A Casebook of Cyberpunk and Postmodern Science Fiction*, ed. Larry McCaffrey (Durham and London: Duke University Press, 1991), pp. 182–93.

6 Larry McCaffrey, 'An Interview with William Gibson', in *Storming*, p. 266.

7 Ibid.

8 Ralph Cohen, 'Do Postmodern Genres Exist?', *Genre* 20, 3/4 (Fall–Winter 1987) p. 246.

9 At a still later stage, the direction of the 'trickle' is reversed, and artistically ambitious writers take up the by now broadly diffused minimalist prose style and use it once again for high art purposes. Examples representing a very wide range of possibilities include Donald Barthelme, Kurt Vonnegut, Richard Brautigan, Robert Stone, Don DeLillo, Raymond Carver, Clark Coolidge, Ron Silliman, and Lyn Hejinian.

10 Cf. Teresa L. Ebert, 'The Convergence of Postmodern Innovative Fiction and Science Fiction: An Encounter with Samuel R. Delaney's Technotopia', *Poetics Today* 1 (Summer 1980), pp. 91–104; Kenneth Mathieson, 'The Influence of Science Fiction in the Contemporary American Novel', *Science Fiction Studies* 12, 1 (March 1985), pp. 22–31; Brian McHale, *Postmodernist Fiction* (London: Methuen, 1987).

11 Cf. 'Forum', *Mississippi Review* [special issue on cyberpunk; ed. Larry McCaffrey], 47/48 (1988), pp. 28–35.

12 The approach adopted here reflects, although in a simplified and selective way, the polysystem theory of Itamar Even-Zohar, ed., *Polysystem Studies*, *Poetics Today* 11, 1 (1990).

13 I owe the phrase 'state-of-the-art fiction' to Moshe Run.

14 I am indebted to Thomas Disch for calling my attention to the importance of this leveling-up phase of SF history.

15 See especially Christine Brooke-Rose, 'Science Fiction and Realistic Fiction', in *A Rhetoric of the Unreal: Studies in Narrative and Structure, Especially of the Fantastic* (Cambridge: Cambridge University Press, 1981): 'It is clear that traditional SF at least does take over wholesale and unmodified most of the techniques of RF [realistic fiction]: the postdated narrative in the past tense, the explanatory flashback and the abuse of free indirect discourse for a character's thoughts. . . . [I]t tends to go back to [the] Balzacian narrator – comment and omniscience, i.e., not to eliminate the narrative voice in favor of substitute transmitters' (p. 102).

16 Cf. Mathieson, 'Influence of Science Fiction': '"SF" themes, plots, and characteristic images began to emerge in other places just when writers

defining themselves as SF authors turned increasingly away from stock for-mulas' (p. 22).

17   Poetry is, of course, even less free to interact with popular genres than seri-ous fiction is, so that, to the degree that such a thing as SF poetry exists, it remains fixed by and large at this early postmodernist phase of the interac-tion with SF, without moving on to the next, most recent phase. See for example the SF poetry of Edwin Morgan, the Israeli poet Dan Pagis, or James Merrill (in certain passages of *The Changing Light at Sandover*). An exception is the cyberpunk poetry of Rob Hardin (some of which can be found in *Storming*). I am grateful to Tamar Yaacobi for calling Pagis's SF poetry to my attention.

18   Stanislaw Lem, in a particularly uncharitable footnote (even by Lem's stand-ards), abuses New Wave writers for their pursuit of what he calls 'Upper Realm', i.e., high modernist, models; cf. his 'Science Fiction: A Hopeless Case – with Exceptions', in *Microworlds: Writings on Science Fiction and Fantasy*, ed. Franz Rollensteiner (San Diego and New York: Harcourt Brace Jovanovich, 1984), pp. 93–4, n. 7.

19   Postmodernist texts from this phase that incorporate contemporary SF mo-tifs and materials include Angela Carter's *Heroes and Villains* (1969) and *The Passion of New Eve* (1977), Harry Mathews's *The Sinking of the Odradek Stadium* (1975 [1971–2]), Steve Katz's *Saw* (1972), Sam Shepard's play *The Tooth of Crime* (1972), Carlos Fuentes's *Terra nostra* (1975), Don DeLillo's *Ratner's Star* (1976), Joseph McElroy's *Plus* (1976), Russell S. Hoban's *Riddley Walker* (1980), Alasdair Gray's *Lanark* (1981), Ted Mooney's *Easy Travel to Other Planets* (1981), and Raymond Federman's *The Twofold Vibration* (1982). See McHale, *Postmodern Fiction*, pp. 65–8.

20   Another example, also involving Burroughs, of an element cycled through the feedback loop between SF and mainstream postmodernism is the title 'Blade Runner'. Originally the title of an Alan E. Nourse SF novel, it was appropriated by Burroughs (who acknowledged Nourse on the copyright page) for a 1979 text in the form of a film script. Ridley Scott in turn appropriated it for the title of the proto-cyberpunk film (1982) he based on Phillip Dick's novel *Do Androids Dream of Electric Sheep?* (1968), acknow-ledging Burroughs (but not Nourse) in the film's credits. Further evidence of Burroughs's presence in 1980s SF can be found in Bruce Sterling's use of Burroughs's cut-up technique in his cyberpunk story 'Twenty Evocations', in *Storming*, pp. 154–61. Cf. also McCaffery's interview of William Gibson: 'I started snipping things out and slapping them down, but then I'd air-brush them a little to take the edges off' (p. 281).

21   This is not the only feedback loop in which cyberpunk is involved. There is also the feedback loop between cyberpunk writing and the electronic media, described in essays by Brooks Landon and George Slusser, 'Bet On It: Cyber/video/punk/performance' and 'Literary MTV', in *Storming*, pp. 239–44 and 334–42, and the loop between cyberpunk and rock music, described by

Larry McCaffery in 'Cutting Up: Cyberpunk, Punk Music, and Urban Decontextualizations,' in *Storming*, pp. 286–307.

22 See for example John Shirley's contribution to 'Forum' (hereafter 'F'), p. 58; McCaffery's interview of Gibson; and Bruce Sterling, 'Preface', in *Mirrorshades: The Cyberpunk Anthology* (New York: Arbor House, 1986), pp. viii and xii. A typical move is to make these postmodernists honorary cyberpunks, or cyberpunks *avant la lettre*; thus, for example, David Porush speaks of 'Burroughs-the-first-cyberpunk' ('F', p. 48), and Rudy Rucker calls *Gravity's Rainbow* 'the quintessential cyberpunk masterpiece' ('F', p. 51).

23 Walter John Williams, *Hardwired* (New York: T. Docherty Associates, 1986) is saturated with allusions to Thomas Pynchon, *Gravity's Rainbow* (New York: Viking, 1973) (hereafter *GR*). Apart from Yoyodyne and Pointsman Pharmaceuticals, others include 'zonedancing', an extrapolated future nightclub dance fashion and the 'zoned' (i.e., zonedancers), together with the associated advertising display, which reads 'In the Zone/Yes' (p. 27); multiple instances of the term 'interface', a key word from *GR*; 'buttonheads', addicts who get their fix by plugging directly into electronics (p. 95), recalling the 'Heart-to-Heart, Man-to-Man' passage from *GR* (see below); and an insanely out-of-control corporate executive named Roon, exiled from the orbitals to the surface of the planet, who seems to have been based on Pynchon's Nazi Faust, the manic Captain Blicero.

24 These motifs appear in a cartoon or comedy routine passage, 'Heart-to-Heart, Man-to-Man' in *GR*, pp. 698–9. Another important cyberpunk motif which seems to derive, at least in part, from one of Pynchon's comedy routines, is that of cellular-level intelligence, developed on a large scale in Greg Bear, *Blood Music* (New York: Arbor House, 1985), but already present in Pynchon's episode of intelligent melanocytes (*GR*, pp. 147–9).

25 William Gibson, *Neuromancer* (New York: Berkeley, 1984), p. 3.

26 Thomas Pynchon, *The Crying of Lot 49* (London: Pan, 1979), p. 5. [See Thwaites in the present volume for a detailed discussion of this text; see also my *PomoIntro*, pp. 15–18, for further discussion of Pynchon's novel and Thwaites's reading of it. (NL)]

27 Kathy Acker, *Don Quixote, which was a dream* (New York: Grove, 1986), pp. 69–77.

28 Susan Sontag, 'The Imagination of Disaster', in *Against Interpretation and Other Essays* (New York: Dell, 1966), pp. 209–25.

29 Ellen G. Friedman, 'A Conversation with Kathy Acker', *Review of Contemporary Fiction* 9 (3) (Fall 1989), p. 16.

30 See Gibson, *Neuromancer*, pp. 55–69 and Kathy Acker, *Empire of the Senseless* (New York: Grove, 1988), pp. 31–42. [Cf. my discussion of Acker's novel in *PomoIntro*, pp. 40–1 and 49–57. (NL)]

31 For example, *Neuromancer*: 'A transparent cast ran from her knee to a few millimeters below her crotch, the skin beneath the rigid micropore mottled with bruises, the black shading into ugly yellow. Eight derms, each a different

size and color, ran in a neat line down her left wrist. An Akai transdermal unit lay beside her, its fine red leads connected to input trodes under the case' (p. 78). Cf. *Empire*: 'A transparent cast ran from her knee to a few millimeters below her crotch, the skin mottled by blue purple and green patches which looked like bruises but weren't. Black spots on the nails, finger and toe, shaded into gold. Eight derms, each a different color size and form, ran in a neat line down her right wrist and down the vein of the right upper thigh. A transdermal unit, separate from her body, connected to the input trades under the cast by means of thin red leads' (pp. 33–4). Note: (1) the slight dilution of the SF effect of the original through deletion of 'micropore' and the brand name 'Akai'; (2) the conversion of Molly's bruises into something that, enigmatically, 'looked like bruises but weren't', and the displacement of the colours of the bruises to 'spots' on the fingernails and toenails – the differences here are partially explained by the fact that Gibson's passage describes Molly's bruised condition *after* the raid, while Acker has displaced this passage to *before* the raid, thus losing the narrative motivation for bruises; (3) the erotically charged additional detail, typical for Acker, of derms down the right upper thigh as well as the right wrist (but why the substitution of right for left?).

32   *Neuromancer*, pp. 73–6; cf. *Empire*, pp. 39–41. Here, too, Acker plays variations on verbal details from Gibson. For example, *Neuromancer*: 'Smith sat very still, staring into the calm brown eyes of death across a polished table of Vietnamese rosewood' (p. 75); cf. *Empire*: 'I knew he was a real man because I knew I was staring into the eyes of death' (p. 40).

33   Another possible example of mainstream postmodernism exploiting already 'postmodernized' cyberpunk SF might be Pynchon himself, in his long-awaited new novel *Vineland* (Boston: Little, Brown, 1990). Pynchon's female ninja character (or 'ninjette', to use Pynchon's gag coinage), Darryl Louise ('DU') Chastain, bears a striking resemblance to Gibson's Molly/Sally Slicars, and her adventures in Tokyo, including a bizarrely bungled assassination attempt, might very well echo Molly's Chiba City caper from *Neuromancer*. If this is so, and Pynchon really is exploiting material from Gibson, then the feedback of models has completed another circuit of its loop: from earlier pulp magazine and monster movie SF to Pynchon to cyberpunk SF and *back* to Pynchon again! (Godzilla, incidentally, is an offstage presence in *Vineland*, taking over the role that King Kong had filled in *Gravity's Rainbow*.)

34   Cf. David A. Porush, *The Soft Machine: Cybernetic Fiction* (New York: Methuen, 1985), pp. 157–71; and McHale, *Postmodern Fiction*, pp. 62–5.

35   Precursors of 1980s cybernetic interface fiction include John Barth's *Giles Goat-Boy* (1966) and Joseph McElroy's *Plus* (1976).

36   Ronald Sukenick, 'Thirteen Digressions', in *In Form: Digressions on the Art of Fiction* (Carbondale: Southern Illinois University Press, 1985), p. 25; see also McHale, *Postmodern Fiction*, pp. 197–9.

37   It appears, interestingly enough, that this is not the route by which Gibson

arrived at his SF version of cybernetic interface fiction; see his admission, in conversation with McCaffery, that he did not learn how to use a personal computer until after the publication of *Neuromancer* and the earlier Sprawl stories (McCaffrey, 'Interview', p. 270).

38 Precedents for such double narration include, among others, the end of Faulkner's *Absalom, Absalom!* (1936); *Balthazar* (1958), the second volume of Lawrence Durrell's *Alexandria Quartet*; and Nabokov's *Ada* (1969).

39 Cf. also Burroughs's 'writing machine', a liberalization and *mise en abyme* of his cut-up and fold-in practices, in *The Ticket That Exploded* (New York: Grove, 1967), p. 65; and see McHale, *Postmodern Fiction*, pp. 159–61.

Chapter Twelve Miracles: Hot Air and Histories of the Improbable

Tony Thwaites

A brief false start. For the sake of bedevilment?

(Actually, the story of this paper is a story of false starts. The abstract originally presented in the programme started off as the abstract to what became another paper, which rapidly grew too big to handle. What happens instead is a paper about false starts, which the abstract still serves to describe. Which is perhaps an odd thing about false starts.)

So there will be several false starts here, stammers of the voice in a nervousness that is not entirely mine, or even yours, or vanishings of certain punctuation marks, inverted commas or parentheses which you will no longer of course hear (or perhaps I see), left dangling before they have opened. . . .

* * *

First of all (though perhaps it's already too late for that), a famous simulating demon. Imagine, suggests Descartes in the *First Meditation* (1641),

> that there is not a true God, who is the sovereign source of truth, but some evil demon, no less cunning and deceiving than powerful, who has used all his artifice to deceive me. I will suppose that the heavens, the air, the earth, colours, shapes, sounds and all external things that we see are only illusions and deceptions that he uses to take me in. I will consider myself as having

Tony Thwaites, 'Miracles: Hot Air and Histories of the Improbable', in *Futur*Fall: Excursions into Post-Modernity*, eds E. A. Grosz, T. Threadgold, D. Kelly, A. Cholodenko and E. Colless (Sydney: Power Institute Publications, 1986), pp. 82–96.

no hands, eyes, flesh, blood or senses, but as believing wrongly that I have all these things. I shall cling obstinately to this notion; and if, by this means, it is not in my power to arrive at the knowledge of any truth, at the very least it is in my power to suspend my judgement. That is why I shall take great care not to accept into my belief anything false, and shall so well prepare my mind against all the tricks of this great deceiver that, however powerful and cunning he may be, he will never be able to impose on me.[1]

And now, a version of another famous demon, whose functioning may turn out to be not entirely unconnected with the first.

James Clerk Maxwell . . . had once postulated a tiny intelligence, known as Maxwell's Demon. The Demon could sit in a box among air molecules that were moving at all different random speeds, and sort out the fast molecules from the slow ones. Concentrate enough of them in the same place and you have a region of high temperature. You can then use the difference in temperature between this hot region of the box and any cooler region, to drive a heat engine.

[The] Nefastis machine contained an honest-to-God Maxwell's Demon. All you had to do was stare at the photo of Clerk Maxwell, and concentrate on which cylinder, right or left, you wanted the Demon to raise the temperature in. The air would expand and push a piston. The familiar Society for the Propagation of Christian Knowledge photo, showing Maxwell in right profile, seemed to work best.[2]

The Nefastis machine, of course, doesn't work. As such. That is, the device sitting in inventor John Nefastis's workroom out back – 'a box with a sketch of a bearded Victorian on its outside, and coming out of the top two pistons attached to a crankshaft and flywheel' – doesn't seem to do much no matter how long you stare at James Clerk. Where it does work, though, is everywhere else in this text, which is Thomas Pynchon's 1966 novel *The Crying of Lot 49*. The machinery of its sorting becomes the chiastic motor of a very improbable history.

I have suggested that the links between these demons – between the wretched simulator and the heat/information machine – are not entirely fortuitous. A false beginning is no place to go into these in much detail, so for now I'll only allude to Michel Serres, who goes into the detail in several places in his *Hermés* series (1968–80).[3] Not only in the two or three particular essays I have in mind, but throughout *Hermés*, the Demon acts as a running metaphor for this very type of oblique and unexpected linkage which Serres delights in drawing between quite widely flung discourses. Suffice it to say here that Descartes invokes the Demon in this *First Meditation* as a trope on an argument he had developed earlier, in the *Discourse on Method*. This is the *cogito* argument – 'I *am*, I *exist*, is necessarily true, every time I express it or conceive of it in my mind'.[4] The rudiments of it are sketched out even earlier, in the *Rules for the Direction of the Mind*, where Descartes discusses those two faculties of the understanding, intuition and deduction, which alone permit knowledge without the fear of error. In all three cases, where it is a matter of arriving at an apodictic knowledge out of doubt, the metaphor which fuels the argument is always rather temptingly and proleptically Maxwellian: a *mixture* (of images, impressions, etc.), and a *selection* from this mixture.

The simulator and the generator. What I want to do here, now that this false start is almost over, is taking *The Crying of Lot 49* as a locus for some of these Demonic intersections and interferences – to see what happens when an entropy machine meets a hologram.

*   *   *

In *Lot 49*, Oedipa Maas finds that she has been named executor of the will of a late lover, whose equally conjecturable name is Pierce Inverarity. As she begins to carry out these legal duties – in a series of false starts which may in fact take up all of the narrative – Oedipa finds that she keeps running across strange fragments of information. These fragments may have been planted there precisely for her to stumble into, or they may be just accidental (whatever that might mean here). What is disturbing about them is that they seem to suggest some sort of a plot. What is more disturbing about them is that this plot may involve Oedipa herself (even if only accidentally – whatever *that* might mean here), and may even centre on her (again, even if only accidentally). What is more disturbing *again* is that there would seem to be absolutely no way at all of telling. The more information she finds, first of all by accident, then by design, the more certain it seems that said plot does exist, in one form or another. But the more information she finds, and the more certain the plot becomes, the more preposterous and even totally impossible it becomes. Everything that supports it simultaneously undermines it.

This plot concerns the existence of an underground postal system, which appears to have been around since the last days of the Holy Roman Empire in the Low Countries, at the end of the sixteenth century. Since then, it would seem to have been on the one hand waging secret and tireless war on the established governmental postal monopolies of Europe and America, and on the other delivering its own unauthorized mails in covert competition. The system seems to be known as the Tristero, spelt either with an *i* or a *y* – there are lots of letters which go astray here. Its collection points are what look like municipal garbage cans on the streets of every city. You can tell the difference because the Tristero cans have these tiny full stops separating the letters, making *W.A.S.T.E.* stand for *We Await Silent Tristero's Empire*. Among other things, the Tristero appears to have been involved in the rewriting of certain Jacobean plays to remove disguised references to its own name, a breakaway sect of Puritans known as the Scurvhamites, the Vatican Index, the ownership of at least one large American corporation and perhaps an entire city in California, forgery of stamps, waylaying the Wells-Fargo pony express, Russian incursions into American waters in 1864, a Confederate ship which sailed all the way round the Horn to make a surprise attack on California the year before that, and the very dodgy history of what became of the bones of GIs killed in action in northern Italy. All this and more in about 140 pages. If it exists, Oedipa will come to realize, it is big. *Really* big.

After a few sleepless nights of wandering San Francisco and finding the Tristero and its post horn symbol everywhere, and of realizing that every access route she has to it can somehow be traced back to that estate of former lover Inverarity, Oedipa gives herself four choices:

> Either you have stumbled indeed, without the aid of LSD or other indole alkaloids, onto a secret richness and concealed density of dream; onto a network by which X number of Americans are truly communicating while reserving their lies, recitations of routine, and betrayals of spiritual poverty, for the official government delivery system; maybe even onto a real alternative to the exitlessness, to the absence of surprise to life, that harrows the head of everybody American you know, and you too, sweetie. Or you are hallucinating it. Or a plot has been mounted against you, so expensive and elaborate, involving items like the forging of stamps and ancient books, constant surveillance of your movements, planting of post horn images all over San Francisco, bribing of librarians, hiring of professional actors and Pierce Inverarity only knows what-all else besides, all financed out of the estate in a way either too secret or too involved for your non-legal mind to know about even though you are co-executor, so labyrinthine that it must have meaning beyond just a practical joke. Or you are fantasying some such plot, in which case you are a nut, Oedipa, out of your skull.
>
> Those, now that she was looking at them, she saw to be the alternatives. Those symmetrical four. She didn't like any of them, but hoped she was mentally ill; that that's all it was. (pp. 129–30)

They amount, in short, to this:

(i)   There is a Tristero.
(ii)   Oedipa is fantasizing that there is a Tristero.
(iii) There is a plot.
(iv)   Oedipa is fantasizing that there is a plot.

The symmetry is simple, circular, and closed. Either the signs of the city-text through which a sleepless Oedipa has been stumbling are real, or she is imagining it all. If they are real, there is either a Tristero, or a plot against her. If imagined, a choice of paranoias. 'Ones and zeroes. So did the couples arrange themselves' (p. 138). If there is no plot, if 'Inverarity had only died, nothing else' (p. 136), then wandering this night text is

> now like walking among matrices of a great digital computer, the zeroes and ones twinned above, hanging like balanced mobiles right and left, ahead, thick, maybe endless. Behind the hieroglyphic streets there would either be a transcendent meaning, or only the earth. . . . Another mode of meaning behind the obvious, or none. Either Oedipa in the orbiting ecstasy of a true paranoia, or a real Tristero. For there either was some Tristero beyond the appearance of the legacy America, or there was just America. . . . (p. 138)

There is a plot, or there is a Tristero. This is real, or you are crazy. In any case, two choices, as simple as a light switch: on/off, nothing in between. Perhaps the Tristero itself is 'waiting for a symmetry of choices to break down, to go skew'. Oedipa has 'heard all about excluded middles'; they are 'bad shit, to be avoided' (p. 138).

The symmetry does break down. Tristero and plot are not the mutually exclusive opposites they may seem when presented as a choice: the Tristero, after all, is a plot too, and the plot against Oedipa is one to make her fantasize that there is such a Tristero-plot. Now the choices look like this:

(i)   There is a plot. (*P*)
(ii)   Oedipa is fantasizing that there is a plot. (*PP*)
(iii) There is a plot to make Oedipa fantasize that there is a plot. (*PPP*)
(iv)   Oedipa is fantasizing that there is a plot to make her fantasize that there is a plot. (*PPPP*)

But then, neither is the choice between the reality or fantasy of the Tristero-plot an exclusive one. If Oedipa is merely fantasizing a plot, then she is actively constructing a fiction, a plot of another sort. (Indeed, each of

Pynchon's novels balances on the shifting edge of this world *plot*: in each case, the plot is that someone discovers or suspects that there is a plot. And fictional plots proceed, fittingly enough, by reversals.) So now Oedipa's alternatives are, ridiculously, these:

(i)   There is a plot. (*P*)
(ii)   There is a plot that there is a plot. (*PP*)
(iii) There is a plot that there is a plot that there is a plot. (*PPP*)
(iv)   There is a plot that there is a plot that there is a plot that there is a plot. (*PPPP*)

What began as a symmetric and closed set of four terms, cross-paired according to the mutually exclusive oppositions of *real/fantasy* and *Tristero/ plot* (for whatever they're worth), now looks more like an asymmetric series of successive accumulations of a single term ('there is a plot', or *P*). And this accumulation could clearly be carried on indefinitely, through plots upon plots: ... *PPPPP* ... Within this series, there is no formal reason, at least, for stopping after the fourth term, though it certainly and rapidly gets ever more difficult to keep track of the proposition's looping syntactic stutter, while the effective difference between successive propositions becomes ever more negligible: Oedipa finds four terms quite enough for utter confusion.

The symmetric set and the asymmetric series are both systems of repetition, but in quite different ways. The set is a static and simultaneous representation of all the elements of a combinatory: that is, of all the possibilities for the existence or non-existence of the Tristero (real, fantasized, the effect of a plot, the fantasized effect of a plot). What repeats in each of these possibilities is the Tristero, the set's centre of symmetry and its unity. The series, though, is a dynamic and successive accumulation of a potentially infinite number of terms, where what is repeated throughout these is not a unitary concept (or conceptual unity) but difference. If the first repetition is of the Tristero as question (what is its mode of existence?), then the second is of the plot as problem. The question demands (or begs?) an answer. The problem, on the other hand, serves only to make indeterminate, to problematize: plot hovers undecidably among several quite incompatible senses, none of which can be eliminated without the series ceasing to function. A plot is a piece of ground, or the site for a building: with its immovable solidity it founds and guarantees a structure. Being also the ground plan of that structure or site, a map, a chart, it can thus be a model or origin of the structure as well, even part of the technology and methodology of construction. The word is both substantive and verb, performing itself on itself. *To plot* is to make a plan, map or diagram, or to represent by such, or to lay down a trajectory across such (the course of an action, or of a ship). Literary works may have plots, not only in the senses of outline or plan, but also as the course of a narrative (whose plot reversals serve only to further the plot). Plot may hide as well as display itself, become some sort of secret: perhaps innocent, perhaps sly, wicked, criminal, illegal, conspiratory or subversive. Plot founds, plans and builds, and at the same time pits itself against that very structure, subverting it with stealth from below. It is a wise husbandry, a production, foresight and economic growth, the lanes of sea trade and the occupation of territories, but also an evil which dissembles, a conspiracy concealed in the populace, waste, piracy, gunpowder and treason. Plot subverts plot. Subverting itself, every plot is a marplot and every marplot a plot. The Tristero, as the centre of symmetry of the set to which it belongs, has some sort of unity, even if unknown, and it is the function of the question to find that out, to conceptualize it. But the plot decentred, problematized and problematizing – repeats difference rather than the Same, difference without concept, *differance*. The series' repeating term, 'there is a plot', is no term at all and only pretends to be a proposition; its constative assurance is an empty form which can say nothing and affirm only its differentiation, already an indeterminate spread and regression of plot. Plots of Plots of Plots of Plots. . . .

And in the thick of all this plotting, the Tristero – whose existence was the one urgent question in the original set of alternatives – has vanished from the series. A superfluous hypothesis, it never even needed to put in an appearance. Regardless of whether it exists or not, the Tristero is still a plot. Or not. What the Tristero is in itself, if anything, is completely beside the point: *that* is the plot, and the point. The course the text plots towards a real Tristero is undermined by that very plotting. Is this suspense, or suspension?

At the very beginning of the text, there is a suspension, the enigma of the title: *The Crying of Lot 49*. Follow the course of the plot, or at least the regular progress of a line of type through the volume, and at the very end of the text the enigma is repeated: 'Oedipa settled back, to await the crying of lot 49' (p. 139). Not resolved, but repeated, and even complicated in this repetition. Oedipa remains in suspense, waiting for 'the direct epileptic Word, the cry that might abolish the night' (p. 89) somewhere beyond the last full stop. Instead of being a passage between a question and its answer – endpoints of a single trajectory, which is the parabola of the Same's gravity – the plot is an eddy where every point sinks, is lost, returns newly problematized in difference at every turn. The human skeletons which adorn the lake in Inverarity's Fangoso Lagoons development become the bodies of American troops at the bottom of the Lago di Pieta, become the Lost Guard of Faggio, become the massacred Wells-Fargo riders, or Randolph Driblette walking into the Pacific in his Gennaro suit, or the victims of Trystero brigands by the Lake of Piety as recounted by Diocletian Blobb, or the drowning of Baby Igor and daddy and doggy inside submarine 'Justine' in an old movie on TV, . . . or, or . . . There are no answers, only multiplications of the problem in a resonating network of repetitions, each affirming all the others, and all affirming that plot which separates them and yet binds them as that increasingly impossible and desperate hypothesis, the Tristero. Here, everything is all false starts and false endings which bottom out.

And similarly, too, in all this plotting Oedipa herself disappears from the series. There is no one here in this plot, not even the one person continually present in all of its narrative. As the repetitions accumulate, Oedipa becomes overwhelmed with toothaches, insomnia, headaches, dreams of disembodied voices, as though the simultaneous possibilities of the Tristero's existence or non-existence, the plot's undermining of itself from within, had become fiercely physical in their contraries and differences:

> She would spend nights staring at a ceiling lit by the pink glow of San Narciso's sky. Other nights she could sleep for eighteen drugged hours and wake, enervated, hardly able to stand. . . . Waves of nausea, lasting five or ten minutes, would strike her at random, cause her deep misery, then vanish as if they had never been. (p. 130)

Friendships dwindle, leaving her in a void. 'If I were to dissolve in here,' speculates Driblette from the shower,

> be washed down into the Pacific, what you saw tonight would vanish too. You, that part of you so concerned, God knows how, with that little world, would also vanish. (p. 59)

A drop in the ocean. Oedipa is going under, like that old children's toy used to illustrate Archimedean flotation, the Cartesian Devil.

The paranoid sign can effect reality as a *mise en scène* or a spectacle. The multiple-articulated stratification of the aleatory into its envelope of language and unconscious can effect a fractal limit to that envelope, the *effect of a limit*, a beyond into which language projects its own death and hence that of the referent, and where the real, bereft of the need for any referent other than those its endless repetitions will produce for it, shimmers in the nimbus of its own transparency. Placing itself at the asymptote of language, the real distinguishes itself from all copies of itself, all representations and even all simulacra, while affirming that there is a true representation in which a certain equivalence between the sign and the real exists. The real is what distinguishes itself from all simulacra. But the simulacrum, on the other hand, refuses to distinguish itself from the real in its turn; on the contrary, in its incessant display of itself as visibility and transparency, it incessantly repeats its reality: it sets up for itself exactly the same limits as the real. The simulacrum is what cannot be distinguished from what distinguishes itself from the simulacrum.

The movement is circular, but it is one-directional and allows for no reciprocity from the real. Impasse. The simulacrum invades both sides of the limit, invades the place of the real without possible retort from the real. The return of simulacra.

Now a third demon (or is it fourth?). But perhaps familiar by now. In 'The Precession of Simulacra', Baudrillard isolates four stages in the development of the image, from representation to simulation:

> [Representation] starts from the principle that the sign and the real are equivalent (even if this equivalence is utopian, it is a fundamental axiom). Conversely, simulation starts from the *utopia* of this principle of equivalence, *from the radical negation of the sign as value*, from the sign as reversion and death sentence of every reference. Whereas representation tries to absorb simulation by interpreting it as false representation, simulation envelops the whole edifice of representation as itself a simulacrum.
>
> These would be the successive phases of the image:
> – it is the reflection of a basic reality
> – it masks and perverts a basic reality
> – it masks the *absence* of a basic reality
> – it bears no relation to any reality whatever: it is its own pure simulacrum.
>
> In the first case, the image is a good appearance – the representation is of the order of sacrament. In the second, it is an evil appearance – of the order of malefice. In the third, it *plays at being* an appearance – it is of the order of sorcery. In the fourth, it is no longer the order of appearance at all, but of simulation.[5]

The plot is hatched, and the image-imago leaves the ground, all ground. Not long previously, Baudrillard had attempted to make these 'successive phases of the image' into a history, where each phase ended up as a sort of Foucauldian episteme in disguise.[6] Here, however, the succession appears to be much more involuted than a simple chronological ordering: indeed, how can one speak of succession when what is involved is the precession of the simulacrum over the real? Perhaps, tentatively, as an involution that swallows its own tail – where the 'basic reality' which the image first of all reflects, then masks and perverts, and so on, cannot be seen as anything but *already* simulacrum itself, thus making Baudrillard's own distinction in its turn nothing but a part of the hyperreal engendered by the very process of simulation from which it seeks to disengage itself as analysis. Baudrillard's account of the simulacrum thus has a quite indeterminate status as the simulation of a theory of simulation: it is the very simulacrum it fears.

Which of course raises quite serious and complex problems for it as analysis (or perhaps more accurately, raises problems for that term *analysis*, which is for Baudrillard precisely what the simulacrum would seem to preclude). But that very entanglement is just what we need here: its knots are exactly those Oedipa finds herself in, in trying to unravel the Tristero, with no vantage point from beyond it, and with no logic available which is not already saturated in the simulacrum's hyperreal; and they are also exactly those into which the *reader* of the text is forced. Baudrillard's 'successive phases' are another version – another account, another fiction – of the set of alternatives Oedipa finds she is left with:

(i)   There is a Tristero, and the signs which Oedipa is coming increasingly to read everywhere do in fact reflect – quite faithfully on the whole, even if incompletely as yet – a basic reality. This real Tristero, which offers 'a real alternative to the exitlessness ... that harrows the head of everybody American', offers a salvation in its truth, perhaps even some sort of 'trembling unfurrowing of the mind's ploughshare' (p. 97);

(ii) Oedipa is fantasizing that there is a Tristero, and this fantasy is malevolent because it is a perverse masking of a quotidian reality whose existence it does not seriously put in doubt (but if anything, confirms in the very insistence of its denial). Oedipa fantasizes, but America goes about business as usual;

(iii) There is a plot afoot, possibly but not necessarily initiated by Pierce Inverarity, with the aim of making Oedipa believe that there is a real Tristero. This plot is a type of sorcery, for the signs that it strews around her pretend to lead to a real Tristero, but in reality all they mask is the fact that the Tristero is not real. Now the signs are no longer reflecting a world, either faithfully or mendaciously, but are beginning to sever themselves from any world but the one they are effecting. The legacy America may be this plot;

(iv)   Oedipa is fantasizing that there is a plot. Whereas previously, in (ii), she was 'hallucinating' – with the unreal merely an irruption of a false representation, a momentary occultation of the real – now she can only be 'a nut', 'out of [her] skull' (pp. 129–30), completely severed from the real in 'the orbiting ecstasy of a true paranoia' (p. 138).

And for Oedipa as much as for Baudrillard, the dilemma is ultimately that there can be nothing to choose between these four alternatives, whose very positing is an effect of the Tristero-simulacrum. They suggest the possibility of a time when all was different, now irretrievably past, a nostalgia by which the simulacrum grounds itself. There is no real now, it says, only the effect of a hyperreal which is 'expressed everywhere by the real's striking resemblance to itself': but once, somewhere and sometime, somehow, before representation began its insidious curvature back onto itself as simulation, there might, just might, have been a real upon which the successive negations of the image could act. Or so the story goes. The real is salvaged by a separation in time, by a history which is nevertheless inescapably textual: there can be no guarantee that this history (which is at least a representation), written from the heart of the Age of Simulation, is not just a theory of simulation but the simulation of a theory. It always leaves the possibility that this real, no matter how distanced from the modern – or perhaps indeed precisely because of that distance, which is that of the fictional 'once upon a time' – is still nothing but an elaborate alibi for the simulacrum. The hyperreal invades all of history, and has no 'before' other than that it creates for itself. Oedipa's discovery is not a falling-into the hyperreal, but the discovery that it has been there all along in this California which finds its own image everywhere in an endless narcissism, and where the geographical centre of the plot seems to be nothing but a city without boundaries – San Narciso.

Even before stumbling across the Tristero, and even before meeting Pierce Inverarity, the curvature of Oedipa's life has been that of the hyperreal, with its simultaneous and indistinguishable phases of salvation, malefice, sorcery and the spilling-over of representation into simulation.

As things developed, she was to have all manner of revelations. Hardly about Pierce Inverarity, or herself; but about what remained yet had somehow, before this, stayed away. There had hung the sense of buffering, insulation, she had noticed the absence of an intensity, as if watching a movie, just perceptibly out of focus, that the projectionist refused to fix. And had also gently conned herself into the curious, Rapunzel-like role of a pensive girl somehow, magically, prisoner among the pines and salt fogs of Kinneret, looking for somebody to say hey, let down your hair. When it turned out to be Pierce she'd happily pulled out the pins and curlers and down it tumbled in its whispering, dainty avalanche, only when Pierce had got maybe halfway up, her lovely hair turned, through some sinister sorcery, into a great unanchored wig, and down he fell, on his ass. But dauntless, perhaps using one of his many credit cards for a shim, he'd slipped the lock on her tower door and come up the conchlike stairs, which, had true guile come more naturally to him, he'd have done to begin with. But all that had then gone on between them had never really escaped the confinement of that tower. In Mexico City they somehow wandered into an exhibition of paintings by the beautiful Spanish exile Remedios Varo: in the central painting of a triptych, titled 'Bordando el Manto Terrestre', were a number of frail girls with heart-shaped faces, huge eyes, spun-gold hair, prisoners in the top room of a circular tower, embroidering a kind of tapestry which spilled out the slit windows and into a void, seeking hopelessly to fill the void: for all the other buildings and creatures, all the waves, ships and forests of the earth were contained in this tapestry, and the tapestry was the world. Oedipa, perverse, had stood in front of the tapestry and cried. No one had noticed; she wore dark green bubble shades. For a moment she'd wondered if the seal around her sockets were tight enough to allow the tears simply to go on and fill up the entire lens space and never dry. She could carry the sadness of the moment with her that way forever, see the world refracted through those tears, those specific tears, as if indices as yet unfound varied in important ways from cry to cry. She had looked down at her feet and known then, because of a painting, that what she stood on had only been woven together a couple thousand miles away in her own tower, was only by accident known as Mexico, and so Pierce had taken her away from nothing, there'd been no escape. What did she so desire escape from? Such a captive maiden, having plenty of time to think, soon realizes that her tower, its height and architecture, are like her ego only incidental: and what really keeps her where she is magic, anonymous and malignant, visited on her from outside and for no reason at all. Having no apparatus except gut fear and female cunning to examine this formless magic, to understand how it works, how to measure its field strength, count its lines of force, she may fall back on superstition, or take up a useful hobby like embroidery, or go mad, or marry a disc jockey. If the tower is everywhere and the knight of deliverance no proof against its magic, what else? (pp. 13–14)

What is held in suspension, always somewhere just before the beginning or after the end (before the slamming of the hotel door in Mazatlan, or after the last snap of the lock on the auction room door), is suspension itself. The 'real' is always, even in the past of nostalgia, buffered and insulated from itself (which, of course, it so closely resembles): an endless permutation of the unanchored possible, 'a hyperreal, the product of an irradiating synthesis of combinatory models in a hyperspace without atmosphere'.[7]

After giving herself the four options of the Tristero, Oedipa 'sat for hours, too numb even to drink, teaching herself to breathe in a vacuum' (p. 130). Oedipa has already begun to figure in an intricate weave of plot, where the already must be understood in two senses. One of these is that of the false beginnings, the overt repetition in which the narrative has *already* commenced with her introduction to the Tristero, in the form of the arrival of the legal letter. As beginning, this arrival is already both too late and too early. Too late at several removes, because the machineries which will connect her to the Tristero-plot have long since been in motion: 'Pierce had died back in the spring, and they'd only just now found the will. Oedipa had been named . . . to execute the will in a codicil dated a year ago' (pp. 5–6). And too early at several removes too, for several other dates will also be proposed at various times for the beginning of 'the languid, sinister blooming of Tristero' (p. 38). Perhaps, on one hand, if

> one object behind her discovery . . . were to bring to an end her encapsulation in her tower, then that night's infidelity with Metzger [Oedipa's co-executor of Inverarity's will] would logically be the starting point for it: logically. (p. 31)

Perhaps, on another, it begins with her meeting with Mike Fallopian, who is writing a history of private mail delivery in the US; or perhaps what really begins then is her attendance at some unique performance, prolonged as if it were the last of the night, something a little extra for whoever'd stayed this late . . . ' (p. 38) – in which case, in its turn,

> The beginning of that performance was clear enough. It was while she and Metzger were waiting for ancillary letters to be granted representatives in Arizona, Texas, New York and Florida. . . . (p. 39)

Beginnings shift restlessly and ominously, and become backdated or postponed. Oedipa recalls the last time she heard from Pierce, a 3.00 a.m. phone call conducted in a host of voices (the last of which, Lamont

Cranston – 'the one he'd talked in all the way down to Mazatlan' (p. 6) – intimates that husband Mucho may be due for a visit from The Shadow):

> Its quiet ambiguity shifted over, in the months after the call, to what had been revived: memories of his face, body, things he'd given her, things she had now and then pretended not to've heard him say. It took him over, and to the verge of being forgotten. The shadow waited a year before visiting. But now there was Metzger's letter. Had Pierce called last year then to tell her about this codicil? Or had he decided on it later, somehow because of her annoyance and Mucho's indifference? She . . . didn't know where to begin. . . . (p. 7)

Letters are late, or await further ancillary letters. Wills get lost, or are found with unwelcome codicils. Telephone calls arrive out of hours as a circus of disguised voices (and visited by the Shadow, Mucho too comes on 'like a whole roomful of people' [p. 108]). The Tristero's 'unique performance' for Oedipa is prolonged, its own entrance delayed in 'a plunge toward dawn indefinite black hours long' (p. 38). Whether the Tristero exists as an organization or not, and whatever the mode of its possible existence according to the four alternatives Oedipa finds herself landed with, there are strange things happening in the mails, short circuits in the routes of communications, lapses in the records, revisions of documents, losses of memory, misplacings of the evidence. There are no first or last terms in the series: earlier repeat later, and the captivity in the tower is already a repetition of the entrapment by the Tristero. The Tristero is an endless rehearsal for a delayed presentation. The narrative involutes itself into a potentially endless series of flashbacks and historical recapitulations. And all of these may be duplicitous: all the tales misleading, all the tellers plotters. *The Courier's Tragedy*, the Richard Wharfinger play which provides Oedipa with some of her first major leads (if that is what they are, and if these beginnings too aren't all false) is indeterminable somewhere among a doubtful 'Whitechapel' version from about 1670, a 1687 Quarto edition, an obscene version perhaps done by Scurvhamites (smuggled out of the Vatican library on microfilm, by Emory Bortz in 1961), two conflicting copies of what otherwise pretend to be the same reprint of Bortz's 1957 edition of Wharfinger, Bortz's planned 'updated edition . . . to be out, they tell me, next year sometime', and an atypical performance of an idiosyncratic production of an unauthorized textual variant (pp. 76–7, 117–19, 47–59). It exists as a simultaneous set of possibilities, a maze of chronologies like a detective story where any number of solutions are logically plausible.

That's what would come to haunt her most, perhaps: the way it fitted, logically, together. As if (as she'd guessed that first minute in San Narciso) [yet another beginning] there were revelations in progress all around her. (p. 31)

But there is another, veiled repetition at work here, another sense in which Oedipa has already begun to figure in a weaving of plot. If the first was a horizontal spread of 'revelations in progress all around her', then the second is vertical; if the first is a set of representations of her situation, then the second is a transrepresentative or (ap)presentative series which positions such representations in the involuted space and time it produces.

The captives are 'embroidering a kind of tapestry which spilled out the slit windows' of the tower, and which Escher-like becomes the world. On the one hand, this tapestry *spills* out, disseminated 'into a void, seeking hopelessly to fill the void'. In this endless deferral and differing, the tower is nowhere, a suspension *in vacuo*. On the other hand, 'all the other buildings and creatures, all the waves, ships and forests of the earth were contained in this tapestry, and the tapestry was the world.' The tapestry is the perfect image of the world, its undisseminated reproduction, its complete representation. Except, perhaps, for one thing: the tower itself. The tapestry contains 'all the other buildings . . . of the earth': no mention of the tower, which is thus the indeterminate site of origin. A silence in the text; a gap, indistinguishable from the weave in the tapestry. A stitch is slipped, a run spills out as the void the text cannot fill, the text spills out in(to) difference. The stitch is between the image and the dissemination, linking and separating as repetition.

Oedipa stands in front of the painting, and her tears spill out into the lens space of her bubble shades. The tower is an empty site, to be occupied by a mobile series of captives. To escape may be nothing more than to confirm this mobility; there may be no end to the series, to the trap. Oedipa had

known, then, because of a painting, that what she stood on had only been woven together a couple thousand miles away in her own tower, was only by accident known as Mexico, and so Pierce had taken her away from nothing, there'd been no escape.

The stitch is not only horizontal, across the surface of a world which holds Oedipa captive everywhere, and which will soon begin to turn to her one by one the faces, signs and horizon of a new captivity, the Tristero.

It is also a verticality, a fractal line of repetition and simulation, along which are woven a series of stitches: narrative regressions into the unexpected convolutions of other histories, other stories. On its point of style are stitched the innumerable positions of its own singular readings.

For the Foucault of *The Order of Things*, Velzaquez's *Las Meninas* serves as epitome of 'the representation, as it were, of Classical representation, and the definition of the space it opens up to us.'[8] From the motionless suspension of the painter's brush between canvas and palette, curving around to the large canvas itself, its back to the observer, to the walls lined with other paintings, mirror and doorway in which other figures stand suspended, and finally to the light which floods in from the windows to the right of the painting, a vast spiral traces out 'the entire cycle of representation'. A sweep of the hand through 360 degrees, as if to say that this, laid out here for the eye, is the empire of representation: an invitation to visibility, and the open hand of its freedom. The gaze runs along the horizons of this freedom, hugging the walls, the canvases, in trajectories through the depths made possible by these horizons which it never really leaves. The lever of the arm describes the sweep of planetary orbits: the circle, the great figure of Classical mechanics.

But the circle has no centre. The geometric centre of this space which the spiral opens out is occupied not by the royal couple whose portrait the court painter is caught in the hiatus of producing, but by *las meninas* and the convergence of gaze and gesture on the Infanta Margarita. Instead of the painted image of Philip and Mariana, there is only the reverse of the great canvas, the weave of its fabric and the structure which supports it. The space occupied by the observer is that which should be occupied by the king and queen; the observer's gaze is returned by the painted gazes, and by the painted mirror at the back of this room. At the very moment that this empirical space is postulated, the centre which holds its horizons absents itself from the scene, its overt repetition as the continuous spiral trajectory of the eye giving way to another veiled and fractal repetition of the singular event which scatters itself in constellation over the surface of the painting. Everywhere, the painting contains itself in prismatic reflections which break and scatter the luminosity which bears representation's spiral. Representation becomes event, the occasion of a sitting, or of the suspended actions which fill the foreground of the painting: an irruption, or even interruption like that of the courtier who stands poised on the threshold at the rear of the room. In place of the centre, or rather in the dystopia of centre, threshold repeats itself throughout the spiral's curve. Catastrophe as quiet and as pervasive as that of the motes dancing in the sunlight which floods in through those steep windows pervades this space. Representation is doubled into the representation of representation, folds over onto itself in an endless pleating of its own space: the obliteration of centre, which is reduced to a revenant mirror-obverse playing on the boundaries of the gaze. At and as the very moment of this configuration of Classical representation, the simulacrum is already in play and representation already dissolved.

Pierce is maybe halfway up the tower when Rapunzel's hair turns into a great unanchored wig, and down he falls, on his ass. Dauntless, he slips the lock, credit card for shim, and sets off up the spiral of the conchlike stairs. The courtier is perhaps caught in the act of entering, perhaps that of leaving; one foot up, one down, he stands suspended on that edge. Perhaps, thinks Oedipa, Pierce had taken her away from nothing, there'd been no escape. The tower, the chamber in the Escorial, its height and architecture, are only incidental, like the endlessly replaceable positions stitched onto the fractal spiral which sweeps out the empire. The gazes confirm it: the king and queen are not here, except as the dead centre which haunts the painting. The spiral presents us with the entire cycle of representation: the gaze, the palette and brush, the canvas innocent of signs, the paintings, the reflections, the real man; then the representation dissolves again: we can see only the frames, and the light that is flooding the pictures from outside, through those tall windows that are foreshortened into drastic slits. Heart-shaped faces, huge eyes, spun-gold hair, dwarfs, maids, a dog. The tapestry spills out the slit windows and into a void, seeking hopelessly to fill the void. The cycle closed, something new has already opened, and the stochastic dance of the light dissolves king and queen and thence all of their retinue, who, in this false ending, have never really escaped the confinement of that tower.

Notes

1   René Descartes, *Discourse on Method and the Meditations*, trans. F. E. Sutcliffe (Harmondsworth: Penguin, 1964), p. 100.

2   Thomas Pynchon, *The Crying of Lot 49* (Harmondsworth: Penguin, 1974), pp. 63 and 64; further references are given by page numbers in the text.

3   Michel Serres, *Hermés* (Paris: Minuit, 1968–80). Includes *I: La Communication* (1968); *II: L'Interférence* (1972); *III: La Traduction* (1974); *IV: La Distribution* (1977); and *V: Le Passage du nord-ouest* (1980).

4   Descartes, *Discourse*, p. 103.

5   Jean Baudrillard, 'The Precession of Simulacra', trans. Paul Foss, *Art & Text*

11 (Spring 1983), p. 8. [For further discussion of Baudrillard's ideas concerning simulation, see my *PomoIntro*, esp. pp. 39–41 and 50–3. (NL)]

6 Cf. Jean Baudrillard, *L'échange symbolique et la mort* (Paris: Gallimard, 1976).

7 Baudrillard, 'Precession', p. 4.

8 Cf. Michel Foucault, *The Order of Things: An Archaeology of the Human Sciences*, trans. Alan Sheridan (London: Tavistock, 1970), pp. 3–16.

Part Four **Text**

Chapter 13 **From Work to Text**

Roland Barthes

It is a fact that over the last few years a certain change has taken place (or is taking place) in our conception of language and, consequently, of the literary work which owes at least its phenomenal existence to this same language. The change is clearly connected with the current development of (amongst other disciplines) linguistics, anthropology, Marxism and psychoanalysis (the term 'connection' is used here in a deliberately neutral way: one does not decide a determination, be it multiple and dialectical). What is new and which affects the idea of the work comes not necessarily from the internal recasting of each of these disciplines, but rather from their encounter in relation to an object which traditionally is the province of none of them. It is indeed as though the *interdisciplinarity* which is today held up as a prime value in research cannot be accomplished by the simple confrontation of specialist branches of knowledge. Interdisciplinarity is not the calm of an easy security; it *begins effectively* (as opposed to the mere expression of a pious wish) when the solidarity of the old disciplines breaks down – perhaps even violently, via the jolts of fashion – in the interests of a new object and a new language neither of which has a place in the field of the sciences that were to be brought peacefully together, this unease in classification being precisely the point from which it is possible to diagnose a certain mutation. The mutation in which the idea of the work seems to be gripped must not, however, be over-estimated: it is more in the nature of an epistemological slide than of a real break. The break, as is frequently stressed, is seen to have taken place in the last century with

Roland Barthes, 'From Work to Text' [Fr. 1971], in *Image Music Text*, trans. Stephen Heath (London: Fontana, 1977), pp. 155–64.

the appearance of Marxism and Freudianism; since then there has been no further break, so that in a way it can be said that for the last hundred years we have been living in repetition. What History, our History, allows us today is merely to slide, to vary, to exceed, to repudiate. Just as Einsteinian science demands that *the relativity of the frames of reference* be included in the object studied, so the combined action of Marxism, Freudianism and structuralism demands, in literature, the relativization of the relations of writer, reader and observer (critic). Over against the traditional notion of the *work*, for long – and still – conceived of in a, so to speak, Newtonian way, there is now the require-ment of a new object, obtained by the sliding or overturning of former categories. That object is the *Text*. I know the word is fashionable (I am myself often led to use it) and therefore regarded by some with suspi-cion, but that is exactly why I should like to remind myself of the principal propositions at the intersection of which I see the Text as standing. The word 'proposition' is to be understood more in a gram-matical than in a logical sense: the following are not argumentations but enunciations, 'touches', approaches that consent to remain meta-phorical. Here then are these propositions; they concern method, gen-res, signs, plurality, filiation, reading and pleasure.

1. The Text is not to be thought of as an object that can be computed. It would be futile to try to separate out materially works from texts. In particular, the tendency must be avoided to say that the work is classic, the text avant-garde; it is not a question of drawing up a crude honours list in the name of modernity and declaring certain literary productions 'in' and others 'out' by virtue of their chronological situation: there may be 'text' in a very ancient work, while many products of contemporary literature are in no way texts. The difference is this: the work is a frag-ment of substance, occupying a part of the space of books (in a library for example), the Text is a methodological field. The opposition may recall (without at all reproducing term for term) Lacan's distinction between 'reality' and 'the real': the one is displayed, the other demonstrated;[1] likewise, the work can be seen (in bookshops, in catalogues, in exam syllabuses), the text is a process of demonstration, speaks according to certain rules (or against certain rules); the work can be held in the hand, the text is held in language, only exists in the movement of a discourse (or rather, it is Text for the very reason that it knows itself as text); the Text is not the decomposition of the work, it is the work that is the imaginary tail of the Text; or again, *the Text is experienced only in an activity of production*. It follows that the Text cannot stop (for example on a library

shelf); its constitutive movement is that of cutting across (in particular, it can cut across the work, several works).

2. In the same way, the Text does not stop at (good) Literature; it cannot be contained in a hierarchy, even in a simple division of genres. What constitutes the Text is, on the contrary (or precisely), its subversive force in respect of the old classifications. How do you classify a writer like Georges Bataille? Novelist, poet, essayist, economist, philosopher, mystic? The answer is so difficult that the literary manuals generally prefer to forget about Bataille who, in fact, wrote texts, perhaps continuously one single text. If the Text poses problems of classification (which is furthermore one of its 'social' functions), this is because it always involves a certain experience of limits (to take up an expression from Philippe Sollers). Thibaudet used already to talk – but in a very restricted sense – of limit-works (such as Chateaubriand's *Vie de Rancé*. which does indeed come through to us today as a 'text'); the Text is that which goes to the limit of the rules of enunciation (rationality, readability, etc.). Nor is this a rhetorical idea, resorted to for some 'heroic' effect: the Text tries to place itself very exactly *behind* the limit of the *doxa* (is not general opinion – constitutive of our democratic societies and powerfully aided by mass communications – defined by its limits, the energy with which it excludes, its *censorship?*). Taking the word literally, it may be said that the Text is always *paradoxical*.

3. The Text can be approached, experienced, in reaction to the sign. The work closes on a signified. There are two modes of signification which can be attributed to this signified: either it is claimed to be evident and the work is then the object of a literal science, of philology, or else it is considered to be secret, ultimate, something to be sought out, and the work then falls under the scope of a hermeneutics, of an interpretation (Marxist, psychoanalytic, thematic, etc.); in short, the work itself functions as a general sign and it is normal that it should represent an institutional category of the civilization of the Sign. The Text, on the contrary, practises the infinite deferment of the signified, is dilatory; its field is that of the signifier and the signifier must not be conceived of as 'the first stage of meaning', its material vestibule, but, in complete opposition to this, as its *deferred action*. Similarly, the *infinity* of the signifier refers not to some idea of the ineffable (the unnameable signified) but to that of a *playing*: the generation of the perpetual signifier (after the fashion of a perpetual calender) in the field of the text (better, of which the text is the field) is realized not according to an organic progress of maturation or a hermeneutic course of deepening investigation, but, rather, according to a

serial movement of disconnections, overlappings, variations. The logic regulating the Text is not comprehensive (define 'what the work means') but metonymic; the activity of associations, contiguities, carryings-over coincides with a liberation of symbolic energy (lacking it, man would die); the work in the best of cases – is *moderately* symbolic (its symbolic runs out, comes to a halt); the Text is *radically* symbolic: *a work conceived, perceived and received in its integrally symbolic nature is a text.* Thus is the Text restored to language; like language, it is structured but off-centred, without closure (note, in reply to the contemptuous suspicion of the 'fashionable' sometimes directed at structuralism, that the epistemological privilege currently accorded to language stems precisely from the discovery there of a paradoxical idea of structure: a system with neither close nor centre).

4. The Text is plural. Which is not simply to say that it has several meanings, but that it accomplishes the very plural of meaning: an *irreducible* (and not merely an acceptable) plural. The Text is not a coexistence of meanings but a passage, an overcrossing; thus it answers not to an interpretation, even a liberal one, but to an explosion, a dissemination. The plural of the Text depends, that is, not on the ambiguity of its contents but on what might be called the *stereographic plurality* of its weave of signifiers (etymologically, the text is a tissue, a woven fabric). The reader of the Text may be compared to someone at a loose end (someone slackened off from any imaginary); this passably empty subject strolls – it is what happened to the author of these lines, then it was that he had a vivid idea of the Text – on the side of a valley, a *oued* flowing down below (*oued* is there to bear witness to a certain feeling of unfamiliarity); what he perceives is multiple, irreducible, coming from a disconnected, heterogeneous variety of substances and perspectives: lights, colours, vegetation, heat, air, slender explosions of noises, scant cries of birds, children's voices from over on the other side, passages, gestures, clothes of inhabitants near or far away. All these *incidents* are half-identifiable: they come from codes which are known but their combination is unique, founds the stroll in a difference repeatable only as difference. So the Text: it can be it only in its difference (which does not mean its individuality) its reading is semelfactive (this rendering illusory any inductive-deductive science of texts – no 'grammar' of the text) and nevertheless woven entirely with citations, references, echoes, cultural languages (what language is not?), antecedent or contemporary, which cut across it through and through in a vast stereophony. The intertextual in which every text is held, it itself being the text-between of another text, is not to be confused with some

origin of the text: to try to find the 'sources', the 'influences' of a work, is to fall in with the myth of filiation; the citations which go to make up a text are anonymous, untraceable, and yet *already read*: they are quotations without inverted commas. The work has nothing disturbing for any monistic philosophy (we know that there are opposing examples of these); for such a philosophy, plural is the Evil. Against the work, therefore, the text could well take as its motto the words of the man possessed by demons (*Mark* 5:9): 'My name is Legion: for we are many'. The plural of demoniacal texture which opposes text to work can bring with it fundamental changes in reading, and precisely in areas where monologism appears to be the Law: certain of the 'texts' of Holy Scripture traditionally recuperated by theological monism (historical or anagogical) will perhaps offer themselves to a diffraction of meanings (finally, that is to say, to a materialist reading), while the Marxist interpretation of works, so far resolutely monistic, will be able to materialize itself more by pluralizing itself (if, however, the Marxist 'institutions' allow it).

5. The work is caught up in a process of filiation. Are postulated: a *determination* of the work by the world (by race, then by History), a *consecution* of works amongst themselves, and a *conformity* of the work to the author. The author is reputed the father and the owner of his work: literary science therefore teaches *respect* for the manuscript and the author's declared intentions, while society asserts the legality of the relation of author to work (the '*droit d'auteur*' or 'copyright', in fact of recent date since it was only really legalized at the time of the French Revolution). As for the Text, it reads without the inscription of the Father. Here again, the metaphor of the Text separates from that of the work: the latter refers to the image of an organism which grows by vital expansion, by 'development' (a word which is significantly ambiguous, at once biological and rhetorical); the metaphor of the Text is that of the *network*: if the Text extends itself, it is as a result of a combinatory systematic (an image, moreover, close to current biological conceptions of the living being). Hence no vital 'respect' is due to the Text: it can be *broken* (which is just what the Middle Ages did with two nevertheless authoritative texts – Holy Scripture and Aristotle); it can be read without the guarantee of its father, the restitution of the inter-text paradoxically abolishing any legacy. It is not that the Author may not 'come back' in the Text, in his text, but he then does so as a 'guest'. If he is a novelist, he is inscribed in the novel like one of his characters, figured in the carpet; no longer privileged, paternal, aletheological, his inscription is ludic. He becomes, as it were, a paper-author: his life is no longer the origin of his fictions but a fiction

contributing to his work; there is a reversion of the work on to the life (and no longer the contrary); it is the work of Proust, of Genet which allows their lives to be read as a text. The word 'biography' re-acquires a strong, etymological sense, at the same time as the sincerity of the enunciation – veritable 'cross' borne by literary morality – becomes a false problem: the *I* which writes the text, it too, is never more than a paper-*I*.

6. The work is normally the object of a consumption; no demagogy is intended here in referring to the so-called consumer culture but it has to be recognized that today it is the 'quality' of the work (which supposes finally an appreciation of 'taste') and not the operation of reading itself which can differentiate between books: structurally, there is no difference between 'cultured' reading and casual reading in trains. The Text (if only by its frequent 'unreadability') decants the work (the work permitting) from its consumption and gathers it up as play, activity, production, practice. This means that the Text requires that one try to abolish (or at the very least to diminish) the distance between writing and reading, in no way by intensifying the projection of the reader into the work but by joining them in a single signifying practice. The distance separating reading from writing is historical. In the times of the greatest social division (before the setting up of democratic cultures), reading and writing were equally privileges of class. Rhetoric, the great literary code of those times, taught one to *write* (even if what was then normally produced were speeches, not texts). Significantly, the coming of democracy reversed the word of command: what the (secondary) School prides itself on is teaching to read (well) and no longer to write (consciousness of the deficiency is becoming fashionable again today: the teacher is called upon to teach pupils to 'express themselves', which is a little like replacing a form of repression by a misconception). In fact, *reading*, in the sense of consuming, is far from *playing* with the text. 'Playing' must be understood here in all its polysemy: the text itself *plays* (like a door, like a machine with 'play') and the reader plays twice over, playing the Text as one plays a game, looking for a practice which re-produces it, but, in order that that practice not be reduced to a passive, inner *mimesis* (the Text is precisely that which resists such a reduction), also playing the Text in the musical sense of the term. The history of music (as a practice, not as an 'art') does indeed parallel that of the Text fairly closely: there was a period when practising amateurs were numerous (at least within the confines of a certain class) and 'playing' and 'listening' formed a scarcely differentiated activity; then two roles appeared in succession, first that of the performer, the interpreter to whom the bourgeois public (though still itself able to

play a little – the whole history of the piano) delegated its playing, then that of the (passive) amateur, who listens to music without being able to play (the gramophone record takes the place of the piano). We know that today post-serial music has radically altered the role of the 'interpreter', who is called on to be in some sort the co-author of the score, completing it rather than giving it 'expression'. The Text is very much a score of this new kind: it asks of the reader a practical collaboration. Which is an important change, for who executes the work? (Mallarmé posed the question, wanting the audience to *produce* the book). Nowadays only the critic executes the work (accepting the play on words). The reduction of reading to a consumption is clearly responsible for the 'boredom' experienced by many in the face of the modern ('unreadable') text, the avant-garde film or painting: to be bored means that one cannot produce the text, open it out, *set it going*.

7. This leads us to pose (to propose) a final approach to the Text, that of pleasure. I do not know whether there has ever been a hedonistic aesthetics (eudaemonist philosophies are themselves rare). Certainly there exists a pleasure of the work (of certain works); I can delight in reading and re-reading Proust, Flaubert, Balzac, even – why not? – Alexandre Dumas. But this pleasure, no matter how keen and even when free from all prejudice, remains in part (unless by some exceptional critical effort) a pleasure of consumption; for if I can read these authors, I also know that I cannot *re-write* them (that it is impossible today to write 'like that') and this knowledge, depressing enough, suffices to cut me off from the production of these works, in the very moment their remoteness establishes my modernity (is not to be modern to know clearly what cannot be started over again?). As for the Text, it is bound to *jouissance*,[2] that is to a pleasure without separation. Order of the signifier, the Text participates in its own way in a social utopia; before History (supposing the latter does not opt for barbarism), the Text achieves, if not the transparence of social relations, that at least of language relations: the Text is that space where no language has a hold over any other, where languages circulate (keeping the circular sense of the term).

These few propositions, inevitably, do not constitute the articulations of a Theory of the Text and this is not simply the result of the failings of the person here presenting them (who in many respects has anyway done no more than pick up what is being developed round about him). It stems from the fact that a Theory of the Text cannot be satisfied by a metalinguistic exposition: the destruction of metalanguage, or at least (since it may be necessary provisionally to resort to metalanguage) its calling into doubt, is part of the theory itself: the discourse on the Text should itself be nothing other than text, research, textual activity, since the Text is that *social* space which leaves no language safe, outside, nor any subject of the enunciation in position as judge, master, analyst, confessor, decoder. The theory of the Text can coincide only with a practice of writing.

Notes

1   The Lacanian 'real' exists prior to, and cannot be assimilated into, systems of representation that arise from the imaginary/symbolic split. In short, the real is unrepresentable; 'reality', on the other hand, is precisely what is given to us to experience *through representation*. See Jacques Lacan, *The Four Fundamental Concepts of Psycho-Analysis*, trans. Alan Sheridan, ed. Jacques-Alain Miller (New York: Norton, 1978); see also Krisetva, 'One Identity', n. 15, in the present volume. (NL)

2   See Lyotard, 'Something Like', n. 6, in the present volume. (NL)

Chapter Fourteen Do Postmodern Genres Exist?

Ralph Cohen

Critics and theorists who write about postmodern texts often refer to 'genres' as a term inappropriate for characterizing postmodernist writing. The process of suppression results from the claim that postmodern writing blurs genres, transgresses them, or unfixes boundaries that conceal domination or authority, and that 'genre' is an anachronistic term and concept. When critics offer examples of postmodern novels, for example, they cite omniscient authors who are parodied or undermined. They point to self-conscious addresses to the reader in *If on a Winter's Night* and note the self-conscious foregrounding of literary artifice that undermines the generic assumption that a novel is referential or that it is a construction that bears a real relation to society.[1]

These critics assume that a genre theory of the novel is committed to backgrounding literary artifice, to demanding coherence, unity and linear continuity. But though such an assumption may apply to some generic theories, there are others that are perfectly compatible with multiple discourses, with narratives of discontinuity, with transgressed boundaries. To mention the multiple discourses that Bakhtin defines as characteristic of the novel is to note only one of the modernist theorists who accept multiple discourses and discontinuous structures.[2] Not only are there genre theories based on these premises but there are texts like *Tristram Shandy* and *Joseph Andrews* that exhibit what are now referred to as postmodern features. Ihab Hassan, one of the leaders of postmodernist theorizing, remarks that we now perceive 'postmodern features in *Tristram*

Ralph Cohen, 'Do Postmodern Genres Exist?', in *Postmodern Genres*, ed. Marjorie Perloff (Norman and London: University of Oklahoma Press, 1998), pp. 11–27.

Shandy precisely because our eyes have learned to recognize postmodern features'.[3]

Ihab Hassan is correct in noting that what we call 'postmodern' writing is espied in an earlier time, but eighteenth-century genres exhibited some of the same features. We rename these features in terms of our critical language, but *Tristram Shandy*'s marbled pages were transgressions then as now as were the foregrounding of literary artifice, the nonlinear narration, the insertion into the narrative of sermons, letters and stories. The basis for a genre theory of mixed forms or shared generic features is as old as Aristotle's comparison of tragedy and epic. Rosalie Colie has pointed out that numerous Renaissance writers self-consciously worked with mixtures of generic features, 'self-conscious, carefully worked mixtures, which counterpoint against one another the separate genres Petrarch was trying to reestablish'.[4] And such mixtures were not isolated cases but rather a way of thinking, of assuming that genres, mixed or unmixed, were the appropriate carriers of ancient knowledge. In fact the mixtures found in Homer's works were considered by some critics as the source of all poetic kinds. Colie points out that 'there were many more kinds [genres] than were recognized in official literary philosophy; and it is by these competing notions of kind that the richness and variety of Renaissance letters were assured'.[5]

Postmodern critics and theorists are often unaware of the various generic theories that have been created, and when they attack genre assumptions, they select these most often from modernist critics. Jonathan Culler, for example, in his 1975 essay, 'Towards a Theory of Non-Genre Literature' took as his modernist model the assumption that genre was a set of expectations between reader and text. This was a modernist assumption that could have been derived from Northrop Frye's *Anatomy of Criticism* (1957). By the mid-1970s there were several modernist formulations of a 'set of expectations'. But this phrase is always part of a comprehensive statement or theory. For example, for Hans Robert Jauss the 'set of expectations' form one part of his system of the aesthetics of reception and influence.

> The analysis of the literary experience of the reader avoids the threatening pitfalls of psychology if it describes the reception and influence of a work within the objectifiable *system of expectations* that arises for each work in the historical moment of its appearance, from a pre-understanding of the genre, from the form and themes of already familiar works, and from the opposition between poetic and practical language.[6]

And the relation of expectations to a particular public as addressee was formulated by Maria Corti: 'every genre seems to be directed toward a certain type of public, sometimes even to a specific class, *whose expectations* are directed toward that genre as long as social conditions warrant'.[7]

Culler formulates the concept of expectations as follows: 'genre, one might say, is a set of expectations, a set of instructions about the type of coherence one is to look for and the ways in which sequences are to be read'.[8] This is a reader-based definition, one that can accommodate to many variations within a genre. But it does not take account of how this generic claim actually fits into a genre theory. These theories attend to the historical moment of a work's appearance or to the social conditions that provide a warrant to a particular public for a specific genre.

When a theory of expectations is divorced from its theoretical frame it can be treated as an unstated 'contractual' relation of author to reader although the formulation of such a contract is a legal image, not an actual situation. Culler argues that postmodern novels void the contract because they alter conventions and become 'unreadable'. But this argument presupposes some hypothesis about how conventions begin, how they become commonplace and how they are altered or abandoned. Postmodern genres, as many critics point out, have features that are inherited from modernist genres. Since genres are interrelated, there seems always a basis for some readability. And at the end of the essay Culler seems to concede that even abstruse postmodern novels come to be read because of a basic human capacity for ordering disorder. There is, he writes, an astonishing human capacity to recuperate the deviant, to invest new conventions and functions so as to overcome that which resists our efforts'.[9] In fact Joyce's *Finnegans Wake*, a text often used as an example of postmodern writing, is treated by Frye as an encyclopedic form and ironic epic. The text requires no abandonment of a genre system: on the contrary, it can fit quite readily within it.

Postmodern critics have sought to do without a genre theory. Terms like 'text' and '*écriture*' deliberately avoid generic classifications. And the reasons for this are efforts to abolish the hierarchies that genres introduce, to avoid the assumed fixity of genres and the social as well as literary authority such limits exert, to reject the social and subjective elements in classification. But these reasons apply to a genre theory that Austin Warren calls 'classical' and that argues for the 'purity' of genres. As he points out, modern genre theory is descriptive: 'It doesn't limit the number of possible kinds and doesn't prescribe rules to authors. It supposes that traditional kinds may be "mixed" and produce a new kind (like tragicomedy).'[10] Modernist genre theories minimize classification and maximize clarification and interpretation. Such genre theories are part of semiotic theories of communication that relate genres to culture. Indeed, modernist critics who resort to genre theory – Todorov, Jameson, Fowler, Bakhtin, Gilbert and Gubar[11] – undertake to explain and analyze the relation between trivial or ignored genres and canonized genres. And this is a procedure that seems most applicable to a postmodern inquiry.

The initiation or use of one genre is determined by its relation to others. If writing were always identical, there would be no kinds and no need for generic distinctions about whole works. And if each piece of writing were different from all others there would be no basis for theorizing or even for communication. But since one piece of writing tends to be based on other pieces – some theorists refer to genres as families of texts with close or distant relatives – a genre offers the most extensive procedure for dealing with this phenomenon. It not only inquires into the reasons for intertextuality; it inquires into the significance of the combinatory procedures that result from it. The generic concept of combinatory writing makes possible the study of continuities and changes within a genre as well as the recurrence of generic features and their historical implications. But this particular genre theory is one among many. Theorists who propose genre theories no less than those who oppose them need, therefore, to explore the aims which govern any genre theory. Whether the purpose of a genre system (however constructed) be evaluative, as it was for Aristotle or Dryden or Irving Babbitt, or educative as it was for Renaissance theorists, or evolutionary as it was for [nineteenth-century French critic] Vincent Brunetière, or a system of communication as it is for Maria Corti or an ideological structure as it is for Fredric Jameson or a basis for understanding literary transitions and history as it was for the Russian formalists, genre theorizing is itself a genre. It can be an essay, literary criticism, literary theory, literary history, etc. And writing in genres is demonstrated by a text itself.

When Derrida asks of what genre is genre, he draws attention to the fact that his own essay belongs with essayistic genres like literary theory or philosophical discourse. This is not the place to discuss the issues involved in the naming of genres, but to point out that every text is a member of one or more genres. What needs to be studied are the constituents of a text and what kinds of effects these have or can have upon readers. It is these constituents in a mixed or combinatory form that make some theorists refer to genres as 'blurred'. In this respect, many critics who find postmodern writing non-generic because it is combinatory or reader oriented or discontinuous seem to be unfamiliar with the available generic theories upon which they can draw.

Clifford Geertz's essay, 'Blurred Genres', is a noteworthy example of assuming that the blurring or mixing of genres is indicative of a new way of thinking. Although his essay is directed at studies of social thought, it also refers to literary examples. He describes the phenomenon of blurring as follows:

> scientific discussions looking like belles lettres *morceaux* (Lewis Thomas, Loren Eiseley), baroque fantasies presented as deadpan empirical observations (Borges, Barthelme), histories that consist of equations and tables or law court testimony (Fogel and Engerman, Le Roi Ladurie), documentaries that read like true confessions (Mailer), parables posing as ethnographies (Castenada), theoretical treatises set out as travelogues (Lévi-Strauss), Nabokov's *Pale Fire*, that impossible object made of poetry and fiction, footnotes and images from the clinic, seems very much of the time; one waits only for quantum theory in verse or biography in algebra.[12]

Geertz finds interactions and intertextuality in and out of 'literary' texts. I add to his examples by noting that genres such as ballads, lyrics, proverbs, short stories, etc., become part of other texts – of novels, of tragedies, of comedies. He notes that parts of a genre such as autobiography, can be mixed with a scientific disquisition (James Watson's *The Double Helix*). One can add that a theoretical essay (Annette Kolodny's 'Dancing Through the Minefield: Some Observations on the Theory, Practice, and Politics of a Feminist Literary Criticism') can also contain autobiographical discourses. For Geertz, this procedure represents a refiguration of social theory; he sees it as indicative of a change in social inquiry from one concerned with *what knowledge is* to 'what it is we want to know'.[13] He assumes that 'modernist' inquiry studied the dynamics of collective life in order to alter it 'in desired directions'.[14] Postmodern inquiry studies the anatomization of thought, not the manipulation of behavior. In *The Double Helix*, however, the purpose of mixing laboratory politics with scientific inquiry serves to undermine the 'objectivity' of scientific procedures and the assumption of a unified scientific community. And Kolodny's essay, in its combinatory procedures, describes her actual indoctrination by male critics in order to support her argument urging the need for an adequate feminist criticism. It is an attack on the 'objectivity' of literary criticism, on the need for an overt acknowledgement of the authority implied in such criticism, on the need for recognition of gender as an overlooked or repressed aspect of academic instruction.

In these works, the combination of autobiography, laboratory or class-room practice and politics is related to social and political attitudes. Combinations present not merely the procedures of scientific or literary inquiry, but serve to illustrate the procedures by which they conceal antagonisms, prejudices and disunity. This generic analysis redirects tex-tual analyses: from studying behavior to studying the grounds of behavior; from the overt desire to manipulate behavior to studying the nature of this desire, the actual processes of manipulation.

The texts that I have been describing still fall within accustomed gen-res: the history of a scientific discovery or the theoretical essay about literary study. Nevertheless they do transgress the modernist generic bounds by introducing subjective elements and insisting on the ideological bases governing inquiries. Still, the very concept of transgression presupposes an acknowledgment of boundaries or limits. Such transgressions, as some theorists of postmodernism recognize, presuppose genres, presuppose that postmodern practices have not homogenized writing; rather they con-tinue to introduce distinctions even though these differ from modernist practices. Certain models of modernist literature – Dos Passos's *U.S.A.*, Pound's *Cantos*, Faulkner's *Absalom, Absalom!* – are cited repeatedly as combinations of multiple discourses found in modernist genres. Thus the issue is not a matter of multiple subjects or discontinuous narration, but of the shift in the kinds of 'transgressions' and in the implications of the revised combinations. And Bakhtin, Jameson and other modernist genre theorists do provide insights into the social basis of generic structures.

What alternatives exist if one rejects the study of genres in analysing postmodern texts? One can discuss themes, one can discuss periods, one can discuss rhetorical strategies. None of these, however, is incompatible with generic study. If we conceive of postmodernism as a style, it must be defined or described by being shown to be different from the modernist style. And yet any such change will inevitably call upon similarities or continuing features. If we conceive of postmodernism as a period, such description will have to include genres like tragedy or new mass culture genres like TV sitcoms and the detective or spy story and film. A period study will have to include genres like Shakespeare's plays and Milton's *Paradise Lost* from earlier periods that are kept alive by the curricula of academic institutions and stage or TV productions. A period study, therefore, unless it degenerizes all previous texts within a given chronological segment, will inevitably have to retain the language of genres as a part of the period.

It is one of the ironies of postmodern criticism that critics who are rightly cognizant of the constraints imposed by boundaries, who seek to reveal what boundaries conceal about 'the nexus between knowledge and power', often do so within boundaries they seem not to recognize. In the introduction to an anthology of theoretical essays entitled *Criticism Without Boundaries*, the editor sees boundaries in terms of disciplinary demarcations.[15] But the anthology of essays is itself a genre, a genre that has been practiced by modernist no less than by postmodernist critics. The essays themselves are collected into a fictitious unity, and they are written, each of them, in the linear tradition of the modernist essay with intersections of sociological, educative and Marxist discourses. What this generic combination implies, since the essays were given or intended as lectures, is the disregard of the difference between oral delivery and the written text in an anthology, between the relation of an audience to a speaker in contrast to a reader reading an essay. We have generic continuity of a modernist genre that aims, as Robert Stallman's anthology did, to undermine earlier critical positions.[16] An awareness of this enterprise as generic would have introduced an aspect of cultural continuity requiring explanation. After all, this postmodern enterprise displays a readiness of critics to operate within the academy, using modernist generic conventions to undermine modernism and its values. This generic procedure operates within familiar categories and constituents including the insistence on the need to defamiliarize them and to politicize them.

One can point out that the journal and the anthology as genres present options of beginning with any selection, of providing multiple thematic approaches or variations of one approach. The texts within an anthology call attention to shared features of essays or poems or stories no less than to differences and they thus permit distinctions to be made regarding individual examples. But these combinatory texts, when they deny their generic identity, serve to repress the difference between what they say and what they are. What lurks in the denial of generic combinations while employing them is the fear that boundaries are conservative, that to admit that bounds or limits are inevitable is to submit to them. But as I have pointed out, there need be no such confinement. 'Postmodernist' writing without boundaries is as much a fiction as postmodernist writing fixed by them.

The combinatory nature of genres moves in our time to mixtures of media and to mixtures resulting from the electronic world in which we live. Films,[17] TV genres, university educational programs, our very explanations of identity and discourses all indicate combinations of one kind or another. The precise nature of these combinations differ, but what genre critics and theorists can now study are the interactions within combinations and how these differ from earlier combinations, whether in epic, tragedy, novel, lyric, etc.

This generic procedure, this combinatory genre theory no less than that of the postmodern 'novel' or surfiction, has significant antecedents in the writings of the early eighteenth century. Marjorie Perloff has suggested that this might be the case with postmodern poetics: 'Postmodern poetics, it may yet turn out, has more in common with the performative, playful mode of eighteenth-century ironists than with Shelleyan apocalypse.'[18] Here the recognition of the anthology as a genre reveals a substantial clue for grasping what might be called generic history, the discontinuous recurrence or the continuity of certain genres or features of genres.

To pursue one example of this that is pertinent to postmodern genres, I wish to consider some of the innovative genres that occur at the beginning of the eighteenth century. One of the characteristic features of that species of writing which came to be called the novel reveals a narrator who quite consciously addresses the reader and suggests how the text should be read. The obvious example, *Tristram Shandy*, resists narrative closure, linear narration, includes genres such as the sermon, letter, and story, produces interventions of musical and other non-verbal genres. Certainly with regard to the postmodern palimpsest assumption that each new text is written over an older one,[19] one need only consult a satire like Swift's *A Tale of a Tub*. And Henry Fielding's *Joseph Andrews* announces itself as 'Written in Imitation of Cervantes, Author of Don Quixote'. I am not suggesting that Fielding is Borges or that *Joseph Andrews* is equatable with 'Pierre Menard, Author of the *Quixote*' or that 'imitation' as used in the eighteenth century is anything but resisted and discarded by postmodern critics. What I am arguing is that Fielding's self-conscious addresses to the reader, that his use of inset stories and thus of multiple narrators who result in making the primary characters become secondary while some of the trivial characters become, for the inset story, the primary narrators, that these practices are analogous to some in postmodern genres. When the inset story of Leonard and Paul is interrupted and left uncompleted in *Joseph Andrews* we have a further instance of the discontinuity characteristic of postmodern writing. A generic history will not merely point to these recurrences, but suggest that these are tied to social and cultural no less than literary phenomena. Thus these procedures are not merely engaged in rejecting inherited hierarchial genres, but, by parodying them, they offer a consciousness of certain limited eighteenth-century alternatives.

Since I am proposing a historical linkage between eighteenth-century and postmodern genres, I wish to relate the innovative periodical essay to the postmodern presence of the critical and theoretical essay. My purpose in drawing attention to the prevalence of innovative early eighteenth-century genres and those in our time is to indicate shared features. These reveal relations between generic constituents and societal changes. The eighteenth-century genres that appeared in periodical papers – letters, stories, critical and political essays, etc. – were addressed primarily to a female audience deprived of a university education. They sought to educate a new audience and in so doing helped create in readers a consciousness that some transgressions were an acceptable and even desirable practice. If, as Douwe Fokkema claims, postmodernism is 'the most "democratic" of literary codes',[20] the generic developments of the earlier time sought to provide generic changes that would make it possible to legitimate a bourgeois society. However different a postindustrial society is from one moving into a bourgeois economy, genre theory may indicate that we are dealing with beginnings and endings. If an analysis of eighteenth-century generic instances and intersections reveals that these served to elevate folk genres (or popular genres ignored by critics) then it seems reasonable to inquire what shifts are involved in modern and postmodern critical acts that elevate formerly ignored genres like slave narratives or popular romances so that they merit academic research and critical analyses. In both situations we find the retention of some older genres, whether the sermon or comedy. In both periods there develop popular genres that serve readers not yet a coherent part of a bourgeois class or of a postmodern non-elite audience. The limits imposed by postmodern writing surely narrows its audience, an audience that responds more fully to rock music of the sixties, to TV sitcoms and to other genres current in the modernist period.

Critics and theorists disagree about how to explain the phenomenon of postmodernism; some even believe that such explanations are unnecessary. But it is especially important to observe that by rejecting generic procedures, such critics deprive themselves of explanatory tools. In order to demonstrate the characteristics of postmodern writing, critics need to distinguish these from those found in modernism. Postmodern critics resist the usefulness that generic critics find in discussing entities. But writings of different kinds do begin and stop. Constituent parts require that they be considered both within the text and in connections with other texts that begin and stop differently. Some generic procedures are essential to any such effort. Derrida, in discussing the genre of a text by Maurice Blanchot, declares that it reveals the madness of genre: 'in

literature, satirically practicing all genres, imbibing them but never allowing herself to be saturated with a catalogue of genres, she, madness, has
started spinning Peterson's genre-disc like a demented sun. And she does
not only do so in literature, for in concealing the boundaries that sunder
mode and genre, she has also inundated and divided the borders between
literature and its others'.[21]

But this very attack upon genre falls within the genres of satire, parody
and literary theory. To note that genres are necessary in order to be
rejected is to remain within the discourse of genres. That a short work can
have reference to or be the basis of all other genres is to parody the claim
that Homer's epics included them all (however ironic one treats or parodies this claim).

Derrida's parodic essay does, of course, have an ending regardless of its
'openness'. And it is this writing against genre while being in it that Linda
Hutcheon identifies with parody: 'The collective weight of parodic *practice* suggests a redefinition of parody as repetition with critical distance
that allows ironic signaling of difference at the heart of similarity.'[22] This
definition applies to parody as a constituent of a text as well as a genre of
its own. And it is as a genre that parody displays itself in the playful/
serious text that Derrida has written.

I have emphasized the constituents of generic text, the combinatorial
parts that together produce effects upon readers. But it is necessary, also,
to stress the notion of an entity, of the consequences of particular kinds of
combinations, mixtures, multiple discourses, intertextuality. The language
that critics – modern and postmodern – use in discussing texts implies
images of the human body as a system, as a biological organism (gender),
as a machine. They refer to voice, to sight, to hearing, to smelling, moving, etc. Overtly or implicitly the image of the body of the reader (sometimes of the narrator) is present in the transaction with a text. In drama,
of course, the actor's body is a constituent of the drama whereas in
postmodern fiction the body can be a theme as it is in Sukenick's 'The
Death of the Novel'.[23] But there is another sense in which the image of the
text as a member of a genre is appropriate. Just as a human body has
physically descriptive limits, so, too, does any text. The body is dependent
on oxygen, on drawing into itself and excreting from itself substances
that make it possible to endure as a physical entity, so texts depend upon
the language of generic forms in order to be considered as verbal entities.
These make it possible to distinguish texts that at any one time are considered unknown or even unknowable genres from those that are known.
How does the unknown genre become knowable? That the concept of a

genre changes because its members change is self-evident. What is not self-evident is how the constituents of a text begin to undermine the usefulness of a genre so that critics offer replacements.

Two examples should be mentioned here. One is M. H. Abrams's positing of 'the Greater Romantic Lyric' as a genre. His procedure is to argue that no known genre describes the texts to which he refers. The new genre is a combination of parts from the loco-descriptive poem, the Romantic meditative lyric, the conversation poem. For Abrams, the new genre 'displaced what neoclassical critics had called "the greater ode" . . . as the favored form for the long lyric poem'.[24] Abrams sought to fill a gap in our understanding of Romantic literary invention. He thus proceeded generically in locating the origins of the new genre for which numerous examples existed but remained unnamed or misdescribed.

The second example of generic imitation occurs in an essay by Rosalind Krauss, 'Sculpture in the Expanded Field'. Her argument is that critics have expanded the genre 'sculpture' to include earthworks, 'narrow corridors with TV monitors at the ends; large photographs documenting country hikes', and other structures so that the category has become 'almost infinitely malleable'.[25] The reasons for such inclusion she attributes to the desire to make the new familiar by assuming that the new forms evolved from past forms. In this respect genre serves to avoid discontinuity by expanding the members of the category. Krauss argues that the genre is a 'historically bounded category' with its own internal logic, its own set of rules, which, though they can be applied to a variety of situations, are not themselves open to very much change'.[26] But if the reliance on the internal logic of sculpture is a problematic use of 'logic', her subsequent explanation is much more persuasive. It is that the genre 'sculpture' must be understood in relation to the genres of landscape and architecture (and not-landscape and not-architecture): 'within the situation of postmodernism, practice is not defined in relation to a given medium – sculpture – but rather in relation to the logical operations on a set of cultural terms, for which any medium – photography, books, lines on walls, mirrors or sculpture itself – might be used'.[27] For Krauss, the remapping of genres is the result of forces reshaping history contemporaneous with the new genres. And the durability of these genres, established by ruptures in concepts of history, would seem to be contemporaneous with the history that initiated it.

For Fredric Jameson, the history that initiates postmodern views of sculpture is not a matter of the rational logic of a genre, but what he calls 'cultural logic'. Postmodernism is a historical period concept characteristic of the late stage of capitalism.

In his projection of a 'new systematic cultural norm', Jameson names as the constituents of postmodernism he plans to discuss 'a new depthlessness', 'a consequent weakening of historicity', 'a whole new type of emotional ground tone', 'the deep constitutive relationships of all this to a whole new technology, which is itself a figure for a whole new economic system'.[28] I cannot rehearse here Jameson's remarkable study of sophisticated and complex features that change as a result of economic changes, his distaste for the dominant cultural norm he finds in postmodernism, his desire to replace Hutcheon's key term 'parody' with 'pastiche', a term that makes 'parody' blank, 'a statue with blind eyeballs'.

The very same concept of a cultural 'dominant' is developed by Brian McHale except that the latter finds critics discovering various 'dominants' demonstrating the reciprocal linkages between modernism and postmodernism: 'Clearly, then, there are *many* dominants, and different dominants may be distinguished depending upon the level, scope, and focus of the analysis. Furthermore, one and the same text will, we can infer, yield different dominants depending upon what aspect of it we are analyzing. . . . In short, different dominants emerge depending upon which questions we ask of the text, and the position from which we interrogate it.'[29]

The writings of Jameson and McHale fall into established genres of critical theory and literary criticism. Alterations of views about dominant features do not result in changes of genre. It thus appears that Jameson's Marxist interventions and McHale's formalist interventions still aim at reader persuasion. Thus we can note that the ideology in the linear essay can be seen as resisting postmodernist emptiness of form or aligning some aspects of modernist ideology while others involve an attack upon it. The two texts thus render paradoxical the arguments they make.

The writings of the critics and theorists who argue for 'postmodern' as a turning away from modernism find themselves, with few exceptions, continuing to write in the essay genres that were characteristic of modernism. Whatever thematic discourses of generic interpretations they introduce into their essays, they combine them with the traits of modernist essays. Even an essay that seeks to free itself from the modernist genre does include some modernist devices. Thus an essay by Ihab Hassan entitled 'POSTmodernISM: A Paracritical Bibliography' undertakes the creation of the essay as encyclopedic genre, as a verbal object typographically innovative, deliberately disjunctive, rejecting linear development, including parts that are normally excluded from the text itself (a bibliography), blank lines for the reader to fill in as he wishes and to become an author, participating in the writing of the essay: 'I offer . . . some rubrics and spaces. Let the readers fill them in with their own spaces or grimaces. We value what we choose.'[30]

Yet even as he experiments with the transformation of the essay, Hassan expresses reservations about postmodernism's transformatory characteristics. Is it, he asks, 'somewhat more inward with destiny? Though my sympathies are in the present, I cannot believe this to be entirely so.'[31] This essay was published in 1971; in *The Postmodern Turn* published in 1987, he writes of postmodernism with considerable uneasiness about its usefulness as a category: 'Though postmodernism may persist, like modernism itself, a fiercely contested category, at once signifier and signified, altering itself in the very process of signification, the effort to speak it can not be wholly vain.'[32]

Critics are divided about the constituents of postmodernism and about its relation to modernism. But most essays confine themselves to constituents of texts rather than to texts as examples of genres. Matei Calinescu writes that as long as we compare and contrast postmodernity with modernity, 'modernity survives, at least as the name of a cultural family resemblance in which, for better or for worse, we continue to recognize ourselves'.[33] Even Linda Hutcheon, in her comprehensive attempt to theorize about postmodernism, points out that postmodernism's relation to modernism is typically contradictory. 'It makes neither a simple and radical break with it nor a straightforward continuity with it: it is both and neither'.[34]

Now this description occurs in an essay developed in a linear manner, including, however, some of the discourses of postmodernism in fiction and the other arts as well as discourses from Marxist and other critics, and, in conclusion, arriving at pluralism, at pragmatism, at an understanding of signifying processes (at epistemology) and even (perhaps in a parodic demonstration of postmodernist contradictions) at a version of humanistic aims: 'To move from the desire and expectation of sure and single meaning to a recognition of the value of differences and even contradictions might be a tentative first step towards accepting responsibility for both art and theory *as signifying processes*. In other words, maybe we could begin to study the implications of both our making and our making sense of our culture'.[35]

The critical and theoretical essay – and my essay is another example of this – is a genre that has come to be practiced more frequently in the late modernist and postmodernist periods than at any time previously in English literary history. To recognize it as a kind of writing, as a genre, is to demonstrate some of the functions it has for us. The essay is not merely a part of anthologies; it is a genre of its own and critics have traced its changes from Montaigne to the present. The academic essay serves postmodernism by exemplifying how a genre can embrace discourses that attack genres, how a genre can be the site of contrary ideologies.

Roland Barthes' view of the essay, as quoted by Réda Bensmäia, is that it is a question '"with intellectual things . . . of combining . . . *at the same time* theory, critical combat, and pleasure"'. And Barthes' experimentation with the essay as a unique form offers 'the possibility of a "plural" text made up of multiple networks "that interact without any one of them being able to dominate the others" . . . it has no beginning; it is reversible; we gain access to it by several entrances, none of which can be authoritatively declared to be the main one' (99).[36]

This is a postmodern view of the essay and it does not refer to the essays I have quoted, but it does draw attention to the fact that the theoretical essay is a historical kind. If this is a postmodern definition, then the multiple networks argument is itself a dominant for postmodern essays. Treating the essay as genre is a recognition that discourses cannot be an adequate substitute for the works that encompass them. The rejection of genre falsifies the situation in which entrances are many and exits are many. For it conceals the fact that in different kinds of postmodernist writing, in novels, dramas, essays, entrances and exits are not the same.

Do postmodern genres exist? This question can now be seen in the context I have set for it. If one wishes to trace the relation between modernism and postmodernism, if one wishes to understand the diverse ways of distinguishing postmodern fiction from postmodern surfiction and from the romance and spy story as fictions equally contemporary but not postmodern, then genre study is the most adequate procedure to accomplish this aim.

Do postmodern genres exist? If we wish to understand the proliferation of academic anthologies, journals, collections of critical essays, then we need names for such omnibus volumes and genre theory provides them. If we wish to study these kinds of writing with reference to the social environment of which they are a part, then genre study helps us relate institutions and economics to the production of texts. If we seek to understand the historical recurrence of certain kinds of writing, the rejection or abandonment of other kinds, genre theory provides the most adequate procedure for this inquiry. If we wish to analyze an individual text, genre theory provides a knowledge of its constituents and how they combine. Not only do these actions recognize the value of a genre theory in analysing modernist writing, but they demonstrate that postmodern theorists, critics, authors and readers inevitably use the language of genre theory even as they seek to deny its usefulness.

Notes

1   Cf. Italo Calvino, *If on a Winter's Night a Traveller*, trans. William Weaver (London: Pan, 1982). Like Pynchon's *The Crying of Lot 49* and Borges's *Labyrinths* (see Thwaites and Barth, respectively, in the present volume), Calvino's text, first published in Italian in 1979, has become a standard instance of postmodern writing. (NL)

2   Cf. Mikhail Bakhtin, *The Dialogic Imagination*, trans. Caryl Emerson and M. Holquist (Austin: University of Texas Press, 1981). [See also Kristeva, n. 14, in the present volume. (NL)]

3   Ihab Hassan, *The Postmodern Turn* (Columbus: Ohio State University Press, 1987), p. xvi. [I discuss Hassan at some length in ch. 5 of my *PomoIntro*, esp. pp. 82–94. (NL)]

4   Rosalie Colie, *The Resources of Kind* (Berkeley: University of California Press, 1973), p. 19.

5   Ibid., p. 8; and consider also the following: 'I would like to present genre-theory as a means of accounting for connections between topic and treatment within the literary system, but also to see the connection of the literary kinds with kinds of knowledge and experience; to present the kinds as a major part of the genus universum which is part of all literary students' heritage' (ibid., p. 29).

6   Hans Robert Jauss, 'Literary History as a Challenge to Literary Theory', in *Toward an Aesthetic of Reception*, trans. T. Bahti (Minneapolis: University of Minnesota Press, 1982), p. 22, emphasis added. An earlier version of some sections of this essay was published in 1970 in *New Literary History*.

7   Maria Corti, *An Introduction to Literary Semiotics*, trans. M. Bogat and A. Mandelbaum (Bloomington: Indiana University Press, 1978), p. 118, emphasis added.

8   Jonathan Culler, 'Towards a Theory of Non-Genre Literature', in *Surfiction*, ed. Raymond Federman (Chicago: Swallow Press, 1975), p. 255.

9   Ibid., p. 259. A point similar to Culler's on the unreadableness of some postmodern genres is made by Charles Caramello, 'On Styles of Postmodern Writing', in *Performance in Postmodern Culture*, eds M. Benamou and C. Caramello (Madison: University of Wisconsin Press, 1977). Referring to essays by Edmond Jabes, Ihab Hassan, Campbell Tatham and Raymond Federman, Caramello writes: 'What they *are* is impossible to ascertain. "Impossible to classify these books", Rosemarie Waldrop writes of Jabes's *Le Livre des Questions*. "They have the texture of poetry, but are mostly prose."'

10   Austin Warren, 'Literary Genres', in René Welleck and Austin Warren, *Theory of Literature* (New York: Harcourt Brace, 1949), p. 245.

11   Discussions of this aspect of genre theory can be found in the essays of Jurij Tynjanov and Roman Jakobson in *Readings in Russian Poetics: Formalist and Structuralist Views*; eds. L. Matejka and K. Pomorska (Cambridge, Mass.: MIT Press, 1971); Mikhail Bakhtin, *Problems of Dostoevsky's Poetics*, trans. and ed. Caryl Emerson (Minneapolis: University of Minnesota Press, 1984) and also in his *Speech Genres and Other Late Essays*, trans. V. W. McGee, eds Caryl Emerson and M. Holquist (Austin: University of Texas Press, 1986) and *Dialogic Imagination*; Tzvetan Todorov, *The Fantastic*, trans. Richard Howard (Cleveland: Case Western Reserve University Press, 1973); Alastair Fowler, *Kinds of Literature* (Cambridge, Mass.: Harvard University Press, 1982); Fredric Jameson, *The Political Unconscious* (Ithaca: Cornell University Press, 1981); and Sandra M. Gilbert and Susan Gubar, *The Madwoman in the Attic: The Woman Writer and the Nineteenth-Century Literary Imagination* (New Haven: Yale University Press, 1979).

12   Clifford Geertz, 'Blurred Genres: The Refiguration of Social Thought', *American Scholar* 49 (Spring 1980), pp. 165–6.

13   Ibid., p. 178.

14   Ibid.

15   Cf. J. A. Buttigieg, ed., *Criticism Without Boundaries* (Notre Dame: Notre Dame University Press, 1987).

16   Cf. Robert W. Stallman, ed., *Critiques and Essays in Criticism 1920–1948* (New York: Ronald Press, 1949).

17   See (among others) Rick Altman, *The American Film Musical* (Bloomington: Indiana University Press, 1987); Christian Metz, *The Imaginary Signifier* (Bloomington: Indiana University Press, 1982); and S. J. Solomon, *The Film Idea* (New York: Harcourt Brace Jovanovich, 1972).

18   Marjorie Perloff, *The Dance of the Intellect* (Cambridge: Cambridge University Press, 1985), p. 176.

19   Julia Kristeva: 'every text takes shape as a mosaic of citations, every text is the absorption and transformation of other texts. The notion of intertextuality comes to take the place of the notion of intersubjectivity' (cited in Carmello, 'Styles', p. 224). [Cf. Julia Kristeva, 'Word, Dialogue, and Novel', in *Desire in Language: A Semiotic Approach to Literature and Art*, trans. Thomas Gora, Alice Jardine and Leon S. Roudiez, ed. Leon S. Roudiez (Oxford: Blackwell, 1981), p. 66; see also my *PomoIntro*, pp. 30–5, for a discussion of this text. (NL)]

20   Douwe W. Fokkema, *Literary History, Modernism and Postmodernism* (Amsterdam and Philadelphia: John Benjamins, 1984), p. 48.

21   Jacques Derrida, 'The Law of Genre', *Glyph* 7 (Baltimore: Johns Hopkins University Press, 1980), p. 228.

22   Linda Hutcheon, 'The Politics of Postmodernism', *Cultural Critique* 5 (Winter 1987), p. 185. The entire issue is devoted to the subject 'Modernity and

Modernism, Postmodernity and Postmodernism'.

23   See Ronald Sukenick, *The Death of the Novel and Other Stories* (New York: Dial Press, 1969).

24   M. H. Abrams, 'Structure and Style in the Greater Romantic Lyric', in *From Sensibility to Romanticism*, eds F. W. Hilles and Harold Bloom (New York: Oxford University Press, 1965), p. 528.

25   Rosalind E. Krauss, *The Originality of the Avant Garde and Other Modernist Myths* (Cambridge, Mass.: Harvard University Press, 1985), p. 277.

26   Ibid., p. 279.

27   Ibid., p. 288.

28   Fredric Jameson, 'Postmodernism, or The Cultural Logic of Late Capitalism', *New Left Review* 146 (July/Aug. 1984); an earlier version appeared as 'Postmodernism and Consumer Society', in *The Anti-Aesthetic: Essays on Postmodern Culture*, ed. Hal Foster (Port Townsend: Bay Press, 1983).

29   Brian McHale, *Postmodernist Fictions* (New York and London: Methuen, 1987), p. 6. The concept of the 'dominant' is applied by Todorov to a theory of genres (see *Fantastic*).

30   Ihab Hassan, 'POSTmodernISM: A Paracritical Bibliography', in *From Modernism to Postmodernism: An Anthology*, ed. Lawrence Cahoone (Oxford: Blackwell, 1996), p. 391. (NL)

31   Ibid., p. 400.

32   Hassan, *Postmodern Turn*, p. xii.

33   Matei Calinescu, *Five Faces of Modernity* (Durham: Duke University Press, 1987), p. 312.

34   Linda Hutcheon, 'Beginning to Theorize Postmodernism', *Textual Practice* 1 (1) (Spring 1987), p. 23.

35   Ibid., p. 26.

36   Réda Bensmäia, *The Barthes Effect: The Essay as Reflective Text*, trans. Pat Fedkiew (Minneapolis: University of Minnesota Press, 1987), p. 99. [Bensmäia is quoting from Roland Barthes, *S/Z*, trans. Richard Miller (New York: Hill and Wang, 1974). For a discussion of this text, see my *PomoIntro*, pp. 75–7. (NL)]

Chapter Fifteen The Literature of Exhaustion

John Barth

The fact is that every writer creates his own precursors. His work modifies our conception of the past, as it will modify the future.

Jorge Luis Borges, *Labyrinths*

You who listen give me life in a manner of speaking. I won't hold you responsible. My first words weren't my first words. I wish I'd begun differently.

John Barth, *Lost in the Fun House*

I want to discuss three things more or less together: first, some old questions raised by the new intermedia arts; second, some aspects of the Argentine writer Jorge Luis Borges, whom I greatly admire; third, some professional concerns of my own, related to these other matters and having to do with what I'm calling 'the literature of exhausted possibility' – or, more chicly, 'the literature of exhaustion'.

By 'exhaustion' I don't mean anything so tired as the subject of physical, moral, or intellectual decadence, only the used-upness of certain forms or exhaustion of certain possibilities – by no means necessarily a cause for despair. That a great many Western artists for a great many years have quarrelled with received definitions of artistic media, genres, and forms goes without saying: pop art, dramatic and musical 'happenings', the whole range of 'intermedia' or 'mixed-means' art, bear recentest witness

John Barth, 'The Literature of Exhaustion' [1967], in *The Novel Today: Contemporary Writers on Modern Fiction*, ed. Malcolm Bradbury (London: Fontana, 1977), pp. 70–83.

to the tradition of rebelling against Tradition. A catalogue I received some time ago in the mail, for example, advertises such items as Robert Filliou's *Ample Food for Stupid Thought*, a box full of postcards on which are inscribed 'apparently meaningless questions', to be mailed to whomever the purchaser judges them suited for; Ray Johnson's *Paper Snake*, a collection of whimsical writings, 'often pointed', once mailed to various friends (what the catalogue describes as The New York Correspondence School of Literature); and Daniel Spoerri's *Anecdoted Typography of Chance*, 'on the surface' a description of all the objects that happen to be on the author's parlour table – 'in fact, however . . . a cosmology of Spoerri's existence'.

'On the surface', at least, the document listing these items is a catalogue of The Something Else Press, a swinging outfit. 'In fact, however', it may be one of their offerings, for all I know: The New York Direct-Mail Advertising School of Literature. In any case, their wares are lively to read about, and make for interesting conversation in fiction-writing classes, for example, where we discuss Somebody-or-other's unbound, unpaginated, randomly assembled novel-in-a-box and the desirability of printing *Finnegans Wake* on a very long roller-towel. It's easier and sociabler to talk technique than it is to make art, and the area of 'happenings' and their kin is mainly a way of discussing aesthetics, really; illustrating 'dramatically' more or less valid and interesting points about the nature of art and the definition of its terms and genres.

One conspicuous thing, for example, about the 'intermedia' arts is their tendency (noted even by *Life* magazine) to eliminate not only the traditional audience – 'those who apprehend the artists' art' (in 'happenings' the audience is often the 'cast', as in 'environments', and some of the new music isn't intended to be performed at all) – but also the most traditional notion of the artist: the Aristotelian conscious agent who achieves with technique and cunning the artistic effect; in other words, one endowed with uncommon talent, who has moreover developed and disciplined that endowment into virtuosity. It's an aristocratic notion on the face of it, which the democratic West seems eager to have done with; not only the 'omniscient' author of older fiction, but the very idea of the controlling artist, has been condemned as politically reactionary, even fascist.

Now, personally, being of the temper that chooses to 'rebel along traditional lines', I'm inclined to prefer the kind of art that not many people can do: the kind that requires expertise and artistry as well as bright aesthetic ideas and/or inspiration. I enjoy the pop art in the famous

Albright-Knox collections a few blocks from my house in Buffalo, like a lively conversation for the most part, but was on the whole more impressed by the jugglers and acrobats at Baltimore's old Hippodrome, where I used to go every time they changed shows: genuine virtuosi doing things that anyone can dream up and discuss but almost no one can do.

I suppose the distinction is between things worth remarking – preferably over beer, if one's of my generation – and things worth doing. 'Somebody ought to make a novel with scenes that pop up, like the old children's books', one says, with the implication that one isn't going to bother doing it oneself.

However, art and its forms and techniques live in history and certainly do change. I sympathize with a remark attributed to Saul Bellow, that to be technically up to date is the least important attribute of a writer, though I would have to add that this least important attribute may be nevertheless essential. In any case, to be technically out of date is likely to be a genuine defect: Beethoven's Sixth Symphony or the Chartres Cathedral if executed today would be merely embarrassing. A good many current novelists write turn-of-the-century-type novels, only in more or less mid-twentieth-century language and about contemporary people and topics; this makes them considerably less interesting (to me) than excellent writers who are also technically contemporary: Joyce and Kafka, for instance, in their time, and in ours, Samuel Beckett and Jorge Luis Borges. The intermedia arts, I'd say, tend to be intermediary too, between the traditional realms of aesthetics on the one hand and artistic creation on the other; I think the wise artist and civilian will regard them with quite the kind and degree of seriousness with which he regards good shoptalk: he'll listen carefully, if noncommittally, and keep an eye on his intermedia colleagues, if only the corner of his eye. They may very possibly suggest something usable in the making or understanding of genuine works of contemporary art.

The man I want to discuss a little here, Jorge Luis Borges, illustrates well the difference between a technically old-fashioned artist, a technically up-to-date civilian, and a technically up-to-date artist. In the first category I'd locate all those novelists who for better or worse write not as if the twentieth century didn't exist, but as if the great writers of the last sixty years or so hadn't existed (*nota bene* that our century's more than two-thirds done; it's dismaying to see so many of our writers following Dostoevsky or Tolstoy or Flaubert or Balzac, when the real technical question seems to me to be how to succeed not even Joyce and Kafka, but those who've *succeeded* Joyce and Kafka and are now in the evenings of their own careers). In the second category are such folk as an artist-neighbour of mine in Buffalo who fashions dead Winnie-the-Poohs in sometimes monumental scale out of oilcloth stuffed with sand and impaled on stakes or hung by the neck. In the third belong the few people whose artistic thinking is as hip as any French new-novelist's, but who manage nonetheless to speak eloquently and memorably to our still-human hearts and conditions, as the great artists have always done. Of these, two of the finest living specimens that I know of are Beckett and Borges, just about the only contemporaries of my reading acquaintance mentionable with the 'old masters' of twentieth-century fiction. In the unexciting history of literary awards, the 1961 International Publishers' Prize, shared by Beckett and Borges, is a happy exception indeed.

One of the modern things about these two is that in an age of ultimacies and 'final solutions' – at least felt ultimacies, in everything from weaponry to theology, the celebrated dehumanization of society, and the history of the novel – their work in separate ways reflects and deals with ultimacy, both technically and thematically, as, for example, *Finnegans Wake* does in its different manner. One notices, by the way, for whatever its symptomatic worth, that Joyce was virtually blind at the end, Borges is literally so, and Beckett has become virtually mute, musewise, having progressed from marvellously constructed English sentences through terser and terser French ones to the unsyntactical, unpunctuated prose of *Comment C'est* and 'ultimately' to wordless mimes. One might extrapolate a theoretical course for Beckett: language, after all, consists of silence as well as sound, and the mime is still communication – 'that nineteenth-century idea', a Yale student once snarled at me – but by the language of action. But the language of action consists of rest as well as movement, and so in the context of Beckett's progress, immobile, silent figures still aren't altogether ultimate. How about an empty, silent stage, then, or blank pages (an ultimacy already attained in the nineteenth century by that *avant-gardiste* of East Aurora, New York, Elbert Hubbard, in his *Essay on Silence*) – a 'happening' where nothing happens, like Cage's 4'33" performed in an empty hall? But dramatic communication consists of the absence as well as the presence of the actors; 'we have our exits and our entrances'; and so even that would be imperfectly ultimate in Beckett's case. Nothing at all, then, I suppose: but Nothingness is necessarily and inextricably the background against which Being etcetera; for Beckett, at this point in his career, to cease to create altogether would be fairly meaningful: his crowning work, his 'last word'. What a convenient corner to paint yourself into! 'And now I shall finish', the valet Arsene says in *Watt*, 'and you will hear my voice no more.' Only the silence *Molloy* speaks of, 'of which the universe is made'.

After which, I add on behalf of the rest of us, it might be conceivable to rediscover validly the artifices of language and literature – such far-out notions as grammar, punctuation . . . even characterization! Even plot! – if one goes about it the right way, aware of what one's predecessors have been up to.

Now J. L. Borges is perfectly aware of all these things. Back in the great decades of literary experimentalism he was associated with *Prisma*, a 'muralist' magazine that published its pages on walls and billboards; his later *Labyrinths* and *Ficciones* not only anticipate the farthest-out ideas of The Something Else Press crowd – not a difficult thing to do – but being marvellous works of art as well, illustrate in a simple way the difference between the fact of aesthetic ultimacies and their artistic use. What it comes to is that an artist doesn't merely exemplify an ultimacy; he employs it.

Consider Borges's story 'Pierre Menard, Author of the Quixote': the hero, an utterly sophisticated turn-of-the-century French Symbolist, by an astounding effort of imagination, produces – not *copies* or *imitates*, mind, but *composes* – several chapters of Cervantes's novel.

> It is a revelation [Borges's narrator tells us] to compare Menard's *Don Quixote* with Cervantes's. The latter, for example, wrote (part one, chapter nine):
>
> > . . . truth, whose mother is history, rival of time, depository of deeds, witness of the past, exemplar and adviser to the present, the future's counsellor.
>
> Written in the seventeenth century, written by the 'lay genius' Cervantes, this enumeration is a mere rhetorical praise of history. Menard, on the other hand, writes:
>
> > . . . truth, whose mother is history, rival of time, depository of deeds, witness of the past, exemplar and adviser to the present, the future's counsellor.
>
> History, the *mother* of truth: the idea is astounding. Menard, a contemporary of William James, does not define history as an enquiry into reality but as its origin . . .

Et cetera. Now, this is an interesting idea, of considerable intellectual validity. I mentioned earlier that if Beethoven's Sixth were composed today, it would be an embarrassment; but clearly it wouldn't be, necessarily, if done with ironic intent by a composer quite aware of where we've been and where we are. It would have then potentially, for better or worse, the kind of significance of Warhol's Campbell's Soup ads, the difference being that in the former case a work of art is being reproduced instead of a work of nonart, and the ironic comment would therefore be more directly on the genre and history of the art than on the state of the culture. In fact, of course, to make the valid intellectual point one needn't even re-compose the Sixth Symphony any more than Menard really needed to recreate the *Quixote*. It would've been sufficient for Menard to have *attributed* the novel to himself in order to have a new work of art, from the intellectual point of view. Indeed, in several stories Borges plays with this very idea, and I can readily imagine Beckett's next novel, for example, as *Tom Jones*, just as Nabokov's last was that multivolume annotated translation of Pushkin. I myself have always aspired to write Burton's version of *The 1001 Nights*, complete with appendices and the like, in twelve volumes, and for intellectual purposes I needn't even write it. What evenings we might spend (over beer) discussing Saarinen's Parthenon, D. H. Lawrence's *Wuthering Heights*, or the Johnson Administration by Robert Rauschenberg!

The idea, I say, is intellectually serious, as are Borges's other characteristic ideas, most of a metaphysical rather than an aesthetic nature. But the important thing to observe is that Borges doesn't attribute the *Quixote* to himself, much less re-compose it like Pierre Menard; instead, he writes a remarkable and original work of literature, the implicit theme of which is the difficulty, perhaps the unnecessity, of writing original works of literature. His artistic victory, if you like, is that he confronts an intellectual dead end and employs it against itself to accomplish new human work. If this corresponds to what mystics do – 'every moment leaping into the infinite', Kierkegaard says, 'and every moment falling surely back into the finite' – it's only one more aspect of that old analogy. In homelier terms, it's a matter of every moment throwing out the bath water without for a moment losing the baby.

Another way of describing Borges's accomplishment is in a pair of his own favourite terms, *algebra* and *fire*. In his most often anthologized story, 'Tlön, Uqbar, Orbis Tertius', he imagines an entirely hypothetical world, the invention of a secret society of scholars who elaborate its every aspect in a surreptitious encyclopaedia. This *First Encyclopaedia of Tlön* (what fictionist would not wish to have dreamed up the *Britannica*?) describes a coherent alternative to this world complete in every aspect from its algebra to its fire, Borges tells us, and of such imaginative power that, once conceived, it begins to obtrude itself into and eventually to supplant our prior reality. My point is that neither the algebra nor the fire, metaphorically speaking, could achieve this result without the other. Borges's algebra is what I'm considering here – algebra is easier to talk about than fire – but any intellectual giant could equal it. The imaginary authors of the *First Encyclopaedia of Tlön* itself are not artists, though their work is in a manner of speaking fictional and would find a ready publisher in New York nowadays. The author of the story 'Tlön, Uqbar, Orbis Tertius', who merely *alludes* to the fascinating Encyclopaedia, is an artist; what makes him one of the first rank, like Kafka, is the combination of that intellectually profound vision with great human insight, poetic power, and consummate mastery of his means, a definition which would have gone without saying, I suppose, in any century but ours.

Not long ago, incidentally, in a footnote to a scholarly edition of Sir Thomas Browne (*The Urn Burial*, I believe it was), I came upon a perfect Borges datum, reminiscent of Tlön's self-realization: the actual case of a book called *The Three Impostors*, alluded to in Browne's *Religio Medici* among other places. *The Three Impostors* is a non-existent blasphemous treatise against Moses, Christ, and Mohammed, which in the seventeenth century was widely held to exist, or to have once existed. Commentators attributed it variously to Boccaccio, Pietro Aretino, Giordano Bruno, and Tommaso Campanella, and though no one, Browne included, had ever seen a copy of it, it was frequently cited, refuted, railed against, and generally discussed as if everyone had read it until, sure enough, in the *eighteenth* century a spurious work appeared with a forged date of 1598 and the title *De Tribus Impostoribus*. It's a wonder that Borges doesn't mention this work as he seems to have read absolutely everything, including all the books that don't exist, and Browne is a particular favourite of his. In fact, the narrator of 'Tlön, Uqbar, Orbis Tertius' declares at the end:

> . . . English and French and mere Spanish will disappear from the globe. The world will be Tlön. I pay no attention to all this and go on revising, in the still days at the Adrogué hotel, an uncertain Quevedian translation (which I do not intend to publish) of Browne's *Urn Burial*.

(Moreover, on rereading 'Tlön', etc., I find now a remark I'd swear wasn't in it last year: that the eccentric American millionaire who endows the

Encyclopaedia does so on condition that 'the work will make no pact with the impostor Jesus Christ'.)

This 'contamination of reality by dream', as Borges calls it, is one of his pet themes, and commenting upon such contaminations is one of his favourite fictional devices. Like many of the best such devices, it turns the artist's mode or form into a metaphor for his concerns, as does the diary-ending of *Portrait of the Artist as a Young Man* or the cyclical construction of *Finnegans Wake*. In Borges's case, the story 'Tlön', etc., for example, is a real piece of imagined reality in our world, analogous to those Tlönian artifacts called *hronir*, which imagine themselves into existence. In short, it's a paradigm of or metaphor for itself; not just the *form* of the story but the *fact* of the story is symbolic; 'the medium is the message'.

Moreover, like all of Borges's work, it illustrates in other of its aspects my subject: how an artist may paradoxically turn the felt ultimacies of our time into material and means for his work – *paradoxically* because by doing so he transcends what had appeared to be his refutation, in the same way that the mystic who transcends finitude is said to be enabled to live, spiritually and physically, in the finite world. Suppose you're a writer by vocation – a 'print-oriented bastard', as the McLuhanites call us – and you feel, for example, that the novel, if not narrative literature generally, if not the printed word altogether, has by this hour of the world just about shot its bolt, as Leslie Fiedler and others maintain. (I'm inclined to agree, with reservations and hedges. Literary forms certainly have histories and historical contingencies, and it may well be that the novel's time as a major art form is up, as the 'times' of classical tragedy, grand opera, or the sonnet sequence came to be. No necessary cause for alarm in this at all, except perhaps to certain novelists, and one way to handle such a feeling might be to write a novel about it. Whether historically the novel expires or persists seems immaterial to me; if enough writers and critics feel apocalyptical about it, their feeling becomes a considerable cultural fact, like the feeling that Western civilization, or the world, is going to end rather soon. If you took a bunch of people out into the desert and the world didn't end, you'd come home shamefaced, I imagine; but the persistence of an art form doesn't invalidate work created in the comparable apocalyptic ambience. That's one of the fringe benefits of being an artist instead of a prophet. (There are others.) If you happened to be Vladimir Nabokov you might address that felt ultimacy by writing *Pale Fire*: a fine novel by a learned pedant, in the form of a pedantic commentary on a poem invented for the purpose. If you were Borges you might write *Labyrinths*: fictions by a learned librarian in the form of footnotes, as he describes them, to imaginary or hypothetical books. And I'll add, since I believe Borges's idea is rather more interesting, that if you were the author of this paper, you'd have written something like *The Sot-Weed Factor* or *Giles Goat-Boy*: novels which imitate the form of the Novel, by an author who imitates the role of Author.

If this sort of thing sounds unpleasantly decadent, nevertheless it's about where the genre began, with *Quixote* imitating *Amadis of Gaul*, Cervantes pretending to be the Cid Hamete Benengeli (and Alonso Quijano pretending to be Don Quixote), or Fielding parodying Richardson. 'History repeats itself as farce' – meaning, of course, in the form or mode of farce, not that history is farcical. The imitation (like the Dadaist echoes in the work of the 'intermedia' types) is something new and *may be* quite serious and passionate despite its farcical aspect. This is the important difference between a proper novel and a deliberate imitation of a novel, or a novel imitative of other sorts of documents. The first attempts (has been historically inclined to attempt) to imitate actions more or less directly, and its conventional devices – cause and effect, linear anecdote, characterization, authorial selection, arrangement, and interpretation – can be and have long since been objected to as obsolete notions, or metaphors for obsolete notions: Robbe-Grillet's essays *For a New Novel* come to mind. There are replies to these objections, not to the point here, but one can see that in any case they're obviated by imitations-of-novels, which attempt to represent not life directly but a representation of life. In fact such works are no more removed from 'life' than Richardson's or Goethe's epistolary novels are: both imitate 'real' documents, and the subject of both, ultimately, is life, not the documents. A novel is as much a piece of the real world as a letter, and the letters in *The Sorrows of Young Werther* are, after all, fictitious.

One might imaginably compound this imitation, and though Borges doesn't he's fascinated with the idea: one of his frequenter literary allusions is to the 602nd night of *The 1001 Nights*, when, owing to a copyist's error, Scheherezade begins to tell the King the story of the 1001 nights, from the beginning. Happily, the King interrupts; if he didn't there'd be no 603rd night ever, and while this would solve Schcherezade's problem – which is every storyteller's problem: to publish or perish – it would put the 'outside' author in a bind. (I suspect that Borges dreamed this whole thing up: the business he mentions isn't in any edition of *The 1001 Nights* I've been able to consult. Not yet, anyhow: after reading 'Tlön, Uqbar', etc., one is inclined to recheck every semester or so.)

Now Borges (whom someone once vexedly accused me of inventing) is interested in the 602nd night because it's an instance of the story-within-the-story turned back upon itself, and his interest in such instances is threefold: first, as he himself declares, they disturb us metaphysically: when the characters in a work of fiction become readers or authors of the fiction they're in, we're reminded of the fictitious aspect of our own existence, one of Borges's cardinal themes, as it was of Shakespeare, Calderón, Unamuno, and other folk. Second, the 602nd night is a literary illustration of the *regressus in infinitum*, as are almost all Borges's principal images and motifs. Third, Scheherezade's accidental gambit, like Borges's other versions of the *regressus in infinitum*, is an image of the exhaustion, or attempted exhaustion, of possibilities – in this case literary possibilities – and so we return to our main subject.

What makes Borges's stance, if you like, more interesting to me than, say, Nabokov's or Beckett's is the premise with which he approaches literature; in the words of one of his editors: 'For [Borges] no one has claim to originality in literature; all writers are more or less faithful amanuenses of the spirit, translators and annotators of preexisting archetypes.' Thus his inclination to write brief comments on imaginary books: for one to attempt to add overtly to the sum of 'original' literature by even so much as a conventional short story, not to mention a novel, would be too presumptuous, too näive; literature has been done long since. A librarian's point of view! And it would itself be too presumptuous, if it weren't part of a lively, passionately relevant metaphysical vision and slyly employed against itself precisely, to make new and original literature. Borges defines the Baroque as 'that style which deliberately exhausts (or tries to exhaust) its possibilities and borders upon its own caricature'. While his own work is not Baroque, except intellectually (the Baroque was never so terse, laconic, economical), it suggests the view that intellectual and literary history has been Baroque, and has pretty well exhausted the possibilities of novelty. His *ficciones* are not only footnotes to imaginary texts, but postscripts to the real corpus of literature.

This premise gives resonance and relation to all his principal images. The facing mirrors that recur in his stories are a dual *regressus*. The doubles that his characters, like Nabokov's, run afoul of suggest dizzying multiples and remind one of Browne's remark that 'every man is not only himself . . . men are lived over again.' (It would please Borges, and illustrate Browne's point, to call Browne a precursor of Borges. 'Every writer,' Borges says in his essay on Kafka, 'creates his own precursors.') Borges's favourite third-century heretical sect is the Histriones – I think and hope he invented them – who believe that repetition is impossible in history and therefore live viciously in order to purge the future of the vices they commit: in other words, to exhaust the possibilities of the world in order to bring its end nearer.

The writer he most often mentions, after Cervantes, is Shakespeare; in one piece he imagines the playwright on his deathbed asking God to permit him to be one and himself, having been everyone and no one; God replies from the whirlwind that He is no one either; He has dreamed the world like Shakespeare, and including Shakespeare. Homer's story in Book IV of the *Odyssey*, of Menelaus on the beach at Pharos, tackling Proteus, appeals profoundly to Borges: Proteus is he who 'exhausts the guises of reality' while Menelaus – who, one recalls, disguised his own identity in order to ambush him – holds fast. Zeno's paradox of Achilles and the Tortoise embodies a *regressus in infinitum* which Borges carries through philosophical history, pointing out that Aristotle uses it to refute Plato's theory of forms, Hume to refute the possibility of cause and effect, Lewis Carroll to refute syllogistic deduction, William James to refute the notion of temporal passage, and Bradley to refute the general possibility of logical relations; Borges himself uses it, citing Schopenhauer, as evidence that the world is our dream, our idea, in which 'tenuous and eternal crevices of unreason' can be found to remind us that our creation is false, or at least fictive.

The infinite library of one of the most popular stories is an image particularly pertinent to the literature of exhaustion; the 'Library of Babel' houses every possible combination of alphabetical characters and spaces, and thus every possible book and statement, including your and my refutations and viridications, the history of the actual future, the history of every possible future, and, though he doesn't mention it, the encyclopaedias not only of Tlön but of every imaginable other world – since, as in Lucretius's universe, the number of elements, and so of combinations, is finite (though very large), and the number of instances of each element and combination of elements is infinite, like the library itself.

That brings us to his favourite image of all, the labyrinth, and to my point. *Labyrinths* is the name of his most substantial translated volume, and the only full-length study of Borges in English, by Ana Maria Barrenechea, is called *Borges the Labyrinth-Maker*. A labyrinth, after all, is a place in which, ideally, all the possibilities of choice (of direction, in this case) are embodied, and – barring special dispensation like Theseus's – must be exhausted before one reaches the heart. Where, mind, the Minotaur waits with two final possibilities: defeat and death, or victory and freedom. Now, in fact, the legendary Theseus is non-Baroque in the

Borgesian spirit, and illustrates a positive artistic morality in the literature of exhaustion. He is not there, after all, for kicks (any more than Borges and Beckett are in the fiction racket for their health): Menelaus is *lost*, in the larger labyrinth of the world, and has got to hold fast while the Old Man of the Sea exhausts reality's frightening guises so that he may extort direction from him when Proteus returns to his 'true' self. It's a heroic enterprise, with salvation as its object – one recalls that the aim of the Histriones is to get history done with so that Jesus may come again the sooner, and that Shakespeare's heroic metamorphoses culminate not merely in a theophany but in an apotheosis.

Now, not just any old body is equipped for this labour, and Theseus in the Cretan labyrinth becomes in the end the aptest image of Borges after all. Distressing as the fact is to us liberal Democrats, the commonality, alas, will *always* lose their way and their souls; it's the chosen remnant, the virtuoso, the Thesean *hero*, who, confronted with Baroque reality, Baroque history, the Baroque state of his art, need not rehearse its possibilities to exhaustion, any more than Borges needs actually to write the *Encyclopaedia of Tlön* or the books in the Library of Babel. He need only be aware of their existence or possibility, acknowledge them, and with the aid of *very special* gifts – as extraordinary as saint- or hero-hood and not likely to be found in The New York Correspondence School of Literature – go straight through the maze to the accomplishment of his work.

Chapter Sixteen Writing Against Simulacrum: The Place of Literature and Literary Theory in the Electronic Age

Jenaro Talens

Und wozu Dichter in dürftiger Zeit.
Friedrich Hölderlin, Brot und Wein

L'albero delle ideologie è sempre verde.
Norberto Bobbio, Destra e sinistra

In his recent book *Destra e sinistra*, Norberto Bobbio insists on the necessity to maintain the distinction between 'right' and 'left' in politics, since these two antithetical terms imply two different models of managing and dealing with everyday life in the real world, based upon the opposed concept of equality inherent to each of them. Published just a few weeks before the general elections that brought the TV mogul Silvio Berlusconi to Italian government, the reflections of the old philosopher remind us how the so-called end of ideologies is, in itself, ideological.

> [and] then left and right do not indicate ideologies only. Reducing them to pure expressions of ideological thought would be an undue simplification:

Jenaro Talens, 'Writing Against Simulacrum: The Place of Literature and Literary Theory in the Electronic Age', *boundary 2*, 22, 1 (Spring 1995), pp. 1–21.

they indicate contrasting programmes with respect to many problems whose solution normally pertains to political action, conflicts not only of ideas but also of interests and valuations regarding the direction to give to society, conflicts which exist in every society, and which are difficult to imagine fading away. [trans. NL and Floriana Perna][1]

It is important to underline that the crisis of Marxism, the fall of the Berlin Wall, and the disappearance of the USSR are seen as demonstrations of the *un*usefulness of critical theory, to which they were related. How to theorize in a world where theory seems to be out of tune? Is there a place for writing as a reflection about the world in this supposed new paradise born from the ashes of what Fukuyama called the end of history?[2] If we think of how that end was celebrated with the invasion of Panama, Desert Storm, the ex-Yugoslavia civil war, the genocide in Rwanda, and so on, it seems to me that if theory – as a discourse able to explain the way things happen – has no place at all, then we will have to find a new discourse, and find it fast.

Within this contradictory mess, even literature appears as the spy who came in from the cold, something that can only teach us how to interpellate the world, but not how to change it. On one occasion, during the early seventies, one of today's best-known writers of my generation, Félix de Azúa, who was, at the time, beginning to shift from poetry to fiction, said in an interview that poets, like other species in the past, are perhaps in the process of extinction.[3] This seems to be the assumption of readers and television junkies twenty-five years later. In fact, and at least in Spain, to be known as a writer usually does not necessarily mean to be read but to appear on TV shows or to be quoted in newspapers, and the circulation of names and/or titles through the mass media has been substituted for the dialogic familiarity with texts. In this sense, the displacement operated in the literary practice from institutionalized social activity to bodiless commodity does not allow poetry to compete with other commodities inside a market that is not an equal opportunity space anymore. Nevertheless, I do not believe that literature is an unuseful work or that writers have to be dealt with as living anachronisms.

* * *

The topic of this essay, as defined by its title, seems perhaps odd and extravagant. Writing and simulacrum are notions that belong to different pragmatic and epistemological worlds, and are not necessarily connected.

However, as we enter into the analysis of the new media that technology has created during the last four decades, the connection between both concepts, and the spaces they refer to begins to appear with relative easiness.

Indeed, the appearance of new technologies (cable TV, private television, telex, fax, modem, and, in general, everything related to the computer world) means something more than a simple technological step forward. Firstly, it seems to imply a radical change in the redistribution of power taking place in the modern world, although such a redistribution – as I will try to discuss in this essay – is more apparent than real. On the one hand, the massive, and almost simultaneous, access to information produces an effect of 'informative democratization' that apparently should make possible the control of information by some groups in power. From this point of view, the amount of information in the offer, as well as the rapid access to what is considered not 'interpretation' but fact, would make more difficult, as an effect, a selective occultation. This is the thesis maintained by many sociologists, political analysts, and communication scholars, for whom, literally, the generalized access to the media, with the increase in the number of information sources – more editorials, more journals, more radio and TV stations – would prevent the manipulation exerted by these sources when they are too few or too concentrated. Such a hypothesis does not take into account some aspects I would like to highlight: (1) on the one hand, the nominal increase in sources does not necessarily mean a dissemination of the original source, because, in fact, the publishing houses and large corporations chaperon under their economic structure an enormous quantity of enterprises with different names but without a real independence from the central power that controls and designs the global functioning from the top of the pyramid; (2) such a democratic illusion does not attach to the media any specific ideological function, apart from their utility in the hands of responsible persons or groups. The media, as such, would be no more than a simple intermediary, totally aseptic and without any ideology, whose function would be to stock, transmit, and circulate contents that they do not control. I believe, on the contrary, that the media's function is to *produce* the sense of these contents, *to establish* the rules of the communication interchange, and *to create* typologies of readers and/or spectators, or predetermined social individuals. This is not to say that the media are good or bad (reserving the negative role to both the users and the controllers) simply because they are based on manipulation; this is not a formal judgement but a datum: it is simply impossible for them *not* to manipulate. What is important is to know how the manipulation is exercised, from where and to the service of what interests it is functioning, and only then can we decide which position to take in relation to the media within the discursive and social framework they are part of and have helped to create. If we switch from television to the editorial world, the new technologies – personal computers and laser printers – have also changed everything. Their accessibility and easy manipulation have breached the industrial monopoly of books by big editorial enterprises. It is not only possible to reduce the cost of publishing but to publish what was once technologically unthinkable. In addition, communications via modem enable elaborate magazines and books on-line, without paper, which reach the interested reader in less than sixty seconds, provided he or she is connected to the network. In such a case, the manipulation of the text, printed as electric impulses onto a diskette and easily altered by the user, introduces an important question in relation to the notion of the closed text and, also, to the copyrighted one, which is the unique mark that justifies the existence of the notion of author as the 'private owner' of a discourse.[4]

Not only have these changes modified the technological media as such but – and this is what matters – they have also changed the perception of the world by the traditionally passive user, who, for the first time, perceives the possibility of being an active part in the process. This could be considered positive, but, first, one should clarify what it means to be an active part, and whether this is possible in a context that gives the technological media such extraordinary power, that evokes fascination, mystery, and omnipotence, inherent to a universe that presents itself as scientific but that is experienced almost as a religion. Indeed, the supposed infallibility of machines is not unlike the written word of the past (let us remember Berceo's *Los milagros de Nuestra Señora*), as a testimony beyond any discussion. Faith is fashionable again. In fact, there is not much difference between the Islamic fundamentalists who kill in the name of God, and this other fundamentalism of technology that kills in the name of computer efficacy, although in the second case, we speak not of barbarism but of rationality. For that reason, we are dealing with an important distinction. These are not abstract or theoretical matters pertaining to the territory of discourse but practices concerning the political and ideological universe.

What place could literature occupy in this universe, where the question is neither to consolidate the relation between culture and state, nor to distinguish between true (history) and false (myth), but to deal with both of them in terms of narration? How to establish both its limits and its function in a context wherein the very existence of literary discourse is systematically put on trial? The following pages do not pretend to give a definitive answer to these questions but will, I hope, briefly analyse some of the epistemological propositions that could help clear the way.

During the last thirty years, there has been some talking about the 'death of literature' – to paraphrase Nietzsche's well-known thesis of the 'death of God' – to such a point that, as Alvin Kernan writes,[5] the appearance in 1982 of a book entitled *What Was Literature?* did not surprise anyone. In his book, Kernan explains how the traditional literary values of romanticism and modernism have been reversed from within. The notion of author, whose creative imagination was considered at the origin of literature, has given way to the idea of a simple assembling of several languages and cultural elements, placed in relation to each other within determined writings that no longer enjoy the status of 'work of art' but the simpler one of 'texts' or 'collages'. From without, radical analyses as those put forward by Terry Eagleton and John Beverley,[6] have even attacked the very existence of literature, considering it an elitist and repressive phenomenon. All this leads one to realize that what was once defined in terms of 'serious literature' nowadays has a minor influence in comparison to the electronic discourses that have replaced it as a more attractive and respected source of information, and that its presence, outside of the university departments that make it the object of their daily work, is almost nonexistent.[7] David Lodge seems to be addressing the same phenomenon when he writes about the discipline of literary theory, whose function, at least in the WASP world – especially the North American one – is more business than epistemology.[8]

However, neither Kernan's lucid and often thought-provoking book nor Lodge's amusing pamphlet try to explain the circumstances, even though they offer testimony of what is happening. We find in Kernan a kind of nostalgia for the lost referent of a time when things were clear: literature was literature, literary criticism was literary criticism, and everyone knew where to stand in relation to them. Lodge, apart from the settling of accounts with an academic universe he had already attacked with an intelligent sense of humor in his novel *Small World*, continues to be clear about what continues to be important (literature) and what secondary (theory) when he underlines that many of the great scholars devoted to theory (Jacques Derrida among them) would really prefer to write novels. The problem, therefore, is still not tackled from its roots, and, consequently, the theoretical debate remains blurred behind the mask of multiplicity conceived as pure and simple confusion.

The present impossibility of a general theory of literature has to be contextualized in order to explain its sense. Mark Poster's concept of 'mode of information'[9] could be of help in this respect. Poster bases his reasoning on the Marxian notion of 'mode of production'. In *The German Ideology*, Marx uses such a concept in two different senses: (1) as a historical category dividing and periodizing the past in accord with the variation in the combinations between means and relations of production; and (2) as a metaphor of the capitalist period that privileges economic activity as determinant of its functioning. Following the first of these two Marxian notions, Poster understands 'mode of information' as a historical category that allows him to periodize history depending on the structural variations of symbolic interchange.

According to this concept, Poster notes that every epoch uses symbolic interchanges containing both internal and external structures, means, and relations of signification. In that sense, he classifies the different historical stages according to three irreducible models: (1) face-to-face relation, by way of oral exchange – equivalent to what Juri Lotman calls 'non-textualized cultures'; (2) written relation, by way of printed exchange – equivalent to Lotman's 'textualized cultures'; and (3) electronic exchange.[10] The first would be characterized by the symbolic; the second by the representation with signs; and the third by informatic simulation. In each one, the relation between language and society, idea and action, identity and alterity are different. Besides that, and because we are dealing not with 'real' stages, traceable in documents of the epoch, but theoretical constructions destined to produce knowledge about the historical process, such stages do not form a temporal sequence, wherein every stage substitutes for the previous one, but coexist in the same time and at the same place – even if one of them articulates and clarifies the others.

For our purpose, the concept of 'mode of information' is important because it produces typologies of the different social subjects. If, indeed, the birth of printing meant a substitution of the 'auditor' by the reader and, consequently, the appearance of what we historically know as 'literature' and the displacement from theatricality to writing,[11] how to conceive the literary and the theories that constituted it from a paradigm that nowadays is not based anymore on the relation of exchange that made them possible?

In order to illustrate the concept of 'mode of information', the example of musical reproduction given by Poster could allow us to clarify this panorama. Live musical execution would respond to the stage of 'face-to-face exchange' (the first stage). The position of the 'auditor' in a concert hall is that of a co-participant in the event. The first recordings in paste

records and the more recent ones in vinyl support the idea of the reproduction of the real concert – that is of the copy as a representation (the second
stage). Sitting in the solitude of his room, the 'melomane' could imagine the
spatial place of each and every one of the instruments, perceive the tones,
and enjoy the solos foreseen in the score *as if* he had been present in the
'real' act. Such an *as if* implied, in any case, the necessity to continue
considering the event, the 'live concert', as an obligatory reference, the final
warrant of what was explicitly received in terms of representation. The
introduction of the stereophonic technique already used in vinyl records by
allowing to select carefully the individual components for their subsequent
mix – initiated, however, a curious process of displacement toward the
conception of the reproduced event as an *improved* copy. Subsequent effects as a result of the development of technology – the rise of filters to
avoid noises, digital recording, and so on – have permitted, for instance, a
Mozart symphony to sound better in the record than in the concert hall, by
determining the disappearance of the minimal, yet technically perceptible,
interferences of ambient noise. Nevertheless, at least in the world of so-
called classical music, the reference continued to be the live performance.

Things changed radically with the introduction of electronics (the third
stage) into the world of rock and roll. The rapid evolution of this kind of
music during the sixties contributed to the fact that records started to be
produced essentially to be listened to at home on the record player. Their
execution as a phenomenon of the real world existed only through their
reproduction. 'Copies' without 'live' originals, particularly *Revolver* (The
Beatles, 1966), but above all, *Sgt. Pepper's Lonely Hearts Club Band*
(The Beatles, 1967) or *We're In It Only for Money* (The Mothers of
Invention, 1967), meant the simulacrum of a representation, because they
referred to a nonexistent performance. It is curious that the progressive
handling of electronics made it more and more difficult to 'reproduce' live
what was created in the laboratory.

Apart from other considerations, this process implied a fundamental
change of paradigm: representation had been substituted by simulation,
and then it was the live concert that needed to sound like the recording.
This is something that, with the invention of the videoclip,[12] has reached
limits that were unthinkable only two decades ago. In the age of technology, to copy an original means, in fact, to produce a simulacrum.[13]

Of course, the implications of this epistemological change are enormous and go beyond the existence of new media to do the same thing,
because *it is no longer the same thing*. The typology of social subjects as
receptors of the messages produced by the new stage does not correspond

with the one congruent with modernity, in whose bosom was born what we know as 'literature', and a reflection on the place of the literary cannot escape this circumstance.

We could enunciate the theoretical problem that is posed as follows: How to conceive of literature from a place where what made it possible does not have a place anymore? First, such a hypothesis implies that literature did not always exist but was born as a discursive form inside a determined mode of information. From this stand, to ignore that its status is historical would not make any sense: its 'social' character comes not – at least fundamentally – from its 'representative' character but instead from the exchange model of communication that constitutes it as 'literature' and allows it to be conceived as such. This model includes forms of emission, transmission, circulation, reception, interpretation, and so on, inside circuits not 'natural' at all but produced and constructed culturally from a system of Cartesian origin that gives them validity and coherence. If it happens that this system is in crisis, its products will be, too.

The well-known Foucauldian thesis of the death of man[14] must be understood in this context: The gap between things and words and the objectification of meanings effecting mass language were both a transparent vehicle and a weapon for action. In that system, the theorist of discourse (literary or otherwise) constitutes him- or herself as a subject of knowledge separated from his/her objects of study, as a subject that utters words more or less univocal in order to define, to explain, and to transmit an objective field different from his/her own subjectivity.[15] Then, the theorist's discourse structures itself as a direct representation of his/her mind. On the contrary, language is understood as existing at a different level from theory. Besides, the spoken language (the world of opinions, of daily opinions, of ideology) is different from the world of action.[16]

In the universe articulated around the appearance of electronic language, however, things function differently. It will be clear if we focus on the Gulf War as an example. News of the first bombardments over Iraq were broadcast to the United States and Canada as prime-time entertainment. In front of a camera and a reporter, a pilot said that the bombing mission from which he had just returned had been like 'the movies' (the Indians having been replaced by Arabs, they were extras anyway and, for that reason, gallows birds). Another pilot, clearly excited, said that the raid had been so easy and enjoyable that he was going to have breakfast and a shower before his next flight, a mission he was anticipating with enthusiasm. A third pilot compared the attack to a football game, in which the other team had suffered a severe defeat due to the superior skill of its opponent. At another moment, a reporter for English Canadian TV interviewed a young marine whose father had given him a video camera just before the Panama invasion, in which he had participated as a member of the 'salvation forces'. In the faraway sands of the Persian Gulf, the proud and improvised soldier-reporter wanted to repeat his exhilarating experience in the Isthmus.

Such a degree of frivolity was surprising. The real problem, however, is that almost no one seemed to perceive these facts as frivolous or obscene. The apparati for perception – which, like any other apparati, are learned and assumed – had transformed the effect of 'live' into the effect of 'truth'. Technology, presented as fair apparatus, became the warrant and not the simple transmitter, of what was being communicated.

These interviews, offered as if they were the last première at Hollywood Boulevard's Chinese theater, alternated with interventions even more obscene, if such a thing is possible: press conferences and opinions by experts in everything, without the slightest desire to simulate a documentary effect. Representatives for the Secretary of Defense and from the Pentagon – clearly taking up their roles as protagonists of the film – gave an excellent lesson on applied technology. Indeed, according to their accounts, their weapons had functioned perfectly, showing the high technological standards of the national industry, even if they had only been tested in mock wars (that is to say, even if, before the Gulf War, they had not yet killed anybody). Someone even had the nerve to say that there was no other country in the world capable of doing things with such efficacy, speed, and cleanliness (perhaps, by 'cleanliness', he was trying to say that no blood splashed on the fighters while they were flying). The problem, however, was not that these speakers spoke with the utmost coolness but that the television media gave their logistic support to these manifestations, taking up the role of truth sanctioner with their very presence. Along with the spokesmen, there were live interviews with international political analysts, economists, strategists, military men, and, even more unusual, technology specialists, who explained how their missiles and fighters with special radars functioned, all this as if they were talking about washing machines. In such a context, as Rey Chow has written, 'The mediatization of both information and life has reached a point where "realities" are interchangeable. To kill someone is as electronic as to write with a computer. Some of the American adolescents who used to stay home manipulating video games on the screens of their TV sets found themselves flying over Iraq during the Cult War. The simulacra they were used to at home appeared in their cockpits, requiring from them the same moves as the games. Many kilometers away from land where people were dying, the clean and cohesive video play became a persuasive substitution for war.'[17] The dirty and bloody part of the bombings *was not* a part of the play. In fact, it substituted reality for the 'virtual reality' exposed in front of the soldier-spectator.

The correspondence between word and thing, proper to the stage of orality, which had been substituted by the notion of representation of the thing by the word after the invention of printing, gave way to the creation of simulacra. Such a production takes place from a language whose power does not come from the exteriority as a structure. This auto-referentiality means that the laws that supposedly regulate the truthfulness or the falsehood of a discourse depend not on their relationship with the world but on the internal coherence of the message.

Representativity still exists in such a language, but only as a sense effect. This has been called the crisis of representation and has effects on the social subjects receiving messages; for them the objects have the tendency not to materialize into language but into the very flow of significants. Jesus González-Requena has studied this crisis formation with respect to television discourse,[18] but we can extend it to almost the totality of discourses, even the literary one, circulating in the contemporary world An anecdote whose implications I have developed elsewhere[19] can serve as an example of it: In October 1990, Sadam Hussein agreed to give a ninety-minute interview with CNN, intended for the North American public. Many wanted to hear how the Iraqi leader would justify the military action – the annexation, by force, of Kuwait – that, a few months later, would begin the Gulf War. I watched his long speech. The following morning, I wanted to discuss it with my North American students in order to analyse both the tricks and the reasoning of the speaker as a practical mechanism for persuasion. My idea was to compare such a mechanism with that used by then President Bush. To my surprise, not one of the students had watched more than the beginning of the interview, and not because they were contrary to its contents but because of the length of the shots and the poor editing. For an audience accustomed to the speed and the concentration of the hegemonic model of discourse – that is, the video clip – the temptation to change the channel was too strong to be resisted during the ninety-minute discourse in Arabic with overimpressed voice-over. These were the same students who complained about their obligation to read novels or essays of more than 150 pages about or from the Spanish classics, but who considered it normal to spend the same amount of time watching *Ghostbusters* or *Indiana Jones and the Temple of Doom.*

Marshall McLuhan's famous axiom 'the media is the message' already pointed toward the same, but centered on the subject as a receptor, leaving aside his quality as an interpreter of the perceived. Chow has written that 'the obsession with visuality signifies also the obsession with some comprehension of visuality, that is to say that it exposes truth'.[20] What I want to stress here is that electronic language questions not only the function of the perceptive apparatus but also, fundamentally, the very status of subjectivity: how to relate with the objects of the world, what perspective to adopt concerning the world. According to Poster, what electronic language outlines is not the passage from a 'hot' medium to a 'cold' one but the destabilization of the subject, a subject that is not fixed anymore in a space and a time, in a privileged and stable position from which to calculate his options.[21] From arboreal beings, with roots in time and space, we have become rhizomatic nomads – as coined by Gilles Deleuze and Félix Guattari[22] – wandering across the incorporeal universe of hertzian waves.

The more the *practice of language* moves away from the context of the communicative situation of daily life within a stable culture, wherein relationships are reproduced by dialogue, the more the *monologic language* of the electronic media has to produce this context within its own structure.

In the face-to-face exchange of orality, the subject constitutes himherself as a member of a community, establishing ties between individuals; in the so-called Gutenberg Galaxy, the subject constitutes him- herself as a rational being, autonomous, as a stable interpreter of the world, capable of establishing logical relationships between symbols, from within his isolation and solitude; in the exchange of simulation, the languages as such occupy the place of the community of speakers and undermine the referentiality of discourse so necessary to the rational being. As no one speaks with the person who is listening, and as the existence of an external world is no longer necessary to confront the validity – or the absence of validity – of the flow of meanings, the subject does not find a clear identity facing his/her conversation.[23] From this perspective, the subject of the electronic era cannot base him- herself on the Cartesian 'I think, therefore I am', but assumes his fragility with a Lacanian 'they think of me, therefore "I" is not'.

The example of what has happened in Italy since the March 1994 general elections can be helpful in showing that discourses 'about reality' were, in fact, discourses 'about themselves as such discourses', and that politics is no longer a question of analysis but of performance. The goal at stake, for the coalition Forza Italia Lega Nord MSI, was not to convince people about what they were saying but to sell themselves as 'legitimate'. Ideas and programs, if any, were sources for the things said. Social imaginary consensus[24] substituted political debate on the basis of an internal coherence of the show-biz flow of the ad-like emptiness of the campaign.[25]

It is of some significance that, in such a horizon, the theoretical reflection has been displaced from the field of study of the supposedly general laws of discourse to the analysis of the places that made possible such a conception of the problem – we called them 'institutions' – and that discursive practices and forms of existence marginalized within a stable universe – defined beforehand – find now a place to grow and develop: feminism, ecology, gay and lesbian studies, cultural studies. This new type of theoretical reflection not only illuminates the present but, at the same time, also tries to disassemble the supposed solidity of 'general' theories in order to substitute for them partial approaches, spatially, socially, and culturally localized. Apart from the social claim inherent to some of those movements, what interests us here is their revulsive function in the territory of discourse. If, as Ferruccio Rossi-Landi has pointed out,[26] the significant plus-value interchange works as the interchange of merchandises in a free market economy, this interchange would produce power relations in concrete social situations. In fact, discourses, while circulating, produce new forms of praxis that, in their turn, produce new plus-values in the territory of significance within the institutions where these discourses exist and circulate and where, finally, interchange takes place. This would explain why theoretical debate about discourses belongs to the space of politics.

Let us focus, for instance, on the notion of literary history. As a field of research and an object of analysis – and from a 'modern' point of view – 'literature' precedes the discipline that narrates its development in time ('history of literature') as well as the one having the role of explaining its 'objective' function ('theory of literature'). But who decides what is and what is not literature?

Someone said once that history is made by the people but is written by the masters. This could be applied to any discourse pretending to give an account, to *narrate*, the course and development across the time of any human activity. The history of literature is not an exception. Indeed, when the study of so-called literary texts is instituted as an academic discipline, such an institutionalization is not so much associated with the desire of an analytical approach of a patrimony previously accepted as artistic or cultural as it is with the necessity to cooperate in the constitution of a clearly established political and social structure. In other words, we do not institute texts to recuperate the past but to constitute and justify the present. Consequently, the election of the 'corpus' object of the study, the establishment of criteria to make coherent the inclusion/exclusion of works and authors, as well as the periodization and taxonomy of the material, would not respond to the existence of a verifiable external truth but to the desire to *construct a custom-made referent*, capable of justifying the way our present society lives and thinks the world, and wrapped with the argument of its authority. Obviously, everyone speaks from a position, be it theoretical, political, or ideological. What I find remarkable is that, concerning this discussion, such a canon was established that pretended to be objective and 'scientific', in complete accord with the system of values of the class who created it: the enlightened bourgeoisie.

The criteria were articulated around three basic concepts: (1) the value of tradition as a model; (2) the notion of 'nationality'; and (3) the assumption that history has a central, individualized subject.

The constant quest for an essentialism, consubstantial with the literary phenomenon as well as classic rhetoric's normative character, derives from the first concept. Such a canonicity can be transgressed or reversed but never discussed.

From the second concept arises the notion of the history of literature as an artistic correlation of the political history of a 'national' community at a moment coincidental with the birth of liberation movements, based on the idea of nation and national tongue as hand in hand. The instrumentalization of such a correlation has played a progressive ideological role in many instances (e.g., in Latin America) but has persisted as a general premise in an ambiguous and equivocal way. The example of Spanish literature is paradigmatic. On the one hand, it is founded on the idea of Spain as a unitary concept; on the other, on the use of the Spanish language. First, there is a projection toward the past of a concept that, strictly speaking, began its existence with the Catholic kings. How, then, could we speak of a medieval Spanish literature if, in the so-called Middle Ages, neither Spain, nor what we now call 'literature' existed? And even if these did exist, why has literature been generally reduced to the practices in Castilian? Obviously, works written in other languages – Latin, Hebrew, Arabic, Catalan, Galician – are omitted, but, at the same time, there is no explanation for the absence of Spanish American literature in light of such a history of Spanish literature. If the reason is due to the necessity of articulating language and political structure, why the exclusion of colonial literature? Besides, what is the so-called Spanish American literature but an invention by Menéndez y Pelayo, cast upon the unquestionable idea of a Hispanic world? More than an integrating will, the decision by the Santander polygraph shows a tendency to neutralize what is different, interpreting it from a thinking model articulated in connection with the geographic peninsula. Besides, by that time, writers such as Goethe had already emphasized the conception of what should be a *Weltliteratur* against what they considered the reductionism of romantic nationalism.

From the third concept derives the never discussed tendency to divide into periods and to approach the literary phenomenon from the point of reference of the author as a private owner of his text's sense. The further displacement of interest toward the notions of 'literary movements', 'schools', or 'generations' did not mean any epistemological change, because the underlying and inevitable concept of individual author continues to function as an articulation point. According to this conception, the analysis of the history of literature can be approached by considering who its subject is (or who the subjects of 'histories of literatures' are), instead of centering on its motor, as Marx had already claimed for social history.

For our purpose, it is important to remember that all this historical process functions as if its inception had been natural, so erasing the concrete historical and ideological implications that made possible the birth of a chronicling methodology such as this one. This methodology, without any logic, continues to be used in order to define and to explain a corpus. Consequently, by being established as a subject of study in secondary schools and universities, the discipline 'history of literature' accomplishes an ideological role that goes far beyond the mere analysis of works and authors. To accept the way of teaching and studying the so-called *literary canon* means to accept the very existence of such a canon, whose consistency has been warranted by the force of tradition. Which authors to study, how to deal with the texts, and according to which explanatory principles are questions put aside as unnecessary by the unquestionable presence of the canon. Not to raise them, however, means to assume the ideological distortion serving as a basis and epistemological foundation.

This, of course, has generated more than a habit, and the resistance to challenge the very validity of the canon also has professional and economic reasons. The appearance of the history of literature as an academic discipline has generated subsequent ways of specialization. It is easy to accept that it would be difficult to dissolve today the notions of 'Generation of 98', 'Realism', 'Naturalism', or 'Generation of 27' as operative concepts for the academic criticism – supposing this dissolution was accepted as scientifically correct – when there is such a cultural industry and so many people depending, economically speaking, on their very existence. It is also easy to understand the suspicion of the so-called national literatures – that is to say, the university departments or the research organizations officially created to guard them, to clean them, and to give them splendour – when they confront the existence of such disciplines as theory of literature, comparative literature, and cultural studies. The suspicions seem to articulate around the assumption of ownership of spaces even more than epistemological discussions; and it is well known how important the maxim 'respect the other's goods' is in our world. This, however, is another matter. Or maybe not.

Of course, the canon is something more than a method to catalogue and classify history; it basically consists of a mode to confront reality and, therefore, to write (that is, to remake) history. But it is far from having an immutable presence. The history of literature as an academic discipline describes the obvious fact of a metamorphosis, but neither does it reveal the framework of changes nor the motives articulating its structure.

By approaching the problem from this perspective, it is easy to understand that 'literature' cannot be considered an autonomous object, reducible to the objects grouped under its explanatory etiquette, but rather an ensemble of practices, including writing, reading, interpretation, commercialization, distribution, teaching, and so on. This ensemble, historically defined in different ways within different cultural traditions, constitutes what we know as 'literature', and constitutes it as a matter to be theorized. It is theory, however, that, by protecting its hypothesis over that matter, constructs the theoretic object called 'literature', which is neither reducible to the former nor coincidental with it. As such, literature is analyzable only with respect to value models presented as 'eternal' and 'essential' if we erase the traces of its historicity – that is, the fact that it is a discourse that has been socially *produced, read, and consumed*.

The practice of what we call, historically, 'literature' not only exists in its relationship with nonliterary and symbolic phenomena but depends as well on parallel discursive formations. Every enunciation lies immersed, whether we want it or not, in the multitudinous space of discursivity. To chronicle its development implies the confrontation of the system of contradictions crossing it, defining it, and constituting it. In these contradictions the collapse of the symmetry of significant and signified is a corollary to the annulment of aesthetic autonomy. The death of both principles makes inoperative both the 'formal' study of texts and a description of their very canonical existence, if it does not challenge the historical conditions that made it possible.

The history of literature, as any history, is the result of projecting on the past a previous analytical model that constructs it as an object. If we want to redefine such a history from a materialist point of view – against the ideological position of considering it a 'natural' fact – it will be necessary to substitute the notion of *succession of centres* (authors, periods, styles, etc.) by the notion of *process without a centre*. Literary texts are only *knots in a discursive network*. This will lead us to consider that literary history is but a specific parcel within a history of the dialogic relation between (1) the different discourses composing a culture, and (2) the different 'institutions' – not taken as a 'thing' but as a 'process designed to give stability to the objects constituting it'.[27] This will oblige us to approach it in terms of a double relationship: *cultural intertextuality* and *literary intertextuality*. With regard to the first, a literary discourse is only approachable as a segment or concatenation of discursive segments within a network of interarticulated discourses. As for the second – only analyzable within the first – a literary discourse establishes horizontal (syntagmatic) relationships with the global discourse of literature in its own language and with the literary discourse in other languages; and vertical (paradigmatic) relationships with the ensemble of discourses – political, religious, economic (that is to say cultural) – composing a culture spatially and temporally determined.[28]

It is not the same thing to analyse the sense of a poem in an articulated universe regarding the word as it is to approach it from a perspective accustomed to the television flow of interchange and advertising. Even if it is possible to speak of the permanence of rhetorical or stylistic constants in the 'official' history of literature, such a permanence implies not an inherent quality of the discourse but the continuity of a 'function', which is only a value historically offered to these constants by determined cultural traditions and within equally determined social formations. That is, their analysis is a question not of syntax or semantics but of pragmatics. Consequently, *the history of literature is only the history of the process of the social institutionalization of a discursive practice.* Displacing the articulation point from the process of production of the object to the process of reproduction – that is, the reading of it – the literary can be analysed from the *inside* of a social formation in its present. If we regard the 'institution' as the process of institutionalization/stabilization of separate discourses, the institutionalization of literature emerges in a determined historical moment.[29] More recently, Samuel Weber[30] has established a distinction between the functioning *institutional* intellectual, who accomplishes what Paul de Man calls the 'correction of mistakes', and the *institutionalizer*, which is what the intellectual mind does when acting blindly, establishing a path 'where nothing existed before'.[31] These are the two conceptions that, in one way or another, cross the debate that seems to exist between the so-called crisis of theory: a crisis that his been understood not as a necessary symptom of the end to its function, but rather as a challenge to the role it has been playing until now.

What is at stake is the renunciation of the false idea of the undifferentiated totality of the object 'literature'. By centering the scope in partial approaches, spatially and temporally localized – that is, in approaches to the world as it is – we can not only rewrite its history but give back explicitly to literature its political function, the one it always had, even if it was under the evasive mask of the 'aesthetic'.

The announced 'end of theory' that Walter Benn Michaels and Steven Knapp[32] exposed as predictable, given the supposed apoliticism generated by deconstruction,[33] can be read in a reversed sense: the end of theory (or theories) that considers the unstable character of its object and the dependency it has on its concrete inscription within a determined cultural tradition. This could lead to comparative propositions (such as that by Milner),[34] which, even if they assume genre taxonomic categories at large, dissolve the notion of literature into the broader and more complex field of cultural studies. In any case, and paradoxically, this displacement gives literature a privileged place from which to reflect on the contemporary world.

A few decades ago, Pier Paolo Passolini affirmed that the consumer's society (that is, what we now could translate as the society) would be the worst of dictatorships, because older dictatorial forms such as fascism were based on the church or the military, which are nothing if compared to television. If this is true, there is no need to look for reasons to explain why an image has more influence than the dissuasive capacity of either a tank or a missile, other than by the efficacy of images to justify the use of weapons. This is why the study and the discussion over the relationship between reality and simulacrum is an urgent and unavoidable task. In my opinion, it is here that the political role of writing and theory continues to be important against those who think that the predominance of the images will make the discourse of words disappear. We should recall that only the discourse of words has, until now, allowed us to think and to theorize the world. Concerning Baudrillard's thesis about the disappearance of 'sense' and 'politics',[35] Paul Virilio warned:

Until World War II – until the concentration camps – societies were societies of incarceration, of imprisonment in the Foucaultian sense. The great transparency of the world, whether through satellites or simply tourists, brought about an overexposure of these places to observation, to the press and public opinion which now ban concentration camps. You can't isolate anything in this world of ubiquity and instantaneousness. Even if some camps still exist, this overexposure of the word led to the need to surpass enclosure and imprisonment. This required the promotion of another kind of repression, which is disappearance. (Gangsters had already invented it by making bodies disappear in cement.)[36]

But even if its place is more and more a no-place, the reflection and the analysis proper to such a theoretical practice are essential today, more than ever, if only to permit us to be conscious of where we stand. Literature can be understood, in this sense, as a place of resistance.

This resistance is twofold: (1) against the nostalgia of representation – that is to say, the idea of a centered subject whose life the literary text refers to – by writing *from* oneself instead of *about* oneself, and (2) against the bodiless subject of the simulacrum, by allowing the otherness that constitutes us to freely circulate through a texture that, paraphrasing Roland Barthes, will no longer be 'dominated by the superego of continuity, a superego of evolution, history [and] filiation'.[37]

On the other hand, since in the world of simulacra discourses become more and more 'real', the political arena will shift more and more toward a discursive space, one in which, as Paul Bové has pointed out, 'the historical specificity of a high-tech, information-based society, in which even the most advanced industrial economies are subect to the operation of the law of value, needs not "organic" intellectuals to provide leadership but specific intellectuals to provide expertise and to decode and control the discourses and technologies dominant in such a society'.[38]

This political practice could be defined in terms of a semiotic one, a practice understood as a way not only to describe but to de-construct what I called above the social imaginary consensus. This is the challenge the electronic age puts in front of us at the end of the millennium.

Notes

1 Norberto Bobbio, *Destra e sinistra: Ragioni e significati di una distinzione politica* (Roma: Donizelli Editore, 1994), p. 5.
2 Cf. Francis Fukuyama, *The End of History and the Last Man* (New York:

The Free Press, 1992). For a very different reading of recent global events, one which is directly at odds with Fukuyama's triumphalism, see Jacques Derrida, *Specters of Marx: The State of the Debt, the Work of Mourning, and the New International*, trans. Peggy Kamuf (New York and London: Routledge, 1994); and for a discussion of Derrida's cautionary approach to Fukuyama's 'end of history' thesis, see my *PomoIntro*, esp. ch. 8. (NL)

3   From an interview included in Federico Campbell, *Infame turba* (1970; rpt, Barcelona: Lumen, 1994). Azúa has readdressed his argument in a recent article, 'Antes de que se extingan', *El Pais* 10 July 1994, p. 11.

4   See, related to this topic, John Frow, *Timeshifting: Intellectual Property and the Means of Reproduction* (Valencia: Eutopias/Working Papers, 1994).

5   Alvin Kernan, *The Death of Literature* (New Haven: Yale University Press, 1990), pp. 1–2.

6   Terry Eagleton, *Literary Theory: An Introduction* (Oxford: Blackwell, 1983). See also his *The Significance of Theory* (Oxford: Blackwell, 1990); and John Beverley, *Against Literature* (Minneapolis: University of Minnesota Press, 1993).

7   Kernan, *Death of Literature*, pp. 2–3.

8   David Lodge, *After Bakhtin* (London: Routledge, 1990). Lodge speaks about the position of the literary critic in the United States in terms of 'a kind of business', analysing the transformation of the place of theory in a kind of academic gloss of the 'Top 20', useful in the battlefield of the different universities, in order to obtain the better academic positions according to a strict market logic; see esp. pp. 175–84.

9   Mark Poster, *The Mode of Information: Poststructuralism and Social Context* (Chicago: University of Chicago Press, 1990).

10 Juri M. Lotmann, *Consideraciones sobre las tipologias de las culturas* (Valencia: Eutopias/Documentos de trabajo, 1993).

11 See my *La escritura como teatralidad* (Valencia: Universidad, 1977). According to Patil Zumthor (*Éssai de poétique mèdiévale* (Paris: Seuil, 1972)), I define as 'author' he or she who received the information on a mouth-to-ear basis during the live performance of the minstrel, as opposed to the reader, who had to receive it on a page-to-page basis.

12 See L. Puig and J. Talens, *Rocking, Writing, and Arithmetic: Too Postmodern to Rock'n'Roll, too Modern to Die* (Valencia: Eutopias/Working Papers, 1993).

13 This possibility already appeared to be at work in silent cinema, when Lev Kuleshov, for instance, wrote about how to create a nonexistent reality out of film through editing (see Silvestra Mariniello, *El cine y el fin del arte* (Madrid: Cátedra, 1992)), but the paradigm of sign as representation was still strong enough at that time to accept his proposals in their deep radicality. More recently, a very well-known star of the opera sent a tape to the studio with an aria he couldn't perform seven months before during the live recording sessions. The producer mixed it with the other material, and now the

album offers itself as a 'live recording'.

14 Michel Foucault, *The Order of Things: An Archaeology of the Human Sciences*, no trans. specified (London: Routledge, 1970).

15 Cf. Louis Marin, 'La dissolution de l'homme dans les sciences humaines: modèle linguistique et sujet signifiant', *Concilium* 86 (June 1973), pp. 27–37.

16 For the relationship between Cartesian thinking as 'masculine' and as a mechanism of production of determined social subjects, see Susan Bordo, *The Flight into Objectivity: Essays on Cartesianism and Culture* (Albany: State University of New York, 1987), and Giulia Colaizzi, *La construccion del imaginario socio-sexual* (València: Eutopias Documentos de trabajo, 1993).

17 Rey Chow, 'Media, Matter, Migrants' (Valencia: Universidad Internacional Menèndez Pelayo, Valencia (mimeo)). Published in Spanish as *Media, materia, migraciones*, trans. Manuel Talens (València: Eutopias Documentos de trabajo, 1994).

18 Jesus Gonzáles-Requena, *El discurso televisivo* (Madrid: Cátedra, 1988).

19 'Velocidad y comunicación' (Valencia: Universidad Internacional Menéndez Pelayo (mimeo)).

20 Chow, 'Media, Matter, Migrants'.

21 Poster, *The Mode of Information*, p. 15.

22 Gilles Deleuze and Félix Guattari, *A Thousand Plateaus: Capitalism and Schizophrenia*, trans. Brian Massumi (Minneapolis: University of Minnesota Press, 1987).

23 Poster, *The Mode of Information*, pp. 46ff.

24 I borrow the notion of 'social imaginary consensus' from Giulia Colaizzi's unpublished paper, 'Genderizing Politics,' discussed at the seminar on History and Narration, University of Valencia, April 1994.

25 As Rossanna Rossanda has pointed out (Berlusconi y television, *El Pais*, 30 April 1994, p. 14), Silvio Berlusconi could do what Ross Perot could not during the 1992 US presidential campaign, because Perot only *appeared* on TV, but Berlusconi *was* the TV. This shift from *using* the media to *being* the media is what defines, probably better than any other characteristic, the structure of the new electronic world. As it is said in the so-called Thomas theorem (quoted in A. Schutz, *El problema de la realidad social* (Buenos Aires: Amorrortu, 1974), p. 340), if people define certain situations as 'real', these situations become 'real' in their consequences. Let us remember how the narrator in Samuel Beckett's *Molloy* ironically states that after habitually calling what happened to him HIS OWN LIFE, he would finally come to believe that his life really was his own.

26 Ferruccio Rossi-Landi, *Linguistics and Economics* (The Hague/Paris: Motitori, 1975).

27 Samuel Weber, 'Caught in the Act of Reading', in *Glyph: Textual Studies 1, Demarcating the Disciplines: Philosophy, Literature, Art* (Minneapolis:

University of Minnesota Press, 1986), pp. 181–214. Weber, commenting on *The Act of Reading*, by Wolfgang. Iser, cites the German sociologist Niklas Luhmann when he defines the concept of 'institution' in terms of a process that immobilizes the world around a system by the 'institutionalization of particular forms of experience (perception habits, interpretations of reality, values). The variety ... of the possible modes of conduct is reduced and secures the complementarity of expectations' (p. 195). See also Susan R. Horton, 'The Institution of Literature and the Cultural Community', in Joseph Natoli, ed., *Literary Theory's Future* (Urbana: University of Illinois Press, 1989), pp. 267–320.

28 See, for example, Wlad Godzich and Nicholas Spadaccini, eds, *Literature Among Discourses* (Minneapolis: University of Minnesota Press, 1986), where the revision of the very concept of 'literature' leads us to consider what we call a 'masterwork' as 'the nexus of a network of themes, motives, verbal tools, narrative models, etc., present in other texts, of whatever status in the epoch' (p. xiii).

29 See, for our cultural context, Wlad Godzich and Nicholas Spadaccini, eds, *The Institutionalization of Literature in Spain* (Minneapolis: The Prisma Institute, 1988).

30 Samuel Weber, *Institution and Interpretation* (Minneapolis: University of Minnesota Press, 1987).

31 Wlad Godzich, 'Religion, the State, and Post(al) Modernism', in Weber, *Institution and Interpretation*, pp. 155–6.

32 Walter Benn Michaels and Steven Knapp, 'Against Theory,' *Critical Inquiry* 8, 4 (1982), pp. 732–42.

33 See, concerning this debate, the suggestive postface written by Wlad Godzich for Weber's *Institution*.

34 Earl Milner, *Comparative Poetics: An Intercultural Essay on Theories of Literature* (Princeton: Princeton University Press, 1990).

35 See, for example, *For a Critique of the Political Economy of the Sign*, trans. Charles Levin (St Louis: Telos, 1981); *Simulations*, trans. Paul Foss, John Johnson, Paul Patton, and Philip Beitchman (New York: Semiotext[e], 1983); and *Seduction*, trans. Brian Singer (New York: St. Martin's Press, 1990).

36 Paul Virilio and Sylvée Lotringer, *Pure War*, trans, Mark Polizzotti (New York: Semiotext[e], 1983), p. 88. See also Paul Virilio, *Live Show*, Spanish trans. Manuel Talens (Valencia: Eutopias Working Papers, 1994).

37 Roland Barthes, *The Grain of the Voice: Interviews, 1962–1980* (New York: Hill and Wang, 1977), p. 132.

38 Paul A. Bové, 'The Literary Critic in the Postmodern World', in *In the Wake of Theory* (Hanover: Wesleyan University Press, 1992), 25–47, esp. pp. 40–1. [The terms 'organic intellectual' and 'specific intellectual' are borrowed, respectively, from the work of Antonio Gramsci and Michel Foucault. For Gramsci, a political activist who was imprisoned by Mussolini in the 1920s, every social group creates – organically – its own various orders of intellec-

tual who are responsible for the social self-identity of the group in political and cultural terms; see *Selections from the Prison Notebooks of Antonio Gramsci*, trans. and ed. Quinton Hoare and Geoffrey Nowell-Smith (New York: International Publishers, 1978). On Foucault's notion of the specific intellectual – whose professional knowledge can be put to good political effect, although that is not its necessary function – see esp. his 'Truth and Power', trans. Colin Gordon, in *Power/Knowledge: Selected Interviews and Other Writings 1972–1977*, ed. Colin Gordon (New York: Pantheon, 1980), pp. 131–3. (NL)]

Part Five **Post**

Chapter Seventeen
Postmodern Value

Catherine Burgass

There has been an irredeemable slur cast upon value by postmodernism. Colluding with poststructuralism, postmodernism has invalidated the metanarrative and dissolved the autonomous subject, thus apparently disabling the construction of any new object- or subject-centred ethics, aesthetics or axiology. However, in spite of this comprehensive threat, a campaign to revive and raise the status of value is gathering force. This enterprise is proceeding under the aegis of postmodernism, and continues to engage selectively with poststructuralist theories. Its profile was raised in America in 1988 with the publication of Barbara Herrnstein Smith's *Contingencies of Value* and John Fekete's *Life After Postmodernism*. The programme for these theorists of postmodern value is to retrieve some sort of status for value without asserting an absolute or truth value for their own claims. The strategy invoked in order to evade the disallowed metanarrative is not to posit the inherent value of value, nor to ascribe positive value to any particular entity such as literature, but rather to vindicate the *activity of evaluation*.

There has more recently been a further development in this area, building upon the project of the first, but distinct in its actualization of a literary-critical practice. This development is marked by the publication of Steven Connor's *Theory and Cultural Value* (1992), which functions partly as a critique of the earlier movement. The general revival of interest in questions of value follows a period in twentieth-century literary studies referred to by Smith as the 'The Exile of Evaluation'.[1] The origins of this displacement can be traced back to the Enlightenment split of sciences and humanities: fact and value. The struggle of Anglo-American literary

Catherine Burgass, 'Postmodern Value', in *Postmodern Surroundings*, ed. Steven Earnshaw, *Postmodern Studies* 9 (Amsterdam: Atlanta, 1994), pp. 23–37.

studies for 'scientific' rigour during the first half of the twentieth-century foregrounds the derogation of evaluative criticism as the poor relation of interpretative literary scholarship. The advent of postmodernism apparently bridges the Enlightenment schism; with the dissolution of the metanarrative, fact can no longer claim precedence over value. However, certainly within cultural studies, this in itself has not occasioned the reinstatement of value judgement; even Connor's engagement with questions of value *together with* the literary text is marked by a curious unwillingness to make explicit statements of value. Before investigating more fully the continuing stigma on value, I am going first to address some postmodern problems of definition, and then briefly touch on the order of value in two accounts of the postmodern.

Much is made of the difficulty of defining postmodernism. Andreas Huyssen claims that 'the amorphous and politically volatile nature of postmodernism makes the phenomenon itself remarkably elusive, and the definition of its boundaries exceedingly difficult, if not per se impossible.'[2] Ihab Hassan concurs, noting that there is 'no clear consensus about its meaning . . . among scholars'.[3] We are nevertheless provided with a neat enough axiom by Jean-François Lyotard, who describes the '*postmodern* as incredulity toward metanarratives'.[4] The problem of definition is perhaps not as disabling as some theorists of the postmodern would have us believe. The prime difficulty, according to Fredric Jameson, is the direct result of our historical and physical location in the postmodern:

> distance in general (including 'critical distance' in particular) has very precisely been abolished in the new space of postmodernism. We are submerged in its henceforth filled and suffused volumes to the point where our now postmodern bodies are bereft of spatial coordinates and practically (let alone theoretically) incapable of distantiation.[5]

We are necessarily without the vantage point of temporal perspective with which to categorize our own experience, but to suggest, as Jameson does, that postmodernism, with its bewildering architectural and urban spaces, physically disorientates and annihilates entirely the perspective necessary for identification, interpretation or evaluation, is mistaken, even at the time of his writing. For one thing, our postmodern minds still have the existential choice of various narratives *including* the apparently obsolescent Enlightenment metanarrative. The postmodern is no more difficult to define than any other concept; considered to be a historico-cultural phe-nomenon, the postmodern is precisely what it says: post-modern(ism). As a term 'postmodernism' is not fully adequate to its object, but functions nevertheless; the very existence of a label marks at least *some* critical dis-tance, and with it the space for evaluation. There is, however, a facet of the postmodern less assimilable to the account of value, and that is postmodernism as a cultural style. Jameson makes a pertinent distinction in his essay between postmodernism as a historical phenomenon, 'the cul-tural dominant of the logic of late capitalism',[6] and postmodernism merely as a stylistic category. He disapproves of the latter as giving rise to a 'complacent (yet delirious) camp-following celebration of this aesthetic new world'.[7] This qualification is one that I would endorse, and I shall distinguish here between 'postmodernity' or 'the postmodern', referring to the historical era, and 'postmodernism' as the stylistic category. A prime example of stylistic anti-aesthetics is to be found in the work of Baudrillard, with its hysterical celebration of a postmodern utopia of empty significa-tion. For Jameson, the physical disorientation caused by postmodern archi-tectural style is analogous with the 'incapacity of our minds'.[8] The postmodern and postmodernism are obviously linked, but I would suggest that even Jameson's account of the abolition of critical distance is informed at times by a wilful conflation of the two.

Moving on to the second preliminary point, the concept of value is inte-gral to the Marxist account of postmodernism. While the shift from use-value to exchange-value is one of the defining features of capitalism, art and aesthetic production have previously been thought of as inhabiting at least a semi-autonomous realm. However, writing in 1984, Jameson suggests that

> What has happened is that aesthetic production today has become inte-grated into commodity production generally: the frantic economic urgency of producing fresh waves of ever more novel-seeming goods . . . at ever greater rates of turnover, now assigns an increasingly essential structural function and position to aesthetic innovation and experimentation.[9]

Paradoxically, art has been transformed from being intrinsically valuable to being immediately quantifiable in terms of exchange-value. Baudrillard takes a less sober-minded but not incompatible view of the effect of commodification:

> the commodity form is the first great medium of the modern world. But the message that the objects deliver through it is already extremely simplified,

and it is always the same: their exchange value. Thus at bottom the message already no longer exists; it is the medium that imposes itself in its pure circulation. This is what I call (potentially) ecstasy. One has only to prolong this Marxist analysis ... to grasp the transparence and obscenity of the universe of communication, which leaves far behind it those relative analyses of the universe of the commodity. All functions abolished in a single dimension, that of communication. That's the ecstasy of communication.[10]

In the postmodern era, commodification has apparently short-circuited both meaning and value. As I have already stated, Baudrillardian postmodernism represents that irresponsible revelling in the floating signifier and loss of value: 'The pleasure is no longer one of manifestation, scenic and aesthetic, but rather one of pure fascination, aleatory and psychotropic. This is not necessarily a negative value judgment.'[11] It is here that the intersection between postmodernism and certain 'extreme' deconstructions occurs. The relation between poststructuralism and the postmodern is complex and symbiotic: poststructuralism is not a historical era and there is no postmodernist 'theory' as such, but certain central themes of postmodern discourse are provoked by the epistemological and ontological problems raised by deconstruction. Poststructuralist theory therefore often underpins postmodern discourse and the deconstruction of metaphysics undoubtedly contributes to our conception of the postmodern. As a schizophrenic identity, postmodern/ism also has its counterpart in poststructuralist theory; the thoughtful study carried out by Jameson corresponds to the philosophical questions worked through by Derrida, while the ecstasies of Baudrillard are comparable to those of such notorious proponents of textuality as Geoffrey Hartman.

Stuart Sim takes the whole poststructuralist-postmodernist project to task in a book which takes as its starting premiss the notion that the grand masters of deconstruction and postmodernism, Derrida and Lyotard, have 'as their goal the creation of the conditions for a post-aesthetic realm beyond the reach of value judgement.'[12] Sim wrongly attributes the desire to 'pass beyond metaphysics'[13] to Derrida, a charge which would fall better on Baudrillard who posits, with apparent relish, 'the end of metaphysics'.[14] Sim is frankly beholden to a socialism which is undoubtedly threatened by anti-teleological elements of certain postmodernisms, but this leads him to underplay real differences. There is a distinction to be made between the philosophically tenable discourses of Lyotard and Derrida, and those which revel in the wilfully incomprehensible and extra-aesthetic. Sim is aware of this distinction: 'It is stretching a point . . . to damn Derrida and Lyotard through Baudrillard, but. . . .'[15] This 'but' is telling. Of course, the question of difference is complicated by the fact that Derrida's writings incorporate a stylistic or performative element, but it is the wholesale identification of historical and hysterical postmodernisms, and philosophical and solely stylistic poststructuralisms, which has resulted in the protraction of the exile of evaluation, even among those who self-consciously promote its reinstatement.

The postmodern retrieval of value is part of a larger concern to repoliticize postmodern discourse after the radical relativism perceived as a necessary apolitical and quietistic consequence of deconstruction. This radical relativism has made deconstruction problematic for those who wish to recruit it for postmodern issues of gender and race. Nevertheless, all factions in the postmodern debate on value are keen to recruit poststructuralist theory, particularly Derridean deconstruction, for their project. It is apparent, however, that many of these postmodern theorists, like Sim, continue to subscribe to the received idea that poststructuralism is hostile to value. The weight of this idea needs to be assessed.[16] As it was initially received in the Anglo-American academy, poststructuralism heralded the inevitable de(con)struction of empirical evaluative criticism, with its proclaimed subversive effects on structures of power, structure itself, and value systems as implicated in and complicit with these structures. All metaphysical discourse is reliant on the fallacy of presence as, according to Derrida, 'truth is agreement . . . a relation of resemblance or equality between a representation and a thing (unveiled, present) even in the eventuality of a statement of judgment.'[17] As in Jameson's account of the postmodern, the critical distance necessary for identification and evaluation is removed. The loss of the guaranteed presence of meaning in the signifier, as represented by the concept *différance*, apparently underpins the assumption that deconstruction advocates and invokes the possibility of value-free discourse by disallowing closure. However, it is a mistaken assumption that *différance* points to the loss of closure simply because it is inimical to particular structures, although it is easy to see how this misconception has been engendered:

> *différance* is not. It is not a present being. . . . It governs nothing, reigns over nothing, and nowhere exercises any authority. It is not announced by any capital letter. Not only is there no kingdom of *différance*, but *différance* instigates the subversion of every kingdom. Which makes it obviously threatening and infallibly dreaded by everything in us that desires a kingdom.[18]

That *différance* theoretically demolishes fixed meaning by stressing the temporal is not contentious. There is no reason, however, to suppose that the potentially infinite regression of meaning should negate the power or violence operational in the activity of closure in individual instances of interpretation and evaluation. The theory of *différance* accounts for the infinite displacement of meanings, and thus for the constant operation of power. This infinite displacement simply replaces the static violence of structuralism with the dynamic violence of poststructuralism. Derrida is concerned with the essential limitations of deconstruction, marked in his refusal to award *différance* the capital. These limitations indeed might be said to constitute the essential antinomy of deconstruction:

> The movements of deconstruction do not destroy structures from the outside. They are not possible and effective, nor can they take them *in a certain way*, because one always inhabits, and all the more when one does not expect it. Operating necessarily from the inside, borrowing all the strategic and economic resources of subversion from the old structure . . . the enterprise of deconstruction always in a certain way falls prey to its own work.[19]

The key to this sang froid is perhaps the willingness to relish rather than decry the ambiguity and paradox associated with postmodernism. However, an irresponsible revelling in textuality is emphatically not a feature of Derridean philosophy. As Derek Attridge puts it 'there has always been an ethico-political dimension to Derrida's writing, manifesting itself particularly in a respect for *other-ness*.'[20]

Arkady Plotnitsky, in *Life After Postmodernism*, notices those qualifiers in Derridean philosophy which should temper the wilder excesses of textuality, and which are appropriate to the postmodern recuperation of value. Plotnitsky initially criticizes Derrida's reading of Nietzsche for paying little overt attention to what he perceives as integral questions of value, but finally suggests that Derridean deconstruction is not as hostile to evaluation as has been previously asserted. Plotnitsky sequesters the Derridean concepts of trace and closure in the service of an analysis which identifies interpretation and evaluation as part of the same activity: 'It follows . . . that in so far as one reappropriates the Derridean matrix – the emergence of trace – as the emergence of value, one then cannot. claim that interpretation is primary or precedes evaluation.'[21]

Plotnitsky rightly posits both termination and infinity as a condition of *différance* in Derrida's own work. His account is informed by the practical streak common to the theorists of postmodern value, and represents

an attempt to mediate between, or incorporate, a deconstructive antinomy, that is, the idea of infinity and the operation of closure:

> deconstruction points toward 'the necessity of interminable analysis.' But
> one must also account for the necessity of termination, for any analysis or
> interpretation is *necessarily* terminated at some point. At the very least,
> death of one kind or another . . . will terminate an analysis.[22]

It is the false ideal of *différance* as absolute, or infinite play of signification, properly qualified by Plotnitsky, that has led to the inhibition of
literary criticism, as both evaluation and interpretation have been perceived as constituting proscribed closure. (I shall indicate this concept by
use of the capital – *Différance*.) Fekete et al. represent a new strain of
'hyper-pragmatism', which maintains epistemological limitations and allows at least for the activity of the metanarrative. This sort of pragmatism
is already identifiable in Lyotard's affirmation of the continuing, if repressed, action of the metanarrative:

> the older master-narratives of legitimation no longer function in the service
> of scientific research – nor by implication anywhere else. . . . This seeming
> contradiction can be resolved . . . namely to posit, not the disappearance of
> the great master-narratives, but their passage underground as it were, their
> continuing by now *unconscious* effectivity as a way of 'thinking about' and
> acting in our current situation.[23]

This insistence on the continued action of the metanarrative in the
postmodern era is analogous to Derrida's acknowledgement of the operation of deconstruction within metaphysical constraints. The effects of the
loss of the ultimate referent are moderated with the admission that any
critical practice necessarily involves a hidden metanarrative. Metanarratives
do still 'exist' *by virtue of what they do*. This stress on functionality and
activity indicates the starting point for the account of evaluation, and
Connor actually evokes Lyotard by suggesting that value and evaluation
have not been 'exiled' as Smith claims, but have rather been 'driven into
the critical unconscious, where they continue to exercise force but without being available for analytic scrutiny.'[24]

The postmodern undertaking to retrieve and dust down evaluative activity after its battering by deconstruction is protean and fraught with
difficulties. Poststructuralist theory, while containing much of interest
and relevance to literary criticism, does not authorize the construction of
any specific methodology or critical programme other than a general

reflexivity. In seeking to lift the ignominy from evaluation, postmodern theorists cannot regress to an unselfconscious evaluative discourse. This restriction informs a characteristic circumspection pervasive within postmodern value theory, evident particularly in the American reluctance to construct any potentially totalitarian theory. Fekete, for instance, states that he is 'not talking about a unified axiology, of a single discipline, of an abstraction from specialized studies' but of 'an emerging intertextual discursive field.'[25] Smith similarly declares that rather than actually conduct a self-conscious, historically locatable enquiry into value, her own study 'is designed to suggest a theoretical framework for such an enquiry'.[26] She defines her mission as neither 'to discover grounds for the "justification" of critical judgments or practices', nor to create a 'literary axiology', but rather to 'account for the features of literary and aesthetic judgments in relation to the multiple . . . conditions to which they are responsive.'[27] Fekete is peculiarly smug about these self-imposed limitations: 'I will conclude as professionally as I began: my wish here has been only to contribute some preliminary considerations toward a research agenda and a discourse on value.'[28]

A collective point of departure for the postmodern 'axiologists' is the assertion that evaluation is a necessary condition of human existence: 'for a responsive creature, to exist is to evaluate';[29] 'we live, breathe, and excrete values'[30]; 'value and evaluation are necessary as a kind of law of human nature'.[31] However, in spite of this obvious consensus regarding the necessity of evaluation, and a common desire to retrieve value from the black hole of infinite regress, positive or explicit value judgement is, to say the least, somewhat sparse in the pages of their texts. Fekete takes care to stress that his revisionist venture should not be identified with an attempt to re-elect the Deity:

> postmodernism may be at last ready – or may, at least, represent the transition to a readiness – unneurotically, to get on without the Good-God-Gold Standards, one and all, indeed without any capitalized Standards, while learning to be enriched by the whole inherited inventory once it is transferred to the lower case.[32]

Arguably, it was from America that *Différance* was disseminated, and it is apparent that traces of this virus linger in the critical system. Fekete's statement arguably has little connection with Derridean *différance*. Geoffrey Bennington, in his recent account of Derrida's work, maintains that *différance* 'does not, for example, amount to announcing once again the death of God'.[33] It is possible also that Fekete's confidence in the ability of postmodernism 'to get on' is misplaced. The tentative nature of the early approaches to postmodern value can be interpreted sympathetically as a diffidence born of the loss of certainty. However, that actual value judgement is absent from this work is perhaps not only a practical limitation of the project at its inception, but a repressed desire to inhabit the postmodern utopia. The cause of the inability to grasp the nettle is a lingering theism, in spite of Fekete's protestations to the contrary. Although there is a drive to account for the actual conditions which produce value, these postmodern theorists continue to afford *Différance* an unhealthy degree of respect. The postmodern project as presented so far connives with critical inaction.

It is only with the publication of Connor's *Theory and Cultural Value* that a revised postmodernist/poststructuralist literary-critical practice is undertaken. First, in order to redress the limiting effects of the previous 'institutionalization of value theory' (which he suggests may account for recent evasions), Connor formulates a postmodern axiology of *différance*:

> The imperative of value may . . . be thought of as the Derridean *différance* of value, not only because it defers the arrival of ultimate value (though it is always necessarily oriented towards it), as *différance* defers the arrival of meaning, but because of the reflexive structure . . . in which every value is itself subject to the force of evaluation.[34]

He goes so far as to support the imperative of value (the value of value itself, which he suggests Smith promotes but cannot account for. This, however, does not in itself mark a progression from the earlier phase of postmodernism. Connor proposes to resolve the apparent impasse between poststructuralist theory and political responsibility or action through 'the difficult task of thinking absolutism and relativism together rather than apart and antagonistic',[35] like Plotnitsky accepting the antinomy of deconstruction without rejoicing in a limitless and removed textuality. In fact it is not especially difficult to *think* the absolute and relative together; the problem comes when one is required to put this dictum into *practice*. Although Connor's paradigm is suggestive of that sort of dubious performative deconstruction where every term is interrogated and no 'statement' actually made, he finally outsteps his predecessors by taking advantage of the theoretical framework constructed by Smith et al., and initiating a critical practice – a breakthrough after the previous coyness surrounding this activity. Texts by Beckett and Joyce are discussed in conjunction with those of Bataille, Nietzsche, Levinas and Derrida. However, by no means can this be seen as the *practising* of relativism and absolutism together; this remains an impossibility by virtue of the necessary agency of closure. When it comes down to it, Connor disappointingly shies away from explicit value judgement. For example, following a reading of Beckett's *Worstword Ho*, he is obliged to admit that the text fulfils the positive criterion of choice: 'my own reading here evidently and inescapably predicates value in the play of value and non-value in *Worstword Ho*'.[36] But postmodern squeamishness triumphs when this statement is followed by the remark that 'this is a value that cannot without violent abbreviation be . . . transmitted by critical discourse'.[37]

It should be recorded that Derrida, one of the cited causes of this fastidiousness, does make positive value judgements. In 'The Double Session', as well as describing the metafictive nature of Mallarmé's *Mimique* through which 'everything describes the very structure of the text and effectuates its possibility', Derrida also refers to 'the chiseled precision of the writing, its extraordinary formal or syntactical felicity'.[38] This propriety is admittedly attributed to the anti-Platonic representation or mimesis in Mallarmé's text, 'this imitator having in the last instance no imitated, this signifier . . . no signified, this sign . . . no referent'.[39] However, the very fact of value judgement conflicts directly with Sim's assertion that 'value judgement is studiously avoided by Derrida'.[40] Sim's earlier accusation that 'Thinkers like Derrida and Jean-François Lyotard have, by their rejection of conventional methods of constructing value judgements . . . succeeded in problematizing the whole area of aesthetics' is tenable, but has no necessary connection with his other central claim that such deconstructive writings have 'as their goal the creation of the conditions for a post-aesthetic realm beyond the reach of value judgement'.[41] Derrida does not claim to supplant conditions of metaphysics or aesthetics but rather to demonstrate, as well as interrogate, their mechanics. Connor does not discuss Derridean 'criticism', and it is debatable whether his work represents any significant development in terms of evaluation, some twenty years later. Both poststructuralism and postmodernism allow for evaluation and this is particularly obvious in the seminal texts; advocates of the extra-aesthetic promulgate extreme and ultimately untenable positions. Although Connor's paradigm approaches the spirit of Derridean *différance*, intervening poststructuralisms and postmodernisms have irredeemably sapped critical self-confidence.

The attempt to practise the ideal of relativism still lingers in the academic institution. Smith notes a critical hesitancy which is undoubtedly born of the undermining of truth value by deconstruction and postmodernism. She describes the 'scrupulously qualified professional precision, in which one has heard one's colleagues or oneself saying things like: "well it seems to me that, in a sense, it might be possible, under certain circumstances. . . . " '[42] She relates these assertions in anecdotal fashion, but they do point to the methodological paradox which seeks to incorporate relativism in critical discourse. Such critical practice as Smith describes is well-intended, but problematic; it is an attempt to demonstrate the contingency of critical judgement, to integrate and voice a postmodern antinomy which actually resists such integration and articulation. The converse of such a practice is, however, equally unsatisfactory and could be formulated thus: once we are aware that value judgements are contingent, which is the general consensus amongst the authors cited, a statement of value is consequently received by a sceptical audience. It is no longer necessary to foreground a statement of value because such statements are already conceptually foregrounded. This is, of course, potentially politically dangerous; the rejection of the textual and discursive qualifier could lead to regression into the dark age of Enlightenment, where concepts of truth and value go unexamined and the structures of power are once again institutionalized and concealed. It is unlikely, and on the face of it, undesirable that full recovery from this type of postmodern neurosis should occur, but trepidation in the face of value judgement has been an unfortunate symptom. The readmission of positive value judgement to a postmodern critical practice represents an objective not yet achieved.

Although we still inhabit the era of 'multinational capitalism',[43] certain stylistic postmodernisms are reaching the end of their natural life. 'The new architecture . . . stands as something like an imperative to grow new organs, to expand our sensorium and our body to some new, as yet unimaginable, perhaps ultimately impossible, dimensions.'[44] This new architecture, product of the postmodern, and producer of 'postmodern hyperspace',[45] is already beginning to look as superannuated as the avant-gardism of high modernism. This is significant as it undoubtedly marks a new perspective on the postmodern itself. Jameson does foresee this eventuality with his remark that the physically disorientating effect of postmodern space is analogous with 'the incapacity of our minds, *at least at present*, to map the great global multinational and decentred communicational network in which we find ourselves caught as individual subjects.'[46] At least some facets of Jameson's 'present' are now past, and with this past returns the 'critical distance' (which I do not believe was lost but only disclaimed by those bewitched by certain postmodern discourses), necessary to identify, classify, and assess the postmodern experience and our representations of it. This will allow for the fastidious selection of those elements of the postmodern appropriate to any new (historically locatable) project of ethics or aesthetics. In time value will accrue to postmodernism, less by virtue of its inherent qualities, rather through its future significance and use.

Notes

1 Barbara Herrnstein Smith, *Contingencies of Value: Alternative Perspectives for Critical Theory* (London: Harvard University Press, 1988), p. 17.
2 Andreas Huyssen, *After the Great Divide: Modernism, Mass Culture and Postmodernism* (London: Macmillan, 1988), p. 58.
3 Ihab Hassan, 'The Culture of Postmodernism', *Theory, Culture and Society* 2 (3) (1985), p. 121.
4 Jean-François Lyotard, *The Postmodern Condition: A Report on Knowledge*, trans. Geoff Bennington and Brian Massumi (Manchester: Manchester University Press, 1984), p. xxiv.
5 Fredric Jameson, 'Postmodernism, or the Cultural Logic of Late Capitalism', *New Left Review* 146 (1984), p. 87.
6 Ibid., p. 85
7 Ibid.
8 Ibid., p. 84.
9 Ibid., p. 56.
10 Jean Baudrillard, 'The Ecstasy of Communication', in *Postmodern Culture*, ed. Hal Foster (London: Pluto Press, 1983), p. 131.
11 Ibid., p. 132.
12 Stuart Sim, *Beyond Aesthetics: Confrontations with Poststructuralism and Postmodernism* (London: Harvester Wheatsheaf, 1992), p. 1.
13 Ibid., p. 34.
14 Baudrillard, 'Ecstasy', p. 128.
15 Sim, *Beyond Aesthetics*, p. 134.
16 For a discussion of what I regard as important distinctions between postmodernism and poststructuralism, see my *PomoIntro*; and for an argument against the charge of deconstruction's alleged apoliticism, see my *Debating Derrida* (Melbourne: Melbourne University Press, 1995), esp. ch. 4. (NL)
17 Jacques Derrida, *Margins of Philosophy*, trans. Alan Bass (Brighton: Harvester Press, 1982), p. 179.
18 Ibid., p. 22.
19 Jacques Derrida, '[from] Of Grammatology', in *A Derrida Reader: Between*

the Blinds, ed. Peggy Kamuf (London: Harvester Wheatsheaf, 1991), p. 41.

20 Derek Attridge, 'Introduction', in *Jacques Derrida, Acts of Literature*, ed. Derek Attridge (London: Routledge, 1992), p. 5.

21 Arkady Plotnitsky, 'Interpretation, Interminability, Evaluation: From Nietzsche Toward a General Economy', in *Life After Postmodernism: Essays on Value and Culture*, ed. John Fekete (London: Macmillan, 1988), p. 129.

22 Ibid., p. 126.

23 Lyotard, *Postmodern Condition*, pp. xi–xii.

24 Steven Connor, *Theory and Cultural Value* (Oxford: Blackwell, 1992), p. 14.

25 John Fekete, 'Introductory Notes for a Postmodern Value Agenda', in *Life After Postmodernism*, p. xiv.

26 Smith, *Contingencies*, p. 29.

27 Ibid., p. 28.

28 John Fekete, 'Vampire Values, Infinitive Art, and Literary Theory: A Topographic Meditation', in *Life After Postmodernism*, pp. 83–4.

29 Smith, *Contingencies*, p. 42.

30 Fekete, 'Introductory Notes', p. i.

31 Connor, *Theory and Cultural Value*, p. 8.

32 Fekete, 'Introductory Notes', p. xi.

33 Geoffrey Bennington and Jacques Derrida, *Jacques Derrida*, trans. Geoffrey Bennington (London: University of Chicago Press, 1993).

34 Connor, *Theory and Cultural Value*, p. 3.

35 Ibid., p. 1.

36 Ibid., p. 89.

37 Ibid.

38 Jacques Derrida, 'The Double Session', in *A Derrida Reader*, p. 181.

39 Ibid.

40 Sim, *Beyond Aesthetics*, p. 66.

41 Ibid., p. 1.

42 Smith, *Contingencies*, pp. 7–8.

43 Jameson, 'Postmodernism', p. 55.

44 Ibid., p. 80.

45 Ibid., p. 83.

46 Ibid., p. 84; emphasis added.

Chapter Eighteen In Search of the Lyotard Archipelago, or: How to Live with Paradox and Learn to Like It

William Rasch

Postmodernist critics and critics of postmodernism are like a bickering couple in a dance contest. They tirelessly circle, locked in a dance they no longer enjoy, but also no longer know how to stop. The postmodernist keeps accusing her partner of stepping on her feet, but the critic of postmodernism pleads his innocence, maintaining that his partner repeatedly and unknowingly steps on her own feet. And so they go on, each confident that it is the other who does not know how to dance. The judges, if there ever were any, have left the hall long ago, the spectators are filing out, but the band, though thoroughly sick of this tiresome two-step, plays on.

In the eyes of the rationalist critic of postmodernism, postmodernists cannot help but trip over their own feet in maintaining their radically ungrounded and therefore paradoxical positions. The classical version of this critique is articulated in the Habermasian contention that it is impossible to use critical reflection to critique reflection without falling into contradiction.[1] Once the rationalist critic makes the central contradiction visible for all to see, the postmodern utterance is said to collapse under its own weight. Yet this critique has been remarkably ineffectual. Postmod-

William Rasch, 'In Search of the Lyotard Archipelago, or: How to Live with Paradox and Learn to Like it', *New German Critique* 61 (Winter 1994), pp. 55–75.

ernist critics continue to perform paradoxically; they continue to imply, through their persistence, that self-referential paradoxes are not careless oversights and not merely banal 'You Are Here' signposts. Rather, they say, the presence of paradox makes a claim about the inescapably self-referential nature of language and therefore of efforts to understand the world. In this paper I will look at some of the self-referential paradoxes that crop up in the work of Jean-François Lyotard and which at times seem to embarrass him. My observations are largely informed by certain aspects of the work of Niklas Luhmann, who, as we shall see, appears far less embarrassed by the presence of paradox in his writings.

In his critique of judgement in *Just Gaming*, Lyotard claims to locate a paradox, based on logical contradiction, in the traditional Western notion of justice. At the same time, he seems to enact the very paradox he locates in his analysis. According to Lyotard, a traditional 'scientific' notion of justice (which could be characterized as Platonic, Marxist, or in a variety of other ways) assumes it is able to describe an essence of justice which can then serve as the model and ground for actualizing a just society. A description of such an essence operates on two levels: on the one hand, it serves as 'a theoretical operation that seeks to define scientifically . . . the object the society is lacking in order to be a good or a just society; on the other hand, plugged into this theoretical ordering, there are some implied discursive orderings that determine the measures to be taken in social reality to bring it into conformity with the representation of justice that was worked out in the theoretical discourse.' In Lyotard's view, traditional notions of justice thereby conflate and confuse the workings of two radically incommensurate language games – the theoretical or descriptive game and the practical or prescriptive one. It is in this confusion of games that Lyotard finds a paradox. 'The paradox is as follows: what is implied in the ordering in question is that the prescriptive call be derived from the descriptive'. Using Aristotle's notion of classes of statements and 'a very schematic logical analysis' that could, he assures us, 'easily be refined', Lyotard claims that commands cannot be derived from propositional statements.[2] 'This passage from one [class of statements] to the other is, properly speaking, unintelligible. There is a resistance, an incommensurability, I would say an irrelevancy, of the prescriptive with respect to the functions of propositional logic . . . ' In short, 'all this thought is actually futile, inasmuch as a command cannot find its justification in a denotative statement' (*JG*, p. 22).

Lyotard opposes to this 'Platonic' notion of justice a 'pagan' one, uttered in Kantian terms, in which judgements are not made in conformity with a concept of justice, that is, 'not regulated by categories', but are rather made 'without criteria' (*JG*, p. 14). But this command – 'Let us be pagan' – violates the proposition he is at pains to demonstrate – that is, 'To be Platonic is to commit a logical fallacy.' In offering judgements without criteria as a model of justice, Lyotard performs the very paradox he claims to diagnose. He utters a simple descriptive statement – that is, that a prescriptive statement cannot be logically derived from a descriptive one – and then uses this descriptive to justify the prescriptive statement that one *ought* not to derive or claim to derive prescriptions from descriptions. That is, because there is a radical discontinuity or incommensurability between language games, one cannot logically derive a statement in one game from a statement in another, therefore prescriptions which in some way claim as their ground a descriptive statement are illegitimate and should not be uttered. So stated, Lyotard's prescription violates its own principle, for it uses the theoretical (descriptive) assertion – that theoretical assertions cannot logically justify more (prescriptive) ones – to justify itself. The situation is rich in irony. In *The Postmodern Condition*, Lyotard invokes Gödel's incompleteness theorem to stress that all formal systems, including logic, have 'internal limitations' and therefore allow for 'the formation of paradoxes'.[3] Thus, older forms of legitimation based on truth as internal consistency have given way to legitimation through performativity or parology, i.e., the quest for new moves 'played in pragmatics of knowledge' and the assumption of 'a power that destabilizes the capacity for explanation'.[4] In *Just Gaming*, he defends his notorious *The Libidinal Economy* by stating that its rhetorical violence is nothing more than a strategy for producing effects. Far from attempting to control and constrain opinion, prevent dialogue or present insurmountable problems of negotiation, he insists that this book, like all his others, was sent off like a 'bottle tossed into the ocean' (*JG*, p. 6). The reader of these messages in a bottle is not thought of as an arbiter of intentions or logical consistencies, but as an 'addressee' of effects. Yet, with regard to systems of justice, the wave of effects on the sea of performance are given up for the solid ground of logical analysis, and Lyotard's strategy for delegitimation reverts to a quintessentially rationalist tactic: the hunting down and elimination of contradiction and paradox, coupled with the denial that his hunt engenders its own paradoxes.[5]

As Samuel Weber has noted, the web of paradox in which Lyotard finds himself ensnared is a result of his insistence on the strict autonomy of language games. It is a manifestation of the anti-foundationalist's contradictory and unstated desire for a perspective from which the particularity and singularity of all perspectives can be guaranteed. As a result, the discourse which claims that no discourse enjoys a special status enjoys a special status. Weber writes, '[T]he concern with "preserving the purity" and singularity "of each game" by reinforcing its isolation from the others gives rise to exactly what was intended to be avoided: "the domination of one game by another", namely, the domination of the prescriptive.'[6] 'The great prescriber' – the title which Thébaud bestows on Lyotard at the end of their seven day discussion – in fact proscribes, 'while at the same time obscuring the necessity for proscription. . . . He guards over the multiplicity of the games as if that multiplicity could be delimited without exclusion – while at the same time excluding himself from the field he thus claims to dominate' (*JG*, p. 104–5). The paradox Weber locates is generated by self-reference. In what way can a discourse, which claims that no hierarchy of discourses exists, give a description of the field of discourses without implying that it exists on a 'higher' level of explanatory power than the discourses it describes?

In *The Differend*, Lyotard discusses self-referential paradox in connection with his first example of a 'differend', the dilemma or 'double bind' which victimizes one party in a legal dispute. Protagoras demands that a fee be paid by one of his students, Euathlus, who refuses, stating that he does not owe his teacher any money because he has never won a case he has argued. Protagoras confronts his former student with the following dilemma. He will take him to court and if he, Protagoras, wins, then Euathlus will owe him the money, but if Euathlus wins, then the latter still owes Protagoras the money, because by winning, Euathlus can no longer say that he has never won a case. 'The paradox', Lyotard writes, 'rests on the faculty a phrase has to take itself as its referent. I did not win, I say it, and in saying it I win.'[7] Lyotard formulates the problem serially. Protagoras's pupil has unsuccessfully argued n litigations; the 'litigation between master and pupil is added to the preceding ones, $n + 1$. When Protagoras takes it into account, he makes $n - n + 1$' (*TD*, p. 7).

This solution works, but only by compounding the original injustice. In the first instance, Protagoras's aggressive use of paradox effectively silences Euathlus, and in the second, the use of logic juridically silences Protagoras. Logic presents itself as the arbiter of difference. It insists that all phrases, if they are to be ordered in a meaningful universe, must be translatable into propositions, so that all discourse may be regulated by one single meta-discourse: logic (*TD*, p. 65). But this regulation is not mediation. What Lyotard diagnoses as the differend does not disappear, it is merely rendered invisible. If in the first instance, one partner of the litigation is made to fall silent, in the second, not only is the second partner silenced, but, since the outcome is labelled a 'solution', the very act of being made to fall silent is silenced. One discourse cannot be translated into the terms of another discourse without loss. The space where that loss occurred is called the differend. If, then, a third discourse claims to be able to adjudicate successfully between the first two discourses, the differend – that original sense of loss – is itself lost. Paradox is not eliminated by logic. It and its effects are rendered invisible although they still exist. Euathlus still says, 'I've never won', in the very moment that he wins.

Self-referential paradox is not the major focus of *The Differend*, the differend is. They are related, however, and given the nature of Lyotard's philosophical project, self-referential paradox is every bit as inevitable as the differend. In his preface, he argues that with the '"linguistic turn" in Western philosophy' and with the 'decline of universalist discourses', the 'time has come to philosophize' (*TD*, p. xiii). With the linguistic turn, traditional problems of philosophy, specifically problems of thought, reflection, and consciousness, are re-written as problems of language. Therefore, since philosophy is a particular discourse, or genre, or 'use' of language, philosophy becomes the linguistic observation of linguistic phenomena, that is, a field of linguistic self-observation. How is this self-observation organized? One can conceive of a universalist, meta-linguistic discourse such as the one which ruled against paradox above – that is able to analyze other discourses without including itself in that which is analyzed. As is well known, however, Lyotard has steadfastly questioned the validity of such a discourse on two grounds. Descriptively, he has questioned the *possibility* of fashioning a meta-discourse which can extricate itself from the field of its observations – as if a discourse could somehow rise above and remain untouched by the language it uses. Prescriptively, he has questioned the *result* of the use of meta-languages, i.e., the formation of differends and their attendant victims. By consistently raising both objections, Lyotard indicates that self-reference and self-referential paradoxes cannot be avoided as easily as the meta-discursive Russellian sleight of hand would have us believe. Lyotard acknowledges that his are meta-linguistic moves – he makes them continually just as I have been making them here – but he gives them 'no logical status' (*TD*, p. 69). He sees them as 'part of ordinary language' (*TD*, p. 76). Therefore, any metalinguistic reference to ordinary language is also a self-reference. If language is subdivided into genres or language games, and in any single language game utterances purport to speak of language as a whole, then they necessarily speak of themselves as well. They may be meta-linguistic utterances by virtue of their claim to speak of the entire entity called language, but they are not meta-linguistic in the sense that they can claim to be above or beyond the consequences of their phrasing. They cannot assert that they are exempt from the rules they utter about language, and they cannot dictate to others without dictating to themselves.

This problem of self-reference is not merely a logical problem, nor is it new. It continually presents itself as the defining problem of modernity. Once the apparently solid, external ground of tradition, God, and the monarchy was replaced by the exercise of rational self-grounding, self-reference in the guises of historicism (all statements, including this one, are historically conditioned), psychoanalysis (all intellectual achievements, including this one, are the result of sublimation), political philosophy (all philosophy, including this one, is ideological), and theoretical analysis (all statements, including this one, are rhetorical) becomes unavoidable. Of course, the 'including this one' clause has generally been excluded: all *other* philosophies are ideological, etc. But if postmodernity can be distinguished from modernity, it is in the various ways that the self-inclusive clause has entered discourses purporting to describe the universe of which they are incontestably a part.

But if discourses are horizontally, not vertically or hierarchically ordered, and if each discourse phrases a distinct universe, independent of and on an equal footing with each other, and if a discourse creates differends whenever it attempts to communicate with another, then what role is left for the discourse of philosophy? By definition, it has no meta-narrative role. It cannot use the traditional rationalist tools of logic, argument, and the assumption of meta-discursive norms to establish the relative validity of other discourse, because in so doing it suppresses – according to Lyotard – what it should not be allowed to suppress. Yet despite philosophy's past claims to preeminence and its affiliations with the politically hegemonic discourse of intellectuals, Lyotard does not shy away from assigning philosophy a specific role. It is no longer the science of all sciences, as speculative idealism would have it, nor the theoretically guided determinant of political action, but rather the guarantor of the inviolability of discursive boundaries. It is designed to protect discourses from being encroached upon by other, self-aggrandizing discourses, and to preserve the evidence of differends – exclusions, silences, victimizations, incomprehensibilities – from obliteration. 'One's responsibility before thought', he concludes in *The Differend*, 'consists . . . in detecting differends and in finding the (impossible) idiom for phrasing them. This is what a philosopher does. An intellectual is someone who helps forget differends ... for the sake of political hegemony' (*TD*, p. 142). At this point, the self-referential paradox Weber located in *Just Gaming* comes back around to bite Lyotard in his rhetorical tail. At the very moment he maintains the radical incommensurability and radical, horizontally-structured autonomy of discourses, he seems to remove one such discourse from the field of play. One does not need to make the deductive, logical move Weber makes to arrive at this conclusion. It is suggested by Lyotard's famous image of the archipelago in his third Kant notice. In this archipelago, Lyotard reports:

> Each genre of discourse would be like an island; the faculty of judgement would be, at least in part, like an admiral or like a provisioner of ships who would launch expeditions from one island to the next, intended to present to one island what was found (or invented, in the archaic sense of the word) in the other, and which might serve the former as an 'as-if intuition' with which to validate it. Whether war or commerce, this interventionist force has no object, and does not have its own island, but it requires a milieu – this would be the sea – the Archipelagos or primary sea as the Aegean was once called. (*TD*, 130–1)

Why does the faculty of judgement not have an island of its own? Is not the exercise of judgement an exercise of language (after the 'linguistic turn'), and therefore is it not a genre, or at least a 'concatenation' of genres, that is, an island, or at least a cluster of islets? Why is this particular language game – judgement – not subject to the same limitations – immobility – as the others?

Lyotard's apparent privileging of the genre of philosophy and the faculty of judgement (over speculative and intellectual modes of discourse) points to a weakness that has often been noticed and variously commented on, either as a hidden nostalgia for unity, or as a self-condemning performative contradiction.[8] The anti-postmodernist critic asks: from what place is this denial of meta-linguistic capabilities uttered if not from a place endowed with meta-linguistic capabilities? Lyotard astonishingly (inadvertently?) answers: from a ship which navigates (impossible?) passages between the islands of discourse. The critic responds: by postulating a discourse which navigates passages between other discourses, you privilege what you say cannot be privileged. Furthermore, you commit a performative contradiction. You can only maintain the inevitability of differends by counterfactually presupposing unity. By defining the stakes of your philosophical project with verbs like 'convince', 'refute', 'defend and illustrate', 'show', and theologically tinged 'bear witness' (*TD*, pp. xii and xiii), you reaffirm the validity of rational argumentation, moral persuasion, and consensus, or at least a consensus about dissonance, difference, and the inevitability of differends. With this disclosure of a performative paradox, the critic closes his or her case. Lyotard's project is exposed as internally incoherent, and no further discussion is deemed necessary. Indeed, his use of the archipelago metaphor can be taken as evidence that he recognizes the inevitable contradictions of a consistently self-referential position. He confronts self-reference – and flinches. He does not seek refuge in a universalist discourse, but he also fails to 'consistently' maintain a self-referential position; as a result, wearing his admiral's cap, he flounders in mid-ocean, fending off the sharks of modernism.

Such, at any rate, is the picture painted of all postmodernist thought by James L. Marsh. In light of the unavoidability of self-contradiction, he writes:

> The post-modernist . . . has the option of either remaining silent or joining fully in the philosophical community. If he opts for the former and moves into a post-rational, post-metaphysical solitude, then there is nothing we can do for him. If he opts for the latter, then we can welcome him back as a Prodigal returned. In making such a return, however, he has to cease being a post-modernist.[9]

Postmodernist discourse, then, is a truly impossible (not just parenthetically impossible) discourse; so impossible, in fact, that it is commanded to disappear. Either speak our language, Marsh declares, or sit down and shut up. But what is meant by Marsh to be a devastating indictment of postmodernism can of course easily be deflected and turned back on itself, for do we not find in his own words a telling enactment of what Lyotard defines as a differend? Doesn't Marsh want to silence his opponent, or at least force 'him' to renounce 'his' heresy and speak the correct idiom? And if Marsh, in the name of Reason, thereby enacts what Lyotard describes, doesn't he affirm the chief postmodernist suspicion about the terrorism of rationalism in the very act of refuting postmodernism? If so, doesn't he come perilously close to performing a contradiction which, by his own criteria, could be construed to condemn him and, by extension, the entire 'philosophical community' to silence? With such an outcome, wouldn't Marsh's postmodernist critic be justified in dusting 'himself' off and smugly saying, 'It takes one to know one!' But where does that leave us? At the gravesite of philosophy? The junkyard of used contradictions?

Lyotard's archipelago can be seen as a snapshot catching the post-modernist in his paradoxical act. In making a global claim about the impossibility of global claims, it depicts the special status enjoyed by the one discourse which claims that no discourse has a special status. The task at hand, then, is to go beyond, on the one hand, mere negation, and on the other, the mere noting of paradox and an accusatorial stance. Any denial of universality utters a truth that falls prey to self-referential paradox and, therefore, given the current climate, to potential paralysis. To get a glimpse of a universe which thrives on self-reference, one can formulate, by developing Luhmann's observations on observation, a contingent universality, which, as the oxymoronic phrase indicates, does not try to avoid paradox, but rather tries to avoid the avoidance of paradox.

The modern European (since about 1600) claim to envision a universal perspective is predicated on distinguishing between thought and thing, mind and matter, spirit and body, the realm of freedom and the realm of necessity. Classical notions of observation assume a clear separation of the human observer from observed nature, and this separation implies that the observer observes from a level distinct from and higher than that which is observed. The human observer is part of nature only in body, not in mind, and mind is the agent of observation. The early twentieth-century logical resolution of paradox is one form of this observational hierarchy. The logician wishing to extricate Euathlus from his dilemma institutes a hierarchical relation between the series of litigations to be observed (n) and the litigation $(n + 1)$ which will observe (and judge) that series. Without this distinction, a clear judgement, valid for all observers, cannot be made. The hierarchical distinction defines a (meta-)language into which all other languages can be translated, a perspective from which all observers may see the same thing. Thus, the logical solution to the problem of self-referential paradox formalizes the model of early modern science, in which the physicist/astronomer is able to determine with God-like precision a discrete and closed system (the solar system, say) with the aid of a few basic mathematical operations, operations which are not applied to the thoughts which manipulate them. The observing mind remains apart from the matter observed. This distinction allows the observer to be thought of as standing quasi-divinely outside of nature and as attaining, in theory, absolute knowledge of it. That the light of the mind may never be able to illuminate every nook and cranny of the universe is blamed on human fallibility, not on the constitutive limits of observation.

Following Luhmann, one might use the term first order observation for this level of empirical observation of an external universe. Kant would argue that it is dogmatic to assert or to reject assumptions based strictly on direct observation. His task, then, is to subject them to a transcendental critique by introducing a second level of observation, an observation of the constitutive nature of observation. He accomplishes this by reproducing the basic observer/observed distinction within the realm of the observer, thereby making self-observation a component of all observation. Kant's analysis of the conditions for the possibility of knowledge is not a simple regress of reflection. In his discussion of the formative media of space and time and the category of causation, he notes how our observation of sense perceptions constitutes the world that these sense perceptions are said to reflect. It is not that observation (mind) creates nature (matter) *ex nihilo*, but that what we know of nature is the observational grid we place on it. Nature is intelligible, not because of a given congruence between mind and nature, but because mind imposes intelligibility on nature by way of fundamental categories. The intelligibility of nature arises because mind (by way of rational reflection and not immediate intellectual intuition) has privileged access to itself, not privileged access to nature. Thus nature, in and of itself, thought of as something essentially separate from us, is in a profound sense unintelligible. We impose intelligibility, but we do this by watching ourselves watch our sense perceptions, without knowing precisely whence these sense perceptions come.

By displacing our knowledge of how we know the world, however, Kant did not alter the accepted scientific knowledge of his day. He speaks in the assured tones of Newtonian mechanics and Euclidean geometry. More to the point, he continues to use the observer/observed distinction to fix the ontological realms of freedom and necessity. It is only in the realm of freedom that self-observation is introduced. The observing mind is not part of the realm of necessity – nature – and nature cannot observe itself – it remains inert. Though consciousness is no longer able to view nature as a simple object standing over and against itself – it knows its own complicity in the construction of the object – it still struggles to free itself from its entanglement with materiality, that is, from the consequences of this complicity, and this struggle is victoriously marked by the construction of a 'transcendental' meta-perspective. In the immediately post-Kantian writings of Schiller, Fichte, and Humboldt, this struggle is not construed as a total denial of the body – though monastic imagery sometimes prevails – but as a triumphant taming of it. The mind/body distinction is reproduced in the realm of mind, where mind overcomes the 'body' of nature by overcoming its own 'body', by purging itself of the influence of materiality, of that which can only be observed. Thus, necessity is brought into conformity with freedom, and the observed universe is stripped of its mute recalcitrance.

If, in the words of Warren Weaver, pre-twentieth-century science was 'largely concerned with two-variable *problems of simplicity*', in which observation was defined as the strict, mathematical determination of the velocity and position of individual bodies, then the philosophical consequences of early twentieth-century science's 'disorganized complexity',[10] in which observation presents itself as the statistical average of large bodies of randomly moving (sub-atomic) particles, plays havoc with the self-assurance of the all-controlling, observing eye. Perhaps more than anything else, Heisenberg's uncertainty principle has come to symbolize this change in the nature of observation. Briefly stated, Heisenberg demonstrated that the precise velocity and position of an individual, sub-atomic particle cannot be measured simultaneously, because the measurement of its position affects its velocity, and the measurement of its velocity affects its position, and that in both cases these changes are unpredictable. This impossibility is not the result of the imperfection of our measuring instruments. It is, as Stephen Hawking puts it, 'a fundamental, inescapable property of the world'. Therefore:

> The uncertainty principle signaled all end to Laplace's dream of a theory of science, a model of the universe that would be completely deterministic: one certainly cannot predict future events exactly if one cannot even measure the present state of the universe precisely! We could still imagine that there is a set of laws that determines events completely for some supernatural being, who could observe the present state of the universe without disturbing it. However, such models of the universe are not of much interest to us ordinary mortals.[11]

Relinquishing the belief in classical determinism does not, of course, mean relinquishing faith in discoverable laws governing the universe. Quantum physics has impressed on us, however, that observation is a physical process using physical tools (such as light waves and neurons) to observe physical processes, and that natural laws govern their mortal, physical discoverers in the same way that they govern the observed universe. If physical processes are said to be physically determined but unpredictable, then the physical processes involved in observation are just as determined but unpredictable as those involved in that which is observed. A complete theory of the universe would then have to account not only for the workings of the universe, but also for the conditions of its own possibility.[12] The picture of observation here becomes undeniably circular. Observers lose their quasi-divine status since the distinction between mind and nature no longer holds in an unqualified manner. Therefore, the aspect of self-observation introduced by Kant cannot be limited to the self-reflection of a consciousness safely embedded in its material base, but must rather encompass a universe no longer neatly divided into distinct domains. As the following passage by the mathematician George Spencer Brown indicates, the universe can thus be envisioned as an amorphous entity straining to see itself from as many angles as possible:

> Let us then consider, for a moment, the world as described by the physicist. It consists of a number of fundamental particles which, if shot through their own space, appear as waves and are thus . . . of the same laminated structure as pearls or onions, and other wave forms called electromagnetic which it is convenient, by Occam's razor, to consider as travelling through space with a standard velocity. All these appear bound by certain natural laws which indicate the form of their relationship.
>
> Now the physicist himself, who describes all this, is, in his own account, himself constructed of it. He is, in short, made of a conglomeration of the very particles he describes, no more, no less, bound together by and obeying such general law as he himself has managed to find and to record.
>
> Thus we cannot escape the fact that the world we know is constructed in order (and thus in such a way as to be able) to see itself.
>
> This is indeed amazing.[13]

Thought of in this way, the observer/observed distinction no longer delineates ontological realms of freedom and necessity, or of thought and physical reality. Rather, it becomes a formal tool the universe uses to observe itself. As Spencer Brown notes, in order to see itself the universe 'must first cut itself up into at least one state which sees, and at least one other state which is seen.' But such self-deformation for the sake of self-observation is of necessity accompanied by blind spots and is therefore incomplete:

> In this severed and mutilated condition, whatever it sees is only partially itself. We may take it that the world undoubtedly is itself (i.e. is indistinct from itself), but, in any attempt to see itself as an object, it must, equally undoubtedly, act so as to make itself distinct from, and therefore false to, itself. In this condition it will always partially elude itself.[14]

It is as if contemporary science has taken the step from Kant to Hegel by incorporating the latter's 'originary paradox' of a consciousness that has to objectify itself – refer to itself as other – in order to become aware of itself.[15]

No matter how aesthetically pleasing and Escher-esque this collapsing of levels may be, however, it can be epistemologically quite unnerving. If one accepts the incompleteness and circularity of observation, how can one frame a theory that can account for its ability to formulate observations on the incomplete and circular nature of observation? Any observation about observation is self-referential and yet, in the form that it takes, implicitly universal. If the claim made by Spencer Brown and others is true – namely, that all observation contains at least implied or collateral aspects of self-observation and is thereby 'false' to itself and will 'always partially elude itself' – how can this claim be made, based as it is on observation? What claim to authority can observation make when observation does not (or does not just) find observables, but creates them, by way of the formal observer/observed distinction. Under these circumstances, is anything that could be called universality still possible?

Although the sciences have only come to thematize self-reference in the twentieth century,[16] the problem of circularity is the basic problem of the self-grounding of modernity. What Lyotard sees, linguistically, as the demise of the grand narratives and the proliferation of incommensurable language games or genres of discourse, Luhmann describes as the shift from a hierarchically structured, stratified society to a horizontally structured, functionally differentiated one. Whereas formerly one part of society – that is, the 'top' part, the aristocracy or the court – assumed the privilege and responsibility of representing the whole, since the eighteenth century this claim has lost its force. In Luhmann's view, as in Lyotard's, the social world has been 'flattened', not in the sense of a general egalitarianism, but in the sense that no single social entity or system enjoys a fixed relationship of hierarchical dominance over all the others as in pre-modern, 'feudal' societies. That is to say, each system is irreducible. No system can take over the functions of any other system, nor can a system subordinate the functioning of any other system to its own. 'We live,' Luhmann writes,

> in a society which cannot represent its unity within itself, because this would contradict the logic of functional differentiation. We live in a society without a top and without a centre. The unity of society no longer appears within this society.[17]

Luhmann would, then, agree with Adorno that we live in an 'administered' society, if we can read 'administered' to mean functionally differentiated. He would not agree, however, that everything can be reduced to the economic as a 'commodity', nor would he grant that the aesthetic, or any other social system or mode of communication, provides an outside, i.e., a non-administered, non-functionally differentiated perspective from which to critique society:

> Even the criticisms of society must be carried out within society. Even the planning of society must be carried out within society. Even the description of society must be carried out within society. And all this occurs as the criticism of a society which criticizes itself, as the planning of society which plans itself and always reacts to what happens, and as the description of a society which describes itself.[18]

This loss of a hierarchical top or perspective from which to write universal narrative, as found not just in contemporary philosophy but also in the philosophy of science, serves as a springboard for Lyotard's war on totalizing theory.[19] Luhmann nevertheless agrees that the only way to come to terms with the paradox of observing and describing the system from within the system is to pursue the project of universal theory, but to accept self-reference as an unavoidable conceptual cornerstone and methodological procedure. For Luhmann, the explicit acknowledgment of self-reference distinguishes theories which can make claims to universality from those which cannot. Universal theories do not claim absolute vision, as if a totality of systems could be seen from somewhere outside that totality, but rather include themselves in the domain they observe. For example, a sociological theory of social systems must acknowledge and examine the social subsystem of sociology in its investigations, just as a physical theory of the universe must acknowledge the physical basis of the system (brain/mind) which derived the physical laws governing the universe.[20] In other words, universal theories subject themselves to their own laws.

The discipline of sociology has had to grapple with the problem of self-reference almost from its inception. It surfaced as the problem of historicism and is usually found under the heading of the sociology of knowledge. Even so, theories of the social construction of knowledge have, in the past, evaded exploring their own social constructedness. Notions of the free-floating intelligentsia, the historical subject, the critique of ideology, communicative action, and even, to a certain extent, the Foucauldian power/resistance distinction have provided an explicit or implicit promise of an unblemished perspective from which to perceive the blemishes of others.[21]

As a social philosopher unabashedly interested in the possibility of a general theory of social systems,[22] Luhmann has been inexorably pushed to consider the recurrent epistemological problem of paradox.[23] Therefore, he is concerned with devising a sufficiently abstract, universal theory that is capable of acknowledging, on a formal level, the constructed – that is, 'blemished' or limited – nature of radically constructivist theories. Since self-reference, or self-observation, is that which both limits and universalizes theoretical considerations, Luhmann has increasingly focused on the nature of observation in his most recent writings. His discussions can be read both as an elaboration of Spencer Brown's contention that the universe 'cuts itself up' in order to observe itself and as a more detailed account of Lyotard's notion that a phrase 'presents' a universe, a universe which includes the addressor of that phrase as a construction of the phrase.

Following Spencer Brown's operational logic, Luhmann defines observation[24] as the ability to mark and label unmarked space, to make left/right, inside/outside, foreground/background distinctions and label them in such a way as to construct an observable universe.[25] These distinctions enable observables to materialize, but they cannot be perceived by the observers who use them. They serve as blind spots, the unseen ground from which a world can be seen. Observers can be aware of the contingency of their activity. They can know *that* there is something they cannot know, but, as Luhmann is fond of saying, they cannot know *what* they cannot know.

With this relatively simple and not unfamiliar model,[26] Luhmann hopes to show that organized complexity can evolve and be observed without an appeal to logically or metaphysically determined hierarchies of perspective. There are 'levels' of observation, but these levels are not distinguished qualitatively. Second order observers can observe the blind spots of other observers by utilizing their enabling distinctions, with the result that a social network of observers of observers evolves, observing what other observers cannot observe, and having what they cannot observe be observed. But no matter whether we are dealing with first order, 'naïve' observation (of 'objects'), or observation of observation, or observation of observation of observation and so on *ad infinitum*, the mechanism of observation remains the same.[27] Observation – the construction of a visible universe – proceeds by way of enabling distinctions and exclusions, that is, by way of what constitutively remains invisible. The 'angle' or 'perspective' achieved, the particular universe which is thus 'presented,' is determined by what remains latent.

The problem of observing latencies, Luhmann maintains, has been *the* – at times unrecognized, at times disowned – epistemological problem of the past two hundred years. It has manifested itself as the Marxist critique of ideology, as Freudian psychoanalysis, and as the sociology of knowledge, but in such manifestations latencies have not been seen as the necessary, enabling blind spot for the production of knowledge. Rather, they have traditionally been interpreted in Enlightenment fashion as *error*, as a deformation of knowledge which can be cleared up, illuminated, brought to the light of day and cured.[28] Once one understands the nature of observation, however, one is forced to recognize, formally, the contingent nature of such universal models. The original procedure – Spencer Brown's command, 'Draw a distinction. . . . Call it the first distinction'[29] – is itself made within a space marked by the unseen and unseeable distinction which allows for the conceptualization of observation to begin with. The phrase which calls forth the observable world is already made within that world. Observation, from its very 'beginning', can only be carried on within the field of observation. It can never observe the unmarked space that is constructed as its origin.[30] Once one accepts that the injunction to observe from its very inception is enmeshed in a paradox that unfolds over time but never resolves or becomes transparent to itself, then one is forced to acknowledge that the Enlightenment, simple-system, Newtonian ideal of observation gives way to more complex, statistical, and 'uncertain' models in which the illumination of shadows casts its own shadow and every gain in information, every gain in order is accompanied by loss and increased disorder.[31]

All of which causes Luhmann to wonder why Lyotard, who appeals to the same critique of Enlightenment science and of Enlightenment presumption to an Archimedean perspective, is still tempted to think the 'unity of the difference' and phrase his version of the inevitability of latency in terms of a 'victimology'. From Marx to Lyotard, Luhmann writes, 'the excluded is determined as a class or in some other way observed as human, mourned, and reclaimed for society. Were society to respond, as demanded, to this complaint, it would still not become a society that excluded nothing.'[32] It would always produce further 'silences' and further exclusions, for exclusions cannot be thought except by way of exclusion. Any attempt to think the unity produces an excess that cannot be contained in the unity of thought. 'If one wants to observe unity', Luhmann writes, 'difference appears. Whoever pursues goals produces side effects.'[33] In a word, bearing witness to the differend produces its own differend. In response, Lyotard would bemoan the lack of a sensitivity to the singularity of loss, the lack of feeling for the sublime. 'The sublime', Lyotard notes, 'does not exist for Luhmann. And if it did exist, it would in any case be destined to become incorporated.'[34] For

Luhmann, paradoxical circularity cannot be avoided by appeals to the outside; what escapes the system can only be observed, and therefore communicated, from within the system, and that which can be communicated is, by definition, part of the system. The 'sublime', once it is distinguished and designated, becomes an element of the space from which it is observed. For the systematizer, no matter how the system may be conceived, there is no 'call', no prescriptive, no obligation which is not marked by the immanent distinctions that confine us. But Lyotard fears that without such an unmediated reminder coming from the unknown and unmarked space beyond the realm of communication, a morally and politically worthwhile sense of justice is impossible.

So, what distinguishes Lyotard and Luhmann can be best described by what is at stake – to frame it in Lyotard's terms – in their arguments. Given the collapse of the grand narrative of knowledge, originally built on an ontology which claimed to provide a solid ground for physical reality, Luhmann is in search of an epistemologically consistent – and that means unavoidably paradoxical – theory of the evolution and function of social systems. Lyotard, on the other hand, celebrates and mourns the collapse of the grand narrative of emancipation by searching for a non-foundational foundation for political action. It is this search for a viable politics in a 'post-political' world that has led him to at once stray into and shy away from the minefield of self-referential paradox. These stakes make for a certain incommensurability between their two discourses, but for those observing the contemporary quarrels between the 'project of modernity' and the 'postmodern condition', perhaps any future Franco-German debate worth having in the 1990s (and beyond) will *not* be the one between hermeneutics and deconstruction, *nor* the one between rational consensus and anarchical resistance, but the one between an epistemologically correct, self-referential, constitutively incomplete systematicity and a politically correct, negatively theological, fragmented asystematicity, the one between a contingent universality and an impossible particularity. So far this debate has only taken place obliquely, in fragments and asides. May it, in the future, develop more systematically.

Notes

1   See, for example, Jürgen Habermas, *Theory and Practice*, trans. Jeremy Shapiro (London: Heinemann, 1974) and *Communication and the Evolution of Society*, trans. Thomas McCarthy (London: Heinemann, 1979). (NL)

2   Jean-François Lyotard and Jean-Loup Thébaud, *Just Gaming*, trans. Wlad Godzich, *Theory and History of Literature* 20 (Minneapolis: Minnesota University Press, 1985), p. 21. Hereafter cited parenthetically in the text as *JG*.

3   Jean-François Lyotard, *The Postmodern Condition: A Report on Knowledge*, trans Geoff Bennington and Brian Massumi, *Theory and History of Literature* 10 (Minneapolis: Minnesota University Press, 1984), p. 43. [The 'incompleteness theorem' refers to an essay published in 1931 by the German mathematician Kurt Gödel, entitled 'On Formally Undecidable Propositions of Principia Mathematica and Related Systems'. (NL)]

4   Ibid., p. 61.

5   Acknowledging that in his analysis he starts from a description, he denies that he draws any prescriptions from it. Referring to the Kantian notion of 'Idea' (of reason, as opposed to concept of the understanding), he writes: 'I start with a description, and what one can do with a description . . . is to extend, or maximize, as much as possible what one believes to be contained in the description. . . . And the idea that emerges is that there is a multiplicity of small narratives. And from that, "one ought to be pagan", means "one must maximize as much as possible the multiplication of small narratives"' (*JG*, p. 59). Why the imperative to maximize is not a prescription is not altogether clear. [For more on this point, see the discussion of Lyotard in my *PomoIntro*, esp. pp. 57–94. (NL)]

6   Samuel Weber, 'Afterword: Literature – Just Making It', *JG*, p. 104.

7   Jean-François Lyotard, *The Differend: Phrases in Dispute*, trans. Georges Van Den Abbeele, *Theory and History of Literature* 46 (Minneapolis: Minnesota University Press, 1988), p. 6. Hereafter cited parenthetically within the text as *TD*.

8   For Derrida's critique of a reconstituted 'we' in Lyotard, and for the general nervousness shared by both Derrida and Lyotard over the issue of nostalgia see *The Lyotard Reader*, ed. Andrew Benjamin (Oxford: Blackwell, 1989), pp. 386–9. See also Alain Badiou's critique and Lyotard's response in *Témoigner du différend: quad phraser ne se peut*, ed. Pierre-Jean Labarrière (Paris: Osiris, 1989), pp. 109–13, 118–21. (My thanks to Andreas Michel for pointing this source out to me.) The most thoroughgoing critique of Lyotard in the Habermasian vein can be found in Manfred Frank's *Die Grenzen der Verständigung: Ein Geistergespräch zwischen Lyotard and Habermas* (Frankfurt/Main: Suhrkamp, 1988), but see also John McGowan, *Postmodernism and Its Critics* (Ithaca: Cornell University Press, 1991), pp. 180–91.

9   James L. Marsh, 'Strategies of Evasion: The Paradox of Self-Referentiality and the Post-Modern Critique of Rationality', *International Philosophical Quarterly* 29 (1989), p. 349.

10 Warren Weaver, 'Science and Complexity', *American Scientist* 36 (1948), p. 537.

11 Stephen Hawking, *A Brief History of Time: From the Big Bang to Black Holes* (New York: Bantam, 1990), p. 55.

12 Ibid., p. 12.

13 George Spencer Brown, *Laws of Form* (London: Allen and Unwin, 1969), pp. 104–5.

14 Ibid., p. 105.

15 See Howard P. Kainz, *Paradox, Dialectic, and System: A Contemporary Reconstruction of the Hegelian Problematic* (University Park: Pennsylvania State University Press, 1988), pp. 22–34 and 109–10, where Kainz refers to Hegel's philosophy as 'the most massive and sustained instance in the history of philosophy of the systematic dialectical development of a conceptual paradox.'

16 On self-reference in twentieth-century mathematics and physics and its relationship to literature, see N. Katherine Hayles, *The Cosmic Web: Scientific Field Models and Literary Strategies in the 20th Century* (Ithaca: Cornell University Press, 1984), esp. the introduction and first chapter, pp. 15–59.

17 Niklas Luhmann, 'The Representation of Society Within Society', in *Political Theory in the Welfare State*, trans. John Bednarz Jr. (Berlin: Walter de Gruyter, 1990), p. 16.

18 Ibid., p. 17. See also his 'Tautology and Paradox in the Self-Descriptions of Modern Society', in *Essays on Self-Reference* (New York: Columbia, 1990), pp. 123–43.

19 His attack on Habermas in *The Postmodern Condition* is by now familiar to all. For a critique of Lyotard's use of science, see N. Katherine Hayles, *Chaos Bound: Orderly Disorder in Contemporary Literature and Science* (Ithaca: Cornell University Press, 1990), pp. 215–16. [Moreover, for a critique of Lyotard's use of art, see my *PomoIntro*, pp. 172–82. (NL)]

20 Niklas Luhmann, *Soziale Systeme: Grundriß einer allgemeinen Theorie* (Frankfurt/Main: Suhrkamp, 1984), pp. 9–10, 33–4 and esp. 650–3. Luhmann makes reference to the same passage in Spencer Brown cited above.

21 Niklas Luhmann, *Die Wissenschaft der Gesellschaft* (Frankfurt/Main: Suhrkamp, 1990), pp. 68–72.

22 Luhmann, *Soziale Systeme*, pp. 7–14.

23 See Niklas Luhmann, 'The Cognitive Program of Constructivism and a Reality that Remains Unknown', *Selforganization: Portrait of a Scientific Revolution*, eds. W. Krohn et al. *Sociology of the Sciences* 14 (Dordrecht: Kluwer, 1990), p. 64; see also his 'Sthenographie und Euryalistik', *Paradoxien, Dissonanzen, Zusammenbüche: Situationen offener Epistemologie*, eds Hans Ulrich Gumbrecht and K. Ludwig Pfeiffer (Frankfurt/Main: Suhrkamp, 1991), pp. 58–63.

24 For a brief overview in English of Luhmann's notions of observation, see his *Ecological Communication*, trans. John Bednarz, Jr. (Chicago: Chicago University Press, 1989), pp. 22–7. For a more comprehensive view, see *Wissenschaft*, pp. 68–121.

25   Referring to communication, the medium for the self-reproduction of all social systems, Lumann writes: 'Therefore, self-reference is nothing but reference to this distinction between hetero-reference and self-reference. And whereas auto-referentiality could be seen as a one-value thing and could be described by a logic with two values only, the case of social systems is a case of much higher complexity because its self-reference (1) is based on an ongoing auto-referential (autopoietic) process which refers to itself (2) as processing the distinction between itself (3) and its topics. If such a system didn't have an environment it would have to invent it as the horizon of its auto-referentiality.' 'The Autopoiesis of Social Systems', *Essays on Self-Reference*, p. 4. See also his *Wissenschaft* (for example, pp. 407–8 and 412) and his *Beobachtungen der Moderne* (Opladen: Westdeutscher Verlag, 1992), pp. 26–7 and *passim*.

26   Though Luhmann relies on Spencer Brown's operational logic and Heinz von Foerster's second order cybernetics for his operational distinctions, his affinity with certain strains of poststructural thought is apparent. The terminology of 'blind spots' calls Paul de Man immediately to mind, but see also Stanley Fish, 'Critical Self-Consciousness, Or Can We Know What We're Doing?', in *Doing What Comes Naturally: Change, Rhetoric, and the Practice of Theory in Literary and Legal Studies* (Durham: Duke University Press, 1989), pp. 436–67. For Luhmann's affinities with Derrida, see Robert Platt, 'Reflexivity, Recursion and Social Life: Elements for a Postmodern Sociology,' *The Sociological Review* 37 (1989), pp. 636–67. [For more on the Luhmann–Derrida connection, see Drucilla Cornell, *The Philosophy of the Limit* (New York and London: Routledge, 1992), esp. ch. 5. (NL)]

27   Luhmann, *Wissenschaft*, pp. 87 and 110.

28   Ibid., pp. 90–1.

29   Brown, *Laws*, p. 3.

30   See Luhmann, *Wissenschaft*, pp. 84 and 189–94. See also Luhmann and Peter Fuchs, *Reden und Schweigen* (Frankfurt/Main: Suhrkamp, 1989), pp. 23–6, on the impossibility of thinking transcendence except from within immanence.

31   For a dramatic image of the loss which accompanies every gain in order, see Hawking, *Brief History*, pp. 152–3.

32   Luhmann and Fuchs, *Reden*, p. 20.

33   Luhmann, *Wissenschaft*, p. 194 (author's translation).

34   Jean-François Lyotard and Christine Pries, 'Das Undarstellbare – wider das Vergessen: ein Gespräch zwischen Jean-François Lyotard und Christine Pries', *Das Erhabene: Zwischen Grenzerfahrung und Größenwahn*, ed. Christine Pries (Weinheim: VCH, Acta Humaniora, 1989), p. 338 (author's translation). Luhmann concurs with Lyotard's assessment: see Luhmann, Frederick D. Bunsen, and Dirk Baecker, *Unbeobachtbare Welt: Über Kunst und Architektur* (Bielefeld: Haux, 1990), p. 66.

Chapter Nineteen Preface to *Anti-Oedipus*

Michel Foucault

During the years 1945–1965 (I am referring to Europe), there was a certain way of thinking correctly, a certain style of political discourse, a certain ethics of the intellectual. One had to be on familiar terms with Marx, not let one's dreams stray too far from Freud.[1] And one had to treat sign-systems – the signifier – with the greatest respect. These were the three requirements that made the strange occupation of writing and speaking a measure of truth about oneself and one's time acceptable.

Then came the five brief, impassioned, jubilant, enigmatic years. At the gates of our world, there was Vietnam, of course, and the first major blow to the powers that be. But here, inside our walls, what exactly was taking place? An amalgam of revolutionary and anti-repressive politics? A war fought on two fronts: against social exploitation and psychic repression? A surge of libido modulated by the class struggle? Perhaps. At any rate, it is this familiar, dualistic interpretation that has laid claim to the events of those years. The dream that cast its spell, between the First World War and fascism, over the dreamiest parts of Europe – the Germany of Wilhelm Reich, and the France of the surrealists – had returned and set fire to reality itself: Marx and Freud in the same incandescent light.

But is that really what happened? Had the utopian project of the thirties been resumed, this time on the scale of historical practice? Or was there, on the contrary, a movement toward political struggles that no longer conformed to the model that Marxist tradition had prescribed? Toward an experience and a technology of desire that were no longer

Michel Foucault, 'Preface' to Gilles Deleuze and Félix Guattari, *Anti-Oedipus: Capitalism and Schizophrenia*, trans. Robert Hurley, Mark Seem and Helen R. Lane (Minneapolis: University of Minnesota Press, 1983), pp. xi–xiv.

Freudian. It is true that the old banners were raised, but the combat shifted and spread into new zones.

Anti-Oedipus shows first of all how much ground has been covered. But it does much more than that. It wastes no time in discrediting the old idols, even though it does have a great deal of fun with Freud. Most important, it motivates us to go further.

It would be a mistake to read *Anti-Oedipus* as *the* new theoretical reference (you know, that much-heralded theory that finally encompasses everything, that finally totalizes and reassures, the one we are told we 'need so badly' in our age of dispersion and specialization where 'hope' is lacking). One must not look for a 'philosophy' amid the extraordinary profusion of new notions and surprise concepts: *Anti-Oedipus* is not a flashy Hegel. I think that *Anti-Oedipus* can best be read as an 'art', in the sense that is conveyed by the term 'erotic art', for example. Informed by the seemingly abstract notions of multiplicities, flows, arrangements, and connections, the analysis of the relationship of desire to reality and to the capitalist 'machine' yields answers to concrete questions. Questions that are less concerned with why this or that than with *how* to proceed. How does one introduce desire into thought, into discourse, into action? How can and must desire deploy its forces within the political domain and grow more intense in the process of overturning the established order? *Ars erotica, ars theoretica, ars politica.*

Whence the three adversaries confronted by *Anti-Oedipus*. Three adversaries who do not have the same strength, who represent varying degrees of danger, and whom the book combats in different ways:

1. The political ascetics, the sad militants, the terrorists of theory, those who would preserve the pure order of politics and political discourse. Bureaucrats of the revolution and civil servants of Truth.

2. The poor technicians of desire-psychoanalysts and semiologists of every sign and symptom – who would subjugate the multiplicity of desire to the twofold law of structure and lack.

3. Last but not least, the major enemy, the strategic adversary is fascism (whereas *Anti-Oedipus*' opposition to the others is more of a tactical engagement). And not only historical fascism, the fascism of Hitler and Mussolini – which was able to mobilize and use the desire of the masses so effectively – but also the fascism in us all, in our heads and in our everyday behavior, the fascism that causes us to love power, to desire the very thing that dominates and exploits us.

I would say that *Anti-Oedipus* (may its authors forgive me) is a book of ethics, the first book of ethics to be written in France in quite a long time (perhaps that explains why its success was not limited to a particular 'readership': being anti-oedipal has become a life style, a way of thinking and living). How does one keep from being fascist, even (especially) when one believes oneself to be a revolutionary militant? How do we rid our speech and our acts, our hearts and our pleasures, of fascism? How do we ferret out the fascism that is ingrained in our behavior? The Christian moralists sought out the traces of the flesh lodged deep within the soul. Deleuze and Guattari, for their part, pursue the slightest traces of fascism in the body.

Paying a modest tribute to Saint Francis de Sales,[2] one might say that *Anti-Oedipus* is an *Introduction to the Non-Fascist Life*.

This art of living counter to all forms of fascism, whether already present or impending, carries with it a certain number of essential principles which I would summarize as follows if I were to make this great book into a manual or guide to everyday life:

- Free political action from all unitary and totalizing paranoia.
- Develop action, thought, and desires by proliferation, juxtaposition, and disjunction, and not by subdivision and pyramidal hierarchization.
- Withdraw allegiance from the old categories of the Negative (law, limit, castration, lack, lacuna), which Western thought has so long held sacred as a form of power and an access to reality. Prefer what is positive and multiple, difference over uniformity, flows over unities, mobile arrangements over systems. Believe that what is productive is not sedentary but nomadic.
- Do not think that one has to be sad in order to be militant, even though the thing one is fighting is abominable. It is the connection of desire to reality (and not its retreat into the forms of representation) that possesses revolutionary force.
- Do not use thought to ground a political practice in Truth; nor political action to discredit, as mere speculation, a line of thought. Use political practice as an intensifier of thought, and analysis as a multiplier of the forms and domains for the intervention of political action.
- Do not demand of politics that it restore the 'rights' of the individual, as philosophy has defined them. The individual is the product of power. What is needed is to 'de-individualize' by means of multiplication and

displacement, diverse combinations. The group must not be the organic bond uniting hierarchized individuals, but a constant generator of de-individualization.

• Do not become enamored of power.

It could even be said that Deleuze and Guattari care so little for power that they have tried to neutralize the effects of power linked to their own discourse. Hence the games and snares scattered throughout the book, rendering its translation a feat of real prowess. But these are not the familiar traps of rhetoric; the latter work to sway the reader without his being aware of the manipulation, and ultimately win him over against his will. The traps of *Anti-Oedipus* are those of humour: so many invitations to let oneself be put out, to take one's leave of the text and slam the door shut. The book often leads one to believe it is all fun and games, when something essential is taking place, something of extreme seriousness: the tracking down of all varieties of fascism, from the enormous ones that surround and crush us to the petty ones that constitute the tyrannical bitterness of our everyday lives.

Notes

1 On this point, see my *PomoIntro*, p. 194; for a discussion of Foucault's 'Preface', see also pp. 192–3 and 204–10. (NL)

2 A seventeenth-century priest and Bishop of Geneva, known for his *Introduction to the Devout Life*.

Chapter Twenty Analytic Ethics

Alec McHoul

This investigation turns to the question of effective semiotics as a social-historical practice and, in particular, it attempts to find the limits of (or the possibilities of) an ethics for semiotic analysis. So far in *Semiotic Investigations*, there has been very little concern with questions of ethics. This is because its effective semiotics has been grounded in the idea of providing empirical *descriptions* of community-based forms of semiosis. It has, precisely, refrained from such generalizing questions as those concerning 'meaning' and 'community', let alone 'the good', 'the right' or 'the proper'. However, at the end of the previous chapter ('Converse Communities'), a particular problem arose from the analysis of *inter*-communitarian communications. That is, it becomes difficult in such cases not to position oneself as analyst in relation to the radical differences which such forms of communication display. In that chapter, while analysing one of Coulter's transcripts, in which a mental welfare officer attempted to have a prospective patient admitted to a mental hospital against his wishes,[1] I placed myself clearly on the side of the patient, against the welfare officer. Bogen and Lynch, referring to an earlier version of that analysis, it seems, were quite right to point out that I probably would not have placed myself so easily on the side of a 'recalcitrant witness' testifying before Joint Committees of Congress concerning his role in 'US covert operations'.[2] But on what grounds? – how, then, to choose between the anonymous patient and (if that's what he is, as he is for Bogen and Lynch) the infamous Oliver North?

That is, if effective semiotics is to make (or at least supply an analytic

Alec McHoul, 'Analytic Ethics', in *Semiotic Investigations: Towards an Effective Semiotics* (Lincoln and London: University of Nebraska Press, 1996), pp. 191–211. (The present version has been slightly revised by the author.)

basis for) political interventions, can it afford, in Bogen and Lynch's words, to be completely 'libertarian'? Would it, that is, be happy to place itself at the disposal of any forms of transgression and resistance no matter what? I think not – but I do not yet have any grounds for making the distinction. Purely intuitively though, it seems right, good and proper to see how Coulter's patient might have used tactical talk to resist incarceration; and so for me to promote and disseminate information to others about his strategies – and it seems equally wrong, bad and improper to align myself with the resistances of such persons as Oliver North and to promote and disseminate information about how *they* might manipulate the semiotics of the courtroom to good advantage. The same problems might occur on a larger political scale. Thus it seems to me intuitively right to support Jewish activists who face religious oppression from the extreme Right. Yet it seems equally wrong for the Australian, Canadian and German governments to deny the historian, David Irving, the right to enter their countries to speak sceptically of the historical basis for this oppression. (It seems even worse, to me, that one of those countries should make holocaust scepticism a criminal offence.) And it seems equally right to support the Palestinian people in their struggles against an invading Israeli state war-machine, without condoning any and every action that might be undertaken towards that end. But where, today, are the ethical grounds on which we make such decisions? The problems of an analytic ethics, then, seem to be but a sub-version of general ethics.

If we turn to philosophical ethics today, we find a paradox or a series of them. To begin with – and this will be a general theme in what follows – Caputo reminds us of the dangers and problems surrounding so-called 'postmodern' ethics. Having previously supported such a position, Caputo goes on to construct an argument against philosophical ethics altogether:

> I have up to now always tried to strike a more respectable pose [than being 'against ethics']. Having consorted in the past chiefly with mystics and saints, I have always made it my business to defend ethics, a more originary ethics, an ethics of *Gelassenheit* and letting be, an ethics of dissemination, a veritable postmodern ethics. I have always protested that if I traffic with anarchy, it is a very responsible anarchy.[3]

A 'responsible anarchy'? This is a paradox in itself. What Caputo calls 'postmodern ethics' continually ceases to be a positive ethics as it yo-yos out towards anarchism and letting be, so that anything goes, but then reels itself back in again as it encounters fascism, patriarchy (and a host of other insupportables) and realizes that 'anything goes' can also mean that 'everything stays', that 'responsible anarchy' means conservatism, non-intervention and a politics of zero transgression. But this is only part of the paradox.

If we turn to the last works of Foucault, we find there an historical argument about the positioning of morality and ethics today.[4] Although the first volume of the *History of Sexuality* is quite different from the two following it, comparing all three opens a stark contrast between ancient Greek and Roman ethics and post-nineteenth century morality. Today, and since the early nineteenth century at least, Foucault argues, we have been in the grip of an increasing legislation of personal practice. In relation to sexuality in particular, a whole host of legal, social scientific, medical and criminological discourses have divided bodily acts into categories with values. An array of sexual and perversionary types has come into being to define and police our conduct. This is a morality in the true sense while, at the same time, its bases are far from absolute or fixed. Instead, the forms of power are distributed and diversified; but all the more to intensify the grip of corporeal control over the minutest of practices and thoughts. (So it's hard to resist the thought that relativist resistance plays right into the hands of modern relativist power.)

By contrast, there was very little direct legislation in ancient Greece over sexual and other forms of personal comportment. At least for 'free men', as opposed to women and slaves, it would seem as if – legislatively at least – all were free to practise sexual acts as they saw fit. However, they did not see fit to act in just any way. A 'culture' of ethics – considered as the relation which a man bore towards himself in terms of his relations with others (boys, his wife, the household and the body politic of the city itself) – grew up. Hence, free men in ancient Greece regulated their conduct in truly *ethical* ways – there is no need to give the full details here – rather than by the coercion of moral codes. Only with Christianity (which Foucault shows to have misread many of the ancient teachings on chastity, virtue, and so on) did there arise an intense focus on sexual acts themselves. Only then did the catalogues of correct and incorrect behaviours come to be written as moral manuals. In this sense, according to Foucault, today we have perfectly knowable and complex forms of scientific regulation (for example, what Foucault calls the *scientia sexualis*), but we have lost the art of governing ourselves, an *ars erotica*.

If we put this into the picture which Caputo draws of philosophical ethics today – a picture which confronts *inter alia* the positive ethical traditions of Kant, Hegel and Levinas – we can begin to see the larger paradox I mentioned earlier. Everywhere there is (philosophical and pseudo-philosophical) ethics, forming mostly as an emergent pluralist-relativist 'responsible anarchy', a postmodern ethics which celebrates the absence of absolutes and ethical positivities. Yet, practical or effective ethics in Foucault's sense (as a positive relation of the self to the self and others) is almost completely absent and has been displaced by moral legislation forming around highly diverse loci of power and resistances to power. This has led to some quite peculiar situations of which I'll mention only two.

At one stage, Foucault himself began to embrace a radically liberal ethics, arguing that all forms of criminal legislation (including laws against rape) should be abolished. According to one of his biographers, after 1982, he even entered into regular discussions with the French justice minister, Robert Badinter, on proposals for officially reforming the Penal Code along these lines – in fact, proposals for its abolition.[5] Earlier still, he had supported the Iranian revolution as a great popular uprising against the repressions of the Shah's régime – and he continued to support the Khomeini government after the revolution despite its own (arguably much more vicious) forms of oppression and genocide.[6] He saw in Iran 'one of the greatest populist explosions in human history'.[7] What these allegiances show is that an ethics resistive to moral legislation in all and any of its forms, an ethics based on 'the will not to be governed', runs into all of the paradoxes and problems of, again very loosely, postmodern ethics.[8] If French rapists and murdering Mullahs are included under the general umbrella of such liberal populism, then again anything goes and all sorts of barbarity remain. The return to an extreme ethics of individual liberty (which is the logical end of Foucault's investigation) is simply that: a return to the possibility of an absolute morality. But, to reiterate the paradox: in the absence of absolute canons of action, can any ethics at all (and especially, for us here, an ethics of analysis) be constructed?

My second practical instance of ethical paradoxy arises in some fields of feminism. Jane Flax puts the problem succinctly when she asks how it's possible to be both a feminist and what she too calls a 'postmodernist'.[9] To be a feminist, she argues, requires a positive ethics of opposition to patriarchal forms, in all of their diversity. It requires something essential in terms of a view of the world which stops short of *laissez faire* politics. On the other hand, as we have seen, what is known as postmodernism points in the opposite direction: towards 'letting be', tolerance of whatever happens. So can she be a feminist and yet tolerate everything, including patriarchal oppression? No easy solution to the paradox is available –

and Flax does not offer us one. However, Rosi Braidotti argues that the feminine, as a positive destiny for women, must be asserted and essentialized, against her own better 'philosophical' judgment.[10] It's necessary as a purely practical and pragmatic 'essence', for without it, feminism will be directionless as a political movement for social change. Hence another paradox: this version of feminism uses relativist ethics as a first step towards surmounting patriarchal normativity and then reinstalls a different normativity without applying the same ethical critique to it.

From these two brief examples, we can begin to see a crisis forming in ethics and its relation to that brand of contemporary relativism for which the term 'postmodernism' is one convenient shorthand.[11] What disturbs me most about this situation is that a complete relativism appears to play into the hands of any form of social control (for example, a church, a legislature, a government or a father) which may, itself, be arbitrary and relativist as well as totalitarian.

So, *in extremis*, absolutist ethics (that is, morality) is nothing more than normativity in the form of political-moral legislation; but relativist and resistive ethics has no basis for discerning good from bad conduct and so allows arbitrary and groundless punishments for whatever might, as the situation arises, come to count as a transgression. It can't argue against (and it certainly can't prevent) cutting off the adulterous hand. In ethics today, it seems, indeterminacy is just as 'bad' (or as 'good') as certainty.

One possible solution to the paradoxical positions which postmodern ethics seems to entail would be to give up on 'professional' ethics altogether, and to argue for the complete unspeakability of ethical positivities. This was Wittgenstein's inclination:

> My whole tendency and I believe the tendency of all men who ever tried to write or talk on Ethics or Religion was to run against the boundaries of language. This running against the walls of our cage is perfectly, absolutely hopeless. Ethics so far as it springs from the desire to say something about the meaning of life, the absolute good, the absolute valuable, can be no science. What it says does not add to our knowledge in any sense. But it is a document of a tendency in the human mind which I personally cannot help respecting deeply and I would not for my life ridicule it.[12]

But again there is a further paradox here: any 'tendency in the human mind' which is so deeply respected is presumably, in itself, a good or something very close to good – so that even injunctions against ethics may be read as quasi-ethical precepts and, at the very least, in terms of value. By contrast with Wittgenstein then, my own urge comes from a distrust of tight oppositions; such as those between philosophy and life (or 'professional' and 'private' ethics), practice and analysis, the speakable and the unspeakable and so on. And it is accompanied by the hope that, in ethics, an analytic failure (a necessary failure, if Wittgenstein is to be believed) can show where some important, even if unspeakable, limits and possibilities could possibly lie. Not only this: for the Wittgensteinian dissolution of ethical talk leaves us with no way to clear up any practical ethical case in hand – such as the decision between the cases of Coulter's mental patient and Oliver North's. In this respect, it is of as little use to me as what Caputo and Flax call 'postmodernism'.

Returning then to the term 'postmodernism' and its implication that it should perhaps come 'after' something, Ferenc Feher asks the deceptively simple question: 'After what?'[13] This can be a question about intellectual chronology or, more to the point, it can ask what postmodernism might be *after*, what its goal might be. I assume that behind the question is a concern with the forms – or even the very possibility – of social life after the presumed deaths of God, Man, Culture, Economy, Logos and the rest. That is, for all that these and the other certitudes may have broken down, none of the writers we have looked at so far (Caputo, Foucault, Flax, Braidotti, Wittgenstein) seems to have publicly embraced a total and numbing relativism – none of them has quite given up to the void, or to 'the swarm of particulars' as philosophers once called it. For all that they may flirt with them, radical personalism, let alone solipsism, are by no means popular among these diverse thinkers of twentieth-century ethics. This suggests that a space, a supplement, may still be left over for some kind of positive ethical thesis, or at least for an affirmation. In fact it suggests that it may be impossible to completely delete all traces of essence, centre and positivity from anything which passes by the name of 'ethics', including counter-ethics. But, it has to be admitted, nevertheless, that the prognosis is not good if we are expecting a 'postmodern' ethics (to continue the shorthand) to be a traditional didactic system of moral positivities.

Is it possible that postmodernism's ethical dilemmas stem from its unique onto-epistemological positioning as a general, rather than a specifically ethical, theory? For postmodernism (along with its more respectable cousin, poststructuralism) appears to want to avoid both objectivism and subjectivism when it comes to the questions of what objects *are* (ontology) and how we can *know* them (epistemology). On the contrary, it has a very different position on the relation between objects and concepts generally.

Let's turn, then, to the case of objectivism. An instance would be the kind of Platonic realism we saw Penrose adopting in one of our previous chapters ('Gatekeeping Logic').[14] If we use 'x' to represent any given concept, the objectivist formula is '$x = obj$'. So the mathematical concept of *pi* is presumed to map directly on to a really existing property of the universe (its object). Here the concept is a kind of pure crystal through which the world of material or ideal objects can be known. The knowability of objects is assured through their right and proper concepts and, in turn, the knowability of these concepts themselves is undoubtable. On the objectivist account, man simply is a concept-using being and the concepts he uses (if he uses them aright) give unmediated access to the world. So if we use brackets to mark out the domain of the fully *knowable* (if only to annoy any remaining phenomenologists), the objectivist problematic may be represented thus:

$$\{x = obj\}$$

To repeat: the concept is a kind of crystal, and knowledge (including philosophical knowledge) is akin to a kind of optics.

By contrast, the subjectivist view of the concept (for example, the position known as 'psychological constructionism') sees it not so much as a crystal as a shuttle – the kind used in spinning and weaving. That is, it proposes a mutual relation between the concept and its object, with these construed as opposites. Each is held to constitute the other, reflexively. However, in this case, the object-in-itself is no longer so clearly available to knowledge; for, on a subjectivist account, the world of objects is always grasped indirectly, through the mediation of subjectively-based concepts. And so only the concept, and not 'the object' itself, can be fully knowable. The object comes to be referred to in terms of the 'object-as-presented-to-consciousness', the 'phenomenon', the 'sense datum' and so on, depending on other philosophical variations. Using the same formal conventions then, for subjectivism:

$$\{x\} <=> obj$$

These two formulations, of course, are caricatures of intellectual struggles, not fixed positions or givens and, presumably, no philosopher ever held either in such simplistic forms. What I'm referring to as objectivism, then, is a *striving* towards, rather than the achievement of, a clear vision by which objects become absolutely transparent. As we saw in the case of

Penrose, it is ultimately a *faith* in the existence of ideal mathematical objects, and in the idea that mathematical concepts directly represent them. By contrast, subjectivism problematizes, or tries to show the mechanics of, what it takes to be the illusory ontological transparency on which objectivism depends. But at the same time, it simply transfers positivity across to the human subject as the proper locus of knowledge.

Postmodernism marks itself by a distrust in both of these faiths. Following, perhaps (and it's a big 'perhaps'), Derrida's critique of the 'metaphysics of presence' and his well-known 'deconstruction' of binary oppositions (such as the opposition between concept and object itself), postmodernism tries to think in a way that deletes both originary objects and primordial subjects as guarantors of concepts. Instead, it asks about the conditions of possibility under which we could come to ask *at all* about concepts and objects. It notices that any concept's conditions of possibility must include that which it is not (so that x always depends on not-x). Additionally, if this is the case, neither a concept (x) nor its negation (not-x) can guarantee full knowability. And this will apply equally to objects in terms of their presence or absence. All questions of full, definite and unmediated 'knowability' – whether based in subjectivity or objectivity – would have to be reconsidered.

What, for convenience, we are calling 'the postmodern' radically denies *any* transparency of meaning whether 'direct' and objective or subjective and 'reflexively constituted'. By continually asking what something (concept or object) must be in relation to its negation or absence, positivity as such comes to be doubted as a fundamental premise. Strong or definite boundaries between positivity and negativity, presence and absence, concept and object are precisely what come into question in a postmodern view.

Is this the source of postmodernism's specifically ethical dilemmas – that it cannot settle, that it must always hover or flicker between certainty and uncertainty over questions of the good, just as much as over any conceptual domain? Let us see what happens, then, in a case where a critique of binarism is motivated towards overtly ethical ends.

Above, I noted (with cautious parentheses) that postmodern thinking may work roughly along the lines of Derrida's 'deconstruction' of the metaphysics of presence – hence its positioning outside both sheer objectivism and sheer subjectivism – and with his critique of the kinds of binaristic thinking deriving from that metaphysics. One ethical problem with binarism (for example, as it operates in structuralist thinking) is that it tends to *equate* both terms in any given opposition. Each appears as a merely formal, structural or logical inversion of its other. So on a standard view, it would be the case that if something is defined as the negation of its opposite, then the inverse should also be the case. To give an example (as it happens, one upon which all computers depend), if 'on' is 'not off', then 'off' should be 'not on'. Each should be definable as being not its other. But in plenty of actual cases this simply does not work. In the case of gender difference, to follow Irigaray's example, we know that while the feminine is defined under patriarchy as the negation or absence of the masculine, the reverse does not hold.[15] For present-day Western societies at least, masculinity is not simply the absence of femininity: it is a primary term in a hierarchy. Its primacy, in a sense, is patriarchy.

Irigaray's question, however, is not a formal, structural or logical one, but a qualitative and ethical one: how to think a feminine quality which is not dependent upon its definition as merely the not-masculine? But, at the same time, by *recognizing* that the binaries are not simply formal-structural but already contain values, and then by deciding to take *action* against them on the basis of a possible array of counter-values, how can the position thus taken not be monological and essentialist? Again, we come across the paradoxes of post-ethics. Ultimately a postmodern onto-epistemology at the formal-structural level (and presumably its related ethics at the level of value) requires a positing of the very realm of essentials to which it is opposed – and, more importantly, such that it *defines* itself by that opposition. And this may be among the reasons why the idea of the post-ethical is so fraught with paradox.

Going back to Bogen and Lynch's ethical dilemma: postmodernist relativism will certainly be able to tell us that a particular binary (for example, sane/insane as general categories and regardless of local practices) involves an opposition which is far from equal. But it will not be able to easily advance a positive ethics of 'support' for the side of the binary which is subordinated to its other (in this case the insane). Equally, unless supplemented by a positive feminist ethics, postmodern theory alone cannot produce ethical arguments for a critique of patriarchy and an affirmation of women. There is a crucial difference between identifying victims on the one hand, and making an ethical argument against their victimization on the other. Otherwise an emancipatory analysis could easily be mobilized on behalf of such figures as Oliver North. But in raising the question of this choice, we return (although the distinction is problematic) from the domain of the theoretico-ethical to practical situations of personal-ethical choice.

Or using the gender example: postmodern theory alone would not be able to distinguish between two counter-archives, one enlisted on behalf of a rape victim and the other on behalf of a rapist facing the (no doubt repressive) legal authorities. To this point, a postmodern ethics could not answer the question 'Are there no victims of repression who simply deserve to be just that?' For this would be like asking postmodernism for an originary, definitive and fixed notion of the pure victim as such when it defines itself outside all purities. And indeed, Foucault himself has been criticized along these lines.[16]

But, for all this, I think it is possible to locate a definite theoretico-ethical affirmation in recent critical theory, or at least a struggle for one, a struggle which necessarily eschews strict social–moral norms. Along these lines, Gasché argues for the project he calls 'deconstructive interpretation':

> In *Spurs*, Derrida insists that deconstructive interpretation is affirmative interpretation. . . . The affirmative character of deconstructive interpretation, however, is not to be confused with positivity. Deconstructive interpretation is affirmative in a Nietzschean sense. . . . [T]his means that deconstructive interpretation affirms the play of the positive *and* the negative, and thus it wards off the ethical temptation to liquidate negativity and difference.[17]

For Gasché, the main point is to 'ward off' the ethical tendencies of other theoretical positions. It is not to establish any affirmative position in its own right. And in fact, Derrida tells us *why* no ethical decision can ever run completely or perfectly along the lines of a moral programme, or from cause to effect in an efficient and linear manner:

> Above all, no completeness is possible for undecidability. . . . A decision can only come into being in a space that exceeds the calculable program that would destroy all responsibility by transforming it into a programmable effect of determinate causes. There can be no moral or political responsibility without this trial and this passage by way of the undecidable. Even if a decision seems to take only a second and not be preceded by any deliberation, it is structured by this *experience and experiment of the undecidable*.[18]

Staten's position is less cautious than either Gasché's or Derrida's in this regard – and it is more fraught with risk. He argues for a general, not specifically ethical, affirmation of the accidental against the essential, indeed for a *law* of the possibility of accident. Accident becomes necessary.

And though – since 'at the end of the book I only reach the point at which one first picks up one's pen'[19] – Staten does not fully explore the ethical dimensions of his affirmation of accidence, it may still be worth seeing if his argument can be taken to that point.

If, as Derrida argues throughout his work, originary presences (essences such as 'the good', for example) never simply arrive alone but are always constituted by repetition (accident, what happens to happen), then an ethics along these lines would involve an affirmative ethics-in-struggle, with no guarantee of returning to a fixed origin, or arriving at a final destination. For example, this would mean struggling to think *the necessity* of, say, the masculine as the negation (or absence) of a more primarily given feminine. That would be a gender politics in which men are considered (and in which we consider ourselves) as lacking a femininity derived without reference to an originary 'baseline' of the masculine. Clearly this theoretico-ethical problem is not without its relations to personal-ethical questions. We seem to have reached a point where the two domains begin to touch. It is no longer clear that there's one rule for philosophy and another for life. For example, for a man in any patriarchal society, thinking the necessity of a lacking femininity would be a type of persistent onto-epistemologico-ethical perversity which required, which made essential, the accidental or aleatory *as it actually appears in specific ethico-political techniques, under specific conditions.* For the fact that one side of such a pair as masculine/feminine comes to be negatively valued is in no sense a pure effect of philosophical speculation. It only comes about given the operation of such general ideas within specific conditions, a specific history of gender relations, particular socio-historical communities, the emergence, sedimentation and stabilization over time of particular institutions, including the apparent 'naturalness' of such an unequal relation, and so on.

Accordingly, we might locate a number of sites of the inessential, sites of 'minority communities', sites to which the accidental is currently confined and which would be affirmed by a 'postmodern' ethics. The list would be long but it might include: writing rather than speech; woman rather than man; sign rather than essential meaning (but also spacing rather than sign); contamination rather than purity; margin rather than centre – where each of these would require an analysis of, for example, gender politics, the politics of semiosis, and so on, as a precondition of any affirmative (that is, tactical) ethics.[20]

Because this is a precondition of possible counter-ethical or post-ethical practices rather than an end in itself, it figures as part of a strategy which is more than a mere negation or overturning. The idea of unmarking the typically marked member of ethical-moral binaries has in view their eventual deconstruction – as a practical political and not merely 'theoretical' matter.[21] It acknowledges that the dominant binarism of, say, modernist thought is co-extensive with the whole ethico-political field. Binarism then comes to be seen as a 'crypto-grammar' whose terms must be used (initially negated) and analysed for their intrinsic play (*jeu*) in Derrida's sense, their never being perfectly completable.[22] Binarism will not easily disappear, leaving us with a new ethical field, as it were, overnight. Inversion, then, could not be the end but only the beginning of a counter-ethics or post-ethics.

However – and here we run against the walls of the Wittgensteinian cage – the precise point or site at which any particular analyst might carry out any particular critique would always be a matter of personal ethics. It might, for example, have to do with particular community memberships and allegiances. This is the point – the point of personal and community allegiance – where ethical *theory* as such drops out. It is the point where formal ethical language runs up against Wittgenstein's limits. And this is why Bogen and Lynch's question (Why the helpless madman and not Oliver North? – Why the rape victim and not the rapist?) can never be answered by a single and definitive moral formula which would be somehow 'built in' to semiotics to keep it ethically 'pure'. If I am asked why I choose the first and not the second, I cannot say. I can only say that my history and my forms of life make it quite clear to me. And I can *then* point back to the traditional or historical under-valuing of insane persons and rape victims as a secondary – more arguable, more discussible – empirical *support* for my decision.

Nevertheless the unmasking of such under-valuings of and by generalized binaries has a certain value. Unmasking or 'psychoanalyzing' this 'metaphysics' would, for example, mean more than simply affirming what it negates: the possibility of the accidental. It would mean showing, by a kind of double move, that the conceptual purity of an absolute boundary *between* a concept (x) and its negation or absence (not-x) is itself a matter of faith. If the undervalued negative concept (woman, writing) is first reaffirmed, then the boundary between concept and object, for example, cannot be anchored either *conceptually* or *objectively*. Neither of the terms alone can secure the boundary between them. The proposition that the boundary or spacing must not allow contamination is not self-evidently true. Rather this ethical requirement of conceptual purity is itself merely one of the over-valued positivities of the traditional metaphysics which 'postmodernism' opposes.

Let me put this more formally. As we have seen, while objectivism required a positive relation – {*x* = *obj*} – between a concept and its object, and while subjectivism required a relation of mutual constitutivity between them – {*x*}<=> *obj* – a search for the limits of both finds, in both, a common formula of *presence* of the general form: *a* R *b*. Here: 'R' is the relation which is always a *difference* even when expressed as 'equals', or 'is', or 'is identical to', or 'mutually constitutes'. Every such realization of R requires a faith in one or another form of pure presence. This faith holds that what *is* present (for example, an 'object') is present*ed* (for example, to consciousness) in a 'medium' of pres*ence*. As such, then, both objectivism and subjectivism forget difference, the always-possible non-relation (corresponding to any arbitrarily given relation) between a concept and its other.

The relation, R, always carries or allows, and sometimes even requires, permeability. The project of a post-ethics would ideally show every R to be a perforated membrane as opposed to a watertight seal. Under such a 'deconstruction' (to use an unduly pretentious term), R does not dissolve altogether. The relation of presence is not merely 'cancelled'. Instead we must remember that R can do other than mark identity. For example, it can be the undecidable double of identity-difference, the 'experience and experiment of the undecidable'.

Between *a* and *b*, there is a situation of *always-possible contingency*: the possibility of leakage, contamination, transfer – the threat of wholesale rupture in some cases. This always-possible contingency is the nearest to an affirmative thesis that any formal post-ethics can come. The boundary can, however, in no case whatsoever, be kept ideally intact. Even to imagine such a pure state, we need to be able to imagine its transgression. The strongest ethical positions utterly require and contain their opposites. In this sense, Staten's law of the *possibility* of accidence would never not be in play: there could be no pure case unregulated by it.

The crunch comes when we must ask whether there is anything to be said from this position with respect to ethics, with respect, that is, to the 'regulation of conduct' as it might be put in the more traditional zones of moralism and/or the 'moral sciences'. Here we can begin to discern a number of possible pro-ethical 'maxims' which would follow from postmodernism's paradoxical onto-epistemological positioning.

1. Within conceptual doubles, there is an emerging revaluation of the politically and historically under-valued concept: privation, absence, contamination and so on. This is not so much in order to instigate a new positivity, but is rather a first step towards showing how such oppositions

are always hierarchical in terms of value even though they may appear to have equal positions when only considered logically or structurally. After this first step, however, there is still work to be done. So Derrida writes:

> What must occur then is not merely a suppression of all hierarchy, for an an-archy only consolidates just as surely the established order of a meta-physical hierarchy; nor is it a simple change or reversal in the terms of any given hierarchy. Rather, the *Umdrehung* must be a transformation of the hierarchical structure itself.[23]

2. Even if the post-ethical is not anarchic, it takes on the *style* of refusal. 'Athesis', as refusal, is therefore a definite strategy in so far as it is – and it must be – a material practice at all.[24] A material practice with the style of refusal remains a material practice. In fact, we can discern in the post-ethical a positivity of the material in a domain traditionally reserved for intangible 'principles'.

3. A crucial point, as we have seen, is that the accidental-aleatory becomes positive in the sense that it becomes essentially possible. In this sense, ethics is a form of *invention*. It is no longer a question of pre-given and self-evident principles or formulae. It no longer conceives of freedom as the freedom to invent *practice* on the basis of given (uninvented) moral principles. The post-ethical points to a different state of affairs in which we must invent principles (such as Staten's essential aleatoriness) whilst cut adrift, as it were, in the domain of practice. The 'post' element of the post-ethical points to the ethical arriving *after* the practical. The rules are always formulated after the fact. In this sense these are not discoveries or uncoverings of 'natural' facts or principles.

4. The domain of practice itself, however, is not to be thought of as without any constraint or limit. Absence of a definite, watertight, R-relation between concepts and their opposites does not mean that practice is a swarm of particulars, an infinite celebration of the play of signifiers, a semiotic carnival.[25] Any specific leakage across R, it is important to note, cannot be without its own history and politics, its own customs and conventions, its own techniques and practices, its own relevances to the specific communities or forms of life involved. To this extent, we must say that it is subject to a constitutive outside – which is always 'there' if only because the accidental is always possible, precisely outside any definite prediction. To return to Wittgenstein: the accidental is thinkable as the 'beyond-the-limit', for example, of language. This 'beyond' points to *at least one* area of unknowable constraint, an area of possibility-

conditions which are not specifiable in advance. And this is precisely why formal or professional ethical inquiry is always (if only slightly but, therefore, importantly) different from personal ethics – including the personal ethics of the analyst.

5. Lastly, then, can a post-ethics have a strategy or tactics? In *Speech and Phenomena*, Derrida writes of 'a strategy without finality ... blind tactics [*tactique aveugle*]'.[26] We can read this at least two ways: either as endless accidence as itself a given tactic, or else as the tactic of making, locating, aleatoriness necessarily within the supposedly proper and precise. Either way, this can be read affirmatively.

But what is this rather general affirmation in terms of Foucault's idea of ethics as a relation to oneself in relation to others? And in particular, what can it mean for the semiotic analyst's relation to him- or herself in relation to the various community-based forms of semiosis which she or he analyses and belongs to? By asking these questions we begin to see the limits of any post-ethics that comes down to *tactique aveugle*: for such a blindness gives us no clear way to proceed in terms of deciding how effective semiotic analyses should position themselves in terms of the communities outside them, the communities they subject to empirical analysis. Let us, then, try to consolidate what we have learned from our excursion into the terrors of relativism and see what can be done, today, in the name of a specifically analytic ethics.

All ethical grounds (as absolute grounds) have been shattered, broken into fragmented slabs like a crazy paving. Today, that is, we have a single ethical principle: that all absolute ethics are anathema since they become normative principles. But if we start to look closely at the shattered remains of those once-firm ethical grounds, we can see that many are so precarious as to forbid all construction upon them, while a few still retain sufficient solidity as to allow us at least the idea of a positive analytic ethics. All grounds are shattered – to repeat – yet a small number remain workable or effective nevertheless, even if there are those who would think they are vestiges of an old positivity to be cleared away. The ethical project would then be to identify these (and their flaws) – empirically. Ethics would then be a method of calculation – one methodic practice which effective semiotics might both analyse and contribute to (as theory and practice). Ethics would then be where effective semiotics both does, and describes, methodic practices.

This would mean trying to find a form of empiricism which was not conservative but critical – critical by means of its intervention into the ethical. To this point, my effective semiotics has been conservative in

simply attempting to describe (without judging) methodic practices. That
has left it open to charges of being unable to discriminate between, to
return to our paradigm case, Coulter's mental patient and Oliver North.
So effective semiotics could take this move into criticism (into the space of
the critical) as the start of 'the good', its own good. Then the ethical
question would be: what are the objects of that criticism or critical move?
Evidently, they would have to be empirical objects – so we could never
know their problems in advance. Or: their problems could not be given
by any general form of normativity. By 'problems' we would then have to
mean problem-solutions, except that, now, effective semiotics would be
identifying and proposing them rather than simply describing them. And
this would involve intervening into communities or forms of life – with all
its attendant risks. Principally, the risk is that such a form of critique
would be tendentious in Garfinkel's sense: we would not know its point
of application in advance of the investigation.[27]

In important ways, this tendentiousness would fit not only with Derrida's
'experience and experiment of the undecidable' but also with Foucault's
idea of the dispersal of power in contemporary society. If Foucault is
right, ethics (as a counter to power) is necessarily plural. For effective
semiotics, then, this would involve a calculation in two parts, with each
part corresponding to the first two 'levels' of semiosis. The first part
would mean locating and describing the *intelligibility* of the good in a
particular locale – it would mean asking: what counts, factually, as the
good in this community? The second part of the calculation would move
beyond mere intelligibility or identification and towards critique and intervention. It would ask the question of the *actionability* of the good.
That is, it would begin to ask questions about the ways in which sociological problems and their solutions are formed in the community under
investigation. It would ask: how is the good which this community *sets* as
such carried into action? Then, at both levels of semiosis (intelligibility
and actionability), it would reserve the right of disagreement: the right to
say that it refuses this idea of the good or that it refuses this idea of its
(proper) implementation. Then effective semiotics might begin to realize
its own community status, and so acknowledge its specific positioning
with regard to those other communities which it analyses.

This gives us a positioning for the first two semiotic levels, but what of
the third: *historicity*? If Foucault is right and a genuine ethics of the self
(in relation to itself) has been taken over, today, by a legislated and
normative morality, then an analytic actionability oriented to a return to
ethics (in Foucault's sense) is already an historical move. It would already

be in a position to begin to discern a new art of the self as against an old science of control. It would already be arguing for (and attempting to practise) the installation of a return to self-judgement and the 'will not to be governed'.

There are risks involved in such a position but the possible outcome is a return to the ethical domain as such; the installation of an ethics of the self over the dominance of morality (as socio-political normativity). And this may, in itself, be a form of the good – the first good of a positive ethics of analysis in terms of its own historicity.

Such an ethics as a situationally located form of calculation (of the good outcome?) will always be imperfect since, as Derrida reminds us, the result of the calculation is always still to come. It leaves itself subject to unknowability, to being (potentially) wrong (as Foucault was about Iran and the delegislation of rape). But, on this account, the good is to risk calculation despite this – to risk being wrong while trying, at every step, not to be.

An unethical analytics would then involve either (a) the quietism of failing to calculate at all – leaving history as it is, condoning everything in effect or (b) the retrospectivism of adjusting one's earlier calculations so that they show themselves as having been right all along. In empirical terms, this would be the equivalent of fudging the results. Taking the risks involved in such work is a matter of courage or its lack. As with experimentation in the natural sciences, Derrida's 'experience and experiment of the undecidable' means that one has to be prepared for things to turn out wrongly. These are the stakes in an empiricist ethics.

How then to choose between Coulter's prospective patient (PP) and Oliver North? Why is it that I want to back one and not the other? When I look back at the transcript of PP's attempted incarceration, I see just that – an attempted incarceration. But I see the attempt as happening against PP's own relevances and self-positioning (as a free person without obligation to the mental welfare system). This prompts me to describe the intelligibility of the situation from his point of view (a point of view which he makes clear to all involved in the scene and to any analyst). Then I feel obliged to describe his ethno-analytic strategy, his way of finding an actionable solution to the problem which he has been *put* in. But I can't find any equivalents in the case of Oliver North, no matter how closely I read Bogen and Lynch's paper and no matter how much I share (as, perhaps, an ethnomethodologist) their own community relevances.[28] For it seems that, in the end, the North case is not one of inter-community dissensus. North has worked for the state – albeit via an agreement that he would (on its behalf) appear to work outside it. The appeals he makes against the judgment against him are based on the fact that the state he worked for allowed him (he would say, legally) to act illegally. In whatever way one analyses this, North has already consented to his complicity with the moral norms by which he is judged. None of this is true for PP. He has in no way registered himself as a member of any community which is in agreement with the mental health authorities. In the case of the PP transcript, we are dealing with a definite, direct and genuine case of inter-community difference. A position has to be taken. And I can see no grounds for taking the position of the mental health authorities. North is by no means a victim of such communitarian differences. He is being tried by the very system he has served and, as it were, subscribed to. There is no case of *différend* in his case – and hence no victimization. Ethically we have no choice but to allow others (including North) such choices: everyone has the right to do wrong and no one has the right to take that right away from them. By doing it, they choose, equally, to be judged by the value system they have chosen to be wrong within. Victims only exist when value systems arrive from other communities or idioms and insist that their (exterior) judgements should stand. Then any effective semiotics would analyse and disseminate the complex means by which such victims find artful ways of refusing to be controlled, legislated or judged.

Whether this type of analysis can be collected and publicized in ways which can be reused by (and even mobilized on behalf of) victims of social injustice remains to be seen. In the end, it may only serve to increase the analyst's own understanding of the world and how it operates. What it might change, in this minimal respect, would be who the analyst is, in terms of his or her community positionings and socio-historical allegiances. But this, in itself, may not be the worst of outcomes. Effective semiotics would then be but one possible 'art of existence' or 'technique of the self', to reinvoke Foucault's terms. It would be, at minimum, one way of 'knowing if one can think differently than one thinks, perceive differently than one sees'.[29] And although it has been much quoted elsewhere, what Foucault has to say about such a practice (which he calls 'philosophy') continues to be instructive – one of the few moves towards a positive ethics arising out of poststructuralist thought:

> People will say, perhaps, that these games with oneself would be better left backstage; or, at best, that they might properly be part of those preliminary exercises that are forgotten once they have served their purpose.

But, then, what is philosophy today – philosophical activity, I mean – if it is not the critical work that thought brings to bear on itself? In what does it consist, if not in the endeavour to know how and to what extent it might be possible to think differently, instead of legitimating what is already known? There is always something ludicrous in philosophical discourse when it tries, from the outside, to dictate to others, to tell them where their truth is and how to find it, or when it works up a case against them in the language of naive positivity. But it is entitled to explore what might be changed, in its own thought, through the practice of a knowledge that is foreign to it. The 'essay' – which should be understood as the assay or test by which, in the game of truth, one undergoes changes, and not as the simplistic appropriation of others for the purpose of communication – is the living substance of philosophy, at least if we assume that philosophy is still what it was in times past, i.e., an 'ascesis', *askesis*, an exercise of oneself in the activity of thought.[30]

Perhaps, after all, Wittgenstein found ethical propositions to be inexpressible in his day (and today) because they *are* currently inexpressible – but for historical reasons rather than for reasons which have to do with the essential inexpressibility of ethics.[31] As we have seen, historical thinking was never Wittgenstein's forte. Perhaps it is only *today* that the ethical cannot be spoken: because the relation to the self (*le rapport à soi*), in so far as it exists at all, is currently overshadowed by legal, juridical, religious and other forms of controlling the self – forms which are better thought of as moral codes rather than ethics as such.

In this case, the unspeakability of the ethical today is not a fixed condition. Foucault has shown that things have been quite otherwise and, at least in principle, could be again:

> We have hardly any remnant of the idea in our society, that the principle work of art which one has to take care of, the main area to which one must apply aesthetic values is one's self, one's life, one's existence.[32]

Perhaps, then, the ethical struggle is no more and no less for a return to ethics itself, against mere morality and its associated legislation. And perhaps one way of securing this struggle would be to turn from ethics as a branch of philosophy and towards ethics as an empirical, factical, actional, or effective decision. If so, ethics as (and in) effective semiotics may be a contribution to 'genealogico-deconstructive research.'[33] It may even be the first move towards that branch of it which Derrida has tentatively named 'pragrammatology.'[34] And finally, it would have to agree with Hunter that 'cultural criticism' is ultimately (no more than) a technique of the self. But, with Foucault and against Hunter, it could not condemn it for all that.[35]

Notes

1 Cf. Jeff Coulter, *The Social Construction of Mind: Studies in Ethnomethodology and Linguistic Philosophy* (London: Macmillan, 1979).

2 David Bogen and Michael Lynch, 'Taking Account of the Hostile Native: Plausible Deniability and the Production of Conventional History in the Iran-Contra Hearings', *Social Problems* 36 (3) (1989), pp. 197–224.

3 John D. Caputo, *Against Ethics: Contributions to a Poetics of Obligation with Constant Reference to Deconstruction* (Bloomington: Indiana University Press, 1993), p. 1.

4 Michel Foucault, *The History of Sexuality, Volume One: An Introduction*, trans. R. Hurley (London: Allen Lane, 1979); *The Use of Pleasure: The History of Sexuality Volume Two*, trans. R. Hurley (London: Viking, 1986); and *the Care of the Self: The History of Sexuality Volume Three*, trans. R. Hurley (London: Allen Lane/Penguin Press, 1988).

5 James Miller, *The Passion of Michel Foucault* (London: Harper Collins, 1993), pp. 328–34.

6 Ibid., pp. 306–9.

7 Ibid., p. 307, quoting Richard Cottam, 'Inside Revolutionary Iran', in *Iran's Revolution*, ed. R. K. Ramazani (Bloomington: Indiana University Press, 1990), p. 3.

8 'The will not to be governed' is Miller's paraphrase (*The Passion*, p. 310) of Foucault's position. It amounts to an inversion of the Kantian imperative, and could be expressed as follows: act in such a way that the grounds of your action defy all principles of general legislation.

9 Jane Flax, 'The End of Innocence', in *Feminists Theorize the Political*, eds J. Butler and J. W. Scott (New York: Routledge, 1992), pp. 445–63.

10 Rosi Braidotti, *Patterns of Dissonance* (Cambridge: Polity Press, 1991).

11 See John Frow, *What Was Postmodernism?* (Sydney: Local Consumption Publications, 1991).

12 Ludwig Wittgenstein, 'A Lecture on Ethics', *Philosophical Review* 74 (1965), pp. 11–12.

13 Ferenc Feher, 'Being After: The Condition of Postmodernity', *The Age Monthly Review* 7 (5) (1987), pp. 8–9.

14 Cf. Roger Penrose, *The Emperor's New Mind: Concerning Computers, Minds, and the Laws of Physics* (London: Vintage, 1991). [The earlier chapter in question is not reprinted here. (NL)]

15 My argument here is informed by a (perhaps idiosyncratic) reading of the

work of Luce Irigaray. See her *This Sex Which Is Not One*, trans. Catherine Porter (Ithaca: Cornell University Press, 1985) and *Speculum of the Other Woman*, trans. Gillian G. Gill (Ithaca: Cornell University Press, 1985).

16 See Teresa de Lauretis, *Alice Doesn't: Feminism, Semiotics, Cinema* (Bloomington: Indiana University Press, 1984), p. 94, regarding Foucault's 'paradoxical conservatism'.

17 Rodolph Gasché, *The Tain of the Mirror: Derrida and the Philosophy of Reflection* (Cambridge: Harvard University Press, 1986), p. 154.

18 Jacques Derrida, 'Afterword: Toward an Ethic of Discussion', trans. S. Weber, in *Limited Inc*, ed. Gerald Graff (Evanston, Ill.: Northwestern University Press, 1988), p. 116.

19 Henry Staten, *Wittgenstein and Derrida* (Lincoln: University of Nebraska Press, 1986), p. xvi.

20 For a list of such counter-values, see Ihab Hassan, *The Postmodern Turn: Essays in Postmodern Theory and Culture* (Columbus: Ohio State University Press, 1987), pp. 91–2.

21 On Derrida's turn towards deconstruction as a practical-political formation (as opposed to a merely analytic strategy in philosophy), see his *Specters of Marx: The State of the Debt, the Work of Mourning, and the New International*, trans. Peggy Kamuf (New York and London: Routledge, 1994). [For a discussion of this text, see my *PomoIntro*, pp. 141–62. (NL)]

22 The term 'crypto-grammar' is taken from Terry Threadgold, 'Postmodernism, Systemic-Functional Linguistics as Metalanguage and the Practice of Cultural Critique', paper presented at the Inaugural Australian Systemics Workshop, Deakin University, January 1990.

23 Jacques Derrida, *Spurs/Éperons: Nietzsche's Styles*, trans. Barbara Harlow (Chicago: University of Chicago Press, 1978).

24 On athesis and the athetical, see Alec McHoul and David Wills, *Writing Pynchon: Strategies in Fictional Analysis* (London: Macmillan, 1990), pp. 90ff.

25 Jeff Coulter, 'Is Contextualising Necessarily Interpretive?', *Journal of Pragmatics* 21 (6) (1994), p. 690. [For more on this paper, see my *Debating Derrida* (Carlton: Melbourne University Press, 1995), pp. 86–91. (NL)]

26 Jacques Derrida, *Speech and Phenomena*, trans. D. B. Allison (Evanston, Ill.: Northwestern University Press, 1973), p. 135.

27 Cf. Harold Garfinkel, *Studies in Ethnomethodology* (Englewood Cliffs, NJ: Prentice-Hall, 1967).

28 Bogen and Lynch, 'Taking Account'.

29 Foucault, *Use of Pleasure*, pp. 11 and 8.

30 Ibid., pp. 8–9.

31 If so, it is ironic that the nearest imaginable society to ancient Greece in recent times – a society where 'free men', old and young, composed their own ethics, relatively unhindered by legal restraint – was, arguably, Wittgenstein's Cambridge.

32 Michel Foucault, 'On the Genealogy of Ethics: An Overview of Work in Progress', in *Michel Foucault: Beyond Structuralism and Hermeneutics*, ed. Hubert L. Dreyfus and Paul Rabinow (Chicago: University of Chicago Press, 1982), p. 245.

33 Jacques Derrida, 'Politics and Friendship: An Interview with Jacques Derrida', in *The Althusserian Legacy*, ed. E. Ann Kaplan and Michael Sprinker (London, Verso, 1993), p. 231.

34 Jacques Derrida, 'My Chances/*Mes Chances*: A Rendezvous with Some Epicurean Stereophonies', in *Taking Chances: Derrida, Psychoanalysis, and Literature*, ed. J. H. Smith and W. Kerrigan (Baltimore: The Johns Hopkins University Press, 1984), p. 27.

35 Cf. Ian Hunter, 'Setting Limits to Culture', in *Nation, Culture, Text: Australian Cultural and Media Studies*, ed. Graeme Turner (London: Routledge, 1993), pp. 140–63. [For a discussion of this paper, see Robert Briggs, 'Discipline and Disclaim: Countermanding Orders of (Inter)disciplinarity', in *Philosophy and Cultural Studies*, ed. Niall Lucy, *Continuum* 12, 2 (July 1998), pp. 131–45. (NL)]

Postscript

Chapter Twenty-one Note on the Meaning of 'Post-'

Jean-François Lyotard

To Jessamyn Blau
Milwaukee, May 1, 1985

I would like to pass on to you a few thoughts which are merely intended to raise certain problems concerning the term 'postmodern', without wanting to resolve them. By doing this, I do not want to close the debate but rather to situate it, in order to avoid confusion and ambiguity. I have just three points to make:

1. First, the opposition between postmodernism and modernism, or the Modern Movement (1910–45) in architecture. According to Portoghesi, the rupture of postmodernism consists in an abrogation of the hegemony of Euclidean geometry (its sublimation in the plastic poetics of 'De Stijl', for example). To follow Gregotti, the difference between modernism and postmodernism would be better characterized by the following feature: the disappearance of the close bond which once linked the project of modern architecture to an ideal of the progressive realization of social and individual emancipation encompassing all humanity. Postmodern architecture finds itself condemned to undertake a series of minor modifications in a space inherited from modernity, condemned to abandon a global reconstruction of the space of human habitation. The perspective then opens onto a vast landscape, in the sense that there is no longer any horizon of universality, universalization or general emancipation to greet the eye of

Jean-François Lyotard, 'Note on the Meaning of "Post-"', in *The Postmodern Explained to Children: Correspondence 1982–1985*, trans Don Barry, Bernadette Maher, Julian Pefanis, Virginia Spate and Morgan Thomas; eds Pefanis and Thomas (Sydney: Power Publications, 1992), pp. 87–94.

postmodern man, least of all the eye of the architect. The disappearance of the Idea that rationality and freedom are progressing would explain a 'tone', style or mode specific to postmodern architecture. I would say it is a sort of 'bricolage': the multiple quotation of elements taken from earlier styles or periods, classical and modern; disregard for the environment, etc.

One point about this perspective is that the 'post-' of 'postmodernism' has the sense of a simple succession, a diachronic sequence of periods in which each one is clearly identifiable. The 'post-' indicates something like a conversion: a new direction from the previous one.

Now this idea of a linear chronology is itself perfectly 'modern'. It is at once part of Christianity, Cartesianism and Jacobinism: since we are inaugurating something completely new, the hands of the clock should be put back to zero. The very idea of modernity is closely correlated with the principle that it is both possible and necessary to break with tradition and institute absolutely new ways of living and thinking.

We now suspect that this 'rupture' is in fact a way of forgetting or repressing the past, that is to say, repeating it and not surpassing it. I would say that, in the 'new' architecture, the quotation of motifs taken from earlier architectures relies on a procedure analogous to the way the dreamwork uses diurnal residues left over from life past, outlined by Freud in the *Traumdeutung*. This destiny of repetition and/or quotation whether it is taken up ironically, cynically or naively – is in any event obvious if we think of the tendencies which at present dominate painting under the names of trans-avantgardism, neo-expressionism, and so forth. I will return to this a bit later.

2. This departure from architectural 'postmodernism' leads me to a second connotation of the term 'postmodern' (and I have to admit that I'm no stranger to its misunderstanding).

The general idea is a trivial one. We can observe and establish a kind of decline in the confidence which, for two centuries, the West invested in the principle of a general progress in humanity. This idea of a possible, probable or necessary progress is rooted in the belief that developments made in the arts, technology, knowledge and freedoms would benefit humanity as a whole. It is true that ascertaining the identity of the subject who suffered most from a lack of development – the poor, the worker or the illiterate – continued to be an issue throughout the nineteenth and twentieth centuries. As you know, there was controversy and even war between liberals, conservatives and 'leftists' over the true name to be given the subject whose emancipation required assistance. Yet all these tendencies were united in the belief that initiatives, discoveries and institutions only had legitimacy in so far as they contributed to the emancipation of humanity.

After two centuries we have become more alert to signs which would indicate an opposing movement. Neither liberalism (economic and political) nor the various marxisms have emerged from these blood-stained centuries without attracting accusations of having perpetrated crimes against humanity. We could make a list of proper names – places, people, dates – capable of illustrating or substantiating our suspicions. Following Theodor Adorno, I have used the name 'Auschwitz' to signify just how impoverished recent Western history seems from the point of view of the 'modern' project of the emancipation of humanity. What kind of thought is capable of 'relieving' Auschwitz – relieving [relever] in the sense of aufheben – capable of situating it in a general, empirical, or even speculative process directed towards universal emancipation? There is a sort of grief in the Zeitgeist. It can find expression in reactive, even reactionary, attitudes or in utopias – but not in a positive orientation which would open up a new perspective.

Technoscientific development has become a means of deepening the malaise rather than allaying it. It is no longer possible to call development progress. It seems to proceed of its own accord, with a force, an autonomous motoricity that is independent of ourselves. It does not answer to demands issuing from man's needs. On the contrary, human entities whether social or individual – always seem destabilized by the results and implications of development. I am thinking of its intellectual and mental results as well as its material results. We could say that humanity's condition has become one of chasing after the process of the accumulation of new objects (both of practice and of thought).

As you might imagine, understanding the reason for this process of complexification is an important question for me – an obscure question. We could say there exists a sort of destiny, or involuntary destination towards a condition that is increasingly complex. The needs for security, identity and happiness springing from our immediate condition as living beings, as social beings, now seem irrelevant next to this sort of constraint to complexify, mediatize, numerize, synthesize, and modify the size of each and every object. We are like Gullivers in the world of technoscience: sometimes too big, sometimes too small, but never the right size. From this perspective, the insistence on simplicity generally seems today like a pledge to barbarism.

On this same point, the following issue also has to be elaborated.

Humanity is divided into two parts. One faces the challenge of complexity, the other that ancient and terrible challenge of its own survival. This is perhaps the most important aspect of the failure of the modern project – a project which, need I remind you, once applied in principle to the whole of humanity.

3. I will give my third point – the most complex – the shortest treatment. The question of postmodernity is also, or first of all, a question of expressions of thought: in art, literature, philosophy, politics.

We know that in the domain of art, for example, or more precisely in the visual and plastic arts, the dominant view today is that the great movement of the avant-gardes is over and done with. It has, as it were, become the done thing to indulge or deride the avant-gardes – to regard them as the expression of an outdated modernity.

I do not like the term avant-garde, with its military connotations, any more than anyone else. But I do observe that the true process of avant-gardism was in reality a kind of work, a long, obstinate and highly responsible work concerned with investigating the assumptions implicit in modernity. I mean that for a proper understanding of the work of modern painters, from say Manet to Duchamp or Barnett Newman, we would have to compare their work with anamnesis, in the sense of a psychoanalytic therapy. Just as patients try to elaborate their current problems by freely associating apparently inconsequential details with past situations allowing them to uncover hidden meanings in their lives and their behaviour – so we can think of the work of Cézanne, Picasso, Delaunay, Kandinsky, Klee, Mondrian, Malevich and finally Duchamp as a 'perlaboration' (*durcharbeiten*) performed by modernity on its own meaning.

If we abandon that responsibility, we will surely be condemned to repeat, without any displacement, the West's 'modern neurosis' – its schizophrenia, paranoia, etc., the source of the misfortunes we have known for two centuries.

You can see that when it is understood in this way, the 'post-' of 'postmodern' does not signify a movement of *comeback*, *flashback* or *feedback*, that is, not a movement of repetition but a procedure in 'ana-': a procedure of analysis, anamnesis, anagogy and anamorphosis which elaborates an 'initial forgetting'.

Chapter Twenty-two The Romantic Movement at the End of History

Jerome Christensen

We profess it in our Creed, we confess it in our lives.
Jeremy Taylor, *Holy Living* (1727)

I profess romanticism, I romantically confess. And if I choose a pre-theoretical, pre-revolutionary epigraph from an eighteenth-century divine to enfranchise this essay rather than a phrase from a more timely master such as Paul de Man or M. H. Abrams, it is because I want to use Jeremy Taylor as Samuel Taylor Coleridge chronically used him: to stage a resistance to theory, to ward off revolutionary utterance, and to keep melancholy at bay. In Taylor's terms, professing romanticism is what I do on each occasion of classroom teaching at Johns Hopkins University or of publishing an article in a specialized journal or a book at a university press. My creed, of course, is not to Coleridge, to Byron, or to Wordsworth. I do not commit belief to what is loosely called a canon but to that discipline which the institutions of education and publication collaboratively authorize and reproduce and which in turn certifies the felicity of my professions. If, as Taylor states, confessing is a matter of living, living ought to be imagined as that structuring activity that Anthony Giddens calls 'practical consciousness': an ensemble of repetitive manoeuvres, signature gestures, and obsessive themes.[1] Living is for servants and for critics – for those who do not have *texts* in Edward Said's sense of the term but only what Coleridge calls 'personalities'.[2] This practical,

Jerome Christensen, 'The Romantic Movement at the End of History', *Critical Inquiry* 20 (Spring 1994), pp. 452–76.

pre-textual consciousness assorts the idiosyncratic and the routinized into a compromise formation: something romantic, something like a *biographia literaria*, something which may be at odds or at evens with an institutional warrant. It depends.

I want to address how confessing romantically bears on the profession of romanticism and to argue that its bearing matters. This essay presupposes that romanticism is not an object of study – neither the glorious expression nor the deplorable symptom of a distant epoch and peculiar mentality – but a problem in identification and in practice. As a Christian divine, Jeremy Taylor sought to induce a harmony between creed and life in himself and for others. Romantic writers grandiloquently profess to wish for such a harmony (*poet* is the name that Coleridge gives to the achieved ideal), even as they prosaically confess that what our creeds profess and what our untimely lives confess do not often synchronize.

The advantages of that discrepancy clarify in the light of the 'end of history' argument as it has been influentially advanced by Francis Fukuyama in his interrogatory 1989 article 'The End of History?' and his recent declarative book *The End of History and the Last Man*.[3] Three features of Fukuyama's 'universal history' of the triumph of liberalism are salient here (*EH*, p. 48). First, in line with his all-too-clerical affirmation of the power of ideology to make history, Fukuyama identifies the end of history not with a momentous incident or a sovereign decision but with the prescribed end of what he calls 'ideological evolution', consummated in the freshly consolidated global hegemony of the liberal state. For the sake of developing a romantic argument, I am prepared to accept both aspects of that claim: that history is (or rather was) ideological contestation and that ideological conflict has ended. I conclude that if one is looking for something with the strength to challenge commercialist hegemony here at the end of history one should look for something non-ideological – whatever that may mean.

The second arresting feature of Fukuyama's argument is its unembarrassed repetitiveness. Fukuyama freely acknowledges Hegel as his precursor, who announced the end of history in 1806. And Hegel was not alone, probably because he was somewhat premature. Not Europe in 1806 but Europe in 1815 is the better analogy with the worldquake of 1989. The contemporary scene of imperial break-up, ethnic crack-up, and commercialist mop-up closely, even eerily, parallels the European aftermath of Waterloo, when commerce first conquered conquest. Just as 1989 found its voice in Fukuyama's celebration of 'the triumph of the Western *idea*' over Soviet collectivism and of the completion of the dialectic of history in liberal society,[4] so did 1814–15 find its spokesman in the anglophiliac Benjamin Constant, who, in *The Spirit of Conquest and Usurpation*, celebrated the triumph of British liberty over Napoleonic tyranny and the advent of perpetual commercial prosperity. Let us say that Fukuyama is right. Let us say that Constant and Hegel were right. What do three rights separated by 175 years add up to? Well, history. A history that is indistinguishable from post-history because a history in which, despite the stirring spectacle of wars and revolutions, the same truth has been proven time and time again and where no real change has occurred.

Thus the third feature of Fukuyama's universal history: its relentless synchronicity. A fundamental belief in a prevailing synchronicity encourages Fukuyama, like Richard Rorty, to indulge the notion of the history of philosophy as a series of conversations with dead authors. He can imagine that he enters into intellectual exchange with Hegel and that, in his passage through *The Phenomenology of Spirit*, he can come upon the chapter on lordship and bondage and recognize liberalism's glory. The 'end of history' argument is an 'always already' formation of considerable elasticity. Although Fukuyama begins by speaking of ideological evolution, because all change has always already occurred, he must really mean ideological elaboration. A pallid scientism, evolution imputes a kind of necessity to the discursive process, subjects change to predictability, and allows for the evidence of 'real change' to be stigmatized as monstrous, anomalous, or, worse yet, anachronistic. Constant was succinct. Writing in 1814 after the abdication of the usurper, he not only trumpeted the end of the era of conquest but also announced that, under the reign of commerce, should some savage fool attempt to conquer, usurp, or dictate he would 'commit a gross and disastrous anachronism'.[5] Constant got it right. Only a few months after the publication of his book Bonaparte returned to France and for a hundred days anachronistically suspended the conventions by which monarcho-liberalism ruled. And therefore Constant got it wrong, for the assumption that an anachronism was a mere nothing that would expire in its appearance proved vain. Although an anachronism does not count in the way that clocks and bankers count, *committing* anachronism romantically exploits lack of accountability as unrecognized possibility.[6]

Post-historical liberalism's disdain for the anachronistic is exceeded only by a fear of it, which fuels the postmodern drive to abolish the possibility of anachronism. It is because Fredric Jameson, the best Marxist theorist of postmodernism, shares many of the evolutionary assumptions of the neoliberals (the word *revolution* does not appear in the index to his *Postmodernism, or, The Cultural Logic of Late Capitalism*) and adheres to the epochal model of tidy synchrony ('the postmodern must be characterized as a situation in which the survival, the residue, the holdover, the archaic, has finally been swept away without a trace')[7] that his utopian agenda looks less like a challenge to postmodernism than another elegant variation. Jameson's utopia is insufficiently romantic. Considered as a set doctrines, Marxism does not trouble Fukuyama's reverie, but the emergence of Marx under the Hegelian sun, committing the romantic anachronism of *Das Kapital* in the middle of the nineteenth century, emphatically does.

Immanuel Wallerstein has proposed a useful taxonomy of the dominant ways that historical change has been represented since the Enlightenment. The emergence of 'normal change' in eighteenth-century Europe was answered, he argues, by the formation of three institutions: 'the ideologies, the social sciences, and the movements'.[8] Wallerstein identifies three ideologies: liberalism, which he calls 'the natural ideology of normal change' (*USS*, p. 17); conservatism, which upholds the prerogatives of traditional arrangements; and Marxism, which imagined change 'as something realized not continuously but discontinuously' and which held that the world had yet to realize the 'perfect society' (*USS*, p. 17). Here is Fukuyama's scorecard: Marxism defeated, conservatism absorbed, and liberalism, 'the natural ideology of normal change', triumphant.

Although that verdict has been contested by the losers, such an outcome means neither payoff nor penalty for romanticism, as Jameson indirectly acknowledges:

> I must here omit yet another series of debates, largely academic, in which the very continuity of modernism as it is here reaffirmed is itself called into question by some vaster sense of the profound continuity of romanticism, from the late eighteenth century on, of which both the modern and the postmodern will be seen as mere organic stages. (*PM*, p. 59)

This essay will more or less inhabit the space of that omission: I will settle for 'largely academic', change 'profound continuity' to 'intermittent insistence', and discard the cliché of organic stages. The essay will proceed on the assumption that if we want to discover what possibilities for change remain open now, we might inquire into the untimely back at the beginning of the nineteenth century, when history first ended. Post-historical historiography suggests that romanticism, which, at least in the British instance, has led a kind of phantomized political existence, crossing among professions conservative, liberal, and Marxist, may, as phantom, confess a political life that is a virtual alternative both to what rules and to what would have inverted ruler and ruled. I will be orienting myself in relation to Coleridge's *Biographia Literaria* for contrary reasons: written in 1815, it is decidedly a Waterloo composition with the Constantian ambition of proclaiming a new dispensation; yet because it was afflicted by near-catastrophic miscalculations in the printing office, the book was not published until 1817 and thus appeared as an anachronism, a ghost at the banquet it had set.

British romantic writing, I shall argue, does not belong with the ideologies but with what Wallerstein calls the 'movements', those political associations on the run which attempted to organize spontaneous anti-systemic impulses into an organized 'politics of social transformation' (*USS*, 21). Neither sect nor school the British romantic writers who straggled onto the scene between 1798 and 1802 formed what E. J. Hobsbawm has called a 'primitive' social movement.[9] I shall later take advantage of the re-emergence of the primitive in a post-Jacobin and post-Napoleonic Britain to suggest analogous possibilities for a post-historical America. Matthew Arnold preferred 'prematurity' to primitiveness and diagnosed it in his canonical judgement that Byron and Wordsworth 'had their source in a great movement of feeling, not in a great movement of mind'.[10] Arnold added mind to feeling with the aim of stopping romantic movement altogether; he was successful in so far as he can be credited with growing precocious writers into Victorian worthies, freezing them as eminent pictures at the Oxbridge exhibition. Arnold's verdict has the unintended consequence, however, of aligning primitive romanticizing – turbulent feeling unsubjected by a regulative idea – with Marx's definition of communism: 'Communism is for us not a stable state which is to be established, an *ideal* to which reality will have to adjust itself. We call communism the *real* movement which abolishes the present state of things.'[11] We shall call romanticism the real movement of feeling that challenges the present state of things, including the consensus that would bury it in the past, whether by omission or by labeling it an ideology. We shall do so in the faith that what was premature then may help revive the possibility of prematurity now – if not to force the spring at least, by heralding, to quicken it.

Romanticism and Ideology

Not long ago Jerome McGann stigmatized romanticism as a version of what Marx called the German ideology, which 'turns the world upside down and sees it from a false vantage because its own point of reference is conceptualized within a closed idealistic system'.[12] McGann alludes to Marx's famous metaphor of the *camera obscura*: 'If in all ideology men and their circumstances appear upside-down, as in a camera obscura, this phenomenon arises just as much from their historical life-process as the inversion of objects on the retina does from their physical life-process' (*GI*, p. 14). Given that ideology is inversion, the critic's responsibility is clear: he must labour to turn the world right-side up and restore it to its truth.

Roughly speaking, two takes on ideology prevail. The first, shared by Fukuyama and McGann, regards ideology as a set of ideas that you hold. In this view, ideology is opinion dressed to kill. The second, Althusserian conception of ideology is as a set of representations that holds us, that '*hails or interpellates concrete individuals as concrete subjects*' – concrete subjects being concrete individuals who 'work all by themselves'.[13] Because ideology has no history (or, as Fukuyama would have it, because its history is universal), it need have no 'end' (there is no truth to restore); none the less, there are limits to ideology's scope, for there remain 'individuals' out of range of its call. Where things work, ideology is; where things do not work, ideology is not, and where ideology is not, *cause*, paradoxically, is. Or, as Lacan aphorizes (thinking of Kant, thinking of Hume) 'there is cause only in something that doesn't work'.[14] For Althusser *art*, as for Constant *anachronism*, names one of those things that, like an idiot boy or an ancient mariner or a female vagrant, does not work but that does somehow, occultly, *cause*.

Given Lacan's aphorism, it is notable that Marx's artful image of how ideology works does not itself work. Paul Ricoeur has observed that the 'unfortunate image' of the camera obscura 'is a metaphor of the reversal of images, but it proceeds as a comparison involving four terms. The ideological reversal is to the life-process as the image in perception is to the retina. . . . But what is an image on the retina' is a puzzle, for, as Ricoeur concludes, 'there are images only for consciousness.' There may be an image in itself, but because there is no image *for* itself, Marx's analogy fails to close and in so failing alludes to something like a supervisory consciousness. Ricoeur goes on to echo Althusser's charge 'that the inverted image belongs to the same ideological world as the original. As a result, he claims, we must introduce a notion quite different from inversion, that of an epistemological break'.[15] We may suggest that what appears as something like consciousness is a movement that disrupts the closure of the optical model and makes Marx's camera obscura metaphor unworkable for the systematic purposes to which Marxists have put it.

W. J. T. Mitchell has observed that 'Marx's use of the camera obscura as a polemical device for ridiculing the illusions of idealist philosophy begins to look even more ungainly when we recall that Locke had also used it as a polemical device – in exactly the opposite way.'[16] Ungainlier still. For if the inversion of the camera image belongs to 'the same ideological world' as the original, what are we to make of the common cause of Karl Marx, avowed materialist, and Samuel Taylor Coleridge, supposed idealist? Here is Coleridge's footnoted denunciation of the habits of the contemporary reading public from chapter 3 of the *Biographia*:

> For as to the devotees of the circulating libraries, I dare not compliment their *pass-time*, or rather hill-time, with the name of *reading*. Call it rather a sort of beggarly daydreaming, during which the mind of the dreamer furnishes for itself nothing but laziness and a little mawkish sensibility; while the whole materiel and imagery of the doze is supplied *ab extra* by a sort of mental *camera obscura* manufactured at the printing office, which *pro tempore* fixes, reflects and transmits the moving phantasms of one man's delirium, so as to people the barrenness of an hundred other brains afflicted with the same trance or suspension of all common sense and all definite purpose. (*BL*, 1:48n)

Although both Marx and Coleridge use the camera obscura to illustrate projection of inverted images of reality, it is the so-called romantic idealist who connects the mechanism with a system of commodity production. Mitchell likewise adjusts Marx by gleaning the camera obscura metaphor away from its Lockean parent, invoking instead the nineteenth-century technological context of photography in order to suture Marx's characterization of ideology with his analysis of commodity fetishism. In Mitchell's account,

> the commodity is a 'fantastic' form – literally, a form produced by projected light; these forms, like the 'ideas' of ideology, are both there and not there – both 'perceptible and imperceptible by the senses. The difference from the images projected by the camera obscura is that the fantastic forms of the commodity are 'objective character[s]' in the sense that they are projected outward, 'stamped upon the product of . . . labour.' The evanescent, subjective projections of ideology are imprinted and fixed the way a printing press (or photographic process) stamps the 'characters' of typographic or graphic imagery. (*I*, pp. 189–90)

If Marx echoes Locke, Coleridge, who never saw a photograph, not only anticipates Marx but Mitchell as well by making the connection between

ideology and commodity production in the context of an imaginary apparatus that looks like nothing so much as the apparatus of the imaginary
we moderns know as the cinema. Projecting his light forward as if a light
bestowed, the measure of the distance that Coleridge travels beyond Marx
is the romantic's failure accurately to historicize his camera obscura, a
neglect symptomatized syntactically by his failure properly to tie the transmitted movement to a stable referent. Is the 'moving phantasm' an affecting ghost or the effective flicker of an image on a movie screen? If the
'phantasm', an untimely and unaccountable life, is the *figure* of anachronism, Coleridge's 'moving' *really* moves – and romantically commits that
anachronism to the future.

Whether or not you buy such a fantastic claim, once the fantastic has
been reinscribed in the Marxian mechanism (classically by Walter Benjamin
or recently by Mitchell), it is difficult to see how Coleridge's 'gothic' of the
camera obscura substantively differs from the 'mental operation of materialist reversal and demystification', which, according to Jameson, is alone
the feature by which 'materialism' as such can be identified' (*PM*, p. 358).
That may be because the image of the camera obscura works *as* a camera
obscura, turning upside down reality and dream, idealist and materialist,
Coleridge and Marx, Jameson and Fukuyama. Althusser's lesson – which
he abstracted from the *German Ideology* but which the Russian masses
suffered deep time to learn – would seem to hold: the more the world is
turned upside down, the more it stays the same. Such a world seems suited
for Fukuyama's spin. From the perspective of universal history, once you
wipe off the actors' grease-paint, all change, no matter how professedly
apocalyptic, is normal change. In such a world the camera obscura's 'mechanism of inversion' is not only what Mitchell calls it, 'a figure for the formal
pattern of revolution and counterrevolution' (*I*, p. 178), but a figure for
the reduction of revolution and counter-revolution to mere formality, historical change to the elaboration of some pattern, whether simple like
inversion or fractally complex. Not surprisingly, most readers find
Fukuyama's moral comforting. But some are unreasonably angry at the
message and suspect the messenger. And that's interesting.

Romantic Resistance to Transfer

In the *Biographia Literaria* Coleridge engages the relations among the
mechanism of inversion, the possibility of change, and unreasonable anger in his analysis of the reception of *Lyrical Ballads*. He invokes *Macbeth*

to epitomize the predicament of the readers of Wordsworth's 1800 preface, who suffer an 'unquiet state of mind' and who wonder 'at the perverseness of the man, who had written a long and argumentative essay to persuade them, that

Fair is foul, and foul is fair. (*BL*, 1:71–2)

Explaining his explanation, Coleridge appends a complicated footnote that diagnoses and performs the romantic movement:

In opinions of long continuance, and in which we had never before been molested by a single doubt, to be suddenly *convinced* of an *error*, is almost like being *convicted* of a fault. There is a state of mind, which is the direct antithesis of that, which takes place when we *make a bull*. The *bull* namely consists in the bringing together two incompatible thoughts, with the *sensation*, but without the *sense*, of their connection. The psychological condition, or that which constitutes the possibility of this state, being such disproportionate vividness of two distant thoughts, as extinguishes or obscures the consciousness of the intermediate images or conceptions, or wholly abstracts the attention from them. Thus in the well known bull, '*I was a fine child, but they changed me:*' the first conception expressed in the word 'I,' is that of personal identity – Ego contemplans: the second expressed in the word '*me*,' is the visual image or object by which the mind represents to itself its past condition, or rather, its personal identity under the form in which it imagined itself previously to have existed, – Ego contemplatus. Now the change of one visual image for another involves in itself no absurdity, and becomes absurd only by its immediate juxta-position with the first thought, which is rendered possible by the whole attention being successively absorbed in each singly, so as not to notice the interjacent notion, 'changed' which by its incongruity with the first thought, 'I,' constitutes the bull. Add only, that this process is facilitated by the circumstance of the words 'I,' and '*me*,' being sometimes equivalent, and sometimes having a distinct meaning; sometimes, namely, signifying the act of self-consciousness, sometimes the external image in and by which the mind represents that act to itself, the result and symbol of its individuality. Now suppose the direct contrary state, and you will have a distinct sense of the connection between two conceptions, without that *sensation* of such connection which is supplied by habit. The man *feels*, as if he were standing on his head, though he cannot but *see*, that he is truly standing on his feet. This, as a painful sensation, will of course have a tendency to associate itself with the person who occasions it; even as persons, who have been by painful means restored from derangement, are known to feel an involuntary dislike towards their physician. (*BL*, 1:72–3)

Coleridge develops a correspondence between Wordsworth as physican and the reviewers of *Lyrical Ballads* as patients. Feeling as if they have been turned upside down by Wordsworth's argument, the reviewers blame the 'painful sensation' associated with this revolution in feeling on the author, as patients are wont to blame even that physician who has restored them from derangement. Wordsworth's preface thus made discursive sense where there had been only outlandish poetic sensation but at the cost of transforming everyday sense into the stuff of dream – rough magic guaranteed to antagonize the custodians of conventional wisdom.[17]

Now suppose the direct contrary. Suppose that the 'bull', 'I was a fine child, but they changed me', anticipates Coleridge's own criticism of Wordsworth's ambitious 'Immortality Ode' in the second volume of the *Biographia*. In Coleridge's acknowledged source, Maria and Richard Edgeworth's 'Essay on the Irish Bull', the authors feature this resentful expostulation: '"I hate that woman," said a gentleman, looking at one who had been his nurse, "I hate that woman, for she changed me at nurse".' 'Change' here signifies 'exchange': 'our Hibernian's consciousness', the Edgeworths comment, 'could not retrograde to the time when he was changed at nurse; consequently there was no continuity of identity between the infant and the man who expressed his hatred of the nurse for perpetrating the fraud.'[18] Coleridge queries Wordsworth's 'bull' likewise. He has in mind the eighth stanza, which addresses the 'six years' Darling of the pigmy size':

> Thou, whose exterior semblance doth belie
> Thy Soul's immensity;
> Thou best Philosopher, who yet doest keep
> Thy heritage, thou Eye among the blind,
> That, deaf and silent, read'st the eternal deep,
> Haunted for ever by the eternal mind, –
> Mighty Prophet! Seer blest!
> On whom those truths do rest,
> Which we are toiling all our lives to find,
> In darkness lost, the darkness of the grave.[19]

In 'what sense is a child of that age a *philosopher*?' Coleridge later asks.

In what sense does he *read* the 'eternal deep?' . . . These would be tidings indeed; but such as would presuppose an immediate revelation to the inspired communicator, and require miracles to authenticate his inspiration. Children at this age give us no such information of themselves; and at what time were we dipt in the Lethe, which has produced such utter oblivion of a state so godlike? (*BL*, 2:138–9)[20]

Wordsworth's embedded fiction of a Letheward hand corresponds to the Irishman's fanciful notion of a malignant hand that changed him at nurse. Coleridge's 'I was a fine child, but they changed me' distills the dependence of Wordsworth's notion of change as alteration on an unreasoned synonymity with exchange as substitution. Coleridge's note thus warns the readers of the *Biographia* – Wordsworth chief among them – that Coleridge's antithetical criticism, designed to set Wordsworth's feet back on the ground of true principle, would likely provoke the poet's 'involuntary dislike', which notoriously proved to be the case.

Now suppose we mix in the quotation from *Macbeth*. As physician is to patent, so, it would seem, are the fair-fouling witches (Wordsworth) to Macbeth (reviewers), who, his world overturned, murders the king and usurps the throne. But it is a peculiarity of this matrix that analogies do not multiply symmetrically. In the analogic of Coleridge's note, Macbeth's 'involuntary dislike' ought to have been directed against the hags who persuaded him that fair is foul and foul is fair, not against Duncan, the rightful king. Macbeth's 'mistake' leads to the primitive violence that Constant called usurpation and that Coleridge identified as the trait of the 'commanding genius'. History progresses to contain that violence by preventing such mistakes, which entails rationalizing the *inversio* by means of substitution and condensation. If we take the split between lies and king as the difference between those who know and that one who authorizes, then the modern physician is *one who can authorize because he knows*. Historical progress has the hallmarks of what Freud calls 'transference'. Not only have '"new editions or facsimiles of the impulses and phantasies [been] aroused and made conscious during the progress of analysis; but they ... replace some earlier person by the person of the physician".'[21] Coleridge's note thus assesses the therapeutic possibilities of inversion in the framework of a transition from the feudal era of Macbeth to the modern moment of the professional physician – a transition that reforms the violently discontinuous change of usurpation as the normal change of remediation. History provides a new answer to the question that Macbeth puts to the doctor who comes to treat his maddened Lady: 'Canst thou minister to a mind diseased?' Macbeth's doctor must answer 'no'; the modern psychiatrist professes 'yes'. But even for the latter, ministration occasionally misfires. Although the transition from usurpation to remediation would seem to be an unambiguous good, the persistence of the 'involuntary dislike' – what Wordsworth calls 'Obstinate questionings / Of sense and outward things' ('*II*', ll. 141–4) – is evidence of the holdover of untransferred affect, a movement of feeling that taints the efficiency of the *inversio*. Although the physician has the credentials to summon spirits from the vasty deep of the unconscious, he cannot guarantee that they will heed his call.

That the professional authority of the physician remains as dubious for the modern as monarchical authority had been for Macbeth suggests to the romantic mind that despite history's progress nothing fundamental has changed. Mistaken ideologies fall as the professions rise in a process of substitution without alteration. Progress through Coleridge's topsy-turvy note induces the same moral. Characteristically, Coleridge has shaped his footnote as a chiasmus (sensation : sense :: sense : sensation), a figure indifferent to the cause of truth but well designed to work like a camera lens to invert perception. Both physician and philosophical critic profess to cure. And maybe they do, *generally*. Yet Coleridge's sophistical mimicry of the accredited physician's therapeutic technique supplies a pretext for the outburst of individual hostility directed toward the critic as to the physician: the obtrusion of the rhetorical scheme in the production of the cure confesses a design unavowed and an expertise unshared. Like the post-historian's mimicry of evolutionary change, such gimmicks seem to turn the world upside down only to return us to where we always were. If the camera obscura illustrates that the ideological reduces to the rhetorical, here the impression of rhetoricity figures the underwriting of the remedial by the coercive: the compulsion applied to the patient reader to choose to recognize himself as subject. That compulsion is not overt, as it is with divining witch and commanding king; it is bound up with the pretense inherent in every profession, whether credentialed or not. This pretense is the chief theme of Coleridge's many attacks on the professions.[22] For Coleridge one must always profess to profess – or, to put it in Jeremy Taylor's terms, professions inevitably confess the pretense of their claims to autonomous power. Such confession lives as the compulsion that invariably backs the bid to transfer and that may either reflect the absence of institutional support for the profession to cure (as in the case of the sophist) or it may register the dissembling of the institutional basis of the professional claims to cure (as in the case of the physician/psychiatrist). Either way, the perception of the intimate conjunction between pretense and compulsion is sufficient to trigger a hostile movement of feeling. However arduous, this particular note of Coleridge's hardly qualifies as a critique of professions; for although its rhetorical structure effectively parodies the dialectic of the cure and detonates antagonism, the intention of the note is ultimately as opaque as the formal scheme of the chiasmus – which is to say, its movement of dislike appears involuntary, like an elementary sense of injustice.

Twentieth-century readers are less familiar with this discharge of 'involuntary dislike' than Freud's 'negative transference'. None the less, the concept had long inhabited the British liberal tradition under the names 'negative liberty' and 'the right of resistance'. J. G. A. Pocock has distinguished between the republican, civic, virtue-based tradition, in which possession of real property grounded a citizen's autonomous political existence, and the liberal, juristic, rights-based tradition. In the latter the law alone confers liberty, which is a citizen's right to be safe from political interference but which presupposes no part in the imperium. Legally constituted rights are acquired and exercised through the citizen's 'role in the possession, conveyance, and administration of things', and because those rights are ultimately things as much as any other thing, individuals could be said to have been 'invested with rights [so] that they might surrender them absolutely to the sovereign'.[23] If the type of republican resistance is an act, the liberal resistance is a species of property, as exchangeable as any other.

According to C. B. Macpherson, nineteenth-century liberalism internalized the tension between the republican and the juristic traditions as the distinction between economic liberalism, which stresses the 'maximization of utilities', and democratic liberalism, which aims at the 'maximization of powers'. The democratic ethic prescribes that each person cultivate his 'potential for realizing some human end, [an ethic which] necessarily includes in a man's powers not only his natural capacities (his energy and skill) but also his *ability* to exert them'. Rather than maximize powers, liberal society, obedient to an economic imperative, has consistently promoted a 'net transfer of powers', which it executes by allowing some to deny others access to the instruments with which they might develop their natural capacities.[24]

On Macpherson's account, Freud looks like an economic liberal, concerned to maximize utility not power. When, in his essay 'The Dynamics of the Transference', Freud asks how it comes about 'that the transference is so pre-eminently suitable as a weapon of resistance', his aim is disarmament.[25] He divides in order to conquer. He first distinguishes positive from negative feeling and then divides positive feeling into 'friendly or affectionate feelings as are capable of becoming conscious and the extensions of these in the unconscious. Of these last', Freud inevitably adds, 'analysis shows that they invariably rest ultimately on an erotic basis' ('DT', p. 112). It must be so because 'to begin with we knew none but sexual objects', and only feelings that have objects are recognizable and subject to the cure. He argues that 'the transference to the physician is only suited for resistance in so far as it consists in *negative* feeling or in the repressed *erotic* elements of positive feeling' ('DT', 112). The 'or' registers an uncertainty about what exactly these negative feelings are – whether they are what they seem or whether they are 'ultimately' a repressed element of something else. What the feelings are puzzles because what the feelings *do* is *move*. They elude inspection:

> The unconscious feelings strive to avoid the recognition which the cure demands; they seek instead for reproduction, with all the power of hallucination and the inappreciation of time characteristic of the unconscious. The patient ascribes, just as in dreams, currency and reality to what results from the awakening of his unconscious feelings; he seeks to discharge his emotions, regardless of the reality of the situation. ('DT', p. 114)

As the psychoanalyst tries to turn feelings, which move under their own power, into desires, which posit objects, random discharge becomes anger. 'Involuntary dislike' is the movement by which the 'unconscious feelings strive to avoid the recognition which the cure demands' and the net transfer of power which it entails.

Psychoanalysis, according to Freud, works to rid the patient of a 'cliché or stereotype . . . which perpetually repeats and reproduces itself as life goes on' ('DT', p. 106). Here is the last, terrible sentence of Freud's essay:

> It is undeniable that the subjugation of the transference-manifestations provides the greatest difficulties for the psychoanalyst; but it must not be forgotten that they, and they only, render the invaluable service of making the patient's buried and forgotten love-emotions actual and manifest; for in the last resort no one can be slain in *absentia* or in *effigie*. ('DT', pp. 114–15)

To cure means to bring up occult, conspiratorial, pointlessly reproductive emotions, to recognize them, and to subject them to the guillotine of analysis, thereby adjusting the patient to the ideological world that Freud calls 'real life' ('DT', p. 113).

What Freud called real life, contemporary liberalism has come to call the post-historical. Fukuyama's universal history tries to reclaim the philosophical vagrants and neurotics of the past (for example, Hegel and

Nietzsche) for the 'liberal ascent' by adjusting them to a narrative that legitimates the way things are. He supplements the classical, Hobbesian definition of man as driven by the threat of scarcity, fear of death, and an insatiable desire for accumulation with a Hegelian conception of man as motivated by a 'totally non-economic drive, the struggle for recognition' (*EH*, p. 135). Hobbes is the scion of economics, Hegel the scion of the political – it is the clerical profession of a universal history to wed them. To seal the bond Fukuyama redescribes affect that is not perceptibly acquisitive as inchoate feelings that *seek*, not, as in Freud, avoid, recognition. Inexorably (epistemology is destiny), the universal 'struggle for recognition' is redescribed again as a universal '*desire* for recognition' (*EH*, p. 152, emphasis added). By identifying the 'totally non-economic drive' as desire, Fukuyama surreptitiously renders it as *already economic* because susceptible to the promise of satisfaction that generates those reciprocal exchanges that maximize utility. Fukuyama thus vindicates Macpherson's taxonomy of liberalisms by attempting to engineer the net transfer of power from political men and women to economic man all at once by means of a massive redescription of struggle as desire. Nifty. But without consequences. Nothing changes. Anger, outrage, involuntary dislike, and questionings persist. The power of Freud's account of human motivation inhabits his reluctant acknowledgment of the intransigence of that which resists the cure. For Freud a drive is a drive, not a desire manqué. Nothing resists Fukuyama's redescription, and, as most liberal economists will tell you, nothing is got for nothing.

If Freud circumscribes Fukuyama, Coleridge's account of his early instruction in English composition characterizes Freud. In the *Biographia* he recalls the lessons in Shakespeare and Milton that cost him so much 'time and trouble to *bring up*, so as to escape [his teacher James Bowyer's] censure'. Drilled in the rigorous logic of poems, Coleridge learned that 'in the truly great poets . . . there is a reason assignable, not only for every word, but for the position of every word.' Diction fell under the purview of a hanging judge:

In our own English compositions . . . he showed no mercy to phrase, metaphor, or image, unsupported by a sound sense, or where the same sense might have been conveyed with equal force and dignity in plainer words. Lute, harp, and lyre, muse, muses, and inspirations, Pegasus, Parnassus, and Hippocrene, were all an abomination to him. In fancy I can almost hear him now, exclaiming, '*Harp? Harp? Lyre? Pen and ink, boy, you mean! Muse, boy, Muse? your Nurse's daughter, you mean! Pierian spring? Oh 'aye! the cloister-pump, I suppose!*' [*BL*, 1:9–10]

Such was learning English composition at Christ's Hospital at the end of the eighteenth century. And such is still moral education, at least according to Michael Oakeshott, who argues that

> a morality . . . is neither a system of general principles nor a code of rules, but a vernacular language. . . . What has to be learned in a moral education is not a theorem such as that good conduct is acting fairly or being charitable, nor is it a rule such as 'always tell the truth,' but how to speak the language intelligently.[26]

Because the conversational standard of the vernacular has never been simply a diction, given or found, but always a *jurisdiction*, answerable to the imperative of what Benedict Anderson has called 'the revolutionary vernacularizing thrust of capitalism',[27] which peremptorily determines native intelligence by censoring unruly, demotic speech as gibberish (a tale told by an idiot boy), there is no practical difference between moral and political education nor between political education and legal judgement. For Bowyer, as for Oakeshott, each fact is a 'verdict'.[28] 'Certain introductions, similes, and examples,' Coleridge recalls,

> were placed by name on a list of interdiction. Among the similes, there was the example of Alexander and Clytus, which was equally good and apt, whatever might be the theme. Was it ambition? Alexander and Clytus! – Flattery? Alexander and Clytus! – Anger? Drunkenness? Pride? Friendship? Ingratitude? Late Repentance? Still, still Alexander and Clytus! At length, the praises of agriculture having been exemplified in the sagacious observation, that had Alexander been holding the plough, he would not have run his friend Clytus through with a spear; this tried, and serviceable old friend was banished by public edict in secula seculorum. (*BL*, 1:10)

Coleridge's boyish stereotype reproduced promiscuously.[29] Because it belonged nowhere, the Alexander and Clytus topos could be discharged anywhere. Bowyer interdicted this demotic frenzy by commanding banishment. But, as Freud knows, interdiction is not transference and banishment is not slaying. Having been put away as if the thing of a child, Alexander-cum-Clytus none the less thrusts back into Coleridge's biographical composition, where, in the very excess of his proscriptive zeal, Coleridge involuntarily transforms judgement into stereotype and, resisting the transference he wills, tips piety into parody.

Romantic Politics

As Freud argues, and as my medley of writers illustrates, willful resistance to the cure involves 'an inappreciation of time', which manifests itself in the refusal of the patient to meet the requirement that 'he shall fit these emotions into their place in the treatment and in his life-history' ('DT', p. 114). As fugitive feelings resist recognition, so they resist being narrativized into the formation of an identity, whether of a person, a people, a social class, or, in the case of Coleridge, a philosophical critic. From the progressivist perspective shared by Fukuyama and McGann, inappreciation of narrative time looks like a conservative refusal to recognize history. But for the romantic, inappreciation of time is neither position nor attitude but the willful commission of anachronism, the assertion of the historical as that which could not be over because it has not yet really happened.

Coleridge said much the same thing in his unpacking of Jacobin:

> The word implies a man, whose affections have been warmly and deeply interested in the cause of general freedom, who has hoped all good and honourable things both *of*, and *for*, mankind. . . . Jacobin . . . affirm[s] that no man can ever become altogether an apostate to Liberty, who has at any time been sincerely and fervently attached to it. His hopes will burn like the Greek fire, hard to be extinguished, and easily kindling. Even when he despairs of the cause, he will yet *wish*, that it had been successful. And even when private interests have warped his public character, his convictions will remain, and his wishes often rise up in rebellion against his outward actions and public avowals.[30]

Coleridge's definition unlinks emancipatory ardour from French principles.[31] Attachment to liberty means resisting the cure of historicization, being locked into synchrony with what the vernacular says can be said. Blind to the vicissitudes of parties and programs, *Jacobin* names a wish that can be fulfilled only in a future toward which, in rebellion against the way things are, the ardent soul moves.

Because *Jacobin* none the less imparts the taint of the foreign and ideological, I prefer the term *demotic*. The distinction between vernacular and demotic may be roughly apportioned in terms of the difference between two kinds of disturbance that troubled the social landscape of Great Britain in the 1790s and the early years of the nineteenth century: the riot and the insurrection. A riot involved the hostile, occasionally violent action of the crowd against property or authority, but the rioters observed a traditional protocol that did not, according to John Bohstedt, 'normally challenge the arrangement of local power'. Even in the revolutionary 1790s the authorities responded moderately because 'they recognized the rioters as members of their own community'.[32] The same authorities who countenanced rioting labeled Jacobin the agent of a disturbance who was unrecognizable according to the traditional norms. That agent has, by and large, remained invisible to historians. One might be inclined to blame the ideological investments of individual historians,[33] but the resistance to historicization inhabits the historical field, for to be an *agent* of insurrection meant and means resistance to becoming an object of study, whether by William Pitt or J. C. D. Clark. As Roger Wells has shown in exacting detail, those agents may have been actually strangers, or persons whose motives were unclear, persons whose motives were too clear and patently ideological – or the agent might have been no 'person' at all, just the occulted and achronistic appearance of the '"grip, password, sign, countersign or travelling password"', handed, muttered, or scrawled.[34] If, as Susan Stewart argues, 'graffiti' are considered obscene because such wild autographs are 'utterances out of place', the intricate oaths, furtive handshakes, and cryptic hails of insurrectionaries are signs out of time.[35] The holdover of tradesmen's rituals and memorials of failed revolutionary projects, they are, however, no more nostalgic than a Wordsworthian epitaph, for they save the place of a possible future by performing a social movement without a social vehicle. Unlike the devices of masons, such signs do not certify membership or indicate status but betoken an affiliation that is transitive, but not transferable, illegible according to what, in the advertisement to *Lyrical Ballads* (1798), Wordsworth called 'preestablished codes of decision'.[36] Insurrectionaries can be distinguished from rioters by consciousness, by regional origin, by class, or by anything else you like. They themselves begin to distinguish themselves from rioters as soon as they begin to *produce* their means of resistance, a step that is only conditioned by their symbolic resourcefulness. Demotic utterances challenge traditional systems of social control not with pikes and pistols but with the uncanny repetition of stereotypes circulating without respect to region or kind, resisting protocols of recognition but soliciting acknowledgment of one stranger by another, of United Irishman by United Briton, of United Briton by Yorkshire weaver, of Yorkshire weaver by Lake poet.

The propagation of demotic utterances identifies a species of what Hobsbawm has called 'primitive social movements', which historically had been characterized by a ritualistic formalism of ceremonies and symbolism. In the nineteenth century two kinds of organizations shared these features: 'secret revolutionary societies and orders . . . and trade unions and friendly societies' (PR, p. 153). As 'primitive' suggests, Hobsbawm (whose study appeared in 1959, well before history expired) consigns such archaic groups to a prepolitical stage of development. In the prepolitical (to adapt the Marx of The Eighteenth Brumaire), form exceeded content; in the revolutions to follow, Hobsbawm implies, the content will exceed the form. The problem that Hobsbawm never confronts – the problem that dogs every engagement with insurrectionary Great Britain after the coronation of Bonaparte – is the return of the prepolitical, a formalism that, because it recurs, cannot be branded as primitive and that, because it is involuntary, cannot be stigmatized as sentimental. The return of the prepolitical or (to romantically equivocate Raymond Williams's famous distinction) the *emergence of the residual* is romantic formalism on the move.[37] Because practiced without good reason in the aftermath of utopian dreams, that movement might be called the politics of hope.

Hobsbawm is inclined to criticize British repressiveness of the post-revolutionary era not for its reactionary ferocity but for its redundancy, for he concludes that 'the belief of early nineteenth-century British governments in the necessarily subversive nature of initiations and secret oaths, was mistaken. The outsiders against which the ritual brotherhood guarded its secrets were not only the bourgeois' and not always the government's.' Yet he adds:

> Only insofar as all working men's organizations by virtue of their class membership, were likely to engage in activities frowned upon by employers or the authorities, did the initiation and oath bind their members specifically against these. There was thus no initial distinction between, as it were, legitimately and unnecessarily secret societies, but only between the fraternal activities in which their members were ritually bound to show solidarity, some of which might be acceptable to the law while others were not. (PR, pp. 158–9)

The government's evident overreaction testified not only to a class bias but also to the fact that the initial *in*distinction between the legitimately and the unnecessarily secret societies that was induced by transitive repetition of stereotypes constituted a shared volatility of purpose which *was* insurrectionary without regard to ideology.

That explains why Coleridge's poetry of the late 1790s, which in its supernatural, preternatural, and conversational modes resonates with suggestions of omens and signals ('Frost at Midnight'), strange visitations and conspiratorial understandings ('Christabel'), mysterious symbolism ('The Rime of the Ancient Mariner'), insistent metrical schemes and arbitrary anachronisms (choose your favorite), did nothing to diminish his reputation for radicalism. It explains why such blatantly bullish ballads of Wordsworth as 'We Are Seven', 'Simon Lee', 'The Idiot Boy', and 'The Thorn' could, despite a lack of revolutionary content, seem unsettling, as Coleridge canonically attests in chapter 17 of the *Biographia Literaria*. The production of stereotypes ('Oh misery! oh misery! / Oh woe is me! oh misery!') that initiated strangers into imagined communities unaccountable to the nation-state was dangerous and was branded as such by the Whiggish *Edinburgh Review*. In its inaugural issue of October 1802, which appeared four years after *Lyrical Ballads* but at a time when, as Wells demonstrates, insurrectionary activity had strongly revived,[38] the *Edinburgh* both adopted the Enlightenment pose of debunker of conspiratorial theories of the French Revolution and yet succumbed to making hysterically sarcastic charges of sect and conspiracy in its review of the activities of the Lake poets. The issue was not Jacobinism – despite half-hearted attempts, Francis Jeffrey would ultimately agree with the contemporary practitioners of ideology critique that none was detectable – but a kind of insistent formalism, which, because its ideological mission was inapparent, seemed the pretext for a secret bond that could only be defended against by condemning it as 'sectual' (Jeffrey's favoured ploy) or sexual (the Freudian recourse).

The Edgeworths' 'Essay on Irish Bulls' may be taken as another example of the way the legitimately and the unnecessarily secret could be confused. In the bull the joke is always on the Irishman, and the Edgeworths are at pains to argue that he is victimized by the prejudice that the bull represents. Yet the Edgeworths' project, to prove that the bull is not a 'species of blunder *peculiar* to Ireland', was finally motivated less by a desire to rescue the Irish from English laughter than to dissipate the English suspicion that there is some kind of essential character or form of thought that binds the Irish together, rejects English reason, and is unassimilable to polite society.[39]

The 'depeculiarization' of Irish speech, which meant translating the demotic into the vernacular (both Maria Edgeworth's and Walter Scott's glossaries prosecute the same end), carried forward the Enlightenment project of homogenizing mankind in the guise of the bourgeoisie and, as Mitchell has argued, of restricting character to what can be stamped on a commodity. Yet that strategy could only be partially effective, for insurrectionary signs solicited acknowledgement while eluding recognition by mobilizing borrowed and disposable stereotypes.[40] The difference between the character of the commodity and the character of the demotic is the difference between a trademark, copyrightable and subject to exchange, and what Marx in the *German Ideology* called a 'form of activity'. The difference is between using a printing press and being one. That difference can be illustrated by George Cruikshank's demotic 'The New Man of the Industrial Future', which is both the figure of a figure capable of reproducing stereotypes and a stereotype that I reproduce:

The difference between the commodity and the demotic can be further elucidated by a romanticized Marx (I have substituted *resistance* for *subsistence*):

> The way in which men produce their means of [resistance] depends first of all on the nature of the actual means they find in existence and have to reproduce. This mode of production must not be considered simply as being the reproduction of the physical existence of the individuals. Rather it is a definite form of activity of these individuals, a definite form of expressing their life, a definite *mode of life* on their part. As individuals express their life, so they are. (*GI*, p. 7)

Excepting that by 'actual means' Marx means material conditions and we mean symbolic conditions, this passage captures the way insurrectionaries

Figure 22.1   George Cruikshank from William Hine, *The Political Showman – At Home! Exhibiting His Cabinet of Curiosities and Creatures – All Alive!* (London, 1821)

work with the stereotypes they have on hand, repeating them in a transitive form of activity that binds men and women together in an insurrectionary mode of life, prepolitical but hopeful.

What was truly peculiar to the insurrectionaries was this form of activity. Hobsbawm comments that 'the fantastic nomenclature of brotherhoods was totally non-utilitarian unlike later revolutionary organizations which have normally attempted to pick names indicative of their ideology or programme' (PR, p. 166). 'Non-utilitarian' should not be translated as aesthetic. That the nomenclature was nonutilitarian simply means that it, like the bull, did no work. Because it did no work, professed nothing, it was therefore without value. It could not be inverted or transferred, synthesized or evolved. But because it *did* not work it *remains* a cause in the way that Lacan speaks of cause – a cause untransferred to history's narrative and therefore untouched by history's end.

Rather like the strange creatures captured in the Burgess Shale, which were mistaken by their discoverer and recently reinterpreted by H. B. Whittington. For the evolutionary model embraced by Fukuyama, Jameson, and Hobsbawm, which moves confidently from the archaic to the postmodern, from the prepolitical to the posthistorical, I would substitute one closer to that proposed by the romantic paleontologist Stephen Jay Gould in *Wonderful Life*. There Gould meditates on the implications of the scandal that Whittington's reconstruction of the residue of anomalous multicellular creatures visited on evolutionary biology's faith in the 'cone of increasing diversity'. He urges the application of the thought experiment called 'replaying life's tape' as a means to adjudge the necessity of the way things have turned out. In the cases of the defunct genera *Sidneyia*, *Marrella*, and *Opabinia*, replaying life's tape argues for the contingency of their extinction and therefore the contingency of all that followed.[41] Replaying life's tape confesses the same contingency in the failure of demotic forms of social life, of romantic movements. But replaying the tape is only a thought experiment with organisms that cannot be revived by Gould's song. Because the resources of the demos were and are symbolic, no such barrier cuts the path between then and now. The demotic cause lives just because it did not succeed; the romantic movement is inescapably anachronistic because it is the politics of the future and always will be until something better comes along. And as contingent analogies between phrases of address (grips, passwords, meters, motifs, commonplaces) bound each to each in transient but strong commonalities then, so now as then. Sensitive to the strength of willful analogy in forging a common cause, I ask you to acknowledge that Coleridge's cliché of the Jacobin's 'Greek fire' marks the demotic heat in Wordsworth's contemporary reference to those 'embers' in which there is 'something that doth live' ('*II*', ll. 130–1) and threads through the political unconscious to link that insurrectionary glow by analogy with the volcanic *Prometheus Unbound*, with the fantastically explosive *Don Juan*, as well as with the fire next time of the Greek Revolution or, perhaps, the 1992 insurrection in LA.

In *City of Quartz*, his superb rendering of the postmodern end zone of Los Angeles, Mike Davis recalls one memorable instance:

> during a [civil rights] protest at a local whites-only drive-in restaurant, when the timely arrival of Black gang members saved [activists] from a mauling by white hotrodders. The gang was the legendary Slausons, . . . [who] became a crucial social base for the rise of the local Black Liberation movement. The turning-point . . . was the festival of the oppressed in August 1965 that the Black community called a rebellion and the white media a riot. Although the 'riot commission' headed by old-guard Republicans supported Chief Parker's so-called 'riff-raff theory' that the August events were the work of a small criminal minority, subsequent research . . . proved that up to 75,000 people took part in the uprising, mostly from the stolid Black working class. For gang members it was 'The Last Great Rumble', as formerly hostile groups forgot old grudges and cheered each other on against the LAPD and the National Guard. . . . Old enemies, like the Slausons and the Gladiators . . . flash[ed] smiles and high signs as they broke through Parker's invincible 'blue line'.[42]

From the thin red line poised against uprisings of ragged Yorkshiremen in 1802 to the thin blue line in LA in 1965 – and again in 1992. It is no doubt irresponsible of Davis to embellish his account of a Watts Rebellion, which lacked any recognizable ideology, with such Jacobin stereotypes as the 'festival of the oppressed'; and it is no doubt irresponsible and inappreciative of time, that is, romantic, to stereotype uprisings in different lands and different epochs in order to draw analogies with no workable plan in view except to suggest that although we may have seen the end of history, we have certainly not seen the last rumble.[43] Or the last romantic movement.

In Arnold's time the notion of romantic expectancy was a sentimental idealism; in the 1960s it sounded revolutionary; in the 1970s and 1980s things soured as stern-lipped academics, fortified for history's long haul by strong doses of Marx, denounced romantic hope as an ideological refuge embraced by apostates to the true cause. Now that the long haul has been aborted and Marx's beautiful theory withers, the romantic movement marks time as the reviving possibility of change that is not merely normal, its historicity the willful commission of anachronism after anachronism linked by bold analogy. By promiscuously replicating stereotypes that resist recognition and transfer, the romantic movement rejects the imperial epochalism of the posthistorical as the sign of the naturalization of injustice. At one point in his writings on ideology and literature, Raymond Williams wisely warns against what he calls premature historicization. Until there is justice, all historicization is premature. Until there is justice the untimely slogan of romantic politics will not be 'always historicize' but 'now and again anachronize'.

Notes

My thanks to Peter J. Manning and Neil Hertz for their critical readings of earlier versions of this essay.

1 Anthony Giddens, *The Constitution of Society: Outline of the Theory of Structuration* (Berkeley: University of California Press, 1984), p. xxiii.

2 See Edward Said, *Beginnings: Intention and Method* (Baltimore: Johns Hopkins University Press, 1975), pp. 191–7, and Samuel Taylor Coleridge, *Biographia Literaria*, ed. James Engell and W. Jackson Bate, 2 vols, vol. 7 of *The Collected Works of Samuel Taylor Coleridge*, gen. ed. Kathleen Coburn (Princeton, 1983), 1:41n; hereafter abbreviated *BL*.

3 See Francis Fukuyama, 'The End of History?', *The National Interest* 16 (Summer 1989), pp. 3–18 and *The End of History and The Last Man* (New York: The Free Press, 1992); hereafter abbreviated *EH*.

4 Fukuyama, 'The End of History?', p. 3.

5 Benjamin Constant, *The Spirit of Conquest and Usurpation and Their Relation to Civilization, in Political Writings*, trans. and ed. Biancamaria Fontana (Cambridge: Cambridge University Press, 1988), p. 55.

6 Wisely or not, this essay abandons the security provided by the so-called anachronism test, which contemporary historians of consequence have argued provides an important criterion for determining that the language identified with a historical agent is not the historian's own fabrication. See Quentin Skinner, 'Meaning and Understanding in the History of ideas', *History and Theory* 8 (1) (1969), pp. 3–53, and J. G. A. Pocock, 'Concept of Language and the metier d'historien: Some Considerations on Practice', in *The Languages of Political Theory in Early Modern Europe*, ed. Anthony Pagden (Cambridge: Cambridge University Press, 1987), p. 21. These criteria are explored in the context of interpretations of the language of economics by M. Ali Khan in 'On Economics and Language: A Review Article', *Journal of Economic Studies* 20, 3 (1993), pp. 51–69.

7   Fredric Jameson, *Postmodernism, or, The Cultural Logic of Late Capitalism* (Durham: Duke University Press, 1991), p. 309; hereafter abbreviated *PM*. Diane Elam takes a divergent position in her *Romancing the Postmodern* (London: Routledge, 1992), where she argues that anachronism is an 'inevitable' constituent of the genre she calls 'postmodern romance' (pp. 68–75).

8   Immanuel Wallerstein, *Unthinking Social Science: The Limits of Nineteenth-Century Paradigms* (Cambridge: Polity Press, 1991), pp. 17, 16; hereafter abbreviated *USS*.

9   E. J. Hobsbawm, *Primitive Rebels: Studies in Archaic Forms of Social Movement in the Nineteenth and the Twentieth Centuries* (New York: W. W. Norton, 1959), p. 151; hereafter abbreviated *PR*.

10   Matthew Arnold, 'The Function of Criticism at the Present Time', *Essays in Criticism, First Series*, ed. Sister Thomas Marion Hoctor (Chicago: University of Chicago Press, 1968), p. 13.

11   Karl Marx and Friedrich Engels, *German Ideology, Parts I and III*, ed. R. Pascal (New York: International Publishers, 1947), p. 26; hereafter abbreviated *GI*.

12   Jerome J. McGann, *The Romantic Ideology: A Critical Investigation* (Chicago: University of Chicago Press, 1983), p. 9.

13   Louis Althusser, *Lenin and Philosophy and Other Essays*, trans. Ben Brewster (New York: Monthly Review Press, 1973), pp. 173 and 182.

14   Jacques Lacan, 'The Freudian Unconscious and Ours', in *The Four Fundamental Concepts of Psycho-Analysis*, trans. Alan Sheridan, ed. Jacques-Alain Miller (New York: Norton, 1978), p. 22.

15   Paul Ricoeur, *Lectures on Ideology and Utopia*, ed. George H. Taylor (New York: Columbia University Press, 1986), p. 78.

16   W. J. T Mitchell, *Iconology: Image, Text, Ideology* (Chicago: University of Chicago Press, 1986), p. 169; hereafter abbreviated *I*.

17   Coleridge is picking up on Wordsworth's warning in the 1800 preface to *Lyrical Ballads* that readers might expect 'feelings of strangeness and awkwardness' in their first encounter with the poetry (William Wordsworth, *Wordsworth: Selected Poems and Prefaces*, ed. Jack Stillinger (Boston: Houghton Mifflin, 1965).) [For further discussion of this preface, see my *PomoIntro*, pp. 43–5 and 54. (NL)]

18   Maria and Richard Edgeworth, 'Essay on Irish Bulls', *Tales and Novels*, 18 vols in 9 (New York, 1836), 1:102.

19   Wordsworth, 'Ode: Intimations of Immortality from Recollections of Early Childhood', *Selected Poems and Prefaces*, p. 189; hereafter abbreviated '*II*'.

20   That children do give us such information is the burden of Wordsworth's 'We Are Seven' in *Lyrical Ballads* and of Lacan's version of the bull in 'The Freudian Unconscious and Ours':

  Remember the naive failure of the simpleton's delighted attempt to grasp the little fellow who declares – *I have three brothers, Paul, Ernest and me*. But it is quite natural – first the three brothers, Paul, Ernest and I are counted, and then there is I at the level at which I am to reflect the first I, that is to say, the I who counts. (Lacan, 'Freudian Unconscious', p. 20)

Lacan takes the Edgeworths' moral, that there could be no continuity of identity, and runs with it.

21   J. Laplanche and J.-B. Pontalis, *The Language of Psycho-Analysis* (New York, 1973), p. 457, quoting Sigmund Freud. For a subtle discussion of the rhetorical complexity of Freud's concept of transference, see Cynthia Chase, ' "Transference" as Trope and Persuasion', in *Discourse in Psychoanalysis and Literature*, ed. Shlomith Rimmon-Kenan (New York and London: Methuen, 1987), pp. 211–32.

22   For example:

> Sagacious men and *knowing* in their profession they are not ignorant that even diseases may prove convenient: they remember that Demosthenes, a state-physician, when he wished to finger a large fee from Harpalus, yet was expected by his former connections to speak out according 'to the well-known tendency of his political opinions' found a *sore-throat* very serviceable; and they have learnt from their own experience how absolutely necessary in point of 'selfish policy' is a certain political palsey in the head, 'omnibus omnia annuens'. (Coleridge, 'A Letter to Edward Long Fox, M.D.', *Lectures 1795 on Politics and Religion*, ed. Lewis Patton and Peter Mann, vol. 1 of *Collected Works*, pp. 326–7.)

See also Coleridge, 'Lectures on Revealed Religion', in *Lectures*, p. 207. An important exception to this programmatic derogation occurs in Coleridge's letters home from Germany in March 1799, written after some study of the German university system, where the term professor is treated with uncharacteristic respect.

23   J. G. A. Pocock, 'Virtues, Rights, and Manners: A Model for Historians of Political Thought', in *Virtue, Commerce, and History: Essays on Political Thought and History, Chiefly in the Eighteenth Century* (Cambridge: Cambridge University Press, 1985), pp. 43–5.

24   C. B. Macpherson, *DemocraticTheory: Essays in Retrieval* (Oxford: Clarendon Press, 1973), pp. 5, 9 and 10.

25   Sigmund Freud, 'The Dynamics of Transference', in *Therapy and Technique*, ed. Phillip Rieff (New York, 1963), pp. 113–14; hereafter abbreviated 'DT'.

26   Michael Oakeshott, *On Human Conduct* (Oxford: Clarendon, 1975), pp. 78–9.

27   Benedict Anderson, *Imagined Communities: Reflections on the Origin and Spread of Nationalism* (1983; London: Verso, 1991), p. 75.

28   Oakeshott, *Human Conduct*, p. 2.

29   Not least in my own writing, where, I confess, this is the third time I have pulled out this particular plum.

30   Coleridge, 'Once a Jacobin Always a Jacobin', in *Essays on His Times*, ed. David V. Erdman, 3 vols, vol. 3 of *Collected Works*, 1:368.

31 This unlinking is an attempt to break with the paranoid logic of political debate in the 1790s. For reformers, radicals, and loyalists 'much of the argument and rhetoric of the decade revolve[d] around the presence or absence of a link between principles and practice in France' (Mark Philp, 'The Fragmented Ideology of Reform', in *The French Revolution and British Popular Politics*, ed. Philp [Cambridge: Cambridge University Press, 1991], p. 59). For an interpretation of movements in 1798 as addressing the felt need to break this impasse, see Jerome Christensen, 'Ecce Homo: Biographical Acknowledgment, the End of the French Revolution and the Romantic Reinvention of English Verse', in *Contesting the Subject: Essays in the Postmodern Theory and Practice of Biography and Biographical Criticism*, ed. William H. Epstein (West Lafayette, Ind.: Purdue University Press, 1991), pp. 53–84.

32 John Bohstedt, *Riots and Community Politics in England and Wales, 1790–1810* (Cambridge, Mass.: Harvard University Press, 1983), p. 5.

33 The various investments are on display in Philp, *French Revolution*.

34 See Roger Wells, *Insurrection: The British Experience, 1795–1803* (Gloucester: A. Sutton, 1983). The list comes from *PR*, p. 160.

35 Susan Stewart, 'Ceci Tuera Cela: Graffiti as Crime and Art', in *Life After Postmodernism: Essays on Value and Culture*, ed. John Fekete (New York: St. Martin's Press, 1987), p. 169. Stewart stands in for a vast range of research in cultural studies on the capacity for resistance in contemporary popular culture, most of it indebted to the paradigmatic work done at the Birmingham Centre for Contemporary Cultural Studies and responsive to the intellectual initiatives of Raymond Williams and Stuart Hall. For a fine critical account of the history and controversies surrounding the theory and practice of cultural studies, see Jim McGuigan, *Cultural Populism* (London: Routledge, 1992), especially his chapter, 'Trajectories of Cultural Populism', pp. 45–85. In its anti-economism and its insistence that even in its apparently most arcane mannerisms romantic writing is 'ordinary', this essay is a species of cultural populism in McGuigan's terms. Indeed, although this is not the occasion to negotiate the bearings of, say, Dick Hebdige's and Dave Laing's competing accounts, in *Subculture: The Meaning of Style* (London and New York: Methuen, 1979) and *One Chord Wonders: Power and Meaning in Punk Rock* (Milton Keynes: Open University Press, 1985), of the political implications of 1970s punk for my argument, I shall use the relative obscurity of a footnote to hazard the anachronistic claim, in the spirit of Williams, that in the long view cultural populism is romanticism.

36 Wordsworth, advertisement to *Lyrical Ballads* (1798), *Selected Poems and Prefaces*, p. 443.

37 See Raymond Williams, *Marxism and Literature* (Oxford: Oxford University Press, 1977), pp. 121–7.

38 See Wells, *Insurrection*, pp. 220–52.

39 Edgeworth and Edgeworth, 'Essays on Irish Bulls', p. 100.

40   'Where no other organization existed, as after the defeat of a revolutionary movement, masonic lodges were very likely to become the refuge of the rebels' (*PR*, p. 163).

41   See Stephen Jay Gould, *Wonderful Life: The Burgess Shale and the Nature of History* (New York: W. W. Norton, 1989), pp. 45–52.

42   Mike Davis, *City of Quartz: Excavating the Future in Los Angeles* (London: Verso, 1990), p. 297.

43   Harold Meyerson remarks on the explosive archaism of contemporary Los Angeles: 'LA has come to resemble those premodern cities where the working class lacked both unions and parties, where fear was a constant of daily life and the riot a routine feature of politics' ('Falling Down: LA, City without Politics', *The New Republic*, 3 May 1993, p. 14).

Select Bibliography

1. Romanticism

Abrams, M. H. *The Mirror and the Lamp: Romantic Theory and the Critical Tradition*. Oxford: Oxford University Press, 1953.

Bloom, Harold. *The Anxiety of Influence: A Theory of Poetry*. New York: Oxford University Press, 1997, 2nd edn.

Cranston, Maurice. *The Romantic Movement*. Oxford: Blackwell, 1994.

Lacoue-Labarthe, Philippe and Jean-Luc Nancy. *The Literary Absolute: The Theory of Literature in German Romanticism*, trans. Philip Barnand and Cheryl Lester. Albany, New York: State University of New York Press, 1988.

McGann, Jerome J. *The Romantic Ideology: A Critical Investigation*. Chicago: Chicago University Press, 1983.

Praz, Mario. *The Romantic Agony*. Oxford: Oxford University Press, 1970.

Willson, A. Leslie. *German Romantic Criticism*. New York: Continuum, 1982.

2. Proto-Pomo

Bakhtin, Mikhail, *The Dialogic Imagination*, trans. Caryl Emerson and M. Holquist. Austin: University of Texas Press, 1981.

Bataille, Georges. *Literature and Evil*, trans. Alastair Hamilton. London: Marion Boyars, 1985.

Freud, Sigmund. *Introductory Lectures on Psychoanalysis*, trans. James Strachey, eds James Strachey and Angela Richards. Harmondworth: Penguin, 1973.

Heidegger, Martin. *Basic Writings*, ed. David Farrell Krell. New York: Harper and Row, 1977.

Heidegger, Martin. *The Question Concerning Technology and Other Essays*, trans. William Lovitt. New York: Harper and Row, 1977.

Horkheimer, Max and Theodor Adorno. *Dialectic of Enlightenment*, trans. John Cumming. New York: Seabury, 1972.

Merleau-Ponty, Maurice. *In Praise of Philosophy and Other Essays*, trans. John Wild, James Edie and John O'Neill. Evanston, Ill.: Northwestern University Press, 1988.

Nietzsche, Friedrich. *Beyond Good and Evil*, trans. Walter Kaufmann. New York: Random House, 1966.

Nietzsche, Friedrich. *The Genealogy of Morals*, trans. Walter Kaufmann and R. J. Hollingdale. New York: Random House, 1967.

Wittgenstein, Ludwig. 'A Lecture on Ethics', *The Philosophical Review* 74, 1 (1965), pp. 3–12.

3. The Post in General

Appignanesi, Richard. *Postmodernism for Beginners*. Cambridge: Icon, 1995.

Barthes, Roland. *Image Music Text*, trans. Stephen Heath. London: Fontana, 1977.

Baudrillard, Jean. *Selected Writings*, ed. Mark Poster. Cambridge: Polity, 1988.

Baudrillard, Jean. *Simulacra and Simulation*, trans. Sheila Faria Glaser. Ann Arbor: University of Michigan Press, 1994.

Bové, Paul A., ed. *Early Postmodernism: Foundational Essays*. Durham: Duke University Press, 1995.

Cahoon, Lawrence, ed. *From Modernism to Postmodernism: An Anthology*. Oxford: Blackwell, 1996.

Calinescu, Matei. *Five Faces of Modernity: Modernism, Avant-Garde, Decadence, Kitsch, Postmodernism*. Durham: Duke University Press, 1987, 2nd edn.

Docherty, Thomas, *After Theory*. Edinburgh: Edinburgh University Press, 1996.

Docherty, Thomas, ed. *Postmodernism: A Reader*. New York: Harvester Wheatsheaf, 1993.

Eagleton, Terry. *The Illusion of Postmodernism*. Oxford: Blackwell, 1996.

Frow, John. *What Was Postmodernism?* Sydney: Local Consumption (Occasional Paper no. 11), 1991.

Kaplan, E. Ann, ed. *Postmodernism and Its Discontents: Theories, Practices*. London and New York: Verso, 1988.

Kroker, Arthur and Marilouise Kroker, eds. *Body Invaders: Panic Sex in America*. New York: St. Martin's Press, 1987.

Kroker, Arthur and Marilouise Kroker, eds. *Body Invaders: Sexuality and the Postmodern Condition*. Basingstoke: Macmillan, 1988.

Lyotard, Jean-François. *The Postmodern Condition: A Report on Knowledge*, trans. Geoff Bennington and Brian Masumi. *Theory and History of Literature* 10. Manchester: Manchester University Press, 1986.

Lyotard, Jean-François. *Toward the Postmodern*, eds Robert Harvey and Mark S. Roberts. Atlantic Highlands, NJ: Humanities Press, 1993.

McHoul, Alec and Niall Lucy. 'That Film, This Paper – Its Body', *Southern Review* 27, 3 (1994), pp. 303–22.

Norris, Christopher. *The Truth About Postmodernism*. Oxford: Blackwell, 1993.

Norris, Christopher. *What's Wrong with Postmodernism: Critical Theory and the Ends of Philosophy*. New York and London: Harvester Wheatsheaf, 1990.

Rorty, Richard. *Contingency, Irony, and Solidarity*. Cambridge: Cambridge University Press, 1989.

Rorty, Richard. *Objectivity, Relativism and the Truth*. Cambridge: Cambridge University Press, 1991.

4. Literature and the Post

Barthes, Roland. *S/Z*, trans. Richard Miller. New York: Hill and Wang, 1974.

Barthes, Roland. *The Pleasure of the Text*, trans. Richard Miller. New York: Hill & Wang, 1975.

Cixous, Hélène. *Coming to Writing and Other Essays*, ed. Deborah Jenson. Cambridge, Mass.: Harvard University Press, 1991.

Elam, Diane. *Romancing the Post*. New York and London: Routledge, 1992.

Federman, Raymond, ed. *Surfiction: Fiction Now and Tomorrow*. Chicago: Swallow Press, 1981, 2nd edn.

Hassan, Ihab. *Paracriticisms: Seven Speculations of the Times*. Urbana: University of Illinois Press, 1975.

Hassan, Ihab. *The Postmodern Turn: Essays in Postmodern Theory and Culture*. Columbus: Ohio State University Press, 1987.

Lucy, Niall. *Postmodern Literary Theory: An Introduction*. Oxford: Blackwell, 1997.

McHale, Brian. *Postmodernist Fictions*. London and New York: Routledge, 1987.

McHoul, Alec and David Wills. *Writing Pynchon: Strategies in Fictional Analysis*. London: Macmillan, 1990.

Miller, J. Hillis. 'The Critic as Host', in *Deconstruction and Criticism*, eds Harold Bloom, Paul de Man, Jacques Derrida, Geoffrey Hartman and J. Hillis Miller. London and Henley: Routledge and Kegan Paul, 1979, pp. 217–53.

Newman, Charles. *The Post-Modern Aura: The Art of Fiction in an Age of Inflation*. Evanston, Ill.: Northwestern University Press, 1985.

Perloff, Marjorie, ed. *Postmodern Genres*. Norman and London: University of Oklahoma Press, 1988.

Rice, Philip and Patricia Waugh, eds. *Modern Literary Theory*. London and New York: Arnold, 1996, 3rd edn.

Spanos, William V. *Repetitions: The Postmodern Occasion in Literature and Culture*. Baton Rouge and London: Louisiana State University Press, 1987.

Tanner, Tony. *City of Words: American Fiction 1950–1970*. London: Jonathan Cape, 1971.

Zavarzadeh, Mas'ud. *The Mythopoeic Reality: The Postwar American Nonfiction Novel*. Urbana, Illinois: University of Illinois Press, 1976.

5. Postmodern Culture

Connor, Steven. *Postmodernist Culture: An Introduction to Theories of the Contemporary*. Oxford: Blackwell, 1989.

Connor, Steven. *Theory and Cultural Value*. Oxford: Blackwell, 1992.

Fekete, John. *Life After Postmodernism: Essays on Value and Culture*. New York: St. Martin's Press, 1987.

Frow, John. *Time and Commodity Culture: Essays in Cultural Theory and Postmodernity*. New York: Oxford University Press, 1997.

Frow, John. *Cultural Studies and Cultural Value*. New York: Oxford University Press, 1995.

Grossberg, Lawrence. *We Gotta Get Out of This Place: Popular Conservatism and Postmodern Culture*. New York: Routledge, 1992.

Huyssen, Andreas. *After the Great Divide: Modernism, Mass Culture and Postmodernism*. London: Macmillan, 1988.

Jameson, Fredric. *Postmodernism, or, The Cultural Logic of Late Capitalism*. Durham: Duke University Press, 1991.

Kroker, Arthur and David Cook. *The Postmodern Scene: Excremental Culture and Hyper-Aesthetics*. London: Macmillan, 1988.

Poster, Mark. *Cultural History and Postmodernity: Disciplinary Readings and Challenges*. New York: Columbia University Press, 1997.

Soja, Edward. *Postmodern Geographies: The Reassertion of Space in Critical Social Theory*. London: Verso, 1989.

Vattimo, Gianni. *The End of Modernity: Nihilism and Hermeneutics in Post-Modern Culture*, trans. Jon R. Snyder. Oxford: Polity, 1991.

6. Feminism and Postmodernism

Bray, Abigail and Claire Colebrook. 'The Haunted Flesh: Corporeal Feminism and the Politics of (Dis)Embodiment', *Signs* 24, 1 (1998), pp. 35–67.

Ebert, Teresa L. *Ludic Feminism and After: Postmodernism, Desire, and Labor in Late Capitalism*. Ann Arbor: University of Michigan Press, 1996.

Ellison, Julie. *Delicate Subjects: Romanticism, Gender and the Ethics of Understanding*. Ithaca: Cornell University Press, 1990.

Felski, Rita. *The Gender of Modernity*. Cambridge, Mass.: Harvard University Press, 1995.

Gatens, Moira. *Imaginary Bodies: Ethics, Power and Corporeality*. London and New York: Routledge, 1996.

Kroker, Arthur and Marilouise Kroker, eds. *The Last Sex: Feminism and Outlaw Bodies*. Basingstoke: Macmillan, 1993.

Marks, Elaine and Isabelle de Courtivron, eds. *New French Feminisms*. New York: Schoken, 1981.

Moi, Toril, ed. *The Kristeva Reader*. New York: Columbia University Press, 1986.

Morris, Meaghan. *The Pirate's Fianceé: Feminism, Reading, Postmodernism*. London and New York: Verso, 1988.

Nicholson, Linda J. *Feminism/Postmodernism*. New York: Routledge, 1990.

Whitford, Margaret, ed. *The Irigaray Reader*. Oxford: Blackwell, 1991.

7. Postmodern Ethics

Bauman, Zygmunt. *Postmodern Ethics*. Oxford: Blackwell, 1993.

Caputo, John D. *Against Ethics: Contributions to a Poetics of Obligation with Constant Reference to Deconstruction*. Bloomington: Indiana University Press, 1993.

Chow, Rey. *Ethics After Idealism: Theory, Culture, Ethnicity, Reading*. Bloomington: Indianapolis University Press, 1998.

Eaglestone, Robert. *Ethical Criticism: Reading After Levinas*. Edinburgh: Edinburgh University Press, 1997.

Harpham, Geoffrey. *Getting It Right: Language, Literature, and Ethics*. Chicago: University of Chicago Press, 1992.

Miller, J. Hillis. *The Ethics of Reading: Kant, de Man, Eliot, Trollope, James, and Benjamin*. New York: Columbia University Press, 1987.

Norris, Christopher. *Truth and the Ethics of Criticism*. Manchester and New York: Manchester University Press, 1994.

Wyschogrod, Edith. *Saints and Postmodernism: Revisioning Moral Philosophy*. Chicago and London: University of Chicago Press, 1990.

8. Cyberculture

Landow, George. *Hypertext: The Convergence of Contemporary Critical Theory and Technology*. Baltimore: Johns Hopkins University Press, 1993.

McCaffrey, Larry, ed. *Storming the Reality Studio: A Casebook of Cyberpunk and Postmodern Science Fiction*. Durham and London: Duke University Press, 1991.

Porush, David A. *The Soft Machine: Cybernetic Fiction*. New York: Methuen, 1985.

Rucker, Rudy, R. U. Sirius and Queen Mu, eds. *The Mondo 2000 User's Guide to the New Edge*. New York, 1992.

Tofts, Darren and Murray McKeich. *Memory Trade: A Prehistory of Cyberculture*. North Ryde, Sydney: Interface, 1998.

Wark, McKenzie. *Celebrities, Culture, Cyberspace*. Sydney: Pluto, 1999.

Weiner, Norbert. *The Human Use of Human Beings: Cybernetics and Society*. London: Sphere, 1968.

Woolley, Benjamin. *Virtual Worlds: A Journey in Hype and Hyperreality*. Oxford: Blackwell, 1992.

Index